C000273423

Corporate Finance

Corporate Finance

Concepts and Applications

Julian R. Franks
London Graduate School of Business Studies

John E. Broyles
Templeton College, Oxford Centre for Management Studies

Willard T. Carleton
University of Arizona

Kent Publishing Company
Boston, Massachusetts
A Division of Wadsworth, Inc.

Kent Publishing Company
A Division of Wadsworth, Inc.

Editor: Richard Crews
Text Designer: Outside Designs
Cover Designer: Outside Designs
Production Editor: Pamela Rockwell
Production Coordinator: Linda Siegrist

© 1985 by Wadsworth, Inc., 10 Davis Drive, Belmont, California 94002. All rights reserved. No part of this book may be reproduced, stored in a retrieval system, or transcribed, in any form or by any means, electronic, mechanical, photocopying, recording, or otherwise, without the prior written permission of the publisher, Kent Publishing Company, Boston, Massachusetts 02116.

Printed in the United States of America
    2   3   4   5   6   7   8   9 — 88   87   86   85

To Our Wives

Library of Congress Cataloging in Publication Data
Franks, Julian R.
    Corporate finance.
    Includes bibliographies and index.
    1. Corporations—Finance. I. Broyles, J. E.
II. Carleton, Willard T. III. Title.
HG4026.F69   1985   658.1′5   84-23357
ISBN 0-534-04095-0

About the Authors

JULIAN R. FRANKS, BA, MBA, PhD, is National Westminster Bank Professor of Finance at the London Business School. Publications include several books on corporate finance and articles on the profitability of acquisitions, leasing, debt, and taxes, and the interaction of investment and financing decisions. He is also consultant for a number of public companies and a trade union. He is a visiting professor at the University of Cape Town (SA), at the University of North Carolina, Chapel Hill, and at the University of California at Berkeley. He is an associate editor of the *Journal of Banking and Finance*.

JOHN E. BROYLES, B.Sc., M.Sc, PhD, is Fellow in Finance at the Oxford University Centre for Management Studies. Formerly at the London Business School, he was director of the Corporate Finance Programme and editor of the *London Business School Journal*. He is a member of the editorial board of the *Journal of Business, Finance, and Accounting*. His research and publications are in capital markets, institutional investment policy, corporate financial planning, and acquisitions. He is consultant for a number of public companies and H.M. Treasury.

WILLARD T. CARLETON, AB, MBA, MA, PhD, is Karl Eller Professor of Finance at the University of Arizona. Formerly he taught at the University of North Carolina and at Dartmouth College, Northwestern, and New York universities. He has served as president of the Financial Management Association, as editor of *Financial Management,* and as an associate editor of the *Journal of Finance* and several other journals. He has published very widely in finance and economics and is a noted consultant in the area of public utility regulation.

Preface

This text has been written for the introductory corporate finance course at the MBA level and for second-level undergraduate courses in financial management. While previous exposure to introductory courses in accounting and statistics will help the student to understand some of the appendices, it is not essential: the text is largely self-contained. The book is conceptually up-to-date and internally consistent. Nonetheless, it is readable and predominately nonmathematical. We have based the book upon the results of modern research, with the conviction that contemporary concepts can be explained in common-sense terms. Students are given a sufficiently thorough grounding to enable them to understand not only the power but also the limitations of existing theory.

The text shows the student how managers can increase the value of their companies by obtaining funds at fair prices in a competitive financial market in order to finance commercial activities in less-competitive product markets. We explain why competitive advantage in product markets is the source of the net present value rules used in financial analysis. We show how managers can use the financial markets to measure the rates of return required by the company's stockholders for new investments in risky assets. The relationships between finance and strategy are emphasized throughout the text. Thus the student sees financial decision-making in the wider context of simple rules of microeconomics and business policy. The text helps the instructor to relate finance to the wider issues that often arise in case studies.

A major feature of the book is the focus on large, concrete examples. Each such example is designed to show the student how the principles discussed in the chapter can be applied to a specific financial problem. Thus the instructor can rely on the text to provide the necessary applications that can be developed further in lectures or used in case studies. End-of-chapter review questions and problems are also provided. Answers to selected problems are given in the book, and the remainder are given in the *Instructor's Manual*. Additional pedagogical support is made available in the *Student's Guide*.

In two introductory chapters Part I offers the student an informal overview of financial management and of the financial market. The object is to motivate the student to put financial management into perspective within the context of both the corporation and the financial market and to underline the existing links that the student has and will have as saver, borrower, investor, and manager.

Part II includes four chapters on the principles and applications of project appraisal methods. First we show how to use discounted cash flow for the purpose of appraising an investment opportunity. Then the effects of taxes on cash flow are clearly presented, and a simple example is given of how interactions between tax effects of different projects alter the traditional value additivity principle. We contrast and compare the characteristics and limitations of the other current methods of project appraisal, including payback, net present value, internal rate of return, and accounting rate of return. We also show the link between a project's internal rate of return and its accounting rates of return, thus helping the instructor to impart a better understanding of the relationship between cash flows and accounting numbers. Next we give a thorough coverage of the difficulties that arise in the practical application of DCF methods.

Then in the chapter on cash-flow analysis, we indicate how to define a project's net incremental cash flows, as well as how to relate the net present value of a project directly to the variables reflecting competitive advantage. In the final chapter of Part II we show how corporate taxes, together with changes in the rate of inflation, can affect the profitability of a project. Thus in Part II the student learns how to relate investment decisions to competitive advantage and to the expected economic and fiscal environment.

Part III devotes four chapters to implications of the relationship between risk and the required rates of return in the financial market. First we introduce portfolio theory and show how the capital asset pricing model derives from this theory. We discuss the limitations of the existing evidence in support of the model. Then we provide some of the evidence that has been used to estimate the cost of equity capital for the average listed company relative to the rates of return on government securities, and we relate the capital asset pricing model and the Gordon model to the weighted average cost of capital. Next we explain how to obtain the cost of capital not only for the company as a whole but also for each of its divisions and for different projects within the divisions. Finally we describe how to use the relationship between risk and return in the financial market as a criterion for setting financial targets for divisions and measuring their performance. This topic provides a further opportunity for the student to explore the links between economic and accounting measures of return. Thus Part III shows the student how discount rates can be obtained from the financial market and helps the instructor to show the relationships between alternative methods of obtaining the cost of capital and of relating performance targets and discount rates to the risks of individual assets.

In Part IV the three chapters concern the valuation of listed and unlisted companies. We begin with a discussion of evidence that tests the efficiency of the stock market in providing an unbiased estimate of the value of a listed company's stock and what implications that evidence has for the corporation's financial decisions. Then we outline the advantages and limitations of the various methods for valuing companies that are not actively traded on any stock exchange. Finally we discuss the sources of added value that may occur as a result of acquisitions and mergers between companies. The student gains further insights into the relationships between accounting and economic valuation of assets, earnings, and cash flows and is shown the pitfalls and advantages in each approach to company valuation. Part IV helps the instructor to show how the principles of valuation in efficient financial markets can be used to improve acquisition decisions.

In Part V there are nine chapters that consider dividend and financing decisions. First we discuss what is currently known concerning the relationship between dividend policy and taxes and explain why dividend policy has aroused so much interest in finance. We then have three chapters on long-term financing including one on common stock, one on debt, and one on the economics of interest rates and bond prices. In the following two important chapters we explain option theory in a readily understood manner and show how the concept of an option sheds light on many important issues in corporate finance. The student is provided an easy entrance into the world of options so that he or she can see how the options concept affects many of the relationships in corporate finance.

In the final three chapters in Part V we analyze the controversy surrounding the theory of capital structure and examine the impact of the Miller and the Miller and Modigliani views concerning debt and taxes on capital structure and project valuation. The student learns that finance is not a cookbook subject and sees why the choice of model is important to the values placed on investment and financing decisions. We explain how investment and financing decisions can interact when a company is in a temporary nontax-paying position, and we demonstrate how to estimate the value of a financial lease, taking into account the company's tax-paying position in both the Miller and the Modigliani and Miller worlds. Part IV gives the student a clear and thorough coverage of the major controversies concerning the impact of taxes on dividend and financing decisions and also helps the instructor to explain why investment and financing decisions cannot always be taken in isolation.

In Part VI there are three chapters giving an introduction to the principles of working capital management. The first covers the management of receivables and the second, management of inventories. Finally we discuss cash management and consider the importance of financial planning. We show the student how pro forma cash budgets and projected funds flow statements can be used to plan the financing requirements of the company. We also consider how combinations of uncertain future events can affect these forecasts. This subject provides further analysis of the interaction between investment and financing decisions and gives the instructor an opportunity to relate individual financial decisions within a larger planning context.

Finally in Part VII, we offer an introduction to international financial management. We describe the main factors determining foreign exchange rate movements, and we explain how to obtain the net present value of a capital project when the cash flows are denominated in more than one currency and are subject to taxation in more than one country. We also explain measures that managers can take to minimize the risk of adverse changes in exchange rates in the long term as well as the short term. The purpose of this final chapter is to awaken the student to the international dimensions of contemporary corporate financial activities.

We are grateful for the many useful comments and suggestions from our colleagues and students at the University of North Carolina at Chapel Hill, the London Business School, and Templeton College, Oxford, who are unfortunately too numerous to give a complete list here. For their excellent and thorough reviews we would like to give our special thanks to James Bicksler, Rutgers University; John A. Boquist, Indiana University; Stewart Hodges, University of Warwick; Keith M. Howe, Iowa State University; James Jackson, Oklahoma State University; Dennis E. Logue, Dartmouth College; Paul H. Malatesta, University of Washington; Roger Mesznik, The City University of New York; George S. Oldfield, Cornell University; Robert A. Taggart, Jr., Harvard University; Dwayne Wrightsman, University of New Hampshire. Thanks to Swee Ung for supplying many of the problems and solutions. Among students whose comments on recent drafts were particularly comprehensive were Cynthia Worthington, Alec Weil, Masahiro Kambe, A. Neuberger, J. Daraugh, and R. Williams. Special thanks to our colleagues whose help has been invaluable: Peter Zinkin, Jeanette Rutherford, Pam Peterson, and Jim Miles.

Finally, our thanks to our wives and families for their practical help, moral support, and forebearance.

Julian R. Franks
John E. Broyles
Willard T. Carleton

Contents

III   *Risk and Return*

VII   *International Capital Projects*

Corporate Finance

Introduction

We begin this text in Chapter 1 by stating the objectives of financial management and discussing the functions that financial managers must perform to pursue these objectives. A main objective of financial management is to maximize the market value of the firm to its owners or stockholders while protecting the interests of lenders and employees. Since the value that is being maximized is measured by the prices of the corporation's securities traded in the financial market, we provide a broad-brush introduction in Chapter 2 to the functions the financial market performs in collecting the savings of individuals and making the capital available at competitive rates for investment by companies. The first two chapters provide the background and the context for the framework that we develop in the remainder of the book.

Financial Management: An Overview

In this introductory chapter we paint a broad-brush picture of what finance is about and how financial management is used to help the firm reach its financial objectives. First we describe the financial problems of the small firm, and then we show how the same problems reappear in large corporations. We also demonstrate the way these problems give rise to the functions performed by the principal financial officers of the firm, and show how financial managers assist operating managers to make more profitable decisions. Finally, we discuss briefly the nature of the firm's financial objectives and how they affect the interests of the stockholders. The chapter provides an introduction to the main concerns of financial management.

What Finance Is Really About

If you were to start a small business of your own tomorrow, you soon would be involved in financial management problems. Having first conceived of a unique product or service, perhaps in a market currently without too much competition, you then must develop some plans. The plans require answers to some important questions; for instance, what assets will the business require? That is, what business premises, equipment, and inventories of merchandise and materials will be needed? The purchase of these resources can require substantial funds, particularly in the initial stages before sales revenue can be generated. In other words, you need access to money.

The strategy that you adopt for starting and operating your business will affect the amount of money you will need and when you will need it. If the money is not available at the right time and in the proper amounts, you may have to alter your plans. As a result, your problems are those of the financial manager, or the typical company treasurer. You have to translate the operating plans of your business into a financial plan, which enables you to forecast how much capital you need and when.

At the same time, in your role as treasurer, you have to begin building relationships with sympathetic bankers who will lend you money when you need it. Banks do not like to lend more than half the money that a business needs, because bankers do not like to take too many chances with their depositors' money. Consequently, before you can borrow you must be willing to risk some of your own funds. If you do not have enough personal capital, you must try to find relatives or other people who might be willing to contribute some money. In exchange for their capital, they will want to be part owners of the business and share in its profits. Thus your business will require two kinds of capital: debt (the bank's funds) and equity (the owners' funds). This is one element of financial management: ensuring that your business has adequate funds available to operate efficiently and to exploit its opportunities.

When you have secured the capital that you need to acquire the physical assets required by the business, you face some further choices. Which assets do you need, and how do you choose between competing ones? If two business machines have different revenue-producing capabilities and different operating lives, you need some financial yardsticks to help you make a choice. How much money will each machine make each month, and for how many years? Is this cash income sufficient to justify the price that you would have to pay for each machine? Does the rate of return on the investment in either machine compare favorably with your other investment opportunities? Answers to such questions require analysis, and finance is concerned in part with providing the techniques for this sort of analysis. A large company would employ financial analysts to make such comparisons for the company treasurer.

Once your business is in operation, you will engage in an enormous number of transactions. Sales slips, receipts, and checkbook entries pile up. You cannot rely on memory to handle information in the mounting piles of paper on your desk. Your sympathetic accountant says, "You need a management accounting system." For a fee, he sets up a simple system for you. The system involves a journal, where all transactions are recorded each day, and various ledger accounts where the transactions can be gathered together into meaningful categories. The sums in these accounts help you to get your business under control, or to know whether you are winning the battle between profit and loss. If you are losing, the accounts may provide some clues as to what to do about it, for example, they will show whether your prices cover all your costs.

Such an accounting system proves worthwhile, but it requires effort to maintain. When the business starts generating sufficient cash, you hire a bookkeeper to make the actual entries in the accounts. Still, the system requires some of your time, for you must supervise the bookkeeper and interpret what the accounts may indicate about the health of your business.

Now that you are keeping accounts regularly, you have made your outside accountant's job much easier. At the end of the year the accountant must add up your assets (what you own) and your liabilities (what you owe). Your total assets less your total liabilities represent your "net worth." If your net worth has increased during the year, you have made a profit, and your company may have to pay a tax on the profit.

All this detail requires a great deal of bookkeeping and help from your accountant. As your business grows, you may be able to hire a full-time accountant, who will then become your controller. The controller will keep your accounts, prepare your tax returns, and supervise your bookkeepers. A good controller can also undertake financial analysis of potential investment decisions and help with financial planning and other treasurer's functions, including raising funds. Your controller then deserves the title, vice president–finance, because he or she will be performing or supervising all the main functions of finance:

planning and forecasting needs for outside financing

raising capital

analyzing financial data

financial reporting and control

paying taxes

Financial management mainly concerns planning, raising funds, analysis of project profitability, and control of cash, as well as the accounting functions relating to reporting profits and taxes. A financial manager is an executive who manages one or more of these functions. As we have seen, finance plays a role in many facets of any business. That is why financial managers participate in virtually all the major decisions and occupy key positions at the center of all business organizations.

How Finance Is Organized in Larger Companies

Most companies are begun by individuals or small groups of entrepreneurs in partnership. The owners and the managers are the same people. As their business grows, the owners usually will register the company as a legal entity called a corporation. One advantage of the corporate form is that in law the corporation can be treated as though it were a person, distinct from its owners. This offers the advantage of limited liability, that is, if the corporation cannot pay its debts, the legal owners cannot be forced to pay them from their private wealth. The owners' risk is limited to the amount of money they have already put into the firm. This feature makes it easier for each of the existing owners to sell his or her share in the ownership of the firm.

A share of ownership in a corporation is represented legally on a common stock certificate registered in the name of the owner of the stock. These stock certificates are securities that can be bought and sold by anyone who wishes to exchange a share of ownership in the company. (Stocks are also called "shares" for this reason.) The larger corporations are listed on one or more stock exchanges where their common stocks can be bought and sold readily in a regulated securities market.

Over time, as the original owner-managers retire or leave the company to manage other businesses, it becomes necessary for the company to hire professional managers, who may have little or no investment in the company. Professional managers represent the interests of the shareholders, who gradually become a diverse and somewhat disinterested population of individuals, pension funds, mutual funds, insurance companies, and other financial institutions. Thus we find that in most large corporations the owners and the actual managers are two separate groups of people.

In this situation, you can understand how managers may associate their lives and their careers more with the corporation than would any owner, and how at times there can be conflicts of interest between managers and owners. Corporation law entrusts the interests of the owners or common stockholders to a board of directors appointed by the stockholders at the annual meeting. The board meets periodically to review company affairs and has the ultimate authority to set policy, to authorize major decisions, and to appoint top managers.

The stockholders at the annual meeting elect or reelect members of the board from both outside and inside the company. Outside directors may be drawn from the top ranks of other companies, financial institutions, and professional and academic bodies. The vice president–finance, the president of the company, and some other key officers almost certainly will be among the inside directors on the board.

Thus the vice president–finance is a senior executive who sits on the board of directors and who is responsible for all the financial aspects of the company's activities. Because of the scope and complexity of finance, typically he or she will delegate major responsibilities to a controller and a treasurer. Although their functions may overlap, the controller tends to concentrate on those activities requiring accountants, and the treasurer specializes in maintaining active relationships with investment and commercial bankers and other providers of funds in the financial market including the stockholders. The financial market consists of the banks, insurance companies, and other financial institutions (including the stock market) that compete to supply companies with capital.

THE VICE PRESIDENT–FINANCE

A seat on the board of directors requires the vice president–finance to play an active part in broad strategic and policymaking activities, which usually involve financial considerations. As many board members may lack financial expertise, the vice president–finance often occupies a strong position of influence.

The board relies on the vice president–finance for advice concerning the payment of dividends to stockholders, major capital expenditures for new assets, acquisition of other companies, and resale of existing assets. They may also rely on the finance department for interpretation of economic and financial developments, including the implications of government economic policies and tax legislation.

These responsibilities of the board require that the vice president–finance participate in long-range planning and the preparation of long-term budgets linking expenditures on fixed assets and financing requirements to strategic planning. Advising the board on investments in new assets may require the vice president to head a capital appropriations committee. In this capacity, the vice president budgets funds for investment, screens investment proposals, and he or she must see that an up-to-date manual for the preparation of capital expenditure proposals is available to operating managers. Ultimately, the vice president is responsible for all activities that may be delegated to the controller or to the treasurer (e.g., financial planning and control and credit arrangements with the company's bankers). A typical organization chart is shown in Figure 1.1.

THE CONTROLLER

Primarily, the controller is responsible to the vice president–finance for establishing, maintaining, and auditing the company's systems and procedures, and preparing financial statements and reports for management, the board, the stockholders, and the tax authorities. Partly as a result of the required data collection for management accounting and financial reporting activities, the controller acquires information that makes his or her participation and advice useful to many decisions throughout the firm. The controller also may be in charge of computer facilities, data processing, and related computer applications.

The controller oversees cost control throughout the company. He or she may participate in product pricing and sales credit decisions and supervise collections from customers. Together with staff, the controller consolidates forecasts and related financial analyses and prepares budgets for operating departments. This person may also be responsible to the vice president–finance for all matters relating to taxes, although some companies have a separate tax department reporting directly to the vice president–finance. In

Figure 1.1   *An example of the organization of the finance function*

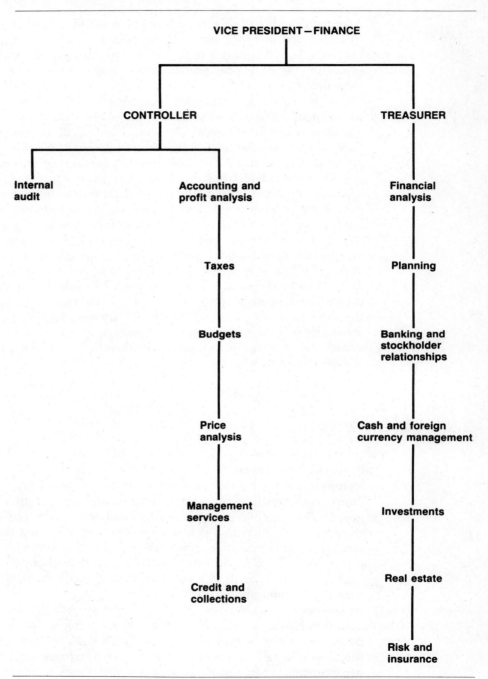

some firms, the controller also performs many of the functions that the treasurer would, as described below.

THE TREASURER

The main functions of the treasurer are to invest surplus funds (often on a daily basis) and to provide sufficient financing to meet all likely contingencies. Thus the treasurer puts together the forecasts of the financial needs of the firm and manages its cash. The treasurer must maintain effective business and personal relationships with the firm's commercial bankers and investment bankers, because he or she is responsible for arranging the external sources of funds that may result from the financial forecasts. The treasurer also is responsible for issuing the firm's corporate securities and for borrowing, paying interest on, and repaying outstanding corporate debt.

The treasurer is the custodian of the company's cash balances and oversees all cashier and payroll activities. He or she therefore is in charge of the company's investments in the financial market and arranges for the management of employee pension funds. The treasurer manages the firm's overseas transactions, taking such measures as may be required to prevent losses due to changes in foreign exchange rates.

The treasurer's department may also manage the company's investment in real estate holdings and insurance arrangements. The treasurer's staff may advise on customer credit through contact with banks and credit agencies. Finally, the treasurer's department is often the center for expertise in financial analysis in the firm, and the treasurer's staff may engage in special projects analyzing, for example, the firm's overall corporate financial plan, proposed major capital expenditures, takeovers and mergers, and different ways of raising new funds. Financial analysts in the treasurer's department are often called upon to participate in training programs designed to make methods of financial analysis more widely known to operating managers.

In summary, the treasurer is the company's main contact with the financial community. He or she plans long-term financing and manages short-term borrowing and lending. The treasurer's prime responsibility is to make certain that there are sufficient funds available to meet all likely needs of the company, both domestic and overseas.

How the Treasurer Raises Funds

Each year a part of the company's after-tax earnings is paid out to the stockholders in the form of dividends, with the remainder retained by the firm to be reinvested in assets. In fact, most funds used by companies are obtained from retained earnings (before depreciation). Retained earnings are treated as equity because they still belong to the stockholders. Frequently, however, additional funds are required, and the treasurer looks to various outside sources of capital to meet the balance of the company's needs. Borrowing has tax advantages, and bank borrowing, the largest single source of external financing to companies in the United States, is easily arranged. Next in importance to bank borrowing is the issue of long-term debt with, say, ten or more years to repay. Long-term debt may take the form of bonds sold publicly in the capital market or placed privately with large financial institutions.

Publicly issued securities, whether they represent debt or equity, entail high transactions costs. As a consequence, most borrowing takes place privately on a one-to-one basis with banks and insurance companies. As dividend payments are not tax-deductible to a corporation, and new issues of common stock involve high transactions costs, new issues are a less significant source of external financing than debt. (Most of the equity dollars raised through stock issues in fact are raised by regulated public utilities.) By law, debtholders have a prior claim on the company's assets, and stockholders can claim only what is left after those claims are satisfied.

The owners' stake in the company is called the equity or net worth. The net worth or equity is the value of all the assets minus the value of the company's liabilities. The stock market makes its own assessment of the values of the assets and liabilities and consequently determines what the equity is really worth. The price of a share of common stock is the market value of the equity divided by the number of shares issued.

When a private company becomes a public corporation, it makes an offering of common stock with the help of investment bankers. The investment bankers usually buy the entire issue at a discount from the issue price and resell the stocks to pension funds, mutual funds, insurance companies, and other financial institutions, or to the general public through stockbrokers.

Once the shares are issued and traded, the treasurer may raise further equity capital from existing shareholders or from the general public, depending in part on what is required in the company's articles of incorporation. A rights issue is an offer of additional shares to existing shareholders. Each shareholder's entitlement is based upon the number of shares already owned. The offer allows shareholders several weeks to exercise their rights to the new shares before a specified date. A stockholder who does not wish to exercise the rights may sell them to someone else. If the rights issue is guaranteed by underwriters, underwriters (usually investment bankers) will have to buy any shares remaining unsold at a price agreed upon in the underwriting agreement. In the United States, most equity issues are made to the general public rather than to the issuing corporation's stockholders.

With sufficient equity capital, the company is in a position to borrow. Lenders wish to be relatively certain of getting their money back. Therefore debt typically represents a smaller proportion of the total financing employed by the firm than equity (mostly generated by retained earnings), which represents the largest part.

Corporate treasurers like to finance their short-term requirements for investments in inventories and accounts receivable with short-term bank loans for up to one year and intermediate-term loans of up to ten years from banks and other lenders. Treasurers finance longer-term requirements with loans from other financial institutions, such as insurance companies and pension funds, or by the public issue of long-term debt securities (called bonds). As short-term requirements for cash change constantly, the treasurer must maintain close and continuing relationships with the company's bankers who supply short-term debt. Long-term loan transactions with such institutions as insurance companies are less frequent, and such transactions are conducted at a less personal level.

The Financial Objectives of the Corporation

Most finance textbooks claim that the appropriate primary financial objective of management is to maximize the value of the corporation's net assets. Value maximization is important for a number of reasons. One of management's responsibilities is to represent the interests of both stockholders and debtholders. The stockholders' main interest is in the preservation or increase of the market value of their investment in the corporation's stock. The debtholders' main interest is in protection of the value of their claims on the corporation and in repayment of all money owed to them when due. Therefore it is an important objective for management to maximize the value of the company's assets in such a way that it increases the wealth of the stockholders, without detriment to debtholders.

For many reasons, conflicts of interest may arise between stockholders and debtholders. Management may invest in speculative ventures that could produce not only large profits but also large losses. These investments may be acceptable to stockholders who are willing to accept high risk for the promise of high reward. Lenders, though, reap their reward in the form of an interest rate that does not rise even if the corporation does unexpectedly well. In contrast, if the corporation does badly, lenders may lose part or all of the value of their loans. Given this asymmetry of reward, it is in the lender's interests to prevent the company from increasing the risk of the business even if the proposed ventures are profitable to stockholders, unless the terms of the loan can be revised. On occasion management may not protect lenders against increases in risks, and the restrictions in loan agreements may not always be effective in obtaining revised terms for loans.

The cash flows that are expected to be generated by an asset together with its cost determine the rate of return that the investment in the asset is expected to earn. In the financial market, different securities have different risks, and investors demand higher rates of return on securities with higher risk. As a result, investors expect managers in a corporation to try to obtain the highest rates of return from those new assets that involve the greatest risks to the stockholders. Unless a proposed new investment in an asset promises a higher expected return than stockholders would require given the asset's risk, then the value of the investment to the stockholders will not exceed its cost, and the proposed investment will not increase the value of the firm's stock in the financial market.

How is the worth of an investment determined given its expected future cash flows, its risk, and the rate of return that investors would require? In principle, stockholders can estimate the worth of the company's investment in an asset by comparing the investment to alternative investments in the financial market. A stockholder would want to know how much it would cost now to buy a portfolio of securities with the same expected future cash flows and the same risk as the asset. The value of such a portfolio indicates the value of the asset. Providing the cost of the asset is less than its value, the investment should take place.

In practice, the financial analyst estimates the present worth of the asset by estimating the present value of each of its expected future cash flows separately and adding up the present values of all the cash flows (using techniques to be described later). Unless the total present value of all the asset's future cash flows exceeds the cost of the asset, investment in the asset cannot be expected to increase the value of the firm. In such a case, management should reject the investment if it wishes to pursue the objective of increasing stockholders' wealth.

The financial market in the United States is very competitive. This competiton also makes the financial market efficient. By "efficient" we mean that the prices of securities reflect almost instantly all price-sensitive information as it becomes available to market participants. One result of such market efficiency is that management normally cannot expect to increase the value of the corporation by raising funds in the financial market and then simply reinvesting the money in the financial market.

The way that management increases the value of the corporation is to raise funds at competitive rates in an efficient financial market and then reinvest the funds in products and services that sell in markets that are not so competitive, and where higher rates of return are obtainable. Managers must seek profitable ventures in product markets where they can expect to enjoy some advantage over competitors. Competitive advantage may derive from new patents or technologies, superior research, well-known brand names, established channels of distribution, superior location, and economies of scale. Value-maximizing investment requires the identification, analysis, and exploitation of such opportunities for competitive advantage.

When management selects investments that it hopes will increase the value of the company, it must find activities that will earn a higher rate of return than the cost of capital. The costs of capital include after-tax interest payments on debt and the level of dividends and capital gains that are required to satisfy the stockholders. The cost of capital is a variable that depends upon the riskiness of the venture. Thus an essential element in the search for value-maximizing investment is measurement of the risks of different kinds of investment. Without an estimate of the risk of each venture, management cannot estimate the cost of capital and would not know whether the rate of return that is expected from an activity may justify the use of capital. For these reasons, part of this book is devoted to ways of measuring risk and to the relationship between the cost of capital and risk.

Summary

Financial management techniques assist operating managers to attain the financial objectives of the firm and to report financial results to the owners, creditors, and employees. For this purpose, the controller's department maintains the financial reporting and control system, and the treasurer's department raises and manages funds and maintains active relationships with institutions in the financial community that are potential sources of capital.

The vice president–finance draws upon the information, analysis, and advice of both financial departments in advising the other members of the board of directors concerning financial planning and policy and major capital investments. The ultimate objective of these activities is to increase the value of the firm to its owners or stockholders while protecting the legitimate interests of debtholders and employees, whose livelihood may depend upon the company.

Review Questions

1. What are the major responsibilities of the chief financial officers of the firm?
2. Describe the different methods of financing the firm and the characteristics of the main financial instruments employed.
3. What are the kinds of competitive conditions in the marketplace for the firm's products that are most likely to increase the wealth of stockholders?
4. Why might conflicts arise between stockholders and lenders?
5. Why is maximizing the value of the firm not necessarily the same as maximizing the value of the stockholders' investment?

6. Would you expect high-risk investments to have higher or lower required rates of return (or costs of capital) than low-risk investments?
7. Should management try to maximize the market value of a corporation or its balance sheet (i.e., accounting) value? What is the difference between the two?
8. How can management find investments that can be expected to increase the value of the corporation?

References

de Butts, John D., "The Treasurer's Function as Viewed by Top Management," in *The Treasurer's Handbook,* J. Fred Weston and Maurice B. Goudzwaard, eds., Homewood, Illinois: Dow Jones–Irwin, 1976.

The Financial Market

American industry requires enormous amounts of capital to modernize, to expand, and to promote new products that will be competitive in both domestic and world markets. The key to financing all this enterprise is the financial market. The costs of finance in the financial market are determined competitively, and the cost of finance is an important benchmark for managers who are contemplating further investment in commercial activities.

What is a financial market, and what is its role? What does it all have to do with any of us as private individuals or as professional managers? In this chapter we describe how the financial market relates to our everyday lives, the roles played by financial institutions such as banks, and where the funds required by companies come from. Finally, we outline the way in which the financial market relates rates of return to the risk of different kinds of assets and how managers can use this relationship to help them decide whether to invest in risky commercial activities.

The Financial Market in Everyday Life

Whenever we make a bank deposit or write out a check, we play a role in the financial market. In product markets, goods such as food, clothing, and cars are bought and sold. In the financial market, money is the commodity, but the money is only for "rent." The rental price is the rate of interest. In the financial market the personal savings of consumers are the ultimate source of supply.

We demand the use of money for home mortgages, consumer credit, and personal bank loans. But the main demand for "rented money" comes from American industry with its requirement for funds to invest in new products, modern plant and machinery, and working capital in order to keep production running efficiently. Thus we are all participants in the financial markets, as the following narrative will help to illustrate.

THE SUPPLY OF FUNDS: JIM SMITH

Jim Smith worked his way through college. Each summer he was employed in an aircraft factory near Los Angeles, and he put as much money as he could into his savings account at his local bank. During the summer he earned more money than he needed; he saved and his account grew. By the end of each summer the bank owed him money, that is, it owed him the amount that had accumulated in his account. During the school year at college, Jim spent more money than he could earn despite having a part-time job, financial assistance from home, and a modest scholarship. His savings account would dwindle to zero by the end of the second semester of each year. By the end of his final year, Jim actually owed the bank money on a student loan, which he agreed to repay in monthly installments when he started a full-time job. Jim did not think of it at the time, but when he was in college he participated in the financial market by borrowing and lending through his bank.

Toward the end of his senior year, Jim was visited by a life insurance salesman who knew Jim's father. Jim agreed to buy insurance, making his mother the initial beneficiary. The monthly premiums would begin when Jim started his first full-time job after leaving college. The policy not only insured Jim's life but also included a long-term savings plan that, together with accumulated interest, would provide Jim with a lump sum when the policy matured.

When Jim left college, he went to work as a management trainee at the aircraft manufacturing company. During the first year, things were a little tight financially, as he needed to buy a car to get to work, and he had life insurance premiums to pay, to say nothing of the cost of food, rent, and clothing, and the repayment of his student loan. Also, the company made deductions from Jim's salary every month, not only for taxes and Social Security contributions but also for a company-sponsored pension plan. For every dollar Jim put into the pension program, the company added two. Jim was aware that the money accumulating in the pension fund was professionally managed and invested in stocks and bonds traded in the financial market. For his car, Jim borrowed money from a local finance company. After a year, however, he was beginning to accumulate cash at the bank again. He thought he might need the money for postgraduate study at a business school a few years later.

The financial market had served Jim very well. In his undergraduate days, when he was earning more money than he was spending during the summers, he was able to put his surplus into the bank where it would earn interest. Later when he needed the money for college, he could withdraw it without fuss. When he required more money than he actually had in his account, the additional money was provided by the bank through a loan. Other people's savings thereby were made available to him by the bank, and for this he was the one who paid the interest. His bank acted as a go-between or **financial intermediary.** Without the help of a financial intermediary in providing funds when they were most needed Jim might not have been able to complete his undergraduate education.

After Jim left college, his contact with financial intermediaries broadened somewhat when he made arrangements for life insurance, a pension, and an automobile loan. In each case, the savings of many thousands of individuals were invested in the life insurance company, the pension fund, the finance company, and the bank. These funds then could be reinvested by these intermediaries in loans to corporations and to individuals like Jim.

Jim did go to business school four years later. The money he had saved added to a large bank loan paid for two years of an M.B.A. program. Jim became a high-salaried management consultant after graduation and quickly repaid his student loans. Still a bachelor, Jim had surplus funds to invest. At business school Jim had become very interested in finance. He was aware that bank deposits represented one of the safer investments that could be made in the financial market, but that if one could afford to take greater risks, higher rates of return were possible (but not guaranteed) elsewhere.

As a bachelor who was able to accept risks, he was willing to put part of his accumulating savings into the stock market. Jim approached an old friend from business school days who was now working for a well-known firm of stockbrokers that were members of the New York Stock Exchange. Jim hoped that his friend would help him to choose some sound investments and to make the necessary transactions for him on the Exchange. If Jim invested $10,000 in different stocks, he could expect to receive dividends paid out of the companies' earnings and also to enjoy capital gains in the form of rising stock prices.

Jim knew the risks of investing in stocks. In bad times dividend payments can be smaller than expected. Worse still, stock prices can actually go down. If he held stocks in sound companies long enough, though, he figured he could expect to earn more money in dividends and capital gains than he would receive if he left the money in a bank deposit account. Jim began reading the *Wall Street Journal* and *Barron's Weekly* regularly and accumulated a portfolio of stocks in twenty different companies. Jim's father died, leaving Jim's mother a modest portfolio of stocks and government bonds, and Jim was able to advise his mother on some of her investments.

Eventually, however, Jim's consulting work absorbed more of his time, and he became less active in the market. He then advised his mother to put her money into a mutual fund, and he did the same. The mutual fund invested funds from people such as Jim and his mother in a wide variety of stocks. When they purchased shares in a mutual fund, Jim and Mrs. Smith bought a proportion of a professionally managed portfolio of stocks, thus releasing Jim from the time-consuming job of following the stock market. Now, he only had to follow the price of their shares in the mutual fund to know how well their investments were doing.

Jim was already thirty when he and Connie decided to marry. He sold his mutual fund shares because he no longer was willing to accept the risks of stock market investment. He wanted to be sure of the money for a down payment on a house. While Jim and Connie were still looking for a house, Jim put the money that he realized from the sale of his mutual fund shares into a money market fund where he knew that it would be invested in safe short-term government securities such as Treasury bills.

Jim and Connie visited several savings and loan associations to find out which one would offer them a mortgage at the lowest interest rate, and they negotiated a thirty-year mortgage for the money they needed. Jim and Connie's future seemed assured, provided that they continued to meet their mortgage payments.

Here we leave the story of the Smiths and their transactions in the financial market. Through their bank accounts, insurance, pension fund, and personal investments, Jim and Connie together with many millions of other people represent the ultimate source of the billions of dollars available for investment by American industry. We now pick up the thread of another story, the story of Frank Greenbuck.

THE DEMAND FOR FUNDS: FRANK GREENBUCK

At the time Jim Smith left business school, Frank Greenbuck was already fifteen years out of college. He was a certified public accountant (CPA) and treasurer of the family firm, a medium-sized manufacturer of farm machinery in the Midwest. His grandfather had founded the business, whose major stockholders were now his widowed mother, two uncles, and a number of cousins. Frank Greenbuck's job was to manage the company's funds. He had to ensure that the company never ran out of money in bad times as well as good, and that he could always find the cash needed for promising new commercial activities. While the company paid substantial dividends, it had been agreed that only about half the firm's earnings were to paid out in this way. The remaining earnings were retained and either plowed back into the business or invested by Frank in the financial market. The company's line of agricultural machinery sold well, although it was exposed to increasing competition from larger manufacturers. Often, Frank found that retained earnings were not adequate to meet the company's financing needs.

Frank Greenbuck maintained close relationships with some Chicago banks. So far he had experienced little trouble raising short-term loans for up to five years when required. When Frank felt he had too much short-term debt (which would have to be repaid relatively quickly), he negotiated a large fifteen-year loan with an insurance company. These measures enabled Frank to meet most of his company's financial requirements.

Five years earlier, Frank's Uncle John had initiated a product development program which was now coming to fruition. The most promising new product was a mechanized cultivator for home gardeners. Early prototypes had been well received, and indications were that the product would sell very well if the price were right. A sufficiently low price would require a high volume of production and a new factory to provide the necessary facilities. Promoting the product would require new channels of distribution for the company and national advertising.

Such a substantial new investment required a thorough financial appraisal. First, Frank and John together with the other managers had to estimate the investment required to initiate the cultivator project. This involved estimating funds required for making final product refinements, constructing and equipping a factory, hiring and training a work force, raising working capital, and financing the launch of the product in a national market. Then Frank and John together with the director of marketing projected annual sales of the cultivator for the next five years. The director of production and the company's management accountant assisted Frank in estimating the fixed and variable operating expenditures required by the projected annual physical volume of sales. Finally, the company's controller projected the effect of the project on the company's taxes. In this way, company officers estimated the net flow of cash into and out of the company each year in the project's life. Frank used an analytical technique called "discounted cash flow" to help him judge whether the expected financial benefits of the project would justify its cost. On this basis the home garden cultivator project looked very attractive.

Still, the required scale of investment called for more funds than the company could possibly generate internally from its existing operations. It was up to Frank as treasurer to see whether it would be feasible to obtain external financing for the cultivator project. Frank's Chicago banking friends raised some troubling questions. They considered that Frank's company already owed as much money as it could prudently afford to borrow. They would be willing to lend more money only if Frank could first raise some additional equity. Frank knew what this would mean: either existing stockholders (his family) would have to put more money into the business, or the company would have to find additional new stockholders. Finding additional equity externally would mean new stockholders who might elect nonfamily directors. Existing family stockholders needed to discuss some fundamental issues if the proposed home garden cultivator project were to be financed.

Frank discussed the financing problems with his Uncle John, who seemed undaunted. At a special meeting of the stockholders, John argued convincingly for the need for the new product before competition sapped the company's strength in existing products. Frank then explained why the company could not borrow more money and that additional equity financing would be required to undertake the cultivator project. It was clear from the start that the family stockholders could not or would not raise the required additional equity, and debate ensued about introducing outside stockholders. Frank estimated that the new stockholders would hold a minority of the voting shares and that the family could still control the company if they acted together. The stockholders voted in favor of issuing new shares to be sold to the public.

Frank sold the entire new issue of stock to a group of investment bankers in Chicago which then resold them to ("placed" them with) a number of insurance companies, pension funds, mutual funds, and individuals at a small margin of profit. These investors represented the **primary market** for the issue of stock and as such they constituted the new nonfamily stockholders in the company. Later some of them would sell their stocks in the **secondary market.** The secondary market for securities not listed on an organized exchange consists of dealers (usually stockbrokers) who keep an inventory of the stock and who stand ready to buy and sell the stock to the general public. This part of the secondary market is known as the over-the-counter market.

The proceeds of the new issue of stock provided the necessary financing for the cultivator project. Plans were still being prepared for the new factory when Frank discovered that he could buy an existing company in the next town that provided almost precisely the production facilities required. Frank and John believed that speed was essential if they were to get the jump on competition. By acquiring an existing company they could obtain almost immediately the necessary facilities and the required labor force for the garden cultivator. The alternative was to delay a year or two in order to plan and build a new factory and to hire, train, and organize a new work force. Frank and John convinced the other managers and, with the approval of the directors, they negotiated the purchase of the company. This action put the cultivator project at least one year ahead of schedule.

When the purchase was successfully negotiated, Frank's family was delighted to see the price of company stock leaping in response to the news. Some began to sell their shares quietly. Frank and John and the rest of the management persevered with the new project and other promising new projects. Frank looked forward to the day when his company's stock might be listed on the New York Stock Exchange.

That is all you need to know of the story of Frank Greenbuck. As a company traeasurer, Frank Greenbuck is one source of the demand for funds in the financial market. In his personal life, Frank Greenbuck is a modest supplier of funds himself through his bank accounts, pension fund, insurance, and his personal investments, just like many others.

The Structure of the Financial Market

The stories of Jim and Connie Smith and Frank Greenbuck illustrate the relationships between the financial market and individuals. They refer to many parts of the financial market, some of which we will describe in more detail in this book. In particular, we shall expand upon those elements of the market that most affect the financial management of companies. For now, let us provide you with an introduction to the structure of the financial market.

Figure 2.1 illustrates the role of intermediaries in the structure of the financial market. The figure shows relationships between savers, intermediaries, companies, and real investment in commercial projects such as new plant and equipment. An intermediary serves as a crucial collection point for the savings of very many individuals and companies. The intermediary may be a commercial bank, an insurance company, or a pension fund. Its role requires it not only to combine the savings of many investors but also, as custodian of their funds, to invest wisely on their behalf. The investments take the form of short- and intermediate-term loans (by commercial banks), long-term loans (by insurance companies), and investment in company stocks (by insurance companies, pension funds, and mutual funds). The intermediary bears the costs of obtaining and analyzing information about possible investments, negotiating loan contracts, and constructing balanced portfolios of investments that minimize risks for a given return or maximize returns for a given risk. Intermediaries take advantage of the large amounts

Figure 2.1   *Role of financial intermediaries*

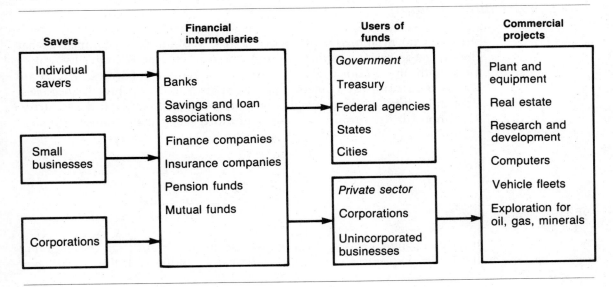

of funds at their disposal and thereby obtain economies of scale from investment. The intermediary helps savers to diversify their risks, because the intermediary's investments are spread across a number of companies.

The intermediary accepts the deposits of many savers, borrowing for different periods at different rates of interest, thus combining funds that can be lent to or invested in companies. The companies in turn invest the funds in commercial activities that they believe to be profitable, for example, building factories or researching new products. The commercial activities generate cash flows that can be used to make dividend and interest payments and to repay loans to the intermediaries. Ultimately, the arrows reverse themselves in Figure 2.1 as dividend and interest payments are made and loans are repaid.

Because there are many intermediaries, and because a company can afford to choose its source of funds, the financial market is very competitive. Intermediaries must exploit economies of scale in order to offer the lowest interest rates to companies, while at the same time paying the highest possible interest rates to savers in order to attract funds. On the other hand, companies sell in product markets that are usually less competitive than the financial market. By obtaining capital at a fair price in the competitive financial market and obtaining favorable product prices in less competitive product markets, a company can try to make profits that not only repay the cost of funds but also provide additional income to be used either for increased dividends to stockholders or for further investment in the business.

Debt and Equity Claims

When the financial market provides a large sum of funds to a company, what does it get in return? In the long run, the market expects to get its money back with an additional appropriate rate of return. Securities, which are claims on a company's assets, can be classified into two broad categories: debt and equity. A claim takes the form of a contract usually called a **security.** Common stocks, corporate bonds, and mortgages are all examples of such securities.

DEBT

If the company takes out a loan, it gives the lender a signed agreement giving the lender a specified claim on the company's future cash flows. The loan agreement is called a **note** or a **bond.** If the loan is secured by property, it is called a **mortgage.** These claims are worth money, and many of them can be bought and sold in the financial market. They are worth money because they entitle the holder to repayment of the loan principal according to a schedule and to regular interest payments (called coupon payments) specified in the loan contract. The original amount borrowed is called the loan's face value or par value. These claims by debtholders must be honored, for if the company fails to meet all its commitments to debtholders, or defaults, the company can be declared bankrupt. If the company becomes bankrupt, some or all of its assets can be sold to raise the funds necessary to meet the debtholders' claims. The legal powers that debtholders possess in the event of default make lending a less risky form of investment for a debtholder than the purchase of common stocks.

The least risky securities of all are United States government **Treasury bills.** They are the least risky because they are short-term claims on the United States Treasury (which has a license to print money) with maturities of up to one year. Of somewhat greater risk are United States government bonds with long maturities, for example, up to thirty years. One reason why the longer-term claims are more risky is that if market interest rates should go up, the market prices of these bonds go down. Of slightly greater risk are debt obligations or securities issued by United States government agencies other than the Treasury or by states and municipalities. State and municipality obligations are more risky, because default is technically possible (for example, consider the near bankruptcy of New York City in the 1970s).

EQUITY

When you buy **common stock** or **equity** in a company, you also have a claim. Common stock gives the stockholder a claim on any dividends that are declared, the claim being proportionate to the number of shares that is held. If the company should be liquidated, the stockholders also have a proportionate claim on the proceeds of the sale of the assets, but only after claims of debtholders and other creditors (including the Internal Revenue Service) have been paid off. If the company is taken over, it is the stockholders who have to agree to the change of control. Thus the stockholders' claim potentially is very valuable, and stocks command a high price in the market when a company's prospects appear favorable. Because the stockholders' claim is paid last after the debtholders' claims, however, common stocks lose their value much more quickly than bonds if the company's prospects become unfavorable. Thus common stocks are relatively risky to their holders compared with debt securities.

The Relationship Between Risk and Return in the Financial Market

On the whole, participants in the financial market are considered to be risk averse. This means that they prefer bearing less risk to more risk. Risk aversion also means that if investors are to be persuaded to hold high-risk securities as well as low-risk securities, they must expect a higher reward or risk premium to induce them to accept the higher risks. At the lowest-risk end of the scale, the reward is relatively clear because it takes the form of a stated interest rate on a debt security such as Treasury bills, where default is virtually impossible. Toward the high-risk end of the scale are dividends and capital gains (or capital losses) on common stock. The combination of dividends and capital gains anticipated on common stock can be expressed as an expected percentage return per year. Such an expected rate of return on common stock must be somewhat greater than the interest rates obtainable on less risky securities if common stock is to attract buyers. Also, as stocks of some sorts of companies are more risky than stocks of others, investors must be able to expect higher rates of return from the more risky stocks. Otherwise, they would not be willing to hold the more risky stocks in their portfolios along with the less risky stocks and bonds.

Figure 2.2 illustrates the relationship between risk and anticipated rates of return on investment in various debt and equity securities. Debt is less risky than equity, and Treasury bills are the least risky form of debt. Therefore, Figure 2.2 shows Treasury bills at the bottom end of the scale of both risk and expected rates of return. Also identified on the scale is a point representing the average common stock. The risk is much higher for equity or common stocks, and so must be the anticipated rate of return on investment. The slope of the line joining the two points is a reflection of the price placed on risk in the financial market.[1] If the expected rate of return on common stock were more than investors required to compensate them for the extra risk, investors would buy equities, and the price of stocks would be bid higher. If stock prices are too high, the anticipated rate of return on an investment in stocks then would be too low to compensate for risk. Investors would sell stocks, and the price of stocks would fall. Only when the price of stocks is at a level where the anticipated rate of return on investment in the stock just pays the market price of risk will investors become indifferent to the choice between Treasury bills and stocks.

The line that joins the two points in Figure 2.2 is called the **capital market line.** Some of the other securities that may be found on the market line in Figure 2.2 (in increasing order of risk) are Treasury bonds, corporate bonds, and corporate preferred equity. The market line is very important in finance because it provides a bench mark for managers to use when determining

---

[1]For example, if the line were horizontal the market price of risk would be zero. The steeper the slope of the line the higher the market's required reward for bearing risk.

Figure 2.2   *Relationship between risk and anticipated rates of return on investment in debt and in equity*

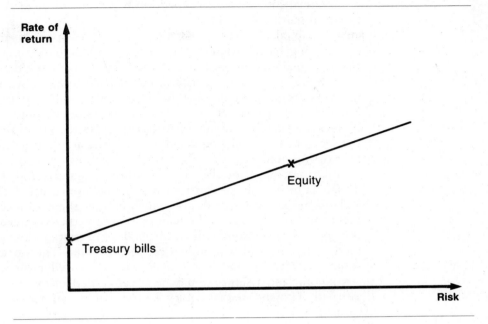

how high a rate of return they should try to earn when investing in risky commercial activities. If the rate of return that can be anticipated from an investment of funds in a commercial activity (for example, a new factory) is below the market line (given its risk), then the funds are better left invested in the capital market.

This raises some important questions. How can the anticipated rate of return on a commercial activity be estimated? How do you measure the risk of investment in a security or in a commercial activity? These questions are among the central issues that we will deal with in subsequent chapters.

Summary

Individual savers provide the supply of funds to the financial market through bank deposits, savings accounts, insurance, pensions, and personal investment. Although individual savers also borrow, the main demand for funds comes from American industry and from federal, state, and municipal governments. Financial intermediaries such as banks, pension funds, insurance companies, and mutual funds gather the savings of a multitude of small investors into the millions of dollars that can be lent to and invested in commercial enterprises. Competition between intermediaries helps make the financial market efficient.

The capital market consists of those sectors of the financial market that deal in long-term corporate finance. The capital market may be divided into primary markets and secondary markets. In primary markets, companies raise money by selling securities to investment bankers who then resell them to investors such as pension funds or individuals. In secondary markets, holders of securities sell them to other investors through a stock exchange or in the over-the-counter securities markets. No new funds are raised in the secondary markets; outstanding securities are merely exchanged for cash by existing holders.

Securities represent claims on a company's assets and future cash flows. These claims may be categorized as either debt or equity. Debtholders receive a claim in exchange for funds, which entitles them to receive interest payments and repayment of the loan on a contractually agreed schedule. If the borrower defaults on payment, the lender can try to obtain payment through the legally enforced bankruptcy of the borrower. The stockholders' claim is subordinate to that of debtholders. The stockholders have a right only to any income and assets that may be left after all debtholders' claims have been satisfied. This means that equity is more risky than debt to the holder of the security.

Because equity is more risky than debt, investors must be able to anticipate a higher average rate of return on investment in equity than on investment in debt. The difference between the expected rate of return on equity and the interest rates obtainable on debt depends upon how the market prices risk. The market price of risk provides a guideline that managers can use when deciding whether the anticipated rate of return from investment in a commercial activity is sufficient to justify its risk. Only if the commercial activity provides a rate of return that is greater than that obtainable on financial securities of equivalent risk can we say that the activity is attractive or profitable.

Review Questions

1. Describe some reasons why individuals and companies use the financial markets.
2. From an investor's point of view, why is common stock riskier than bonds? From the company's point of view (and that of its stockholders), is common stock financing more or less risky than bond financing? Why?

3. Why might you expect common stocks to provide higher returns than Treasury bills?
4. What are the sources and uses of funds in the financial market?
5. Describe the different kinds of financial intermediaries in the market and what they do.
6. How can managers use the financial market to help them judge whether investment in a commercial activity will be profitable?

Appraising Investment Opportunities

One of the most important functions of financial management is the financial analysis and appraisal of proposed investments in assets and new commercial activities. The object of investment appraisal is to determine whether such an investment is worth more to the firm and its stockholders than it actually costs. The basic tool for the analysis of investment opportunities is discounted cash flow. The object of discounted cash flow is to determine what value would be attached by the financial market to the cash flows that a proposed investment is expected to generate. In the next five chapters we shall show you how to define a project and its after-tax future cash flows. We shall describe the difficulties that arise in the practical application of discounted cash flow methods in project appraisal and how inflation affects the analysis. Most importantly, we show how to include strategic factors in the financial analysis and appraisal of a proposed commercial activity. Since discounted cash flow is the basic tool of financial analysis, the skills that you develop in working with the five chapters in Part II are essential to an understanding of the material in the remainder of the text.

Discounted Cash Flow: The Basic Tool of Financial Analysis

The first task of financial management that we shall consider is financial analysis. One purpose of financial analysis is to assess whether an investment in a proposed commercial activity is likely to be profitable from the point of view of the stockholders. Investments in commercial activities are called **capital projects.** They usually involve the purchase of a physical asset, such as a machine or a new factory. A capital project may also involve investment in a less tangible asset, such as a new product or an advertising campaign. One important characteristic of a capital project is that cash is paid out now or in the near term in order to obtain more cash subsequently. In this chapter we shall show how to estimate the value of a project's future cash flows to the corporation. Using discounted cash flow methods, we shall show how to determine whether a project is worth more to the corporation than it costs.

The Capital Budgeting Process

Companies usually follow a capital budgeting procedure for allocating funds to capital projects. The company budgets funds for capital investment in advance for its individual divisions. Budgets are established on the basis of plans for growth in different markets and in response to emerging opportunities for exploiting new products and for reducing costs.

Larger projects, such as chemical plants, are anticipated in budgets often five or more years in advance of the actual expenditure, but funds are also budgeted for smaller investments (machine tools, for example) about which little may be known until the time when they are proposed for formal approval.

In large companies the capital budgets may be drawn up by a high-level capital appropriations committee and then approved by the board of directors. Even if a project can be included in a budget, the money will not be spent until the capital project has been approved formally at the appropriate level of management. For example, one company may permit plant managers to approve projects costing up to $10,000. More costly projects must go to the divisional manager for final approval. Projects costing $50,000 or more must be approved at the board level after having been approved at the lower levels. A formal project proposal report may have to include analysis of how the project fits in with the company's overall commercial strategy, as well as financial analysis.

Capital Market Opportunity Costs

Anyone with spare cash can invest in securities in the financial markets. This opportunity to invest in the financial market is available to corporations as well as to their stockholders. If you were a stockholder in a company and if you could get, say, a 15 percent return each year on investment in securities, would you want your company to invest your money in a capital project that gives a return of less than 15 percent? Surely not, assuming the capital project has the same risk as the alternative investment in securities. You would prefer that the company use stockholders' funds to invest in securities at 15 percent or, alternatively, to pay the money out as a dividend to you the stockholder. Then you could make the investment in securities for yourself, instead of the company investing your money in capital projects that yield lower rates of return.

The question is, how is the company to calculate and compare returns on an investment in a capital project with an alternative investment in the financial market? The major technique that is used in industry to make this comparison is **discounted cash flow** (DCF) analysis. DCF methods can be used in two ways for this purpose. First, you can find out whether the same cash flow income that a project is expected to generate could be obtained with a smaller cash outlay by investing in financial securities that are of the same risk as the project. Second, you can use DCF methods to find out whether a capital project can be expected to earn a higher rate of return than can be obtained by investing in securities of comparable risk. In this sense, the rates of return that can be earned in the financial market represent an **opportunity cost** to investment in capital projects, that is, if cash is invested in the capital project it cannot be invested elsewhere to earn a return. This return in the alternative financial security is the opportunity cost. The two DCF approaches are equivalent and we shall describe both in this chapter.

Actually, discounting is the reverse of the more familiar concept of compounding interest, so we shall describe how compound interest calculations may be done and then describe how cash flows can be discounted. In all subsequent calculations we have used a calculator whose calculations are based upon ten digits. If the reader's calculations are based on a different number of digits there may be small differences in the last digit of a calculation.

COMPOUND INTEREST

In order to make comparisons between capital projects and investments in the financial markets, it will be helpful if we first examine the returns on investments in the financial market. Let us consider some examples.

What happens to a dollar that is invested in an instrument in the financial market (for example, a bank savings account) that earns, say, 10 percent interest per year: How does it grow? Table 3.1 shows how a dollar invested at 10 percent interest grows each year for three years. Column 1 labeled "End of year" in the table shows the elapsed time in years. The period 0 means zero elapsed time or *now,* period 1 means one year later, when the first interest payment is received. Period 2 means one year after that. Now look at the second column. In period 0 $1.00 is invested. After one year $1.00 will have earned 10 percent and will have $0.10 added to it. Thus the

Table 3.1　　　　*Growth of $1.00 invested at 10%*

End of year	Interest earned	Total principal
0		$1.00
	0.10 × 1.00	0.10
1		$1.10
	0.10 × 1.10	0.11
2		$1.21
	0.10 × 1.21	0.121
3		$1.331

initial investment of $1.00 will have grown to a future value of

$$\$1.00 \times (1 + 0.10) = \$1.10$$

We multiply the original investment of $1.00 by a factor of one plus the interest rate (expressed as a decimal fraction), as we expect to have our original investment plus interest at the end of the period. After another year (period 2) the $1.10 will earn another 10 percent. Thus, $0.11 will be added to the $1.10 and the sum invested will have grown to

$$\$1.10 \times (1 + 0.10) = \$1.21$$

Each year the amount of capital will grow in this way, by a factor of $(1 + 0.10) = 1.10$.

It will be useful for us to have a more direct way of calculating the future value of a dollar. At the end of the second year, the original dollar will have been increased twice by the same factor:

$$\$1.00 \times (1.10) \times (1.10) = \$1.21$$

or,

$$\$1.00 \times (1.10)^2 = \$1.21$$

The factor $(1.10)^2$ is called the "two-year compound factor at 10 percent." **Compound factors** can be used to show how much any sum of money will grow when invested at a given interest rate. In general, a compound factor F for N years at $R \times 100$ percent is given by the formula:

$$F_{N,R} = (1 + R)^N$$

where R is the interest rate expressed in decimal form. A dollar invested for two years at 10 percent (or $R = 0.10$), for example, would grow by the factor

$$F_{2,0.10} = (1.10)^2$$
$$= 1.21$$

Going back to the example in Table 3.1, we see that $1.00 will grow to $1.331 in three years. We could have obtained this figure more easily with a three-year compound factor:

$$\$1.00 \times F_{3,0.10} = \$1.00 \times (1.10)^3$$
$$= \$1.331$$

In Table 3.2 we have tabulated compound factors for years 1 through 10 at interest rates of 5, 10, and 15 percent using the formula $F_{N,R} = (1 + R)^N$.

Table 3.2 Compound factors (F)

End of year (N)	Interest rate (R)		
	5%	10%	15%
0	1.00000	1.00000	1.00000
1	1.05000	1.10000	1.15000
2	1.10250	1.21000	1.32250
3	1.15762	1.33100	1.52088
4	1.21551	1.46410	1.74901
5	1.27628	1.61051	2.01136
6	1.34010	1.77156	2.31306
7	1.40710	1.94872	2.66002
8	1.47746	2.14359	3.05902
9	1.55133	2.35795	3.51788
10	1.62889	2.59374	4.04556

Note: $F_{N,R} = (1 + R)^N$

A more extensive table of compound factors (The Future Value of $1.00) has been provided in Appendix A at the end of the book. Of course, if we can obtain the future value of a dollar, we can also determine the future value of any sum of money by using compound factors. We simply multiply the sum invested by the appropriate compound factor.

Another way of analyzing the return on an investment that is closely related to using compound factors is the discounted cash flow approach.

DISCOUNTED CASH FLOW

We have shown how much cash a dollar invested today will generate at any time in the future by using compound factors. We shall also be able to answer another important question by using compound factors in a different way: How much money would we have to invest today to generate a dollar of income in the future? Table 3.3 helps us to find the answer.

Where Table 3.2 showed how $1.00 grows when invested in the financial market at a 10 percent rate of return, Table 3.3 shows how other sums will grow if invested at 10 percent. We have chosen sums that grow to exactly $1.00 after the end of a given number of years. For example, in the third column of Table 3.3, you see that an initial amount of $0.82645 invested at 10 percent is required to produce $1.00 at the end of two years:

$0.82645 \times (1.10)^2 = $1.00

Table 3.3   *Compound growth of a capital sum invested at 10%*

| | Initial sum invested | | |
End of year	$0.90909	$0.82645	$0.75131
0	0.90909	0.82645	0.75131
1	1.00000	0.90909	0.82645
2		1.00000	0.90909
3			1.00000

In the final column you see that an initial investment of $0.75131 invested at 10 percent is required to produce $1.00 at the end of three years:

$$\$0.75131 \times (1.10)^3 = \$1.00$$

Sums of money invested in period "0" that will compound to $1.00 in the future are of special interest and are called the **present values of a dollar.** The present value (at 10 percent) of $1.00 to be received at the end of three years is $0.75131, or just over $0.75. Similarly, the present value (at 10 percent) of $1.00 to be received in just two years is $0.82645, because that is the sum invested at 10 percent annually that will grow to $1.00 in two years. The present value of a future cash flow of $1.00 is a very important figure, because it tells us what each dollar of future cash flow is worth now.

For example, we can say that $2.00 to be received in two years' time has a present value of $2.00 × 0.82645 = $1.6529 when discounted at 10 percent. How did we calculate the present values shown in Table 3.3? How did we know, for example, that $0.75131 is the present value of (or would compound to) $1.00 in three years at an interest rate of 10 percent? We used the following formula:

Present Value × Compound Factor = Future Value

Solving for the present value we get:

$$\text{Present Value} = \text{Future Value} \times \frac{1}{\text{Compound Factor}}$$

For example, the three-year compound factor at 10 percent is given by

$$F_{3,0.10} = (1.10)^3 = 1.33100$$

Thus the present value of $1.00 to be received in three years can be found as follows:

$$\text{Present Value} = \$1.00 \times \frac{1}{1.33100}$$

$$= \$0.75131$$

You can find the present value of any future cash flow in a similar way using your calculator. Simply multiply the future value by the inverse of the compound factor (which is one over the compound factor). The inverse of the compound factor is called the **discount factor** or **present value factor**. In the previous example the discount factor was (1/1.33100) or 0.75131.

Table 3.4 tabulates discount factors for years 1 through 10 at interest rates of 5, 10, and 15 percent. The table is based on the formula

$$P_{N,R} = \frac{1}{(1 + R)^N}$$

where $P_{N,R}$ represents the present value of \$1.00 to be received after N years when the rate of interest is $R \times 100$ percent. You can verify that each number in Table 3.4 is equal to one divided by the corresponding compound factor in Table 3.2. For example, the discount factor for a cash flow occurring at the end of year 5 at an interest rate of 15 percent is 0.49718. You can calculate

Table 3.4   *Discount factors: present value (P) of \$1.00 paid at the end of N years*

End of year (*N*)	Interest rate (*R* × 100%)		
	5%	10%	15%
1	0.95238	0.90909	0.86957
2	0.90703	0.82645	0.75614
3	0.86384	0.75131	0.65752
4	0.82270	0.68301	0.57175
5	0.78353	0.62092	0.49718
6	0.74622	0.56447	0.43233
7	0.71068	0.51316	0.37594
8	0.67684	0.46651	0.32690
9	0.64461	0.42410	0.28426
10	0.61391	0.38554	0.24718

Note: $P_{N,R} = 1/(1 + R)^N$

this number simply by taking the reciprocal of the compound factor for five years at 15 percent. From Table 3.2 you know that the compound factor is 2.01136. Consequently, the corresponding discount factor is

$$\frac{1}{2.01136} = 0.49718$$

A more extensive set of discount factors is presented in the tables called Present Value of $1.00 in Appendix B at the end of the book.

Discount factors represent a very powerful tool. Using discount factors, you can calculate the present worth of a future series of cash flows generated by a capital project. You multiply each future cash flow by the appropriate discount factor and add up the present values of all the cash flows. With this information you should be able to say whether a project is worth more than it actually costs.

What Is a Project Worth?

A capital project involves investment of funds at one or more times for the purpose of generating cash at future times. The purpose of discounted cash flow analysis is to determine whether the project is worth more to the company than it costs. In other words, we ask: is the discounted present value of the cash that will be coming in greater than the discounted present value of the cash that will be going out?

The discounted present value of a future cash flow is found simply by multiplying the cash flow by an appropriate discount factor. The present worth of a sequence of future cash flows is the sum of the present values of the individual cash flows. A project is worth the sum of the discounted net cash flow benefits that result from investing in the project. If the present value of the project's net operating cash flows is more than the present value of its investment expenditures, the project is said to have a positive **net present value.**

Let us consider an example of a capital investment in a machine tool, summarized in Table 3.5. The machine tool costs $1,000 and will be worthless at the end of five years. The reason you would consider buying the machine tool is that it could be used to manufacture a product that would increase the level of annual sales by $800 during the next five years. However, the cash costs of the additional sales (and additional taxes) will be $500 per year. Therefore, the net cash flow benefits given in the final column of the table would be $300 per year. What is it worth to have a net cash flow income of $300 per year for five years? If this net cash flow income is worth less than the $1,000 cost of the project, it would not be profitable. We can make this comparison by using the discounted present value method.

Table 3.5   *Cash flows for an investment in a machine tool*

End of year	Cash cost of investment	Cash sales (Dollars)	Cash cost of sales and taxes (Dollars)	Net cash flow (Dollars)
0	−1,000			−1,000
1		800	−500	300
2		800	−500	300
3		800	−500	300
4		800	−500	300
5		800	−500	300

In Table 3.6 we show the project's cash flows in the second column. To each cash flow we have assigned a discount factor in the third column depending upon the timing of the cash flow. The discount factors are based on a discount rate of 10 percent. The choice of discount rate naturally should reflect the rate of return that could be obtained in the financial market on securities of similar risk to the project. The reason, as we have said, is that management always has the option of investing its cash in the financial market rather than buying such assets as machine tools. (Of course, the choice of discount rate depends upon the risk of the capital project, which we shall discuss in detail in Chapters 9 and 10.)

Table 3.6   *Discounting a project's cash flow at 10 percent*

End of year	Net cash flow (Dollars)	×	Discount factor	=	Present value of cash flow (Dollars)	
0	−1,000	×	1.00000	=		−1,000
1	300	×	0.90909	=	272.73	
2	300	×	0.82645	=	247.94	
3	300	×	0.75131	=	225.39	
4	300	×	0.68301	=	204.90	
5	300	×	0.62092	=	186.28	
			Total present value		1,137.24	1,137.24
			Net present value			137.24

In the fourth column we show the discounted cash flows, which were obtained by multiplying the net cash flow in column 2 by the discount factor in column 3. The sum of the discounted present values of the cash flow benefits of the project is $1,137.24. The fifth column compares the project's present value of net cash inflows of $1,137.24 with its cost of $1,000.00. You find that the project's present value exceeds its cost by $137.24. This difference is called the project's net present value. If the net present value is positive, the project is profitable because it is estimated to cost less than a comparable investment in the financial market. A comparable investment in the financial market in this case would return 10 percent and at that rate would have a zero net present value. As a result, it is more profitable to invest in the positive NPV project than to give the cash back to investors who could invest the funds at a zero NPV in the financial market.

Annuities

For many investment and financing transactions, such as leases, the cash flows are equal in some or all periods. A set of cash flows that are equal in each and every period is called an **annuity.** If the analyst must value these cash flows manually (rather than, say, with a pocket calculator), he or she can use annuity factors as a shortcut.

Table 3.7 illustrates two ways of calculating the present worth of an annuity. The first way of calculating the present worth, with which you are already familiar, is to obtain the present value of each individual cash flow and then to add up all the individual present values as is done in column 4 of the table. The total present worth of the annuity of $100 for three years at 10 percent is found to be $248.685. However, because all the cash flows for an annuity are the same, another more convenient method of calculation is possible. In column 3, we simply add up all the *discount factors,* obtaining

Table 3.7   *Present worth of an annuity calculated in two ways*

End of year	Cash flow (Dollars)		Discount factor		Present value (Dollars)
0					
1	100	×	0.90909	=	90.909
2	100	×	0.82645	=	82.645
3	100	×	0.75131	=	75.131
	100	×	2.48685	=	248.685

a total of 2.48685 as shown in the last line of the table. In the last line of the table we also show that the present worth of the annuity is 100 × 2.48685 = 248.685, which is the same result we obtained with the first method. The total 2.48685 of the discount factors is called the annuity factor for three years at 10 percent. An **annuity factor** is a cumulative sum of discount factors as Table 3.7 shows. You can use a table of annuity factors to obtain the present worth of a set of equal cash flows in only one step, whereas using discount factors requires several steps, one for each cash flow.

The annuity factor is the sum of the present value factors for all the years in which the annuity is received. The annuity factor is usually represented by the symbol $A_{N,R}$, where the subscript N denotes the number of periods in which the annuity is received, and R denotes the discount rate or required rate of return. For the example in Table 3.7,

$$A_{3,0.10} = 2.48685$$

Annuity factors at 5, 10, and 15 percent for annuities lasting up to ten years are given in Table 3.8. You can verify that the annuity factors in Table 3.8 are merely cumulative sums of the discount factors given in Table 3.4. (A more extensive set of annuity factors is provided in the tables called Present Value of $1.00 per Period in Appendix C at the end of the book.) The annuity factor can also be calculated using the formula derived in Appendix 3.1.

The project cash flows in Table 3.5 are an example of an annuity. You can find the total present value in one step by using an annuity table. Appendix C gives the five-year annuity factor at 10 percent as 3.79078,

Table 3.8   *Annuity factors: present value* (A) *of $1.00 per year*

End of year annuity is paid	Interest rate *(R)*		
	5%	10%	15%
1	0.95238	0.90909	0.86957
2	1.85941	1.73554	1.62571
3	2.72325	2.48685	2.28323
4	3.54595	3.16986	2.85498
5	4.32947	3.79078	3.35216
6	5.07569	4.35526	3.78448
7	5.78637	4.86842	4.16042
8	6.46321	5.33492	4.48732
9	7.10782	5.75902	4.77159
10	7.72173	6.14456	5.01877

which multiplied by $300.00 yields a present value of $300 × 3.79078 = $1,137.23. Subtracting the initial capital outlay of $1,000, we obtain the net present value of $137.23 in only one step.

In this calculation we have used a formula that we will use frequently throughout the book:

Present Value of an Annuity = Annual Cash Flow
$$\times \text{ Annuity Factor for } N \text{ Years at Rate } R$$
$$PV = C \times A_{N,R}$$

Consider the example of a company that wishes to know the break-even rental payment for a machine tool that it could either rent (lease) or buy. The machine tool costs $100,000 after tax and has an economic life of five years. Management is considering renting the machine tool for five years instead of buying it. Before asking for rental quotations, management wishes to have some idea as to the maximum annual rental payment that the company should pay, given the alternative of purchasing the machine tool for $100,000. The break-even rental payment can be found by using the previous formula for the present value of an annuity.

What set of annual lease payments (that is, what set of annual cash flows) when discounted at rate R will equal the purchase price of the asset? Inasmuch as the price of the asset equals its present value in a break-even situation, by definition, we can rewrite the formula as:

Purchase Price of the Asset = Break-even Annual Rental Payment
$$\times \text{ Annuity Factor for } N \text{ Years at Rate } R$$

Let us assume that the annual interest rate appropriate for discounting the rental payment is 15 percent. Thus,

$100,000 = Break-even Annual Rental Payment × 3.35216

where 3.3516 is the five-year annuity factor using an interest rate of 15 percent, and $100,000 is the purchase price of the machine tool. We can solve for the annual rental payments by rearranging the equation:

$$\text{Break-even Annual Rental Payment} = \frac{100,000}{3.35216}$$

$$= \$29,831.51$$

Thus, an after-tax annual rental payment of $29,831.51 would make renting break even with purchasing the asset for $100,000 cash. At a larger annual rental payment purchase would be preferred. Often you can use annuity factors in this way to analyze contracts involving equal payments for a given number of periods.

Frequently, cash flows may change in such a way that they can be treated as a combination of annuities. Table 3.9 is an illustration of such a cash flow stream. An annuity of $100 is to be received for three years. Subsequently, an annuity of $200 is to be received for the following two years. The purchase price of the annuity is $350. What is the net present value of these two annuities? Remember that annuity factors are cumulative present value factors, as you can verify by comparing the annuity factors in Appendix C with the present values given in Appendix B. Therefore, you can obtain the annuity factor for years 4 and 5 by subtracting the annuity factor for three years from the annuity factor for five years as follows:

Five-year annuity factor ($A_{5,0.10}$)   3.79078

Minus

Three-year annuity factor ($A_{3,0.10}$)   2.48685

Equals   1.30393

The annuity for the first three periods can be calculated in the usual way with the three-period annuity factor 2.48685.

Perpetuities and Growth

Let us consider the special case of an annuity with an infinite life. An equal sum of money to be paid in each period forever is called a **perpetuity.** Perpetuities are easy to value. To see why this is so, consider the answer to

Table 3.9   *Cash flows treated as a combination of annuities*

End of year	Net cash flow (Dollars)	Annuity factor at 10%	Present value (Dollars)
0	−350	1.0000	−350.00
1	100		
2	100		
3	100	2.48685	248.69
4	200		
5	200	1.30393	260.79
		Net present value	159.48

the following question. At an interest rate of 10 percent, how much income would you receive every year (forever) from an investment of $1,000? The answer is obviously $100:

$$\$1,000 \times 0.10 = \$100$$

Now suppose we turn the question around. What is the value today of $100 to be received every year in perpetuity, if the relevant interest rate is 10 percent? The answer, of course, is $1,000, which can be found by rearranging the equation as follows:

$$\$1,000 = \$100/0.10$$

Thus the present value P of a perpetuity is equal to the sum C to be received per period divided by the discount rate R expressed as a decimal fraction:

$$P = \frac{C}{R}$$

For example, suppose that you are promised a perpetuity of $500 per year and that the interest rate on perpetuities is 15 percent. What price P should you be willing to pay for this income?

$$P = \$500.00/0.15$$

$$= \$3,333.33$$

The present value of the $500.00 perpetuity is $3,333.33, which is the amount you would have to pay if the interest rate on perpetuities were 15 percent.

A variation on the perpetuity formula involves perpetual growth. Suppose that the $500 annual income most recently received is expected to grow by a rate G of 5 percent per year (compounded) forever: How much would this income be worth when discounted at 15 percent? You can find the answer by subtracting the growth rate from the discount rate and treating the first period's cash flow as a perpetuity:

$$P = C\,(1 + G)/(R - G)$$

$$P = 500\,(1 + 0.05)/(0.15 - 0.05)$$

$$= 525/0.10$$

$$= \$5,250$$

These calculations are easy and make tables unnecessary, but they will work only when the growth rate is less than the discount rate. If the growth rate were greater than or equal to the discount rate, the value of the investment would be infinite, a price that you never encounter in financial markets. The growth form of the perpetuity formula will be useful when we discuss the valuation of companies and their securities in later chapters. A more formal derivation of these formulas is given in Appendix 3.1.

Quarterly, Monthly, and Continuous Discounting

Often it is desirable to discount cash flows at more frequent intervals than one year, because the cash flows may be paid out or received on a quarterly or monthly basis. If cash flows are received (and paid out) monthly, you must use a monthly discount rate in order to calculate the net present value of the project accurately. Frequently the financial analyst knows the annual discount rate and monthly cash flows and must convert the annual discount rate to a monthly rate.

Suppose that a company is offered a one-year loan of $1,000. The company is told that it will be charged an annual interest rate of 12 percent compounded quarterly. However, this means that the company will be charged 3 percent per quarter, which when reinvested at three-month intervals will compound to more than 12 percent per year. That is, each dollar borrowed will require interest equal to

$$\left(1 + \frac{\text{Annual Interest Rate}}{\text{Number of Times Compounded}}\right)^{\text{Number of times compounded}} - 1$$

$$= \text{Effective (or Equivalent) Annual Interest Rate}$$

$$\left(1 + \frac{0.12}{4}\right)^4 - 1 = (1 + 0.03)^4 - 1 = 0.12551$$

In other words, 12 percent compounded quarterly (or 3 percent per quarter) equals an effective annual interest rate of 12.551 percent. We can present the previous equation more formally:

$$R = \left(1 + \frac{r}{n}\right)^n - 1 \tag{3.1}$$

where r represents the quoted annual interest rate that is to be compounded n times per year, and R is the effective annual interest rate. Suppose, for example, that the bank was quoting 12 percent annual interest compounded weekly (or $\frac{1}{52}$ of 12 percent per week). Then the effective or equivalent annual rate is

$$R = \left(1 + \frac{0.12}{52}\right)^{52} - 1$$

$$= 0.12734$$

or 12.734 percent compared with only 12.551 percent for quarterly compounding. Using the same equation, the reader should be able to show on his or her calculator that for daily compounding the corresponding equivalent annual rate would be 12.747 percent.

   In principle, the bank could quote an annual interest rate compounded as often as its customer would accept. The number of times n that interest is compounded can be made infinite, and in this case we have what is called *continuous compounding*. If we let n go to infinity the above equation becomes

$$R = e^{rT} - 1 \tag{3.2}$$

where $e = 2.71828$ is (you may recall) the base of the natural logarithm, and T is the period for the effective or equivalent rate, which in our example is equal to one year. Thus an annual interest rate of 12 percent compounded continuously is equal to an equivalent annual interest rate given by

$$R = 2.71828^{0.12} - 1$$

$$= 0.12750$$

or 12.75 percent. You can't compound more frequently than that, so 12.75 percent is the most that the bank can earn annually on loans quoted at 12 percent.

   Frequently, we want to know what rate r compounded n times will equal a known equivalent annual interest rate R. For example, what compounded rate will amount to 12 percent? That is, we solve for r in equation (3.1):

$$r = n((1 + R)^{1/n} - 1) \tag{3.3}$$

   In the case of continuous compounding n goes to infinity, and from equation (3.2) we can solve for r (where $T = 1$):

$$e^r = (1 + R)$$

Taking the natural logarithm of both sides of the equation,

$$r = \ln(1 + R)$$

Suppose, for example, the equivalent annual interest rate R is equal to 12 percent, and we want to know the corresponding quarterly compounded rate $r/4$.

$$r = 4((1 + 0.12)^{1/4} - 1)$$

$$= 0.11495$$

or 11.495 percent (which is 2.874 percent per quarter). (We have raised 1.12 to the 0.25 power, which is easy to calculate on a good calculator.) You can see that this is the correct rate using equation (3.1) since

$$\left(1 + \frac{0.11495}{4}\right)^4 = (1 + 0.02874)^4$$

$$= 1.12$$

In other words, interest of 2.874 percent per quarter compounds to 12 percent per year.

If we let n go to infinity, the continuously compounded rate corresponding to an equivalent 12 percent per year is

$$r = \ln(1 + R)$$

$$= \ln(1.12)$$

$$= 0.1133287$$

or only 11.33287 percent compared with 11.495 percent using quarterly compounding. You can see that this result is correct for continuous compounding since

$$e^r = 1 + R$$

$$2.71828^{0.1133287} = 1.12$$

That is, an annual rate of interest of 11.33287 percent compounded continuously yields an equivalent 12 percent by the end of one year.

Analysts often make approximations by assuming that cash flows received, for example, at quarterly intervals are received at the end of the year. In fact, cash flows for most projects are received (or paid out) at more frequent intervals. Let us see what size of error is made by making such an approximation.

A project consists of an initial capital outlay of $100 and four quarterly cash inflows of $35 each. The annual discount rate for this project is 12 percent, and the quarterly rate $r/4$, using equation (3.3), is $(1.12)^{1/4} - 1 = 0.02874$. If the analyst discounts the cash flows on the exact date of receipt, the net present value is

$$NPV = -100 + \frac{35}{(1.02874)} + \frac{35}{(1.02874)^2} + \frac{35}{(1.02874)^3} + \frac{35}{(1.02874)^4}$$

$$= \$30.49$$

However, if, as an approximation, the sum of the four quarterly cash inflows is assumed to be received as one sum of $140 at the end of the year, the net present value is

$$NPV = -100 + 140/(1.12)$$

$$= \$25.00$$

The error in assuming that quarterly cash flows are received at the end of the year for this project is $30.49 - \$25.00 = -\$5.49$. The error is a little more than 5 percent of the value of the investment, which may be significant.

A better approximation would be to assume that the cash flows are received at mid-year. If the semiannual rate is $(1 + 0.12)^{1/2} - 1 = 0.05830$, the net present value is

$$NPV = -100 + 140/1.05830$$

$$= \$32.29$$

This latter assumption provides a slightly better approximation, and the error has been reduced to $32.29 - \$30.49 = \$1.80$. The error would have been greater at higher annual discount rates or if cash flows were concentrated early in the year.

The Financial Significance of Net Present Value

We can best show the financial significance of net present value with an example. If you wished to borrow on the cash flows of the machine tool project we considered earlier in Table 3.6 what loan today could be repaid (with interest) entirely from the cash flows of the project? In fact, you know exactly how much this loan would be worth: it is $1,137.23, which represents the cost of the machine tool ($1,000.00) added to the net present value of the project ($137.23); you learned this from Table 3.6. We can prove that this is the case by taking out a loan of $1,137.23 at 10 percent. The rate of interest has been chosen to equal the required rate of return on the project.

We can show that the project's net cash flow stream is just sufficient to pay off the principal and the interest on the loan. We show the calculations in Table 3.10.

The initial loan is $1,137.240 and the cash flow stream from the project is $300 at the end of year 1. The project's cash flow for year 1 is used in part to pay the interest on the bank loan (0.10 × $1,137.240 = $113.724), and the remainder ($300.00 − $113.724 = $186.276) is used to reduce the bank loan principal ($1,137.240 − $186.276 = $950.96). In year 2 the project's cash flow of $300 is used in part to pay interest of $95.0964 on the outstanding loan, with the remainder of $204.904 applied to reduce the outstanding loan balance from $950.964 to $746.060, and so on. As a result, the net cash flows of the project will pay off the loan exactly, as indicated by the zero bank balance in year 5 in the last column.

We have shown that the project's income stream is sufficient to pay off a loan of $1,137.24 with a 10 percent rate of interest each year. In this sense, the project's income stream is worth $1,137.24 to the stockholders. As only $1,000.00 of stockholder funds would have to be paid for the capital cost of the project, the net present value of the project to the stockholders is the difference, or $137.24. By accepting the project, management can add $137.24 to the value of the firm.

The analytical approach used in Table 3.10 is called the loan balance method. If you had not found the net present value of the project in Table 3.6 by discounting, you could use the loan balance method to find the NPV of the project. The present value of the project is equal to the initial loan that would be repaid completely and precisely by the cash flow benefits that are generated by the project. The initial loan of $1,137.24 can therefore be found by trial and error. If we had started with an initial loan balance greater than $1,137.24, we would have obtained a positive cash balance at the end of year 5 in Table 3.10. Conversely, if we had started with an initial loan

Table 3.10 *Loan balance method of calculating net present value*

End of year (1)	Net cash flow of project (2)	Interest paid (10% × previous year's bank balance) (3)	Net change in bank balance (column 2 − column 3) (4)	Bank balance (previous year's bank balance − column 4) (5)
0				1,137.240
1	300 =	113.724 +	186.276	950.964
2	300 =	95.096 +	204.904	746.060
3	300 =	74.606 +	225.394	520.666
4	300 =	52.067 +	247.933	272.727
5	300 =	27.273 +	272.723	0

balance less than $1,137.24, we would have obtained a negative cash balance at the end of year 5. By a process of iteration we will converge to the initial loan of $1,137.24 that leaves a zero cash balance at the end of year 5.

Although the loan balance method is more cumbersome to use than discount factors, it has proven to be useful in a number of applications, for example leasing, which are discussed later in the book. In addition, it shows that the mechanics of discounting are equivalent to paying interest and principal on a loan where the rate of interest is equal to the required rate of return for the project.

The Internal Rate of Return

In practice most managers like to look at a project's rate of return as well as its net present value. If the project's rate of return exceeds the rate that could be obtained if the cash flows were invested in financial securities, then the project is considered to be profitable. The usual method of estimating the project's rate of return is to compute the internal rate of return. The **internal rate of return** (IRR) is defined as the discount rate that would make the net present value for the project equal to zero. Such a discount rate would mean that the present value of the cash inflows for the project would equal the present value of its outflows. In this respect the IRR is a break-even discount rate; it tells us the financial market rate of return at which the project is neither more nor less attractive than alternative investment in financial securities.

Let us find the internal rate of return for the example in Table 3.9. At a discount rate of 10 percent, we obtained a positive net present value of 159.48. To obtain a project's IRR you must use a discount rate that produces a net present value equal to zero. Normally, to get a smaller net present value you use a higher discount rate. Table 3.11 shows the results of dis-

Table 3.11   *Net present value of the example in Table 3.9 at different discount rates*

Discount rate (%)	Net present value (Dollars)
0	350
10	159.47
20	37.47
IRR	0.00
30	−44.50

Figure 3.1   *Plot of net present value versus discount rates (data from Table 3.11)*

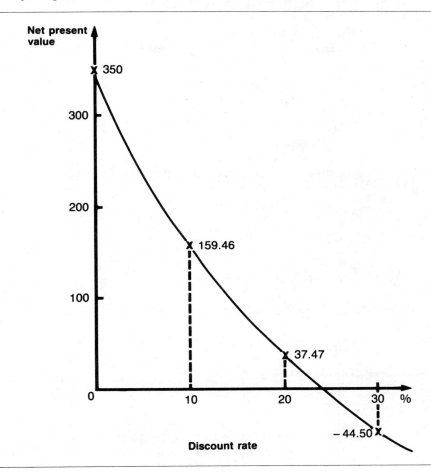

counting the project's cash flows at rates of 10, 20, and 30 percent, and in Figure 3.1 we have graphed the results. The internal rate of return is found where the net present value is equal to zero; that is, where the curve cuts the horizontal axis in Figure 3.1. The internal rate of return is about 24 percent, as you can see from the graph.

A more precise estimate of the IRR is obtained by interpolation. For example, in Table 3.11 we see that the net present value is zero at some discount rate between 20 and 30 percent. The figures show that a difference of 10 percent (when you go from a 20 percent to a 30 percent discount rate) makes a difference of 81.97 in the net present value (37.47 + 44.50 = 81.97). However, we want to change the discount rate only enough to reduce the net present value from 37.47 to 0.00. This change represents a fraction of 37.47/81.97 = 0.457 of the total difference in net present value (81.97) that occurs. This suggests that the discount rate should be increased not by 10 percent but by approximately

$$0.457 \times 10\% = 4.57\%$$

That is, our first estimate of the IRR would be

$$20\% + 4.57\% = 24.57\%$$

This estimate, however, is only an approximation. The reason is that we are assuming a straight line or linear relationship between the NPV and the discount rate. From Figure 3.1 it should be obvious that the relationship is nonlinear. If we repeat the interpolation again and again using discount rates closer and closer to the rate that would make the NPV equal to zero, we will ultimately arrive at the correct value of

$$IRR = 24.11\%$$

   The internal rate of return of 24.11 percent in this example implies that the project will be profitable as long as the rate of return available in the financial market, on securities of equivalent risk, is less than 24.11 percent. At lower discount rates the net present value is positive for this project, as you can see in Figure 3.1.

Summary

Capital projects involve the investment of funds in activities that generate positive net cash flows at future times. Discounted cash flow is the basic tool of financial analysis that permits us to value cash flows no matter when they are expected to occur. Thus we are able to estimate the present value of the cash flow benefits of a project to the stockholders and to compare the worth of these benefits with the project's cost. Discounted cash flow methods permit us to use rates of return that can be obtained in the financial market as a yardstick by which to measure the profitability of a company's investments in capital projects.

Appendix 3.1 Common Formulas Used in Discounted Cash Flow Analysis

Usually it is easier to use discounted cash flow formulas with a pocket calculator than it is to use the tables commonly provided for the purpose.

In general, the problem in DCF involves estimation of the present value (PV) of a stream of expected future cash flows:

$$PV = \frac{C_1}{1 + R} + \frac{C_2}{(1 + R)^2} + \cdots + \frac{C_N}{(1 + R)^N}$$

where C_N is the cash flow assumed to occur at the end of period N, and R is the rate of return available on a comparable investment in the capital market. The net present value (NPV) is the difference between the present value of a project and what the project actually costs. The following formulas are used frequently in financial analysis.

COMPOUND VALUE FACTOR WITH REINVESTMENT AT THE END OF EACH PERIOD

The future value, FV, at time N of an investment I if the proceeds of the investment are to be reinvested at the end of each period at rate R is given by

$$FV = I \times F_{N,R}$$

where

$$F_{N,R} = (1 + R)^N$$

This formula was used to construct the Future Value Tables in Appendix A.

PRESENT VALUE FACTOR

The present value of a series of future cash flows is given by

$$PV = C_1 P_{1,R} + C_2 P_{2,R} + \cdots + C_N P_{N,R}$$

where the present value factor $P_{N,R}$ is given by

$$P_{N,R} = 1/(1 + R)^N$$

Thus the present value factor is equal to the inverse of the compound factor. This formula was used to generate the Present Value Tables in Appendix B.

ANNUITY FACTOR

An annuity is a series of equal cash flows to be received (starting at the end of the first period) for a specified number of periods. The present value of an annuity can be written,

$$P = \frac{C}{1 + R} + \frac{C}{(1 + R)^2} + \cdots + \frac{C}{(1 + R)^N}$$

$$= C(f + f^2 + \cdots + f^N) \tag{A3.1}$$

where $f = 1/(1 + R)$

If we multiply both sides by $1/f$, we obtain

$$P/f = C(1 + f + \cdots + f^{N-1}) \tag{A3.2}$$

Subtracting equation (A3.1) from equation (A3.2),

$$P/f - P = C(1 - f^N) \tag{A3.3}$$

Solving for P and simplifying,

$$P = C(1 - f^N)/R$$

That is, we can obtain the present value of an annuity by multiplying the cash flow C by the annuity factor $A_{N,R}$:

$$P = C \times A_{N,R}$$

where

$$A_{N,R} = (1 - f^N)/R$$

and

$$f = 1/(1 + R)$$

PRESENT VALUE OF A PERPETUITY

A perpetuity is an annuity with an infinite life. The formula for the present value of an annuity of C per period, derived above, is given by

$$P = C(1 - f^N)/R$$

where $f = 1/(1 + R)$

This formula will give us the present value of a perpetuity if we let N go to infinity. Since the discount rate R is finite and greater than zero, the term f is also greater than zero but less than 1.0. This means that the term f^N in the above equation goes to 0 as N goes to infinity. Thus the formula for the present value of a perpetuity is given by

$$P = C(1 - 0)/R$$

$$P = C/R$$

PRESENT VALUE OF PERPETUAL GROWTH

Consider now the case where the first cash flow to be received equals $(1 + G)$ times the cash flow C received in the most recent prior period and is expected to grow at the compounded annual rate G in perpetuity. Equation (A3.1) becomes

$$P = C\frac{1 + G}{1 + R} + C\frac{(1 + G)^2}{(1 + R)^2} + \cdots + C\frac{(1 + G)^N}{(1 + R)^N}$$

$$= C(f + f^2 + \cdots + f^N) \tag{A3.4}$$

where now $f = (1 + G)/(1 + R)$

If R is greater than G and if N goes to infinity, then $f^N = [(1 + G)/(1 + R)]^N$ goes to zero and equation A3.3 becomes

$$P/f - P = C$$

Substituting $f = (1 + G)/(1 + R)$ and rearranging, we obtain

$$P = \frac{C(1 + G)}{R - G} = \frac{C_1}{R - G} \tag{A3.5}$$

where $C_1 = C(1 + G)$ is the cash flow at the end of the first period, G is the annual compound rate of growth in the cash flow, and R is the required rate of return.

CONTINUOUS COMPOUNDING AND DISCOUNTING

Let $r(n)$ be the annual interest rate that, reinvested n times per year, compounds to an equivalent annual rate R. That is

$$\left(1 + \frac{r(n)}{n}\right)^n = 1 + R$$

or

$$r(n) = n((1 + R)^{1/n} - 1)$$

If n goes to infinity then \$1 compounds continuously to

$$\left(1 + \frac{r(n)}{n}\right)^{1/n} = e^r \qquad n \to \text{infinity}$$

$$= 1 + R$$

where $e = 2.71828$

This implies that the continuously compounded annual rate r is given by the natural logarithm of $(1 + R)$. If

$e^r = (1 + R)$ then,

$r = \ln(1 + R)$

If an amount I is invested at a continuously compounded rate r for T periods, then that sum will grow to a sum F:

$F = Ie^{rT}$

Alternatively, if an amount C is to be received in period T and is to be discounted continuously at a rate r, then its present value is P,

$$P = Ce^{-rT}$$

or, $P = C \dfrac{1}{e^{rT}}$

Review Questions

1. How can you estimate whether a capital project is worth more to a company than it costs?
2. How can present value tables and annuity tables be obtained from future value tables?
3. Show that a quarterly discount rate is different from one-fourth of the equivalent annual discount rate.

4. If the annual discount rate is R, how would you determine the discount rate for quarterly cash flows (every three months)?
5. How do you determine the internal rate of return for a capital project?
6. What is the financial significance of net present value?
7. What is the net present value of a security traded in a competitive capital market? Why?
8. Is the continuously compounded interest rate less than or greater than the same rate compounded semi-annually?
9. Explain the loan balance method for calculating a project's net present value. How would you calculate an internal rate of return using this method?

Problems

*1. What is the future value of $5,000 invested at 15 percent annually for five years? What is the present value of the future value? Explain your answer.
*2. Calculate the discount factors to five decimal places for each of a sequence of five future years when the discount rate is 12.5 percent per year.
3. Calculate the net present value for a capital project that has the cash flows below. The company's opportunity cost of capital is 12 percent.

End of year	0	1	2	3	4
Net incremental cash flow (dollars)	−10,000	3,000	4,000	5,000	6,000

*4. Company X is considering the purchase of a machine that would result in the following net cash inflows:

End of year	1	2	3	4	5
Net cash inflow (dollars)	5,000	4,000	3,000	2,000	1,000

The required rate of return for a project of this risk is 15 percent. What would the price of the machine have to be for the company just to break even on the investment?

*5. Use the annuity tables to calculate the net present value of an initial investment of $5,000 that produces annual cash flows of $1,200 for five years, the first payment arising one year after the investment. The opportunity cost of capital is 10 percent. Is the investment profitable?

*6. A company is contemplating a project involving an initial expenditure of $1,200 and thereafter providing an annuity of $250 per year. The riskiness of the project implies a required rate of return of 13 percent. Use the appropriate table at the end of the text to determine what the life of the project would have to be for the project to break even.

7. A mortgage for $10,000 is to be repaid in five equal annual installments, including interest at 8 percent on the declining balance. Calculate the amount of the annual installment, and then figure how much of each installment is interest and how much is applied toward repayment of principal.

*8. What would be the present value of a sum of $1,000 to be received every year forever when the interest rate is 12 percent per year?

*9. Given a quarterly rate of interest of 3.5 percent, what is the annual rate of interest? If the annual rate of interest is 15 percent, what is the quarterly rate?

10. A government bond, redeemable in November 1995 for $100, pays interest at 10 percent annually on the $100 face value of the bond. If the price of the bond is $75 at the end of 1985, what is the yield to redemption (internal rate of return) on the bond?

*11. Calculate the net present value for a capital project with the following (after-tax) net cash flows. The required rate of return is 15 percent. Is the project profitable?

End of year	0	1	2	3
Net incremental cash flow (dollars)	−1,000	200	200	1,200

(a) Use the graphical method to estimate the internal rate of return for the project (see Figure 3.1) between 0 and 30 percent.

(b) Calculate an estimate of the IRR by interpolating between two discount rates.

*12. You have borrowed $10,000 from the bank for five years. The terms of the loan are such that you have to pay equal annual installments over the five years (of principal plus interest). Option (a) requires interest at 12 percent payable annually on the initial size of the loan, while option (b) requires interest to be paid at 14 percent on the declining balance of the principal. Which option is the least costly?

13. Calculate the continuously compounded rate of interest, r, if the annual interest rate is 10 percent.

14. Use the loan balance method (and trial and error) to obtain the NPV of a three-year annuity of $500 per year costing $1,100. Start with an initial loan balance of $1,200 and use a discount rate of 10 percent.

15. Find the IRR for the project in Table 3.6 by trial and error using the loan balance method.

16. A bank offers a depositor the choice of having her interest compounded quarterly at 3 percent per quarter or compounded continuously at a rate of 12 percent per year. How much difference would it make (1) at the end of one year and (2) by the end of two years?

*17. A capital project involving investment in machinery and equipment costs $1,000 after tax. The investment is expected to generate after-tax incremental cash flows of $265 per year for five years. The company uses an annual discount rate of 12 percent for such investments. Compare the net present value for the investment under the following two assumptions:
(a) The cash flows are received at the end of each year.
(b) The cash flows are received and reinvested quarterly.
    How would the assumptions affect the investment decision?

18. A two-year project has the following after-tax cash flows:

End of year	0	1	2
Cash flow	−1000	700	600

Assuming that the cash flows are received at a constant rate within each year, calculate the net present value at 15 percent using
(a) annual discounting
(b) quarterly discounting
Explain the differences in your results.

References

Fisher, I., *The Theory of Interest*, New York: Macmillan, 1930.

Hirshleifer, J., *Investment, Interest, and Capital*, Englewood Cliffs, N.J.: Prentice-Hall, 1970.

How to Appraise a Capital Project

What are the major methods that companies use to appraise business investments? What are the strengths and weaknesses of each of these methods? How do corporate taxes and tax depreciation schedules affect the capital investment decision? In a survey of the *Fortune* 500 companies carried out in 1978, Petty and Scott (1979) found that 59 percent of the responding firms assigned a high level of importance to the internal rate of return. Three other methods, net present value, payback period, and accounting rate of return, were considered highly important by 30 to 33 percent of the respondents. This chapter shows how the net incremental cash flows that are generated by a project arise and how they are affected by corporate taxes. We evaluate the project using all four methods, assessing the advantages and disadvantages of each.

Investment in New Assets: An Example

We will take as our example a proposed investment in machinery and equipment and in working capital costing a total of $1,200,000. The first step is to identify the cash flows of the firm that would be affected by the investment decision. The impact of the project on these cash flows is called the project's net incremental cash flow. To simplify the tables we have rounded the entries to the nearest thousand dollars.

NET INCREMENTAL CASH FLOWS

Table 4.1 shows net incremental cash flows for the project in each period. These cash flows were found by first asking three separate questions:

What are the elements of the company's cash flow that would be affected if the project goes ahead?

What would be the expected level of these cash flows in each period with the project?

What would be the expected level of these cash flows in each period without the project?

The **net incremental cash flow** is the difference between the cash flows for the company with and without the project. In this chapter we make the simplifying assumption that the corporation is all equity financed, therefore there are no interest charges or loan repayments in the project's cash flow statement. The impact of debt financing on cash flows and discount rates will be analyzed in later chapters.

Table 4.1 divides the net incremental cash flows into three parts: investment, operating cash flows, and corporate income taxes. The investment in items 1 and 2 of the table takes place during a period of one year. An initial payment of $200,000 is required in machinery and equipment and the remainder of $900,000 is payable in the first year when the machinery is fully installed and operational. At the end of five years the machinery and equip-

Table 4.1   *Incremental cash flows for the project (thousands of dollars)*

	End of year					
	0	1	2	3	4	5
INVESTMENT						
1. Investment in machinery and equipment	−200	−900				50
2. Investment in working capital		−100				100
OPERATING CASH FLOW						
3. Revenue		525	1100	1150	1200	1100
4. Operating expense		−275	−550	−630	−810	−940
5. Net cash flow (before taxes)	−200	−750	550	520	390	310
TAXES						
6. Net corporate income taxes		32	−145	−137	−77	6
7. Net cash flow (after taxes)	−200	−718	405	383	313	316

ment will have a secondhand market value of only $50,000. In line 2 an investment of $100,000 in working capital is also required at the end of one year at the time the machinery and equipment are put into use. The working capital includes cash investment in raw materials, semifinished and finished goods inventories, and in accounts receivable (less accounts payable). At the end of the project in year 5, cash is realized from the working capital, when inventories are finally depleted and sold, and the remaining accounts receivable are collected.

The operating cash flows in lines 3 and 4 of Table 4.1 represent the increase in cash receipts from sales less operating expenditures that result from the operation of the machinery and equipment. The operating expenditure includes both variable and fixed cash expenditure but not accounting depreciation charges, which are not cash outflows. In line 5 we have calculated the net cash flows before tax. If we were to stop our analysis at this step, the project would look very attractive, because the project generates plenty of net operating cash flow. Taxes, though, are a fact of life and must be included in the analysis.

Line 6 of the table shows the effect of the project on corporate taxes and line 7 the net after-tax incremental cash flows. Note that the project increases the firm's taxes in three of the years (because it generates taxable income), but in two of the years it reduces the tax bill. The tax calculation requires a detailed analysis and understanding of existing tax laws.

Table 4.2 provides a tax statement detailing the calculations behind the income tax figures that appear in Table 4.1. In lines 1 to 4 we estimate the

Table 4.2   Tax statement (thousands of dollars)

	End of year				
	1	2	3	4	5
1. Revenue	525	1100	1150	1200	1100
2. Operating expense	−275	−550	−630	−810	−940
3. ACRS depreciation	−160	−234	−223	−223	−223
4. Residual value in excess of unrecovered ACRS					50
5. Taxable income	90	316	297	167	−13
6. Corporate income taxes at 46%	−41	−145	−137	−77	6
7. Investment tax credit	73				
8. Net corporate income tax effect	32	−145	−137	−77	6

taxable income generated by the project. The **taxable income** is the difference between revenue and tax deductible expenses plus profits on the sale of assets. Sales revenues and operating expenses from Table 4.1 are listed again on lines 1 and 2 of Table 4.2. We are making the simplifying assumption for tax purposes that all the operating expenditures in each year are paid for in the same year. In line 3 of the table we also subtract tax depreciation using the accelerated cost recovery system (ACRS), which we explain below. Although ACRS depreciation is not a cash flow, it is a deduction permitted by the Internal Revenue Service to be set against taxable income, and therefore it reduces taxes. In line 4, the residual value of the asset is $50,000 and assuming the asset is sold, the income is taxable since the asset has been fully depreciated for tax purposes.

The taxable income resulting in line 5 is taxed in line 6 at the 46 percent federal tax rate. Note that in column 5 of line 6 there is an expected net tax saving of $6,000, because in that year the taxable income is expected to be negative. This tax saving is obtained only if there are taxable earnings elsewhere in the company's operations that can be reduced by the net loss attributable to the project in year 5. Line 7 shows a $73,000 reduction in taxes payable in year 1 because the project qualifies for an investment tax credit (ITC). The investment tax credit reduces taxes payable in the year that the machinery and equipment is put into use. As the investment tax credit ($73,000) exceeds the taxes generated by the project in year 1 ($41,000), the remaining credit of $32,000 can be set against taxes payable on operations elsewhere in the company.

INVESTMENT TAX CREDIT

The **investment tax credit** (ITC) is a government incentive that permits a company to reduce its federal tax bill when it invests in an asset used in the business. Direct tax credits are an important feature of the contemporary business environment. These represent Congress's attempt to induce firms to undertake a variety of activities regarded as socially desirable. For most companies the most significant of these is the investment tax credit, which is designed to stimulate business investment and thereby economic growth. The ITC has had a varied life since its origin during the Kennedy administration, and since the Revenue Act of 1978 its basic rate of 10 percent has been "permanent." What this means is that 10 percent of a proportion of the cost of a qualifying asset may be deducted from the income tax otherwise payable during the year in which the asset is purchased. Table 4.3 shows the proportion of the asset's cost qualifying for the 10 percent investment tax credit (as of 1982) and the investment tax credit as a percentage of the original cost of the asset.

The machinery and equipment in our example has a five-year life for tax purposes. An initial payment of $200,000 is required and a further payment

Table 4.3   *Investment Tax Credit (ITC)*

Asset life	Proportion of cost of asset qualifying for ITC	ITC as a percentage of cost
0–2 years	0	0
3–4 years	⅓	3.33
5–6 years	⅔	6.67
7+ years	1.00	10.00

of $900,000 when the asset becomes operational during the first year, so the total investment in machinery and equipment is $1,100,000. As Table 4.3 shows, two-thirds of the cost of an asset with a five-year life for tax purposes qualifies for the investment tax credit of 10 percent. Accordingly, the amount of investment tax credit that can be subtracted from the company's federal tax bill in the first year when the asset is put into use is equal to $0.10 \times$ ⅔ $\times$ $1,100,000, or $73,370.[1] All tax calculations are based upon the rounded figure of $73,000.

CORPORATE TAXES UNDER ACRS

Taxable income in line 5 of Table 4.2 is calculated by subtracting operating expenditures and tax depreciation charges from the sales revenues generated by the project. For assets put into service after 1980, depreciation is determined in accordance with the accelerated cost recovery system (ACRS) provided in the Economic Recovery Act (ERA) of 1981. Under ACRS, depreciation is based upon the life of the asset, defined by the ERA as being either three, five, ten, or fifteen years depending upon the type of asset. For example, machinery and equipment used in research and development are classified in the three-year life category, whereas most other machinery and equipment are treated as having a five-year life. Assets with a ten-year life include public utility property, railroad cars, and mobile homes. Most real estate is treated as having a fifteen-year life.

Table 4.4 shows the percentages provided in the ERA for assets classified in the three-, five-, ten- and fifteen-year life categories. The accelerated

[1]After 1982 the amount of tax liability that could be reduced by the regular ITC in any one year has been limited to the first $25,000 of tax liability, plus 85 percent of any tax liability exceeding $25,000. Changes in tax laws are inescapable. We have used the 1982 law for this chapter.

Table 4.4   *ACRS depreciation schedules for three-, five-, and ten- and fifteen-year assets (%)*

Year	Class of asset			
	Three-year	Five-year	Ten-year	Fifteen-year*
1	25	15	8	7
2	38	22	14	11
3	37	21	12	10
4		21	10	8
5		21	10	7
6			10	7
7			9	6
8			9	6
9			9	6
10			9	5
11				5
12				5
13				5
14				5
15				5
16				2
Total	**100**	**100**	**100**	**100**

*ACRS schedule for 15-year real estate differs slightly depending upon the month in the first year that the property is placed in service.

character of these percentages is more evident in the case of the ten- and fifteen-year life assets than for the three- and five-year assets. The percentages in every case add up to 100 percent. This means that ACRS depreciation schedules treat an asset for tax purposes as if its salvage value is equal to zero. Some depreciation is allowable under ACRS in the first year that the asset is put into use. The amount that is allowable annually does not change, whether the asset is put into service near the beginning of the year or near the end; the exceptions are the fifteen-year assets.

The total cost that can be used as the basis of ACRS depreciation generally is not the full cost of the asset. The basis of the calculation as modified in 1982 is the cost of the asset minus one-half of any investment tax credit that has been taken for it. Thus in Table 4.2 the basis of the ACRS depreciation schedule shown in line 3 is $1,100,000 − ½ ($73,000) = $1,063,500; the latter was rounded up to $1,064,000. The ACRS depreciation figures shown in

Table 4.2 were calculated by multiplying $1,064,000 by the annual percentage rates given for an asset of five-year life in Table 4.4 and rounded.

You might wonder why tax depreciation charges are deductions in the tax statement in Table 4.2 but an accounting depreciation charge does not appear as a deduction in the cash flow statement in Table 4.1. The answer is that the entire cost of the asset ($1,100,000) has already been paid for in the cash flow statement by the end of the first year. To deduct part of the asset's cost again from the project's revenues would be to double count the cost of buying the asset.

In a more precise calculation we would have to show quarterly or even monthly cash flows (as in Chapter 3). In addition, taxes actually are paid quarterly rather than annually as the tables assume.

RESIDUAL VALUES

Under the ACRS system of depreciation, an asset will be fully depreciated by the end of its statutory life; therefore, its value at that time for tax purposes will be zero. If the asset is sold before the end of its statutory life, the firm cannot claim any depreciation for the year in which the asset is sold. The unrecovered value of the asset for tax purposes will then be the total remaining ACRS depreciation outstanding at the end of the preceding year. If the asset is sold for more than its unrecovered value, the difference is taxed as ordinary corporate income.

In the example in Table 4.1, the machinery and equipment are expected to be sold immediately after year 5, so the tax deduction from depreciation can be claimed for that year. At the end of year 5, the asset is fully depreciated, and its unrecovered value is zero for tax purposes. Thus the residual value of $50,000 that is realized (line 1, year 5) when the machinery and equipment are sold is considered by the IRS as part of taxable income. As our analysis is on an annual basis, we have assigned the income to year 5, although the IRS would view the income as being received in the first quarter of year 6.

TAX LOSSES

If taxable income is negative, such losses can be used to offset taxable income from other parts of the business and thereby reduce taxes. If taxable income is not available, losses in one year may be carried back to the three previous years and may be set against the taxable income for those years. Any proportion of the losses not used up in the three carry-back years may then be carried forward to offset taxes in future years. The carry-forward period has been limited (as of 1984) to fifteen years.

CORPORATE TAX RATE

We have assumed that the current federal corporate income tax rate of 46 percent applies to taxable income in all periods. In a real project, state income taxes should be included in the cash flow as well, which could add another 6 to 10 percent to the 46 percent tax bill.

Is the project now sufficiently profitable to be attractive in the light of tax effects? By what criteria should the profitability of projects be judged? First, let us assess the project using the discounted cash flow method, then compare the results with other commonly used methods of assessment, such as the payback period and the accounting rate of return.

Discounted Cash Flow

You will encounter the two discounted cash flow (DCF) methods discussed in Chapter 3 throughout this book. The net present value (NPV) method measures a project's profitability in terms of its estimated incremental effect on the market value of the firm. On the other hand, the internal rate of return (IRR) method seeks to establish a rate of return for the project that can be compared with the rate of return on investments in securities of similar risk in the financial market.

NET PRESENT VALUE

The calculation of net present value represents an estimate of the increase in the market value of the firm that would be attributable to investment in the project. Calculation of a project's net present value requires discounting the project's expected future cash flows using a discount rate that reflects the risk associated with the project. In our example we shall assume that the appropriate discount rate is 15 percent. The net present value of the cash flows of the project in Table 4.1 is calculated in Table 4.5 as $69,000. The net present value of the project is positive, implying that investment in the project will increase the market value of the firm by $69,000, because the project is worth $69,000 more than it costs (in present value terms).

Table 4.5 also shows the net present value of the project assuming a discount rate of 25 percent, with a resulting NPV value equal to −$87,000. This negative NPV suggests that, if the capital market's required rate of return for the project had been as high as 25 percent, investment in the project would have reduced the market value of the firm by an estimated $87,000. Obviously, the choice of the correct discount rate in the calculation

Table 4.5   *Illustration of computation of net present value (in thousands of dollars) for two trial values of the discount rate at 15% and 25%*

Year	Net cash flows	Discount factor at 15%	Discount factor at 25%	Present value at 15%	Present value at 25%
0	−200	1.00000	1.00000	−200	−200
1	−718	0.86957	0.80000	−624	−574
2	405	0.75614	0.64000	306	259
3	383	0.65752	0.51200	252	196
4	313	0.57175	0.40960	179	128
5	316	0.49718	0.32768	157	104
			Net present value =	69	−87

Each year's present value is rounded off to the nearest thousand dollars.

of the NPV is an important issue that shall be discussed in detail in later chapters.

INTERNAL RATE OF RETURN

Many companies use both the net present value and the internal rate of return method when valuing projects. Some managers, however, prefer to obtain a rate of return rather than a dollar net present value figure, so it is important for you to know how to calculate both since both are widely used by financial analysts.

The internal rate of return is defined as that discount rate that would make the net present value of the project equal to zero. The internal rate of return cannot be solved for directly; it must be obtained by a process of trial and error. You can do this manually by the interpolation method shown in Chapter 3 or with a programmable calculator or computer.

The internal rate of return for the project is found to be equal to 18.9 percent. Analysts generally interpret this result to mean that the project earns this rate of return. Actually, this result means that if the market's required rate of return, often referred to as the "cost of capital," for the project were as high as 18.9 percent, the project would only just break even, and its NPV would be zero. For the all-equity financed company a project's cost of capital is equal to the stockholders' required rate of return on financial market securities that have the same risk as the project. If the market's required rate of return is less than 18.9 percent, for example, 15 percent, the project's cash flows would cover more than its cost of capital and the project would therefore be profitable. A caveat: it is not always true that a high IRR means that a project can cover its cost of capital. We shall discuss this particular problem in the next chapter.

The Economic Significance of a Positive Net Present Value or a High Internal Rate of Return

We have said that a project is profitable if it has a positive net present value. Similarly, if the project has an internal rate of return greater than the project's required rate of return, it is also said to be profitable (with some exceptions to be described in Chapter 5). Here we describe the conditions under which a project will have a positive NPV or an IRR in excess of the project's minimum required rate of return.

A positive NPV must derive from a product's competitive advantage, or from a supply shortage of the product that was unanticipated by some producers and that cannot be remedied quickly by extra production. For example, Xerox's copiers have been very profitable for many years because the company has improved its product continually and stayed ahead of its competitors. Of course, high profits, that is, large positive NPVs, attract new entrants into the market. Gradually, competition forces prices down until positive NPVs from new projects become harder to find. As a result, although Xerox is still profitable, its competitive advantage has been gradually reduced, thereby reducing its level of profitability.

An example of a supply shortage producing large positive NPVs is in the oil industry. During the 1970s, the sharply rising price of oil brought large positive NPVs to those countries or companies owning oil fields that were already developed or that could be developed quickly. The high prices of oil were in large part due to the price-fixing arrangements authorized by the Organization of Petroleum Exporting Countries (OPEC). The high prices could not initially be forced down without substantial new oil fields being brought into production, or substitutes for oil being further developed. Since it takes time to explore and develop new oil fields or to produce cheaper oil substitutes, large positive NPVs were being earned. In the 1980s the price of oil declined as new oil fields were discovered, cheaper substitutes were developed, and the OPEC cartel was weakened.

The main point of this background is to demonstrate that the correct justification of a project's profitability does not depend on mechanical forecasts of cash flows, but upon a proper economic assessment of a product's competitive environment and the company's competitive advantage. Without such a justification, a project's NPV may only reflect errors in cash flow forecasts, or the wrong choice of discount rate.

We have suggested that a positive NPV in part must be due to a lack of competition or to a supply shortage that cannot be corrected quickly. What size of NPV would you expect in a highly competitive market where no one company has any competitive advantage? You should not expect new projects to have better than zero NPVs. Such projects may be able to earn a sufficient rate of return to cover the cost of the funds being used (taking into account risk), but no more.

Since a positive net present value reflects either a competitive advantage or scarcity, it is important to ask how long such product market advantages will last. Obstacles such as barriers to market entry, the time lags in introducing substitutes, or cartels may preserve high prices for limited periods. In economies such as that of the United States, however, competition at home and from abroad will combine to reduce high prices. As a consequence, the level of prices and resulting cash flows that produce positive NPVs will tend to be reduced with the passage of time.

The message is clear—even if a company has a great new product which looks as though it is a profit winner, competition eventually is bound to erode market share, prices, and profit margins. The financial analyst should be suspicious of persistently high cash flow forecasts that imply large positive net present value.

The Payback Period—Advantages and Limitations

Most managers like to look at the payback period as well as use DCF. The **payback period** is defined as the length of time expected for the project to generate sufficient cumulative cash flows to repay the initial investment. How long is the payback period for our project example, and how do we calculate it?

Looking at line 7 of Table 4.1 starting from year 0, we add the cash flows until the cumulative sum becomes positive. Our project recovers its initial investment in 3.4 years, which is the project's payback period. In some industries this payback period would be considered attractive, provided there are sufficient positive cash flows after the payback period to make the project profitable. Of course, a rapid return of capital does not of itself constitute profitability because there is no simple yardstick to determine a project's minimum required payback period. Payback usually is perceived within firms as a measure of liquidity, although a short payback period can be a favorable omen of profitability. By liquidity, we mean here the speed with which a project's cash outflows are recovered for redeployment to alternative uses.

The payback measure has a number of limitations. For example, payback ignores cash flows that occur after the payback period. This is an obvious shortcoming, for the existence of additional positive cash flows is a necessary condition for a project to be profitable—that is, to provide returns in excess of the sum of money invested.

Many companies use discounted payback. **Discounted payback** is the payback period that is obtained from a project's cash flow sequence that has first been discounted to present value. The more distant cash flows are reduced by having been discounted; as a result, the payback period is lengthened for most projects. Discounting takes account of the time value of money, which provides an important adjustment to the payback period, particularly at times of high inflation and interest rates.

One problem with payback is that there is no objective minimum payback criterion. In a sense, projects with longer lives can justify a longer payback period, but there is no precise relationship between a project's life and the pattern and risk of its cash flows. Two projects may have the same expected cash flows and the same payback period but very different risks, and therefore are not equally attractive.

Nevertheless, the payback period criterion has sufficient advantages to make it a widely used measure; it usually is employed in conjunction with other criteria more closely identified with profitability. The liquidity implications of payback are clear. Lenders use the payback period as an indicator of when a project loan can be repaid, and companies use it as an indication of how rapidly funds committed to a project will be available for redeployment in the future. Multinational companies use the payback period as a measure of length of exposure to political risks in foreign countries.

One important feature of the payback period is that it is an extra safeguard against biased or exaggerated forecasts. If forecast cash flows are excessively optimistic, the resulting bias is most likely to be concentrated in the years beyond the payback period. Simulation studies by Marsh and Brealey (1974) have indicated that when cash flow forecasting is sufficiently biased upward the use of payback can result in better decisions compared with those made using DCF methods.

For these reasons, the payback period should be considered mainly as a measure of liquidity and as an extra safeguard against the effects of biased forecasting.

The Accounting Rate of Return

Another measure of profitability, and one that is widely used, is the accounting rate of return. This measure is also referred to as the return on capital employed. The **accounting rate of return** (ARR) measure is based upon the accounting earnings of a project and the book value of the assets in each period. These data are not the same as those used in IRR or NPV calculations, which are based upon the net cash flows, including investment costs, that are attributable to the asset.

This section shows how an accounting rate of return may be calculated, and why it may differ from the internal rate of return on the same project. (Appendix 4.2 shows how an internal rate of return can be calculated from a project's accounting rates of return.) The relationship between the two measures is important, not only because both measures are used in industry to appraise new projects, but also because return on capital employed calculations are used to measure the performance of the assets after the investment has taken place.

A typical calculation of the accounting rate of return would follow the conventions below. The rate of return may be approximated by a fraction. The denominator represents the amount of capital employed at the beginning of the year, and the numerator the accounting earnings for the year.

$$\text{ARR} = \frac{\text{Accounting earnings after tax and depreciation}}{\text{Book value of capital employed at beginning of the year}}$$

What is the average accounting rate of return for the five-year project in Table 4.1? First we calculate the accounting rate of return for each year. Then we can calculate a (weighted) average accounting rate of return for all five years. For the purpose of calculating the ARRs we will take the before-tax annual accounting profit from line 5 of Table 4.2. From this we subtract net corporate income taxes given in line 8 to obtain the after-tax accounting earnings as follows:

| | End of year | | | | |
| | 1 | 2 | 3 | 4 | 5 |
		(Thousands of dollars)			
Taxable income	90	316	297	167	−13
Corporate income taxes	32	−145	−137	−77	6
Net income after tax	122	171	160	90	− 7

The net income after tax provides the numerator of the ARR fraction for each year. Now we require an estimate of the capital employed for the denominator.

In Table 4.6 we have calculated the book value of the assets at the end of each period, using numbers obtained from Tables 4.1 and 4.2. In the first column, we begin year 0 with no assets in line 1 but invest $200,000 in line

Table 4.6   *Computation of book value (remaining undepreciated value) of machinery and equipment (thousands of dollars)*

			End of year			
	0	1	2	3	4	5
1. Value of assets at beginning of period		200	903	669	446	223
2. Plus further investment	200	900				
3. Less one-half investment tax credit		−37				
4. Less depreciation		−160	−234	−223	−223	−223
5. Book value of fixed assets at end of period	200	903	669	446	223	0

2. At the end of year 0 we have $200,000 invested in machinery and equipment. This also gives us the investment in machinery and equipment at the beginning of year 1 in line 1. To this we add the additional investment of $900,000 in line 2, less one-half of the investment tax credit (rounded up to $37,000) in line 3. In line 4 we also subtract the ACRS depreciation of $160,000, leaving a net undepreciated value of machinery and equipment of $903,000 at the end of year 1 in line 5. This gives the value at the beginning of year 2 in line 1, and the rest of the table is a straightforward series of deductions for depreciation. At the end of year 5 the residual value under ACRS is zero, as can be seen in line 5 in the last year.

We now have the estimated depreciated book value of machinery and equipment at the beginning of each year in line 1 of Table 4.6. To this value we add the investment in working capital which takes place at the beginning of period 2 (i.e., end of period 1):

	Year				
	1	2	3	4	5
		(Thousands of dollars)			
Book value of machinery and equipment	200	903	669	446	223
Working capital		100	100	100	100
Total capital employed at beginning of year	200	1,003	769	546	323

To obtain the accounting rate of return for each year, divide the net income after tax for each year by the capital employed at the beginning of the year:

		Year				
		1	2	3	4	5
		(Thousands of dollars)				
Accounting Income / Total Capital Employed	=	122 / 200	171 / 1,003	160 / 769	90 / 546	− 7 / 323
ARR (%)	=	61.000	17.049	20.806	16.484	−2.167

The question arises as to how these changing accounting rates of return can be related to the project's internal rate of return. We calculated previously that the internal rate of return for the project was 18.9 percent. If we take a simple average of the accounting rates of return (ARRs) for each period, we obtain 22.634 percent. This average ARR is, as you can see, reasonably close to the project's IRR. However, we could have constructed a different project where the average ARR was very different from the project's internal rate of return. Appendix 4.2 provides such an example and also shows how you can obtain the IRR of a project from a sequence of annual accounting rates of return using a specially constructed weighted average.

An important point to remember is that the accounting rate of return for an individual project may vary a great deal from one period to another. This is because an arbitrary depreciation schedule is used to calculate accounting income and book values. In the previous example the average ARR was 22.634 percent but the annual ARRs ranged from −2.167 to 61.00 percent. You may wonder why any company bothers to use the accounting rate of return at all. The main reason seems to be that many managers are more accustomed to using accounting numbers than cash flows. They are more familiar with accounting numbers because financial objectives and divisional performance usually are measured in terms of accounting income and book value rather than by cash flow and present value. Managers are trying to be consistent in their approach to investment decision making and subsequent performance measurement. Chapter 11 discusses this problem.

Let us summarize the results of the four methods of analysis:

$$\text{NPV (at 15\%)} = \$69,000$$
$$\text{IRR} = 18.9\%$$
$$\text{Payback} = 3.4 \text{ years}$$
$$\text{ARR} = 22.634\%$$

Interaction Between Investment Decisions

Earlier in the chapter in Tables 4.1 and 4.2, we described a project with tax losses in two periods. We assumed then that taxable income was available elsewhere in the company so that tax losses could be used to reduce the corporation's taxes in the same year. The amount of corporate taxes saved as a result of the tax loss generated by the project in year 1 was $32,000, which saving was added to the project's net cash flow stream. An important question arises: What happens if taxable income is not available in the rest of the company, and how would the project's net cash flows (and NPV) be affected? This question is important, because a sizable minority of United States corporations at any one time may have negative taxable income and will not be able immediately to obtain the value of the tax credits as they arise from new projects.

We have constructed an example below called project A which is similar to that analyzed earlier in Tables 4.1 and 4.2. The data are shown in Table 4.7. There are no sales receipts or operating expenditures until year 3, so that there are negative net cash flows in years 1 and 2, and tax losses. The tax losses remain unabsorbed because there is no taxable income from other operations. Thus, the amount of ACRS in year 3 ($617,000) is the cumulative ACRS depreciation for the first three years, based on line 3 of Table 4.2. Similarly, the investment tax credit is carried forward until year 3 when there will be corporate taxes against which the credit can be taken.

Now suppose that the company accepts an additional project B. We shall not show the cash flow details of this project, but report that the project generates sufficient taxable income in years 1 and 2 to enable the company to obtain the benefits of project A's ACRS depreciation and investment tax credit when they arise. Thus the company can use project A's ACRS depreciation as a charge against project B's taxable income in years 1 and 2. Project B will allow the company to obtain the tax benefits from project A's ACRS depreciation earlier, and the present value of the tax saving thereby will be increased. Similarly, the investment tax credit for project A could be set against project B's taxes as soon as project A is put into service rather than later when there are taxes on A's own income.[2] In Table 4.8(a) we calculate the present value of the tax effect of ACRS depreciation and the investment tax credit for project A if project B is not accepted. The present value of these tax effects is $344,830. In Table 4.8(b) we calculate the tax effect of ACRS depreciation and the investment tax credit for project A if project B is accepted. The annual ACRS depreciation is the same as that calculated in Table 4.2. The difference between Table 4.8(a) and Table 4.8(b) is that

---

[2]Note that the ITC can be carried back three years and forward fifteen years if it cannot be used in the year it arises. Thus, A may use B's *past* taxable income as well as its present and future taxable income in order to shelter its tax losses.

Table 4.7   *After-tax net incremental cash flow for Project A*

	Elapsed time (years)					
	0	1	2	3	4	5
CASH FLOW STATEMENT						
Investment cash flows						
1. Investment in machinery and equipment	−200	−900				50
2. Investment in working capital		−100				100
3. Total investment	−200	−1000				150
OPERATING CASH FLOWS						
4. Sales receipts		0	0	2775	1200	1100
5. Operating expenditure		0	0	−1455	−810	−940
6. Net operating cash flow		0	0	1320	390	160
7. Net corporate income tax				−250	−77	6
8. Net cash flow	−200	−1000	0	1070	313	316
TAX STATEMENT						
9. Residual value in excess of unrecovered ACRS						50
10. Revenue	0	0	0	2775	1200	1100
11. Operating expense	0	0	0	−1455	−810	−940
12. ACRS depreciation	0	0	0	−617	−223	−223
13. Taxable income	0	0	0	703	167	−13
14. Corporate income tax at 46%				−323	−77	6
15. Investment Tax Credit				73		
16. Net corporate income tax				−250	−77	6

Table (b) shows project A's depreciation and investment tax credit as being obtained earlier as a result of project B's taxable income and taxes. This causes the present value of the tax benefits to rise to $385,310, for a net increase of $40,480.

We have shown that the net present value of a project can be affected by the tax position of the company. In principle, it is possible for one project to provide taxable income when another project is providing a tax loss. As a result projects A and B considered in combination are worth more than the projects considered separately:

NPV (Projects A + B) > NPV (Project A) + NPV (Project B)

For this reason one project cannot necessarily be considered in isolation from

Table 4.8(a) *Tax benefits of ACRS depreciation and the investment tax credit for Project A if Project B is rejected (thousands of dollars)*

	End of year					
	0	1	2	3	4	5
ACRS depreciation	0	0	0	617	223	223
Tax benefits at 46%	0	0	0	284	103	103
Investment tax credit	0	0	0	<u>73</u>		
Total tax benefit	0	0	0	357	103	103

Present value of tax benefits at 15% = 344.83

Table 4.8(b) *Tax benefits of ACRS depreciation and the investment tax credit for Project A if Project B is accepted (thousands of dollars)*

	End of year				
	1	2	3	4	5
ACRS depreciation	160	234	223	223	223
Tax benefit at 46%	74	108	103	103	103
Investment tax credit	<u>73</u>				
Total tax benefit	147	108	103	103	103

Present value of tax benefits at 15% = 385.31

other projects. Chapters 22 through 26 develop this question of how one project's value interacts with another's.

Summary

We have shown ways in which corporate taxes affect the incremental cash flows of a capital project and how the tax effects of different projects may be interrelated. Using an example, we have compared four of the most widely used capital investment criteria: net present value, internal rate of return, payback period, and accounting rate of return. We found that these criteria may not provide the same signals as to the profitability of a project, because the four criteria do not measure the same thing. The payback period is a measure of project liquidity and does not measure profitability. The accounting rate of return seeks to measure return in terms of the incremental impact of a project on accounting statements but does not measure the economic value of the project. The net present value and the internal rate of return criteria use a project's contribution to the cash flow of the firm to estimate, respectively, its net effect on the value of the firm and its rate of return. Of the four, the net present value and the internal rate of return methods have the better conceptual basis.

In the next chapter we shall discuss pitfalls in the use of rate of return criteria in capital project appraisal. In particular, we will focus on a comparison between the internal rate of return and the net present value methods.

Appendix 4.1 Income Tax Factors in Business Financial Decisions

State and federal taxes have an important impact on business financial decisions. In the first place, the quantitative impact of a 46 percent federal corporate tax rate is significant. Second, tax statutes are complex, they are frequently altered by Congress and state legislatures, and their legal interpretation is not always clear or consistent over time. Taxes may be as inescapable as death, but their form and amount, much as the date of death, are uncertain.

In this Appendix we sketch out in broadest terms the major features of the United States tax laws as they exist at the date of this book. Special features of the tax laws will be dealt with separately in the chapters on bonds and leasing. Our treatment only scratches the surface. You should realize that more detailed information from the statutes, tax guides, and tax specialists is required in practice.

CORPORATE INCOME TAXES

Virtually all large United States business firms are incorporated, and their profits are taxed by the federal government at the progressive rates described in Table A4.1.1.

Corporations use accrual accounting methods for the determination and reporting of taxable income. For some financial decisions this feature can be

Table A4.1.1   *United States corporate tax rates for tax years after December 31, 1982*

Marginal taxable income (dollars)	Marginal tax rate (%)	Marginal taxes (dollars)	Cumulative taxable income (dollars)	Cumulative taxes (dollars)	Average tax rate (%)
25,000	15	3,750	25,000	3,750	15
25,000	18	4,500	50,000	8,250	16.50
25,000	30	7,500	75,000	15,750	21.00
25,000	40	10,000	100,000	25,750	25.75
	46		100,000+		

important, because the economic logic of present value analysis depends on after-tax cash flows, not after-tax accounting income. For purposes of this text, the most important features of the United States corporate income tax law relate to the determination of income and deductible expenses.

INTEREST PAYMENTS. Interest payments are a tax-deductible expense. Preferred and common stock dividend payments are not. This means that corporate profits paid to owners (stockholders) generally have to pass through two rounds of taxes, corporate and individual. The conspicuous exception occurs when individuals own stock indirectly through such financial institutions as pension funds and Individual Retirement Accounts (IRA), where returns are not received and taxed until retirement.

DIVIDENDS PAID TO CORPORATIONS. Generally, 85 percent of the dividends received by a corporation from other domestic corporations is excluded in calculating taxable income. This feature mitigates what otherwise could amount to triple taxation of the same original profit stream. Further, in the case of closely affiliated corporations filing consolidated returns, intercorporate interest and dividend payments are netted out, so that only consolidated net corporate income is taxed.

FISCAL DEPRECIATION. Determination of the corporate income figure subject to tax at the rates in Table A4.1.1 requires a determination of the cost of resources used up in the production of income, notably plant, equipment, and inventory. As these resources may be used up over more than one tax year, their initial outlay has to be allocated in the form of noncash-using depreciation expenses over the years of the assets' useful lives. For fixed assets of any special type, guidelines are provided as to useful life. This figure, along with the asset's initial cost and an estimate of its salvage value, determines the depreciable cost.

The Economic Recovery Act of 1981 requires that either the accelerated cost recovery system or straight-line depreciation be used for tax purposes on assets purchased after 1980. The ACRS system is illustrated in this chapter. For assets purchased before that time, the three most popular methods of depreciation are illustrated in Table A4.1.2. These are the straight-line, sum of the years digits (SYD), and the double declining balance (DDB) methods. Clearly DDB gives the largest first-year tax shield, but it also results in the smallest total depreciation charge over the life of the asset.

We discuss below the main items in the table.

STRAIGHT-LINE DEPRECIATION

In the case of straight-line depreciation, the depreciable book value of an asset is reduced each year by an amount equal to the initial book value multiplied by the fraction 1 divided by the number N of years in the asset's depreciable life. The depreciable book value is equal to the initial book value minus the estimated salvage value at the end of the depreciable life of the asset.

SUM OF THE YEARS DIGITS (SYD)

In the sum of the years digits method of accelerated depreciation, the denominator of the fraction by which the book value of an asset is depreciated is obtained by summing the digits in the years of the asset's depreciable life. The formula for this summation is:

$$1 + 2 + \cdots + n = n \times \frac{(n + 1)}{2}$$

For example, for a ten-year depreciable life the sum used in the denominator is 55. The numerator of the fraction is taken from the year numbers in reverse order. Thus, for a ten-year depreciable life the fractions are:

Year	1	2	...	10
Fraction	10/55	9/55	...	1/55

To obtain the annual amount of depreciation, multiply the fraction for the year by the initial cost of the asset less the salvage value. Thus, in Table A4.1.2 the first year's depreciation is $10/55 \times (\$11,000 - \$1,000) = \$1,818$.

Table A4.1.2
Comparison of depreciation methods

	Straight-line		Sum of the years digits (SYD)		Double declining balance (DDB)	
	Annual depreciation	**Remaining value**	**Annual depreciation**	**Remaining value**	**Annual depreciation**	**Remaining value**
0	$ —	$11,000	$ —	$11,000	$ —	$11,000
1	1,000	10,000	1,818	9,182	2,200	8,800
2	1,000	9,000	1,636	7,546	1,760	7,040
3	1,000	8,000	1,455	6,091	1,408	5,632
4	1,000	7,000	1,273	4,818	1,126	4,506
5	1,000	6,000	1,091	3,727	901	3,605
6	1,000	5,000	909	2,818	721	2,884
7	1,000	4,000	727	2,091	577	2,307
8	1,000	3,000	545	1,546	461	1,846
9	1,000	2,000	364	1,182	369	1,477
10	1,000	1,000	182	1,000	295	1,182
Total	**$10,000**		**$10,000**		**$9,818**	

Cost of Asset (A)　　　= $11,000
Estimated Salvage Value (S)　= $1,000
Estimated Useful Life (n)　= 10 years

Formula: Annual Depreciation, Straight-line

$$D_t, \text{ for year } t = \frac{1}{n} \times (A - S)$$

Formula: Annual Depreciation, SYD

$$D_t = \frac{L}{N} \times (A - S)$$

where N = Total of each year of the asset's depreciable life ($N = 1 + 2 + 3 + 4 + 5 + 6 + 7 + 8 + 9 + 10 = 55$ in this case, and where L = The remaining depreciable life of the asset (Year 1, $L = 10$; Year 2, $L = 9$, . . ., Year 10, $L = 1$).

Formula: Annual Depreciation, DDB

$$D_t = \frac{2}{n} (A - D_1 - D_2 - \cdots - D_{t-1}).$$

Note that the rate is applied to book value, not to book value less 5.

DOUBLE DECLINING BALANCE (DDB)

In the double declining balance (DDB) method, the remaining undepreciated book value is reduced by a fraction represented by 2 divided by the number n of years in the asset's depreciable life.

The Internal Revenue Service permits a onetime switch from the DDB method to the straight-line method during the life of the asset. In the example in Table A4.1.2, the optimum time to switch would be at the end of year 5: the remaining depreciable value of $3,605 would be written off at $721 per year. For assets purchased after 1980, a corporation can use the system, which incorporates a switch to straight-line depreciation, because it provides a faster and therefore more generous write-off for tax purposes in the latter years of an asset's life, and the residual value of an asset is treated as though it is equal to zero.

INVENTORY ACCOUNTING

The cost of inventory used up in production is a question of price levels. If the inflation rate on inventory purchases were zero, all inventory used of the same item would be at the same unit cost. In the presence of inflation, however, it is not clear whether in any given year the inventory used is the most recently purchased (i.e., most expensive), the earliest purchased (i.e., least expensive), or some average. The Internal Revenue Code permits firms to adopt either a "last in, first out" (LIFO) or "first in, first out" (FIFO) procedure. In the case of inflation, LIFO obviously provides better tax shield protection for operating revenues. It is no accident that many companies shift to LIFO accounting in periods of high inflation rates. If there was deflation, with prices falling, FIFO should be preferred.

EXAMPLE OF LIFO AND FIFO INVENTORY ACCOUNTING IN THE PRESENCE OF INFLATION

Suppose that a company's beginning inventory consists of two lots of identical items purchased at different unit costs. The first lot of 100 units costs $50 each. The second lot of 125 units purchased later costs $75 each. Thus the total beginning inventory cost:

100 units at $50	=	$ 5,000
125 units at $75	=	$ 9,375
Total		$14,375

Now suppose that the company sells 150 units. Using LIFO, the cost of goods sold is

125 units at $75	=	**$ 9,375**
25 units at $50	=	**$ 1,250**
		$10,625

and the tax deductible expenses are $0.46 \times \$10,625 = \$4,887.50$.
Using FIFO, the cost of goods sold is

100 units at $50	=	**$ 5,000**
50 units at $75	=	**$ 3,750**
		$ 8,750

and the tax deductible expenses are only $0.46 \times \$8,750 = \$4,025$.

This example illustrates that tax-deductible costs of goods sold are higher under LIFO than under FIFO with inflation. The corresponding tax benefits must also be greater.

TAXATION AND THE LEGAL FORM OF ENTERPRISE

While for many small companies it may pay (in lower taxes) to remain unincorporated, incorporation lends substantial benefits: indefinite life, limited liability of owners, simplification of estate planning, for example. Fortunately, Congress has provided a way to have the best of both worlds. Subject to restrictions, a closely held corporation may elect to be a Subchapter S corporation. Under these provisions the firm is not taxed itself, but all its income is considered to have been distributed pro rata to owners and taxable at their individual rates.

Appendix 4.2 *Calculating the Internal Rate of Return from a Sequence of Accounting Rates of Return*

We shall show here how to calculate the internal rate of return for an asset from a sequence of accounting rates of return (ARR) on the asset. There are two reasons you would want to be able to do this. First, many companies use the accounting rate of return as a profitability measure when investing in capital projects, and they need to be able to compare the sequence of expected ARRs for a project with the cost of the capital. Second, companies use accounting rates of return to measure the performance of their various divisions, and it is important for them to be able to compare this performance measure with the discounted cash flow criteria that are used to make the investment decisions in each division.

The accounting rate of return is defined as the accounting income from an asset divided by its book value, where the accounting income is equal to the cash flow generated by the project minus the asset's depreciation. Using as an example a capital project that has an internal rate of return of 20 percent, first we calculate the accounting rate of return that would be obtained on the asset if economic depreciation were used as the basis of book value and income. In this case the internal rate of return equals the accounting rate of return. Second, we calculate a sequence of accounting rates of return based upon straight-line depreciation rather than upon economic depreciation. Third, we show that a weighted average of the sequence of accounting rates of return equals the internal rate of return for the project.

Table A4.2.1 shows that the economic rate of return is equal to the internal rate of return. The economic rate of return for a period is equal to the accounting rate of return that would be obtained if depreciation is defined as the change in present value of the asset's cash flow over the period. Line 1 of the table shows the cash flows of the project. In line 2 of the table we calculate the present value of the future cash flows remaining after each period, discounted at 20 percent. For instance, the value of $395 (in thousands of dollars) in line 2 at the end of year 2 is the discounted present value at 20 percent of the one remaining cash flow of $474 at the end of year 3. The $725 in line 2 at the end of year 1 is the discounted present value of the two remaining cash flows at the end of years 2 and 3, and so on. We calculate

Table *A4.2.1*   *Calculation of economic rate of return (thousands of dollars)*

	End of year			
	0	1	2	3
1. Cash flow		475	475	474
2. Present value of remaining cash flow (discounted at 20%)	1,000	725	395	
3. Economic depreciation		275	330	395
4. Economic income		200	145	79
5. Economic rate of return (%)		20.0	20.0	20.0

the present value of the project at the end of each period so that we can measure the rate at which the project's economic value diminishes over time. The change in present value over each period is called economic depreciation. For example, in line 3, period 1, the project's economic depreciation is equal to $1,000 − $725 = $275, and in period 2 the economic depreciation is equal to $725 − $395 = $330.

The economic income for a period is the cash flow minus the economic depreciation. For example, in line 4 the economic income for year 1 is $475 − $275 = $200. The accounting rate of return is equal to the accounting income divided by the depreciation value of the assets employed. When we use economic depreciation to calculate the accounting rate of return, the income for year 1 is $200 and the economic (present) value of the asset at the beginning of the period is $1,000. Therefore the accounting rate of return based on economic depreciation for year 1 is equal to 200/1,000 = 20%. The accounting rate of return for years 2 and 3 are also equal to 20 percent. The example demonstrates that if the accounting rate of return is based on economic depreciation and if economic depreciation is based on a discount rate equal to the internal rate of return, then the accounting rate of return will equal the internal rate of return for every period.

Let us now see how our example is changed if we substitute straight-line accounting depreciation for economic depreciation in calculating the accounting rate of return. Table A4.2.2 shows the corresponding calculations (in thousands of dollars). The table is similar to the preceding one, but there is straight-line depreciation of $333 per year in place of economic depreciation. The book value of the asset in line 2 in the table reflects this new depreciation schedule. The accounting income for year 1 is equal to the cash flow minus the accounting depreciation, or $475 − $333 = $142. The book value of the asset at the beginning of year 1 is equal to $1,000. Thus the accounting rate of return for year 1 is equal to 142/1,000 = 14.2%. In year 2 the accounting income is equal to $475 − $333 = $142. The book value of the asset based on straight-line depreciation at the beginning of year 2 is equal to $667.

Table A4.2.2   *Calculation of accounting rate of return (ARR) (thousands of dollars)*

	End of year			
	0	1	2	3
1. Cash flow		475	475	474
2. Remaining book value	1,000	667	333	0
3. Straight-line depreciation		333	333	333
4. Accounting income		142	142	141
5. Accounting rate of return (%)		14.2	21.3	42.2

Therefore, the accounting rate of return for year 2 is equal to 142/667 = 21.3%. Similarly, we obtain an accounting rate of return in year 3 equal to 42.2%. None of the accounting rates of return equals the internal rate of return of 20 percent.

This example demonstrates that when an arbitrary accounting depreciation schedule is used to calculate the accounting income and the book value of an asset, the resulting accounting rate of return will not be equal to the internal rate of return in each period. Nevertheless, you still can obtain the internal rate of return from a weighted average of accounting rates of return if depreciation is based on the cost (and residual value) of the asset.

What type of weighted average should be used to calculate the internal rate of return that is implied by a sequence of accounting rates of return? In other words, we would like to know what should be the values of the weights w_1, w_2, and w_3 used in the following formula:

$$IRR = \frac{w_1}{W} \times ARR_1 + \frac{w_2}{W} \times ARR_2 + \frac{w_3}{W} \times ARR_3 \qquad \text{(A.4.2.1)}$$

where $W = w_1 + w_2 + w_3$.

It has been shown by Kay (1976) that the weight that should be used is the discounted value of the book value of the asset as the basis of the accounting rate of return. The weight for period 2, for example, is based on the book value at the end of period 1. If we let V_1 be the book value for period 1, w_2 for period 2 is given by

$$w_2 = \frac{V_1}{(1 + K)^2}$$

where the discount rate K equals the IRR, the internal rate of return. In our example the values of w_t are

$$w_1 = 1,000/1.2 = 833 \qquad w_2 = 667/(1.2)^2 = 463 \qquad w_3 = 333/(1.2)^3 = 193$$

and $W = 833 + 463 + 193 = 1,489$.

Thus the internal rate of return can be obtained from the ARRs using equation A.4.2.1. Substituting in the numbers from our example we obtain

$$IRR = \frac{833}{1,489} \times 14.2 + \frac{463}{1,489} \times 21.3 + \frac{193}{1,489} \times 42.2 = 20.04$$

The error of 0.04% is due to rounding.

The weights that we use in equation A4.2.1 require an initial estimate of the IRR to be used as the discount rate. The true IRR must be calculated by a process of trial and error. For example, suppose that we had guessed initially that the IRR was going to be 26 percent. This initial guess of 26 percent is equal to the unweighted average of the ARRs in line 5 of Table A4.2.2. Using this rate as the discount rate we would have obtained the following values for the weights:

$$w_1 = 1,000/1.26 = 794 \quad w_2 = 667/(1.26)^2 = 420 \quad w_3 = 333/(1.26)^3 = 166$$

$$W = 794 + 420 + 166 = 1,380$$

Using these initial weights, we obtain the first estimate of the IRR:

$$IRR = \frac{794}{1,380} \times 14.2 + \frac{420}{1,380} \times 21.3 + \frac{166}{1,380} \times 42.2 = 19.73\%$$

Our initial estimate that the IRR is 26 percent is incorrect because the calculated IRR (19.73%) does not equal the initial estimate (26%). The value of 19.73 percent that we have obtained is inaccurate, because the weights used are based on a discount rate that does not equal the calculated IRR. If we let our discount rate in the weights equal 19.73 percent we will approach the true value of the IRR. This process can be repeated as often as necessary to obtain the accuracy that is required.

The formula for the weighted average used here is found in Kay (1976).

Review Questions

1. Comment on the following statement: "Projects should be analyzed on a before-tax basis, because taxes are uncertain."
2. A project's after-tax IRR will always be less than its pre-tax IRR. Is this statement true or false? Explain your answer.
3. If a project's taxable income in a particular year is negative, under what circumstances is the project entitled to a tax shield (on the tax loss) in the year that it occurs?
4. Would an increase in the corporate tax rate always reduce a project's after-tax IRR?
5. Provide some reasons why projects can have positive NPVs. Would you expect positive NPVs to persist for particular products? Give reasons for your answers.
6. Why do companies calculate the payback period for a project?
7. Why do many companies use discounted payback instead of undiscounted payback?

8. Why does the accounting rate of return for a project differ from the project's IRR? Under what conditions would they be equal? (Note: The answer to this question requires some knowledge of Appendix 4.2.)
9. Why is it difficult to value a project's NPV in isolation when a company has unused tax credits from other projects that may be used to absorb the project's tax losses in particular years?

Problems

*1. An investment project is expected to generate the following after-tax net incremental cash flows net of taxes.

End of year	0	1	2	3
Net incremental cash flow (dollars)	−2,400	−500	2,000	2,000

Would the project be financially attractive if the required rate of return considering the project's risk is 15 percent?

*2. The before-tax cash flows from a project are shown below. The initial investment of $2.2 million consists of $2 million in fixed assets and $200,000 in working capital. The project is eligible for the investment tax credit on five-year assets.

End of year	0	1	2	3	4	5
Cash flow (thousands of dollars)	−2,200	800	1,200	1,600	1,400	1,000

Assume that the physical life of the asset is the same as that of the project and that there is no scrap value. The working capital is converted into cash at the end of the project. Assume that the corporate income tax rate is 46 percent and that ACRS is used to calculate taxable income.

The company's required rate of return for the project is 15 percent. Should the company undertake the project? Follow the example illustrated in the text. What impact might this project have on the market value of the company?

3. Calculate the internal rate of return for a capital project with the following expected (after-tax) net incremental cash flows. The required rate of

return for the project's risk class is 15 percent. Is the project financially viable?

End of year	0	1	2	3	4	5
Net incremental cash flow (dollars)	−2,000	200	400	600	800	800

*4. A company is contemplating investment in a project with capital outlays of $20,000. The scrap value is expected to be $2,000 at the end of the fifth and final year of the project. Which depreciation policy (straight-line or accelerated cost recovery) will result in the lowest taxes to be paid, and therefore the highest tax shields? Use a discount rate of 15 percent to compute the present value of the tax shields. Assume a corporate tax rate of 46 percent.

5. Wells, Inc., an all-equity financed firm, is considering a capital project with the following expected after-tax cash flows. It has the cash for the initial investment, and the market value of Wells's common stock is $30.42 million.

End of year	0	1	2	3	4
Incremental after-tax cash flow (thousands of dollars)	−8,500	3,200	5,000	4,500	3,000

Should the company invest in this project? What will be the present value of the project and the resulting market value of the company's equity if Wells, Inc., invests in the project? If Wells did not have the cash for the project and had to raise it from the equity market, how would the market value of the company be affected? The appropriate discount rate for the project is 15 percent.

*6. Why might some companies prefer to use the discounted payback method? A project requiring the following stream of investments provides the after-tax net incremental cash returns indicated below:

End of year	0	1	2	3	4
Net incremental cash flow (dollars)	−5,000	−4,000	−3,000	7,000	10,000

(a) What is the payback period for the project?

(b) What is the discounted payback at 10 percent?

*7. Calculate the average accounting rate of return for the following three-year project of Scove, Inc. The initial investment of $500,000 is expected to give rise to before-tax cash flows of $200,000 for each of the subsequent three years. The investment qualifies for the investment tax credit and ACRS. Assume the corporate income tax rate is 46 percent, and the expected scrap value is zero. Do not deduct the ITC from book value.

*8. Whiz Kid has $15,000 to commit to an investment at the present time. One possibility, a project to supply goods for four years to a large industrial customer, is virtually risk-free, as the prices are fixed and the purchases can also be obtained on a fixed price contract. The alternative is to purchase government bonds paying 10 percent annually (after-tax).

The expected net incremental after-tax cash flows for the project are given below (in dollars).

End of year	0	1	2	3	4
After cash flows	−15,000	4,500	4,500	4,500	4,500

Use the NPV method of investment appraisal to indicate which course of action would be more attractive financially. Determine what payback period for this project is consistent with a required rate of return of 10 percent. What would be the limitations on constructing payback criteria in this way?

9. A company can invest $9,000 in a project that is expected to produce after-tax net annual cash inflows of $4,000 for the next three years. The required rate of return on projects of similar risk is 15 percent.

(a) Calculate the net present value of the project.

(b) Calculate the payback period and the discounted payback period.

10. Using the data for the project in problem 9 answer the following questions:

(a) At what discount rate would the project break even?

(b) What is the minimum amount of after-tax net cash flow that the company would have to receive per year to break even if the required rate of return is 15 percent?

*11. The J-Kart Co. is planning to invest in a project costing $4 million that is eligible for the investment tax credit on five-year assets. The ACRS depreciation is shown below with the pre-tax operating cash flows (all in thousands of dollars).

End of year	1	2	3	4	5
Pre-tax operating cash flow	1,600	2,400	3,200	2,800	2,000
ACRS depreciation	580	850	812	812	812
Investment tax credit	266				

(a) Suppose J-Kart is in a nontaxpaying position now but expects to have sufficient revenues (including cash flows above) in year 3 to absorb the depreciation shields above. Calculate the net present value of the project. Assume there is no scrap value, that the corporate income tax rate is 46 percent, and that the discount rate is 15 percent.

(b) What difference would it make to the NPV of the project if the company were in a taxpaying position now?

12. Calculate the IRR from the sequence of accounting rates of return in Problem 7 (see Appendix 4.2), writing down final book value to zero.

13. A company has on file the information (given below) concerning the accounting book values and the returns on capital employed (ROCE) for an asset. Management has asked you what IRR was earned by the asset over the entire period (refer to Appendix 4.2).

Year ending	0	1	2	3
Book value	1,000	667	333	0
ROCE (%)		14.2	21.3	42.5

14. A company is examining the tax implications of investment in a project that has the following before-tax cash flows:

End of year	0	1	2	3	4
Cash flows	−600	−1,000	2,000	1,000	500

The project qualifies for ACRS depreciation as a three-year asset, but there is no investment tax credit. (a) Assuming the company has sufficient taxable profits elsewhere to shelter any tax losses when they arise, what is the value of the project's NPV? (b) How would the value of the project's NPV alter if the company is expected to have zero taxable profits elsewhere?

15. You are given the following accounting data for an asset (in thousands of dollars):

Year	0	1	2	3
Profit before tax		1,000	2,000	1,000
Depreciation		250	380	370

Net working capital worth $500,000 is required to operate the asset, and it does not qualify for an ITC.

(a) Prepare a table of after-tax cash flows for the project assuming a tax rate of 46%.

(b) Calculate the project's after-tax IRR from the cash flows.

(c) Calculate the project's after-tax IRR from its after-tax profits and book values.

References

Fisher, F. M., and J. J. McGowan, "On the Misuse of Accounting Rates of Return to Infer Monopoly Profits," *American Economic Review* 73, no. 1 (March 1983): 82–97.

Franks, J. R., and S. D. Hodges, "The Use of Accounting Numbers in Target Setting and Performance Measurement: Implications for Managers and Regulators," Paper presented at the American Finance Association Meetings in San Francisco, December 1983.

Kay, J. A., "Accountants, Too, Could be Happy in a Golden Age: The Accountant's Rate of Profit and the Internal Rate of Return," *Oxford Economic Papers* 28, no. 3, 1976: 447–60.

Livingstone, J. L., and G. L. Solomon, "Relationship Between the Accounting and the Internal Rate of Return Measure: A Synthesis and an Analysis," *Journal of Accounting Research* 8, no. 2 (1970): 199–216.

Marsh, P., and R. A. Brealey, "The Use of Imperfect Forecasts in Capital Budgeting," Proceedings of the European Finance Association, Amsterdam: North-Holland, 1974.

Petty, J. W., II, and D. F. Scott, Jr., "Capital Budgeting Practices in Large U.S. Firms: A Retrospective Analysis and Update," in *Readings in Strategy for Corporate Investment,* Eds. F. G. J. Berkunderen and R. L. Crum. Marshfield, Mass.: Pittman Publishing, 1981: 9–29.

Solomon, E., "Return on Investment: The Relationship of Book Yield to Time Yield," in *Research in Accounting Measurement,* ed. R. K. Jaedicke, Y. Ijiri, and O. W. Nielsen, American Accounting Association, 1966.

Stauffer, T. R., "The Measurement of Corporate Rates of Return—A Generalized Formulation," *Bell Journal of Economics and Management Science* 2, no. 2 (1971): 434–69.

DCF Methods: Problems Arising in Application

In the previous chapter we have given some examples indicating why the results of discounted cash flow methods provide different answers to other capital investment criteria such as payback and the accounting rate of return. Over 70 percent of large United States companies use DCF methods, either the internal rate of return (IRR) or the net present value (NPV). In the majority of these firms the internal rate of return appears to have become the most widely used method. This chapter discusses the difficulties that can arise in the use of the IRR and how to avoid them. The problems that can arise usually occur when direct comparisons are made between different projects and when capital is rationed by budgetary constraints.

Limitations of Rate of Return Criteria

Managers usually want to know the rate of return that a new asset is likely to earn in the future. This measure can then be compared with a rate of return offered on funds invested in the financial market and with rates of return being earned on other assets. Under some circumstances, however, the IRR can give ambiguous and even incorrect signals as to whether one project is more profitable than another. One purpose of this chapter is to describe the circumstances when you need to take particular care in interpreting a project's IRR. In these circumstances the NPV method must be used.

MUTUALLY EXCLUSIVE PROJECTS

The company may be faced with many different kinds of mutually exclusive projects; for example, whether to site a factory in one location or another, whether to buy an asset or to rent it, or whether to convert an old machine or purchase a new one. Using the IRR criterion to choose between alternatives is not without difficulty. Let us examine an example.

Suppose that we were to offer you two risk-free investments that are mutually exclusive; that is, you may invest in one or the other but not in both. We impose a further restriction that only one of each of these investments is available. Investment A has a rate of return of 100 percent for one year and investment B offers a rate of return of 30 percent for one year. The required rate of return in the financial market for the risk class of these investments is, let us say, 15 percent. All these figures are after tax. Which is the preferable investment? The rate of return maximizer will take investment A every time: 100 percent is better than 30 percent, and only 15 percent is required for this level of risk. However, the net present value maximizer requires more information before the choice can be made.

We now reveal that investment A requires an investment of only $1,000 and investment B offers the opportunity of investing $1 million. One does not require financial genius to appreciate that a 30 percent return on $1 million is a much better proposition than a 100 percent return on $1,000 even after deducting the 15 percent cost of capital. Investment A provides a dollar revenue of $2,000 while investment B provides a dollar revenue of $1,300,000. With a 15 percent cost of capital, investment A has an NPV of $739 and investment B an NPV of $130,435.

Investment A: $-\$1,000 + \$2,000/1.15 = \$739$

Investment B: $-\$1,000,000 + \$1,300,000/1.15 = \$130,435$

On the face of it, investment A appears to be a better investment than B because it offers a "margin" of 85 percent over and above the 15 percent cost of capital, while investment B offers a margin of only 15 percent above the cost of capital. Nevertheless, investment A has a much lower net present value in spite of its larger margin. The reason that investment A is not so favorable as investment B is that the net dollar returns are smaller. If we multiply the relatively small $1,000 investment in A by its margin of 85 percent, we obtain a profit of $850 net of the cost of capital. However if we multiply the larger investment of $1 million in B by its smaller margin of 15 percent, we obtain the much larger return of $150,000 net of the cost of capital. In other words, the larger scale of investment B more than compensates for its smaller margin. The IRR can only tell us the investment's margin over the cost of the funds. However, the NPV provides different information; it can tell us the margin in dollars discounted to present value.

It should be clear from this example why managers should prefer to maximize the NPV of their investment rather than the IRR. Maximizing NPV provides the largest dollar returns measured in today's value whereas maximizing IRR may not do so as the prior example illustrates.

Such problems with the IRR do not arise only because the two projects have very different capital outlays. Two projects with the same initial investment, the same life, and the same net present values can have very different internal rates of return. To illustrate, let us take the example in Table 5.1 of two mutually exclusive projects A and B, both requiring the same initial investment. Project A's positive cash flows arrive mainly in period 2, and project B's positive cash flows arrive mainly in period 1. Project A's internal rate of return is 72.8 percent, while project B's is 100 percent. Which project would you select?

The IRR for each project in Table 5.1 was calculated by finding the discount rate, *K,* that makes the project's net present value equal to zero. That is, we solved for *K* in the following equation:

$$\text{NPV} = 0 = C_0 + \frac{C_1}{(1 + K)} + \frac{C_2}{(1 + K)^2} + \cdots + \frac{C_N}{(1 + K)^N}$$

where C_N is the net cash flow in period *N*. We solved for *K* using the IRR function on a financial calculator, but you can also solve the equation manually using the interpolation method described in Chapter 3.

If the required rate of return for both projects is 20 percent, you may think that project B is clearly preferable to project A, for the internal rate of return for B is much higher and both require the same initial investment, but this is not the case. At a discount rate of 20 percent, you find that the net present value is the same ($10,000) for both projects, as shown in Table 5.1. Table 5.2 shows the net present value of the project at a 15 percent discount rate and again at 25 percent. At 15 percent the net present value for project A is larger ($11,701) than the net present value of project B ($11,248) even though A's IRR is smaller than B's. Consequently, at a discount rate

Table 5.1   *Evaluation of two mutually exclusive projects*

	End of year			IRR (%)	NPV at 20% (dollars)
	0	1	2		
		(dollars)			
Project A	−10,000	2,000	26,400	72.8	10,000
Project B	−10,000	14,000	12,000	100.0	10,000

Table 5.2   *Effect of changing the discount rate*

	NPV (%)		
	15	20	25
Project A	11,701	10,000	8,496
Project B	11,248	10,000	8,880

of 15 percent the NPV and IRR appear to conflict with one another. At rates above 20 percent, for example 25 percent, they agree. In those circumstances where the IRR and the NPV diverge, the use of IRR as the sole criterion for choosing between mutually exclusive projects leads to lower net present values and therefore to a lower value for the corporation.

Another way to look at the comparison is to note that projects A and B differ only in the profiles of their cash inflows in years 1 and 2: B's total cash inflow is smaller, but a larger proportion is received earlier. As a consequence, when capital markets offer high rates of return, B's earlier cash flows become more valuable, and above some rate (20 percent) B is preferred to A.

A GRAPHICAL REPRESENTATION

The two projects A and B are considered graphically in Figure 5.1. The horizontal axis represents the discount rate and the vertical axis the net present value resulting from each discount rate. Each curve represents the project's net present value at a series of discount rates. Along the horizontal axis, the internal rate of return for each project is found where the project's curve crosses the horizontal axis, that is, where the NPV is equal to zero. As it happens, each project has only one internal rate of return: For project A it is 72.8 percent and for project B it is 100 percent.

Now, it would be tempting to believe that project B is better than project A. If the object of financial policy were to maximize the internal rate of return on projects, you would choose project B, as it cuts the horizontal axis at the larger discount rate. However, one of the objects of financial policy is to maximize the market (dollar) value of the firm; this means maximizing the NPV of the project, which is measured in the vertical rather than in the horizontal direction. If the market discount rate for both projects is 15 percent, we see that the NPV at 15 percent is higher for A than for B, so project A increases the net present value of the firm more than project B. Only when the required rate of return exceeds the point at the intersection

Figure 5.1   *NPV versus discount rates for projects A and B*

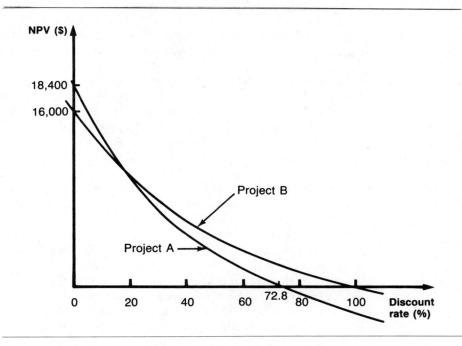

between the two curves at 20 percent is project B preferable to project A, as we have already seen in Table 5.2.

Table 5.1 and Figure 5.1 show that it can be misleading to compare two mutually exclusive projects on the basis of their internal rates of return alone. Projects A and B have the same net present values, the same initial investments, the same lives and the same risk, and yet they have very different internal rates of return because the projects have very different cash flow profiles.

In order to understand why this discrepancy exists, we must return to basic definitions. The **internal rate of return** (IRR) is defined as that discount rate that would make the net present value for a project equal to zero. The internal rate of return should be interpreted as that discount rate at which the project in question would just break even. As a rule, the rate of return that the project earns does not usually equal the break-even rate.

THE INCREMENTAL YIELD METHOD

Some analysts adapt the internal rate of return approach when comparing two projects by using the **incremental yield method**. First, they subtract the cash flows of project B from the cash flows of project A. Then they calculate the IRR on this incremental set of cash flows. If this internal rate of return (or incremental yield) is greater than the required rate of return, project A is considered to be more attractive than project B.

The method is demonstrated in Table 5.3 where you see that the incremental yield on the difference between A's and B's cash flows is 20 percent. Note that the IRR of 20 percent on the incremental cash flows is not equal to the difference between the two IRRs of 72.8 percent and 100 percent. The IRR, or yield on the incremental cash flows, suggests that, if the required rate of return is 20 percent for both projects, we would be indifferent about choosing either one. If the incremental yield of 20 percent were higher than the required rate of return, we would prefer project A. We would come to this conclusion even though the IRR on A's total cash flows is less than the IRR on B's total cash flows. If the incremental yield were lower than the required rate of return, we would prefer project B, subject to some qualifications described below.

In this example the incremental yield method results in the same decision as that indicated by net present value. Why not use the incremental yield method instead of net present value? There are three reasons. First, we assumed that the two projects in Table 5.3 have identical risks and therefore identical required rates of return of 20 percent. Suppose that the two projects had different risks and therefore different required rates of return, say, 15% on project A and 20% on project B. To what required rate of return would we compare the IRR on the incremental cash flow of $(A - B)$? We cannot use A's required rate of return of 15 percent nor B's of 20 percent, because the incremental cash flows $(A - B)$ are a mixture of A's and B's cash flows. We could use a discount rate that reflects the risks and required rates of return of both A and B, but it would be complicated to obtain the correct composite rate. As a result, the incremental yield method is simply too difficult to use correctly in these circumstances.

Table 5.3   *Evaluating two mutually exclusive projects using the incremental yield method*

| | End of year | | | IRR (%) | NPV at 20% (dollars) |
	0	1 (dollars)	2		
Project A	−10,000	2,000	26,400	72.8	10,000
Project B	−10,000	14,000	12,000	100.0	10,000
Difference (A − B)	0	−12,000	14,400	20.0	0

Second, if the cash flows of the two projects are of roughly the same scale, the difference between them is likely to exhibit frequent changes of sign over time. Cash flows that change sign more than once can have more than one IRR and thus there could be more than one incremental yield. We shall look at this problem in the next section.

Third, the NPV always provides the correct answer, and therefore the incremental yield may be regarded as unnecessary.

MULTIPLE INTERNAL RATES OF RETURN

Another difficulty with the internal rate of return as an investment criterion is that there may be more than one discount rate that will make the net present value equal to zero, and therefore more than one internal rate of return for a project. This difficulty arises from the mathematical implications of the definition of the internal rate of return. Remember that we are solving for an unknown discount rate K that makes the net present value equal to zero in the discounting formula:

$$\text{NPV} = 0 = C_0 + \frac{C_1}{(1 + K)} + \frac{C_2}{(1 + K)^2} + \cdots + \frac{C_N}{(1 + K)^N}$$

where C_N is the cash flow in period N. As the unknown discount rate K is raised to powers greater than one, there can be more than one solution for the value of K.

You may recall that the unknown in a quadratic equation can have up to two values. In the quadratic equation, the unknown is squared. In a polynomial such as the one above, the unknown, $K,$ is raised to even higher powers, and it can have correspondingly more values. Fortunately, the maximum number of different real values for K is limited to the number of changes of sign in the cash flow sequence.

In what kinds of projects do multiple rates of return arise? They might well occur with large-scale mining or oil development projects where large negative cash flows arise late in the project's life if the mine has to be closed and the environment landscaped, or where offshore oil wells have to be capped and the equipment removed. Multiple rates of return also arise in some kinds of leasing transactions. Multiple rates of return raise two problems. First, if the analyst does not know that more than one solution exists, all the solutions may not have been found. Second, even if all the solutions have been found it may not be obvious how the multiple internal rates of return should be compared to the required rate of return. The subsequent example will illustrate these problems in more detail.

Consider the example of the net incremental cash flows for the two projects in Table 5.4. Project C has only one change of sign (from −$50,000

Table 5.4   *Net present value and internal rates of return for two projects*

| | End of year | | | NPV at 20% (dollars) | IRR (%) |
	0	1 (dollars)	2		
Project C	−10,000	−50,000	60,000	−10,000	0
Project D	−10,000	50,000	−60,000	−10,000	100, 200

to +$60,000) and therefore can have only one value for the IRR, which happens to be equal to zero. Project D is a similar project in that it has the same cash flows, but the signs of the final two cash flows are reversed. Project D has the same net present value as project C (−$10,000) but it has a large negative cash flow at the end of its life. In this case there are two changes of sign in the cash flow sequence from −$10,000 to +$50,000 and from +$50,000 to −$60,000. Therefore there can be up to but no more than two values for the IRR. In fact the IRR is now equal to both 100 percent and 200 percent for project D.

Clearly, project C is not viable, for its net present value discounted at the project's required rate of return of 20 percent is −$10,000. Furthermore, the project's IRR is less than its required return of 20 percent. As a result, both DCF methods suggest that project C does not compare favorably with a 20 percent rate of return in the financial market. Project C's NPVs are plotted for different discount rates in Figure 5.2.

Project D is no better than project C, as it has the same negative net present value, the same initial investment, and the same life. Nevertheless, project D has the high IRRs of 100 and 200 percent in comparison with project C's zero IRR. You would be deceived if you thought that project D really earns 100 or 200 percent. It would earn these rates of return only if the prevailing rate of return in the financial market for an asset of that risk were either 100 or 200 percent. However, we are told that the required rate of return is only 20 percent, which gives a negative net present value. Remember that the IRR is merely a break-even discount rate. The IRR is a reliable measure of what a project earns only when the project's required rate of return happens to equal the project's IRR.

Project D's NPVs are plotted for different discount rates in Figure 5.3. Project D is just as unattractive as an investment as project C at the 20 percent discount rate and would not become attractive unless the discount rate were to be above 100 percent (but less than 200 percent), as the figure shows. Even within this range the project is barely profitable although the IRRs are high. The graph in Figure 5.3 tells us that if the NPV curve starts

Figure 5.2   *NPV versus discount rate for project C*

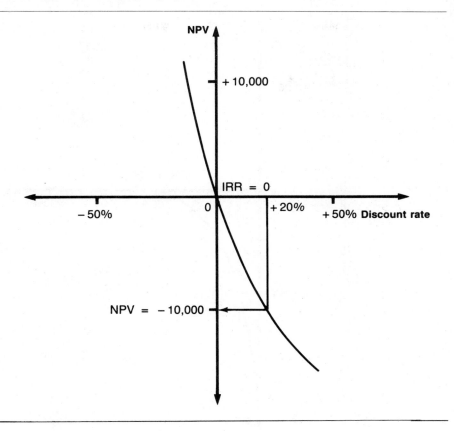

out negative (the sum of the undiscounted cash flows is negative), and if there are two IRRs, the project is not viable unless the required rate of return falls between the two IRRs where the NPV is positive. Obviously the IRR on its own can be an unreliable indicator of a project's attractiveness in comparison to a comparable investment in the financial market.

The contrast between projects C and D raises an additional question concerning multiple internal rates of return. There are two changes of sign in the sequence of cash flows of project D and two IRRs. Remember that the number of changes of sign in the cash flow sequence for a project provides only an upper limit on the possible number of IRRs. The actual number of IRRs can be fewer than this upper bound. How can we tell how many IRRs there really are? One way is simply to plot the NPV at different discount rates as we have done already for projects C and D in Figures 5.2 and 5.3. Each time the curve crosses the horizontal axis (where the NPV is zero), we

Figure 5.3   *NPV versus discount rate for Project D*

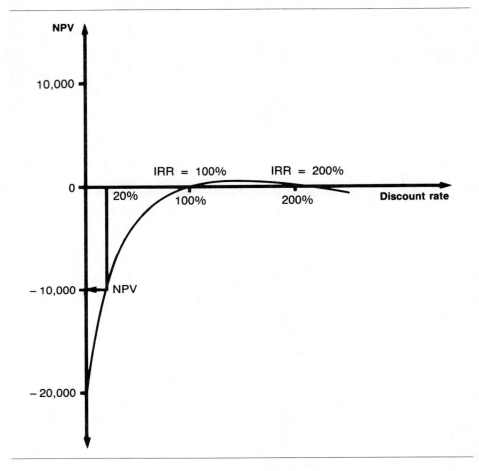

have another value for the IRR. We know that happens twice for project D. It would be useful to know ahead of time just how many IRR values might occur so that we know when to stop plotting. In Appendix 5.1 we discuss a more refined sign sequence rule that can indicate how many different values for the IRR could be found.

You may be wondering why we have devoted so much space to the internal rate of return if on occasions it is a less reliable criterion than net present value and at the same time is more difficult to calculate. We have done so because the IRR is more widely used than NPV in industry. The reason is that managers and analysts find it intuitively more appealing to measure percentage returns than dollar amounts as the NPV does.

ANALYZING PROJECTS INDEPENDENTLY

We have shown that mutually exclusive projects should not be compared on the basis of their internal rates of return alone, as a project with a higher rate of return than another can have a lower net present value. When they are considering projects independently, managers like to compare a project's internal rate of return with the required rate. Projects are treated as eligible for investment if the IRR is greater than the required rate of return.

Normally, this procedure will be satisfactory providing that the project's cash flows do not have multiple sign changes, as in the example of project D. Both project D IRRs are in excess of the 20 percent required rate of return for the project, but we know that the project has a negative net present value at a discount rate of 20 percent. In fact the IRR has given incorrect signals. These criticisms do not mean that analysts should never use the IRR; rather they should know when the IRR provides an ambiguous or incorrect signal as to the accept-reject decision. This suggests that the IRR should not be used as the sole investment criterion, but rather as an addition to the NPV.

Profitability Index

Providing that the correct discount rate is used and that the analyst has an unbiased forecast of net incremental cash flows for the investment, a positive net present value will always indicate whether the investment is a financially favorable one. However, management frequently wishes to relate the net present value of a project to the size of the capital investment. A net present value of $10,000 may be very significant for a project requiring an investment of only $20,000, but it would be trivial for a project requiring an investment of $1 million. The profitability index provides a relative measure of profitability that reflects the scale of investment. The **profitability index** (PI) is defined as the present value (PV) of net cash flows divided by the present value (I) of the investment expenditures:

$$PI = PV/I$$
$$\quad = (NPV + I)/I$$

The profitability index for project A in Table 5.1 is

$$PI = 20,000/10,000$$
$$\quad = 2.00$$

What does this figure mean? It means that the project generates $2 of present value for each $1 of investment.

How shall we interpret the profitability index? Consider two projects. Project 1 and project 2 each has a net present value of $100, and therefore they both look equally profitable. However, project 1 requires an investment of only $500, where project 2 requires an investment of $10,000.

	NPV $	I $	PI
Project 1	100	500	(100 + 500)/500 = 1.20
Project 2	100	10,000	(100 + 10,000)/10,000 = 1.01

Each dollar invested in project 1 generates $1.20 in present value, while each dollar invested in project 2 generates only $1.01 in present value. Clearly, project 2 barely breaks even though its NPV is the same as the NPV of project 1. Financial forecasting is frequently subject to problems of inadequate information and management bias, and in the above example the profitability index of only 1.01 for project 2 makes it clear that there is much less room for forecasting error or bias in evaluating this project than there is for project 1 with a PI of 1.20.

One word of warning should be given. The profitability index could be manipulated by treating part of the capital expenditure as operating expense, thereby reducing the denominator of the profitability index. For example, if $50 of capital expenditure in project 1 were called operating expense, the NPV would be unaffected, but the value of I would be reduced by $50, from $500 to $450. The result would be[1]

Profitability Index = (100 + 500)/450 = 1.333

The index increases from 1.20 to 1.333 merely as a result of reclassifying a cash flow item.

The profitability index can be useful, however, when the funds available for capital investment are rationed (for example, by divisional capital budgets). The profitability index can indicate how to obtain the maximum total net present value from the available capital.

---

[1] In reclassifying the cash flows the numerator is unaffected because the total present value (PV) of the cash flows is unchanged by accounting classifications.

Capital Rationing

The funds available for capital investment are limited for many firms, a condition called **capital rationing.** For example, small companies that are unlisted on any stock exchange and without easy access to the capital market are often unable to raise sufficient funds to finance many large projects. Even if funds are available, they may come at a substantial price. For example, current owners may be unwilling to give up control of the company in exchange for the required capital, or outside investors may not be willing to pay the right price for the new shares. The latter is often the case with smaller companies which are owner-managed and where the owner has more information than investors (and which cannot be easily validated).

Even large companies whose securities are traded in the capital market often behave as though they face capital rationing. In principle, the financial market can finance all projects with positive net present values. In practice, top management may use capital budgeting rules to restrict investment. Given limited managerial and technical manpower, capital budgeting is a device used to force middle management to select the projects of the greatest priority. Budgeting capital across the different divisions of the business is also a means of implementing corporate plans and business strategy. By encouraging growth in promising lines of business and restricting investment in other areas, top management can superimpose its selective view on the growth of the company. This means that funds for capital investment are restricted in those divisions that might like to grow more rapidly than senior management believes is compatible with their view of the divisions' growth prospects.

The profitability index can be used as a criterion for ranking projects under conditions of capital rationing. Projects with the highest profitability index are accepted first until the available funds are used up. The idea is to maximize the total present value from the limited funds available. This problem is really a job for a computerized model, but the profitability index ranking procedure can lead to a reasonable approximation for allocating funds that are limited in a single period.

Table 5.5 shows five projects ranked in descending order by values of their profitability index. Project 5 is listed at the top because its PI value of 3.0 (column 3) is the highest. Its net present value *per dollar* of investment is the best of the five. The final column is the cumulative sum of the investments required in column 2. Thus the first two investments require a total budget of $6,000, the first three investments require $16,000, and so on. The cumulative funds requirement can be matched against the available capital budget, and the budget will determine which of the top ranking projects can be included in the investment program. For example, if the capital budget is $24,000, project 4 must be left out. If the budget is only $22,000, however, project 2 must be left out as it brings the total capital requirement to $24,000.

Table 5.5   *Profitability index rankings (thousands of dollars)*

	NPV	I	PI*	Cumulative sum of I
Project 5	2.00	1	3.00	1
Project 3	2.50	5	1.50	6
Project 1	4.00	10	1.40	16
Project 2	2.80	8	1.35	24
Project 4	0.60	6	1.10	30

* (NPV + I)/I

If both projects 2 and 4 are left out, we need only $16,000 and have $6,000 left. Thus we can fit project 4 into the budget even though we have to leave out the better but larger project 2.

By ranking projects in the descending order of their profitability index values and matching their cumulative funds requirements against the available capital budget in this way, we can maximize the total present value obtainable under capital rationing.

If Table 5.5 had ranked the five projects according to their respective IRRs, we could expect to obtain a somewhat different ordering. As we have shown earlier, if the IRR is inconsistent with net present value, it can also be inconsistent with the profitability index because the latter is based on the NPV. If we had chosen projects according to a different ordering, we would not be able to obtain the maximum total net present value. The IRR should not be used as a criterion for ranking projects when the capital budget limits the number of projects that can be accepted.

We have, however, made an assumption that in some circumstances may be unrealistic. We have assumed that investment in all the projects takes place in the same budgetary period and that funds generated from earlier projects are not added to the capital budget. Thus our assumptions do not permit the cash flows of one project to be invested in another. If a division of the company has a degree of financial autonomy, it may be permitted to use funds generated by previous investments to finance subsequent projects and to carry forward surplus funds for this purpose. In this more complex situation the division still may experience capital rationing, with implications for the choice of projects that are too subtle to be handled by rankings based upon the profitability index. A best choice of projects in this circumstance presents a potentially complex problem for which mathematical programming often offers the best solution.

Table 5.6 illustrates a capital budgeting problem in which the best of four projects beginning in different periods must be selected so as not to exceed the capital budget. The budget shown in the last column is $1 million. In

Table 5.6   *Cash flow of four capital investments and the capital budget (thousands of dollars)*

	Project				
End of year	A	B	C	D	Budget
0	1,000				1,000
1	200	500			
2	200	100	550		
3	200	100	100	660	
4	200	100	100	132	

this case, no further funds are to be allocated to the division, but the division is to be allowed to use funds generated by one project to finance another and to keep surplus funds within the division for this purpose. Surplus funds in one period may be saved and invested in the financial market at 10 percent for investment in subsequent projects in later periods.

It is easy to see in the table that if the initial $1 million of capital were to be used for capital project A, all that would be left for project B would be the $200,000 generated by project A in period 1. As project B requires a minimum of $500,000, insufficient funds would be available for it. Project C could not be undertaken for the same reason. Project D, on the other hand, could be selected as well as A because it does not begin until the end of period 3. By that time, project A will have generated $200,000 per period for three periods. These funds together with interest would be more than sufficient to fund the $660,000 cost of project D. Although we can see that A and D are feasible within the budget, is this combination the only one that is feasible? If not, which feasible combination of projects provides the largest total net present value?

The search for feasible combinations of projects follows the principle that cumulative net commitments to projects must not exceed the cumulative capital budget, after allowing for interest earned from reinvestment of temporarily idle cash in the financial market. Table 5.7 shows the accumulated cash flows of each project in Table 5.6 together with interest compounded at 10 percent earned from reinvestment. Take, for example, the figures shown for project A (in thousands of dollars). The first figure is still −$1,000. The second figure is −$1,000 × 1.1 + $200 = −$900. The third figure is −$900 × 1.1 + $200 = −$790, and so on. These figures show an application of the principle that the cumulative net commitments to projects must not exceed the cumulative capital budget after allowing for opportunities for reinvestment of any temporarily idle cash.

Table 5.7   *Cumulative requirements for funds (thousands of dollars)*

End of year	Project A	B	C	D	Budget
0	−1,000				1,000
1	−900	−500			1,100
2	−790	−450	−550		1,210
3	−669	−395	−505	−660	1,331
4	−536	−335	−456	−594	1,464

By comparing sums from left to right in Table 5.7 with the cumulative budget in the final column, all feasible combinations can be found. Let us apply the method. Project A can be undertaken because the $1,000 required does not exceed the budget of $1,000. Can any other project also be undertaken along with project A? Consider project B. As the combined cumulative net requirements of $900 for A and the investment of $500 for B exceed the cumulative budget of $1,100, the combination of A and B is infeasible. The same is true of A and C. Now let us consider A and D. The cumulative net requirement for A and D is $669 + $660 = $1,329. As $1,329 does not exceed the cumulative budget of $1,331 at that stage, both A and D are feasible within the budget. The profitability of such a combination of projects would be indicated by their combined net present value, both discounted to a common date, period zero. Actually, there may be other feasible combinations of projects that could be more profitable.

Consider next the combination of project B with projects other than A. Project B can be combined with project C, for the cumulative net requirement for funds, $450 + $550 = $1,000, does not exceed the cumulative budget of $1,210. Similarly, project B can also be combined with project D within the cumulative budget. By the same method, we find that projects C and D are also feasible together. Table 5.8 shows the cumulative net requirement for funds for each possible combination of two projects. The only combinations of projects that actually are feasible are those for which the combined cumulative funds requirement is less than or equal to the cumulative budget. The infeasible combinations are indicated by asterisks in the table. Although the table does not show combinations of three and four projects, you can use the information in Table 5.7 to explore these possibilities.

To summarize, projects are feasible in the following combinations within the cumulative budget: A, B, C, D, AD, BC, BD, CD. The immediate decision is whether to invest in project A since investment in that project would prevent investment in any other project but D. If project combinations

Table 5.8   *Cumulative fund requirements for different combinations of projects (thousands of dollars)*

End of year	A	AB	AC	AD	B	BC	BD	C	CD	D	Budget
0	1,000										1,000
1		1,400*			500						1,100
2			1,340*			1,000		550			1,210
3				1,329			1,055		1,165	660	1,331
4											1,464

(header spanning A through D: "Projects")

including B or C were more profitable, we would not invest in A. To make the choice, we simply add the net present values as of period zero for each feasible combination of projects, as we have done in Table 5.9. (The positive net present values for the four projects are accounted for in part by cash flows after year 4 not shown in Table 5.6.) The feasible combination AD has the largest total net present value of $280,000, and therefore is preferred. The discount rate that should be used for each project is the capital market required rate of return which reflects the risk of the project. By maximizing the total net present value obtained in this way, we maximize the increase in the market value of the firm that can be obtained within a limited capital budget.

We have just demonstrated the manual solution of an **integer programming** problem. Application of mathematical programming methods to financial planning problems is discussed further in Appendix 5.2.

One problem with this sort of financial analysis is that we treat projects as though their results are known with certainty. Actually, one does not have

Table 5.9   *Net present values of feasible combinations of projects (thousands of dollars)*

Project	A	B	C	D
A	150			280
B		120	245	250
C			125	255
D				130

(header spanning A through D: "With project")

full information concerning future projects at the outset. Further investment opportunities may be revealed subsequently. (There are ways to make tentative provision for further projects when determining the budget size, but they are beyond the scope of this book.) Also, projects that are anticipated now may be made obsolete subsequently by competitive developments that eliminate assumed competitive advantage. Furthermore, capital budgets may be increased or reduced depending upon success or failure in the business and upon financing in the capital market. Finally, the concept of a capital budget may be too simple in cases where leasing, joint ventures, and mergers provide alternative methods of financing particular projects. For these reasons, mathematical programming methods have not been widely used for project selection. They have been used mainly in broad financial planning situations, in which management policies and/or lender restrictions impose limitations on financial practices such as dividend payments or borrowing. (We will deal with some of these matters in later chapters.)

Nevertheless, the formalized statement of the capital rationing problem helps to describe the problems faced by small companies and by divisions whose growth is being limited by capital budgets. It shows the impact that such restrictions can have on consideration of feasible combinations of projects and on the resulting total net present value. We could use this approach to project selection when project values interact because of taxes, as described in Chapter 4, p. 75.

Summary

The net present value method is the most consistent and straightforward method of financial analysis. The internal rate of return can be an ambiguous indicator of profitability; it is, by definition, a break-even discount rate that does not necessarily reflect the rate of return actually earned by a project. Furthermore, rates of return are of limited use for making comparisons between projects unless the projects are of the same scale. To make life a little easier, however, correctly estimated positive NPVs always imply profitable projects, and where projects are mutually exclusive, the one with the largest NPV is more profitable. The financial aspects of investment decisions can always be based on the net present value method.

The internal rate of return can be calculated in addition, but it should be supplemented by the NPV criterion to ensure that the correct decision is made. In the case of limitations on cash or other resources available for capital investment, the NPV method should still be used. The objective is to maximize the total net present value for the combination of projects selected, subject to limited resources available.

Appendix 5.1 Predicting the Maximum Possible Number of Internal Rates of Return for a Project

A capital project is represented by a sequence of cash flows, which may have one or more internal rates of return. How can one predict the number of internal rates of return that the cash flow sequence might generate? Pratt and Hammond (1979) have provided a number of rules for determining upper bounds on the possible number of IRRs. These rules are based upon a cumulative cash balance method. The cash balance is found by adding the project cash flows cumulatively from left to right. For example, the first row of Table A5.1.1 shows the cash flows for a project, and the second row shows the cumulative cash balance.

Note that in the first row there are four changes of sign in the cash flow sequence but that in the cash balance sequence in the second row there are only two changes in sign. Pratt and Hammond provide the following rules relating to cash balance sequences:

Rule 1

The number of internal rates of return is no greater than the number of sign changes in the cash balance over the life of the project.

Rule 2

The number of internal rates of return is odd if the initial cash flow and final cash balance have opposite signs. It is even, possibly zero, if they have the same sign.

Rule 3

If the cash balance never changes sign over the life of the project, there is no internal rate of return. If it changes sign just once and the final cash balance is not zero, there is exactly one internal rate.

Pratt and Hammond also show that closer upper bounds on the number of IRRs can be found by further stages of cumulation, that is by cumulatively adding the preceding cumulative cash flow from left to right. Often the number of sign changes will be fewer in the final stage. If so, we obtain a closer bound on the possible number of internal rates of return for the original cash flow sequence. Pratt and Hammond give the example reproduced in

Table A5.1.1   *Cumulative cash balance for a project (thousands of dollars)*

Cash flow	−10	50	−30	10	−200
Cash balance	−10	40	10	20	−180

Table A5.1.2. Note that each row is obtained by cumulating the row above. Any number of stages may be used until it is obvious that the number of sign changes in the final stage will not be reduced by proceeding to further stages.

If two or more stages of cumulation are used, the following rule applies:

Rule 4

Count the number of sign changes going across the bottom row to the end of, around the corner, and up the right-hand side of the table of cumulative values (for any number of stages). This number is the upper bound on the number of internal rates of the original sequence of cash flows.

Note that the rule says to count the cumulations themselves and to count around the corner. Note that there is only one sign change for the final stage in Table A5.1.2 (going around the corner) and thus there can be no more than one IRR for the original sequence of cash flows. Changes from -1 to 0 or from 0 to 1 do not count as sign changes. Without their rules we might anticipate up to eight IRRs when in fact we now know there is only one. Pratt and Hammond provide further rules in their article that may be useful in unusual cases. The multistage cumulative cash flow method together with the four rules given here would suffice in the majority of cases to generate very close upper bounds on the possible number of internal rates of return for a cash flow sequence.

Appendix 5.2 Formulating an Integer Program

A more standardized formulation of the problem in Tables 5.6, 5.7, and 5.8 is given in Table A5.2.1. A standardized formulation facilitates computer input. In the first row of the table we show the objective function

Maximize $P_1X_1 + P_2X_2 + P_3X_3 + P_4X_4$

where P_j is the net present value of the project j ($j = 1, 2, 3, 4$). The variable X_j has the value 1 if project j is included in a feasible combination of projects and has the value of 0 if the project is not included. The project's capital requirements are multiplied by X_j (either 0 or 1) for each project and then added. For example, in row 5 we have

$669X_1 + 395X_2 + 505X_3 + 660X_4 \leq 1,331$

This expression says that the total cumulative funds requirement for the projects included in a solution must be less than or equal to ($\leq$) the $1,331,000

Table A5.1.2   *Four stages of cumulation*

CASH	−1	4	−11	20	−20	15	−15	10	−1
CUMULATIONS									
Stage 1	−1	3	−8	12	−8	7	−8	2	1
Stage 2	−1	2	−6	6	−2	5	−3	−1	0
Stage 3	−1	1	−5	1	−1	4	1	0	0
Stage 4	−1	0	−5	−4	−5	−1	0	0	0

Source: John W. Pratt and John S. Hammond, III, "Evaluating and Comparing Projects: Simple Detection of False Alarms," *Journal of Finance* 34 (December 1979): 1234–1242.

cumulative capital budget available by this period. The projects actually included in the optimal combination within this budget will depend upon the values of the X_j (0 or 1) in the solution. For example, when projects A and D are in the solution, the above inequality becomes

$$669 \times 1 + 395 \times 0 + 505 \times 0 + 660 \times 1 \leq 1,331$$

$$669 + 0 + 0 + 660 \leq 1,331$$

or $1,329 \leq 1,331$

This combination obviously satisfies the constraint. Because it also satisfies all the other constraints as well, it is a feasible solution. However, it is not

Table A5.2.1   *Programming formulation based on Table 5.7 (thousands of dollars)*

	Project				
	A	**B**	**C**	**D**	**Budget**
Objective function to maximize	P_1X_1 +	P_2X_2 +	P_3X_3 +	P_4X_4	
Subject to constraints	$1{,}000X_1$ +	$0X_2$ +	$0X_3$ +	$0X_4$ ≤	1,000
	$900X_1$ +	$500X_2$ +	$0X_3$ +	$0X_4$ ≤	1,100
	$790X_1$ +	$450X_2$ +	$550X_3$ +	$0X_4$ ≤	1,210
	$669X_1$ +	$395X_2$ +	$505X_3$ +	$660X_4$ ≤	1,331
	$536X_1$ +	$335X_2$ +	$456X_3$ +	$594X_4$ ≤	1,464
and		$X_j = 0, 1$ $j = 1, 2, \ldots, N$			

the only feasible solution, as we have already seen, and it may not be the optimal solution that maximizes the total net present value. Computerized integer programming algorithms are available that can search systematically for all feasible combinations and find the feasible combination that maximizes the objective function.

The method is easily adapted to reflect constraints other than capital rationing. For example, we could add another row to Table A5.2.1 reflecting constraints on the availability of key management or technical personnel who might be required in each period to implement projects successfully. The coefficient of X_j in a row of Table A5.2.1 could represent the number of man-years available in that period.

If two of the projects are mutually exclusive, we can include the constraint

$$1X_j + 1X_k \leq 1$$

where projects j and k are the mutually exclusive projects. Thus, should X_j take the value 1 in the optimum solution, X_k would have to take the value 0 (and vice versa).

If instead, project j were contingent on project k, that is, if project j could not be undertaken unless project k were undertaken first, we would include the constraint:

$$1X_j - 1X_k \leq 0$$

Note that this constraint is equivalent to

$$X_j \leq X_k$$

and that therefore, if the value of X_k is 0, the value of X_j must also be 0. Only if the value of X_k is equal to 1 can the value of X_j be 1. With this constraint we have ensured that project j will be contingent on project k in the optimal solution.

The coefficients of Xs in Table A5.2.1 are arranged in the format usually required for input to computer programs designed to solve linear optimization problems. Our example includes only four variables, one for each project. Computer programs exist that can solve integer programs for up to around twenty variables, with reasonable efficiency. For many more variables, the linear programming method of solution may be required. A linear programming solution will allow fractional values of X, indicating that only a fraction of a project is required in the optimal solution. Such a solution may not be feasible technically, and the assumed costs and revenues may not apply to projects that are not implemented at full scale. Unfortunately, simply rounding fractions up or down will not, in general, yield the optimum integer combination.

Review Questions

1. Define the IRR. Under what conditions can a project be said to earn a rate of return equal to the IRR?
2. "If a project's IRR is greater than its required rate of return, the project must be profitable." Is this statement true or false? Explain your answer.
3. Discuss the different conditions under which the IRR may not give the correct signal as to whether a project is profitable.
4. Describe the incremental yield method. Why is this method used, and what are its disadvantages?
5. When do multiple rates of return arise? Given a set of net cash flows, can you always tell by inspection how many IRRs or solutions there are? Give reasons for your answer.
6. Why is the profitability index used by companies? In what circumstances is it most useful?
7. Under what circumstances, and for what kinds of companies, would you expect capital rationing to occur?
8. "In a perfect capital market there is no such thing as capital rationing." Is this statement true or false?
9. Why might some companies impose capital constraints on a division's capital expenditures even when the company has unrestricted access to funds?
10. Why is the integer programming method for solving the capital rationing problem preferable to the profitability index approach?
11. Explain how you would use linear (or integer) programming to help solve the problem of interactions between investment decisions and taxes described in Chapter 4.

Problems

*1. Two mutually exclusive projects have identical initial investments. The product manager has forecast the cash flows and suggests that project A, with an IRR of about 80 percent, should be chosen, as project B's IRR is only 60 percent. The projects have the same risk. If the company's required rate of return for these projects is 20 percent, which project should be undertaken? When would a different required rate of return change your decision?

End of year	0	1	2	3
Project A	−25,000	25,000	30,000	10,800
Project B	−25,000	10,000	10,000	60,800

*2. The expected cash flows (in dollars) for two mutually exclusive projects are given below. Both projects have the same risk, and their required rate of return is 10 percent. Obtain the values of the NPV and the IRR for each project, and justify your choice as to which is the best project.

End of year	0	1	2	3	4	5
Project A	−15,000	10,000	8,000	6,000	0	0
Project B	−15,000	6,000	6,000	6,000	6,000	6,000

3. In problem 1 assume project A has a lower risk and a required rate of return of 10 percent, and project B is riskier and therefore requires a rate of return of 15 percent. Can you use the incremental yield method to determine which project is more profitable? If so, complete the calculation. If not, explain your answer.

4. A company involved in the exploration of oil has estimated the after-tax cash flows from an oil field to be as follows for its ten-year life (in millions of dollars):

End of year	0	1	2	3	...	10
Net cash flow	−150	22	22	22	...	22

A cash subsidy of $50 million will be received in year 0.

Calculate the IRR for this investment by plotting the net present value of the project against the discount rates used. Find out what happens to the IRR when:

(a) The subsidy expected in year 0 is not forthcoming; or
(b) There are abandonment costs of $80 million in the last period (year 10) but the subsidy still is received in year 0.

What should the company do if its required rate of return is 15 percent?

*5. Given below are the net incremental cash flows for two mutually exclusive capital projects (in dollars):

End of year	0	1	...	9	10
Project A	−4,750	1,000	...	1,000	0
Project B	−4,572	900	...	900	1,000

(a) Plot the NPV versus the discount rate for each project in the range of 0 to 20 percent.
(b) Plot the NPV versus the discount rate for the difference between the cash flows of A and B for the same range of interest rates.

(c) Explain why obtaining the internal rate of return for the difference between the cash flows of two mutually exclusive projects will not always provide an unambiguous criterion for choice between them.

*6. Plot the net present value versus the discount rate for the following net incremental cash flows (in the range of 0 to 30 percent).

End of year	0	1	2	. . .	9	10
Project	−178	81	81	. . .	81	−919

(a) What is the NPV at 15 percent, 20 percent, and at 30 percent?
(b) What is the internal rate of return for the project?
(c) Explain how the IRR can exceed the required rate of return in some cases, yet the NPV can still be negative and therefore make the project unacceptable.

7. Write the equation for the net present value of the following project, and then solve for the IRR (the discount rate that makes the NPV equal to zero).

End of year	0	1	2
Net cash flow	−350	1,750	−2,100

*8. A firm with total resources of $2,000 has the opportunity of investing in one or more of the projects below, with the net after-tax cash flows shown below.

End of year	0	1	2	3	4
Project A	−2,000	700	700	700	700
Project B	−1,000	380	380	380	380
Project C	−1,000	330	330	330	330
Project D	−900	320	320	320	320

If the discount rate is 12 percent, use the profitability index method to select the project or projects in which the company should invest to maximize profitability. Surplus funds cannot be reinvested, and any project can be undertaken only once.

*9. A division of a large firm is considering four projects for which net incremental cash flows are given in the table below. Also shown in the table is the divisional budget for capital investments that has been approved by headquarters for the current year and for each of the next two years. No external funds are available for years 3, 4, and 5. Cash flows generated by the projects may be included in the budget, and budgeted funds not invested immediately in projects may be held in reserve for later use and invested in securities at 10 percent after-tax. If the required rate of return for each project is 15 percent, which combination of projects should be accepted, subject to the budget constraints? What is the maximum obtainable total net present value? (Use Tables 5.6 to 5.9 as guides.)

End of year	Cash flow for each project (thousands of dollars)				Budget
	A	B	C	D	
0	−900				1,000
1	495	−400	−900		200
2	495	205	495	−1,500	200
3	495	205	495	735	0
4		205	495	735	0
5				735	0

10. A paper manufacturing company has identified three projects in which it wishes to invest. The cash flows are shown below:

End of year	0	1	2	3	4
Project A	−3,500	−14,000	17,500	17,500	—
Project B	−5,000	−5,000	20,000	12,500	—
Project C	−9,000	500	6,000	9,000	12,000

The company has $12,000 to invest now and another $8,000 to invest in the next period. The projects cannot be delayed, and any funds not used can be invested at the risk-free rate of 10 percent per year. However, during period 1, a shortage of a raw material is expected, and only 35,000 tons are available. Projects A, B, and C use 15,000, 12,000, and 20,000 tons of this material, respectively. A fixed overhead of $3,000 per year has to be allowed for, as this will be spent no matter which project is undertaken. The company's required rate of return is 20 percent; the projects are all in the same risk class.

Formulate this problem as a linear program. The objective is to maximize the NPV of the company. (A linear program assumes the projects are divisible.)

What important considerations and assumptions must you make when formulating the linear program?

*11. Estimate the maximum number of IRRs for the cash flow below. Use the Pratt and Hammond method described in Appendix 5.1 to predict the number of IRRs that the following sequence of cash flows below might generate.

End of year	0	1	2	3	4
Cash flow	−25	125	−75	25	−500

12. A company is intending to lease a piece of equipment costing $1,000. Three possible lease agreements require the following rental streams, including an immediate advance rental payment in year 0:

End of year	0	1	2	3	4
Lease 1	362.6	290.1	217.6	145.0	72.5
Lease 2	230.0	230.0	230.0	230.0	230.0
Lease 3	82.5	165.0	247.5	330.0	412.5

Calculate the IRR for the lease versus purchase decision for each of these leases, ignoring all taxes. Calculate the NPV of each lease versus purchase decision using a discount rate of 13 percent. Rank the three leases on the basis of IRR and NPV. Why do the rankings differ? Which lease is the least costly?

13. A firm is examining three projects whose investment and profitability is reproduced below. Which projects would you select if the capital available was restricted to $2,000?

	Size of initial investment	NPV	IRR
Investment A	1,000	200	20%
Investment B	1,000	300	18%
Investment C	1,000	250	22%

14. A company is considering an investment in a new project with the following cash flows:

Year	0	1	2
Cash flows	−1,000	−600	2,000

The state government offers the firm a loan of $750 for three years at an interest rate of 3 percent per annum. The firm would have to repay the loan entirely at the end of three years. The equivalent loan raised by the firm from a bank would cost 12 percent per annum. What is the NPV of the project, if its required rate of return is 17 percent per annum (without the loan)?

References

Alchian, A. A., "The Rate of Interest, Fisher's Rate of Return Over Costs and Keynes' Internal Rate of Return," *American Economic Review* 45, no. 5 (December 1955): 938–43.

Arrow, K. J., and D. Levhari, "Uniqueness of the Internal Rate of Return with Variable Life of Investment," *Economic Journal* 79 (September 1969): 560–66.

Aucamp, Donald C., and Walter L. Eckardt, Jr., "A Sufficient Condition for a Unique Nonnegative Internal Rate of Return—Comment," *Journal of Financial and Quantitative Analysis* 10 (1976).

Broyles, J. E., "Compact Formulations of Mathematical Programmes for Financial Planning Problems," *Operational Research Quarterly* 27, no. 4 (1976): 885–93.

Carleton, W. T., "Linear Programming and Capital Budgeting Models: A New Interpretation,"*Journal of Finance* 24, no. 5 (December 1969): 825–33.

Carleton, W. T., G. Kendall, and S. Tandon, "Application of the Decomposition Principle to the Capital Problem in a Decentralized Firm," *Journal of Finance* 29, no. 3 (June 1974): 815–28.

Chambers, D., "Programming the Allocation of Funds Subject to Restrictions on Reported Results," *Operational Research Quarterly* 18, no. 4 (December 1967): 407–32.

Dorfman, R., "The Meaning of Internal Rates of Return," *Journal of Finance* 5 (December 1981):

Fisher, I., "*The Theory of Interest*," New York: Macmillan, 1930.

Fleming, J. S., and J. F. Wright, "Uniqueness of the Internal Rate of Return: A Generalization," *Economic Journal* 81 (June 1971): 256–63.

Lorie, J. H., and L. J. Savage, "Three Problems in Rationing Capital," *Journal of Business* 28 (October 1955): 229–39.

Pratt, John W., and John S. Hammond, III, "Evaluating and Comparing Projects: Simple Detection of False Alarms," *Journal of Finance* 34 (December 1979): 1231–1242.

Weingartner, H. M., *Mathematical Programming and the Analysis of Capital Budgeting Problems* (Englewood Cliffs, N.J.: Prentice-Hall, 1963).

6

Cash Flow Analysis and Market Factors That Determine the Profitability of Projects

The previous three chapters have been concerned with various methods for appraising the value of projects. Analysis of each example required a cash flow forecast as the basis of our appraisal. In this chapter we examine more closely the underlying assumptions of the cash flow forecasts. First, we show how to define a project's net incremental cash flow in terms of the project's impact on the cash flow of the firm. Then we show why a positive net present value (or an internal rate of return in excess of the project's required rate of return) must have its roots in competitive advantage, either in a superior product that can attract a higher price, or in lower production or distribution costs than that enjoyed by the competition. Because competitive advantage is temporary in nature, an essential part of a project appraisal centers on the length of time that a competitive advantage can last. We show how to relate net incremental cash flow forecasts to temporary competitive advantage. Finally, we describe how decisions by management may change a project's character and its cash flows during its life.

Net Incremental Cash Flow

When managers want to invest in an asset or a new commercial activity, they want to know whether the required capital investment will increase the value of the firm. The financial analyst tries to evaluate such investment proposals by estimating how they would change cash flows throughout the company. A typical project will generate new sets of cash flows but may also alter cash flows that already had been anticipated by the company.

The effect of a decision on a company's cash flow is measured by the **net incremental cash flow.** The net present value of the incremental cash flow tells management how much the value of the company can be expected to change as a result of adopting the project. Estimating the net incremental cash flow requires answers to the following four broad questions:

1. Which of the existing cash flows in the company would be changed by the project, and what new cash flows will occur as a result of the project?
2. If the project is undertaken, what would be the expected level of each of the cash flows defined in (1)?
3. If the project is not undertaken, what would be the expected level of each of the cash flows defined in (1)?
4. What is the difference between the cash flows with the project (2) and without the project (3)?

A common error is simply to discount the cash flows referred to in step 2. Such a procedure is wrong because it does not take account of what will happen to the company's cash flows if the project is *not* undertaken. If the full impact of a decision is to be measured, the net incremental cash flows in step 4 must be estimated and then discounted to present value.

Net Incremental Cash Flows: An Example

A management committee in a manufacturing company meets to discuss whether to continue operating a machine. The company's changing product line makes it unlikely that existing product lines would allow the machine to be operated for more than three additional years. In the meantime, changing product requirements suggest that the machine would not be operating efficiently. The committee consists of the plant manager, a product manager, the production planning manager, a production engineer, and a financial analyst.

The committee's feeling at the beginning of the meeting is that the machine should be disposed of and not replaced. However, the product manager argues forcefully that the machine should be retained, or at least improved, because it "is already paid for" and will continue to make products that will generate a "substantial cash flow for the next three years." Before the meeting he had prepared the following net after-tax cash flow figures with some data from the financial analysis group.

	End of year		
	1	2	3
	(thousands of dollars)		
Operating cash flow from old machine	25	20	15
Resale value	—	—	25
Cash flow	25	20	40

These figures created some initial confusion, as they did not seem to support the general feeling that the machine should be sold. No one doubted that the net cash flows would be lost if the machine stopped operation, but something seemed to be missing. The plant manager said that he knew the machine could be sold for $80,000 today, which ought to carry some weight in the argument. The product manager disagreed, saying that the market value of the machine is not a cash flow, for the company already owns the machine. The financial analyst was asked to resolve the issue.

The financial analyst thought that the confusion arose from trying to reach conclusions on the basis of "cash flows" rather than net incremental cash flows. She pointed out that there were actually two sets of cash flows that needed to be considered in order to obtain the net effect of continuing to operate the machine. She then presented the sets of cash flows given in Table 6.1. In row 1 of the table are the after-tax cash flows that result from operating the machine, and in row 2 is the cash flow arising from the sale of the machine now (period 0) and not operating it. In row 3 is the net incremental cash flow representing the difference between these two choices. The financial analyst pointed out that the $80,000 (in row 3) is a negative figure, as it is the difference between rows 1 and 2. The $80,000 can be

Table 6.1   *Net incremental cash flow from continued operation of old machine (thousands of dollars)*

	End of year				NPV at 10%
	0	1	2	3	
Operating the old machine	0	25	20	40	
Selling the old machine	80	0	0	0	
Net incremental cash flow	−80	25	20	40	−10.69

described as an **opportunity cost,** because the company loses the opportunity of selling the machine now if it continues to operate it.

Discounting the net incremental cash flows at 10 percent, the analyst obtained a net present value of minus $10,690 for keeping the machine. She stated: "The firm would be at least $10,000 better off selling the machine for $80,000 and investing the money in the bank at 10 percent." Most of the committee members felt their initial judgment to be vindicated by this analysis and were somewhat surprised when the product manager came forward with another alternative.

"I agree," he said, "selling the existing machine for $80,000 is an opportunity worth taking, and that money can be put toward a new machine. I am told that a new machine costs $100,000. Therefore, the net incremental cost of selling the existing machine and buying the new one would only be $100,000 − $80,000 = $20,000. The cash flow in year 3 for the new machine consists of $55,000 for the residual value and $15,000 for the net operating cash flows." He presented the following net cash flow representing the difference in incremental cash flows between keeping the existing machine and buying the new one:

	End of year			
	0	1	2	3
		(thousands of dollars)		
New machine	−100	25	20	70
Old machine	− 80	25	20	40
Net cash flow	− 20	0	0	30

He thought the net present value calculated on the difference between the net incremental cash flows for the new and old machines would be positive, and said, "Why not buy a new machine to go on supplying my customers?"

"I don't think I agree with your conclusions," the financial analyst responded. "Sure, the new machine is better than the old one, but both look unprofitable to me." She then substantiated this view with the figures given in Table 6.2, which shows the net present value of each machine separately as well as the net present value of the cash flow differences between the two machines. Row 1 shows the NPV of the new machine to be −$8,150, with the NPV of the old machine even worse at −$10,690. Even though the new machine represents a net improvement in NPV of $2,540 over the old machine, the new one is still unprofitable. Everyone around the table agreed that neither machine was profitable on its own.

As the meeting was drawing to a close, the product manager expressed his position more forcefully. "If we dispose of the machine, we will have to reduce the product line, and we will lose customers that we will need in the

Table 6.2   *Comparison of cash flows for new and old machines (thousands of dollars)*

	End of year				NPV at 10%
	0	1	2	3	
New machine	−100	25	20	70	− 8.15
Old machine	− 80	25	20	40	−10.69
Difference	− 20	0	0	30	2.54

future. There must be another alternative." The production planning manager agreed that it would be necessary to eliminate some items in the product line. The production engineer then suggested that they could alter the existing machine to a better specification, which would "cost money," but would produce future cost savings. The committee decided to meet again the following week when the production engineer could produce some costs for this new alternative.

At the next meeting the production engineer presented the following figures:

	End of year			
	0	1	2	3
	(thousands of dollars)			
Cost of alterations	−10			
Cost savings	____	10	10	10
Net savings	−10	10	10	10

The others around the table expressed interest in this alternative, seeing that the estimated cost savings were obviously large in comparison to the cost of the alterations.

The analyst seemed wary of the new proposal at first. "This is an example of a contingent project," she said. "Altering the machine is contingent upon whether we really want to keep it. In other words, the alternative may not improve the machine sufficiently to make us want to keep it." While the others discussed the proposed alterations in more detail, the analyst prepared the figures given in Table 6.3.

Table 6.3 shows that not only does the alteration have a positive net present value on its own, the net present value is sufficiently large to make the altered machine acceptable. Without alteration, the machine has an NPV

Table 6.3   *Cash flows for machine alteration as a contingent project (thousands of dollars)*

	End of year				NPV at 10%
	0	1	2	3	
Operating the machine as it is	−80	25	20	40	−10.69
Alteration	−10	10	10	10	14.87
Operating the altered machine	−90	35	30	50	4.18

of −$10,690; the alteration adds an NPV of $14,870. The existing machine with improvements has an NPV of $4,180. Consequently, the improved machine would be profitable to operate. The committee was impressed with these figures and devoted the rest of the meeting to examining more closely the nature of the alterations and the plausibility of the cost savings. In the end, the committee decided to continue operating the machine after making the proposed alterations.

In this example we have seen three applications of net incremental cash flow measures: first, in the abandonment decision (sale of the existing machine); second, in the choice between alternative projects (replacement of the existing machine); and finally in the valuation of contingent projects (alteration of the existing machine). These are typical applications about which we can generalize. As most capital investments are contingent projects, we shall comment on contingent projects first.

Contingent Projects

Some projects cannot be undertaken independently of other assets. Such projects are called **contingent projects.** For example, investment in a new machine may be contingent upon an extension being added to the factory. Such an investment should take place only if the following two questions can be answered positively:

Do the net incremental cash flows of the contingent project have a positive net present value?

Do the two projects when taken together (i.e., the contingent project and the project on which it depends) have a positive net present value?

Except for completely new activities, most investment projects are contingent projects. If a project is contingent on the use of other assets, the analyst must be satisfied that it would not be more profitable to abandon one or more of the other assets than to undertake the project. An example would be an investment made in converting an oil-fired boiler to a coal-fired boiler for a factory, when a complete analysis might have revealed that the most profitable action would have been to cease manufacturing and dispose of the factory. The net incremental cash flow concept requires that contingent projects should be analyzed along with any assets or activities on which they depend.

Abandonment Decisions

Knowing when to liquidate a project can be as important as knowing when to invest. For example, a project's profitability may have been estimated on the basis of expectations that do not materialize fully. Even if management regrets the investment, this does not have to mean that the time has come for abandonment. The resale or liquidation value of the project may be even less now than the present value of the remaining cash flows, and immediate abandonment may not be profitable. The analysis of abandonment follows in many respects the same principles as any other investment analysis. Two questions must be asked:

If we keep the asset, what is the present value of the after-tax cash flows?

How does this present value compare with the after-tax cash flows that can be realized from liquidation?

If the present value of the asset's future cash flows is less than its resale value, management should consider selling the asset. The cash that would be generated by the disposal of the asset represents the effective investment in the proposal "not to abandon." The abandonment decision is more important than is often supposed, because most capital investments are contingent upon the continuation of an existing activity of which the project is a part.

In principle, management should not consider further investments in existing activities until it is established that abandonment is unlikely in the foreseeable future. The abandonment of major activities can take a long time to accomplish. A job for the financial analyst is to determine how the various phases of abandonment should be carried out. If the assets are not readily salable, it may be prudent to extract as much cash as is possible from operations. During this period, expenditure on new machinery and maintenance can be budgeted strictly in accordance with plans for phasing out the operation. The net present value of the phaseout can often exceed the net present values either of continuing a normal operation or of immediate liquidation.

While in some respects the analysis of the abandonment decision follows the same principles as any other investment analysis, it differs in others. Consider an example of a coal mine developed some years ago that is producing operating losses due to a recent fall in the price of coal. Management asks the financial analyst to produce an appraisal of the prospects of closing down the mine. The analyst calculates the cash flows from continued operation of the mine and compares them with the cash flow costs of shutting the mine down. In this particular case, the analyst reports that closure is the least costly course of action. What the analyst has done is to assume that the option to close the mine is available today and only today. In fact, if the mine is kept open, the option to close is still alive and can be exercised in the future.

Why might a company be willing to continue operating the mine even though it is making losses? One explanation might be that coal prices may rise next year, making the mine profitable, and reopening the mine could be more costly than keeping it open. Actually, the option to abandon the mine should not be exercised simply when the present value of the expected operating losses under current conditions is greater than the current closure costs. This explains why many businesses are kept operating at a loss during a recession. The valuation of the abandonment option has been analyzed by Myers and Majd (1983) and by Brennan and Schwartz (1983).

The Optimum Replacement Period

In our first example, the product manager proposed to replace an existing machine with a new one. Analysis in that case was simplified by the fact that the proposal was to abandon the product line and to resell the machine at the end of three years. Many commercial activities, however, are expected to be carried out longer than the individual machines or equipment employed in the activity are expected to last. In this circumstance management can almost certainly expect to replace machines with similar or improved models in the future. A key question is when to replace the machine. If we cannot estimate when the machine would be replaced, we do not know for how many years the project's net incremental cash flows will continue, and we would have no sound basis for calculating net present value for an individual machine. Therefore it may be necessary to make some estimate of the optimum time to replace the machine.

In Table 6.4 we have the capital investment, operating costs, and residual value for a machine to be replaced after two years, after three years, and after four. Which replacement period is best? The present value of costs

Table 6.4   *Net of tax costs and residual values for machines with two-, three-, and four-year lives (thousands of dollars)*

		End of year			
	0	1	2	3	4
TWO YEARS					
Capital investment	−1,000				
Operating cost		−200	−300		
Scrap value			200		
Present value at 10%	−1,264.46				
THREE YEARS					
Capital investment	−1,000				
Operating cost		−200	−300	−400	
Scrap value				+100	
Present value at 10%	−1,655.15				
FOUR YEARS					
Capital investment	−1,000				
Operating cost		−200	−300	−400	−650
Scrap value					50
Present value at 10%	−2,140.09				

increases as the assumed life becomes longer and includes more periods in which there are costs. Operating costs also increase, and the residual value is reduced with each additional year that the machine is operated, so the figures in the table are not comparable for the different lives.

The costs for the different lives in the table can be made comparable if they are each converted to an equivalent annuity. For the two-year life the present value of the costs (in thousands of dollars) is $1,264.46, and the life is two years. We wish to determine the equivalent annual costs C_2 for the machine. In Chapter 3 we described the following formula:

$$\frac{\text{Present Value}}{\text{of Costs}} = \frac{\text{Equivalent Annual}}{\text{Cost}} \times \frac{\text{Annuity Factor}}{\text{for N years at R\%}}$$

Solving for the equivalent annual cost, we have,

$$\text{Equivalent Annual Cost} = \frac{\text{Present Value of Costs}}{\text{Annuity Factor for 2 years at 10\%}}$$

Taking the data from Table 6.4,

$$C_2 = \frac{1,264.46}{1.73554} = 728.57$$

where 1.73554 is the two-year annuity factor at 10 percent annually.

The equivalent annual costs for the three- and four-year lives are obtained in a similar way: $C_3 = 665.56$ and $C_4 = 675.14$, respectively. As C_3 is the lowest equivalent annual cost, we conclude that a three-year replacement cycle is optimum (to the nearest year) for identical machinery. You should recognize, however, that this analysis assumes identical cash flows and risks in each replacement period; that is, inflation and new technology have not been considered.

The option to replace an asset resembles in many respects the option to abandon an asset. Often it is better to delay exercising the option. One reason might be to avoid commitment to a technology that soon may become obsolete. We expand on this theme in Chapter 19.

Determining the Expected Economic Life of the Project

The expected **economic life** of most assets is limited by several factors. Consider, for example, a multipurpose machine. The operating life of the machine will end when increasing maintenance costs make it too costly to operate. However, the profitable portion of the machine's operating life will end when the present value of the incremental cash flows attributable to the machine during its remaining operating life becomes less than the machine's resale value. An asset's profitable operating life ends when it becomes more advantageous to abandon or to sell the asset than to operate it.

However, if operation of an asset is contingent upon the continued operation of other assets or activities, the expected economic life of the asset may be determined by the life of another activity. For example, suppose a specialized machine can make only one product. Its expected economic life may be determined by the product's life where the product's life is shorter than the machine's expected profitable operating life.

The expected economic life of an asset may be even shorter if it is anticipated that the asset will be replaced by a more profitable machine. If a machine is profitable in a commercial activity that should not be abandoned, management may still find it advantageous to replace the machine with a newer or technologically better model before the end of its profitable operating life. In this case, the optimum replacement period for an asset determines its expected economic life.

The expected economic life of a project will be determined by the shortest of the following lives:

profitable operating life of the asset

economic life of assets or activities on which continued operation of the asset is contingent

optimum expected replacement period for the asset

Clearly, the estimation of the economic life of a project requires analysis of the alternatives available in the future.

Net Present Value and Market Imperfections

If we lived in a world where all markets, including product and labor markets as well as capital markets, were perfect, competition would quickly bid prices down or costs up to a level where all net present values were equal to zero. That is, competitors would continue to enter the market until prices would allow them no more than the minimum acceptable return on capital. In other words, for an investment to have positive net present value, market imperfections must exist.

In a very competitive financial market such as that in the United States, it is not easy to generate positive net present values by investing in financial securities. If managers wish to generate positive net present values, they must look to product and/or labor markets that are less competitive. The **market imperfections** that generate net present value most frequently include scarcity of the product, unique advantages in quality or cost (which may be due in part to the special abilities of the firm's workers and management), and legally imposed barriers to would-be competitors (such as patents). A capital project appraisal should include an analysis of the market imperfections and the unique capabilities of the firm that justify an estimate of positive net present value.

Because unanticipated competition can reduce the expected net present value, barriers to competitors entering the market are required to ensure that a project can remain profitable. A project's positive net present value can be maintained only during the limited period of time before effective competition finds a way through the barriers. Therefore, an analysis of barriers to entry is an important part of a thorough project appraisal.

Barriers to entry may include one company's ability to provide consistent technological leadership by offering products covered by comprehensive patents. Also, large-scale investment may discourage smaller competitors from entering the field, and the resulting economies of scale can provide the larger company with a continuing product cost advantage. A large and well-established distribution and service system together with a known brand and trusted product warranties can provide a degree of consumer loyalty that new competitors cannot match quickly. Geographical position can also provide links to local markets and transportation cost advantages that potential competitors cannot duplicate easily. All such barriers can delay the response of competitors to new initiatives, while providing opportunities for the established company to capture net present value before competition drives prices down to less profitable levels.

BREAK-EVEN ANALYSIS AND PRODUCT MARKET IMPERFECTIONS

If the market requires a new or improved product, sales revenue forecasts must reflect strategies that exploit competitive advantages, presumably behind barriers to entry. The analysis should indicate in which market segments the company can maintain substantial market strength in relation to competitors and should demonstrate the cost or quality advantages upon which the market strength will be based. The analysis must include estimates of the trend of total demand in each market segment, the company's changing share in that demand, the anticipated response of competitors, and the implied pricing strategy. Market requirements, together with manufacturing technology, dictate the design of the project, and the design determines the required investment and operating costs. The capacity required to produce the product and the estimated demand for it will affect estimated prices and resulting sales revenues.

The degree of uncertainty in market projections must also be assessed, for the design of the project requires commitment to a specific capacity. What range of product demand and market share is projected in the relevant market segments in each period, and how costly would it be if too much capacity is installed? Should capacity be built up in stages as market uncertainty is resolved? How low might prices have to be to generate the demand necessary to fill each alternative level of capacity that could be provided?

The scale of the investment also affects economies of production and costs per unit of product. What are the anticipated initial operating costs, and how quickly can these be reduced as experience is gained with the production technology? Will advances in technology mean that competitors can subsequently enter the 'market with a lower-priced product? What will be the pricing implications of the anticipated costs for eventual competitors? Will they shelter under our price umbrella, or will they cut prices to increase their market share?

These considerations suggest that the most important facets of the analysis are the size of the company's competitive advantage, in cost or revenue terms, and the length of time that advantage will last. A project's net present value is equivalent to the present value of the cash flows that can be attributed to the project's competitive advantage. Analysis of a new project can be defined around the following two broad questions:

What break-even level of the project's cash flows would prevail under highly competitive conditions? In other words, what level of incremental cash flows would be consistent with a zero net present value for the project?

What additional cash flows in excess of the break-even level can be expected as a result of imperfect competition?

Figure 6.1 illustrates this process. The cash flows in the unshaded area are the break-even cash flows. The shaded area represents the predicted abnormal cash flows from the project, often referred to as **economic rents.** The present value of the cash flows represented by the shaded area is the net present value of the project.

The break-even level for the project can be defined as those cash flows under competition that would correspond to a zero net present value. If we assume that all competitors have the same costs, and begin and end their projects simultaneously, we can estimate the break-even point from the

Figure 6.1   *Graphical representation of net present value*

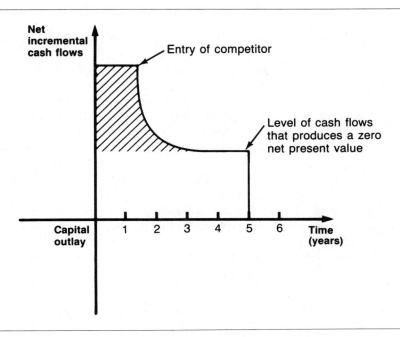

following formula:

$$\text{Present} \atop \text{Value} \left[\left(\begin{matrix} \text{Price per} \\ \text{Unit} \end{matrix} - \begin{matrix} \text{Variable Cost} \\ \text{per Unit} \end{matrix} \right) \times \text{Quantity} \times \left(1 - \begin{matrix} \text{Tax} \\ \text{Rate} \end{matrix} \right) \right.$$

$$\left. + \begin{matrix} \text{Tax Shields} \\ \text{from Depreciation} \end{matrix} - \begin{matrix} \text{Fixed Expenditure} \\ \text{after Taxes} \end{matrix} - \text{Investment} \right] = 0$$

That is,

$$\text{PV} \left[(p - v) \, Q \, (1 - T) + TD - F \, (1 - T) - I \right] = 0 \qquad (6.1)$$

where p is the price per unit of output
         v is the variable cost per unit
         Q is the expected quantity (units) to be sold under competitive
                conditions
         T is the corporate tax rate
         TD is the tax shield from depreciation
         F is the fixed operating expenditure, and
         I is the capital investment expenditures

Equation (6.1) provides an important tool that can be used to analyze the interrelationships between financial variables at the break-even level.

BREAK-EVEN ANALYSIS

Break-even analysis is the analysis of the interrelationships between price, volume and costs near the break-even point. The break-even model in equation (6.1) is based on the distinction between fixed and variable costs. By definition, variable costs are proportional to the physical volume of sales, whereas fixed costs are not. The break-even point is the expected level of sales at which the net present value is just equal to zero. Beyond this level the net present value is positive. The break-even point is an important strategic variable because commercial activities that operate above the break-even point tend to attract competition.

Figure 6.2 is a break-even chart illustrating these relationships. The horizontal axis represents the physical volume of sales, and the vertical axis represents the present value of sales revenues and (cash) costs. The upward sloping line that begins at zero on both axes represents the present value of after-tax sales revenue.

$$\text{PV} \left(\begin{matrix} \text{After-tax} \\ \text{Sales Revenue} \end{matrix} \right) = \text{PV} \left[pQ(1 - T) \right]$$

$$= \text{PV} \left[p(1 - T) \right] \times Q$$

Figure 6.2   *Net present value break-even chart*

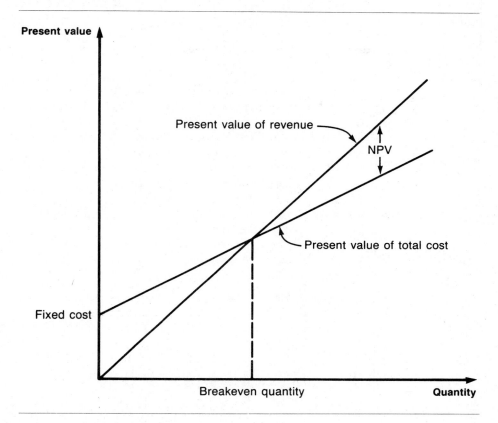

At zero physical volume the present value of revenue is equal to zero. The higher the volume Q (and the higher the price) the higher the present value of sales revenue.

The second upward sloping line represents the present value of total costs (after-tax). The line begins on the point of the vertical axis which represents the present value of after-tax fixed expenditure including tax savings on the depreciation, which does not change with increased sales. As we move to the right towards higher physical volumes of sales the line moves higher as variable cost is added to the fixed expenditure.

PV (After-tax) Cost = Present Value of After-Tax Fixed Expenditure
+ Present Value of After-tax Variable Cost

The break-even point is located where the total cost line crosses the revenue line. To the left of this point, the NPV (the difference between the present values of the revenue and total cost) is negative. To the right of the break-even point, the net present value is positive.

In the numerical example that follows, we shall show how break-even analysis may be used to help isolate a project's competitive advantage.

A NUMERICAL EXAMPLE

In Table 6.5 we have provided the data for an example to illustrate how the problem can be analyzed. Using the data in the table, we can solve for the break-even price given values of the remaining variables. The capital cost has been depreciated for tax purposes. The annual fixed cash costs (e.g., rent, local taxes, minimum labor costs) are $10 per unit, while the variable costs (e.g., overtime payments, raw materials) are $5 per unit initially. The estimated quantities of unit sales are also provided. The tax rate is 50 percent and the annual required rate of return for the project is 20 percent. Initially, we wish to solve for the price p per unit that would produce a zero net present value for the project on the basis of these estimates.

Table 6.5   *An example of break-even analysis*

End of year	Price	Variable cost	Quantity	Depreciation	Fixed cost*	Investment
0						−150
1	p	5	30	50	10	
2	p	5	35	40	10	
3	p	4	40	30	10	
4	p	4	35	20	10	
5	p	4	20	10	10	

* Fixed cost does not include depreciation in this analysis.

Step 1: Solve for Break-even Price That Would Produce a Zero NPV
The problem is to solve for the price (p) per unit of sales that provides a net present value of zero at a discount rate of 20 percent. The cash flows in each year, using Equation (6.1), will be as follows:

End of year	$(p-v) \times Q \times (1-T) + (TD)$	$-F \times (1-T)$	$-I$
0			−150
1	$(p-5) \times 30 \times (1-0.5) + (0.5 \times 50) - 10 \times (1-0.5)$		
2	$(p-5) \times 35 \times (1-0.5) + (0.5 \times 40) - 10 \times (1-0.5)$		
3	$(p-4) \times 40 \times (1-0.5) + (0.5 \times 30) - 10 \times (1-0.5)$		
4	$(p-4) \times 35 \times (1-0.5) + (0.5 \times 20) - 10 \times (1-0.5)$		
5	$(p-4) \times 20 \times (1-0.5) + (0.5 \times 10) - 10 \times (1-0.5)$		

The process can be simplified by expanding the brackets and adding up the cash flows:

End of year	Cash flows		
0	-150	$=$	-150.0
1	$15.0p - 75.0 + 25 - 5 = 15.0p -$		55.0
2	$17.5p - 87.5 + 20 - 5 = 17.5p -$		72.5
3	$20.0p - 80.0 + 15 - 5 = 20.0p -$		70.0
4	$17.5p - 70.0 + 10 - 5 = 17.5p -$		65.0
5	$10.0p - 40.0 + 5 - 5 = 10.0p -$		40.0

We are now in a position to discount the cash flows on the right-hand side of the equations above and solve for the price (p) that would produce a zero net present value:

$$p \left(\frac{15}{1.2} + \frac{17.5}{(1.2)^2} + \frac{20}{(1.2)^3} + \frac{17.5}{(1.2)^4} + \frac{10}{(1.2)^5} \right) - 150$$

$$- \frac{55}{1.2} - \frac{72.5}{(1.2)^2} - \frac{70}{(1.2)^3} - \frac{65}{(1.2)^4} - \frac{40}{(1.2)^5} = 0$$

These cash flows reduce to

$$48.69p - 334.11 = 0$$

$$p = \$6.86$$

Therefore, the break-even price per unit equals $6.86.

Step 2: Forecast Product Prices and Calculate Differences Between Competitive Prices and Forecast Prices

In order to compute the net present value of the project, we must estimate the prices that management believes can be obtained in the marketplace. If such prices are higher than the break-even price p ($6.86), the difference must be attributed to the market imperfections that the project is intended to exploit. It is to be expected that this price differential will diminish over the course of time as competing companies catch up. The following table shows the expected additional price (p') per unit in each year. The price p' is the difference between the forecast unit prices p^* for the product and the expected break-even price p. The forecast unit prices can only be obtained by analyzing the demand and supply conditions for the particular product.

End of year	p^*	−	p	=	p'
1	10.00	−	6.86	=	3.14
2	9.00	−	6.86	=	2.14
3	8.00	−	6.86	=	1.14
4	7.50	−	6.86	=	0.64
5	7.00	−	6.86	=	0.14

Step 3: Calculate NPV of Project

The NPV of the project can be calculated by taking the difference p' between the competitive price ($p = \$6.86$) and the price to be charged (p^*) and multiplying by the quantity sold in each period and subtracting taxes. The resulting cash flow is then discounted:

End of year (n)	$[p' \times Q \times (1-T)]/(1+r)^n$	= Present value of incremental cash flow
1	$[(3.14) \times 30 \times (1-0.5)]/1.2$	= $39.25
2	$[(2.14) \times 35 \times (1-0.5)]/1.2^2$	= $26.01
3	$[(1.14) \times 40 \times (1-0.5)]/1.2^3$	= $13.19
4	$[(0.64) \times 35 \times (1-0.5)]/1.2^4$	= $ 5.40
5	$[(0.14) \times 20 \times (1-0.5)]/1.2^5$	= $ 0.56
	Net Present Value	**$84.41**

This analysis requires some comment. First, we have assumed that competition is expected to erode prices and profit margins. As a consequence, you see that revenues are expected to decline, not only because unit sales are expected to fall eventually but also because prices are expected to fall (ignoring inflation) due to increasing competition. Also, we have assumed that the competitors' costs and break-even price are the same as one's own. We could use different costs when appropriate.

Second, throughout the example we have used only one forecast of quantities to be sold. This assumption could be a crucial one, for forecasts of demand usually are subject to a wide margin of error, especially where new products are concerned. Such forecasts depend not only upon forecasts of the size of the market but also upon the company's market share.

The example does emphasize that financial analysis requires more than an understanding of techniques such as discounted cash flow. Estimating a project's profitability requires a study of the markets in which the product is going to compete. Project appraisal forms and the capital budgeting process should reflect this fact. One of the important objectives of the project appraisal system should be to encourage the manager to identify the source of a project's NPV. For instance, our example focused on a project's price, when we might have assumed instead that the product's competitive advantage lay in lower operating costs. In that case, we would have calculated a break-even cost per unit. Then we would obtain the NPV by discounting the cash flows attributable to the difference between the forecast cost per unit and the break-even cost per unit.

Why have we gone to so much trouble to isolate the difference between a product's break-even price and forecast prices? Why not just discount the forecast net cash flows of a project, as in previous chapters? Actually, we could have done just that; and, with the same assumptions, we would obtain exactly the same answer. However, we analyzed the break-even price so we could estimate the effect of competition on the product price. This analysis supplied additional information that permitted us more accurately to reflect the effects of expected competition on prices in the cash flow.

ANNUAL BREAK-EVEN PROFIT ANALYSIS

Many managers define break-even analysis in terms of a single-period profit rather than in terms of the asset's net present value. We can see whether this approach works using our previous example. Equation (6.1) becomes

$$(p - v) \, Q \, (1 - T) + TD - F \, (1 - T) - I^* = 0 \qquad (6.2)$$

Note that in equation (6.2) we no longer are discounting. The conventional (undiscounted) approach is to use the fraction I^* of the initial investment that is represented by accounting depreciation. This has the effect of converting net cash flow into accounting earnings. Break-even now occurs where accounting profit is equal to zero. How would this approach compare in practice with the discounted cash flow formulation in equation (6.1)?

Returning to our example in Table 6.5, we must choose which period's break-even point to analyze. Suppose we want to know the break-even price for period 1. We shall assume $I^* = D = 50$. Equation 6.2 becomes

$$(p - 5) \times 30 \times (1 - 0.5) + (0.50) \, 50 - 10 \times (1 - 0.50) - 50 = 0$$

Solving the equation, we obtain $p = \$7.00$. The break-even prices for the other periods are calculated in the same way and are given below.

Period	1	2	3	4	5
Price (p)	$7.00	$6.43	$5.00	$4.86	$5.00

With the exception of the first period, when the depreciation D is greatest and volume Q is low, the break-even prices based on accounting profit are much lower than the NPV break-even price of $6.86 that we obtained using equation (6.1). Why are break-even prices based on profit so low?

The profit break-even prices are almost uniformly too low because equation (6.2) omits one very important cost, the cost of capital. The earlier equation (6.1) allowed for the cost of capital in the discount rate. Many managers would insert after-tax interest payments on borrowing as an additional cost in equation (6.2), and this would increase the break-even price for each period. However, the costs of borrowing do not ordinarily cover the full cost of capital for a project because it does not include the full premium for risk.

While it is possible to calculate a break-even point for each individual period in the life of an asset, our example illustrates that the break-even point for a single period may not be representative for the project during the whole of its life. Also, the example shows that the use of accounting numbers in place of discounted cash flow may not allow for the full cost of capital for the asset and can result in optimistically low break-even points.

Contingent Decisions and Project Valuation

Usually a project is valued on the basis of a most likely set of future events. For example, managers make assumptions on when competitors will enter the market. However, one set of events represents an incomplete picture of the many possible combinations of events that could occur in the future and the resulting decisions that might affect the value of the project. If the project is undertaken, and future events do not conform to original expectations, what corrective actions could management take in response to these events? Corrective actions are taken with the intention of increasing the project's net present value. Therefore, the possibilities of such action should be included in the original design and financial analysis of the project.

Table 6.6 shows net incremental cash flows for a project whose design management can alter if future circumstances change. The cash flows shown are predicted on the assumption that a technologically superior competitive product will enter the market at the end of the second year of this project. Thus the project's design permits a two-year profitable operating life. An investment of $1 million generates net operating cash flows of $610,000 each year for two years and a residual value of $100,000 at the end of the second year. With this set of events the net present value of the project at a discount rate of 10 percent is $141,320. This is not the end of the story, however, for we need to consider the implications of alternative sets of events.

What would happen if competition entered the market one year earlier, causing our expected net operating cash flow in year 2 to be cut from $610,000 to $305,000? Table 6.7 compares continuing to operate the project for two

Table 6.6   *Expected net incremental cash flows for a project assuming a two-year product life (thousands of dollars)*

| | End of year | | | NPV at 10% |
	0	1	2	
Capital cost	−1,000		100	
Net operating cash flow		610	610	
Net incremental cash flow	−1,000	610	710	141.32

years (with net operating cash flows reduced by competition from $610,000 to $305,000 in the second year) with abandonment and sale for $500,000 at the end of the first year. The net present value of the project at time zero associated with continued operation is −$110,740. If the project is abandoned after one year, its net present value (inclusive of the effect of the optimal abandonment decision) would be $9,090. What else, though, could happen?

A third possible event that should be considered is that the entry of competition could be delayed beyond two years, because of technological

Table 6.7   *Analysis of abandonment as a response to competition at the end of the first year for the two-year project (thousands of dollars)*

| | End of year | | | NPV at 10% |
	0	1	2	
CONTINUED OPERATION				
(with competition in year 2)				
Capital cost	−1,000		100	
Net operating cash flow		610	305	
Total	−1,000	610	405	−110.74
ABANDONMENT AFTER YEAR 1				
Capital cost	−1,000	500		
Net operating cash flow		610		
Total	−1,000	1,110		9.09
Net incremental cash flow	0	−500	405	−119.83

problems, for example. What would management do in this event, and how would its actions affect the net present value of the project? At present the project is designed to operate for only two years, but an additional expenditure of $490,000 at the end of year 2 would make it possible to operate the project one additional year at the same $610,000 level of net operating cash flow. Table 6.8 shows that, with no competition in the third year, the three-year operation has a net present value of $187,150 which is $45,830 greater than that for a two-year operation.

Suppose that we attach a probability of 4 chances in 6, or 4/6, to competition entering at the end of the second year and a probability of 1/6 each to competition entering at the end of the first and third years, respectively. In this case the probability-weighted average net present value would be given by

Event	NPV × probability of occurrence = expected value		
Entry of competition at the end of the first year	9.09 ×	1/6	= 1.52
Entry of competition at the end of the second year	141.32 ×	4/6	= 94.21
Entry of competition at the end of the third year	187.15 ×	1/6	= 31.19
		Net present value	126.92

The example illustrates how the net present value for a project can be changed substantially under different assumptions as to what will happen and how the project will be managed. In this case the largest impact would come from the possible early entry of competition. This possibility, even with the relatively small probability of 1/6, significantly reduces the net present value of the project. A project is more valuable to a company if its design permits management to adapt its operation to a changing industrial environment. The true value of its design is not revealed unless analysis includes those alternative circumstances in which management is most likely to exercise options to change the project.

Contingent decisions have several important implications in investment projects:

Most large corporate projects involve a sequence of outlays over more than a single period. To the extent that the future outlays are not irrevocably committed at the start, there may be opportunities to modify and/or abandon a project.

Other things being equal, the project that offers contingent decision opportunities is more valuable than one that does not.

Table 6.8   *Analysis of extending the operation of a two-year project to three years in the absence of competition (thousands of dollars)*

	End of year				
	0	1	2	3	NPV at 10%
THREE-YEAR OPERATION					
Capital cost	−1,000		−490	100	
Net operating cash flow		610	610	610	
Total	−1,000	610	120	710	187.15
TWO-YEAR OPERATION					141.32
NPV advantage of three-year operation					45.83

The NPV of a project that offers opportunities for contingent decisions is affected by management's skill in making such decisions. Management capabilities in this context may be a source of net present value.

We have illustrated the analysis of alternative events in valuing a project that is subject to change. In more complex situations involving sequences of interdependent decisions contingent upon uncertain future events, decision tree analysis can provide a more systematic means of evaluation. In a similar vein, the capital project itself may be regarded by management as only the first of a sequence of investments, each contingent upon the success of the earlier one. For instance, a project in a new field of commercial activity for the company offers the opportunity for experience in unfamiliar technologies and markets. The company may invest in exploratory projects, later making further investments in those areas that prove to be the most promising. Analysis of alternative future sets of events can suggest where such exploratory investments might best be made.

Summary

The financial analyst plays an important role in helping other managers to define the net incremental cash flows that result from investment in a new asset or activity. The net incremental cash flow is the difference between those cash flows that will exist for the firm if the project is undertaken and those cash flows expected to occur if the project is not undertaken. This means that if the project, for example, is to improve the profitability of an existing asset such as a machine, one of the cash flows that must be considered is the money that would be realized if the machine were sold as is rather than improved. An asset should not be improved if it can be shown that it can be sold for more than the present value that would result from continued operation. It can be dangerous to subtract the cash flows of one project from another before discounting them, as this may indicate only which project is preferable, when both may be unprofitable. We have also indicated the importance of identifying when a project is contingent upon other assets or activities that may already be overdue for abandonment and how such projects should be analyzed.

The net present value of a project can be affected by the number of years that the asset is expected to remain in use. The life of the assets or activities upon which the project depends may be shorter than the length of time that the project otherwise might last. Also it is often possible to anticipate that a technologically advanced machine will be replaced by even better models prior to the end of its life.

Net present value depends upon the existence of imperfections in product markets. We have described some imperfections in terms of competitive advantages and shown how to link cash flow forecasts directly to such advantages. Finally, we have discussed how decisions that may be made during the life of an asset that depend upon future events can contribute to the project's net present value.

While forecasting future cash flows accurately may be difficult, it is important to give careful consideration to the estimation of the net incremental cash flows that are to be attributed to a decision to invest in a project. Incorrect definition of incremental cash flow can lead to even greater errors than the more familiar problems that we have in forming unbiased forecasts.

Review Questions

1. What questions would you ask before considering investment in a new product?
2. How would you treat fixed assets already owned by the company when you are analyzing a project using those assets?
3. Provide a working definition of net incremental cash flow.
4. Define the economic life of a capital project.
5. Describe the factors determining the optimal replacement period for machinery and equipment.
6. What is the distinction between mutually exclusive and contingent projects? How are they analyzed?
7. Explain the conditions that permit positive net present values to exist.
8. Describe a method for linking cash flow analysis to product market imperfections.
9. Explain how future decisions contingent on a project's future outcomes can increase the net present value of the capital project.

10. Why is the abandonment option valuable? Give some other options that would be valuable.
11. Why might management not wish to close an operation that is unprofitable?

Problems

*1. Mr. Jay, who has become a consultant working from his home, has obtained offers of some regular contracts for work for the next three years. The expected after-tax cash flows are shown below; his initial investment is to be spent on the conversion of a room and the purchase of some equipment. Securities of equivalent risk earn 13 percent.

End of year	0	1	2	3
Cash flow	−15,000	6,000	8,000	10,000

Another proposal Mr. Jay could accept would generate after-tax annual cash flows of $4,000 for the next three years. However, for this contract, he would need a computer costing $8,500 and existing cost would be increased by $800 per year. Should he accept the new contract?

*2. STU, Inc., makes 20,000 units per year of component A for use in its own manufacturing. These components cost the company $64,000 per year before-tax to make. The components are used in a product with an expected life of five years.

One of STU's suppliers has offered to provide the components for only $3 each on an annual contract for 20,000 units. If STU, Inc., buys the component outside, it must carry $10,000 of additional inventory, which will be liquidated at the end of year 5. Partially offsetting this fact is the possibility of selling machinery that would no longer be required for $5,000 before-tax. The machinery was purchased for $25,000 and has been fully written off, although it has a useful life of another five years.

In five years' time, however, the machinery will become worthless, as its scrap value will not exceed the removal costs. The company's required rate of return for the product is 20 percent. The company pays federal and state taxes at a combined rate of 46 percent.

Should STU, Inc., buy component A from this supplier? What other considerations not included in your analysis should enter into the decision?

3. A machine belonging to EZ Company has worn out. It can be overhauled completely at a cost of $1,000 and will produce net after-tax cash flows

of $800 per year for another five years. If it is sold without being overhauled, the asset would bring in cash of $500. A brand-new machine can be purchased for $2,500. The economic life of the new machine is the same as that of the overhauled machine, and it will be depreciated on a straight-line basis over this period. The required rate of return is 15 percent. What should the management of EZ Company do? The new machine does not qualify for the investment tax credit, and corporate tax is paid at 46 percent.

*4. An engineer has come up with a way of adapting a machine that will cut waste of raw materials and thereby reduce costs. The cost of adapting the machine is estimated to be about $5,000, with cost savings of $1,500 expected in the first two years and $1,800 in the subsequent six years, after which the machine will be scrapped (without any salvage value). Assume the corporate tax rate to be 46 percent and the discount rate to be 10 percent. The capital expenditure is to be depreciated on a straight-line basis and does not qualify for the investment tax credit. As a financial analyst, what would your recommendation be?

5. The machine in Problem 4 has been depreciated over the last three years and the book value is now $25,000. It could be sold for the same amount if the decision to scrap it is taken now. The net after-tax cash flows from products made by this machine are expected to be $4,500 per year for the next eight years. The rate of return required from these products is 10 percent. Is it profitable for the alteration to be made on this machine, given the cost of alteration and the cost savings in Problem 4?

*6. Molux, Inc., sells a number of specialized products. Sales of one product, X, have been falling because of increased competition in the market. The main competitor has offered to purchase the equipment for manufacturing this product for $60,000. You, as an analyst, have been asked to evaluate this offer in the light of projected net incremental after-tax cash flows for the next three years. The discount rate for this product is 16 percent.

End of year	1	2	3
Cash flow (in dollars)	35,000	25,000	10,000

7. A product introduced three years ago has proven to be less popular than expected, and the product manager is considering withdrawing the product. It is not sold in conjunction with other products, but there will be some redundancy costs for some of the factory and distribution staff, which will amount to $80,000. The equipment used in the production has a written-down book value of $200,000 and could be sold in the immediate future for $300,000 if the decision to withdraw the product is made now. If the product is kept, increased advertising will be re-

quired. The revised expected net cash flows (after-tax) for the next five years (the life of the equipment) are as follows:

End of year	1	2	3	4	5
Product cash flow	100,000	80,000	60,000	40,000	20,000

The rate of return required for this product is 18 percent. Should the product be abandoned, or should the company continue producing it? Combined federal and state taxes amount to 46 percent. There will be no scrap value if the equipment is used for another five years. What would you recommend the company to do?

*8. Eastdox, Inc., is reviewing the equipment it uses to manufacture clocks. Basic equipment required for the manufacturing process is not expected to change in the future, and it needs to be kept in good condition and repair. The scrap values for this specialized equipment are low, so management policy is to keep the equipment for as long as possible. Each unit costs $50,000, and the company is planning to acquire five units. Operating and maintenance costs in the first year will be $12,000 per unit, annually increasing at 20 percent for the next three years and 30 percent in the last two years. The scrap value of each unit at the end of three years is $10,000, which is reduced by 25 percent each subsequent year it is kept in operation. What is the optimal replacement period of these units of equipment? The company's required rate of return is 15 percent. The physical life of the equipment is six years. Ignore tax on the sale proceeds and the depreciation tax shield, as the company expects to continue to be in a nontaxpaying position.

*9. Addison, Inc., is planning the introduction of a new product that has proven to be very popular in another state. The forecasts of sales and costs are shown below; sales are expected to fall from year 4 onward, as competitors enter the market.

End of year	Investment	Fixed cost	Variable cost	Quantity
0	−600			
1		30	8.0	80
2		30	7.5	90
3		40	7.0	100
4		40	6.0	80
5		40	6.0	60

The company adopts a straight-line depreciation policy, and there is no scrap value at the end of five years. The ITC is not available, and the

combined rate for federal and state taxes is 46 percent. The project is deemed to be riskier than the normal operations of the company, and the required rate of return for this project is 25 percent.
   (a) What prices would be charged in each year if the company can get 20 percent more than the break-even price in the first three years and only 10 percent more than break-even in the last two?
   (b) Calculate the NPV of the project.
   (c) Discuss the effect of ACRS depreciation on the project NPV.
10. Sunny, Inc., is planning to introduce a new sun bed. Market tests have shown that the product has 80 percent probability of success. New equipment and related costs will amount to a $3 million initial investment. Sales (units) are expected to be as follows depending upon success or failure:

End of year	1	2	3	4
Success	10,000	15,000	20,000	15,000
Failure	6,000	10,000	8,000	8,000

The selling price is expected to be $200, with variable costs of $80 per unit; overhead production costs are fixed at $400,000 per year for the first year and $300,000 per year after that. The project has an economic life of four years, after which the entry of a technologically superior product is expected.
   Assume all cash flows arise at the end of the year. The discount rate for this project is 20 percent, reflecting the higher risk entailed in introducing a new product.
   (a) Calculate the NPV of the project; ignore taxation in your calculations.
   (b) What would happen to the NPV of the project if competition entered the market earlier than expected, with sales in years 3 and 4 reduced to half the expected levels?

References

Bower, J. L., *Managing the Resource Allocation Process,* Cambridge, Mass.: Harvard University Press, 1976.

Brennan, M. J., and E. S. Schwartz, "Evaluating Natural Resource Investments," Working Paper, University of British Columbia, May 1983.

Dyl, E. A., and H. W. Long, "Abandonment Value and Capital Budgeting: Comment," *Journal of Finance* 24, no. 1 (March 1969): 88–95.

Franks, J. R., and H. Scholefield, Chapter on Replacement of Capital Equipment in *Corporate Financial Management,* 2nd Ed., London: Gower Press, 1977.

Kensinger, J., "Project Abandonment as a Put Option: Dealing with the Capital Investment Decision and Operating Risk Using Option Pricing Theory," Working Paper 86–121, Edwin L. Cox School of Business, Southern Methodist University, 1980.

King, P. F., "Is the Emphasis on Capital Budgeting Theory Misplaced?" *Journal of Business Finance and Accounting* 2, no. 1 (Spring 1975): 69–82.

Myers, S. C., and Saman Majd, "Calculating Abandonment Value Using Option Pricing Theory," Working Paper MIT No. 1462-83, revised August 1983.

Robichek, A. A., and J. C. Van Horne, "Abandonment Value and Capital Budgeting," *Journal of Finance* 22, no. 4 (December 1967): 577–70.

7

Inflation and the Investment Decision

In this chapter we discuss ways in which changes in the rate of inflation can affect the profitability of capital investment. We consider the effects of inflation on interest rates and on a project's discount rate, and we show how inflation affects the cost of holding inventories and other working capital. We discuss how the prices of production inputs and outputs may change relative to one another and why it is necessary to forecast the impact of inflation on taxes. Also, we consider how uncertainty about future rates of inflation may affect interest rates. Finally, we discuss ways in which progressive personal taxes can redistribute wealth during periods of inflation and how this income effect can change project cash flow forecasts.

Inflation and Interest Rates

The relationship between interest rates and inflation is important to any system of investment appraisal, because inflation may have a significant effect on an investment's revenues and costs and on the cost of money. To avoid error, the financial analyst must ensure that the assumptions about inflation that enter into forecasts of revenues and costs are consistent with those that enter into the cost of capital (and therefore the project's discount rate).

How are discount rates for a project affected by inflation? A discount rate for a project can be expressed as a (risk-free) interest rate plus a premium for risk.[1] If inflation affects other costs in the economy, surely it must affect interest rates and therefore discount rates as well. Consider that when interest rates in Israel were roughly ten times greater than interest rates in the United States, the Israeli rate of inflation also was roughly ten times greater than the American rate of inflation. Was this a coincidence, or is there really a significant relationship between a country's interest rates and its rate of inflation? It may help to look at some other countries as well.

Table 7.1 provides a comparison between average before-tax short-term interest rates and inflation for the entire 1967–1978 period in the United States and in eight other countries. The first column in the table gives the average short-term interest rate in each of the nine countries for the twelve-year period. The second column shows the average realized rate of inflation in each of the nine countries for the same period, measured using the country's retail price index. The third column provides an estimate of the average real rate of interest in each of the countries for the period. The real rate of interest is the nominal or money rate of interest adjusted for changes in purchasing power due to inflation. Roughly speaking, the real rate of interest is equal to the difference between the nominal or money interest rate and the rate of inflation. (A more precise method of calculation was used in the table.)

A comparison between the first two columns in the table reveals that higher average interest rates have been associated with higher rates of infla-

Table 7.1   *Annualized interest rates, realized inflation rates, and estimated real interest rates, 1967–1978*

Country	Nominal interest rate*	Realized inflation rate	Estimated real interest rate
Belgium	7.31	6.19	1.01
Canada	7.43	6.41	1.00
France	9.13	7.60	1.32
Germany	4.95	4.16	0.80
Italy	11.43	9.53	1.54
Netherlands	5.88	6.77	−0.93
Switzerland	4.08	4.30	−0.22
United Kingdom	10.08	9.97	0.09
United States of America	7.24	6.05	1.19

*Eurocurrency market rates of interest.
Source: Kaveh Alamouti, "An Analysis of the International Relationship Among Real Rates of Return," Unpublished Ph.D. Thesis, London Business School, 1981.

[1] We can use the rate of interest on short-term government securities, for example Treasury bills, as a proxy for the risk-free rate of interest.

tion for the various countries. For example, Germany had a lower rate of inflation than France, and it also experienced lower average interest rates. While nominal interest rates differed considerably across countries, the third column reveals that the average estimated real rates of interest were reasonably close among the nine countries, in a band between -0.22 percent and $+1.54$ percent. As the average real rate of interest was roughly the same for all the countries, we could assume that differences in the average nominal rates of interest largely reflected differences in the average rates of inflation.

THE FISHER EFFECT

This evidence provides some support for the proposition attributed to Irving Fisher (1930) that interest rates fully reflect anticipated rates of inflation. This proposition has come to be known as the **Fisher effect.** Fisher proposed the following equation relating the nominal rate of interest to the real rate of interest and the rate of inflation: If the real rate of interest is unaffected by changes in the rate of inflation, the nominal rate of interest is given by the equation

$$\left(1 + \frac{\text{Nominal Rate}}{\text{of Interest}}\right) = \left(1 + \frac{\text{Real Rate}}{\text{of Interest}}\right) \times \left(1 + \frac{\text{Expected Rate}}{\text{of Inflation}}\right)$$

Suppose that the real rate of interest is expected to remain equal to 1 percent and that the rate of inflation is expected to be 15 percent. According to Fisher, the nominal or money rate of interest r would have to be:

$$(1 + r) = (1 + 0.01) \times (1 + 0.15)$$

$$r = 0.1615$$

That is, the nominal rate of interest would equal 16.15 percent.

If the nominal rate of interest were below 16.15 percent in the above example, and the real rate of interest remained unchanged, what would happen? Consumers would tend to borrow relatively more money and start buying more goods. The increased borrowing would tend to push interest rates up toward 16.15 percent.

Of course, Fisher's relationship between interest rates and inflation could not be perfect for a number of reasons. The markets for some commodities, consumer goods, and assets may not be very competitive; there are storage costs and transactions costs for goods. Also, many consumers may fear that inflation could reduce economic activity and make them less well-off in real terms. If such uncertainties cause consumers to save proportionately more of their incomes and cause companies to reduce their capital investment, real interest rates may decline. Therefore, even if interest rates fully reflect changes in the rate of inflation, changes in the real rate of interest may occur, particularly in the short term. Fisher had assumed that real interest rates are unaffected by changes in the expected rate of inflation.

ARE REAL INTEREST RATES STABLE OVER TIME?

While the estimated short-term real rate of interest averaged only 1.19 percent in the United States during the years 1967 through 1978, actually it changed a great deal throughout this period. Figure 7.1 compares annualized monthly interest rates for the period and shows the degree to which the difference between the short-term interest rate and the rate of inflation has fluctuated. You can see from the figure that the relation between the interest rate and the rate of inflation fluctuates a great deal from one period to the next. For example, in 1969 the rate of inflation was much lower than the rate of interest; as a consequence, the real rate of interest was very high. However, during 1973 the rate of inflation raced ahead of interest rates, and therefore the estimated short-term real interest rate was negative. Beginning in the middle of 1979 (after the period in the figure) the position changed dramatically. For example, from the middle of 1980 to the middle of 1984 the estimated short-term real interest rate averaged about 4.8 percent and continued to be quite variable on a quarter-to-quarter basis.

Do the fluctuations in estimated short-term real interest rates disprove Fisher's proposition? Not necessarily. One explanation for the differences in real interest rates over time may be that we are comparing nominal interest rates with actual rather than expected rates of inflation. Apparent changes in the difference between inflation and interest rates may be due to actual rates of inflation being different from the rates of inflation that were expected when market interest rates were set. However, it does not seem plausible that errors in short-term inflation forecasts could be large or persistent enough to explain the differences that we observe between interest rates and the actual rate of inflation. Indeed, constancy of real interest rates would imply stability in the real growth of the economy. In fact some instability has been a prominent characteristic of developed economies.

In the longer term, real interest rates are harder to estimate in the United States: although we can obtain the yields on long-term government bonds, we cannot estimate easily the expected long-term rate of inflation. In Britain the government sells a series of long-term index-linked bonds. The final redemption value (the principal amount that is to be repaid) for these bonds is tied to the retail price index, and the quoted interest rates are thus real rates. Currently the bonds sell at a price that provides an annual long-term real rate of interest that has been under 4 percent. Because these bonds are long-term, their prices fluctuate with changes in the real interest rate, and so the bonds are moderately risky. In the United Kingdom the real long-term

Figure 7.1

Figure 7.1   *United States inflation and nominal interest rates annualized monthly*

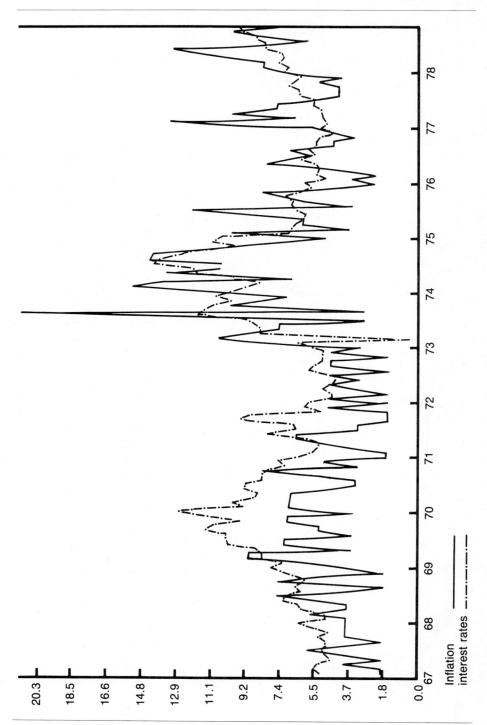

Source: Kaveh Alamouti, "An Analysis of the International Relationship Among Real Rates of Return," Unpublished Ph.D. Thesis, London Business School, 1981.

rates of interest on these bonds have fluctuated between 2 and 4 percent. These data strongly suggest that both short-term and long-term real interest rates can change quite significantly over time.

WHAT DETERMINES REAL INTEREST RATES?

The real rate of interest is determined by the demand for borrowing and the supply of lendable funds. As a result, the real rate of interest will change until the demand for funds equals the supply. For this reason the demand for funds should be determined by the **marginal productivity of capital,** which is the rate of return that would be obtainable from marginal investment in capital projects. As long as the rate of return that would be available from additional (equivalent risk-free) projects is greater than the interest rate, demand for funds will tend to increase the interest rate until the real rate of interest equals the (real) marginal productivity of capital. Similarly, if the real interest rate on the marginal loan were greater than the real return on the funds invested in the marginal project, it would not be worthwhile or profitable to borrow, and the real rate of interest would fall. In the United States the average rate of growth in productivity during the post-war years has averaged around 1.5 percent per annum. As a result we might have expected real interest rates to be no more than 1.5 percent. In 1984 the current short-term real interest rate was estimated to be around 4.5 percent, which appeared excessively high by historical standards. If in 1984 you were analyzing a project with a short life, say one or two years, you would have used one- or two-year bond interest rates and corresponding expected rates of inflation, implying real interest rates of 4.5 percent. However, if you had been analyzing a twenty-year project, you should have questioned whether estimated real interest rates of around 4.5 percent would be sustainable over a long period of time, unless you expected growth in productivity to increase from the historical level of 1.5 percent to around 4.5 percent. If you did not believe that such a high rate of growth would be sustainable for more than a few years, then you should have used an estimated real interest rate more closely approximating your expectation for the growth in productivity in the economy, for example something nearer the historic 1.5 percent. Of course if you had rejected the long-term real rate of interest implicit in the market prices of long-term government bonds, you would have been rejecting the market's expectations for the long-term rate.

In all the numerical examples in this chapter we assume that Fisher's proposition holds.[2] We make this assumption not necessarily because we believe that it holds, but rather as a working approximation. It is very useful to assume a relationship between interest rates and inflation so that we can isolate other effects of inflation on a project's profitability. Evidence is ac-

---

[2] In fact we have assumed that Fisher's relationship holds before taxes.

cumulating, however, that real interest rates do change with changes in the expected rate of inflation. Estimates of such a relationship will certainly affect a project's calculated profitability, and can be incorporated in the calculation of a project's discount rate.

Net Present Value and Inflation

Analysts sometimes assume that a change in the expected rate of inflation should have no effect on the before-tax profitability of a capital project. According to this argument, the adverse effect of an increase in the interest rate (and the resulting discount rate) due to inflation would be offset exactly by the favorable effect of an increase in the expected cash flow. As a result, a project's NPV would remain unchanged, irrespective of the rate of inflation. This argument would be true if we could assume that inflation affected all cash flows in the same proportion in a way that we shall now describe. Inflation does not affect all cash flows equally, however, as we shall show later in the chapter.

Suppose that the expected rate of inflation during the life of a project was 10 percent and that the real required rate of return for the project was 9 percent. This real rate of return consists of two parts, a real rate of interest (which we shall assume for the moment to be equal to 1 percent), plus a real risk premium of 8 percent.

Real Required Rate of Return = Real Rate of Interest + Real Risk Premium

Real Required Rate of Return = 0.01 + 0.08

$$= 0.09$$

We shall assume that the risk premium must increase sufficiently to protect the security holder's buying power. Otherwise, the profitability of risky projects would be altered as inflation rates change. We can use Fisher's equation to provide the necessary adjustment:

$$\left(1 + \frac{\text{Nominal Required}}{\text{Rate of Return}}\right) = \left(1 + \frac{\text{Real Required}}{\text{Rate of Return}}\right) \times \left(1 + \frac{\text{Rate of}}{\text{Inflation}}\right)$$

$$= (1 + \text{Real Interest Rate} + \text{Real Risk Premium}) \times (1 + \text{Rate of Inflation})$$

$$(1 + R) = (1 + 0.01 + 0.08) \times (1 + 0.10)$$

solving for the required rate of return R, we obtain

$R = 0.10 + 0.011 + 0.088$

$\quad = 0.199$

The effect of inflation has been to increase the interest rate from 1 percent to a nominal rate of 11.1 percent as Fisher suggested, and to increase the risk premium from 8 percent to 8.8 percent. Thus the total required rate of return becomes $11.1 + 8.8 = 19.9$ percent.

Table 7.2 gives the cash flows of a capital project assuming zero inflation. A sum of $320,000 is invested to obtain $100,000 per year for four years. The real required rate of return or discount rate is 9 percent for this example. The net present value at 9 percent for the project is $397,000, with rounding.

In Table 7.3, we show how the project is affected if the expected rate of inflation changes from 0 to 10 percent per year. The capital expenditure is still $320,000 (because the capital expenditure is assumed to be made immediately), but the subsequent operating cash flows are assumed to increase at a compound rate of inflation of 10 percent.

How is the net present value affected? If the required rate of return increases to 19.9 percent in the way Fisher suggests,

$1 + 0.199 = (1 + 0.09)(1 + 0.10)$

the increase in the discount rate just cancels the effect of inflation on the project's cash flows. As a result, the NPV is still $397,000.

Consider for example, the $100,000 to be received at the end of year 1 in Table 7.2. The present value of $100,000 discounted at 9 percent is

$100/1.09 = 91.743$

Table 7.2 *Expected cash flow for a capital project with zero inflation (thousands of dollars)*

		End of year			
	0	1	2	3	4
Capital investment	−320				
Operating cash flow		100	100	100	100
Net cash flows	−320	100	100	100	100
		NPV at 9% = 3.97			

In Table 7.3 both the cash flow of 100 and the denominator of 1.09 (representing the present value factor) have been increased in the same proportion, to 110 and 1.199, respectively:

$$110/1.199 = (100 \times 1.10)/(1.09 \times 1.10)$$

$$= 91.743$$

If the cash flows and the discount rate are changed by the same factor, the factor cancels out and the fraction remains the same at 91.743. Thus, the present value of the period's net cash flow remains unchanged. The present values of the project's other net cash flows remain unchanged as well. Clearly, if a project's net incremental cash flows increase at the same rate as the general rate of inflation and if the required rate of return increases in line with Fisher's proposition, then the project's net present value will be unaffected by changes in the expected rate of inflation, as shown in Table 7.3.

However, many projects have characteristics that prevent cash flows from increasing at the same rate as the general rate of inflation. In the remainder of the chapter we shall discuss the variables that could cause changes in a project's net present value.

Why Cash Flows Do Not Change at the Rate of Inflation

An example will show two ways that inflation can affect the profitability of a capital project adversely. First, even if revenues and costs before taxes were

Table 7.3   *Expected cash flow when the expected rate of inflation equals 10% for the capital project in Table 7.2 (thousands of dollars)*

	End of year				
	0	**1**	**2**	**3**	**4**
Capital investment	−320				
Operating cash flow		110	121	133.10	146.41
Net cash flows	−320	110	121	133.10	146.41
		NPV at 19.9%* = 3.97			

*0.199 = (1 + 0.09) (1 + 0.10) − 1

to increase in line with the general rate of inflation, taxes increase even more rapidly, thereby reducing the project's NPV. Second, inflation requires increased investment in working capital, and the resulting negative cash flow reduces the net present value of the project. The total loss in net present value due to inflation can be substantial, as our example will illustrate.

In Table 7.4 we show a capital project's profits, taxes, and cash flows in the absence of inflation. With zero inflation the project makes an NPV of

Table 7.4   *After-tax net incremental cash flow for project without inflation (thousands of dollars)*

	End of year					
	0	**1**	**2**	**3**	**4**	**5**
CASH FLOW STATEMENT						
Investment						
Machinery and equipment	−2,800					100
Inventory	−1,000					
Other working capital	− 300					300
	−4,100					400
Operating cash flow						
Revenues		2,000	2,000	2,000	2,000	2,000
Operating expenditure		−1,000	−1,000	−1,000	−1,000	0
Net operating cash flow		1,000	1,000	1,000	1,000	2,000
Net corporate taxes		−86	−186	−199	−199	−245
Net cash flow	−4,100	914	814	801	801	2,155

Net present value at 9% = 10.23

TAX STATEMENT						
Residual value in excess of unrecovered ACRS						100
Revenues		2,000	2,000	2,000	2,000	2,000
Operating expense		−1,000	−1,000	−1,000	−1,000	−1,000
ACRS depreciation		−406	−595	−568	−568	−568
Net taxable income		594	405	432	432	532
Corporate taxes at 46%		−273	−186	−199	−199	−245
Investment tax credit		187				
Net corporate taxes		−86	−186	−199	−199	−245

only $10,230 at a discount rate of 9 percent. Table 7.5 following shows the same project with annual inflation at 10 percent. This rate of inflation is reflected uniformly in increases in the revenues and the costs of the project. Nevertheless, the NPV drops from +$10,230 to −$453,050 if the discount rate is increased in line with Fisher's proposition, to 19.9 percent. Why?

Although revenues, costs, and the discount rate have all increased in line with inflation in Table 7.5, corporate taxes have increased at a higher rate

Table 7.5   *After-tax net incremental cash flow for project with 10% inflation (thousands of dollars)*

			End of year			
	0	**1**	**2**	**3**	**4**	**5**
CASH FLOW STATEMENT						
Investment						
Machinery and equipment	−2,800	0	0	0	0	161
Inventory	−1,000					
Other working capital	−300	−30	−33	−36	−40	439
	−4,100	−30	−33	−36	−40	600
Operating cash flow						
Revenues		2,200	2,420	2,662	2,928	3,221
Operating expenditures		−1,100	−1,210	−1,331	−1,464	0
Net operating cash flow		1,100	1,210	1,331	1,464	3,221
Net corporate taxes		−132	−283	−351	−412	−834
Net cash flow	−4,100	938	894	944	1,012	2,987
Net present value at 19.9%	−453.05					
TAX STATEMENT						
Residual value in excess of unrecovered ACRS						161
Revenues		2,200	2,420	2,662	2,928	3,221
Operating expenditure under LIFO		−1,100	−1,210	−1,331	−1,464	−1,000
ACRS depreciation		−406	−595	−568	−568	−568
Net taxable income		694	615	763	896	1,814
Corporate taxes at 46%		−319	−283	−351	−412	−834
Investment tax credit		187				
Net corporate taxes		−132	−283	−351	−412	−834

than the rate of inflation. Also, investment in working capital is increased. As a result, the net present value for the project has fallen by a total of $463,280. Obviously, with potential losses of this magnitude, it is important to be able to analyze the impact of inflation on a project's profitability. In analyzing Tables 7.4 and 7.5 in more detail we can show how the expected changes in NPV due to inflation can be measured.

INVESTMENT TAX CREDIT

In the example in Table 7.4, the investment tax credit of $187,000 is a deduction from corporate taxes at the end of the first year. The credit is granted for the $2,800,000 expenditure on machinery and equipment in year zero. The present value of the investment tax credit at 9 percent is $187,000/ 1.09 = $171,560. In Table 7.5 the rate of inflation rises to 10 percent, and the discount rate is 19.9 percent, but the $187,000 investment tax credit remains the same. The present value of the investment tax credit is now only $187,000/1.199 = $155,963. Thus the one-year lag in the use of the investment tax credit to reduce corporate taxes results in a net loss in present value of nearly $16,000 with 10 percent inflation.

DEPRECIATION

Comparing the tax statement in Table 7.4 with the tax statement in Table 7.5, we note that the ACRS depreciation tax shield is unchanged with changes in the rate of inflation. If the discount rate is 9 percent when there is no inflation (Table 7.4) and rises to 19.9 percent when inflation is 10 percent per year, the present value of the tax benefit of ACRS depreciation must be lower. Table 7.6 shows that this effect alone contributes a loss of $228,650 to the total loss of $463,280 in net present value for the project when inflation rises from zero to 10 percent per year. Thus nearly half the loss is attributable to the original or historic cost basis for ACRS depreciation.

INVENTORIES

In Table 7.4 an investment in inventory equal to $1 million takes place in year 0. The liquidation of this investment in inventory generates a positive cash flow at the end of the project's life in year 5. The cash flow from inventory is reflected in a reduction in operating expenditure in year 5. An operating expenditure that would have been $1 million in year 5 in Table

Table 7.6   *Effect of changes in rate of inflation on the present value of a project's tax shield (thousands of dollars)*

	End of year						PV
	0	1	2	3	4	5	
Depreciation	0	−406	−595	−568	−568	−568	
Tax shield (depreciation × tax rate of 46%)	0	187	274	261	261	261	
ZERO INFLATION							
Present value of tax effect at 9%							958.25
10% INFLATION							
Present value of tax effect at 19.9%							729.60
Reduction in project's present value if inflation rises to 10%							228.65

7.4 has been reduced by that amount to zero because inventories worth $1 million are used up.

The same thing happens under inflation in Table 7.5. At 10 percent inflation the operating expenditure rises by year 5 to $1,000,000 × 1.10^5 = $1,610,510 which represents an additional $610,510 due to inflation. As the value of the inventory has also increased by $610,510, operating expenditure in year 5 has been reduced by $1,610,510 (to zero in this case) because inventories are not replaced at the end of the project's life. The resulting effects of the inventory investment on the project's net present value are analyzed in Table 7.7.

In the upper portion of Table 7.7 we show the value of the inventory with zero inflation. The investment takes place in period 0 and is liquidated in period 5 at the end of the project's life. The net present value of the investment in inventory equals −$350,070. Since there is no inflation, there are no inventory gains and no resulting tax effects. In the lower portion of Table 7.7 we show the corresponding figures under 10 percent inflation when taxes are calculated on the basis of LIFO (last in, first out). If the physical volume of inventory is held constant, its book value under LIFO remains unchanged with inflation, as indicated in the first row. The book value remains unchanged because the more recently purchased goods (at inflated prices) are charged to cost of goods sold while the originally purchased goods are treated as though they were still in inventory. The inventory investment has increased in value in nominal terms, an increase recognized under LIFO only when the physical inventory is reduced (in year 5 in our example).

When the inventory is no longer being replaced in year 5, inflated costs

Table 7.7   *Effect of inflation on taxes paid on inventory gains under LIFO (thousands of dollars)*

	End of year						NPV
	0	1	2	3	4	5	
ZERO INFLATION							
Book value of inventory investment	−1,000	0	0	0	0	1,000	
Net present value at 9%							−350.07
10% INFLATION							
Book value of inventory investment	−1,000	0	0	0	0	1,000.00	
Effect of inventory gains on (LIFO) taxable earnings						610.51	
Corporate taxes on increased earnings						−280.83	
Cash flow	−1,000	0	0	0	0	1,329.68	
Net present value at 19.9%							−463.40
Change in net present value due to inflation							−113.33

can no longer be charged to cost of goods sold. Rather, the existing inventory, at its original cost, is charged to cost of goods sold. The lower cost results in higher taxes. The net effect is that the entire increase in the nominal value of the inventory from $1,000,000 to $1,610,510 is taxed in the final year when the inventory is depleted. The result in Table 7.7 is a tax of $280,830 in year 5, and the total net present value of the inventory investment and of the eventual tax falls to −$463,400. Thus the net loss of present value to the project resulting from the effects of 10 percent inflation and the $1,000,000 inventory investment is $113,330 under LIFO.

The effect of using FIFO for the project in Table 7.5 is analyzed in Table 7.8. Note that with inflation the book value of the inventory investment is increased year by year, for under FIFO goods sold are costed at their oldest and thus lowest (under inflation) value; goods remaining in inventory are thus costed at their most recent and therefore most inflated values. Since FIFO costs are lower under inflation, the increasing book value of inventory investment is exactly counterbalanced by a corresponding increase in taxable earnings. Therefore, the only net difference in cash flow between FIFO and LIFO is the effect each method has on the timing of tax payments.

Under FIFO the tax on inventory appreciation is paid year by year. Under

Table 7.8   *Effect of inflation on taxes paid on inventory gains under FIFO (thousands of dollars)*

	End of year						NPV
	0	1	2	3	4	5	
ZERO INFLATION							
Book value of inventory investment	−1,000	0	0	0	0	1,000	
Net present value at 9%							−350.07
10% INFLATION							
Book value of inventory investment	−1,000					1,610.51	
Effect of inventory gains on (FIFO) taxable earnings		100	110	121	133.1	146.41	
Corporate taxes on increased earnings		−46	−50.6	−55.66	−61.23	−67.35	
Cash flow	−1,000	−46	−50.6	−55.66	−61.23	1,543.16	
Net present value at 19.9%							−512.73
Change in net present value due to inflation							−162.66

LIFO the same total tax applies, but payment is delayed until the inventory is actually reduced or liquidated. In Table 7.8 we see that the net present value of the inventory investment would fall by almost $162,660 under FIFO with 10 percent inflation. This loss of present value to the project is $49,330 greater than the $113,330 loss under LIFO shown in Table 7.7. For this reason, many companies change to LIFO accounting in periods of inflation.

You may wonder why inflationary increases in the value of inventories do not require further investment of cash. The reason is that inventories, just like land and buildings, are real assets that can increase in value without further investment. Monetary assets such as accounts receivable cannot increase in nominal value without further investment of cash.

OTHER WORKING CAPITAL

So far we have shown the effects of inflation on net present value of the investment in inventory. Inflation also influences investment in working capital other than inventory. The other working capital investment of

$300,000 in our example consists of accounts receivable less accounts payable. As prices of both materials and products increase, the cash value of investment in payables and receivables can be expected to rise correspondingly. Thus an increase in the investment of cash in other working capital appears in each year in row 3 of Table 7.5. In the first year the initial $300,000 investment is increased by 10 percent or $30,000. In the second year the increase is $33,000 or 10 percent of $330,000 and so on. These changes in value are analyzed separately in Table 7.9. The table shows that under zero inflation the net present value of the investment in receivables less payables is −$105,020. In the presence of 10 percent inflation, the present value drops to −$211,100. The annual increase in cash required for investment under inflation therefore produces a net loss of $106,080 in present value to the project.

The corporation might react to the increase in the costs of its investment in receivables in one of two ways. It might be able to raise prices at a greater rate than the rate of inflation. Alternatively, the company simply might reduce the length of the credit period allowed as a way of reducing the total investment in receivables. The extent to which the company can implement such measures depends upon the degree of competition in the industry.

Table 7.9   *Effect of inflation on present value of investment in receivables and payables (thousands of dollars)*

			End of year				
	0	1	2	3	4	5	NPV
ZERO INFLATION							
Investment in receivables and payables	−300					300	
Net present value at 9%							−105.02
10% INFLATION							
Investment in receivables and payables	−300					483.15	
Further investment required*		−30	−33	−36.3	−39.93	−43.92	
Cash flow	−300	−30	−33	−36.3	−39.93	439.23	
Net present value at 19.9%							−211.10
Change in net present value due to inflation							−106.08

*Additional nominal investment required to maintain the same real investment.

A RECONCILIATION

For our example we inflated both revenues and costs at the same annual 10 percent rate, and thus the net present value of revenues and costs would not change if the discount rate is increased from 9 percent to 19.9 percent in line with Fisher's proposition. The net present value in our example, however, declines with 10 percent inflation. This means that the total drop in present value between Tables 7.4 and 7.5 must be accounted for by the impact of inflation on other items in the cash flow. We have already analyzed the separate effects of 10 percent inflation on (1) the present value of the investment tax credit, (2) the present value of the tax effect of depreciation, (3) the present value of taxes on inventory appreciation, and (4) the present value of the investment in other working capital. Table 7.10 shows that these four items together account for the entire loss in net present value for the project and that each of the last three items contributes substantially to the total.

The effects of inflation on a project's profitability that we have measured with our example can work in two directions. When the expected rate of inflation increases, the effect on a project's net present value is adverse or negative. However, as the expected rate of inflation decreases, these negative effects are reduced, and a project that has been unprofitable at high expected rates of inflation may well become profitable. In our example the project has a net present value of −$453,050 when the expected rate of inflation is 10 percent. However, if the rate of inflation is reduced to zero, the project's net present value becomes a positive at $10,230.

An important assumption we have made throughout is that increases in corporate tax obligations caused by inflation are not neutralized by changes in tax legislation. If the government does not require the additional revenues, it will have to return the money to the corporate sector or, alternatively, to the personal sector by, for example, reducing corporate tax rates, personal tax rates, or both.

Table 7.10

Comparison of net present values of inflated and uninflated project cash flows (thousands of dollars)

Net present value of uninflated cash flows		**10**
Contribution to changes in NPV due to 10% inflation:		
Tax effect of delayed ITC	**−16**	
Tax effect of depreciation	**−229**	
Tax effect of LIFO	**−113**	
Increased investment in other working capital	**−106**	
Total effect of 10% inflation on NPV	**−464**	**−464**
Net present value of inflated cash flow*		**−454**

*Reflects rounding error

Differential Price Changes

Changes in the pattern of demand will change product prices and costs relative to one another. Relative changes in prices and costs can have a significant effect on net present values. Because forecasts of such differential price changes could be crucial to the outcome of the analysis, they must be justified on sound economic grounds. Unfortunately, frequently we do not have the necessary information to make forecasts of differential changes in prices and costs. One approach is to assume that inflation affects prices and costs uniformly and then to analyze the sensitivity of the project's net present value to possible differences in the rates of change for prices and costs. (Such sensitivity analysis is described in more detail in Chapter 10.)

Even in the absence of inflation we may have reason to believe that some prices and costs will change relative to others. For example, increases in the productivity of labor in the economy can be expected to result in real increases in wage rates relative to other costs and prices. Such an increase in price is determined in the labor markets and can affect a capital project whether or not changes in the productivity of the labor used in the project justify the higher labor costs, and the net present value of the project can be affected as a result.

Commodities, such as certain natural resources that can be expected to be in short supply during the life of the project, may increase in cost more rapidly than the general rate of inflation. The supply of crude oil was restricted in the early 1970s by the Organization of Petroleum Exporting Countries (OPEC) cartel, and massive increases in the prices of crude oil occurred in both real and in nominal terms. For industries that rely on cheap oil, such as the chemical and automobile industries, forecasts of the price changes for oil are essential in capital project appraisals.

Obviously, an analyst can make the net present value of a project come out to almost any figure by forecasting that product prices will rise at one rate and costs will rise at a different rate. Consequently, the analyst must take great care when incorporating differential price and cost changes in a capital project. In the absence of better information, a sensible practice may be to assume that prices and costs will inflate at the same rate.

Real Versus Nominal Cash Flow Analysis

As mentioned early in the chapter, it is commonly stated that inflated nominal cash flows must be discounted at a nominal discount rate (which would reflect expected inflation) and that real cash flows should be discounted using a real discount rate. The two approaches will lead to the same net present value only if the effect of inflation on taxes and on the real changes in investment in working capital are included in the analysis. Some companies like to express their required rates of return in real terms, "9 percent real," for example. This gives them a target rate of return or **hurdle rate** that does not change with changes in inflation and interest rates, providing that the real rate of interest does not alter. The problem is how to use a constant real discount rate and still obtain correct net present values.

Table 7.11 illustrates the problem in terms of our project example. Row 1 of Table 7.11 shows the annual inflated nominal after-tax cash flows of the project from Table 7.5. Because the cash flows are inflated, they are discounted at the nominal rate of 19.9 percent, and we obtain a net present value of −$453,050 as the last column indicates. In row 2 of Table 7.11 we have deflated the nominal cash flows by discounting each of them using the 10 percent annual rate of inflation as the discount rate. Once the cash flows are deflated we can no longer use the nominal discount rate of 19.9 percent. We must now discount the deflated cash flows at the real rate of 9 percent, and we obtain the correct net present value of −$453,050. The first two rows of the table demonstrate that if a company wishes to use real discount rates, it can obtain correct net present values if it uses them to discount deflated nominal after-tax cash flows. The nominal cash flows must correctly reflect the tax and working capital changes under inflation in the ways that we have shown.

An incorrect procedure is illustrated in row 3 of Table 7.11. Here we have simply used the real discount rate of 9 percent to discount the uninflated cash flows from Table 7.4. The resulting net value of $11,230 is incorrect if inflation at 10 percent is expected. The tax and working capital estimates in Table 7.4 were only correct in the case of zero inflation. A direct comparison between rows 2 and 3 in the table illustrates the great difference that can exist between deflated nominal cash flows and uninflated real cash flows.

Another potential error in financial analysis is to discount real cash flows

Table 7.11   *Example of size of errors possible (thousands of dollars)*

	End of year						NPV at	
	0	1	2	3	4	5	19.9%	9%
Inflated nominal cash flow (Table 7.5)	−4,100	938	894	944	1,012	2,987	−453	
Deflated nominal cash flow	−4,100	853	739	709	691	1,855		−453
Uninflated cash flow (Table 7.4)	−4,100	914	814	801	801	2,155		10

The NPVs reflect small rounding errors.

at a nominal discount rate. Needless to say, this inconsistency incorrectly measures net present value when market interest rates and resulting nominal discount rates reflect expected inflation, and the real cash flows do not.

If real discount rates are to be used, the following procedure should be followed:

Forecast each item of incremental cash flow, including changes in working capital, taking into account the effect of the forecast general rate of inflation and any relative price changes.

Calculate expected taxable earnings from the project for each future period, and estimate the resulting corporate taxes.

Deflate each item of cash flow (including taxes) by discounting with the expected rate of inflation as the discount rate.

Discount the deflated cash flow by expected real rates of interest plus the risk premium.

As this approach ensures that the forecast nominal interest rate reflects the rate of inflation, it minimizes one source of inconsistency frequently encountered in practice. That is, it prevents the discounting of real cash flows at nominal discount rates or the discounting of nominal cash flows at real discount rates. Of course, it cannot stop managers from making inappropriate assumptions concerning future rates of inflation. The effects of such errors, however, will be confined to those cash flow items such as taxes that change at a rate different from the forecast inflation rate.

How Uncertain Inflation Affects Interest Rates

Until now we have assumed that future changes in the rate of inflation are known with certainty. Forecasts of future rates of inflation are by no means certain, and it is important to understand how uncertainty about expected rates of inflation can affect the level of interest rates. Since Treasury bills have very short horizons, uncertainty about the rate of inflation usually has little effect on Treasury bill rates. In the case of longer-term government bonds, however, uncertainty about future rates of inflation during the life of a bond may have a more significant effect on the bond's yield.

Since future rates of inflation are uncertain, we may describe the nominal interest rate on a fixed-interest bond as made up of three components:

$$\text{Long-term Nominal Interest Rate} = \text{Real Rate of Interest} + \text{Risk Premium for Uncertain Inflation Rate}$$

As the example will show, the real returns from investing in one two-year bond at a fixed interest rate are more volatile than the real returns from investment in a sequence of two one-year bonds. As a result, the interest rate on a two-year bond should reflect a larger premium for uncertain inflation than the interest rate on a one-year bond.

Suppose that an investor has $1,000 available for investment in a two-year bond or in a sequence of two one-year bonds. In Figure 7.2 we have assumed that in year one there are only three possible rates of inflation: 6, 8, and 10 percent. Whatever the inflation rate turns out to be in year 1, we posit that the rate of inflation will remain the same in year 2. If the inflation rate for year 1 is 6 percent, the rate of inflation in year 2 will also be 6 percent.

Table 7.12 compares the real dollar returns from each of the two strategies. We have assumed here that the real rate of interest is 2 percent annually. Thus, nominal interest rates are 2 percent higher than the expected inflation rate. In year 1, the expected rate of inflation is 8 percent as indicated by the central branch of the tree in Figure 7.2. As a consequence, the rate of interest on a one-year bond will be $8 + 2 = 10$ percent, and the one-year bond pays off $1,100 at the end of the first year, as indicated in the third column of the table. The rate of interest obtainable on a one-year bond bought at the beginning of the second year will depend upon the expected inflation rate for the second year. If the inflation rate in year 1 was 10 percent, the inflation rate for year 2 is expected to continue at 10 percent, so the interest rate on the one-year bond (in the second year) will be 12 percent. If the inflation rate for the first year had turned out to be 8 percent, the inflation rate for the second year also would be 8 percent, the interest rate would be 10 percent, and so on.

In the fifth column we have calculated the final payoff from reinvesting the proceeds of the first one-year bond at the three possible interest rates for

Figure 7.2   *Assumed behavior of inflation*

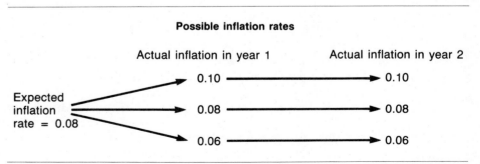

Source: R. A. Brealey and S. C. Myers, *Principles of Corporate Finance* (New York: McGraw-Hill, 1981), p. 465.

Table 7.12   *Real payoff of two bond investments*

	Inflation rate	Invest at (%)	Year 1 nominal cash flow (dollars)	Reinvest year 1 cash flow at (%)	Final nominal payoff (dollars)	Final real payoff (dollars)
Invest $1,000	0.10	0.10	1,100	0.12	1,232	1,018
in two one-year	0.08	0.10	1,100	0.10	1,210	1,037
bonds	0.06	0.10	1,100	0.08	1,188	1,057
Invest $1,000	0.10	0.10	100	0.12	1,212	1,002
in one two-year	0.08	0.10	100	0.10	1,210	1,037
bond	0.06	0.10	100	0.08	1,208	1,075

Source: R. A. Brealey and S. C. Myers, *Principles of Finance* (New York: McGraw-Hill, 1981), pp. 464–65.

the second year. To convert the nominal (money of the day) dollar returns into real returns, we have deflated them by the respective inflation rates. Thus, the nominal payoff of $1,232 in column 5 is the result of inflation of 10 percent for two years and 12 percent interest rates. If we deflate the nominal amount by the inflation rate, the real payoff is $1,232/(1.1)^2 = $1,018. We have completed similar calculations at 8 and 6 percent inflation rates for the first strategy as shown in the table.

The second strategy requires the investor to invest in a two-year bond at a fixed interest rate, set currently at 10 percent because the expected rate of inflation is 8 percent per year, and the real interest rate is 2 percent. Cash flow at the end of year 1 from the $100 coupon is reinvested in a one-year bond. The nominal and real payoffs at the end of year 2 are provided in the last two columns.

What can be seen in the table is that the spread of real returns is greater under the second strategy ($1,075 − $1,002 = $73) than under the first strategy ($1,057 − $1,018 = $39). Therefore, the second strategy is more risky in real terms. If the two-year bond is more risky in real terms than the purchase of a sequence of two one-year bonds, we would expect investors to demand a risk premium on the longer bonds to compensate them for the greater risk.

Why should the financial analyst be interested in the effect of uncertain inflation on interest rates? Previously, we have described a simple model of a project's required rate of return. The required rate of return was made up of a risk-free nominal rate of interest plus a premium for risk. However, if the project has cash flows occurring over more than one period, it is possible that nominal rates of interest and, therefore, discount rates may differ over the periods. The differences may be due to different expected rates of real interest, different expected rates of inflation for each period, and to inflation uncertainty.

DO BORROWERS ALWAYS GAIN IN INFLATIONARY PERIODS?

An understanding of the previous example provides some important lessons. Because historically borrowers have gained from inflation, some analysts believe that borrowing is in itself a good thing in inflationary conditions. At long-term fixed interest rates, borrowing was very profitable in the 1960s and 1970s only because inflation had increased unexpectedly. For example, suppose that a borrower had taken out a ten-year loan at an annual interest rate of 7 percent when inflation was expected to be 5 percent annually. If the expected rate of inflation were to rise to 7 percent, we might expect interest rates on ten-year bonds to increase to 9 percent. The original borrower would feel very pleased at having taken out a loan at 7 percent when interest rates rose subsequently. However, if inflation had been reduced unexpectedly instead, fixed interest rate borrowers would have had to continue paying high fixed interest rates after inflation and market rates of interest fell. Borrowing does not automatically confer a gain on the borrower or the lender under inflation. Of course, after the rate of inflation has been revealed, either lenders or borrowers at fixed rates of interest may have gained depending upon whether there was an unexpected decrease or increase, respectively, in the rate of inflation.

SHOULD WE BORROW SHORT-TERM WHEN SHORT-TERM RATES ARE LOWER THAN LONG-TERM RATES?

A second lesson of our analysis can be illustrated by answering the following question: If the interest rate for one year is 10 percent and for two years 11 percent, is it cheaper to keep borrowing for one year at a time? Not necessarily. If short-term rates are lower than long-term rates, it may be merely because inflation and short-term interest rates are expected to be higher in the second year than in the first year. The decision to borrow either short- or long-term at fixed rates of interest should depend upon the nature of the company's cash flows rather than upon forecasts of market rates of interest. For example, a company with cash flows that are fixed by contract in nominal terms might wish to borrow at fixed rates of interest to match the fixed cash flows. Other companies with cash flows that can be expected to change in line with changes in inflation may prefer to borrow short-term so that changes in interest rates match more nearly changes in nominal cash flows. These issues are discussed further in Chapter 16.

Income Effects of Inflation

A uniform change in the general level of wages and prices should not alter consumer behavior in a world without taxes if each consumer's buying power remains unchanged. However, in a progressive income tax system where higher pay means that individuals move into higher tax brackets, inflation may increase the taxes being paid. Even if inflation were to keep before-tax incomes in step with prices, some consumers would be worse off as they move into higher tax brackets. Also, some people, such as senior citizens, live on incomes that are fixed or adjust slowly to changes in the rate of inflation. As a consequence, consumers must alter either their savings or their purchases of goods and services. Demand for luxury goods can be expected to change in a different way from demand for necessities. The resulting shifts in demand for specific products can affect revenues and costs of individual projects in significant ways that project analysts should try to anticipate.

Now project appraisal is not the only activity that requires firms to monitor inflation. Appraisal of the profitability of ongoing projects and products must also reflect changes in the rate of inflation. Furthermore, prices and credit terms should be adjusted to reflect anticipated inflation. This adjustment is all the more important when price changes cannot be made at frequent intervals. Monitoring inflation also helps the analyst to forecast changes in government economic policies regarding interest rates, taxes, profits, and price controls. Such policies can affect demand, growth, and ultimately the cash flows of the firm. In this sense one cannot separate financial analysis from forecasts of either inflation or the level of economic activity.

Summary

Inflation affects a capital project's discount rate as well as its cash flows. Even if interest rates and corresponding discount rates fully reflect changes in the expected rate of inflation, cash flows may change less than proportionately with changes in the expected rate of inflation. As inflation results in real increases in taxation and real increases in working capital investment, the net present values of capital projects can be reduced significantly by increases in the rate of inflation. On the other hand, reductions in the rate of inflation may increase the profitability of capital investment. We have shown how to incorporate the effects of inflation in a project's nominal cash flows and taxes. The resulting after-tax nominal cash flows can be discounted at nominal discount rates or, alternatively, they can be deflated and then discounted at real discount rates. We shall adopt the practice of discounting nominal after-tax cash flows at nominal discount rates for the remainder of the book.

Inflation may also redistribute income and wealth and thereby affect demand for different products and services, and ultimately a project's cash flows. If inflation reduces economic growth, the profitability of capital investment in the private sector must be affected adversely. Changes in the economic environment, such as those associated with inflation, should be reflected in the analysis of individual capital projects.

Review Questions

1. In a taxless world, how would changes in the expected rate of inflation affect the value of a project? How would the existence of taxes change your answer?
2. Discuss ways in which the federal government could alter the tax system to neutralize the tax effects of inflation on a project's values.
3. Explain why many United States firms have changed to the LIFO method of valuing inventories over the past ten years. Can you think of any reason why some firms have not changed to LIFO?
4. Which items of working capital involve additional cash investment when inflation is increasing? Assume that the volume of sales is constant and that the current tax system operates. Explain why one type of working capital does not require additional cash investment under increased inflation.
5. Give reasons why companies might wish to cast project appraisal in real terms or nominal (money of the day) terms. Briefly describe the calculation procedures in each case.
6. Give the circumstances in which the prices of commodities might be expected to change at a different rate from the expected rate of inflation. Would you classify the price of oil in this category? Explain your answer.
7. Why might long-term interest rates be different from short-term interest rates?
8. If long-term interest rates are above short-term interest rates, corporations should borrow on a short-term basis. Comment.

Problems

*1. If the expected rate of inflation is 8 percent, and the real rate of interest is 2 percent, what is the nominal interest rate?
*2. Suppose that the rate of interest is 12 percent, the expected rate of

inflation is 15 percent, and the investors' required real rate of interest is 1 percent. Explain carefully why you would not expect such conditions to continue indefinitely. How would equilibrium be restored?

3. ATL, Inc., aims to achieve an annual nominal rate of return on its investments of 20 percent. Inflation in the economy has been constant at 5 percent annually. The general rate of inflation for the next year is expected to increase to 12 percent. What effect will this have on ATL's required rate of return?

*4. An asset costing $1,000 today is estimated to have a scrap value of $100 after five years if there is no inflation. However, the expected rate of inflation is 8 percent and the nominal interest rate is 9 percent. What is the present value of the asset's residual value after-tax if the asset is fully depreciated on a straight-line basis over five years? Combined federal and state taxes are 46 percent; ignore the ITC.

*5. A company invests $500 in inventory and keeps the physical level of inventory constant. At the end of the fifth year the inventory will be used up when a particular project is ended. The expected rate of inflation is 10 percent, and the nominal discount rate is 19 percent. Using the following valuation rules for tax purposes, calculate the present value of the taxes paid under (a) FIFO, and (b) LIFO. Assume combined corporate taxes are paid at 46 percent.

*6. A company expects to pay no taxes and has forecast cash flows (in real terms) for a project under consideration. Inflation is expected to be 10 percent per year, and the nominal required rate of return is 19 percent. Show how these real cash flows can be discounted at the real required rate of return, and also how they can be adjusted for inflation and discounted at the nominal required rate of return.

End of year	0	1	2	3	4
Real cash flow (after-tax)	−1,500	450	600	750	500

7. Using the cash flows in Problem 6, show what happens to the NPV when (a) the Fisher effect holds, and inflation increases to 13 percent, and (b) the Fisher effect does not hold, and the nominal rate is still 19 percent when inflation is 13 percent.
Explain the differences in NPV for (a) and (b).

8. The real cash flows of a project are shown below. The initial investment of $1,200 is written-off using a straight-line depreciation policy over the six years, without any salvage value at the end of its life. The company will not pay tax in the first year but will do so from year 2 (inclusive) onward at a combined rate of 46 percent.

Given the expected real rate of return of 3 percent, calculate the NPV when (a) the inflation rate is 5 percent, and (b) the inflation rate is 15 percent.

Explain why the differences in NPV occur.

End of year	0	1	2	3	4	5	6
Net incremental cash flow	−1,200	400	400	400	400	400	400

*9. A company is considering a proposal to invest in a new product expected to earn economic rents in the first five years. The forecasts for sales and costs (in real terms) are shown below, together with the expected rates of price increase for each category. Assume that the economic life of the asset is five years and that the sum-of-the-years digits depreciation method is used, with a nominal salvage value at the end of the asset's life of $10,000. The controller's department estimates that the nominal opportunity cost of capital for this project and others of similar risk is 20 percent. No investment tax credit will be received. As a financial analyst, you are asked to evaluate the financial feasibility of the project, taking the various price changes into consideration.

End of year	0	1	2	3	4	5	Rate of annual increase (%)
Capital investment	−160,000						
Sales		114,000	125,125	138,000	101,875	91,000	12
Operating cost		−22,800	−25,025	−27,600	−20,375	−18,200	10
Labor cost		−7,600	−8,600	−9,000	−9,000	−8,000	12
Other costs	−20,000	−5,000				−4,000	10
Depreciation		−50,000	−40,000	−30,000	−20,000	−10,000	
Pre-tax profit	−20,000	28,600	51,500	71,400	52,500	50,800	
Tax at 46%	9,200	−13,156	−23,690	−32,844	−24,150	−23,368	
Profit after-tax	−10,800	15,444	27,810	38,556	28,350	27,432	
Incremental investment in inventories	0	−5,700	−6,256	−6,900	−5,000	0	10

*10. Wailing, Inc., is planning to build a new complex of buildings, which it will rent in the future. The complex will take five years to build, with capital expenditure of $150 million immediately and the remaining $200 million at the end of the second year. Labor costs are expected to be $50 million each year starting in the first year of construction. Material and other expenses should be in the region of $100 million each year. Assume all costs arise and are payable at the end of the year.

All the costs are expressed in present-day prices; labor costs are expected to increase at an annual rate of 15 percent and material and other costs at 10 percent per year for the first two years and at 13 percent thereafter. It is thought that the annual price increases for capital expenditures will be in line with the general rate of inflation, which is 12 percent. The company's required real rate of return is 8 percent, and it would like to achieve this rate with this project.

The company plans to lease the fifty buildings immediately after completing the whole complex; 60 percent of the buildings in the complex should command one and one-half times the annual rentals of the rest. The initial rental periods will be for fifty years. The company wants to recover all costs during this fifty-year period. What annual rental for both types of buildings (in real terms) should the company be aiming for, in order to achieve its required real rate of return if the inflation rate remains at about 12 percent for this period? Ignore taxation. (*Hint:* As an approximation treat the annual rental stream as a perpetuity. How good an approximation is it?)

References

Brealey, R. A., and S. C. Myers, *Principles of Corporate Finance,* Second Edition, New York: McGraw-Hill, 1984.

Brealey, R. A., and S. M. Schaefer, "Term Structure and Uncertain Inflation," *Journal of Finance* 32, no. 2 (May 1977): 277–90.

Carsberg, B., and A. Hope, *Business Investment Decisions Under Inflation,* London: The Institute of Chartered Accountants in England and Wales, 1976.

Fama, E. F., "Short-Term Interest Rates as Predictors of Inflation," *American Economic Review* 65, no. 3 (June 1975): 269–82.

Fisher, I., *The Theory of Interest,* New York: Macmillan, 1930 (reprinted 1967).

Franks, J. R., and J. E. Broyles, "Inflation and the Investment Decision," in *Inflation: A Management Guide to Company Survival* (C. West, Ed.). London: Associated Business Programmes, 1976, 114–26.

Geske, R., and R. Roll, "The Fiscal and Monetary Linkage Between Stock Returns and Inflation," *Journal of Finance* 38, no. 1 (March 1983): 1–33.

Gultekin, N. Bulent, "Stock Market Returns and Inflation: Evidence from Other Countries," *Journal of Finance* 38, no. 1 (March 1983): 49–65.

Ibbotson, R. G., and R. A. Sinquefield, *Stocks, Bonds, Bills and Inflation: The Past and the Future,* Monograph No. 15, Financial Analysts Research Foundation, 1982.

Jaffe, J., and G. Mandelker, "The Fisher Effect for Risky Assets: An Empirical Investigation," *Journal of Finance* 31, no. 2 (May 1976): 447–58.

Kessel, R. A., "Inflation-Caused Wealth Redistribution: A Test of Hypothesis," *American Economic Review* 46, no. 1 (March 1956): 128–41.

Miles, J. A., "Taxes and the Fisher Effect: A Clarifying Analysis," *Journal of Finance* 38, no. 1 (March 1983): 67–77.

Modigliani, F., and R. A. Cohn, "Inflation, Rational Valuation and the Market," *Financial Analysts Journal* 35 (March/April 1979): 24–45.

Nelson, C. R., "Information and Rates of Return on Common Stocks," *Journal of Finance* 31, no. 2 (May 1976): 471–83.

Solnik, B., "The Relation Between Stock Prices and Inflationary Expectations: The International Evidence," *Journal of Finance* 38, no. 1 (March 1983): 35–48.

III

Risk and Return

In the next four chapters we address the problem of how to determine required rates of return on assets within the company using returns on assets of equivalent risk in the financial market as a benchmark. In Chapter 8 we show how the corporation's stockholders reduce the risks of their investments by holding diversified portfolios of securities in different companies. Because portfolio diversification does not eliminate all the risk, we show how the financial market's required rates of return reflect the risk that the stockholders cannot eliminate through diversification. In Chapters 9 and 10 we show you how to obtain the cost of capital not only for the company but also for its divisions and its individual assets. We do so by estimating the nondiversifiable risk for each level and type of asset and by obtaining the corresponding required rate of return in the financial market. We show you how to estimate the nondiversifiable risk for different assets so that you can obtain discount rates for new investments and establish performance targets for the different divisions of the company. Finally, in Chapter 11 we show how to relate the accounting performance targets for a division to the economic required rates of return that are consistent with the division's risk.

8

Portfolio Theory and the Capital Asset Pricing Model

Up to this chapter, our choice of a discount rate to be used for valuing a project's cash flows has been arbitrary. We have, however, suggested that a project can only be profitable for investors if the project provides a greater return than they could obtain on an asset of similar risk traded in the capital market. For example, AT&T should only invest in new communications equipment if the returns are greater than those that investors could obtain by investing in financial securities whose returns are of the same risk. Assume that the risk of the communications equipment is the same as the risk of the common stock of AT&T. If we could measure the returns investors expect on AT&T's common stock, we could use that rate of return as the discount rate for the project's cash flows.

In this chapter, we describe a theory of risk and return that allows us to measure the risk and expected returns on investments in common stocks. The theory of risk and expected return on collections or portfolios of securities is known as **portfolio theory,** and the model that allows us to relate the rate of return that investors expect from an individual stock given its risk is known as the **Capital Asset Pricing Model** (CAPM). We shall show how the CAPM can be derived from portfolio theory.

The Investor's Dilemma

Investors invest in common stocks in order to obtain dividend income and increases in the capital value of their investments. That is, during any period of time that they hold an investment, investors wish to maximize their expected **holding period rate of return,** which can be defined as

Holding Period Rate of Return = Dividend Yield + Expected Capital Gain

where the dividend yield is the dividend expected for the next period expressed as a percentage of the price of the stock at the beginning of the period, and the capital gain is the change in value, also expressed as a percentage of the initial price.

However, every investor knows that expected dividends and capital gains are not the only factors to be considered; something called risk lurks in the background of every investment decision, whether the investment is being made by investors or by management on their behalf. Most decisions involve a large element of uncertainty about the future, and they are taken in the expectation of returns that might not materialize fully, or that might result in losses. The investor's dilemma is how to maximize returns from investments and at the same time minimize the associated risk.

The first step that most investors take is to reduce risk by holding a diversified portfolio of investments. A **portfolio** represents an investment in a collection of different securities or other assets. A **diversified portfolio** of securities is a portfolio in which the investment has been divided among different securities in a manner that makes the risk of the portfolio as a whole less than the risk of the average security in the portfolio. By holding many different securities in the portfolio, the investor can hope that when some of the securities go down in value, others may go up. In the language of the man or woman on the street, investors put their eggs into many baskets. Portfolio theory shows us how best to select such investments so that we do not end up putting all the eggs into the same basket. The theory enables us to minimize the risk for a given rate of return on the portfolio, or to maximize the rate of return for a given level of risk. In this way portfolio theory resolves the investor's dilemma.

Although portfolio theory explains how large reductions in risk can be obtained through diversification, it also shows us why all the risk cannot be eliminated by holding portfolios of risky securities. The characteristics of the risky securities that are available for selection are not sufficiently different that they enable all risk to be eliminated from a portfolio. The risk that remains in a well-diversified portfolio is called **nondiversifiable risk.** How can the risk of a portfolio be measured, and what is the best way to measure nondiversifiable risk? How large a rate of return should an investor expect from his investments to justify the nondiversifiable risk? In this chapter we shall show how we arrive at answers to such questions.

Measuring Risk

In earlier chapters we did not fully define or measure risk, and we have suggested only briefly how the capital market might discount it. Because the element of risk is so important in investment decisions, we must take at least as much care in the definition of risk as we have in the definition of the holding period return. What is risk? Mathematicians and statisticians measure risk in terms of variation from the mean or expected return; that is, how wrong could our best estimate be? Investors, on the other hand, think of risk as the probability of having to take an unacceptable loss. These two aspects of risk are closely related.

In Table 8.1 we describe the **probability distribution** of rates of return for a particular investment. The first column shows various ranges for the rates of return, and the second column provides the **frequency distribution,** or number of times a return in each range is expected to occur. In the third column we express that frequency in the form of a probability of occurrence. The probability can be estimated by dividing the frequency by the total number of trials (in this case, forty). For example, a frequency of six out of forty (for the range of $x = -10\%$ to 10%) is equivalent to an estimated probability of occurrence of 0.15. The probability of earnings equal to minus 10 percent or less is 0.05 (two chances out of forty) and the chance of earning 10 percent or less is $0.05 + 0.15 = 0.20$. The probability distribution provides a means of estimating risk. The greater amount of probability concentrated in the extremes of the distribution (lowest and highest returns), the greater the risk of extreme loss and the greater the chance of extreme gain.

If an investor is offered a choice between two investments, both offering an uncertain return of 20 percent but having different probability distributions, how would the investor choose between them? In Table 8.2 we show the probability distributions of the two investments. Both have an expected

Table 8.1   *Probability distribution of return*

Rate of return x (%)	Frequency (chances out of 40)	Probability
$-30 \leq x < -10$	2	0.05
$-10 \leq x < 10$	6	0.15
$10 \leq x < 30$	14	0.35
$30 \leq x < 50$	10	0.25
$50 \leq x < 70$	6	0.15
$70 \leq x < 90$	2	0.05
	40	1.00

Table 8.2   *Probability distribution of returns for two investments*

Rate of return x (%)	Probability	
	Investment A	Investment B
$-30 \leq x < -10$	0	0.16
$-10 \leq x < 10$	0.16	0.21
$10 \leq x < 30$	0.68	0.26
$30 \leq x < 50$	0.16	0.21
$50 \leq x < 70$	0	0.16

Mean rate of return for investment A = 20%

Mean rate of return for investment B = 20%

return of 20 percent, but you can see that B's probabilities are dispersed over a wider range of returns than investment A's probabilities. Therefore, although investment B offers the chance of getting a higher return than A does, it also shows a probability of making a larger loss. If the investor were indifferent to risk, that is risk-neutral, he would have difficulty in choosing between investments A and B, as both investments offer the same expected return of 20 percent. The fact that investment A is less risky than investment B would make no difference to the risk-neutral investor. It is assumed more commonly that investors do not like risk, that is, that they are risk-averse. If an investor is risk-averse, he or she gives more weight to the possibility of loss than to the possibility of gain. Although investment B offers a better chance of extreme gain than A, the **risk-averse investor** attaches greater weight to the fact that investment B also has the greater possibility of extreme loss. The risk-averse investor would prefer investment A to investment B because investment A is less risky than B. (The concept of risk aversion is explained in more detail in Appendix 8.1.)

How much more risky is B than A? Risk can be measured in terms of the degree to which possible outcomes may deviate from the mean or expected outcome. The most common measure of the degree to which the possible outcomes deviate from the mean is the **standard deviation** of the probability distribution. For the most common distributions, most of the probability falls within plus or minus one standard deviation from the mean return, and nearly all the probability is contained within two standard deviations from the mean return. Tables are available to tabulate the relationship between probability and standard deviations for a variety of distributions.

For the **normal distribution,** more than two-thirds of the probability (68 percent) is contained within plus or minus one standard deviation, and 95 percent of the probability is contained within plus or minus 1.96 standard deviations. In Table 8.2 the standard deviation of the rate of return on investment A is approximately 10 percent, as 68 percent of the probability is contained within the range 10 percent to 30 percent, which is + or − 10 percent from the mean of 20 percent. In contrast the standard deviation for investment B is approximately 30 percent since 68 percent of the probability is contained within the range of −10 to +50 percent which is + or − 30 percent from the mean of 20 percent. These standard deviations are only approximate, because the probabilities in Table 8.2 are only approximately normally distributed.

How is the standard deviation from the mean rate of return more accurately calculated? The standard deviation is defined in terms of the **variance** of the distribution. The standard deviation is the square root of the variance, which is calculated for investment B in Table 8.3 (the formula for calculating the standard deviation is given in Appendix 8.2). In the first column of Table 8.3 we have listed the mean rate of return for each of the ranges given in the first column in Table 8.2. For example, the first range of rates of return listed in Table 8.2 is −30 to −10 percent. In Table 8.3 we have estimated the mean of this range by its midpoint or −20 percent, and so on for the other values.

In the second column of Table 8.3 we calculate the amount by which the returns in the first column deviate from the mean rate of return for the project. As the mean of the distribution is 20 percent, we obtain the deviations in column 2 by subtracting 20 from each of the figures in column 1. In column 3 we square all the deviations in the preceding column. Then we multiply the squared deviations by the probabilities (from Table 8.2) in column 4 to obtain the products in column 5. Finally, the sum of the products in the fifth column gives us the variance, which is 680. The **variance** is the probability-weighted average of the squared deviations from the mean. We obtain the standard deviation by taking the square root of the variance. The square root of 680 is just over 26, and therefore the standard deviation of the distribution of returns for investment B is approximately 26.

Table 8.3   *Calculation of the variance of returns for investment B*

Rate of return (%)	Deviation	Squared deviation	Probability	Probability × squared deviation
−20	−40	1600	0.16	256
0	−20	400	0.21	84
20	0	0	0.26	0
40	20	400	0.21	84
60	40	1600	0.16	256
			Variance	680

We had guessed earlier that the standard deviation would be 30, if the probabilities could be approximated by the normal distribution. We have obtained a slightly smaller standard deviation than would have been obtained from a normal distribution, because the probabilities in the table for investment B are more concentrated toward the mean than would be the case for the normal distribution. For example, the table does not show any possibility of returns below minus 30 percent or above 70 percent.

Risk Reduction Through Portfolio Diversification

If risk can be reduced by diversification, the standard deviation of returns for a single investment may overstate its risk when it is part of a diversified portfolio. Portfolio theory enables us to adjust the risk of an individual security for the effects of portfolio diversification. To the extent that the dividends and capital gains on stocks tend to move independently of each other, diversification will reduce the amount of risk the security contributes to the portfolio. The key question, then, is to what extent are returns on the individual security correlated with the returns on other securities in the portfolio?

CORRELATION: THE KEY TO EFFECTIVE DIVERSIFICATION

If the prices of two securities always move together, they do not provide effective diversification when combined in a portfolio. If, on the other hand, there is a likelihood that one security may increase in value when the other declines, combining the two securities will reduce risk without affecting their average returns. For this reason it is important to be able to measure the degree to which returns (dividends and capital gains) on investments in different securities move together. A convenient way to measure the comovement between security returns is by means of the **correlation coefficient**.

Figure 8.1(a) illustrates the correlation pattern between two hypothetical securities that could be combined into a portfolio. The expected annual return on each security is 20 percent, or 1.53 percent compounded monthly. If we put half our money into each security, we would still expect to obtain 1.53 percent per month on average from the portfolio. However, both securities are risky, and their monthly holding period returns deviate substantially from the mean of 1.53 percent. To what extent might the holding period returns *on the portfolio* deviate from 1.53 percent per month?

Ideally, we would want the two securities to be perfectly negatively correlated; in this case the portfolio could be balanced in such a way that there would be no risk. **Perfect negative correlation** occurs when one

Figure 8.1(a)   *Comparison between holding period returns on two securities*

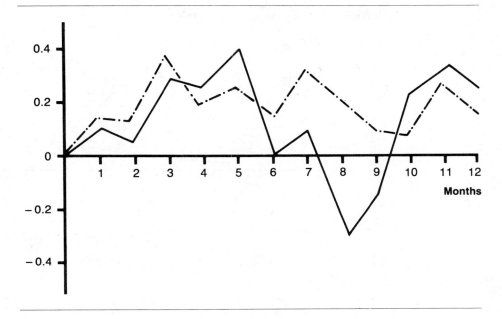

security's returns deviates in the negative direction while the other's always deviates a corresponding amount in the positive direction. Figure 8.1(b) illustrates the special case where a deviation in the monthly holding period return on one security is always matched by an equal deviation in the opposite direction by the other security. In this case we would put half our money into each security, and the portfolio would always earn 1.53 percent per month (the dotted line in the figure). Because the returns on the portfolio would not deviate from the expected return of 1.53 percent per month, there would be no risk. Unfortunately, the returns on pairs of common stocks are negatively correlated only occasionally.

A convenient way to measure the degree to which security returns move together is by means of the **correlation coefficient.** In principle, the correlation coefficient can take on any value from $r = -1.00$ to $r = +1.00$ where the value -1.00 indicates perfect negative correlation and the value $+1.00$ indicates perfect positive correlation. While perfect negative correlation between the returns of different securities could make portfolio diversification 100 percent effective in eliminating risk, perfect positive correlation would make portfolio diversification totally ineffective as a method of risk reduction.

In Figure 8.2(a) we show a scatter diagram illustrating perfect positive correlation. Returns on security 1 are measured on the horizontal axis. Returns on security 2 are measured on the vertical axis. Each point in the

Figure 8.1(b)   *Holding period returns on two negatively correlated securities*

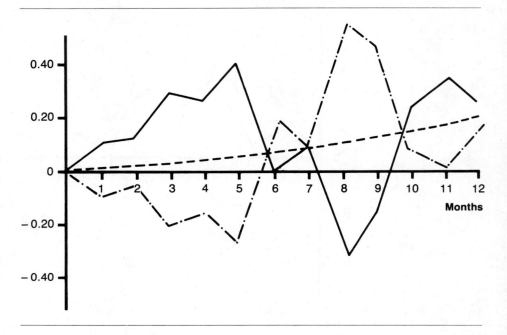

diagram represents returns on the two securities for one month. If the points fall on a straight line and if the line has a positive slope, the returns on the two securities are perfectly positively correlated ($r_{1,2} = 1.00$). Portfolios composed of such securities cannot reduce risk, for the returns always move together.

At the opposite extreme, when a decline in the return on one security is always accompanied by a corresponding rise for the other security, the two securities are perfectly negatively correlated, and $r_{1,2} = -1.00$. This situation is illustrated in Figure 8.2(b), where we see that all the points fall on a straight line, but now the slope of the line is negative. As discussed earlier, if we could find securities that are perfectly negatively correlated, we could eliminate all risk from portfolios composed of such securities.

Figure 8.2(c) illustrates an example of zero correlation ($r_{1,2} = 0$) between the returns on two securities. The points are scattered at random, and it is not possible to find a line that would describe a significant relationship between the returns on the two securities. Even though we no longer have negative correlation, effective diversification is obtainable by combining a sufficient number of securities with uncorrelated returns. Diversification still reduces risk in this case, for when one security's return declines there is a 50 percent chance that the other's may simultaneously increase, thus reducing the combined risk.

Figure 8.2   *Correlations between pairs of securities*

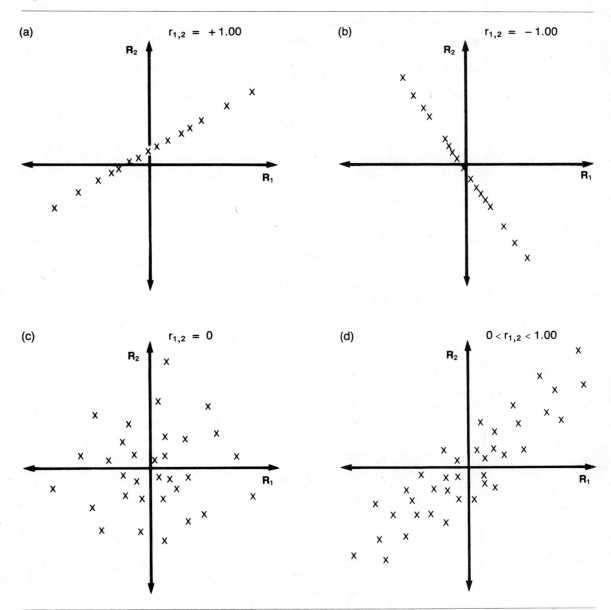

The more usual case of imperfectly positively correlated securities is represented in Figure 8.2(d). Although the relationship is not perfect, corresponding returns tend to fall along an upward-sloping straight line. The correlation coefficient is positive but less than one ($0 < r_{1,2} < 1.00$). As the correlation is less than perfect, portfolio diversification will still reduce risk, although by a smaller amount than when the correlation coefficient is zero or negative.

These arguments suggest that the degree of correlation between the returns on pairs of securities in a portfolio provides the key to the effectiveness of diversification in reducing risk. The higher the value of the correlation coefficients, the greater the number of different securities that would be required in a portfolio to achieve a given level of risk reduction.

Because the returns on most securities move somewhat independently, we cannot predict the standard deviation of a portfolio from the standard deviations of the individual securities in the portfolio alone. In order to predict the standard deviation of the portfolio, we also need to know the correlation coefficients that measure how closely returns on the individual securities in the portfolio are related. The correlation coefficients together with the standard deviations of returns for individual securities can be used to obtain the risk of a portfolio. Now we can see more precisely how portfolio diversification reduces risk.

THE TWO-SECURITY PORTFOLIO

We shall first consider the easiest case, a portfolio composed of only two securities. The standard deviation of the returns on the portfolio is equal to the square root of the variance of the portfolio's returns. The variance, s_p^2, of the returns on a portfolio composed of two securities is given by the following formula:

$$s_p^2 = (x_1 s_1)^2 + (x_2 s_2)^2 + 2r_{1,2}(x_1 s_1)(x_2 s_2) \tag{8.1}$$

where x_1 = proportion of the value of the portfolio p invested in security 1
   x_2 = proportion of the value of the portfolio p invested in security 2 ($x_2 = 1 - x_1$)
   s_1 = standard deviation of the returns on security 1
   s_2 = standard deviation of the returns on security 2
   $r_{1,2}$ = correlation coefficient for the comovement between the returns on securities 1 and 2.

Equation 8.1 shows that the variance of a two-security portfolio is the sum of three parts as represented by three terms on the right-hand side of the equation. The first part, represented by the term $(x_1 s_1)^2$, is the contribution that security 1 makes independently to the total variance of the portfolio. The second part, represented by the term $(x_2s_2)^2$, is the contribution that security 2 makes independently to the total variance of the portfolio. The third part represents the contribution to the total variance of the portfolio made by the two securities together as a result of any tendency for their returns to be correlated (as reflected in the correlation coefficient $r_{1,2}$). The factor 2 in the last term $2r_{1,2}(x_1s_1)(x_2s_2)$ reflects the fact that if security 1 is correlated with security 2, security 2 must also be correlated with security 1 to an equal degree. This final term is really the sum of two identical terms.

If we assume in the previous formula that the correlation coefficient between securities 1 and 2 is +1.00, equation 8.1 for the variance of returns for a portfolio simplifies to

$$s_p^2 = (x_1s_1)^2 + 2(x_1s_1)(x_2s_2) + (x_2s_2)^2 \qquad (8.2)$$

The standard deviation of returns for such a portfolio is

$$s_p = x_1s_1 + x_2s_2$$

as you can easily prove by squaring the equation.[1]

For example, suppose that the standard deviation of the returns on security 1 is $s_1 = 0.30$ and for security 2 it is $s_2 = 0.50$. If the two securities are perfectly positively correlated, the standard deviation of the portfolio would be given by

$$s_p = x_1(0.30) + x_2(0.50)$$

As the proportions x_1 and x_2 add up to one ($x_1 = 1.0 - x_2$), we can substitute for x_1 in the equation above to get

$$s_p = (1 - x_2)(0.30) + x_2(0.50)$$

$$s_p = 0.30 + 0.20\,x_2$$

where the proportion x_2 in security 2 can have any value between 0 and 1.00. This equation shows that risk is not reduced by holding these two securities in combination, because the standard deviation of the portfolio is merely a linear combination of the standard deviations of the two securities. That is, s_p is merely proportional to the fraction x_2 that is invested in security 2 in the above equation. If we were to divide our money equally between the two securities, x_2 would equal 0.5, and the formula would give us

$$s_p = 0.30 + (0.20 \times 0.50)$$

$$= 0.40$$

[1]You can prove this if you remember that $(a + b)^2 = a^2 + 2ab + b^2$.

The standard deviation of the portfolio would equal 0.40, which is just midway between the standard deviations of the two securities—but no less.

You can see the situation graphically in Figure 8.3 where we have plotted the expected returns versus the risks of the two securities and of all portfolio combinations of the two securities. Point 1 represents security 1, with a standard deviation of 0.30 and an expected holding period return of 0.15. Point 2 represents security 2, with a standard deviation of 0.50 and an expected holding period rate of return of 0.25. The straight line between the two points represents all possible portfolio combinations of the two securities when their returns are perfectly positively correlated. If we were to hold only security 1 in the portfolio, we would find ourselves at point 1 in the figure. If we were to hold only security 2 in the portfolio, we would be at point 2. However, if we put half our money into each security, we would be at point A on the straight line midway between the two points. If the returns on the two securities were not perfectly positively correlated, point

Figure 8.3   *Risk and expected return for a portfolio composed of two perfectly positively correlated securities*

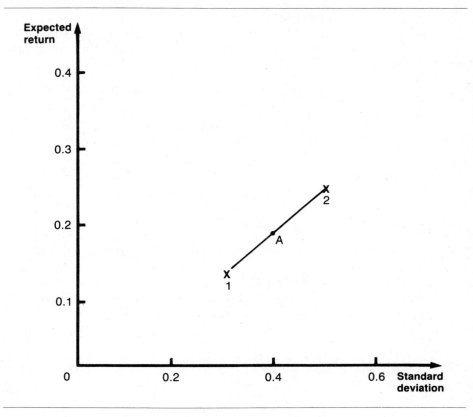

A would have been to the left of the straight line, because in that situation diversification would succeed in reducing risk. Similarly, all other portfolio combinations that include both securities would fall to the left of the straight line joining securities 1 and 2.

This example is the simplest case but also the least interesting one, as risk cannot be reduced when securities are perfectly positively correlated. Now let us consider the case where the two securities' returns are completely uncorrelated ($r_{1,2} = 0$). In this case the portfolio formula becomes,

$$s_p{}^2 = (x_1 s_1)^2 + (x_2 s_2)^2 + 0$$

The equation is no longer linear if $r_{1,2} = 0$. The standard deviation of the portfolio is now the square root of the sum of the squares in the equation. Suppose that the value of the standard deviation of security 1 is still $s_1 = 0.30$ and for security 2 it is still $s_2 = 0.50$; how will the standard deviation of portfolios composed of the two securities change as the weights x_1 and x_2 change?

The portfolio equation provides the answer, which we have tabulated in Table 8.4. The table compares the two cases $r_{1,2} = 1.00$ and $r_{1,2} = 0$. It shows that when $r_{1,2} = 0$, the standard deviation of any portfolio combination of the two securities has a smaller value than when $r_{1,2} = 1.00$. The first two columns show the portfolio proportions, x_1 and x_2 of securities 1 and 2, respectively. The third and fourth columns compare the portfolio returns when the correlation between the two securities' returns is, respectively, 1.00 and 0.

First note that in column three (where $r_{1,2} = +1.00$) the portfolio standard deviations are merely weighted averages of the standard deviations of securities 1 and 2 as we saw in Figure 8.3. That is, no risk reduction is taking place. However, in column four (where $r_{1,2} = 0$), all the portfolio standard

Table 8.4   *Standard deviation of returns on a two-security portfolio*

Proportion in security 1 x_1	Proportion in security 2 x_2	Correlation between returns on securities 1 and 2	
		$r_{1,2} = +1.00$	$r_{1,2} = 0$
		Standard deviation of returns of portfolio	
0	1.00	0.50	0.500
0.25	0.75	0.45	0.382
0.50	0.50	0.40	0.292
0.75	0.25	0.35	0.257
1.00	0	0.30	0.300

deviations are either less than or equal to the portfolio standard deviations in column three. Thus portfolio diversification is reducing risk when $r_{1,2} = 0$.

These results are plotted in Figure 8.4, where we see that the straight line corresponding to $r_{1,2} = 1.00$ becomes a curve bending toward lower standard deviations when $r_{1,2} = 0$. You might like to consider how the line would be drawn if $r_{1,2} = -1.0$.

So far we have shown that a portfolio composed of only two securities can reduce risk if the two securities' returns are not perfectly positively correlated. Further diversification using three or more securities can reduce risk even further, as we shall see.

PORTFOLIOS OF MORE THAN TWO SECURITIES

The portfolio formula is similar for portfolios that contain more than two securities. However, there are more terms corresponding to the extra securities and to the many additional correlations corresponding to the paired

Figure 8.4   *Risk and expected return for a two-security portfolio of uncorrelated securities*

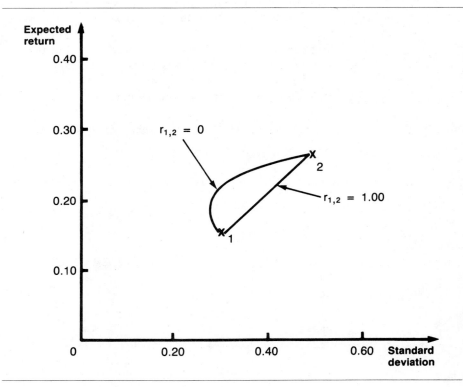

combinations of securities. For example, for portfolios of three securities the portfolio formula is now,

$$s_p{}^2 = (x_1s_1)^2 + (x_2s_2)^2 + (x_3s_3)^2 + 2r_{1,2}(x_1s_1)(x_2s_2)$$
$$+ 2r_{1,3}(x_1s_1)(x_3s_3) + 2r_{2,3}(x_2s_2)(x_3s_3)$$

The variance of a portfolio of three securities is shown in the formula to be made up of six parts. The first three parts represented by the first three terms on the right-hand side of the equation are the contributions that each of the securities makes independently to the total variance of the portfolio. The remaining three terms represent the additional variance contributed as a result of the correlations between pairs of securities. The extent to which the returns on pairs of securities are correlated is reflected in the values of the correlation coefficients $r_{1,2}$, $r_{1,3}$, and $r_{2,3}$. There are three terms that contain these correlation coefficients, because there are just three possible combinations of correlated pairs of securities in a three-security portfolio. In larger portfolios there are many more possible combinations of pairs of securities. For example, in a portfolio of four securities there are six possible pairs of correlated securities. In a portfolio of N securities there would be $N(N - 1)/2$ different possible correlations between pairs of securities. In a portfolio of only 50 securities there can be 1,225 such pairs.

The effect of increasing the number of securities in a portfolio on the portfolio's risk can be seen more clearly with a simple example. Suppose that all the securities were to have the same standard deviation equal to s and that all correlations between the holding period returns are equal to r. For an equal investment x in each of N securities, the portfolio formula simplifies to

$$s_p{}^2 = N(xs)^2 + N(N - 1)r(xs)(xs)$$

The first term on the right-hand side represents the independent contributions of the N securities to the portfolio's total variance, and the second term represents the additional variance contributed as a result of correlations between the $N(N - 1)/2$ different pairs of securities in the portfolio. The fact that we invest an equal amount in each of the N securities means that the proportion x invested in each security is $x = 1/N$. Substituting for x in the equation, we have

$$s_p{}^2 = \frac{s^2}{N} + \frac{(N - 1)\ rs^2}{N} \tag{8.3}$$

Now we can see how the risk of the portfolio changes as we increase the number N of securities in the portfolio. For example, as we let N get larger, the first term s^2/N gets smaller, and the second term approaches rs^2. As N goes to infinity, the first term disappears and all we have left is the term rs^2, which represents the nondiversifiable risk of this portfolio.

Nondiversifiable risk is defined as that portion of a portfolio's risk that cannot be reduced further by increasing the number of securities in the portfolio. In the portfolio represented by equation (8.3) we saw that non-diversifiable risk is equal to rs^2 when we let the number N of securities in the portfolio go to infinity. That is, the nondiversifiable risk of the portfolio is equal to a proportion of the risk s^2 of a single security, and that proportion is given by the correlation coefficient r. If the correlation coefficient r is equal to 1.00, the portfolio variance equals $1.00 \times s^2$, i.e., the variance of the one security, and therefore risk is not diversifiable. If, however, the correlation coefficient is equal to 0, the minimum variance of the portfolio equals $0 \times s^2 = 0$, and all the risk is diversifiable.

The degree to which portfolio diversification can reduce the variance of holding period returns thus depends upon the number N of securities in the portfolio and the degree of correlation r between them. We illustrate this relationship in Figure 8.5, where we plot equation (8.3) for different values of r and N. It is clear that increasing the number of securities in the portfolio from one to ten securities sharply reduces the variance of the portfolio. Beyond ten securities, the risk reduction is very much less steep. The figure also makes clear that the value of the correlation coefficient sets the extent to which portfolio diversification can reduce risk. For example, if the correlation coefficient equals $r = 0.25$, the variance of the holding period returns on the portfolio cannot be reduced to less than 0.25 times the variance for one security, no matter how many securities are added to the portfolio.

In our example we invested equal sums in each security in the portfolio, and all the securities had the same variance. Also, all correlations between holding period returns for pairs of securities were the same. If we relax these assumptions and permit unequal investments in the different securities, different variances for the securities, and different correlation coefficients for different pairs of securities, we must use the portfolio formula to obtain the variance of the portfolio. The computation becomes more tedious than it was for the simple example, but the general principles remain the same. The first ten or fifteen securities that are added to the portfolio (in significant proportions) eliminate most of the diversifiable risk. The nondiversifiable risk that remains is determined by the amount of correlation between the holding period returns on the different securities in the portfolio. If the standard deviations of the holding period returns for the securities and the correlations between them are all different, how shall we determine the optimum proportions to invest in each security?

Efficient Portfolios

Securities can be selected in virtually an infinite number of alternative portfolio combinations. How shall we choose among them? The investor faces

Figure 8.5 *Portfolio variance and diversification*

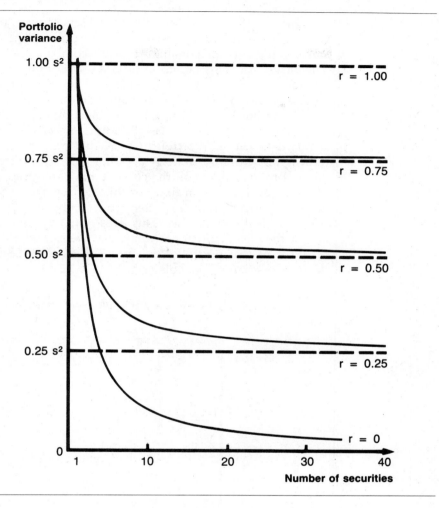

a dilemma: How is he or she to get the maximum expected return from a portfolio while minimizing risk? It cannot be had both ways. The investor must compromise, and the best compromise is to be found among efficiently diversified portfolios.

The **efficient set** of portfolios consists of those portfolios that minimize the risk for each level of expected return, or (equivalently), maximize expected return for each level of risk. Of all the possible portfolio combinations that could be chosen from a given set of securities, only a very limited proportion represents an efficient set of portfolios. If a rational risk-averse investor prefers more expected return to less expected return and prefers less risk to more risk, he or she will always try to select a portfolio from among the efficient set of portfolios.

Figure 8.6 illustrates three alternative sets of ways that securities 1, 2, and 3 can be combined into two-security portfolios. The curve joining points 1 and 2 represents all possible portfolio combinations of securities 1 and 2. The curve that joins points 1 and 3 represents all possible portfolio combinations of securities 1 and 3. Likewise, the curve that joins points 2 and 3 represents all possible portfolio combinations of securities 2 and 3.

Is portfolio A, consisting of a combination of securities 1 and 3, efficient? No, because portfolio B has the same expected return as A but a lower standard deviation. Portfolio C has the same risk but a higher expected return. Therefore portfolio A does not belong to the efficient set. Similarly, none of the portfolios on the curve joining securities 2 and 3 belongs to the efficient set, for we can find portfolios consisting of securities 1 and 3 with lower risk for the same expected return and portfolios with higher expected return with the same risk. This does not, however, imply necessarily that any of the two-security portfolios that we can see in Figure 8.6 is efficient. Could it be that portfolios consisting of all three securities dominate some of the two-security portfolios?

Figure 8.6   *Risk and return for two-security portfolio combinations selected from three securities*

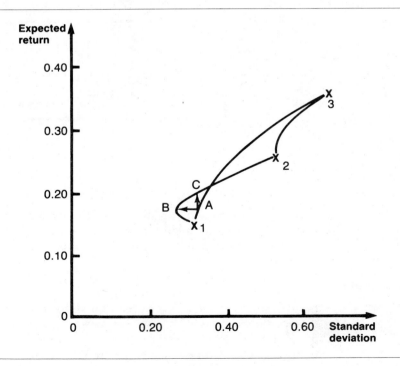

In Figure 8.7 we illustrate just one set of portfolios that can be constructed from all three securities. Let portfolio A represent a combination of securities 1 and 2. For every $1 invested in security 2 in portfolio A, $3 are invested in security 1. The curve between point A and point 3 represents all portfolios that can be constructed by combining portfolio A with security 3. In other words, the line joining points A and 3 represents a set of three-security portfolios. For example, at point B half the funds are invested in security 3 and half in portfolio A. This means that for every $1 invested in security 2, $3 are invested in security 1 and $4 in security 3. It should be clear from the figure that the set of three-security portfolios on the solid curve is more efficient than all the two-security portfolios that lie below it.

However, we have not considered all possible three-security combinations that might be even more efficient than those on the solid line, nor have we considered portfolios selected from the thousands of other securities that could be included in a portfolio. Thus we have not yet found the efficient set, which must lie above any of the portfolio combinations considered so far.

The boundary or envelope in Figure 8.8 encloses the opportunity set of all feasible portfolio combinations from *N* common stocks. The heavy dark

Figure 8.7   *Comparison of efficiency of some three-security portfolios with two-security portfolios selected from three securities*

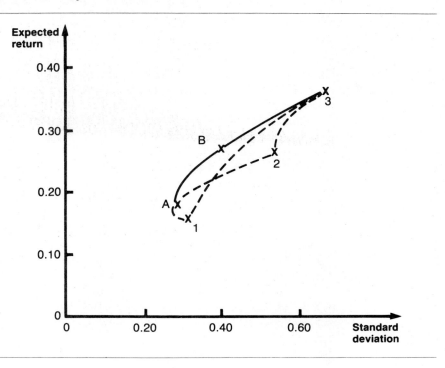

Figure 8.8   *Opportunity set and efficient set of portfolios selected from N securities*

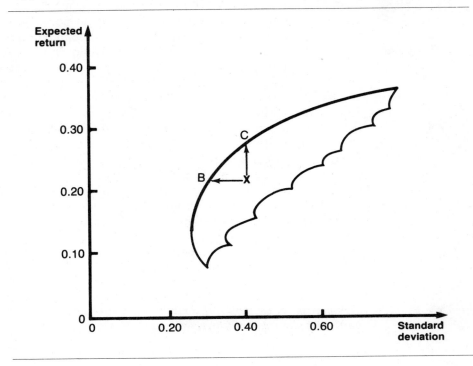

line on the upper left boundary of the opportunity set represents the efficient set often called the **efficient frontier,** that is, the subset of the feasible portfolios that is efficient. As can be seen, portfolio combinations in the efficient set dominate all other feasible portfolios, as there are no other portfolios that have less risk for a given expected rate of return or a greater expected return for a given level of risk. For example, consider the feasible portfolio X, which lies within the opportunity set. Portfolio X is not efficient, because another portfolio B has the same expected return but a lower risk. Also, portfolio C has the same risk but a higher expected return.

For any number of securities for which we are able to estimate the expected returns, standard deviations, and correlations, it is possible to construct the corresponding efficient set of portfolios. In his original exposition of portfolio theory, Markowitz (1959) developed a mathematical method that, with the aid of a computer, can be used to solve for the efficient set. The efficient set still represents an enormous number of possible portfolio combinations. Which of all the possible efficient portfolios would a rational investor choose? This question has a remarkable answer: As a rule, there is only *one* optimal portfolio in the efficient set, as we shall demonstrate.

The Optimal Portfolio of Risky Securities

The efficient set affords an enormous choice of combinations of risky securities. The choice of an optimal portfolio of risky securities from the efficient set depends upon the investor's opportunities to lend and to borrow.

The average investor may hold some short-term government bonds; if so, he or she is lending to the government. Lending may be regarded as holding a riskless security in the portfolio. The introduction of the possibility to invest in a riskless security has crucial implications for the portfolio of risky securities that the investor should hold. This point can be seen graphically in Figure 8.9. Point D represents the risk ($s_D = 0.00$) and the expected return (interest rate) on riskless lending. The tangent line between point D and the efficient set of risky securities at point E represents all possible combinations of lending and the risky portfolio at point E. The line is

Figure 8.9   *Efficient set of portfolios including both borrowing and lending*

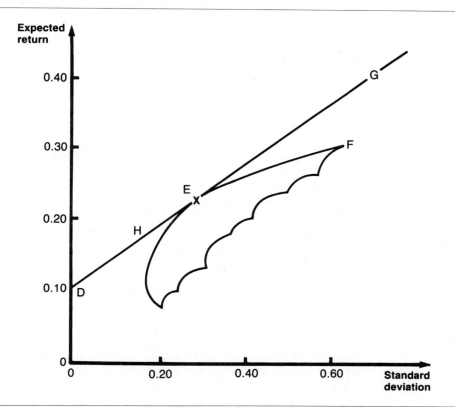

straight, as we can prove by applying the portfolio formula:

$$s_p^2 = (x_D s_D)^2 + (x_E s_E)^2 + 2r_{D,E}(x_D s_D)(x_E s_E) \qquad (8.4)$$

The first term on the right-hand side of the equation is the independent contribution that asset D makes to the combined portfolio's variance. However, asset D is riskless lending, and thus the first term is equal to zero. The second term on the right-hand side is the independent contribution that asset E (the efficient portfolio at the point of tangency) makes to the combined portfolio that includes lending. The third term is the contribution to the combined portfolio's variance that the two assets would make together as a result of any correlations between the returns on D and E. However, since the lending is riskless, s_D equals zero, and there can only be a zero correlation between the holding period returns on riskless lending and risky securities. Thus the third term is equal to zero. Consequently, the equation reduces to

$$s_p^2 = (x_E s_E)^2$$

or $s_p = x_E s_E$

Suppose we were to put half our money into the efficient portfolio at point E and half our money into Treasury bills (the riskless asset) at point D. What would be the standard deviation on the combined portfolio?

$$s_p = x_E s_E$$

$$= 0.50 \times s_E$$

The standard deviation on the portfolio consisting of one-half portfolio E and one-half Treasury bills is equal to one half the standard deviation of the returns on portfolio E. As the expected returns will also lie halfway between, the combined portfolio is to be found on a line halfway between D and E at point H in Figure 8.9. All such combinations of the risky portfolio at E and riskless lending at D fall on this same straight line.

The line D,E has an important property. As it is a line that is tangent to the efficient set, we cannot obtain a steeper line that would combine risky securities with lending. Therefore, we now have a new efficient set, which follows the path D,E, where all points on the line offer expected returns that are at least as great as portfolios of the same risk on the efficient frontier.

Now let us suppose that the investor can borrow at the same rate at which he or she can lend. Borrowing is the opposite of lending. For this reason borrowing can be represented by the line from E through G in Figure 8.9. The line from E through G represents all leveraged portfolios that can be formed by borrowing and buying more of portfolio E on the efficient frontier. For example, suppose an investor placed all her funds totaling $1,000 in the market portfolio, which provided an expected return of 16 percent and had an annual standard deviation of 18 percent. What would happen if she decided to lever up by borrowing $500 at an interest rate of 10 percent, and to invest the additional funds in the market portfolio? The expected return R on the portfolio, net of interest expenses, would be

$$R = \frac{(1{,}500 \times 16\%) - (\$500 \times 10\%)}{\$1{,}000}$$

$$= 19\%$$

where the $1,500 is the total amount invested in the market portfolio, and $500 is the amount borrowed. We have expressed this dollar return as a proportion of the investor's equity to obtain a return of 19%. The standard deviation of return s on the portfolio is

$$s = \frac{(\$1{,}500 \times 18\%) - (\$500 \times 0\%)}{\$1{,}000}$$

$$= 27\%$$

where the standard deviation on the riskless loan is zero. Thus, leverage has increased the risk from $s = 18\%$ to $s = 27\%$, while the expected return has risen from $R = 16\%$ to $R = 19\%$. Note that all points on line E,G are efficient, because no other portfolios have higher expected returns for the same level of risk. If the investor can borrow and lend, the set of portfolio opportunities has widened considerably. Now the efficient set has become the line from D through E and G. Except at point D, all investment strategies in this new efficient set have one thing in common: holding portfolio E. Therefore, portfolio E is an optimal portfolio of risky securities. The combination of risky securities in portfolio E is the combination that the rational investor would choose if he or she has the opportunity to borrow and to lend at the same interest rate.

An investor disliking risk will hold more Treasury bills and less of portfolio E. One who is more prone to take some risk will move up the line from D toward E by concentrating a larger proportion of wealth in portfolio E. A risk-taker can "lever up" by borrowing and investing the money in portfolio E, and thus move up the line beyond E toward G. Whether the investor lends by buying government securities or borrows to lever up the portfolio, he or she still holds the same portfolio E of risky assets. The investor's choice from among the efficient portfolios is not affected by lending or borrowing. The investor's attitude toward risk determines how much is loaned or borrowed, but portfolio E is still the risky portfolio chosen.

That there is a distinction between the investor's choice of risk and return and the optimal choice among the efficient portfolios of risky securities is called the **separation theorem.** The separation theorem is important, because it shows us how we can most easily adjust the risk of our optimum portfolio of risky securities: by changing the level of lending or borrowing rather than by changing the composition of the risky portfolio E. An important theoretical implication of the separation theorem is that all investors hold the same efficient portfolio of risky securities E. Investors with different risk preferences still hold the same risky portfolio but with different combinations of lending and borrowing. Investors who wish to take high risks lever up and invest the borrowed funds in E; investors with low risks invest (lend) part of their funds in the riskless asset and the remainder in portfolio E.

The Capital Asset Pricing Model

Suppose that all investors were to agree on the expected distribution of returns and correlations between returns for all securities traded in the capital market. Suppose also that all investors can lend or borrow at the same risk-free rate. What would be the implications of these assumptions for the prices of risky securities traded in an efficient capital market?

We have already seen that investors who can borrow and lend at the same interest rate and who face the same portfolio opportunity set will hold the same efficient portfolio of risky securities. If all securities must be held by someone, and everyone chooses the same optimal portfolio, each investor would hold some fraction of the market portfolio of all securities and portfolio E in Figure 8.9 becomes the market portfolio M. As the market portfolio offers maximum diversification, all risk capable of being diversified virtually disappears.

These simplifying assumptions that all investors hold the market portfolio, that only the nondiversifiable portion of total risk can be of any concern to them, and that they can all borrow or lend at the same risk-free rate of interest underlie the capital asset pricing model (CAPM) illustrated in Figure 8.10. The figure illustrates the relationship between risk and expected rates of return that is implied by the capital asset pricing model. As investors are assumed to be efficiently diversified, the model relates expected returns to nondiversifiable risk, and the horizontal axis in Figure 8.10 represents the nondiversifiable risk $c_{i,M}$ that a security i contributes to the market portfolio M. The nondiversifiable risk of an individual security i is the weighted sum of its covariances with all the other securities in the market portfolio and is thus equal to its covariance with the market portfolio given by

$$c_{i,M} = r_{i,M} s_i s_M \qquad (8.5)$$

Figure 8.10   *Capital asset pricing model in covariance form*

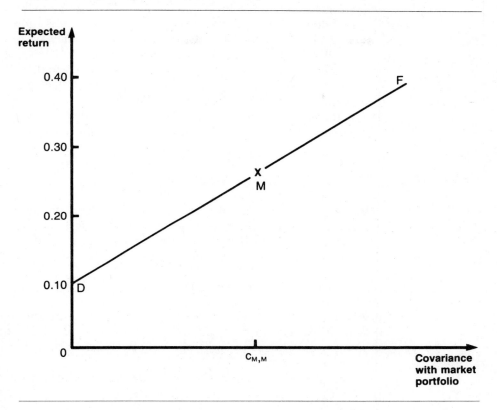

The covariance between the holding period returns on a security and the corresponding holding period returns on the market portfolio is defined as the correlation $r_{i,M}$ between its returns and the returns on the market portfolio multiplied by the product of the standard deviations of the returns on the security and the returns on the market portfolio, respectively.

The straight line from the risk-free lending rate D through point M in Figure 8.10 represents investor opportunities to combine lending or borrowing with the optimal efficient portfolio of risky securities (the market portfolio). An implication of the capital asset pricing model is that all individual securities fall on the capital market line D,M,F in Figure 8.10. If a security i were overpriced and its expected return were below the line, there would be no demand for it. Investors would agree that they could obtain a higher expected return at the same level of risk $c_{i,M}$ by holding the combination of the risk-free security (at D) and the market portfolio at M that would have the same risk but a higher rate of return (as it would be on the capital market line). Similarly, any securities that found their way above the capital market line quickly would be brought back onto the line by increased demand.

An alternative way of looking at covariance risk is more appealing intuitively. The **beta coefficient** measures the tendency of a security's returns to change with changes in the returns on the market portfolio. The beta coefficient equals 1.00 for the market portfolio, is less than 1.00 for less risky securities, and is more than 1.00 for securities that are more risky than average. The beta coefficient is closely related to the covariance risk $c_{i,M}$. In fact, the beta coefficient for any security i is estimated statistically by dividing its covariance $c_{i,M}$ by the variance s_M^2 of the returns on the market portfolio:

$$\beta_i = \frac{c_{i,M}}{s_M^2} = \frac{r_{i,M} s_i s_M}{s_M^2} = \frac{r_{i,M} s_i}{s_M} \tag{8.6}$$

We can easily estimate the beta of a portfolio from the betas of the securities that are in the portfolio, as the linear relationship between risk and return of the CAPM implies that the beta β_p of a portfolio is just the weighted sum of the betas β_i of its constituent securities. That is,

$$\beta_p = x_1\beta_1 + x_2\beta_2 + \cdots + x_N\beta_N \tag{8.7}$$

where the weights x_i ($i = 1, 2, \ldots, N$) are proportional to the market value of each security i held and add up to a total weight of 1.00. Thus an investor can choose the portfolio beta β_p desired and construct the portfolio using equation (8.7).

In Figure 8.11 we have shown the **capital market line** as it relates to beta risk. To obtain this figure, we divided the risk scale in Figure 8.10 by a constant, the variance s_M^2 of the return on the market portfolio. While the beta risk of lending at the risk-free rate is still equal to zero, the risk of the market portfolio has been scaled down to a value of 1.00 (as would be expected, for by definition the beta of the market portfolio is equal to 1.00).

The equation for the capital asset pricing model is an equation for a straight line. The expected return $E(R_i)$ on a security is given by

$$E(\tilde{R}_i) = R_f + \beta_i\,[E(\tilde{R}_M) - R_f] \tag{8.8}$$

where $R_f =$ risk-free rate of return
$E(\tilde{R}_M) =$ expected rate of return on the market portfolio
$\beta_i =$ beta of security i

The line intercepts the vertical axis at the risk-free rate R_f. As we move to the right toward higher levels of beta risk β, the line moves up because investors expect a premium for higher risk. How much premium per unit of higher risk do they expect? The slope $[E(\tilde{R}_M) - R_f]$ of the market line is the market price for risk given by the expected difference between the return

Figure 8.11   *Capital asset pricing model measuring nondiversifiable risk by the beta coefficient*

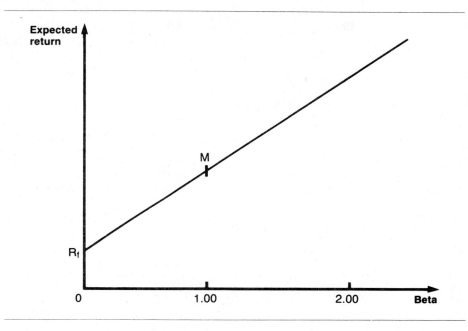

$E(\tilde{R}_M)$ on the market portfolio and the risk-free rate R_f. This difference is usually referred to as the risk premium on the market. We shall estimate the value of the risk premium in Chapter 9.

Tests and Limitations of the CAPM: The Good News and the Bad News

An important issue is whether the capital market behaves as if investors were evaluating securities in the manner suggested by the CAPM. This issue is not yet resolved. Figure 8.12 presents the evidence of Black, Jensen, and Scholes (1972).

They measured beta values each year for each of 1,200 shares traded on the New York Stock Exchange. They then created ten portfolios. The first portfolio contained the 10 percent of securities with the highest β values. The second portfolio contained the 10 percent with the next largest β values,

Figure 8.12   *Historical relationship between risk and return on the New York Stock Exchange between 1935 and 1965 based on ten portfolios of different risks (after Black, Jensen, and Scholes, 1972)*

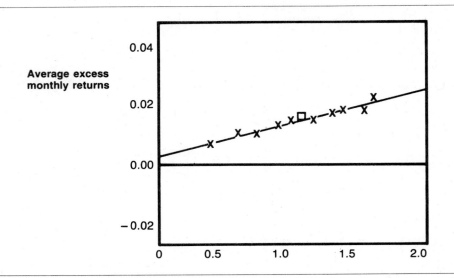

and so on. On the graph are plotted the excess returns over the risk-free rate against the β value for each of the ten portfolios for the period 1935–1965. A straight-line relationship appears to exist between risk and portfolio returns. This would be evidence that shareholders obtained proportionately higher excess returns on portfolios with higher betas over a thirty-year period.

However, Roll (1977) has pointed out deficiencies in existing tests and evidence. He shows the importance of constructing a market portfolio of assets that truly represents all the risky assets available in the economy. For example, the Dow Jones Industrials and the Standard & Poor's indexes of stock market prices do not include samples of risky assets, such as land, antiques, small firms, and above all, human capital (where returns accrue to people). Roll showed that, in order to test the capital asset pricing model, it would be necessary to show that the market portfolio of all assets in the economy is efficient. Such a test is obviously impractical since many such assets are traded infrequently. Roll shows that even if Black, Jensen, and Scholes chose the incorrect market index, they might still obtain a linear relationship between risk and return. As a result, Roll concluded that existing methods are not powerful enough to test the CAPM.

It is useful to examine Roll's point in a practical way. Banz (1981) examined holding period returns on stocks over the period 1936–1975, finding, on average, that firms with a small market value earned higher risk-adjusted returns than the CAPM would predict. The implication of this study is that either an incorrect index is being used to measure the betas of individual stocks, providing incorrect measures of performance, or that the CAPM is an inadequate model for explaining a security's returns. For example, we know that some small stocks are not traded very frequently or in very large blocks. As a result, the market in these stocks may not be very liquid, and buyers and sellers may have to pay a premium (or sell at a discount) if they wish to deal in large blocks of such shares. The CAPM does not contain any term that reflects the inability to liquidate stocks without lowering prices; some people would call this a liquidity effect.

The strength of the capital asset pricing model is that it emphasizes the likely impact of nondiversifiable risk on investors' required rates of return. It assumes, however, that market returns on securities are generated in a very simple way, that they are related only to the market index, and that the only other determinants of returns are unique to the individual company and can be diversified away. This model of the returns generating process may be too simple. Returns on a security may be affected by other indexes than the market index. Examples might be the **industry index** (an average of the returns on stocks of companies in the industry in which the company operates) and indexes based upon such factors as company size, the rate of inflation, oil prices, exports, and foreign exchange rates.

A successor to the capital asset pricing model is called the **arbitrage pricing model.** While the arbitrage pricing model is derived in a different way from the CAPM, it takes a very similar form, except that the model can include additional explanatory variables with a different beta for each, instead of only one market index:

$$E(\tilde{R}_i) = R_f + \beta_{i1}\lambda_1 + \beta_{i2}\lambda_2 + \cdots + \beta_{in}\lambda_n \qquad (8.9)$$

where R_f is the risk-free rate

                $\lambda_1, \lambda_n, \ldots$, are market prices for the n risk factors

                $\beta_{i1}, \beta_{in}, \ldots$, are the "beta" values for security i, one for each index

Note that in the case of $\lambda_2, \ldots, \lambda_n = 0$ and $\lambda_1 = E(\tilde{R}_M) - R_f$ then the arbitrage pricing model reduces to the capital asset pricing model. Thus the capital asset pricing model can be regarded merely as a special case of the arbitrage pricing model. Arbitrage pricing theory (APT) is more robust than the CAPM because it requires fewer assumptions. For example, the APT makes no assumptions regarding the empirical distribution of asset returns and no strong assumptions about individuals' utility functions other than greed and risk aversion. The APT applies to any subset of assets and does not require a market portfolio embracing the entire universe of assets. Thus, the arbitrage pricing model avoids Roll's most important criticism of the capital asset pricing model since it does not depend upon the existence of an efficiently diversified market portfolio.

Current research is working toward developing valid tests of the arbitrage pricing model identifying the additional variables that may be of significance to different companies. However, since the market index appears to be the most important variable for the majority of firms, the CAPM continues to be a useful model for representing the relationship between risk and required rates of return on securities that are actively traded in the financial market.

Summary

In this chapter we have shown how portfolio theory can be used by investors who wish to minimize the risk that they take for a given expected return or to maximize the return that they expect for a given level of risk. We have used the theory to show how increasing the numbers of different risky securities in a portfolio reduces the risk, and how this risk reduction is limited by the degree of correlation between the different securities' returns. As a portfolio becomes more efficiently diversified, that part of the risk that is diversifiable is eliminated leaving only the risk that is nondiversifiable. For this reason investors are primarily interested in the nondiversifiable risk that a security adds to their portfolios, which can be measured in terms of the covariance of the security's returns with the returns on the market portfolio.

We also showed that only a subset of all possible portfolios of risky securities is efficient, in the sense that these portfolios have the lowest risk for a given expected return or the highest return for a given level of risk. When we introduce the opportunity to lend and to borrow, we find as a rule that only one of the possible efficient portfolios of risky securities is optimal. The investor's risk preferences may affect an individual's propensity to lend or to borrow but not the choice of an optimal portfolio of risky securities.

We then discussed the implications of portfolio theory for the trade-off between risk and expected return in a competitive capital market. If we assume that the optimal portfolios of individual investors approximate the market portfolio of all securities, we can derive two broad and useful generalizations. The first is that the nondiversifiable risk attributable to a security can be measured in terms of the covariance of the security's returns with the returns on the market portfolio. The second is that there is a simple, straight-line relationship between expected returns on the security and its nondiversifiable risk. This relationship has become known as the capital asset pricing model (CAPM). Another approach is to assume that investors eliminate risk through arbitrage transactions.

Appendix 8.1 Utility Theory and Risk

An individual with wealth W expects some satisfaction, or utility, $U(W)$, from the consumption possibilities that wealth W affords. It is usually assumed that the individual always prefers more wealth to less (nonsatiation) and that therefore $U(W)$ is an always increasing function of W.

If this individual is an investor, he or she may anticipate that wealth W will increase to an amount W with a degree of uncertainty depending upon the riskiness of the portfolio of investments that he or she chooses to hold.

Suppose that an investor is offered a choice between future wealth W made secure by a safe investment and an uncertain future wealth, which for simplicity we shall assume would be either $W - h$ or $W + h$ with equal probability of 0.5 for each.

The risk-averse investor will prefer the certain outcome; that is, the utility from the consumption of a known future wealth W is greater than the expected utility from the same wealth (on average) but that is uncertain:

$$U(W) > 0.5\ U(W - h) + 0.5\ U(W + h)$$

Multiplying the above relation by two and rearranging terms, we find

$$U(W + h) - U(W) < U(W) - U(W - h)$$

That is, utility increases less rapidly at higher levels of wealth than at lower levels of wealth. Thus the risk-averse investor displays diminishing marginal utility for wealth. For the risk-averse investor, it is nice to win but it really hurts to lose. The gain in utility from an increase in wealth does not make up for the loss in utility from an equal loss of wealth, if the investor is risk-averse.

The shape of a typical utility function is given in Figure 8.A1. Wealth, W, is measured along the horizontal axis, and utility is measured along the vertical axis. The slope of the curve is always positive (the first derivative $U' > 0$), signifying that the investor always obtains increasing utility from increasing wealth. However, the slope of the curve becomes more horizontal or less positive (the second derivative $U'' < 0$) with increasing wealth; that is, absolute increases in wealth become less useful as the individual becomes more wealthy.

Note that, as a result of this shape, if we move to the left of wealth W_0 in Figure 8.A1, more utility is lost than is gained if we move a corresponding amount to the right. If, as a result of risky investments, W is allowed to deviate randomly around W_0, there will usually be a net loss of utility on average because of the steeper slope of the utility curve for negative deviations than for positive deviations.

If one thinks of the standard deviation as a measure closely associated with the range of possible outcomes in the above expressions, one can begin to

Figure 8.A1   *A utility function displaying properties of nonsatiation and diminishing marginal utility for wealth*

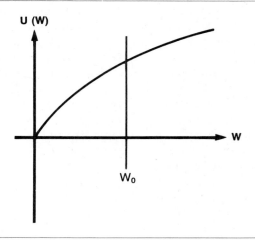

appreciate the connection between standard deviation and risk aversion in the theory of portfolio selection. Whether the standard deviation alone is adequate to describe risk for portfolio-building purposes depends upon the precise shape of the utility function $U(W)$ and the probability distribution of future returns. The probability distributions that are actually used to describe stock market returns and for many utility functions commonly employed in economics, the standard deviation provides an adequate measure of risk for portfolio-building purposes.

For a more detailed discussion of risk, utility theory, and risk aversion, see Arrow (1971) and Markowitz (1959).

Appendix 8.2 Calculation of the Standard Deviation

The standard deviation is a measure of the degree to which a random variable, such as a monthly holding period return on a security, deviates from its expected value. For practical implementation of portfolio analysis it is necessary to assume that standard deviations measured from historic time series of stock returns can be used as a valid estimate of standard deviations of the next period. Under usual circumstances this assumption works fairly well. It is acceptable to estimate the standard deviation of a security's return from samples of five or more years of monthly data. Since the distribution of these returns tends to be approximated by the lognormal distribution, we usually work with the natural log of the holding period returns. This device enables us to treat the resulting returns as though they were normally distributed. The log holding period returns are calculated by the following formula:

$$R_t = \ln(P_t + D_t)/(P_{t-1})$$

where P_t is the price of the security in period t, and P_{t-1} is the corresponding price in the previous month. D_t represents the value of any dividends paid during the period. The resulting value of R_t represents the capital gain and dividend for period t in log form. Most of the research results reported in this book were obtained on the basis of monthly log holding period returns calculated in this way.

The standard deviation s_i of returns on security i is obtained by taking the square root of the variance. The value of the variance s_i^2 is found from:

$$s_i^2 = \frac{1}{n-1} \sum_{t=1}^{n} (R_{i,t} - R_i)^2$$

where n is the number of observations

$\displaystyle\sum_{t=1}^{n}$ denotes the sum for $t = 1$ to n

$R_{i,t}$ is the holding period return on security i for period t

R_i is the mean of the returns $R_{i,t}$

The first step is to compute the mean R_i by adding up the $R_{i,t}$ for all periods t and dividing by n. The second step is to calculate all the deviations $(R_{i,t} - R_i)$ by subtracting the mean from each of the holding period returns $R_{i,t}$. The third step is to square all the deviations, add them up, and divide by $n - 1$. This gives the variance of the observations from the mean. The standard deviation of the returns is obtained by taking the square root of the value of the variance.

Appendix 8.3 Calculation of the Correlation Coefficient

The correlation coefficient $r_{i,j}$ can be used to measure the degree of linear relationship between the holding period returns (see Appendix 8.2) on investment in securities i and j. The correlation coefficient may have any value from -1.00 to $+1.00$. The value for the correlation between the holding period returns on two securities is usually somewhat less than 1.00 but greater than 0.

The value of the correlation coefficient for returns on two securities i and j can be obtained with the following formula:

$$r_{i,j} = \frac{(1/(n-1)) \sum_{t=1}^{n} (R_{i,t} - R_i)(R_{j,t} - R_j)}{s_i s_j}$$

where n is the number of observations in the sample

$R_{i,t}$ is the observed holding period return for security i (j) in period t

s_i is the standard deviation of the holding period returns for security i (j)

The standard deviations can be obtained by the method given in Appendix 8.2.

The formula says that we should calculate the differences $(R_{i,t} - R_i)$ between each return $R_{i,t}$ on security i and the mean or average R_i of all n of the returns $R_{i,t}$. Similarly, we calculate the differences $(R_{j,t} - R_j)$ for all n time periods. For each time period t we multiply the pairs of differences $(R_{i,t} - R_i) \times (R_{j,t} - R_j)$ and add them up. We then divide this sum by the number of observations (time periods minus 1). Finally, we divide by the product $s_i s_j$ of the standard deviations of $R_{i,t}$ and $R_{j,t}$.

Review Questions

1. If asset A had a larger standard deviation of returns than asset B, would you expect it to have a lower or higher expected rate of return?
2. "If all securities are imperfectly correlated with one another, the risk of a portfolio can be reduced to zero." Is this statement true? Explain your answer.
3. Explain why a portfolio of holdings in all risky assets in the United States economy would not reduce risk to zero.
4. How many common stocks does an investor need to hold in order to obtain most of the gains from diversification?
5. What are the implications of the separation theorem for portfolio management?
6. What is the relationship between risk and return described by the capital asset pricing model?

7. How would we obtain the beta of a security if we knew the standard deviation of its holding period returns, their covariance with the returns on the market index, and the standard deviation on the market index?
8. How does the arbitrage pricing model differ from the capital asset pricing model?

Problems

*1. The following table provides monthly returns from investment in Americana Investment Corporation common stock during the twelve months of 1983. Estimate the variance and standard deviation of AIC's returns based upon the twelve months' data.

	Returns (%)		
January	1.08	July	0.84
February	1.43	August	−0.36
March	0.76	September	1.24
April	−1.80	October	1.29
May	−0.54	November	0.88
June	2.20	December	1.07

2. In the previous exercise twelve months' returns are given for Americana Investment Corporation common stock. During the same twelve months the returns on American Food Company's common stock were as given below. Estimate the variance of returns for AFC common stock. Then estimate the correlation coefficient and the covariance between the returns on AFC and AIC common stock.

	Returns (%)		
January	2.12	July	0.50
February	−1.43	August	1.48
March	0.64	September	2.12
April	0.50	October	1.75
May	−1.20	November	−2.50
June	0.84	December	2.64

*3. What is the expected return and the risk of the two-security portfolio constructed from equal investments in the following two securities?

	Expected return	Standard deviation
Security A	0.10	0.30
Security B	0.12	0.40

Correlation between the returns on the two securities is $r_{A,B} = 0.20$

*4. An investor has bought some shares in two indexed mutual funds, one in each of two countries, X and Y. The correlation between the funds is 0.3.

	Country X	Country Y
Risk-free rate of interest	0.05	0.08
Risk premium	0.07	0.10
Standard deviation %	0.20	0.50

If the investor has an equal investment in each fund, what is the expected return and standard deviation for the resulting portfolio? Explain why the risk of the portfolio is reduced.

5. What would be the expected return and variance of returns on the three-security portfolio constructed from equal investments in securities A and B (from Problem 3) and security C? Data for security C are as follows:

	Expected return	Standard deviation
Security C	0.15	0.50

The correlations between the returns on security C and securities A and B are given by $r_{C,A} = 0.15$ and $r_{C,B} = 0.30$

*6. The portfolio manager of the Rocketing Growth Mutual Fund is deciding whether to invest in the common stock of Space Medical Electronics Corporation. The correlation between the returns on Space Medical's common stock and returns on the market index is equal to only 0.15, but the standard deviation of the returns has been very high at 0.75. The corresponding standard deviation of returns on the market index was only 0.25. In comparison, the correlation between the mutual fund's returns and the returns on the market index is 0.30, and the standard deviation is 0.30. The correlation between the returns on Space Medical's common stock and the returns on the mutual fund is equal to 0.30.

(a) What is the value of beta for units in Rocketing Growth Mutual Fund and for Space Medical common stock? (b) What will be the value of beta for Rocketing Growth if 5 percent of its assets are invested in Space Medical? (c) What will be the new standard deviation of returns on the fund after the investment in Space Medical?

7. The expected returns and standard deviations of returns for portfolios composed of different combinations of securities D and E are given below. Using an appropriate graph, plot the data, and estimate the optimum portfolio when the thirty-day Treasury bill rate is 10 percent. The correlation cofficient $r_{D,E} = 0.30$.

Proportion in D	Proportion in E	Expected return on portfolio	Standard deviation of portfolio returns
0.0	1.0	0.30	0.350
0.2	0.8	0.28	0.294
0.6	0.4	0.24	0.210
0.8	0.2	0.22	0.193
1.0	0.0	0.20	0.200

*8. The respective values of the beta coefficients for the monthly returns on three securities are 1.0, 0.5, and 0.8 when the variance on the market portfolio is equal to 0.0625. (a) What are the respective values of the covariance between each security's returns and the returns on the market portfolio? (b) What would be the value of beta for a portfolio composed equally of the three securities? (c) What would be the value of the covariance between the portfolio's returns and the returns on the market portfolio?

*9. The risk-free rate is 0.10, and the risk premium on the market is expected to be 8.25 percent.

(a) Investor A is risk-averse and does not want his portfolio beta value to exceed 0.80. What respective proportions should he invest in Treasury bills and in a mutual fund with beta equal to 1.20 if he wishes to maximize his expected return, given the constraint on the value of the beta for his portfolio? What rate of return would he expect?

(b) Investor B is less risk-averse than the average. She can tolerate beta values up to 1.50. Nevertheless, she dislikes holding individually risky stocks and prefers to lever up her holdings in an indexed mutual fund (beta = 1.0). If she has $10,000 of her own money to invest in the fund, how much additional money should she borrow to invest in the fund to maximize the expected return on the levered-up investment? What rate of return should she expect?

10. Orchard Computers, Inc., a recently established manufacturer of personal computers, has just made its first public issue of common stock at a time when the Treasury bill rate is 10 percent and the risk premium on the market portfolio is expected to be 8 percent. Dividends for next year are expected to be only $1.00 per share but are expected to grow at an annual rate of 30 percent for the foreseeable future. The newly issued shares are actively traded in the market at $100 per share.

   Use Gordon's model to estimate the market's required rate of return, and use the capital asset pricing model to estimate the value of the beta coefficient for Orchard common stock. (Gordon's model says that the required rate of return equals the dividend yield plus the growth rate.)

References

Arrow, K. J., *Essays in the Theory of Risk-Bearing,* Amsterdam: North-Holland, 1971.

Banz, R. W., "The Relationship Between Return and Market Value of Common Stock," *Journal of Financial Economics* (March 1981): 3–18.

Black, F., "Equilibrium in the Creation of Investment Goods under Uncertainty," in *Studies in the Theory of Capital Markets,* M. C. Jensen, ed., New York: Praeger, 1972, 249–65.

Black, F., M. C. Jensen, and M. Scholes, "The Capital Asset Pricing Model: Some Empirical Tests," in *Studies in the Theory of Capital Markets,* M. C. Jensen, Ed., New York: Praeger, 1972, 79–121.

Cho, D. Chinhyung, Edwin J. Elton, and Martin J. Giruber, "On the Robustness of the Roll and Ross APT Methodology," *Journal of Financial and Quantitative Analysis,* Forthcoming.

Dhrymes, Phoebus J., Irwin Friend, and N. Bulent Gultekin, "A Critical Reexamination of the Empirical Evidence on the Arbitrage Pricing Theory," *Journal of Finance* 39 (June 1984): 323–46.

Ibbotson, R. G., and R. A. Sinquefield, "Stocks, Bonds and Inflation: Year-by-Year Historical Returns (1926–1974)," *Journal of Business* 49 (January 1976): 11–47.

Jensen, M. C. (ed.), *Studies in the Theory of Capital Markets,* Praeger: New York, 1972.

Lintner, J., "Security Prices, Risk and Maximal Gains from Diversification," *Journal of Finance* 20, no. 4 (December 1965): 587–615.

Markowitz, H. M., *Portfolio Selection: Efficient Diversification of Investments,* New York: Wiley, 1959.

Mossin, J., "Equilibrium in a Capital Asset Market," *Econometrica* 34, no. 4 (October 1966): 768–83.

Reinganum, M. R., "A Direct Test of Roll's Conjecture on the Firm Size Effect," *Journal of Finance* 37, no. 1 (March 1982): 27–35.

Roll, R., "A Critique of the Asset Pricing Theory's Tests," *Journal of Financial Economics* 4, 1977: 129–76.

Roll, R., "A Possible Explanation of the Small Firm Effect," *Journal of Finance* (September 1981): 879–88.

Roll, R., and Stephen S. Ross, "An Empirical Investigation of the Arbitrage Pricing Theory," *Journal of Finance* 35 (December 1980): 1073–103.

Ross, Stephen A., "The Arbitrage Theory of Capital Asset Pricing," *Journal of Economic Theory* 13 (December 1976): 341–60.

Sharpe, W. F., "Capital Asset Prices: A Theory of Market Equilibrium under Conditions of Risk," *Journal of Finance* 19, no. 3 (September 1964): 425–42.

Estimating the Investors' Required Rate of Return on a Company's Assets

In this chapter we show how to calculate the investors' required rate of return on a company's assets. We describe this calculation in three stages. First, we show how to measure the rate of return that is required on a broadly diversified portfolio of common stocks as represented, for example, by the Standard & Poor's Composite Index of 500 large companies. Second, we use the capital asset pricing model, introduced in Chapter 8, to calculate investors' required rates of return on the common stocks of individual companies. Third, we show how to adjust investors' required rate of return on a company's common stock in order to obtain the required rate of return on the underlying assets of the company.

Why a Company Needs to Know What Rate of Return Its Investors Require

In the earlier chapters of this book we valued capital projects in order to determine whether investment in a project would increase the value of the company. If a project had a positive net present value, we said that it was profitable and therefore could be undertaken. Conversely, if the project had a negative net present value, it was unprofitable and should be rejected. The net present value for a project is obtained by subtracting the discounted present value of the investment expenditures for the project from the discounted present value of the project's operating cash flows, all after tax. In order to carry out such calculations, one requires a discount rate; this is a principal reason why a company needs to know its shareholders' required rates of return for assets of different risks.

Suppose that a company is financed only with common stock, it has only one kind of asset, and all its assets are equally risky. How could it choose the correct discount rate to value a new project? If you could determine from the stock market what rate of return the investors require on the company's common stock, you could use that rate of return to discount the cash flows of a new project, if its risk is the same as the risk of the existing assets. In this way, the investors' required rate of return on the company's common stock (if the company has no debt) is used as a yardstick by which to measure a project's profitability. This measure is known by a variety of names: the company's cost of capital, the company's required rate of return, and the risk-adjusted required rate of return. All these terms are attempts to capture the significance of one of the principal valuation rules: If a project's cash flow can provide a return in excess of what investors require on financial securities of the same risk as the project, that project will have a positive net present value and may be accepted.

Knowledge of the investors' required rate of return is useful for a variety of purposes, although the underlying objective in each case is to measure net present value. Figure 9.1 shows numerous decisions that require the use of

Figure 9.1   *Financial circumstances requiring an estimate of investors' required rate of return*

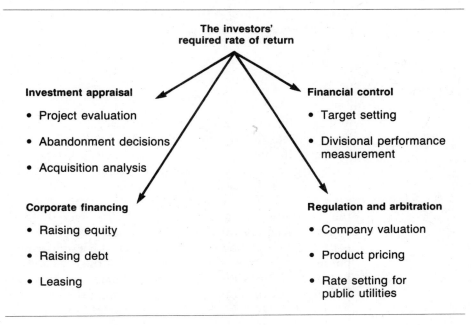

a discount rate to reflect the investors' required rate of return. These activities include investment appraisal, financial control, corporate financing, and dealings with regulatory bodies.

INVESTMENT APPRAISAL

A required rate of return is needed not only for the appraisal of capital projects but also for abandonment decisions and acquisitions analysis. An abandonment decision involves the discontinuance of a project, often accompanied by the sale of assets. If the discounted present value of the cash flows expected from the use of an existing asset is less than its resale value, the asset should be sold.

A company interested in the acquisition of another company can use discounted cash flow analysis to estimate the value of the acquisition. Choice of the discount rate has an important effect on the estimated value.

FINANCIAL CONTROL

One of the functions of financial management is to set financial targets and to monitor divisional performance to see if the targets are being met. Such targets often take the form of a rate of return on capital employed. A required rate of return can be estimated for each division and then translated into accounting earnings targets that divisional managers understand and know how to use.

CORPORATE FINANCING

When a company makes a public offering of its common stock for the first time, it needs to know at what price it should sell the stock to the investment bankers. If there has been no previous market for the stock, how is the company to know what the price should be? First, the value of the whole company can be estimated by discounting the cash flow forecasts for its assets. The difference between the total worth of the company's assets and the company's debt and other liabilities gives the economic value of the company's equity (or its common stock). The economic value of the company's equity divided by the total number of shares to be issued either publicly or privately gives an estimate of the expected market price per share for the company's stock. Discount rates are important both for valuing future cash flows of the company and for valuing the company's liabilities.

REGULATION AND APPRAISAL

When government agencies or other official bodies wish to acquire or to sell assets in the private sector, the values or prices of the assets are often determined by appraisers. Experts are called in to give evidence based on financial analysis; such analysis frequently includes the use of discounted cash flow methods. Although some controversy always surrounds the cash flow forecasts used, the price of the asset also depends very much upon the discount rate that is used.

When companies such as public utilities enjoy some degree of monopoly in the market, the prices or rates that they charge for goods and services are usually regulated by state or federal government agencies. Hearings are held periodically to adjust the prices charged, and expert testimony is used to establish when a price or rate can be increased. Such hearings consider financial analyses based upon the various costs incurred in providing the goods and services, where one significant cost includes the investors' required rate of return on the capital invested.

Four Steps to Estimate the Required Rate of Return on a Company's Assets Using the CAPM

In the previous chapter, we described the capital asset pricing model given below:

$$\begin{array}{c} \text{Expected Return} \\ \text{on an Asset} \end{array} = \begin{array}{c} \text{Risk-free Rate} \\ \text{of Interest} \end{array} + \text{Beta} \times \begin{array}{c} \text{(Expected Excess Return} \\ \text{on the Market)} \end{array}$$

$$E(\tilde{R}_j) = R_f + \beta_j[E(\tilde{R}_M) - R_f)] \tag{9.1}$$

where

$E(\tilde{R}_j)$	=	investors' expected return on asset j
R_f	=	risk-free rate of return
β_j	=	beta (or risk index) for asset j
$[E(\tilde{R}_M) - R_f)]$	=	expected excess return on the market index of risky assets (risk premium on the market)

There are four steps for obtaining the investors' required rate of return on the assets of the company.

Step 1: Obtain an Estimate of the Riskless Rate of Return

The riskless rate of return R_f has been defined as the rate of return that could be earned on a portfolio that has a beta value equal to zero. The rate of interest on Treasury bills is often used as an approximation to the risk-free rate. Treasury bills are government debt obligations with maturities of up to six months. Although there is virtually no possibility of the government refusing to pay its debts when they fall due, the returns on Treasury bills are not risk-free in real (or purchasing power) terms. For example, if inflation proves to be higher than anticipated at the time the investor purchases a Treasury bill, the fixed interest rate would not compensate for the extra inflation. As a result, the investor would receive an amount that was worth less in real terms than had been anticipated when the Treasury bill originally was purchased.

It is easy to find the rate of interest on Treasury bills in the *Wall Street Journal*. Thus it is easy to obtain an estimate of the riskless rate of return.

Step 2: Estimate the Excess Return on the Market Index

In the second term on the right-hand side of equation (9.1), $[E(\tilde{R}_M) - R_f)]$ represents the expected excess return on the market portfolio of risky assets. We can obtain an estimate, for example, by calculating the average difference between historical returns on a broadly based market index, for example, the Standard & Poor's Composite Index of 500 large companies and historical returns on Treasury bills. The average excess return on the market index is employed as an estimate of the risk premium on the market portfolio.

Step 3: Calculate the Beta of the Common Stock

In the previous chapter we described why the risk of an individual common stock may be different from the risk of other common stocks. We measured a common stock's individual risk by comparing the volatility of its returns (dividends plus capital gains) with the volatility of the returns on the market portfolio represented by a market index. If the individual security were as risky as the market index, its beta would be equal to one. If the common stock were less risky (i.e., less volatile) than the market index, its beta value would be less than one, and if it were more risky, its beta value would be greater than one. We shall describe how to calculate the value of a common stock's beta in more detail in a subsequent section.

Step 4: Calculate the Value of Beta for the Company's Assets

To the extent that a company has debt and preferred stock outstanding, the beta value of the common stock is "levered up" or increased. By unlevering the beta of the common stock, we are able to readjust the common stock's risk and thereby obtain an estimate of the value of beta for the company's assets.

We have briefly described how values for each term in equation (9.1) can be calculated so that we may obtain the required or expected rate of return on the company's assets. We shall now describe two ways for estimating the excess returns on the market $[E(\tilde{R}_M) - R_f)]$.

Historical Estimates of the Excess Returns on a Common Stock Index

One way to estimate the excess returns on an index of common stocks is to use historical data. The Dow Jones Industrial Average consists of only 30 stocks in large industrial companies. The Standard & Poor's Composite Index contains 500 common stocks and is much more representative of the companies making up the United States economy, although most of the companies in the index are of medium to large size. Ibbotson and Sinquefield (1982) have calculated annual historical rates of return (dividends and capital gains) for the Standard & Poor's Index over the period 1926–1981 and annualized returns on Treasury bills over the same period. Subtracting the annualized return on Treasury bills in each year from the annual return on the Standard & Poor's Index gives the excess return for the year.

$$\text{Annual Excess Return} = \text{Annual Dividends and Capital Gain} - \text{Annualized Return on Treasury Bills}$$

The annual return on the Standard & Poor's 500 includes both the capital gain (or capital loss) and any dividends paid during the year. Ibbotson and Sinquefield assume that, in the long run, stockholders obtain the rate of return that they expect. Only if this is the case can we use historical data as a proxy for estimates of the future. Although in individual years stockholders might make unexpectedly large gains or losses, the long-term average is assumed to equal their required rate of return on equity capital. Adopting this assumption as an approximation, some analysts use an historical average as the estimate for what stockholders currently require as a reward for bearing risk.

In Table 9.1 we have reproduced the Ibbotson-Sinquefield results for different (overlapping) periods. We have reported both the (arithmetic) average return in excess of the Treasury bill return for the period and the standard error associated with the use of the average excess returns as an estimate of the risk premium. For example, in the period 1926–1981 the average annual rate of return in excess of the prevailing Treasury bill return was 8.28 percent, with a standard error of 2.95 percent. The standard error of 2.95 percent means that 68 percent of the time we would expect the true risk premium to be within the range of 8.28 percent + or − 2.95 percent. As we change the time period, the average risk premium alters. For example, the postwar period (1951–1981) provided excess returns of 7.04 percent, and more recent periods provided substantially lower excess returns. The question is, which period of years should we use to obtain our estimate of the risk premium?

Table 9.1   *Historical estimates of excess returns on United States equities*

Overlapping periods	Excess returns (%)	
	Average	Standard error
1926–1981	8.28	2.95
1931–1981	8.28	3.03
1941–1981	8.70	2.85
1951–1981	7.04	3.38
1961–1981	3.01	3.70
1971–1981	1.49	5.87

Source: Original data from R. G. Ibbotson and R. A. Sinquefield (1982).

In general, when you are using a sample of data to make estimates, the larger the sample, the smaller the degree of error. For example, if a gambler wanted to know whether a roulette wheel was biased, he or she might observe the turning of the wheel ten times and record the results. If black came up six times and red four times, what conclusions could be drawn? The wheel might be biased toward black, but the sample number of turns is so small that the difference between the outcomes of red and black could have taken place purely by chance. On the other hand, if the gambler observed the wheel turn one hundred times, with black coming up sixty times, we could conclude with more confidence that the wheel was biased in favor of black. The relationship between sample size and the size of the error in Table 9.1 is similar. The more years over which the excess returns are observed, the more the standard error tends to diminish. The excess returns for the eleven-year period 1971–1981 averaged 1.49 percent, but the standard error for that estimate is 5.87 percent, almost twice as large as the estimate for the fifty-six-year period 1926–1981. As a result, we have much greater confidence in the estimate of the risk premium based upon data from the fifty-six-year period. However, there are qualifications.

One concern is that the risk of the companies traded on the New York Stock Exchange may have changed during the period of Ibbotson and Sinquefield's study. If risks change, we can assume that the stockholders' required rates of return will change as well. As a result, changes in the excess returns from one period of years to another may not be due to chance. For example, it may be argued that stockholders perceived greater risks in 1929 at the beginning of the last depression, in 1939 at the beginning of World War II, and during the oil crisis of 1974 than at other times.

In Table 9.2, we have provided the excess returns and standard errors for

Table 9.2   *Historical estimates of excess returns on United States equities*

Periods	Excess returns (%)	
	Average	Standard error
1931–1940	6.58	10.98
1941–1950	13.84	5.03
1951–1960	15.52	6.55
1961–1970	4.68	4.58
1971–1980	3.36	6.15

Source: Original data from R. G. Ibbotson and R. A. Sinque-field (1982).

selected subperiods. If risk has been stable over time we would expect the excess returns in each period to be the same. Although the excess returns are not the same, the standard errors are large enough that it is difficult to conclude that there are any differences in the true value of the underlying excess returns that we are attempting to measure. However, our statistical tests may not be sufficiently powerful to detect underlying changes.

The results in Table 9.1 based on historical data suggest that the average excess returns of 8.3 percent (rounded) for the longest period provide the best estimate of the market's risk premium. Using this figure we are now able to calculate an estimate of the current required rate of return on investment in the average common stock in the Standard & Poor's Composite Index. If the current three-month Treasury bill rate is 10 percent, the risk premium is 8.3 percent, then according to equation (9.1) the required rate of return for the market portfolio is 10 + 8.3 = 18.3 percent. It is important to understand how stockholders would actually receive this rate of return. The expected dividend yield plus the expected rate of capital gain must equal the estimate of what shareholders require. If the dividend yield on the average common stock is expected to be 7 percent, shareholders must be expecting annual capital gains of about 11.3 percent for a total of 18.3 percent.

An Estimate of Excess Returns Based Upon Analysts' Forecasts of Dividends and Growth

The fact that required rates of return on common stocks take the form of a dividend yield plus capital growth suggests another method of estimating required rates of return for common stocks using analysts' forecasts of growth. This second method also has been used to estimate the risk premium on an index of common stocks.

As the only cash flow that a stockholder receives prior to selling common stock is some pattern of dividend payments, it would be reasonable to suppose that an investor's required rate of return on stock is related to dividend yield plus any expected growth in dividends. The Gordon model, which is based upon such a relationship, offers a potentially useful way of estimating shareholder required rates of return on company stocks.

THE GORDON MODEL

The Gordon and Shapiro (1956) model, which we shall call the **Gordon model**, is based upon the principle that the price of a stock must be equal to the discounted present value of the cash flows that the stockholders expect to receive. The market's required rate of return for the stock then would represent the discount rate that equates the present value of the expected future cash flows from dividends with the current share price. This discount rate is the internal rate of return (IRR) that the stockholder expects to earn by holding the stock over a period of time. If the IRR were lower than the required rate of return, investors would sell the stock, the price would fall, and the resulting IRR would rise. The Gordon model assumes that stock market prices are in balance (or in equilibrium) when the IRR just equals the investors' required rate of return. Thus the financial analyst should be able to use this IRR based upon dividend forecasts as an estimate of the investors' required rate of return for the stock. The Gordon model provides a means of making such estimates.

Suppose that a stock pays one dividend D_t at the end of each period t. If an investor holds his stock for only one period, he receives one dividend D_1 plus a capital gain (or loss) for the period. The expected rate of return for the period is given by

$$\text{Expected Rate of Return} = \frac{\text{Expected Dividend}}{\text{Initial Price}} + \frac{\text{Expected Change in Price}}{\text{Initial Price}}$$

This can be rewritten as

$$R_1 = \frac{D_1}{P_0} + \frac{P_1 - P_0}{P_0} \tag{9.3}$$

Thus the internal rate of return R_1 expected by the stockholder who intends to hold the stock for only one period is given by the expected dividend yield D_1/P_0 plus the expected capital gain expressed as a rate of return $(P_1 - P_0)/$

growth

P_0, which we shall represent by the symbol g_1. Thus,

$$R_1 = \frac{D_1}{P_0} + g_1 \tag{9.4}$$

A similar expression can be constructed for every other period.

The rate of capital gains can be shown to be equal to the dividend growth rate, for the price of a stock increases in line with the level of dividends. This is so because the price is the discounted present value of the dividends. Assuming that the expected growth rate of dividends is constant for every future period and equal to g and that the required rate of return R is the same for each year, Gordon obtained the following formula for the internal rate of return from a perpetual stream of dividends beginning with D_1 and growing at a constant rate g.

$$R = \frac{D_1}{P_0} + g \qquad (g < R) \tag{9.5}$$

A formal derivation of this formula is provided in Appendix 9.1.

Assuming that market prices are in balance, the Gordon model says that the investors' required rate of return equals the expected dividend yield for the first period plus the market's estimate of the annual rate of growth for dividends. This expression is important because it describes the shareholders' required rate of return in a form that is capable of measurement. If the analyst can obtain an estimate of the market's expectation of the dividend growth rate, he can calculate an estimated required rate of return for the stock.

One problem with this formula is that it requires a constant perpetual growth rate g for dividends. If the growth rate for the stock is expected to be the same as the rate of growth of the economy, the problem is not too great. However, suppose that the firm is a growth stock with dividends currently growing three times as fast as the United States economy. Can we assume that this growth will be constant and perpetual? Obviously not, as perpetual growth at such a rate would mean that the firm would eventually own a major and increasing proportion of all assets in the country. Either competition or antitrust action by the government eventually would put a stop to such growth. Thus the simple Gordon formula will be most appropriate in an economy that is growing steadily and for a company that is expected to continue growing at a rate that is not too different from the rate of growth of the economy.

Formulas can be derived that assume one rate of growth for a limited period and another (average) rate of growth thereafter. In fact, any pattern of dividend growth can be assumed for the early years, and we can still obtain the internal rate of return for the resulting dividend cash flow stream in the usual way (as in Chapter 3). These more complex models of course are more difficult to use.

ESTIMATING THE REQUIRED RATE OF RETURN FOR THE AVERAGE FIRM
USING THE GORDON MODEL

What required rates of return on investment in common stock does the Gordon model suggest? Carleton (1984) and Harris (1984) employed the average five-year earnings growth rate forecasts by securities analysts for leading securities firms collected each mid-month by Lynch, Jones & Ryan, a New York securities firm. For each company in the Standard & Poor's 500 Index currently paying dividends, the current indicated annual dividend was multiplied by $(1 + g)$, where g was the average growth rate forecast, to estimate D_1 in the Gordon model described in equation (9.5). D_1 was divided by the daily average stock price during the first half of the month to produce D_1/P_0. Each company's $R = D_1/P_0 + g$ was weighted by its proportionate total market value to produce a value-weighted estimate of the market (or S&P 500 company) cost of equity capital. The results, for each month from January 1982 to December 1983, are given in column 1 of Table 9.3. Carleton subtracted the yield on twenty-year U.S. government bonds (as an estimate of the long-term risk-free rate), given in column 2, to produce the estimated market excess return for each of the twenty-four months in column 3. The average, 6.75 percent, is an estimate of the stock market's risk premium in excess of the long-term interest rate. If Carleton had used Treasury bills, the resulting market risk premium would have been 8.45 percent.

How to Measure the Value of Beta for a Company's Common Stock

The beta factor is a measure of an asset's risk relative to the risk of the market portfolio of all investments in the market. For the average common stock the value of beta is equal to 1.00 if a stock market index is used to represent the market portfolio. If the value of a common stock's beta is 2.00, its risk premium is twice as large as the risk premium for the market portfolio. When the risk premium on the market portfolio is scaled up or down by an individual company's beta factor in this way, we obtain the risk premium for the individual company's stock. When the risk premium for the company is added to the risk-free rate, we obtain the CAPM's estimate of the required rate of return on the company's stock.

In order to use the capital asset pricing model, we need estimates of the risk-free rate, the risk premium on the market portfolio, and values of beta factors for individual companies. We have already suggested using the Treasury bill rate as an estimate of the risk-free rate of interest. Also, Ibbotson and Sinquefield have provided an estimate of the excess returns on the market

Table 9.3   *Estimates of the cost of equity capital and risk premium for S&P 500*
companies using the Gordon model and twenty-year United States
government bond yield

	Estimated cost of equity (1)	Yield on 20-year U.S. government bonds (2)	Estimated risk premium (1) − (2) = (3)
January 1982	.2061	.1457	.0604
February	.2052	.1448	.0604
March	.2094	.1375	.0719
April	.2069	.1357	.0712
May	.2034	.1346	.0688
June	.2060	.1418	.0642
July	.2060	.1376	.0684
August	.2058	.1291	.0767
September	.1925	.1216	.0709
October	.1878	.1097	.0781
November	.1832	.1057	.0775
December	.1839	.1062	.0777
January 1983	.1810	.1078	.0732
February	.1800	.1103	.0697
March	.1785	.1080	.0705
April	.1785	.1063	.0722
May	.1756	.1067	.0689
June	.1765	.1112	.0653
July	.1768	.1159	.0609
August	.1797	.1196	.0601
September	.1780	.1182	.0598
October	.1795	.1177	.0618
November	.1792	.1192	.0600
December	.1724	.1202	.0522
Average		.1213	.0675
Range		.1057–.1457	.0522–.0781

Sources: W. T. Carleton, Testimony before the Vermont Public Service Board, Docket No. 4865 (January 1984) as updated and corrected, and R. S. Harris, "Analyst Forecasts and the Cost of Equity Capital," unpublished paper (1984); and *Federal Reserve Bulletin.*

equal to 8.3 percent using the Standard & Poor's Composite Index to represent the market portfolio. Now suppose that the relative risk of a company's stock is 30 percent greater than the average, that is, its beta factor is equal to 1.30. Using equation (9.1) the required rate of return on its stock would be:

Required Rate of Return $= 0.10 + (1.30 \times 0.083)$

$$= 0.2079$$

The risk premium on the market is thus scaled up by nearly a third by the company's beta factor, and the resulting required rate of return on the stock is estimated to be equal to 20.79 percent compared to 18.3 percent for investment in the market index where beta equals 1.00 by definition.

Many analysts would accept that share prices tend to move with the market. Because the stock market index can be used as an indicator of expected future economic activity for the economy as a whole, and as the price of a stock can be regarded as the corresponding indicator for the economic prospects of the firm, it would not be surprising to find that a firm's stock price changes are correlated with changes in the stock market index. In other words, if activity in the economy is expected to increase, so might most companies' revenues and profits. As a result, the market values of companies' stocks will change more or less together. The monthly rate of return R_j on stock in a company (designated j) is measured in terms of any dividends paid plus the price change for the month, all divided by the price at the beginning of the month (adjusted if necessary for any capitalization changes). For example:

Return on Common Stock (R_j)

$$= \frac{\text{Dividend} + (\text{Price at End of Month} - \text{Initial Price})}{\text{Initial Price}} \quad (9.6)$$

Dividend paid during month $= \$\ \ 5$

Price at the end of month $= \$110$

Price at the beginning of month $= \$100$

Hence,

$$R_j = \frac{5 + (110 - 100)}{100} = 0.15$$

The monthly rate of return, R_M, on the market portfolio can be approximated by a similar computation using the Standard & Poor's Composite

500 Stock Index as a proxy for the market portfolio. The riskier the stock, the larger we can expect the returns on the stock to be in relation to the returns on the market index. For example, when R_M is negative, R_j will tend to have an even greater negative value if the share is of above-average risk.

The volatility of monthly returns R_j for the share in relation to corresponding monthly returns R_M for the market can be seen more readily if we plot them in a scatter diagram, as illustrated in Figure 9.2. Each point in the scatter diagram represents a month's return for the stock plotted against the return on the market portfolio in the same month. For example, Point A in the diagram represents a month in which the return for the stock was 12 percent when the return on the market portfolio was 15 percent. Point B represents a month when the stock return was −3 percent with a return on the market portfolio of −4 percent. Notice that such monthly returns reflect capital gains (or losses) and dividends actually paid.

In order to obtain an adequate picture of the pattern in the data, it is usual to work with returns for sixty consecutive months. Over such a period the points tend to scatter upward to the right. The line drawn through the points

Figure 9.2   *A scatter diagram of monthly returns on an individual security with corresponding monthly returns on the market index, together with the regression line relating the two*

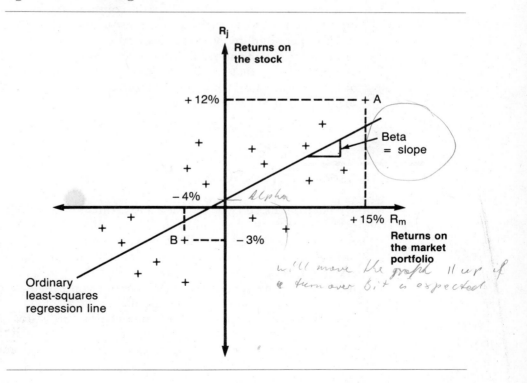

represents the average or mean of the relationship between the points in the scatter diagram. The line in Figure 9.2 should be drawn so that the sum of the squared deviations of points from the line is minimized. The slope of this least squares line in the scatter diagram is called the beta coefficient. The steeper this line is, the more the price of the security tends to move when the market index moves up or down. If the slope of the line is greater than 45 degrees (beta is greater than 1.00), then the stock will tend to be more risky than the market index.

Let us assume that the market falls 10 percent (after subtracting the risk-free rate of interest). If the value of a security's beta coefficient is 0.50, we would expect the security's price to fall only 5 percent (after subtracting the interest rate). Similarly, if the security has a beta coefficient of 2.0, we would expect its price to fall twice as far as the market, i.e., 20 percent.

If we constructed a portfolio that consisted of all the securities in the market index, the line in Figure 9.2 would pass through the origin and slope upward at 45 degrees. All points would be on the line. We can say this with certainty since both axes would represent the same thing. The value of beta would be equal to one. Has risk been eliminated when the scatter about the line is eliminated and the value of beta is equal to one? No, for the risk of the portfolio then would be the same as the risk of the market as a whole. The risk of the market portfolio reflects all the uncertainties about the future of the companies that are part of the United States economy.

Values of the beta coefficient for the common stocks of corporations traded on the major stock exchanges are estimated regularly and published by stockbrokers and by various financial services. Thus the beta coefficient represents a useful and readily available measure of the riskiness of individual common stocks that can be employed in the capital asset pricing model to obtain an estimate of investors' required rates of return on stocks in many major United States companies.

The Gordon Model and the CAPM Compared

We have discussed two approaches to estimating shareholders' required rates of return, the Gordon model and the capital asset pricing model (CAPM). The two models can provide alternative approaches to estimating both an individual company's cost of equity capital and the market's risk premium, and both models frequently are used for these purposes. Since these two models can generate different estimates of a company's cost of equity capital, a further comparison would be useful.

Both models assume that the market price on a stock adjusts to a level where the expected subsequent return from investment at that price precisely equals the rate of return that investors require. Conceptually, the cost of equity that is obtained by using the CAPM is a single-period, risk-adjusted rate of return. Strictly speaking, its use to value multiperiod cash flows requires the assumption that both future risk-free rates and future risk premiums on the market portfolio be known with certainty. In comparison, the cost of equity that is obtained by using the Gordon model represents a risk-adjusted rate of return for a perpetuity. Strictly speaking, use of the Gordon model requires that the same discount rate be applicable to every period in an asset's life. As shown in Appendix 10.1, the use of a constant discount rate implies that more distant cash flows have greater risk, and such a relationship between risk and time will not apply to all projects. Given that short-term and long-term interest rates (and, by implication, risk-free rates) generally are different and that the risk premium on the market portfolio may change with time, neither model fully captures reality. As we have already seen, the two models can result in different estimates of the risk premium on the market portfolio, although the difference (8.28 percent for the CAPM compared to 8.45 percent for the Gordon model) was small when returns on Treasury bills were used to represent risk-free rates. Under some circumstances involving long-term projects analysts may wish to express equity risk premiums relative to long-term bond yields, and this will usually give different results.

The CAPM makes the additional assumption that shareholders use diversified portfolios to reduce risk and thus only that part of the risk (measured by beta) which cannot be eliminated by portfolio diversification is important. The Gordon model takes no explicit account of risk but does make use of data that implicitly reflect risk. Thus the Gordon model contains no assumptions about how risk should be measured. It is for this reason that we employ the CAPM as our principal framework for discussing the relationship between risk and required rates of return when evaluating financial decisions in this text.

When we come to consider required rates of return for individual capital projects within the firm in Chapter 10, the Gordon model can provide no conceptual help because it contains no theory of how asset risk is priced in the financial market. However, the CAPM can be used to help estimate required rates of return for the company's individual assets and capital projects.

Some Implications of the CAPM

The CAPM has some implications for the discount rates that should be used to value the assets of a company that are to be acquired by another company. Also, it can be used to choose discount rates for projects whose risks are significantly different from the average for the firm.

DISCOUNT RATES FOR ACQUISITIONS

In Figure 9.3 we illustrate the relationship between the required rate of return on a stock and its risk as described by the CAPM. The model represents this relationship as a straight line. We have also plotted three points representing the risk and the corresponding required rate of return on the common stocks of three companies, A, B, and C, which we shall assume are all-equity financed companies. Company C wishes to acquire company A or company B. Company C believes that it can manage A and B better than they are being managed currently, and so it expects that returns from A and B will be above what the capital market requires, considering their risk. Company C wishes to know whether it should use its own required rate of return to discount the cash flows of companies A and B. Figure 9.3 suggests that, as company A's assets have a lower risk than company C's assets, it has a lower required rate of return. If company C uses its own somewhat higher required rate of return for discounting the cash flows of company A, it will undervalue company A's stock. What company C should do is to use company A's required rate of return to discount the cash flows of company A.

You might respond that if company C acquires company A the combined rate of return on the merged company will be below the pre-merger rate of return for company C. Although this conclusion is correct, the risk of the equity of the combined company will also be below the risk of the equity

Figure 9.3   *Relation between risk and return described by the CAPM*

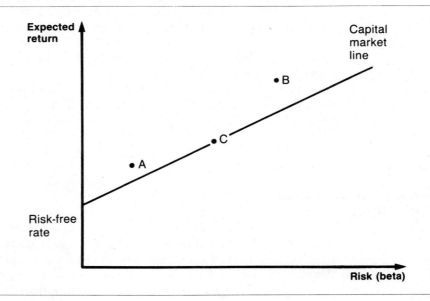

of company C; therefore, the required rate of return for the merged company will be lower than that of company C.

What discount rate should company C use to value the cash flows of company B? If company C uses its own required rate of return, it would overvalue the stock of company B. The overvaluation would take place because the assets of company B have a higher risk than the assets of company C, and therefore the more risky assets in company B require the higher discount rate.

DISCOUNT RATES FOR INDIVIDUAL CAPITAL PROJECTS

If company C should not evaluate acquisitions using a discount rate that reflects the risk of its own assets, a similar circumstance exists when the company tries to value its own assets, because some of them are more or less risky than others. Should the company use a different discount rate for each capital project?

To answer this question we must understand the relationship between the risk of the assets of a whole company and the risks (or beta values) of the individual assets in the company's "portfolio." Because of the linear relationship between the expected return on an asset and its beta the capital asset pricing model implies that the risk (beta) of a portfolio of assets is a value-weighted average of the risks of the individual assets in the portfolio. Suppose that an entirely equity-financed company has only two assets, asset 1 and asset 2. Let PV_1 and PV_2 represent the discounted present values of assets 1 and 2, respectively. Then the company's asset beta would be given by the following weighted average:

$$\text{Beta of Assets} = \text{Beta of Asset 1}\left(\frac{PV_1}{PV_1 + PV_2}\right) + \text{Beta of Asset 2}\left(\frac{PV_2}{PV_1 + PV_2}\right)$$

This relationship underlines the contribution of the risk of each individual asset to the weighted average risk of the assets of the firm and raises an important question of practical significance for most companies. Can a company use just one average required rate of return for all its capital projects and still make the right investment decisions on average? This question can be answered easily with the aid of an example illustrated in Figures 9.4 and 9.5.

In Figure 9.4 we have once again illustrated the relationship between risk and required rates of return, assuming that the financial market behaves in the way that the CAPM suggests. We have marked the respective risks and rates of return of two projects X and Y on the diagram. Project X promises a rate of return of 17 percent and project Y a return of 22 percent. Should the company accept both projects, or one of them, or neither of them?

Figure 9.4   *Risk and return on two projects compared with equivalent investment opportunities in the capital market*

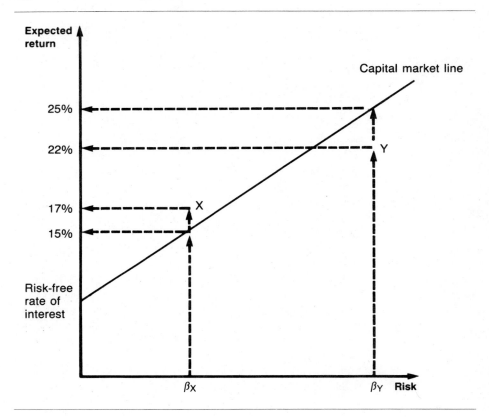

You should be able to recognize immediately that project X is a profitable one and project Y is unprofitable. The reason that project X is profitable is that on the capital market line a financial security of the same (beta) risk as project X provides a lower return of only 15 percent compared with project X's 17 percent. Because the project offers the company and its investors a greater return than could be obtained on financial securities of the same risk, the project will have a positive net present value. Conversely, project Y is unprofitable because it offers a return of 22 percent compared with a higher return of 25 percent offered by financial securities of the same risk. The capital market line provides a bench mark for the company to use to compare the profitability of its projects.

Would we have come to the same decision if we had used the investors' required return on the common stock as the same bench mark for both projects? Figure 9.5 is illustrative. It is identical to Figure 9.4 except for the addition of the horizontal broken line that represents the required rate of

Figure 9.5   *Risk and return on two projects*

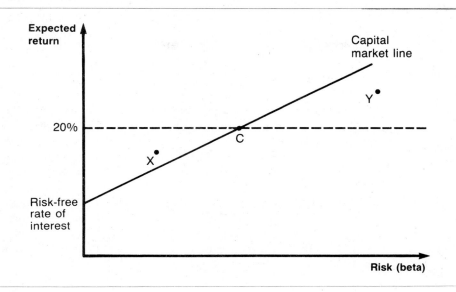

return on company C stock, which happens to be 20 percent. If we adopt the 20 percent line as the standard or **hurdle rate,** we find that we would reject project X, which should be accepted, and accept project Y, which should be rejected.

This example shows that a company cannot count on making the right decisions if it uses a single required rate of return or discount rate for all its capital projects. If it uses only one such hurdle rate, it will tend to reject profitable, safe projects and accept unprofitable, risky projects. In Chapter 10 we show how to estimate the risks and required rates of returns for individual capital projects.

How Debt Financing Affects the Value of Beta for a Company's Equity

In much of the previous analysis we have assumed that the company was financed only with shareholders' equity or common stock. As a result, the beta of the common stock was the same as the beta of the company's assets. However, most United States companies are financed with debt and (perhaps) preferred stock as well as by common stock. As a result, the beta of the company's common stock is not the same as the beta of the company's assets, so we must adjust the beta of the common stock in order to obtain the beta of the company's assets. We shall assume in this analysis a world without taxes.

Debt financing is often called **leverage** because it increases or levers up the risk and required rate of return on common stock. Let us see how leverage works. If the company were to be all equity financed, the value of beta for its common stock would be equal to the beta of its assets, for equity would represent the only claim on the assets. However, if the company uses debt financing as well, the effect is to lever up or increase the beta value of the common stock. The reason for this effect is that debtholders take relatively less risk, leaving the common stockholders to bear almost all the commercial risks. Because debt financing reduces the relative dollar amount of equity financing, the risk per dollar of equity for common stockholders is increased, thereby raising the value of beta for the common stock.

We can quantify this leverage effect in the following way. Because of the straight line or linear relationship between risk and return, the CAPM implies that the weighted average of the betas of all the financial (debt and equity) claims on the firm must equal the value of beta for the firm's assets. That is,

$$
\begin{array}{c} \text{Beta of} \\ \text{Assets} \end{array} = \left(\begin{array}{c} \text{Beta of} \\ \text{Debt} \end{array} \times \begin{array}{c} \text{Proportion} \\ \text{of Debt} \end{array} \right) + \left(\begin{array}{c} \text{Beta of} \\ \text{Equity} \end{array} \times \begin{array}{c} \text{Proportion} \\ \text{of Equity} \end{array} \right) \qquad (9.7)
$$

In this formula the proportions of debt and equity are measured in terms of the market value of the debt and equity. If the debt is riskless we can assume that the value of beta for the debt is equal to zero, we have,

$$
\text{Beta of Assets} = 0 + (\text{Beta of Equity} \times \text{Proportion of Equity}) \qquad (9.8)
$$

where

$$
\text{Proportion of Equity} = \frac{\text{Market Value of Equity}}{\text{Market Value of Equity} + \text{Market Value of Debt}}
$$

In fact the beta of debt would not be zero if there is a chance of the company defaulting on its debt obligations. We relax this assumption in the next chapter.

This formula can be used in two ways: to obtain the value of beta for a company's assets from the beta of its common stock, and to show how the value of the company's equity is affected by debt financing.

For example, the value of the beta coefficient for XERAT Corporation's common stock was estimated to be equal to 1.21 over a period of sixty months. During the same period the average value of XERAT's debt was equal very nearly to 20 percent of the total market value of XERAT's common stock and debt. What was the beta value of XERAT's assets? The answer is obtained easily from the previous formula:

$$\text{Beta of Assets} = \text{Beta of Equity} \times \text{Proportion of Equity}$$

$$= 1.21 \times \frac{0.80}{0.80 + 0.20}$$

$$= 0.968$$

The formula can also be used to show how debt levers up the value of beta for the company's equity as follows. If we solve for the value of beta of the equity in equation (9.8), we obtain

$$\text{Beta of Equity} = \frac{\text{Market Value of Equity} + \text{Debt}}{\text{Market Value of Equity}} \times \text{Beta of Assets} \quad (9.9)$$

The fraction on the right-hand side of the formula above can be regarded as a leverage factor. If the value of debt is equal to zero, the fraction is equal to 1.00, and the beta of the equity or common stock equals the beta of the company's assets. As the value of the debt increases, so does the beta of the equity. For example, when the debt is equal in value to the equity, the value of the leverage factor is equal to 2.00, and the beta of the common stock is twice as large as the beta of the underlying assets.

Why should we want to know the beta of the assets rather than the beta of the equity? The reason is simply that we wish to find the rate of return that investors require on proposed new projects. When those new projects are evaluated, it is the total cash flows of the project that are forecast and discounted, not just those cash flows accruing to the common stockholders. Thus, we use the value of the unlevered (or asset) beta in the CAPM in order to obtain the rate of return that is required on assets. In Appendix 9.2 we provide an alternative (weighted average cost of capital) approach to obtaining the discount rate. The weighted average cost of capital (WACC) is also examined in later chapters.

Summary

We have discussed why firms need to estimate what rate of return investors require on their capital. When analyzing problems relating to investment appraisal, financial control, corporate financing, and regulation, we require an estimate of investors' required rates of return on assets of different risks. We showed how we might calculate the rate of return that investors require on an average common stock equal in risk to the market index. Then, using the CAPM, we showed how the required rate of return may be calculated for a common stock of different risk to the market index. Finally, we showed how to obtain a required rate of return on the assets of a company rather than simply on its equity. In the following chapter we show how the required rates of return on individual assets within the company can be related to their individual risks.

Appendix 9.1 Derivation of the Gordon Model

The Gordon formula for the required rate of return on common stock derives from two assumptions. The first assumption is that the price of a stock is equal to the discounted present value of the dividends that are expected to be paid to the holder of the stock:

$$P_0 = \frac{D_1}{1 + R} + \frac{D_2}{(1 + R)^2} + \cdots + \frac{D_t}{(1 + R)^t} \qquad t \to \infty \qquad \text{(A9.1)}$$

where
P_0 = price per share at time $t = 0$
D_t = dividends per share at times t $(t = 1, 2, \ldots, \infty)$
R = shareholders' required rate of return

The second assumption is that the dividends D_t grow at a constant rate g:

$$D_t = D_0 (1 + g)^t \qquad \text{(A9.2)}$$

Combining equations (A9.1) and (A9.2) we obtain

$$P_0 = \frac{D_0(1 + g)}{(1 + R)} + \frac{D_0(1 + g)^2}{(1 + R)^2} + \cdots$$

$$= \frac{D_0(1 + g)}{(1 + R)} \left(1 + \left(\frac{1 + g}{1 + R}\right) + \left(\frac{1 + g}{1 + R}\right)^2 + \cdots\right)$$

$$P_0 = \frac{D_1}{1 + R} (1 + f + f^2 + \cdots) \qquad \text{(A9.3)}$$

where $f = (1 + g)/(1 + R)$

The expression in the parentheses in equation (A9.3) is the sum of an infinite geometric series that is equal to $1/(1 - f)$, if f is a fraction between 0 and 1. Therefore,

$$P_0 = \frac{D_1}{(1 + R)(1 - f)}, \qquad (0 < f < 1)$$

Substituting for f we obtain

$$P_0 = \frac{D_1}{R - g} \qquad (-1 < g < R) \qquad (A9.4)$$

By solving for R in equation (A9.4) we obtain the Gordon formula for the required rate of return:

$$R = \frac{D_1}{P_0} + g \qquad (-1 < g < R)$$

Appendix 9.2 The Weighted Average Cost of Capital

In many finance text books the required rate of return on a company's assets is calculated using the weighted average cost of capital (WACC). We shall describe how to calculate the WACC, although we shall leave a fuller discussion and critique to later chapters.

The most direct way to obtain an estimate of the overall cost of a company's capital is to use the weighted average of the company's debt and equity financing. The cost of debt for a company is easily measured. It is the rate of interest that the company pays on its borrowing after tax;

Cost of Debt after Tax = Interest Rate × (1 − Corporate Tax Rate)

The cost of a company's equity can be estimated by measuring the riskiness of its common stock. Measuring the risk and estimating the cost of a company's common stock requires several steps, which were described in detail in this chapter.

The weighted average cost of capital (WACC) for a company is calculated from the measured costs of debt and equity using the following formula:

WACC = (Cost of Debt after Taxes × Proportion of Debt Financing)
   + (Cost of Equity × Proportion of Equity Financing)   (A9.5)

levered

The WACC is a weighted average of the costs of debt and equity (common stock) where the weights are equal to the proportions of each type of financing that are used. The proportion of debt financing in the WACC formula is given by

$$\text{Proportion of Debt Financing} = \frac{\text{Market Value of Debt}}{\text{Market Value of Debt and Equity}}$$

The market value of a firm's debt that is used in the above ratio is composed of two parts: traded debt securities or bonds and nontraded debt. The current market value of all the traded debt securities is the price of each security multiplied by the number that have been issued. Nontraded debt, on the other hand, includes outstanding bank loans and privately placed bonds. An estimate of the market value of nontraded debt is obtained by discounting the future interest payments and repayments of principal of the debt using the current rates of interest for the remaining maturity of the debt as the discount rate. The market value of the firm equals the total market value of both the debt and the equity.

The proportion of equity financing in the WACC formula is given by

$$\text{Proportion of Equity Financing} = \frac{\text{Market Value of Equity}}{\text{Market Value of the Firm}}$$

$$= (1 - \text{Proportion of Debt})$$

The market value of the equity in the above ratio is the market price per share multiplied by the number of shares that have been issued. For simplicity, we have assumed that a company has only debt and common stock outstanding. In fact, companies use other sources of finance, such as convertible bonds and preferred stock. Let us look at an example.

Suppose that a corporation borrows at a 10 percent rate of interest and that the stockholders' required rate of return on the company's stock is estimated to be 20 percent. The corporate tax rate is 46 percent, and the proportion of debt financing that has been used by the company is 15 percent (based on market values of debt and equity). What is the company's weighted average cost of capital? Using the WACC formula in equation (A9.5) we have

$$\text{WACC} = [0.10 \, (1 - 0.46) \times 0.15] + (0.20 \times 0.85)$$

$$= 0.1781$$

The weighted average cost of capital for this company is 17.81 percent. Therefore, the discount rate that the company should use for discounting the cash flows for an asset that is of identical risk to the company would also be 17.81 percent. An identical risk asset is one with risk equivalent to the average risk of the company's assets. The discount rate would be higher for prospective assets of higher than average risk and lower if the asset's risk is lower than average for the company.

The weighted average cost of capital formula provides a method of obtaining the cost of capital for the firm. The formula requires an estimate of the cost of equity capital as well as the cost of debt.

Using the capital asset pricing model together with published values of the beta coefficient, we can obtain estimates of the cost of equity capital. The following example will illustrate how to use the capital asset pricing model in the weighted average cost of capital. For purposes of simplicity, we shall assume that there are no taxes.

The published value of the beta coefficient for XERAT Corporation's stock is equal to 1.20. The beta value has been estimated from sixty months' returns on XERAT common stock. During the same period the market value of the company's debt equaled 20 percent of the value of its debt plus equity. It paid an interest rate of 8 percent on its borrowing. The Treasury bill rate was also 8 percent. We have assumed that the corporation's debt is risk-free. If the debt were risky, the interest rate would be greater than 8 percent, but the beta of debt would not be zero. What is XERAT Corporation's weighted average cost of capital?

First we can estimate XERAT's cost of equity capital with the CAPM:

$$\frac{\text{Cost of}}{\text{Equity Capital}} = \frac{\text{Risk-free Rate}}{\text{of Interest}} + \left(\frac{\text{Beta of}}{\text{Equity}} \times \frac{\text{Excess Returns on}}{\text{the Market Index}} \right)$$

$$= 0.08 + (1.20 \times 0.083)$$

$$= 0.1796$$

The cost of equity capital for XERAT is 17.96 percent. However, the cost of equity capital represents the stockholders' required rate of return on their investment in the company's common stock. It does not equal the discount rate that should be used for the company's assets which are financed with both debt and equity. In order to obtain that discount rate, we can calculate the weighted average cost of capital using equation (A9.5):

$$\text{WACC} = (0.08 \times 0.20) + (0.1796 \times 0.80)$$

$$= 0.1597$$

The estimated weighted average cost of capital for XERAT Corporation is equal to 15.97 percent. For a capital project that is of average risk for the company, a discount rate of 15.97 percent would be appropriate if the project (like the company) were to be financed 20 percent by debt and 80 percent by equity. For projects of different risk from the average, the discount rate must be altered in the manner that we shall describe in Chapter 10.

We could have obtained exactly the same rate of return for the firm's assets by unlevering the observed equity beta in order to obtain an asset beta, and then calculating the required return on assets using the CAPM. We shall use the previous example to demonstrate the point.

We can accomplish the unlevering process by using the formula that relates the asset beta to the equity beta (equation (9.8) in the text).

Beta of Assets = Beta of Equity × Proportion of Equity

If the equity beta is 1.2, the asset beta is 0.96 assuming the proportion of equity is 0.8. Using the asset beta in the CAPM we can calculate the required rate of return on assets:

$$\text{Required Rate of Return on Assets} = \text{Risk-free Rate} + \left(\text{Beta of Assets} \times \text{Excess Return on Market Index} \right)$$

$$= 0.08 + (0.96 \times 0.083)$$

$$= 0.1597$$

Thus, the required return on assets is 15.97 percent, which is identical to the WACC calculated previously.

If we introduce taxes, the formulas become a little more complicated, but we can still obtain a required rate of return on assets either using the WACC or by unlevering the equity beta and calculating the required rate of return on assets using the CAPM.

Review Questions

1. Why does a company's management need to know the rate of return required by investors?
2. Describe each component of the formula for the capital asset pricing model. What are the possible sources of data for each component in order to make the model operational?
3. What are the advantages and disadvantages of using historical data to calculate the risk premium on the market index?
4. How could you measure the risk premium on the market index using analysts' forecasts? What are the strengths and weaknesses of this approach?
5. Under what conditions can a company use its cost of capital as the discount rate for a new project?

6. What is the relationship between the beta of a firm's assets and the beta of a firm's equity when there is debt outstanding? How would you adjust the formula given in the text to include preferred stock?
7. Under what conditions would you expect the beta of debt to be zero? Why might it be not zero? Could the beta of a firm's debt be greater than the beta of the equity? Explain your answer.
8. In a taxless world, does the unlevered cost of equity equal the weighted average cost of capital? Explain your answer. (Familiarity with Appendix 9.2 is required to answer this question.)

Problems

*1. Estimate the shareholders' required rate of return on holdings in the average common stock when the current yield on a ninety-day Treasury bill is 10 percent. State your assumptions and refer to the source of any additional data that you use to obtain your result.

*2. The required rate of return on the common stock of GHI, Inc., as determined by the capital asset pricing model is 15 percent. The dividend yield on GHI common currently is 5 percent. Show how you would obtain the expected average growth rate for dividends implied by this information.

3. Meretricious Products Company, Inc., expects dividends to grow at the rate of 14 percent per year indefinitely. The shareholders' required rate of return is 19 percent per year. Show how Gordon's model can be used to estimate the resulting price per share if the next annual dividend is widely expected to be $2.00 per share.

*4. The value of the beta coefficient of the common stock of U.S. Goldmines, Inc., is equal to 0.50. The ninety-day Treasury bill rate currently is 5 percent. Estimate the shareholders' required rate of return on their holdings of U.S. Goldmines' common stock. Describe the method used.

*5. The ninety-day Treasury bill rate is 10 percent. The beta coefficient for company A equals 1.20 and for company B equals 0.90. Estimate the required rate of return for company A, and also estimate the difference between the required rates of return for the two companies. Plot your results on a graph, and label it appropriately. Refer to any additional data that you use.

6. Estimate the value of the beta coefficient for an actively traded company quoted on the New York Stock Exchange. Use one year's monthly data. If you are not familiar with Ordinary Least Squares Regression, you may plot a scatter diagram and estimate the value of beta visually. Normally, the most recent five years data are used. What would be the effect of increasing the amount of data used?

*7. Advanced Projects, Inc., is all-equity financed. Its common stock is of average risk. The company has two major assets. Asset A is believed to have twice the systematic risk as asset B. Both assets are of equal value. If the ninety-day Treasury bill rate is 10 percent, what are the required rates of return for assets A and B?

8. ROTO, Inc., has no debt. The beta value of its common stock is equal to 1.20. The company has three assets summarized in the following table. Fill in the missing information.

Asset	A	B	C
Value	150	100	200
Beta	1.30	0.9	

*9. The Conservative Company has no debt finance, and its common stock has a beta value of 0.80. The company's stock is capitalized in the market at $100,000,000. The company's treasurer has decided to raise $50,000,000 in long-term bonds. The money will be used to buy replacements for existing assets. What will be the value of beta for the common stock after the bond issue? What will be the value of beta for the company's assets after the bond issue?

10. The treasurer of Frugalman, Inc., has decided to repay $10,000,000 of the company's $20,000,000 outstanding debt. The company's common stock is capitalized in the market at $40,000,000, and the value of the beta coefficient for its stock is equal to 1.00.

(a) What is the value of beta for the company's assets both before and after the debt has been redeemed (repaid)?

(b) What will be the value of the equity beta after the $10,000,000 has been repaid?

*11. Elban, Inc., has $40,000,000 of outstanding debt, which is priced in the market at $85 for each $100 bond. The issued stock of 5,000,000 shares is valued in the market at $36 per share. The quoted beta value is 1.32; what is the value of the asset beta?

12. Molteno, Inc.'s $80,000,000 9 percent debt is quoted in the market at $100 (at par) for each bond. The issued share capital of 10,000,000 shares is quoted at $42 per share. The dividend, which has just been paid, was $2 per share, and the rate of growth of dividends is expected to be around 8 percent for the foreseeable future.

Assume the company pays corporate tax at 46 percent. Calculate the weighted average cost of capital for Molteno, Inc.

References

Brealey, R. A., and E. Dimson, "The Risk Premium on UK Equities: 1919–1975," *Investment Analyst* 52: 14–18.

Carleton, W. T., Testimony before the Vermont Public Service Board, Docket No. 4865 (January 1984).

Carleton, W. T., D. R. Chambers, and J. J. Lakonishok, "Inflation Risk and Regulatory Lag," *Journal of Finance,* no. 38 (May 1983): 419–31.

Fama, E. F., "Risk-adjusted Discount Rates and Capital Budgeting Under Uncertainty," *Journal of Financial Economics* 5 (August 1977): 3–24.

Gordon, M. J., and E. Shapiro, "Capital Equipment Analysis: The Required Rate of Profit," *Management Science* 3 (October 1956): 102–110.

Harris, R. S., "Analysts' Forecasts and the Cost of Equity Capital," Unpublished paper, University of North Carolina, 1984.

Ibbotson, R. G., and R. A. Sinquefield, *Stocks, Bonds, Bills and Inflation: The Past and the Future,* 1982 edition, The Financial Analysts Foundation, 1982.

Officer, R., "The Variability of the Market Factor of the New York Stock Exchange," *Journal of Business* 46 (1973): 434–53.

Rubinstein, M., "A Mean Variance Synthesis of Corporate Financial Theory," *Journal of Finance* 28, no. 1 (March 1973): 167–81.

Risk-adjusted Discount Rates for Divisions and Capital Projects

In the two preceding chapters we showed how the risk of a company's common stock can be measured, how the required rate of return on the stock is related to its risk, and how this required rate of return can be adjusted to obtain a required rate of return on the assets of the company. However, if the risk of an individual asset is different from the risk of the average of all the firm's assets, a correspondingly different discount rate should be used for the individual asset. In this chapter we illustrate a method for obtaining a required rate of return (or cost of capital) for each division of the company. Then we show how to estimate a required rate of return for each type of asset or project within the division depending upon its risk.

How Companies Apply Different Discount Rates to Different Classes of Assets

In Chapter 9 we showed why a company will not make the correct investment decisions on average if it uses a single cost of capital as the discount rate for all projects regardless of their different risks. If a company uses the same discount rate for all projects, it will tend to reject low-risk projects that are profitable and invest in some high-risk projects that are unprofitable.

For this reason many companies use different discount rates for different kinds of assets depending on their risks.

Figure 10.1 illustrates three levels at which a company may calculate different costs of capital as discount rates. At the uppermost level is the cost of capital for the company as a whole. The company's cost of capital can be used as a discount rate for projects or assets that are of average risk for the company.

At the second level in the figure are divisions of the company. If the various divisions engage in activities that differ significantly in risk, management should use different average discount rates in each division. For example, if an oil company engages in exploration as well as in refining and marketing, usually it will use a higher discount rate for its exploration division than it does for its marketing or refining divisions. The rationale would be that the value of beta of assets used in the exploration division is higher than the value of beta of assets used in marketing or refining.

At the lowest level in the figure are the individual assets and projects

Figure 10.1   *Discount rates at three levels in a company*

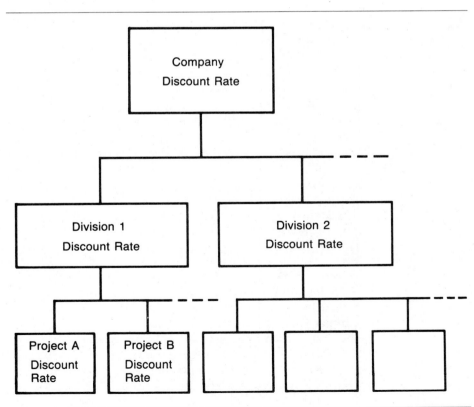

within each division. It may be that the risks of the individual assets and projects within the division differ much more widely than the average risks of the various divisions. Therefore, it is at the project level where the use of different discount rates for different risk classes of assets can be most important.

In the following sections we shall first review how to estimate the cost of capital at the company level. Then we shall show how the cost of capital for an individual division can be estimated if the risk of the division's assets differs from the risk of the company's assets. Finally, we shall show how the riskiness of assets within the division can be related to the risk of the division as a whole. In this way a cost of capital can be obtained for each class of assets or projects. The reason why we estimate the risk of the company and the division first, instead of directly estimating the risk of the individual assets, is that market data is often available for the former but not for the latter. As a result, our estimates of the required rate of return for the company and divisional levels are more easily obtained than for the individual asset.

Estimating a Company's Cost of Capital

In Chapter 9 we showed how to calculate a cost of capital for a company. The cost of the company's equity depends upon the systematic risk of its stock. As we have discussed in the preceding two chapters, the systematic risk of the company's stock is measured by the value of its beta coefficient. The beta risk of any asset is often referred to as the asset's market risk, since beta reflects the sensitivity of the asset's returns to changes in the general economy, represented by the market index of common stocks. In Table 10.1 are listed the equity beta values, the leverage adjustment factors, and the corresponding asset beta values of six major United States oil companies. The estimates of the stock beta values in the table were obtained using share price data over the five-year period 1977–1981. Assume that one of the companies, Gulf Oil, has hired us to determine the cost of capital for the assets of the company and for one of its divisions. In order to obtain the cost of capital for the assets of the company we must be able to obtain an estimate of its asset beta to be used in the capital asset pricing model. Similarly, to obtain an estimate of the cost of capital for a division of the company, we will need to estimate the value of the division's asset beta. We shall now discuss the method in more detail.

Table 10.1 tells us that the estimated value of Gulf's equity beta is 1.158. As the value of Gulf's equity beta is not far from 1.0 (the average for all common stocks), we have little reason to believe that the value of beta for Gulf in the table has been affected significantly by statistical error. Therefore we shall use the corresponding value of Gulf's asset beta coefficient in the

Table 10.1   *Equity and asset betas of United States oil majors (1977–1981)*

Company	Equity beta	×	Leverage adjustment factor*	=	Asset beta
Exxon	0.906	×	0.822	=	0.745
Gulf	1.158	×	0.805	=	0.932
Mobil	1.018	×	0.715	=	0.728
Sohio	1.227	×	0.825	=	1.012
Standard Oil of Indiana	1.187	×	0.811	=	0.963
Texaco	1.188	×	0.721	=	0.857
Equally weighted portfolio	1.114				0.873

$$* \text{ Leverage Adjustment Factor} = \frac{\text{Equity}}{(\text{Debt} + \text{Equity})}$$

Source: K. Alamouti and I. Cooper, Unpublished Manuscript, London Business School, 1982.

capital asset pricing model to obtain an estimate of its cost of equity capital. The beta values that we measure from returns on common stock such as those in the second column of the table reflect not only the risk of the oil business but also the financial risks that are induced by each company's borrowing. Suppose, for example, there are two exploration companies that are identical in every respect except for their capital structures. That is, although the risks of their operations are the same, one company has more debt than the other. The company with more debt will have earnings after interest charges that are more variable, for it has greater fixed costs due to higher interest payments. If the earnings are more volatile for the company that has greater debt, its share price will be more volatile, and the measured value of the beta coefficient for its stock should reflect this higher volatility. As the first step toward obtaining a cost of capital for Gulf we need to have an estimate of the beta coefficient for its assets.

Since debt and equity (common stock) represent all the financial claims on the firm, they reflect all the risks of the firm's underlying assets. We can obtain an estimate of the asset beta of a company because it is simply a weighted average of the betas of the company's equity and debt securities.

$$\text{Beta of Assets} = \left(\begin{matrix} \text{Beta of} \\ \text{Equity} \end{matrix} \times \begin{matrix} \text{Equity} \\ \text{Proportion} \end{matrix} \right)$$

$$+ \left(\begin{matrix} \text{Beta of} \\ \text{Debt} \end{matrix} \times \begin{matrix} \text{Debt} \\ \text{Proportion} \end{matrix} \right) \quad (10.1)$$

The proportions of debt and equity in the capital structure should be based on the market values of the securities, as explained in Chapter 9.

Reilly and Joehnk (1976) found an average beta equal to 0.17 for bonds of industrial corporations based on the Standard & Poor's Composite Index. Sharpe (1973) found an average bond beta value of 0.286 using an index composed of both bonds and stocks. Friend and others (1978) report an average bond beta value of 0.362 and an average common stock beta value of 1.569 using a market index of stocks, corporate bonds, and government securities.

It seems reasonable from the evidence for us to assume that the average beta value for bonds is about 0.2, because the market index used to obtain the betas in Table 10.2 included no bonds. To make the calculations simple, however, we shall assume that the company's capitalization includes only debt and common equity and that the beta for debt is equal to zero. Thus we can obtain an estimate of the value of beta for a firm's assets by multiplying the value of its equity beta by the leverage adjustment factor Equity/ (Debt + Equity).[1] The values of the asset betas of the six United States oil companies listed in the final column of Table 10.1 were obtained in this way. For example, Gulf Oil's asset beta is obtained from

$$\text{Asset Beta for Gulf Oil} = \text{Equity Proportion} \times \text{Equity Beta for Gulf Oil}$$

$$= 0.805 \times 1.158$$

$$= 0.932$$

We can calculate the required rate of return or cost of capital for Gulf's assets by using this asset beta value estimate in the CAPM:

$$\begin{aligned} \genfrac{}{}{0pt}{}{\text{Required Rate of Return}}{\text{on Gulf's Assets}} &= \genfrac{}{}{0pt}{}{\text{Risk-free Rate}}{\text{of Interest}} \\[6pt] &\quad + \left(\genfrac{}{}{0pt}{}{\text{Beta}}{\text{of Assets}} \times \genfrac{}{}{0pt}{}{\text{Excess Returns on}}{\text{the Market Index}}\right) \quad (10.2) \end{aligned}$$

---

[1]Note that there is no tax term in this formula, even though interest is tax-deductible. The reason is that the asset beta obtained by this formula is contingent on the firm maintaining its existing capital structure. If we had wanted to calculate an unlevered equity beta for the firm (equal to the value of the asset beta for the case where the firm had no debt), the corresponding equation would be:

$$\text{Unlevered Beta} = \left(\frac{\text{Equity}}{\text{Equity} + (\text{Debt} \times (1 - \text{Tax Rate}))}\right) \times \text{Beta of Equity}$$

This equation is derived in Rubinstein (1973).

Table 10.2   *Equity and asset betas of United States oil exploration companies (1977–1981)*

Company	Equity beta	×	Leverage adjustment factor	=	Asset beta
General American Oil	1.814	×	0.969	=	1.758
Louisiana Land and Exploration	1.289	×	0.882	=	1.137
Mesa Petroleum	2.355	×	0.628	=	1.479
Murphy Oil	1.602	×	0.729	=	1.168
Natomas	1.840	×	0.593	=	1.091
Oceanic Exploration	1.526	×	0.774	=	1.181
Superior Oil	1.350	×	0.843	=	1.138
Equally weighted portfolio	1.682				1.279

Source: K. Alamouti and I. Cooper, Unpublished Manuscript, London Business School, 1982.

To solve, we shall assume that the risk-free rate is 10 percent and that the expected excess return on the market index is 8.3 percent:

$$\text{Required Rate of Return on Gulf's Assets} = 0.10 + (0.932 \times 0.083)$$

$$= 0.177$$

Therefore, the cost of capital for Gulf's assets is 17.7 percent.

If we had felt that Gulf's beta value was affected significantly by measurement error, we could have obtained an estimate of the asset beta in one of two other ways. We could have selected another of the six companies in the table whose operations most resembled those of Gulf and used its asset beta value as a proxy for Gulf's in the CAPM. Alternatively, we could have used the average asset beta of 0.873 for the six companies given on the bottom line of the table.

Estimating a Division's Cost of Capital

As the exploration division of Gulf Oil does not have securities that are traded in the market, we cannot measure the risk of the exploration division directly. We must measure the risk indirectly by using the stocks of exploration companies that are traded in the stock market. In the first column of Table 10.2 are listed the equity beta values of seven United States oil exploration companies. In Chapter 9 we showed how to obtain an estimate of the beta coefficient for a company's assets by adjusting the value of beta for the company's stock, which you see in columns 2 and 3. The reason we need to obtain the value of the beta coefficient for each company's assets is that their equity betas are not directly comparable because the companies employ different proportions of debt capital.

Table 10.2 shows the asset beta values for the seven United States oil exploration companies. Consider, for example, Louisiana Land and Exploration in the table. The value for the asset beta was obtained from the value of the equity beta as follows:

$$\text{Beta of Assets} = \text{Equity Proportion} \times \text{Beta of Equity}$$

$$= 0.882 \times 1.289 \tag{10.3}$$

$$= 1.137$$

The average of all the asset betas for the oil exploration companies shown in the table is equal to 1.279, so we could use this value as a proxy for the value of the asset beta for Gulf Oil's exploration division. (Alternatively, we could use the value of the asset beta for the company that resembles Gulf's exploration division most closely.) This value for the exploration division is very different from the value of the asset beta for the Gulf Oil Corporation as a whole, which we found to be only 0.932. Because the estimated value of the asset beta for the exploration division (1.279) is so much higher than the value of the asset beta for Gulf as a whole, management should use a higher than average discount rate for the exploration division.

We can calculate the required rate of return for Gulf's exploration division, based upon the estimated value of the asset beta for exploration companies, by using the CAPM in equation (10.2). To solve, we shall assume (as before) that the risk-free rate is 10 percent and that the expected excess return on the market index is 8.3 percent:

$$\text{Required Rate of Return on Exploration Assets} = 0.10 + (1.279 \times 0.083)$$

$$= 0.206$$

The required rate of return or cost of capital on new projects in the exploration division is therefore 20.6 percent. It is useful to compare this rate with the required rate of return of only 17.7 percent that we obtained on Gulf's total assets.

Table 10.3 shows the equity and asset betas of the exploration companies for each of the five years from 1977 through 1981. The results indicate that

Table 10.3   *Equity and asset betas for United States exploration companies for different subperiods between 1977–1981**

Company		1981	1980	1979	1978	1977
General	Equity	1.829	1.211	0.804	0.407	1.241
American Oil	Asset	1.811	1.184	0.785	0.394	1.160
Louisiana	Equity	1.609	1.414	0.747	1.108	1.277
Land and Exploration	Asset	1.250	1.328	0.710	0.974	1.105
Mesa	Equity	2.172	1.887	0.750	1.287	1.469
Petroleum	Asset	1.188	1.434	0.493	0.710	0.914
Murphy	Equity	1.816	1.714	1.351	1.194	1.899
Oil	Asset	1.531	1.436	0.946	0.801	1.126
Natomas	Equity	1.807	1.922	1.502	1.230	1.402
	Asset	0.951	1.405	0.946	0.652	0.758
Oceanic	Equity	1.695	1.813	1.318	1.148	1.538
Exploration	Asset	1.593	1.487	0.895	0.797	1.135
Superior	Equity	2.539	1.704	1.412	1.075	1.392
Oil	Asset	2.059	1.482	1.196	0.830	1.277
Equally weighted portfolio	Equity	1.924	1.666	1.126	1.064	1.460
	Asset	1.483	1.394	0.853	0.737	1.068

*Annual betas are based upon weekly data.

Source: K. Alamouti and I. Cooper, Unpublished Manuscript, London Business School, 1982.

both the equity and the asset betas have been increasing with time. In 1977 the equity and asset betas of the average exploration company were 1.460 and 1.068, respectively. In 1981 estimates of both had risen to 1.924 and 1.483, respectively. If such increases were due to the changing business risk of exploration, the implication would be that the discount rate for exploration projects should be increased as a result.[2]

Estimating a Project's Cost of Capital

In a survey published in 1975, Brigham found that nearly half of a sample of United States industrial firms used a single hurdle rate or required rate of return to evaluate investment proposals. As we pointed out in the last chapter, a single discount rate for all projects regardless of their individual risks will bias investment away from safe projects that are profitable toward

[2]You should treat estimates of beta that differ significantly from 1.0 with some caution. There are many statistical problems associated with the measurement of estimates of beta.

risky projects that are unprofitable. Obviously, it is highly desirable to identify the factors that determine the systematic risk of an individual capital project and to be able to use the factors to estimate the project's risk.

PROJECT RISK CLASSIFICATION

Most companies using risk-adjusted discount rates employ a risk classification scheme. Typical projects are classified into, say, four categories, each with a different level of risk and a different risk premium. The discount rate becomes

$$\text{Required rate of return} = \text{Risk-free Rate of Interest} + \text{Risk Premium for the Project's Risk Class}$$

If there are only four risk classes, there are only four discount rates used at a time. Figure 10.2 is a graphical representation of a typical relationship between required rates of return and risk classes. Class B in the figure represents projects of average risk for the division, and replacement projects for typical assets might fall into this category. The risk premiums for Classes A, C, and D are scaled relative to Class B on the horizontal axis. The scalings shown in the figure are arbitrary and may be altered, if appropriate, for the actual relative risks of each risk class in the division. The more risk classes a company can use, the less the likelihood of investing in unprofitable projects or rejecting profitable ones because of the use of inappropriate discount rates.

While risk classification provides a convenient means of assigning a discount rate for a project, it cannot provide as accurate a discount rate as you might calculate by estimating an individual discount rate for each project depending upon its risk. The reasons for using risk classification are largely organizational ones. An analyst can preassign likely projects to risk classes and determine the risk premium that is to be used for each risk class in the division. Less well qualified personnel do not have to estimate a separate risk premium for each project. A further benefit of risk classification is that it minimizes bias in project evaluation within divisions. If the salary and promotion system of the company rewards short-term growth, for example, there otherwise might be an implicit temptation for each division to assign low discount rates so as to encourage project acceptance.

To assign a project to a risk class we must be able to identify the factors that make projects risky. We shall consider two such factors that contribute to the systematic risk of most projects. The first, which we may call **revenue sensitivity,** measures the degree to which a project's cash income is affected by general economic conditions. The second factor is a project's **operating leverage,** which measures the degree to which the cost structure of the project may magnify the effect of its revenue sensitivity on the net cash flow and the present value of the project.

Figure 10.2   *An example of the relationship between the costs of capital and risk classes*

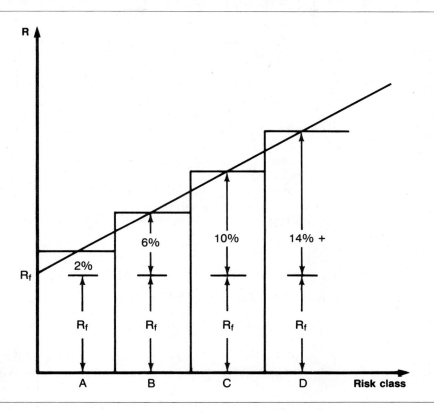

REVENUE SENSITIVITY AND PROJECT RISK

Most managers would agree that the following four sorts of projects, all of which may arise in a single division, can have very different risks:

reduction of operating expenditure

replacement of existing assets

expansion

new products or markets

The single factor that best characterizes the differences in risk in these four categories of capital projects is the relative sensitivity of their revenue cash flows to changes in business conditions. Savings in operating expenditure (particularly fixed operating expenditure) are regarded as the least sensitive to unanticipated changes in sales volume and therefore are the least risky.

The revenues generated from replacement of typical existing assets are regarded generally as of average sensitivity for the division but of greater sensitivity than the revenues for projects intended to reduce operating expenditure. Expansion of existing product markets involves still higher revenue sensitivity, for marginal increments in market share usually are more vulnerable to changes in general business conditions. Sales revenues from new product markets may be the most sensitive to changes in economic conditions.

Although revenue sensitivity is likely to be one of the most important factors affecting the risk of a project, there are others to be considered. For example, the degree to which the project's cost structure is fixed can have an important impact on the extent to which net cash flows are sensitive to unexpected changes in sales volume. Fixed operating costs usually are referred to as operating leverage. Operating leverage is similar to financial leverage, because fixed operating expenditures resemble interest charges and repayments in that they do not change as a result of changes in output or sales.

OPERATING LEVERAGE AND PROJECT RISK

Table 10.4 provides a numerical example of how operating leverage affects a project's risk. The rows represent four possible outcomes, each implying a different level of sales and related variable costs. The first two columns are, respectively, the possible sales outcomes and the corresponding variable costs. Column 3 shows the unlevered net cash flow, which is merely the difference between the figures in columns 1 and 2 when there is no fixed operating expenditure. Column 4 represents operating leverage in the form of fixed operating expenditure equal to 10 per period. In the second line, if

Table 10.4   *Comparison between unlevered and levered net cash flows for four different possible outcomes*

Sales	−	Variable cost	=	Unlevered net cash flow	−	Fixed operating expenditure	=	Levered net cash flow
100	−	50	=	50	−	10	=	40
50	−	25	=	25	−	10	=	15
20	−	10	=	10	−	10	=	0
0	−	0	=	0	−	10	=	−10

sales should be 50 the unlevered net cash flow is expected to be 25, and the levered net cash flow is expected to be only 15 with a fixed operating expenditure of 10. If sales drop unexpectedly by 30 to only 20 in the third line, the net cash flow in both the unlevered and levered cases drops by 15 to 10 and 0, respectively. While a drop of 15 represents only 60 percent (15/25) in the unlevered case, it represents a 100 percent drop (15/15) for the levered cash flow. Thus operating leverage has increased beta by the ratio of 100%/60%, or 1.67. This effect on beta could have been predicted by dividing the expected unlevered net cash flow 25 by the expected levered net cash flow 15 or 25/15 = 1.67.

The joint effect of revenue sensitivity and operating leverage on the systematic risk of a project can also be explained by separate consideration of the components of a project's cash flow and the risk of each component. The net cash flows are generated by revenues minus expenditures:

Net Cash Flow = Revenue − Variable Cost − Fixed Expenditure

The project's revenue can be expressed as the sum of three parts: the net cash flow, the variable cost, and the fixed expenditure. Rearranging the equation, we have

Revenue = Net Cash Flow + Variable Cost + Fixed Expenditure

If we discount these components of cash flow, we have

$$R = A + V + F \tag{10.4}$$

where R, A, V, and F represent the present values of revenues, net cash flow, variable cost, and fixed expenditure. The capital asset pricing model implies that the value of the beta coefficient for the term on the left-hand side of the equation must be the value-weighted average of the betas for the terms on the right-hand side of the equation:

$$\beta_R = \beta_A \frac{A}{R} + \beta_V \frac{V}{R} + \beta_F \frac{F}{R} \tag{10.5}$$

We can simplify this equation by assuming that the value of beta for variable costs equals the value of beta for revenues, because variable costs are directly proportional to revenues. The equation simplifies further if we assume that the value of beta for fixed expenditure is equal to zero.[3] These simplifications give us:

$$\beta_R = \beta_A \frac{A}{R} + \beta_R \frac{V}{R} \tag{10.6}$$

Solving for the beta of the present value of the net cash flow we obtain

$$\beta_A = \beta_R \frac{R - V}{A} \tag{10.7}$$

or, because $R - V = A + F$ from equation (10.4),

$$\beta_A = \beta_R \times \frac{A + F}{A} \tag{10.8}$$

This shows that the value of beta (β_A) for the project is equal to the beta (β_R) of the project's (after-tax) revenues scaled up by the factor $(A + F)/A$. This factor is called the **operating leverage factor.** In words, the factor is given by

$$\text{Operating Leverage Factor} = \frac{\text{Asset} + \text{Fixed}}{\text{Asset}}$$

where Asset and Fixed represent the present values of the project and of the fixed operating expenditure, respectively.[3]

The equations above show that the systematic risk for a project is equal to the systematic risk of its revenues scaled up by the operating leverage factor. Revenue sensitivity and operating leverage are therefore two principal factors affecting the systematic risk of a capital project. We shall now show how these two factors can be used to assign projects to risk classes.

Risk Classification

We wish to be able to assign a capital project to one of four risk classes A, B, C, or D in a division where A represents the class of least risky projects and D represents the most risky projects. Assume that we wish to assign projects typical of average risk for the division to class B. This would imply that the cost of capital for the division overall is a good approximation to the correct discount rate for class B projects. Our problem is how to assign projects that are significantly more or less risky than average to the other risk classes and how to choose appropriate discount rates for these risk classes.

[3]Note that the calculation of Asset in the operating leverage factor requires the use of the very discount rate that we are looking for. We can solve for the correct discount rate using iterative methods, although problems of convergence and uniqueness may remain.

RELATING PROJECT RISK TO DIVISION RISK

The easiest way to assign a project to a risk class is first to relate its risk to that of a typical (class B) asset in the division. If we can compare the project's revenue sensitivity and operating leverage to that of the typical asset, we shall be able to obtain a measure of its risk relative to that of the typical class B asset. We can then use the project's relative risk as a criterion for assigning the project to a risk class.

The average asset for a division is the asset that most typifies the risk of the division and one that can provide a convenient reference point against which to compare the risk of other projects. In Gulf Oil's refining division, a typical asset might be, for example, a fifteen-year-old oil refinery. The risk of proposed projects for the division may then be compared with the risk of the refinery.

We can compare other projects to the reference asset by estimating the relative risk of the project, defined as the ratio of the beta for the project to that of the reference asset for the division. The beta for the project would be given by equation (10.8) as follows:

$$\text{Beta of Project} = \frac{\text{Beta of Project}}{\text{Revenues}} \times \frac{\text{Project Operating}}{\text{Leverage Factor}} \tag{10.9}$$

Similarly, the beta for the reference asset for the division would be obtained from

$$\text{Beta of Asset} = \frac{\text{Beta of Asset's}}{\text{Revenues}} \times \frac{\text{Asset's Operating}}{\text{Leverage Factor}} \tag{10.10}$$

Using the two equations above, we can obtain a formula for the ratio (Beta of Project/Beta of Asset) that measures the relative risk of the project. Dividing the first equation by the second we obtain,

$$\frac{\text{Beta of Project}}{\text{Beta of Asset}} = \frac{\text{Beta of Project Revenues}}{\text{Beta of Asset's Revenue}}$$

$$\times \frac{\text{Project Operating Leverage Factor}}{\text{Asset Operating Leverage Factor}}$$

$$\text{Project Relative Risk} = \text{Project Relative Revenue Sensitivity}$$

$$\times \frac{\text{Project Operating Leverage Factor}}{\text{Asset Operating Leverage Factor}} \tag{10.11}$$

The resulting combined equation tells us that the project's estimated relative risk is equal to the project's revenue sensitivity relative to that of the reference asset multiplied by the ratio of the project's and the reference asset's operating leverage factors.

AN EXAMPLE

Determining the values of the operating leverage factors that are used in the ratio above is a straightforward problem in discounted cash flow. For the project or asset we simply calculate the present value of the net operating cash flow (excluding investment expenditures), add to this the present value of the fixed operating expenditure, and divide this sum by the present value of the net operating cash flow. For a first approximation, the divisional cost of capital can be used as the discount rate for the project as well as for the reference asset in order to estimate the values of the operating leverage factors. By dividing the operating leverage factor for the project by the operating leverage factor for the reference asset, we can obtain the ratio required for the relative risk of the project.

All that remains is to estimate the project's relative revenue sensitivity factor for the equation. The relative revenue sensitivity factor can be estimated with the aid of the sensitivity analysis techniques described in more detail toward the end of this chapter. In short, management must make a judgment on how much more sensitive the project's expected revenues are to changes in assumed general economic conditions than the expected revenues of the reference asset are. For example, if management feels that general economic outcomes that could cause a 15 percent drop in the revenues for the project would cause only a 10 percent drop in the revenues for the reference asset, the project's relative revenue sensitivity would be equal to $15\%/10\% = 1.50$. If the operating leverage factors for the project and the reference asset are equal to 1.20 and 1.15, respectively, using equation (10.11) we can obtain the value of the project's relative risk:

$$= 1.50 \times \frac{1.20}{1.15}$$

$$= 1.57$$

The combined effect of the project's relatively high revenue sensitivity and high operating leverage compared with that of the reference asset for the division raises its relative risk factor to a value of 1.57. The systematic risk of the project is therefore 57 percent higher than that of the reference asset for the division; and, in principle, the risk premium for the project should be 57 percent larger than the risk premium for class B projects.

PUTTING PROJECTS INTO RISK CLASSES

The procedure outlined above could be used to obtain a different risk premium and therefore a different discount rate for every project depending upon its relative risk factor. However, you can see how cumbersome it would be to use different discount rates for each project, so a risk-class approach is generally preferred. We can use the estimated value of the relative risk factor to assign projects to risk classes and then use one risk premium for all projects that are in the same risk class.

Each risk class can be defined in terms of a range of values for the relative risk factor. For example, the following ranges for the different risk classes are typical of those that might be used:

Risk Class	Relative Risk Factors	
	Midpoint	Range
A	0.33	0 − 0.67
B	1.00	0.68 − 1.33
C	1.67	1.34 − 2.00
D	2.33+	2.01 − 2.67+

The ranges that are given above correspond to the arbitrary scale that was used for the risk classes shown in Figure 10.2. Other more appropriate ranges based upon natural groupings of projects can be selected. For example, it may be found that cost reduction projects, expansion projects, or new product projects for a division typically have relative risk factors that cluster into different sets of ranges than those given above, and the ranges for the risk classes can be adjusted accordingly.

It remains only for us to assign the appropriate discount rate to each risk class. The midpoint of the range of relative risk factors for each risk class provides a criterion for selecting a discount rate for the risk class. The discount rate for an asset is given by

$$\text{Required Rate of Return} = R_f + \text{Risk Premium}$$

where R_f is the cost of capital for a risk-free asset. The risk premium now depends upon the asset's risk class. Therefore, the risk premium is given by

$$\text{Risk Premium} = \frac{\text{Relative Risk for}}{\text{the Class}} \times \frac{\text{Risk Premium for}}{\text{the Division}}$$

Suppose that the risk premium for the division is 8 percent and that we have a cost saving project that falls into class A. The value of the midpoint for class A suggested earlier was equal to 0.33. Therefore, the risk premium for the cost-saving project is equal to,

Risk Premium $= 0.33 \times 0.08$

$= 0.0264$

The risk premium for the division's class A projects would be only 2.6 percent on these assumptions.

We have shown how to classify a project's risk by analyzing its revenue sensitivity and operating leverage. Now we shall discuss some of the problems that make risk measurement a very inexact science.

Difficulties in Measuring Project Risk and Discount Rates

The general approach we have taken to risk measurement in our extended illustration has been based upon four important assumptions:

that the capital asset pricing model is an adequate representation of the cost of capital

that the risk of the market portfolio and the risk (beta) of individual securities can be obtained by using historical data

that project risk can be estimated by simply relating the revenue sensitivity and operating leverage of a project to that of other assets

that a suitable risk-free rate can be obtained

These assumptions permit the use of a single discount rate for the cash flows in all periods for a capital project.

In Chapter 8 we referred to some evidence that supported the validity of the CAPM. Evidence, however, is certainly limited at this stage. Consequently, our use of the model is based upon the principles of first approximation. However, it is important to appreciate some of the practical problems associated with risk measurement, so that you understand when the model is not applicable or when some adaptation must be made. Some of the general problems were discussed in Chapter 9. Others are discussed below.

WHEN SHAREHOLDERS OR MANAGERS ARE NOT DIVERSIFIED

A critical assumption of the CAPM is that shareholders hold diversified portfolios of shares and that through diversification shareholders are able to reduce risk until only the risk relating to the economy is left. However, in some companies the shareholders own large dominating interests (frequently the owners are also the managers), and they do not have sufficient capital to invest in many other companies. This policy may be sensible if the shareholders wish to retain control or if they believe that the business itself will provide them with a superior return on capital. In this situation, diversifiable risk is still important, but the beta coefficient understates the risk taken by the undiversified shareholders.

Undiversified shareholders should demand higher required rates of return from new projects. This may cause the company to invest in fewer projects than its competitors if its shareholders are less diversified than its competitors' shareholders. Indeed, any acceptable investment would be worth more in the hands of a company with diversified shareholders, as the diversified shareholders require a lower discount rate. Consequently, it will always pay an owner-managed firm to diversify in order to reduce the owners' risk and required rates of return.

What about undiversified managers? Managers are frequently undiversified, because much of their wealth is either in assets such as their houses or in their human capital (the ability to produce wealth from their own labor), which cannot be turned into cash readily. The reason that human capital cannot be turned into cash readily is that banks and other lenders charge higher rates of interest on loans secured by intangible assets, and personal guarantees are much less secure than real estate or even plant and machinery. If the manager is undiversified, obviously he will face risks that are greater than the risks borne by shareholders.

How should such a manager evaluate projects? We still suggest that the manager should determine the value of cash flows discounted at rates that reflect nondiversifiable risk, not total risk. If the project is profitable to shareholders on this basis, then the manager can consider whether the total risk of the project is too risky for the managers. If so, several choices are available. The manager can try to reduce a project's risk to the firm by starting a joint venture with another company or by drafting contracts that share risk (for a price) with customers or suppliers. Other possibilities would include postponing the project or selling the opportunity to another company. However, the manager must appreciate that if projects are rejected because they are too risky for managers and other employees, notwithstanding the fact that they are profitable for shareholders, the company may be in danger of becoming uncompetitive. Finally, it may pay the company's directors to devise a compensation scheme that encourages management to accept risks that shareholders can diversify.

It also may be worthwhile for the firm to diversify its own product range in order to reduce risks, especially if cash flows are very volatile and there are risks of the firm not being able to meet its loan payments. Strictly speaking, the capital asset pricing model makes no distinction between the company's assets and the company as a going concern. However, the essence of a going concern lies in continual generation of positive net present values. If the threat of bankruptcy impairs an organization's capacity to do this, diversified shareholders may find corporate diversification to be worthwhile as a safeguard against financial distress. The possibility of such financial distress can be very costly to shareholders; for example, if managers demand higher salaries and customers demand lower prices (perhaps because of fear that warranties will not be honored). In 1980 Chrysler's sales were affected adversely by the company's financial problems. Many customers were under the impression that car warranties might prove difficult to enforce, and Chrysler was forced to cut its car prices sharply as a consequence.

IS THE RISK OF THE PROJECT OR THE COMPANY EXPECTED TO REMAIN CONSTANT?

In our description of risk estimation, we assumed that the object was to find a single discount rate for a project. One discount rate would be used to discount all the net cash flows of a project irrespective of the length of its life. There are a number of reasons why such an approach may be inadequate. First, a project's risk may be concentrated mostly in one event. For example, the future level of cash flows from an expansion project may be contingent on the outcome of the project's first year. Afterward, the level of subsequent cash flows will have been established and may represent relatively low risk. In principle, the first year's cash flow would be much riskier than subsequent cash flows in this case. However, the constant discount rate approach does not reflect these differences in the rate of increase in risk. Indeed, the mathematics of a constant risk-adjusted discount rate is based on an assumption that the project's risk increases through time. A proof of this proposition is provided in Appendix 10.1.

A related problem, and a more subtle one, is that we do not understand how risk is affected by time. For example, suppose that you are offered two computers that do similar jobs, but one lasts longer than the other and is, as a consequence, more expensive. In any analysis of the computer purchase one would want to take account of the fact that technological change may produce better and cheaper computers in the future. The computer with the longer life will be riskier, for there is a greater chance it will prove obsolete. Clearly, one would be willing to pay less for the cash flows in the final years of the longer-lived computer than for those in the earlier years.

Finally, a third problem arises in measuring the beta of a growth company. A company's value and risk are determined not only by the current investment set but also by the expectation of possible future investments. However, the net present values of future investment opportunities are very volatile, and as a result they have high beta values. Thus, when one measures the equity beta of a firm that has substantial growth opportunities, the measured beta value overestimates the risk of the existing investments. Analysts must realize that the measured beta values of high-growth companies may be too high to use in estimating the cost of capital for assets already in place.

Traditional Risk Measurement

A number of methods are used for evaluating project risk. The most widely used method has been **sensitivity analysis,** whose object is to obtain an estimate of the possible range of net present values for a project given a range of possible cost and revenue conditions. Cost and revenue variables may be changed one at a time or in combination.

Sensitivity analysis is a valuable and necessary complement to the appraisal of important projects. Even if you have obtained a satisfactory estimate of a project's risk premium and discount rate, and you can compute its net present value, it is still important to carry out a sensitivity analysis. Such an analysis permits you to identify the variables to which the project's profitability and risk are most sensitive.

One problem in using sensitivity analysis is that usually little distinction is made between nondiversifiable and diversifiable risks. This distinction may not be important if the purpose of the sensitivity analysis is to gauge the financial needs of the company or to plan for contingencies if a project goes wrong. However, if sensitivity analysis is used to measure the effect of risk on the profitability of the project, only systematic or nondiversifiable risks should be included in the analysis, according to the CAPM. One way to focus on nondiversifiable risk is to base sensitivity analysis on different possible economic outcomes in the future. Managers should develop alternative optimistic and pessimistic sets of outcomes for the growth of the economy and industry and analyze each set of sales, variable costs, and fixed operating expenditures for each set of outcomes. Unique events, such as a strike, are treated separately if they are diversifiable by shareholders (if not by managers and employees).

Figure 10.3 illustrates values of the profitability index of a project for three different outcomes at different discount rates. You will recall that the profitability index is the present value of a project divided by the present value of its investment expenditures. Analyzing projects and divisions on the basis of the same sets of outcomes makes it possible to compare their respective ranges in profitability more consistently. The vertical distance on the graph between the values of profitability indexes for different sets of outcomes represents the range. At each discount rate the analyst identifies the possible range in profitability. The greater the range, the greater the systematic risk. Higher discount rates should be applied to the projects with the greater risk. Projects falling significantly below a profitability index of 1.00 for the pessimistic outcome require special attention to see if there may be means of reducing unnecessary risks.

In estimating the value of a project's beta or systematic risk, we have used operating leverage and revenue sensitivity. In fact we have measured risk in relation to the sensitivity of a project's present value to economic change. The resulting estimate measures the risk associated with the mean or expected outcome for the project. An analyst, however, can provide three cash flows

Figure 10.3   *Sensitivity analysis: Graph of profitability index versus discount rate for a project under three scenarios*

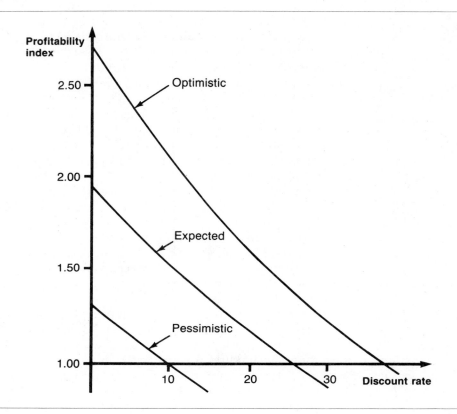

based upon most likely, optimistic, and pessimistic future outcomes. Should the same discount rate be used for each set of outcomes? Usually not. Take for example the optimistic outcome. If business turns out to be very favorable, sales volume and variable costs will be relatively large in relation to the fixed operating expenditure for the project. The operating leverage of the project will be lower, reducing the project's beta value and its discount rate in the optimistic case. Conversely, for the pessimistic outcomes where sales are lower than expected, sales revenues and variable costs are low in relation to fixed operating expenditure, making the operating leverage ratio high and thus increasing the discount rate.

An alternative approach would be to forecast the project's net cash flows for each possible outcome and then obtain the certainty equivalents (see Appendix 10.1) of risky cash flows. The analyst would then use the risk-free rate to obtain their present value. For example, if in the optimistic outcome a cash flow of $1,000 is forecast, then if management would accept a risk-free cash flow of $800 in exchange for that risky cash flow, the risk-free sum is called the certainty equivalent cash flow. The net present value of the project for each outcome would then be based upon the discounted value of the certainty equivalent cash flows.

Sensitivity analysis has several benefits. First, it allows managers to gather more information and thereby narrow the range of uncertainty about those variables to which the project's net present value is most sensitive. Second, managers may be able to insure against the risk of certain things going wrong by entering into contracts that shift risk to other parties (for a price). Also, it may be possible to prepare contingency plans so that, if a project goes wrong suddenly, management has a plan for limiting the losses. Finally, management should be aware of the full range of possible economic outcomes so that financing arrangements may take into account the worst plausible ones. In the last resort, management may even postpone or reject a project that seems to expose the company to the serious possibility of financial distress. All the ways of sharing or otherwise reducing project risk should be considered.

Summary

The use of a single discount rate for all projects regardless of their systematic risk can lead to underinvestment in profitable low-risk projects and encourage investment in high-risk projects that are not profitable. We have suggested a procedure for obtaining a measure of the systematic risk of the assets of a product division by comparing the unlevered beta values of similar listed companies competing in the same product market. Using this value for the asset beta of the division, one can estimate an average cost of capital for the division that can be used as the discount rate for projects that are of average risk for the division. Projects not typical of the division with significantly greater or lesser nondiversifiable risk fall into different risk classes and have correspondingly higher or lower discount rates. A method of assigning projects to risk classes was suggested, based upon analysis of the project's revenue sensitivity to economic change and upon its operating leverage. We then discussed reasons why project risk measurement is a very inexact science. Finally, we compared traditional methods of sensitivity analysis to the other methods suggested in this chapter.

Appendix 10.1 A Single Risk-adjusted Discount Rate Assumes Risk Increases with Time

We shall show that when we use a single risk-adjusted discount rate we make the implicit assumption that risk associated with expected future cash flows increases with time.

Suppose that cash flows C_t are expected with uncertainty at times t ($t = 1, 2, \ldots, N$) for a capital project with economic life N. Let C_t^* be a corresponding set of certain or risk-free cash flows at times t. If the investor is indifferent between the risk-free cash flows C_t^* and the corresponding risky cash flows C_t, the risk-free cash flows C_t^* are said to be the **certainty equivalents** of C_t, and we can define certainty equivalent factors that adjust cash flows C_t to the equivalent risk-free cash flows C_t^*:

$$C_t^* = a_t C_t$$

If the investor dislikes risk, then $a_t < 1.0$.

Now let us suppose that the investor's risk preferences can be captured by a single risk-adjusted discount rate R. The present value of the uncertain cash flows C_t obtained with the risk-adjusted discount rate R would be equal to the present value of the certainty equivalent cash flows C_t^* discounted at the risk-free rate R_f:

$$\frac{C_t}{(1 + R)^t} = \frac{C_t^*}{(1 + R_f)^t} = \frac{a_t C_t}{(1 + R_f)^t}$$

Solving for the certainty equivalent factor a_t we obtain,

$$a_t = \left(\frac{1 + R_f}{1 + R}\right)^t$$

We can rewrite this expression for the certainty equivalent factor as follows:

$$a_t = a_1 a_{t-1} \qquad (t = 1, 2, \ldots, N)$$

where $a_1 = \dfrac{(1 + R_f)}{(1 + R)}$

If a_1 corresponds to the increase in risk between periods $t = 0$ and $t = 1$, it also corresponds to the increase in risk between times $t - 1$ and t for all times $t = 1, 2, \ldots, N$, implying that risk increases over time at a constant rate, or alternatively a_t decreases over time by a constant factor, a_1. The important question is, does the risk profile of a project's cash flows over time correspond to this assumption?

Review Questions

1. At what levels in a company might different costs of capital prevail? Why might it be useful to distinguish between these different levels?

2. How might a company go about estimating its required rate of return or cost of capital?
3. How would you obtain an estimate of the beta coefficient for a company's assets from the beta coefficient of the company's equity when the beta of the company's debt is greater than zero?
4. How would you estimate the value of the beta coefficient for the assets of a division within a company?
5. If the risk of an individual asset within a division is significantly different from the average for the division, what is the simplest way of estimating the cost of capital for its class of risk?
6. Name three types of projects which are likely to have risk that is of significantly more or less risk than the average for a division.
7. What are two of the most important factors that determine the risk class of an individual capital project? Can you explain their relationship to each other?
8. What scaling factor might be used to obtain an estimate of the risk of an individual project relative to the risk of a typical asset in the division? How can this scaling factor be used as an aid for assigning projects to risk classes?
9. What assumptions underlie the use of the capital asset pricing model as a means of obtaining discount rates for capital projects?
10. What are three reasons that risk measurement is more of an art than a science?
11. Describe the method that traditionally has been used to measure the riskiness of a capital project. Give some reasons why this method is still useful.
12. Describe some means by which managers can reduce the riskiness of projects.
13. How can certainty-equivalence factors be used to allow for changes in risk during the life of a project? What does the certainty equivalence approach tell us about the assumptions concerning risk and time underlying the use of a single risk-adjusted discount rate for a project?

Problems

*1. Nisa, Inc.'s common stock has a beta of 1.36. The company is considering investment in a new project that is much riskier than existing projects of the company; the beta of this new project is estimated to be 1.5 times that of the company's existing projects. The company has a debt/equity ratio of 1:4. If the annual risk-free rate is 8 percent and the annual market risk premium is 10 percent, calculate the required rate of return for the new project.

*2. A firm is considering three projects A, B, and C, which have beta values of 0.5, 0.7, and 1.5, and expected returns of 10.0, 12.5, and 14.0 percent, respectively. Given a risk-free rate of interest equal to 5 percent and a risk premium on the market portfolio of 9 percent, illustrate graphically the trade-off between risk and return for the three projects. Show how the firm would accept or reject each project on the basis of:

(a) A single required rate of return based on the average beta for the three projects
(b) Estimated required rates of return for each project
(c) What are the implications of using one required rate of return for all projects? Does this practice ever permit net present value maximization?
(d) What will happen to a firm if it persistently accepts only investments of the sort that project C represents?

*3. Given the following information, calculate the asset beta of the company on both book value and market value bases.

	Book value	Market value
	(thousands of dollars)	
Common stock	1.0	17.2
Reserves	8.5	
Long-term debt	1.5	1.3
β of common stock = 1.2		

Which asset β would you use? Explain why.

4. Given the information in Problem 3, and the additional data that the market value of preferred stock issued is $2.5 million, what would be the value of the asset β? Common stock dividends cannot be paid unless specified preferred stock dividends are paid first. Explain your treatment of preferred stock.

*5. Moateno, Inc., is considering an investment in some manufacturing equipment. It has narrowed the choice down to two pieces of equipment, for which it has the following estimates of operating costs. Use the information to suggest which piece of equipment might be preferable, given that the demand for the products manufactured by this equipment is unlikely to increase. Estimates are based on projected production levels.

	Equipment	
Present value	A	B
Revenue	24.26	24.26
Variable cost	15.58	17.84
Fixed operating expenditure	5.32	3.20

6. Moateno's marketing director, analyzing the project in Problem 5 in greater detail, has estimated that if there were a downturn in the economy and the division's revenues dropped 10 percent, the project's revenues would drop by 12 percent. The division's operating leverage factor is 1.4. Calculate the risk of the project (if either piece of equipment, A or B, were purchased) relative to the risk of the division.

*7. FLOPO, Inc., has fixed annual operating expenditure of $100,000 and variable cost of $1.00 per unit for its Fixit product, which is priced at $2.00.

 (a) Plot the break-even chart, and determine the cash flow break-even point for the Fixit product. What is the operating leverage factor if forecast sales are 150,000 units?

 (b) If forecast sales increase to 200,000 units, and fixed operating expenditure increases to $150,000 per year, by what proportion will the operating leverage factor of the Fixit product change?

*8. An investment to reduce waste in a production operation gives an expected rate of return of 18 percent, while a project to expand the scale of production to achieve increased market share promises a rate of return of 21 percent. If the average cost of capital for the company is 20 percent, which project or projects should the company undertake?

*9. Using your judgment about the characteristics of the following projects that a company might invest in, group them into the four risk classes A, B, C, and D (as defined in the chapter).

 1. Marketing new product
 2. Installing manufacturing robots using established technology
 3. Scale expansion
 4. Variable cost saving
 5. Replacement of asset
 6. Energy saving
 7. Entering new market
 8. Fixed operating expenditure saving
 9. Research project on cost saving
 10. Development of new product
 11. Marketing new product in new market
 12. Minerals prospecting
 13. Leasing contract
 14. Loan

10. For the previous question, estimate the risk premium that an average company might use in the discount rates for each risk class. Use your judgment based on the data in Chapter 9 and the risk class framework in Chapter 10.

11. The following table provides two outcomes for the cash flows for a typical project for a division and for a new project. The cash flows for each are discounted at different rates to provide a range of net present values. If the risk premium for the division is 6 percent, estimate the risk premium for the project. The Treasury bill rate is 9 percent.

Discount rate (%)	Typical project's outcomes		New project's outcomes	
	1	2	1	2
5	116,475	51,532	159,770	29,885
10	89,540	32,678	127,448	13,724
15	67,610	17,327	101,132	−566
20	49,530	4,671	79,436	−10,282
25	34,465	−5,874	61,358	−19,321

(Note: This data can be analyzed by drawing graphs. The spread between outcomes measured relative to present values should be different for the two projects implying different risks. Different risks imply different discount rates, which means the spread would be measured at different discount rates.)

*12. Calculate the certainty equivalence factors over a four-year period implied when the risk-free rate is 4 percent, and the risk-adjusted discount rate is:

(a) 12 percent

(b) 18 percent

Explain what is implied in the relationship between the certainty equivalence factors and the risk-adjusted discount rate. What does the use of a constant discount rate approach assume about risk through time?

References

Bildersee, J., "Some Aspects of the Performance of Non-Convertible Preferred Stocks," *Journal of Finance* 28, no. 5 (December 1973): 1187–1201.

Brigham, E. F., "Hurdle Rates for Screening Capital Expenditure Proposals," *Financial Management* 4, no. 3 (Autumn 1975): 17–26.

Carleton, W. T., D. R. Chambers, and J. Lakonishok, "Inflation Risk and Regulatory Lag," *Journal of Finance* 38, no. 2 (May 1983): 419–31.

Conine, R., "Corporate Debt and Corporate Taxes: An Extension," *Journal of Finance* (September 1980):

Copeland, T. E., and J. F. Weston, *Financial Theory and Corporate Policy,* Second edition, Reading, MA: Addison-Wesley, 1983.

Fama, E. F., "Risk-Adjusted Discount Rates and Capital Budgeting under Uncertainty," *Journal of Financial Economics* 5, no.1 (August 1977): 3–24.

Franks, J. R., and J. E. Broyles, "Capital Project Risk and the Discount Rate" in *Modern Managerial Finance,* New York: Wiley, 1979.

Friend, I., R. Westerfield, and M. Granito, "New Evidence on the Capital Asset Pricing Model," *Journal of Finance* (June 1978):

Fuller, R., and H. Kerr, "Estimating the Divisional Cost of Capital: An Analysis of the Pure-Play Techniques," *Journal of Finance* (December 1981):

Hamada, R., "The Effect of the Firm's Capital Structure on the Systematic Risk of Common Stocks," *Journal of Finance* (May 1972):

Hertz, D. B., "Risk Analysis in Capital Investment," *Harvard Business Review* 42, no. 2 (January–February 1964): 95–106.

Ibbotson, R. G., and R. A. Sinquefield, "Stocks, Bonds, Bills and Inflation: Year-by-Year Historical Returns (1926–1974)," *Journal of Business* 49 (January 1976): 11–47.

Myers, S. C., and S. Turnbull, "Capital Budgeting and the Capital Asset Pricing Model: Good News and Bad News," *Journal of Finance* 32 (May 1977): 321–36.

Reilly, F., and M. Joehnk, "The Association Between Market-Determination Risk Measures for Bonds and Bond Ratings," *Journal of Finance* (December 1976):

Robichek, A. A., and S. C. Myers, "Conceptual Problems with the Use of Risk-adjusted Discount Rates," *Journal of Finance*, no. 21 (December 1966): 727–30.

Rubinstein, M. E., "A Mean-Variance Synthesis of Corporate Financial Theory," *Journal of Finance* 28, no. 1 (March 1973): 167–81.

Sharpe, W. F., "Bonds versus Stocks: Some Lessons from Capital Market Theory," *Financial Analysts Journal* 29 (November–December 1973): 74–80.

Weinstein, M., "The Systematic Risk of Corporate Bonds," *Journal of Financial and Quantitative Analysis* 16, no. 3 (September 1981): 257–78.

Target Setting and Performance Measurement for Divisions

In this chapter we explain why companies need to measure the financial performance of their assets. We show how the performance of a project or a division can be measured using an asset's cash flows and the resulting economic values. We compare this approach with the one usually adopted by management, which is to base performance measurement on accounting earnings and book values of assets. We explain why accounting numbers usually are used to set targets and measure performance instead of the cash flow numbers that are used to appraise capital projects. Subsequently, we show how the internal rate of return can be calculated from accounting rates of return for one or more periods. We show that we can calculate the internal rate of return from accounting numbers only if cash flow data are available. Finally, we discuss some of the lessons that can be drawn from this analysis.

Why Management Needs to Measure a Division's Financial Performance

In previous chapters we have described how a risky project's cash flows can be defined, forecast, and valued. The cash flow that is discounted is the mean or expected cash flow derived from a probability distribution of outcomes (see Chapter 8, Table 8.1, for an example). However, the actual cash flows for a project usually turn out to be different from what had been expected. There could be two reasons why actual performance differs from that expected. The first is explained by chance or conditions that are outside management's control. The American economy may be performing differently from what had been expected. Or, the demand for the particular product may be greater (or less) than predicted because of an unexpected change in consumer tastes. A change in interest rates may alter the required rate of return against which a division's performance should be evaluated. The change in discount rate may not be compensated for fully by a change in net cash flows. Such chance occurrences generally are outside the control of management. A second reason for the difference between forecast and actual performance may lie in managerial efforts. For example, management may have implemented better methods of production or distribution, and found ways of reducing costs and increasing revenues.

Why is it important for management to measure actual against forecast performance? If capital is to be committed to a division or to a product group, performance measurement becomes an important means of managerial control. The monitoring of divisional performance serves three purposes. First, it provides useful feedback on how general economic and industry conditions are affecting costs and revenues. For example, if revenues are less than forecast, management can put contingency plans into effect. Such plans may include limiting further expenditures, making management changes, selling some parts of the business, or even closing a division.

Second, monitoring performance provides important information to the capital appropriations committee or other top management groups who are responsible for allocating funds for investment to products, divisions, regions, or countries. Why should management look at past performance before allocating capital? Without examination of recent performance of products and divisions, top management will find it more difficult to assess whether the forecasts being made for future divisional earnings and cash flows are realistic. If a division requesting a substantial budget for capital expenditure has made forecasts that have proven wrong in the past, it must explain the errors if its new forecasts are to be believed. Even if the performance of the industry has deteriorated because of an unanticipated downturn in the economy, management still will want to ask whether the division has performed well relative to the industry: For example, did the division lose market share to competing companies? Unless such questions can be answered satisfactorily, it will be difficult for divisional management to support the forecasts of profits necessary to justify further capital investment.

The third motive for monitoring performance is to collect the information that is necessary if incentives are to be provided and management is to be rewarded for superior performance. In order to measure managerial performance, we must be able to separate out management's contribution to divisional performance from the effects of unanticipated changes in economic and industry conditions on profits. The problem of divisional performance measurement is understood better when one considers how the performance of a portfolio (or mutual fund) manager should be measured.

Divisional Performance: A Portfolio Analogy

The measurement of the financial performance of a division is analogous to the measurement of the performance of a portfolio of common stocks. In portfolio performance measurement, we want to know what the returns on the portfolio have been. We also want to see how the portfolio has performed relative to the stock market. The returns on the portfolio consist of both dividends and capital gains (or capital losses) as a percentage of the market value of the portfolio at the beginning of the period. Similarly, in divisional performance measurement, we must ask not only what earnings were realized during the period but also how the economic value of the division's assets has changed over the period. The division's earnings are like the portfolio's dividends, and the change in the economic value of the division is like the capital gain or capital loss of the portfolio. In addition, we must know whether the division has performed well relative to an industry or economywide index. After all, if a division has exceeded its forecast, but other companies in the industry have done even better, managers actually may not have performed very well. Such inferior performance may reflect that the division has lost market share or that profit margins are lower compared with other companies in the industry. In this situation the division may be the first to become unprofitable if industry conditions deteriorate.

In calculating a division's earnings to appraise performance, we would want the earnings to include changes in the value of the assets in the same way that returns on a portfolio of common stocks reflect capital gains or losses. Calculating the capital gains or losses on assets from one period to another requires that assets be revalued regularly. However, if the assets do not have active second-hand markets and market values are not available, present values (based upon cash flow forecasts) may have to be calculated. This measurement problem usually does not occur in portfolio performance measurement because common stocks are traded at known prices; therefore, the change in the value of the securities can be measured more easily.

Measuring Asset Values and Setting Targets

A division's performance can be measured using the present value of its cash flows as the division's asset value. Normally, divisional performance is measured using accounting values instead of present values of expected future cash flows. We show the nature of discrepancies that result from using each approach, and describe how accounting numbers may be interpreted to provide economically meaningful signals.

When we described how to measure portfolio performance in Chapter 8, we included the capital gains or capital losses in the returns on the portfolio for the period. These capital gains (or losses) reflected the change in the value of the assets in the portfolio over the period. As suggested above, we can think of a division as a portfolio of real assets whose values also change. How would we measure changes in the values of divisional assets such as plant and machinery?

THE BASIS OF ASSET VALUATION

When measuring performance or setting targets a company must estimate the economic value of its assets. Economic value may be represented by either cost or present value. If the assets are new, their current cost is simply their purchase price. However, as the assets are used over time, their economic values also change. If such assets have a second-hand market, we can obtain current costs for the assets from market prices. For example, the cost of a three-year-old car can be found from the market prices of three-year-old cars in active second-hand markets. However, if the assets do not have active second-hand markets and we cannot obtain current prices, we must make some estimates. These estimates are usually made by adjusting the original purchase price of the asset for the fact that inflation tends to increase the second-hand value, and age and usage tend to diminish it. This attempt to measure the current cost of an asset that is already in use can be described as calculating the written down replacement cost of the asset.

An alternative measure of economic value is the present value of the assets' remaining net cash flows. The present value will be higher than the assets' estimated costs if the assets are expected to generate positive net present values.

Which basis for calculating economic value should we use, costs or present values? The answer depends upon the purpose—whether we are setting the targets or measuring performance. For example, when government agencies regulate the rates charged by utilities and measure their performance, they use cost-based asset values. They do not use present values, because they wish to ensure that assets do not earn either positive or negative net present values. If present values were used and they were, for example, higher than the assets' replacement costs, regulators would be allowing returns to be earned on the assets' positive net present value. Managers also may wish to use costs in measuring the performance of a division to determine if the assets are earning more than their required rate of return, and if it would be worthwhile to invest more money in the division.

Alternatively, management may want to know whether the division has done better or worse than expected. In this case the present value of the assets should be used since present values include the positive or negative net present values that are expected.

In the succeeding analysis we shall show how to set targets and measure performance using both definitions of economic values: costs and present values.

CALCULATING TARGET ECONOMIC INCOME

On line one of Table 11.1 is a forecast of expected cash flows for a group of projects. (For simplicity's sake, we have omitted taxes from this example, but we will introduce tax effects later in the chapter.) The assets cost $900, and three annual net cash flows are expected. In the second line of the table we have calculated the present value at the end of each period of the remaining future cash flows. At time 0 the present value of the assets' future net cash flows is $1,000.

$$\$1,000 = \frac{475}{(1 + 0.20)} + \frac{475}{(1 + 0.20)^2} + \frac{474}{(1 + 0.20)^3}$$

These assets, which cost $900, have a present value equal to $1,000. At the end of period 1, the present value of the cash flows expected in periods

Table 11.1   *Calculating target economic income based on the present value of the project (dollars)*

	End of year			
	0	1	2	3
Net cash flow	−900	475	475	474
Present value of future cash flow at 20%	1,000	725	395	0
Change in present value (economic depreciation)		−275	−330	−395
Target economic income		200	145	79
Target economic rate of return		0.20	0.20	0.20

2 and 3, discounted at 20 percent, is equal to $725.

$$\$725 = \frac{475}{(1 + 0.20)} + \frac{474}{(1 + 0.20)^2}$$

Similarly, $395 is the present value at the end of period 2 of the cash flow expected in period 3. The 20 percent discount rate reflects prevailing interest rates and a premium for the risk of the project. The third line of Table 11.1 shows the change in present value from one period to the next. For example, the difference between the present value of the assets at the end of period 0 (i.e., beginning of period 1) and the end of period 1 is equal to $1,000 − $725 = $275. In fact, $275 can be said to be the assets' **economic depreciation** for the period, or the amount of the assets' present value or economic income used up during the period's operations.

It should be easy for you to derive the fourth line of the table, Target economic income: it is simply the cash flow less economic depreciation for the year. Because the change in the present value of the asset is negative, we subtract economic depreciation from the cash flow; for example, in year 1, target economic income is $200, which is found by subtracting economic depreciation of $275 from $475.

There are two further points worth noting from the example in Table 11.1. First, economic income targets are based initially on the $1,000 present value of the assets' cash flows rather than on the $900 cost of the assets. This means, in principle, that management should have been given credit for the forecast net present value of $1,000 − $900 = $100 in period 0. As a result, in period 1 economic income will be based on the asset's present value of $1,000, not its cost. Second, the target economic rate of return in each year (20 percent in this example) always will be equal to the discount rate used to calculate economic depreciation, because economic income is based on present value of future cash flows. (This would not be the case if economic value was based on costs.) In this approach, managers are given credit not only for the cash flows ("dividends") of the period but also for capital gains or losses in the form of economic depreciation. Such gains or losses are similar to the capital gains or losses on a portfolio of common stocks.

COMPARING ACTUAL AND TARGET ECONOMIC INCOME

Now let us step back from the calculations and ask how we are going to use them. In Table 11.1 we calculated our forecast or target economic income so that when we come to monitor the performance of the assets (or the division) we can compare the actual economic income of the period with the forecast economic income. Let us suppose that we are now at the end of period 1. The actual cash flows of the division turn out to be only $375 (instead of the forecast $475), and the forecast cash flows for periods 2 and 3 have been downgraded to $375, as shown in Table 11.2. In addition, a change in interest rates in the capital market has reduced the required rate of return from 20 to 18 percent.

Table 11.2 gives a comparison between the forecast and the actual cash flows for the assets as of the end of year 1. The first line of the table shows the original forecast that was made in year 0 for the three future years. Next are the actual cash flows to date up to the end of year 1 and the revised forecast cash flows for years 2 and 3. Now we can calculate the change in present value for years 1, 2, and 3, in the same way as in Table 11.1, except with a discount rate of 18 percent. The change in present value (economic depreciation) is calculated for each period in the fifth line of the table, and we obtain the corresponding economic income in the next line.

The economic income of −$37.88 for year 1 is made up of actual cash flows of $375 minus economic depreciation of $412.88. This economic depreciation represents the difference between the original forecast present value of $1,000 in year 0 and the newly calculated present value of $587.12 at the end of year 1. Alternatively, we can describe year 1's economic depreciation of −$412.88 as being made up of the original forecast economic depreciation of $275 (Table 11.1) plus the unanticipated decrease in the economic value of the assets by the end of year 1 ($137.88). The latter amount ($137.88) reflects the reduction in years 2 and 3 of the forecast cash

Table 11.2 *Realized economic income for year 1 and revised target economic income for years 2 and 3 (dollars)*

	End of year		
	1	**2**	**3**
Net cash flow forecast in period 0	475.00	475.00	474.00
Actual cash flow at the end of period 1	375.00		
Revised forecast at the end of period 1		375.00	375.00
Present value of revised forecast at 18%	587.12	317.80	0
Change in present value (economic depreciation)	−412.88	−269.32	−317.80
Target economic income	−37.88	105.68	57.20
Target economic rate of return		0.18	0.18

flows valued at a reduced discount rate of 18 percent. The revised target economic income levels for years 2 and 3 reflect the new cash flow forecasts and the new discount rate.

While the realized economic income for year 1 is a loss of $37.88, the new target economic income (and rates of return) for years 2 and 3 is based on the revised present value of the cash flows. The principle here is that the economic income that is realized for the year reflects not only the cash flow for the year but also any revisions in present value of the cash flow forecasts for the future. As a result, after unexpectedly good or bad performance is reported for the year, management starts the next year with a clean slate.

WHY MANAGERS PREFER TO USE ACCOUNTING NUMBERS

Companies customarily do not calculate the economic rate of return when measuring the past performance of individual projects or divisions. They prefer to calculate a rate of return based upon accounting earnings and book values of assets. There are two possible reasons for this approach. First, nonfinancial managers are more accustomed to working with accounting numbers, such as those in monthly and quarterly profit reports, than with cash flows and economic earnings. The number of managers who know the definition of economic depreciation and how it should be calculated may be small. In contrast, most managers understand accounting depreciation. The second reason why managers use accounting numbers is that they sometimes believe that data about asset values and future cash flows that are required for the measurement of economic income are not available.

You will see from Appendix 11.1 that it is not possible to draw very meaningful economic interpretations from accounting numbers unless sufficient information is available to determine the cash flows and the economic value of the assets. We shall return to this point subsequently.

CALCULATING ACCOUNTING TARGET INCOME AND THE TARGET ACCOUNTING RATE OF RETURN

Table 11.3 summarizes how the cash flows in Table 11.1 would be reported to management in accounting terms. In the first line we calculate the book value of the asset assuming straight-line depreciation. We could have used the accelerated cost recovery system (ACRS) depreciation (see Chapter 4), but instead have used straight-line depreciation for clarity of presentation. If the assets cost $900, the depreciation charge in each year will be $300. Thus the book value at the end of the first year is $900 − $300, or $600. To obtain the book value at the end of the second year we subtract another year's depreciation charge of $300 from the book value of $600 for a book

Table 11.3   *Calculating target accounting income and the target accounting rate of return (dollars)*

	End of year			
	0	1	2	3
Book value of asset (using straight-line depreciation)	900	600	300	0
Net cash flow		475	475	474
Depreciation (straight-line)		300	300	300
Accounting income (cash flow minus accounting depreciation)		175	175	174
Accounting rate of return		0.1944	0.2917	0.5800

value of $300. In the second line of the table is the cash flow, from which we subtract book depreciation in order to obtain accounting income. The accounting rate of return or **return on capital employed** (ROCE) is calculated by dividing the accounting income by the book value of the asset at the beginning of the period. It is apparent that the annual ROCE based on the book values need not be constant. In fact, ROCE rapidly increases in our example. It is easy to see why: Accounting income is constant from one period to another, whereas book values are declining.

It is interesting to compare the assets' accounting depreciation with their economic depreciation. In year 1, economic depreciation is $275, while accounting depreciation is $300. Because the division is overdepreciating its assets, the target accounting rate of return (19.44 percent) is below the economic rate of return (20 percent) in the first year. In year 2, economic depreciation is $330, which compares with accounting depreciation of $300. Because the division is now underdepreciating its assets, the accounting rate of return (29.17 percent) is now higher than the economic rate of return (20 percent). In year 3, the difference really is striking, for accounting depreciation of $300 is far below economic depreciation of $395. As a result, the accounting rate of return (58.00 percent) is far above the economic rate of return (20 percent). If we had used ACRS for depreciation, the contrast with economic depreciation would have been even more pronounced.

Unless management understands the relationship between economic rates of return and accounting rates of return, it might interpret the numbers in Table 11.3 to mean that the division's forecast performance is poor in year 1, adequate in year 2, and very good in year 3. Such an impression would be false. The division's expected economic performance actually does not change from year to year, as we have already shown in Table 11.1.

Companies that set a minimum level of ROCE to be achieved by a division in each period must recognize that the accounting ROCE can vary from one period to another, simply because book values do not reflect accurate estimates of economic depreciation. Even if the division consists of many projects starting and ending in different periods, the resulting ROCE will not necessarily be constant, for two reasons. First, divisions and companies frequently invest not on a continuing basis but in large lumps or in uneven flows. Second, some divisions include major units of plant whose depreciation schedule represents a dominant proportion of the division's depreciation charges. In both cases we would not expect the book value of the assets to be constant unless capital expenditures equaled book depreciation.[1]

The example in Table 11.3 describes the forecast earnings of the assets. But, just as in the case of economic income, earnings forecasts can be proven to be in error after the fact. Table 11.4 shows what the realized accounting rate of return for the project in Table 11.3 is in period 1, when the assets' cash flow turns out to be $375 instead of $475. Year 1's realized accounting rate of return turns out to be 8.33 percent rather than the targeted 19.44 percent. Because income is related to depreciated book value of the assets rather than to their economic value, the fluctuations in realized accounting rates of return derive entirely from changes in cash flow.

How to Obtain the Realized Internal Rate of Return from Accounting Data

In the previous section, we showed how a company can calculate economic income and set targets based on economic rates of return. Using the same

Table 11.4   *Comparison of actual accounting income with target for year 1 (dollars)*

	End of year 1
Cash flow (actual)	375
Depreciation (straight-line)	300
Accounting income	75
Accounting rate of return (75/900)	0.0833

[1]Solomon and Laya (1966) show that ROCE will be constant and equal to the cost of capital only when the rate of investment grows at a rate equal to the cost of capital. This condition will hold when a corporation's net inflow (or outflow) of cash is exactly zero.

data, we demonstrated how many companies actually set targets and measure performance. If performance calculations use accounting numbers, under what conditions can we determine the internal rate of return that actually was earned? It is necessary to be able to obtain the internal rate of return from accounting information if we are to link the accounting rate of return (ROCE) data in a company's management information system with the targets that have been set in terms of discounted cash flow and required rates of return for new capital investment. In practice, a measurement problem arises from the fact that investment decisions usually are made because the forecast internal rate of return on an investment exceeds the required rate of return. A significant danger of inconsistency exists when, subsequent to investment in an asset, management measures the financial performance of the asset using accounting rates of return and does not know how to compare performance in accounting terms with the target required rate of return based upon market costs of capital. Management should be able to calculate an internal rate of return from the accounting performance data, so that this internal rate of return can be compared with the target required rate of return that has been set for the asset (or group of assets, or division).

We shall show that there is a weighted average of the accounting rates of return earned by an asset that is equal to the asset's internal rate of return to date. Thus it is possible to use accounting data to calculate the economic performance of an asset or division. However, to do so it is necessary for management to be able to calculate the economic value of the asset at the end of the period over which performance is being measured. This requires an estimate of the present value of the expected cash flows for the project's remaining life. Without this additional information, economic performance cannot be measured correctly from the accounting performance data.

Table 11.5 continues the example from Tables 11.1 through 11.4, showing accounting data for the division after it has been operating for a period of three years. The first line gives book values of the division at the end of each year. The initial cost of the assets remains at $900, representing the initial book value. The second line shows market values (not present values in this application), assumed in this case to be zero in the final period. Also shown are actual accounting income (not known previously) and ROCE for each period. The question that we wish to answer is, what is the IRR on the division's assets over the past three years? You might be tempted to average the ROCEs, and hope that the average ROCE of 22.22 percent equals the IRR. In fact the average ROCE of 22.22 percent is above the IRR, which we shall show to be 19.789 percent.

Obtaining the IRR from a sequence of ROCEs requires the solution to the following equation for the IRR:

$$k = \frac{ROCE_1 w_1 + ROCE_2 w_2 + ROCE_3 w_3}{w_1 + w_2 + w_3} \tag{11.1}$$

Table 11.5 *Deriving the actual cash flows from the accounting data and calculating the IRR from ex post data (dollars)*

	End of year			
	0	**1**	**2**	**3**
Book value	900	600	300	0
Economic value of asset	900	not required	not required	0
Book value depreciation		300	300	300
Accounting income		75	250	50
Net cash flow		375	550	350
ROCE		.0833	.4167	.1667

where k is the internal rate of return, $ROCE_1$ is the accounting rate of return in period 1, and w_1 is the book value of the assets at the beginning of period 1 discounted for one period at the rate k. This formula is derived in Appendix 11.1. Substituting into equation (11.1) the values for the accounting rates of return calculated in Table 11.5,

$$k = \frac{8.33w_1 + 41.67w_2 + 16.67w_3}{w_1 + w_2 + w_3} \tag{11.2}$$

where the weights are $w_1 = 900/(1 + k)$, $w_2 = 600/(1 + k)^2$, and $w_3 = 300/(1 + k)^3$.

The internal rate of return (IRR) is found by iteration. Let us assume initially (and arbitrarily) that $k = 0$ on the right-hand side of equation (11.2), and that we wish to calculate k on the left-hand side.

$$k = \frac{(8.33 \times 900) + (41.67 \times 600) + (16.67 \times 300)}{900 + 600 + 300}$$

$k = 20.83\%$

The object is to obtain a value for k on the left-hand side that equals the value for k substituted on the right-hand side. Because our initial estimate of $k = 0$ on the right-hand side does not equal $k = 20.83\%$ on the left-hand side, our initial estimate of k was incorrect. We can obtain a better estimate by substituting $k = 20.83\%$ on the right-hand side to obtain

$$k = \left(\left(8.33 \times \frac{900}{(1 + 0.2083)}\right) + \left(41.67 \times \frac{600}{(1 + 0.2083)^2}\right)\right.$$

$$\left.+ \left(16.67 \times \frac{300}{(1 + 0.2083)^3}\right)\right) \bigg/ \left(\frac{900}{(1 + 0.2083)} + \frac{600}{(1 + 0.2083)^2}\right.$$

$$\left.+ \frac{300}{(1 + 0.2083)^3}\right) = \frac{26,164.239}{1,325.868}$$

$k = 19.73\%$

Because the estimate of $k = 0.2083$ on the right-hand side once more is not equal to the calculated value of $k = 0.19789$ on the left-hand side of the equation, we must continue the iteration process. By continuing in this fashion, we converge rapidly on the internal rate of return of 19.789 percent. Note again that the IRR of 19.789 percent is different from the simple average of the ROCEs in Table 11.5 of 22.22 percent.

There is of course another way of deriving the IRR from the accounting data. We could use the cash flows given with the accounting data in Table 11.5 to calculate the IRR directly. The initial cost of the assets ($900) is the initial investment. To obtain the cash flows of years 1, 2, and 3 we have added the depreciation charge to the accounting income of the year. In year 1 the depreciation charge is $300, which, when added to the accounting income of $75, makes a total cash flow of $375. In year 2 the total net cash flow is $550, and in year 3 it is $350. The internal rate of return on this set of net cash flows is 19.789 percent.

We have shown how to obtain an IRR from accounting data in two ways: first by calculating a weighted average of the ROCEs, and second, the much simpler way, by using cash flows directly.

Why bother to provide two methods of finding the internal rate of return when one is so much simpler than the other? Kay (1976), and in a simpler form Franks and Hodges (1983), showed that, in order to obtain an internal rate of return from a sequence of accounting rates of return, one requires the cost and economic value, respectively, of the assets in the initial and final periods. The economic value is based on the present value of the assets' future cash flows. Since using economic values in the formula requires sufficient information to calculate the cash flows (as in Table 11.5), one could calculate the IRR directly from the cash flows. This point is important, for some financial analysts may not realize that economically meaningful information cannot be obtained from accounting numbers unless the numbers contain sufficient information to provide the corresponding cash flows.

If accounting rates of return only give meaningful signals of profitability when we have the cash flow figures available, why don't managers work with the cash flows instead of the accounting numbers? The simple answer is that many managers do not understand cash flow data. The previous analysis shows them how to interpret accounting data in an economically meaningful way if they feel uncomfortable with cash flow data.

Setting Accounting Targets Based on Economic Criteria

In our previous analysis we ignored taxes and for the sake of simplicity and clarity treated them as though they did not exist. Of course, tax cash flows have a significant impact on the financial performance of the assets of most companies. If we can calculate the incremental corporate taxes attributable to an asset or a division, we can calculate the after-tax ROCEs for the asset. A weighted average of these after-tax ROCEs then can be used to calculate the asset's internal rate of return, which can be compared with the (after-tax) required rate of return. Similarly, if we are given the after-tax required rate of return, we can calculate the equivalent after-tax period-by-period ROCEs for the asset by including the corporate tax effects attributable to the assets in the calculations in, for example, Table 11.3.

Let us address the problem of how to set the appropriate before-tax accounting target that is consistent with a desired after-tax economic rate of return. Some companies evaluate new investment on an after-tax cash flow rate of return basis (IRR), then proceed to set financial performance targets on the basis of before-tax (ROCE) accounting rates of return. Why would they do this? Because the corporate tax is assessed on a companywide basis, some companies believe that it is too complex to allocate precisely the amount of tax attributable to each division. As a result, managers in such companies tend to focus on before-tax accounting earnings when setting targets and analyzing past performance. If management can set its before-tax accounting earnings targets in a way that is consistent with (although usually different from) the required after-tax cash flow rates of return, all may be well. Let us examine a familiar example to see how consistent targets can be defined.

In Chapter 4 we described the cash flows for a five-year project, which you see reproduced in Table 11.6, although slightly modified. This example assumes depreciation based upon the accelerated cost recovery system; an investment tax credit of 6.7 percent; and payment of taxes at the end of each year on a cash basis.

Management wants to set before-tax accounting rate of return targets that, if attained, would cause the project to generate the after-tax IRR of 18.90 percent. In this example the required accounting targets are easy to obtain.

Table 11.6   Cash flow and ACRS depreciation for a project (dollars)

	End of year					
	0	1	2	3	4	5
INVESTMENT						
1. Investment in machinery and equipment	−200	−900				50
2. Investment in working capital		−100				100
OPERATING CASH FLOW						
3. Revenue		525	1100	1150	1200	1100
4. Operating expenditure		−275	−550	−630	−810	−940
5. Net cash flow (before tax)	−200	−750	550	520	390	310
TAXES						
6. Net corporate income tax (see Table 4.2)		32	−145	−137	−77	6
7. Net cash flow	−200	−718	405	383	313	316
ACRS depreciation		160	234	223	223	223

We know that the cash flows in Table 11.6 generate the expected IRR of 18.90 percent, and we only need to calculate the before-tax accounting rates of return for the project based upon the same figures.

Table 11.7 shows the necessary calculations to obtain the before-tax accounting rates of return that are consistent with the cash flow data in Table 11.6 (with an 18.90 percent IRR). The relevant investment and income figures come from Table 4.1 in Chapter 4. We calculated the book value of investment in plant and working capital in each period and then calculated the ratio of before-tax reported income in each period to the book value of investment at the beginning of the same period. These results demonstrate that if management sets the before-tax accounting rate of return targets for each period given at the bottom of Table 11.7, and reaches these targets, the project will earn an after-tax internal rate of return of 18.90 percent, as described in Table 11.6.

The example shows that the required after-tax internal rates of return can be converted to the corresponding before-tax accounting rates of return that can be used as performance targets. The example also demonstrates that the appropriate accounting target is different in each period of the asset's life, even though the internal rate of return is constant.

Table 11.7   *Accounting earnings reported on a before-tax basis (dollars)*

	End of year					
	0	1	2	3	4	5
Investment in plant and equipment (book value)	200	940	706	483	260	
Investment in working capital (book value)		100	100	100	100	
Total investment (book value)	200	1040	806	583	360	
Revenue		525	1100	1150	1200	1100
Operating expenditure		−275	−550	−630	−810	−940
Depreciation		−160	−234	−223	−223	−223
Before-tax reported income		90	316	297	167	−63
Accounting rate of return		0.45	0.30	0.37	0.29	−0.18

The size of the difference between accounting targets and the economic rates of return varies with the type of asset, the speed with which it can be depreciated, the pattern of cash flows, and the resulting pattern of tax payments. What is most important to note is that a before-tax target cannot be obtained without knowing the incremental taxes attributable to an asset or a division. This is a difficult problem to solve when setting targets for an asset or a division if the firm pays taxes as a whole, not for each division. One division may have a tax loss at the same time that another has a taxable profit. Because the loss in one division may shield the profit in the other, the company's overall tax bill may be very different from the sum of the tax bills of the individual divisions as separate entities. The implication of this simple analysis is that it may be difficult to obtain accurate estimates of before-tax returns for divisions of a company when taxes are paid at the corporate level. This problem also exists when targets are set for a profit center within a division.

We have analyzed the relationship between accounting and cash flow rates of return, because management uses both in financial control systems. Some financial analysts believe that there is no connection between the rates of return calculated on the two sets of numbers, while others believe that they are comparable numbers that need no further adjustment. Both conclusions are wrong. However, to obtain a required return on capital employed in accounting terms requires us to start with the required rate of return for the asset (or group of assets) given its risk, and then to determine the accounting rates of return period-by-period that are consistent with the required rate of return. If management wants to use a before-tax ROCE performance target that corresponds to the appropriate after-tax required rate of return, it must know not only the cash flow profile of the asset (or division) and the accounting conventions used to report earnings, but also the incremental tax effects that the division has on the corporation.

Some Lessons from the Measurement of Economic Income

The comparison we have made between the characteristics of economic income and accounting income has revealed some important lessons concerning performance measurement, four of which we review next.

ECONOMIC VERSUS ACCOUNTING NUMBERS

Management can use cash flows (and economic values) or accounting numbers to set targets and measure performance. The data requirements are the same in each case, as we showed in earlier examples. In order to obtain meaningful economic numbers from accounting numbers, it is necessary to have sufficient information to be able to calculate cash flows and economic (present) values.

As many operating managers are accustomed to dealing with accounting numbers, it may be easier for them to continue using such numbers. However, if accounting depreciation is very different from economic depreciation, the accounting rate of return may vary significantly from one period to another, even if the division's economic performance is unchanged from one period to the next. The example in Tables 11.1 through 11.5 demonstrates this point.[2] One way to remove these potentially confusing variations is to adopt accounting depreciation schedules that are closer to economic depreciation. Economic depreciation schedules require forecasts of the way in which cash flows are expected to change during the remaining life of an asset. This is fine if information is available from the cash flow patterns of similar previous assets. In practice, cash flows on specific assets ordinarily are not recorded separately in most information systems, although often they can be deduced from accounting information for a profit center.

If discounted cash flow is used in the investment decision for the new asset, the cash flow forecasts that were used in the project appraisal can also be used to calculate economic depreciation schedules. If the asset performs as expected, the economic depreciation schedule remains valid. If perfor-

[2]In 1983 AT&T acknowledged the difference between accounting and economic depreciation by writing off $5.5 billion of under-depreciated assets.

mance does not meet targets, however, and forecasts must be changed, economic depreciation schedules may have to be recalculated to go with the resulting new cash flow forecasts, as we did in Table 11.2.

THE ECONOMIC VALUE OF ASSETS: COSTS OR PRESENT VALUES?

In Table 11.1 the initial value of the asset was based on present value, while in Table 11.3 it was based on cost. Which basis of valuation is chosen depends upon the objectives of the performance measurement system. If management wishes to determine if the division's performance provides an adequate return on assets, the cost of the assets should be used. Alternatively, if management wishes to determine if the division has increased in value over the period, present values of the division should be used. In this latter case, the principle is the same as in evaluating a portfolio of common stocks. Performance should be based on the present value or market value of the common stocks, not their original cost, if one wishes to know whether the portfolio has increased in value.

TARGET SETTING AND PERFORMANCE MEASURES SHOULD REFLECT RISK

If a target ROCE for a period is to be set for a division, the target should reflect the relative risks of the division's assets. The target ROCE that a division needs to earn should be consistent with the risk-adjusted required rates of return for the group of assets whose performance is being measured. The ROCEs should be consistent with an IRR for the assets that is greater than or equal to the assets' required rate of return, given their risk.

MEASURING THE MANAGER'S PERFORMANCE

Merely comparing actual profit with the forecast will not reveal whether management has done well or badly. Management's profit forecasts are contingent upon various other forecasts for the economy and the industry regarding factors such as economic growth or consumption. It is unlikely that the average or mean of any such forecasts will be realized. If demand has altered in the economy, a division's revenues also will be affected. Measurement of divisional performance must take account of unexpected economic change, including changes in interest rates and required rates of return. The greater the risk reflected in the divisional target rate of return, the greater the deviation from the target that can occur through no fault of divisional management. Variations from target performance standards always require interpretation and diagnosis.

Diagnosing Performance Variances

Calculating the economic income of a project or of a division is only the first stage in measuring performance. Let us suppose that we have calculated the division's economic income for the year, and it exceeds the forecast economic income. Has the division performed well? In fact we cannot answer this question without further information. Unless we know how the economy and industry have performed, we cannot know whether the division has underperformed or overperformed. This reveals two important aspects of performance measurement. We are interested in the division's performance because this information can influence future investment decisions. We are also interested in individual managerial performance, however, and to measure that we must know if the division has outperformed the competition.

This approach to performance involves the same criterion that we applied to our mutual fund manager. We wanted to know if the returns on the portfolio exceeded the returns on the market index, after taking into account differences in risk between the portfolio and the market index. Measuring divisional performance, though, is much more difficult than measuring portfolio performance. After all, we do not have a market index to compare with divisional income. An alternative is to compare the company's profit performance with the industry's profit performance or with that of selected companies in the industry. In addition to looking at rates of return on capital, we could compare changes in other corporate data, such as market share. Measurement of managerial performance actually cannot be limited to consideration of financial data. What is required is a management audit that will reveal efficiency or inefficiency in terms of real variables over which managers have direct control in the operation of the business. Financial performance data represent only one of the important diagnostic tools that may help to highlight potential problems. (See D. Solomons for a detailed discussion.)

The Role of Forecasting

In much of our discussion of performance measurement we have required the calculation of the present value of future cash flows. To compute such present values, cash flows must be forecast over some time period. Clearly, forecasting horizons will vary from one company to another depending upon the product life cycle. For extractive industries such as coal and oil, the forecasting period may be more than ten years, whereas for consumer goods industries probably it will be less than five years. The forecasts that are required to calculate economic income are useful not only to measure actual income against forecasts, but also to enable management to identify those areas of the business where expansion or contraction may be necessary.

Forecasting cash flows is most useful when the firm considers it has a competitive advantage, or when it believes a scarcity will continue. Beyond that point, the best guess should be that profits will be earned to provide only a fair rate of return. Such profits should be based upon anticipated product prices that allow the firm to earn the risk-adjusted required rate of return on the asset—but no more. In this sense, firms need to make forecasts only for the periods when they still expect to be making abnormally high profits; profit estimates for subsequent periods can be based upon a fair rate of return.

Summary

The financial analyst should understand the link between the investment decision and subsequent reported performance. A company that uses discounted cash flows to appraise an investment and afterward evaluates the profits of such investments using an accrual accounting system may be introducing serious inconsistencies. Similarly, in a company that evaluates investments on an after-tax cash flow basis but monitors results on a before-tax basis, additional inconsistencies may arise.

Target accounting rates of return should be as consistent with target internal rates of return as possible. The relationships between the two can be measured, and internal rates of return can be translated into the corresponding accounting rate of return targets. These targets will differ from one division to another because of differences in risk. Accounting profit targets characteristically differ over time, even if the underlying cash flows do not vary. The range of permissible performance variations from target must reflect the basis of the forecasts and the underlying risk of the assets.

When measuring performance we seek the answers to two principal questions. The first is: Has the division outperformed the industry after adjustment for any differences between the division and the rest of the industry? The second question is: Has management performed as well as could be expected under the circumstances? These two questions cannot be answered using financial input alone. Such judgments require an audit of operating performance as well as evaluation of financial performance variables.

Appendix 11.1 Proof That the IRR Is a Weighted Average of the Accounting Rates of Return

We shall prove that the internal rate of return (IRR) on an asset can be obtained from a weighted average of the returns on capital employed (ROCEs), using the following variables:

V_t = book value of assets at time t

y_t = accounting income in period ending at time t

a_t = accounting rate of profit (ROCE) for time t ($a_t = y_t/V_{t-1}$)

c_t = cash flow occurring in time t, assumed to occur at the end of the period

Assume that an accountant's definition of income y_t is such that the following identity is always satisfied:

$$c_t = y_t + V_{t-1} - V_t \tag{A11.1.1}$$

Note that in this definition all surpluses or deficits on revaluations and extraordinary items are passed through the income statement. Also we must assume that initial book value V_0 is equal to either the asset's cost or its present value. In addition, the final period's asset value V_N equals the corresponding market value or its present value. The internal rate of return (k) is defined by the equation

$$-V_0 + \frac{c_1}{(1 + k)} + \frac{c_2}{(1 + k)^2} + \cdots + \frac{c_N + V_N}{(1 + k)^N} = 0 \tag{A11.1.2}$$

If we substitute our basic accounting identity (A11.1.1) for c_t in equation (A11.1.2) we obtain

$$\sum_{t=1}^{N} \left(\frac{y_t}{(1 + k)^t} - k \frac{V_{t-1}}{(1 + k)^t} \right) = 0 \tag{A11.1.3}$$

We can rearrange equation (A11.1.3) to obtain

$$k = \frac{\displaystyle\sum_{t=1}^{N} a_t V_{t-1}/(1 + k)^t}{\displaystyle\sum_{t=1}^{N} V_{t-1}/(1 + k)^t} \tag{A11.1.4}$$

In other words, the IRR is a weighted average of the ROCEs, where the weights are the book values for the previous period discounted at the IRR.

Despite the apparent circularity of equation (A11.1.4), it does provide a well-defined iterative procedure for calculating an IRR (although one that naturally is subject to the usual problems of calculating IRRs if there is a multiplicity of roots).[1]

Review Questions

1. What is economic depreciation? How can it be measured?
2. Why is it that accounting depreciation rules usually do not provide good estimates of economic depreciation?
3. Explain why economic income usually does not equal accounting income.
4. "Accounting income measures of performance are more convenient to use than economic income measures because fewer data are required." Is this statement correct?
5. Under what conditions will the accounting rate of return for a project be constant and equal to the internal rate of return?
6. The arithmetic average ROCE for a sequence of accounting rates of return will equal the IRR. Is this statement true or false? Give reasons for your answer.
7. What difficulties does the presence of taxes produce in setting targets and measuring the performance of a division of a company?
8. What are the reasons economic income may differ from what had been forecasted?
9. Why do many firms measure the accounting return on capital employed (ROCE) for a division or company? How useful is this measure as an indicator of managerial efficiency?

Problems

*1. An individual invests $1,000 in a mutual fund whose portfolio is made up entirely of equities. The equities are concentrated in the electronics industry, which was estimated to be about 50 percent more risky than the Standard & Poor's 500 index. At the end of the year, the investment is worth $1,350, while the S & P 500 index has risen 30 percent during the same period. The risk-free rate is 10 percent.

[1]This proof is taken from Franks and Hodges (1983).

(a) How would you measure the portfolio manager's performance? Make any assumptions necessary to answer the question.

(b) Why is it difficult to measure a portfolio manager's performance over only one year?

*2. An asset costs $1,000 and has a five-year life. The forecast cash flows are $335 per year, and the asset's IRR is 20 percent (rounded).

(a) Compare the asset's book value at the end of each year (using straight-line depreciation and assuming a zero residual value) with its economic value at the end of each year; ignore taxation for the sake of simplicity.

(b) Calculate the asset's forecast accounting ROCE for each year.

3. An asset costs $1,000 and has a five-year life. Its forecast after-tax cash flows are given below, and its IRR is 34 percent (rounded).

End of year	0	1	2	3	4	5
Cash flow	−1,000	840	420	210	120	85

(a) Compare the asset's economic value with its book value at the end of each year (using sum-of-the-year's-digits depreciation and assuming a zero residual value); no ITC is available.

(b) Calculate the asset's forecast accounting ROCE for each year. Why are the forecast ROCEs different from the asset's IRR?

*4. The expected cash flows of a project are given below. Calculate the IRR, the economic depreciation, and the economic income for each year of the project's life. Calculate the economic ROCE in each year.

End of year	0	1	2	3	4	5
Cash flow	−5,000	1,200	1,500	1,800	2,168	2,168

*5. Calculate the economic values and book values of the following project, given a required rate of return for the project of 15 percent and a straight-line depreciation policy (with no scrap value). Plot these values against time.

End of year	0	1	2	3	4	5	6
Net cash flow	−18,000	7,000	6,000	5,000	2,000	1,000	5,663

Explain the differences that you observe between the book value and the economic value of the asset. Calculate the accounting rate of return and discuss what would be the most appropriate form of accounting depreciation to use.

6. Using the cash flows in Problem 5, calculate the depreciation on a sum-of-the-year's digits policy. Plot the book value of the asset in each period, and compare this with the economic values calculated in Problem 5. Compare the accounting ROCE on the basis of sum-of-the-year's digits with the accounting ROCE using straight-line depreciation.

*7. A project's expected before-tax cash flows are given below:

End of year	0	1	2	3
Expected cash flow	−1,000	587	587	587

(a) Calculate the before-tax IRR.
(b) Calculate the after-tax cash flow assuming corporate taxes at 50 percent, straight-line depreciation, and no residual value or ITC.
(c) Calculate the after-tax IRR.
(d) Obtain the before-tax accounting performance targets.
(e) Compare the before-tax accounting performance targets with the after-tax IRR and the before-tax IRR. Explain the differences.

8. Wave, Inc., has purchased an asset for $1,000 that will produce the following net cash flows.

End of year	0	1	2	3	4
Net cash flow	−1,000	350	450	450	280

The company uses straight-line depreciation to calculate the accounting rate of return. Use the weighted average method illustrated in the chapter to calculate the IRR from the annual accounting rates of return. Ignore tax (for simplified calculation).

9. Asset beta values of companies competing with the Roto Division are given below. These beta values already have been adjusted to eliminate the effects of financial leverage in the manner described in Chapters 9 and 10. The risk-free rate is 8 percent, and the risk premium on the market portfolio is 9 percent.

Company	A	B	C	D	E
Beta value	1.00	1.15	1.12	1.17	1.06

(a) What should be the target nominal (economic) rate of return for the division?

(b) What are the implications if the accounting ROCE falls 5 percent below the target for the year? State any assumptions needed to answer the question.

(c) What are the implications if the economic ROCE falls 5 percent below the target for the year? State any assumptions needed to answer.

*10. The sales, quantities, and variable and fixed operating expenditures and depreciation of Division X are given below. The division currently is able to charge a premium on its product prices because of unpatented product advantages; this premium is reflected in the cash flow. A competitor would have to pay $0.8 million for similar assets. The expected economic life of the division's assets is ten years, without inflation the real after-tax required rate of return in the industry is 5 percent.

End of year	1	2	...	10
		(thousands of dollars)		
Sales	430	430	...	430
Variable operating expenditure	100	100	...	100
Fixed operating expenditure	167	167	...	167
Depreciation	100	100	...	100
Quantity (units)	300	300		300

Calculate the NPV of the division if the corporate tax rate is 50 percent.

References

Fisher, F. M., and J. J. McGowan, "On the Misuse of Accounting Rates of Return to Infer Monopoly Profits," *American Economic Review,* 73, no. 1 (March 1983): 82–87.

Franks, J. R., and S. D. Hodges, "The Use of Accounting Numbers in Target Setting and Performance Measurements: Implications for Managers and Regulators," presented at the Meeting of the American Finance Association, San Francisco, December 1983.

Kay, J. A., "Accountants, Too, Could be Happy in a Golden Age: The Accountant's Rate of Profit and the Internal Rate of Return," *Oxford Economic Papers,* 28, no. 3 (November 1976): 447–60.

Lerner, E. M., and W. T. Carleton, *A Theory of Financial Analysis,* New York: Harcourt, Brace Jovanovich, 1966.

Peasnell, K., "Some Formal Connections between Economic Values and Yields and

Accounting Numbers," *Journal of Business Finance and Accounting,* 9, no. 3 (Autumn 1982): 361–81.

Solomon, E., and J. C. Laya, "Measurements of Company Profitability: Some Systematic Errors in the Accounting Rate of Return," *Financial Research and Its Implications for Management Decisions,* edited by A. A. Robichek, New York: Wiley, 1966.

Solomons, D., *Divisional Performance: Measurement and Control,* New York: Financial Executives Research Foundation, 1965.

Stauffer, T. R., "The Measurement of Corporate Rates of Return: A Generalized Formalization," *Bell Journal of Economics,* 2, no. 2 (Autumn 1971): 434–69.

Treynor, J. L., "The Trouble with Earnings," *Financial Analysts Journal,* 28, no. 5 (September–October 1972): 41–43.

Valuation of Companies

One of the principal objectives of financial management is to maximize the value of the firm to its shareholders. In the next three chapters we discuss in more depth the means by which the value of the firm is determined. In Chapter 12 we first discuss the evidence that the stock market sets stock prices that reflect all available information concerning the value of a company's assets and liabilities. The fact that the market has been found to be relatively efficient in this respect means that discounted cash flow can be used by managers to estimate the effect of a capital investment decision on the market value of the firm's securities. However, the securities of many companies are not actively traded in the financial market. In Chapter 13 we show how the value of such a company can be estimated by comparing it with comparable companies that are traded in the financial market and by discounting the cash flows expected to be generated by the company. Finally, in Chapter 14 on acquisitions and mergers we discuss the economic and financial benefits attributable to the merging of companies' operations and show how the value of such benefits affects the prices that are offered and paid for companies.

12

The Efficiency of the Stock Market

In this chapter we consider some of the evidence concerning the efficiency of the stock market. "Efficiency" does not refer to the administrative or organizational efficiency of the stock market, but to the ability of the market to price securities quickly and fairly. An **efficient capital market** (or, alternatively, an informationally efficient financial market) is a market in which current securities prices reflect all available relevant information. The analysis of preceding chapters suggests that the market value of the firm should reflect the present value of all existing assets plus the net present value of the firm's growth opportunities that investors expect management to undertake. It follows that, if the stock market is efficient, equity prices will fully reflect the favorable effect of profitable capital investments in fixed assets. Conversely, unwise or unprofitable capital investment decisions will reduce the market value of the firm.

The volatility of stock market prices may give the impression that the market is somehow irrational. In fact, it would be surprising if the market were not volatile. The market for long-term government bonds may be volatile, but few would argue that it is irrational. Interest payments and redemption values are known with certainty in this market. Nevertheless, movements in the interest rates being used by investors to discount future bond cash flows are reflected simultaneously in movements in bond prices. Volatility of the bond market is a reflection of the efficiency of the market in translating changes in required rates of return into bond prices.

Similarly, changes in the discount rates that stockholders use to price stocks reflect changes in interest rates, but they also reflect changes in expectations concerning the future income stream (dividends and capital gains) to shareholders. Thus, we would expect that, in a rational stock market where investors seek returns that compensate for risk, stock prices will be volatile and change rapidly in response to changes in cash-flow risk as well as to changes in interest rates and expected income.

How quickly do individual share prices respond to new information that would imply a change in the economic value of the firm? In an efficient market, prices will respond to information quickly enough that investors cannot expect on average to make profits from dealing in the securities, after taking into account transactions costs. In other words, the net present value of expected returns in an efficient stock market would be zero.

Characteristics of the Capital Market

We shall review some of the characteristics of the capital market that we touched upon in Chapter 2, as well as consider the conditions that produce an efficient capital market.

PURCHASE AND SALE OF SECURITIES

EQUITY. An individual who wishes to buy or sell common stocks usually completes such a transaction through a broker. If the stock is not listed on a stock exchange, it may be traded "over the counter." That is, the stock may be bought from or sold directly to a securities firm that holds an inventory and "makes a market" in the common stock. (Although most securities are traded over-the-counter, the more active stocks in the largest companies are traded on the major exchanges. Approximately 90 percent of the dollar volume of trading on exchanges takes place on the New York Stock Exchange and the American Stock Exchange (which also is in New York City), while the remainder takes place on regional exchanges.) Dealers quote a **bid** price at which they are willing to buy the stock and a higher **asked** price at which they are willing to sell the stock. The difference between these two prices is called the **spread.** This spread is the source of the dealer's gross revenues, from which are deducted operating expenses to leave a profit.

If the security is listed on an organized exchange such as the New York Stock Exchange, the broker telephones the order to a member of his firm on the floor of the Exchange. The member proceeds immediately to the

trading post at which the security is traded. At the trading post he or she may encounter a **trading crowd** of floor brokers buying and selling the stock among themselves. If the member does not encounter another floor broker at the trading post, the order can be executed by buying from or selling to the **specialist,** who is a member of the exchange acting as a dealer quoting bid and asked prices for the stock. Generally, brokers prefer to deal directly with one another in the trading crowd, for in this way they may be able to avoid paying the specialist's profit which is reflected in the bid–ask spread. In contrast, when one is buying securities over the counter, there is no way of avoiding the spread.

Generally speaking, the size and the amount of trading activity determine whether a firm's shares will be listed and traded on a major stock exchange. Forces are at work, however, to reduce differences in the ways in which shares of large and small firms are traded. The first depends on regulation: Since May 1975, brokerage firms have not been allowed to charge fixed commissions for making transactions. Consequently, investors can shop around for the lowest cost of transacting a purchase or sale. Technology also affects the industry. The Securities and Exchange Commission has required the stock exchanges to make their stock price quotations available in a combined quotation system since 1978. The electronic availability of this information reduces the cost to brokers of searching several markets to find the best terms. The final stage of this evolution could well be a single national market for common stocks, electronically linked.

Besides actually executing trades, brokers perform many services for their clients, including securities analysis and provision of various technical and economic information services. While these services are provided at nominal charges and often are free, the broker expects to be compensated by commissions that are received for the execution of orders to buy and sell securities. Present-day commissions are negotiated between the broker and the client. One can expect to pay between 1 and 2 percent of the value of the transaction. While these costs are not high by international standards, it should be obvious that frequent trading of a security will cause a client to incur substantial cumulative costs. Thus many investors adopt a "buy and hold" strategy.

DEBT. Over 95 percent of bond transactions take place in the over-the-counter market, although the bonds of the larger companies can be traded on the New York Stock Exchange. The dealing spreads on bond transactions average about one half of one percent. The dealing spreads on bonds and stocks reflect a number of factors, including the amount traded (actively traded issues provide greater revenue to dealers to cover the fixed costs of their operations) and liquidity. Actively traded issues involve a smaller spread because incoming buy and sell orders are less likely to produce large price changes and hence involve less risk to the value of the dealer's inventory of securities.

PRIMARY AND SECONDARY SECURITIES MARKETS

A market in securities performs two important functions. The first function, that of a **primary market,** is to provide both existing listed companies and new companies with the facility for raising new capital. The second function is to permit existing holders of securities to sell their holdings speedily and preferably at low cost. This latter function is usually described as the **secondary market.** In this chapter we shall be concerned with the secondary market for common stocks.

The secondary market functions of a stock exchange often are described in critical terms, as if providing a facility for exchanging ownership does not contribute to the creation of wealth in the economy. Without a secondary market, however, it is doubtful whether individuals or institutions would subscribe as much new capital to companies, because it would be more difficult to sell the securities in order to rebalance portfolios or to increase consumption. In Table 12.1 we have reproduced statistics for the market value of United States securities listed on the stock exchanges at the end of 1979. The total value was slightly under $1.5 trillion. The majority of these securities are owned by individuals or their trustees (Table 12.2), and such relatively widespread holdings of securities generally are attributed to the existence of a very active secondary market.[1]

The fact that securities are marketable allows them to be used by investors as collateral for borrowing. Also, marketability helps shareholders to reduce risks by holding a diversified portfolio of securities. It should be clear that if risk can be reduced by diversification, the cost of finance to industry will be lower when shareholders can trade securities in order to increase diversification and reduce risk.

Table 12.1   *Analysis of company securities listed on exchanges at December 31, 1979*

Classification	Number of securities	Market value (millions of dollars)
Bonds	3,212	465,269
Preferred stocks	870	27,326
Common stocks	2,539	994,945
Total	6,621	1,487,540

Source: Securities and Exchange Commission, *Annual Report,* 1980.

[1]The totals in the two tables do not agree because over-the-counter stocks are not included in Table 12.2.

Table 12.2   *Market value of common and preferred stockholdings by investor type at December 31, 1979 (billions of dollars)*

Private nonsecured pension funds	123.7
Open-end investment companies	34.8
Other investment companies	1.8
Life insurance companies	40.5
Property and liability insurance companies	24.8
Personal trust funds	106.4
Common trust funds	NA
Mutual savings banks	4.7
State and local retirement funds	37.1
Foundations	40.3
Educational endowments	10.2
Subtotal	424.3
Less: Institutional holdings of investment company shares	8.5
Total institutional investors	415.8
Foreign investors	80.2
Other domestic investors (including individuals)	652.6
Total stock outstanding	1,148.6

Source: Securities and Exchange Commission, *Annual Report,* 1980.

Conditions Conducive to Efficiency in the Capital Market

In this chapter we wish to establish whether the financial markets that we have described are efficient. The securities market can be described as efficient if prices in the market behave as though they were obtained in a perfect market. First, we shall compare the concept of an efficient market to the model of a perfect market that is used in economic theory.

DEFINITION OF EFFICIENCY

The model of a perfectly competitive market requires a number of assumptions: that there are many buyers and sellers in relation to the volume of transactions, that all participants are "price takers" rather than "price makers" (that is, no one participant deals in the market in sufficiently large scale to influence prices), that all participants can obtain all the relevant information that they need costlessly, and that there are no barriers to entry, transactions costs, or taxes. Under such ideal conditions, competition among market participants would ensure that security prices reflect virtually instantaneously the information that is available to all.

All the strict assumptions that define perfectly competitive markets need not be met for there to exist an efficient capital market. It is only necessary that dealing costs are not too high, that the relevant information is available to a sufficiently large number of investors, and that no individual participant is of sufficient wealth to dominate the market in any sense. As such conditions are not very stringent, it should not be too surprising if the evidence indicates that United States capital markets are efficient.[2]

A market is defined as efficient if transactions prices reflect fully and in an unbiased way all relevant information available to market participants at the time. It is important to know whether a market is efficient for a number of reasons. First, we cannot expect to obtain positive net present values (on average) from transactions in markets that are efficient. If prices reflect fully all relevant information available to investors, no one investor can obtain the competitive advantage necessary to obtain positive net present values systematically from market transactions. If capital markets are shown to be efficient, financial managers cannot expect to profit from speculating in capital markets. Instead, they should seek investments in *inefficient* product markets where they can earn returns in excess of the cost of capital, or positive net present values, while meeting their capital needs at competitive costs in the financial market.

If securities are priced efficiently, their prices reflect forecasts of expected benefits from owning future cash flows capitalized at appropriate discount rates. Of course, individuals can disagree on forecasts, and it is this disagreement that results in transactions. The resolution of expectations in the transaction process produces an unbiased valuation in an efficient market. Fama (1965) describes such a market as a fair game in which all participants have an equal opportunity for gains. Information emerging subsequent to transactions may prove the market valuation to have been incorrect, and some investors may be seen with hindsight to have experienced unusual gains or losses. However, no individual relying only on foresight can expect unusual gains (or losses) on average if the market is a fair game.

Thus we have the **efficient markets hypothesis:** that prices of securities rapidly reflect all available price-sensitive information. Such a hypothesis should be subject to various tests. Although a proposition cannot be proved by statistical tests, it can be disproved in the sense that evidence of market behavior may be inconsistent with either the hypothesis itself or its major implications.

Statistical research on this subject is now substantial. The University of Chicago has produced a data base containing monthly share prices for all companies listed on the New York and American Stock Exchanges for over

---

[2]Grossman and Stiglitz (1980) point out that if there are costs to obtaining information such costs inevitably must reduce the efficiency of the market.

fifty years. These data have been available to numerous other universities and have been used in scores of tests. In the main, results of these tests support the efficient market hypothesis. At the same time, there are a number of studies providing results that do not appear to be consistent with efficiency.

SOME IMPLICATIONS OF EFFICIENCY FOR FINANCIAL MANAGERS

The question of market efficiency is of fundamental importance to financial managers. Consider a few of the reasons. First, and most important, the net present value investment criterion for projects assumes an efficient financial market. We use the rates of return available in the financial market as a bench mark against which to compare project profitability. Remember that projects can be considered profitable only if they provide an expected return greater than the returns on financial securities of equivalent risk. The assumption is that financial securities of equivalent risk are fairly priced and therefore provide an expected rate of return equal to what investors require given the risk. Securities that are priced in this way represent zero NPV investments. If such securities were not priced properly and provided either a negative or positive NPV investment, we could no longer use such securities as a bench mark for projects. For example, suppose that securities used as a bench mark have a negative NPV. Even if a project has a positive NPV compared with the negative NPV securities, it still might not provide investors with a sufficiently large NPV to compensate for the wrong bench mark.

A second implication of market efficiency for financial managers concerns the timing of financing decisions. Some financial managers believe that there is a right time and a wrong time to raise funds by new issues of common stock. Such timing decisions, they believe, depend on the overall level of stock market prices. When market prices are low, new issues should not be made; when market prices are high, new issues should be made. However, if financial markets are efficient, managers have no way of knowing whether common stock prices tomorrow will be higher or lower than they are today. As a consequence, there is no "right" or "wrong" time to issue common stock. Indeed, if the financial manager could forecast where the market is going, he or she really should be managing a mutual fund rather than directing the financial affairs of nonfinancial companies.

A third implication of financial market efficiency concerns mergers and acquisitions. If financial markets are efficient, financial securities are fairly valued and properly priced. If one company wishes to acquire another, it may have to pay a bid price for the acquired company's common stock that is well above the market price in order to obtain control. If the market price is fair, a bid price premium can be justified only if the acquiring company can increase the value of the assets of the acquired company. If the bid premium cannot be justified by benefits from merging that will increase the value of the acquired company's assets, the merger will result in a transfer of wealth from the acquiring company's shareholders to the acquired company's shareholders. The bid price will prove to have been too high, because the company's stock was fairly priced in an efficient financial market in the first place.

Tests of Market Efficiency

Broadly speaking, evidence on the efficiency of the stock market can be divided (Roberts (1967)) into three categories:

weak form hypothesis, that current stock prices already reflect all information that can be gleaned from past price changes

semistrong form hypothesis, that current stock prices reflect not only the information implied by historical price changes but also information implied by all publicly available information relevant to a company's securities

strong form hypothesis, that current stock prices reflect all relevant information including information available only to company insiders or other privileged groups

These three categories of hypotheses classify levels of market efficiency according to the amount and the availability of information reflected in share prices. Let us consider some of the better-known tests of each hypothesis.

WEAK FORM TESTS OF MARKET EFFICIENCY

Weak form tests of market efficiency have to do with any information that may be implied in past price changes. Some investors and analysts (called "chartists") believe that by plotting past price changes for an individual stock or for the market as a whole they can make better predictions of future price changes. If the market is efficient, analyzing past price patterns for the purpose of prediction is useless, because all information that could be gleaned from such analyses already is reflected in the current price.

Suppose that one share of IBM common stock sells for $100 per share on Monday and that it is expected confidently that the price will be $125 on Friday. How would the price of the stock change during the week? Figures 12.1 (a), (b), and (c) illustrate three possible price patterns. In Figure 12.1(a) we see a last-minute change in the price. In Figure 12.1(b) we see the price

Figure 12.1   *Three hypothetical expected stock price patterns*

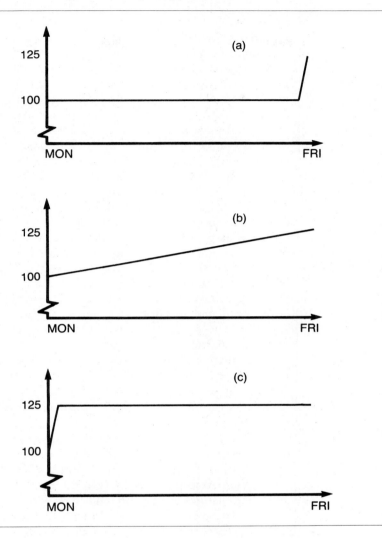

changing gradually over the week from $100 to $125. Finally, part (c) of the figure shows an almost instantaneous change in the price to $125 on Monday. Which of these price patterns is consistent with an efficient market?

It takes only a little reflection to realize that Figure 12.1 (c) represents the correct pattern for the price in a competitive market. If the other two patterns were to represent the behavior of the market for IBM stock, speculators would find it easy to grow rich by selling stock on Friday that they had purchased earlier during the week. This profitable game would attract more competition among speculators, so combined demand would drive the price up to $125 before Friday. Only those speculators who bought the stock first would profit from their transactions. With sufficient competition, the price would rise to $125 on Monday within minutes after market participants confidently expected that the price was going to be $125 by Friday.

Samuelson (1965) and Mandelbrot (1966) prove that if there were no transactions costs in a speculative market, if all relevant information were freely available to all market participants, and if all investors shared the same expectations over a common time period (as in Figure 12.1), price changes would reflect new information instantaneously and therefore would be random. By random, we mean that it is impossible to predict tomorrow's price change on the basis of today's price change. For example, if prices rise today, this will have no bearing on tomorrow's price change, if price changes are random. The reason that prices change randomly in an efficient market is that if the price level reflects all available information at the time, subsequent changes to the price level must reflect new information. By definition, new information is unpredictable; therefore, the resulting price changes are unpredictable and random. Obviously, the assumptions made by Samuelson and by Mandelbrot when they showed that price changes in speculative markets are random cannot be satisfied completely in reality. Fama (1970) has argued, however, that it would be sufficient for a speculative market to be efficient and for price changes in the market to be random if two assumptions hold: Transactions costs are not excessive and there is no group of market participants with consistently superior information.

Share price changes are said to follow a **random walk** if all future prices represent a random departure from the current price. In a random walk, changes in price would be unrelated to past price changes. A relationship between successive price changes can be measured statistically in terms of the correlation between successive changes (measured by the serial correlation coefficient). If share prices were to follow a trend, and price changes during one period were positively related to price changes in the preceding period, the measured value of the correlation coefficient would tend to be positive on a scale between 0 and +1. On the other hand, if the market overreacts, and price changes in a period tend to reverse changes in the preceding period, the correlation coefficient would tend to exhibit a value between 0 and −1. If, however, current prices reflect all available information, the market would exhibit neither trend nor reaction; the value of the correlation coefficient would be equal to zero.

There have been many tests of serial correlation in stock market prices, of which we can review a few examples. Kendall in his early study (1953) observed that various United Kingdom economic indexes including common stocks and commodities appeared to follow a random series through time. In 1965 Fama reported similar results for New York Stock Exchange prices. Table 12.3 gives Solnik's (1973) measurements of average serial correlation coefficients for daily, weekly, and monthly price changes in nine countries. If there were no transactions costs, it would be possible to profit from serially

Table 12.3   *Average serial correlation of returns in nine countries*

Country	Daily returns	Weekly returns	Monthly returns
France	−0.019	−0.049	0.012
Italy	−0.023	0.001	−0.027
United Kingdom	0.072	−0.055	0.020
Germany	0.078	0.056	0.058
Netherlands	0.031	0.002	−0.011
Belgium	−0.018	−0.088	−0.022
Switzerland	0.012	−0.022	−0.017
Sweden	0.056	0.024	0.140
United States of America	0.026	−0.038	0.009

Source: Bruno H. Solnik, "Note on the Validity of the Random Walk for European Stock Prices," *Journal of Finance,* 28, no. 5 (December 1973): 1156.

correlated price changes. However, taking into account the costs of buying and selling securities, Solnik's results indicate that it would not be possible to make money, as the serial correlation coefficients are close to zero. Thus we might conclude that price changes in these markets can be described for all practical purposes as following a random walk.

If the results had suggested that price changes were strongly correlated over time (e.g., correlation of +0.5), what would investors do? They would buy securities when prices started to go up, with the expectation that they would rise again in the following period. Solnik's results are what the weak form of the efficient markets hypothesis would predict. This lends support to the view that capital markets in these countries are efficient, at least for the major companies on which these studies are based.

Some analysts have raised the objection that serial correlation tests are insufficiently sophisticated to measure the complex patterns in prices that are supposed to convey the relevant information. In answer to this argument, researchers have proposed the ultimate weak form test. Those who believe that the stock market is inefficient must demonstrate a trading rule based on historical price patterns that will systematically make money for the investor. That is, a set of rules governing the timing of purchases and sales of shares must be shown to earn a return, after transactions costs, superior to a simple buy and hold strategy for shares of equivalent risk. One such strategy proposed by Alexander (1961) was shown by Fama and Blume (1966) to be ineffective. Of course, if any profitable strategy were to become known, it should self destruct immediately, because investors following it would drive prices up (or down) until the possibility of extra profit was eliminated.

On reflection, the hope that profitable predictions of share price changes can be made on the basis of limited information about past prices is, of course, naive, while information from so many other sources relating to the future of the firm is of more fundamental significance. For this reason, brokers and institutions employ thousands of investment analysts to comb through annual reports and other relevant economic information about a company, an industry, and the economy. A stronger definition of market efficiency would state that all publicly available information is reflected fully in stock market prices. Tests appropriate for measuring market response to other forms of publicly available information also have been constructed.

SEMISTRONG FORM TESTS OF MARKET EFFICIENCY

STOCK SPLITS. Fama, Fisher, Jensen, and Roll (FFJR) in a 1969 study of stock splits devised an ingenious method for testing market response to the introduction of publicly available information. FFJR wished to examine the average behavior of equity prices of firms announcing a stock split. For example, suppose a company with 1,000 shares outstanding announces a stock split whereby each existing share is split into two shares. There are now 2,000 shares outstanding. Each investor retains the original proportional claim on the company's assets and earnings, and by definition the split has involved no change in the company's operating and investment decisions. A stock split changes the number of shares outstanding but not the earning power of the firm.

FFJR adjusted proportional changes in prices before and after the stock split for capitalization changes and for dividends. Price changes were also adjusted for the effect of general market movements around the period of each stock split and for the volatility of each share relative to corresponding changes in the market index. Adjusted in this way, returns for 940 stock splits between January 1927 and December 1959 were calculated. Since FFJR wished to examine the price performance before and after each stock split, the date of each split was designated as month 0 (irrespective of its calendar date). Any abnormal returns were measured in relation to the number of months before and after the stock split (month 0). Every month the returns of each stock were calculated, with returns adjusted for movements in the market index and for the systematic risk (beta) of the stock. In this way, a stock's monthly abnormal returns were calculated. The abnormal returns on all stocks for each month were averaged and then accumulated over time. A plot of the average *abnormal returns* (Figure 12.2) accumulated over time shows virtually no average movement at all within the thirty months after the announcement; therefore, it can be concluded that the stock splits added no information that was not reflected already in share prices. However, in the thirty months prior to the stock splits, the cumulative average returns

Figure 12.2   *Abnormal returns for companies announcing stock splits*

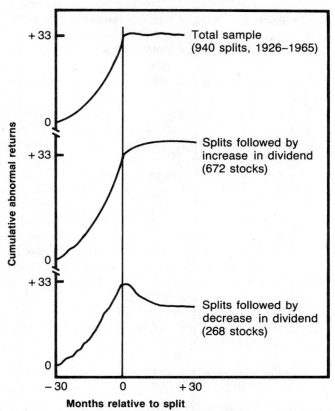

Source: E. F. Fama, L. Fisher, M. C. Jensen, and R. Roll, "The Adjustment of Stock Prices to New Information," *International Economic Review,* 10, no. 1 (February 1969): 1–31.

rose rapidly, and stockholders received a return substantially in excess of those for other securities of equivalent risk.

There is no theoretical reason why share prices should respond favorably to the announcement of a stock split unless the split is considered to be confirmation of other evidence that the prospects of the firm are improving. Other corroborating evidence might include a dividend increase, an event that often coincides with stock splits. FFJR divided their sample into companies that increased their dividends and companies that did not. As Figure 12.2 illustrates, firms that did not increase their dividends suffered a loss in valuation in the ten months following a stock split announcement, while firms that increased their dividends as expected experienced very little additional gain.

This latter result suggests that abnormal price changes prior to stock splits actually reflect the market's expectation of future dividend (and therefore earnings) behavior. The fact that the abnormal price changes take place before such events rather than after supports the semistrong form of the efficient markets hypothesis that current prices already reflect all publicly available information relevant to the value of a company's securities.

MERGERS. Similar tests have been devised for measuring share price movements before and after the announcement of a takeover or merger between two companies. As acquirers usually have to pay a substantial premium over market value to the acquiree's shareholders in order to induce enough of them to sell their shares, one might expect investors to try to anticipate such windfall gains. If the market is efficient, prices will reflect virtually instantaneously any such expectations held by investors. Prices of shares in companies thought to be candidates for a takeover therefore will begin to reflect the expected bid premium even before any public announcement is made concerning the bid. Mandelker (1974) found positive average abnormal returns for a merger sample beginning as early as eight months before the completion of mergers. More importantly, after a merger announcement was made, no further average abnormal price changes took place. By that time investors could not have made money by, for example, buying shares of a potential acquisition and selling shares of an acquiring company. If public information about the bid was only slowly reflected in market prices, it would be possible to make money by buying the shares of some and selling the shares of others.

The evidence indicates that the stock market rapidly reflects the economic benefits of mergers in the valuation of securities even before mergers are announced publicly. Because a takeover may be viewed as a capital investment, these results are of particular significance. We would expect a similar market response to apply to other forms of capital investment. In other words, the net present value of a capital project should be reflected in the market price of the securities of the firm undertaking the project.

One may conclude from these results that share prices seem to reflect investors' expectations of significant company developments even before the public disclosure of corroborating information by the companies involved. Therefore, these tests provide further evidence consistent with the semistrong form of the efficient markets hypothesis.

SECONDARY DISTRIBUTIONS. While it may be that share prices tend to anticipate company announcements, we might wonder still whether the resulting prices can be distorted by temporary excesses of supply or demand. It is often accepted without question that the sale of large blocks of shares by institutions or individuals can depress the price of a company's stock temporarily. What is the evidence? Scholes (1972) examined the effect of large block sales of shares or **secondary distributions** (which must be reported to the SEC) on the returns of a sample of 345 companies in the years 1961–1965.

A secondary distribution is handled by a broker in combination with other members and nonmembers of the Exchange who place enough of the shares with clients to permit sale of the entire block off the floor of the Exchange. The sale is usually negotiated (after trading has finished) at a slight discount on the last price recorded for the share on the Exchange. The buyer pays no commission, but the seller of the block pays twice the normal rate.

Figure 12.3 shows the impact of secondary distributions on the average abnormal returns for the shares in Scholes's sample running from twenty-five days before to fifteen days after the distribution. The negative impact on stock prices during that period was between −2.5 and 0 percent. These are relatively small abnormal returns. If an investor knowing that a secondary distribution was about to be made sold the shares short (i.e., without actually owning them), then purchased them subsequently, he or she would just about cover brokerage costs on the total transaction.

Would not the largest secondary distributions result in larger negative abnormal returns? Scholes found no discernible pattern between the abnormal return on the day of distribution and the size (value) of the secondary distribution. He also found no relationship between the abnormal return and the size of the distribution as a percent of the company's total equity capitalization. What Scholes did find was a slight difference in abnormal returns

Figure 12.3   *Relative price performance of stocks around dates of secondary distributions*

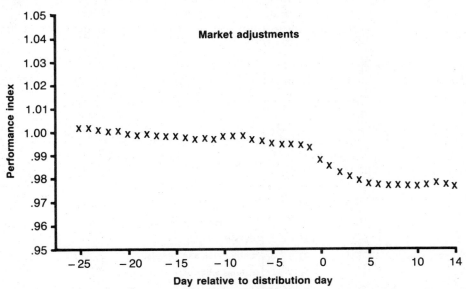

Source: M. Scholes, "The Market for Securities: Substitution vs. Price Pressure and the Effects of Information on Share Prices," *Journal of Business,* 45, no. 2 (April 1972): 193.

depending on who was selling the block of shares. The largest price decline was associated with sales by corporate insiders. (See Table 12.4.) The declines also were largest when the secondary distributions were not registered with the SEC in advance and therefore were unannounced previously. Thus the abnormal returns accompanying secondary offerings appear to be more closely identified with the implied informational content of insider selling and unregistered block sales than with any supply effects.

Kraus and Stoll (1972) in a more complete study of all block trades of 10,000 or more shares executed on the NYSE between July 1, 1968, and September 30, 1969, found comparable results based on daily price data. Using prices occurring within each day, however, they found clear evidence of price pressure effects. The study found evidence of small negative returns measured from the day before block trades to at least a month after. The price pattern is reproduced in Figure 12.4. Finally, Dann, Mayers, and Raab (1977) measured these price pressure effects minute by minute, using continuous transactions data. They found that immediately after a block trade prices fell by an average of 4.5 percent, but recovered completely within fifteen minutes.

These results are important when companies issue common stock to new investors in order to finance new capital investment. If the new issue could not be sold at the current prevailing market price because an increased supply of shares would depress the market price of the common stock, the reduction in price would be a cost to be included as part of the costs of external financing. Such added cost might encourage the company to seek a different way of financing the new investment, such as borrowing. Alternatively, the company might consider retaining a greater proportion of earnings and limiting the proportion of earnings that is paid out as dividends. Evidence

Table 12.4   *Abnormal performance index for secondary distributions partitioned by seller*

| | | Abnormal returns | |
| | | −10 to +10 days % | 0 to +10 days % |
Number of observations	Category		
192	Investment companies and mutual funds	−2.5	−1.4
31	Banks and insurance companies	−0.3	−0.0
36	Individuals	−1.1	−0.7
23	Corporation and officers	−2.9	−2.1
50	Estates and trusts	−0.7	−0.5

Source: Myron Scholes, "The Market for Securities: Substitution vs. Price Pressure and the Effects of Information on Share Prices," *Journal of Business*, 45, no. 2 (April 1972): 202.

Figure 12.4   *Price impacts of block trading*

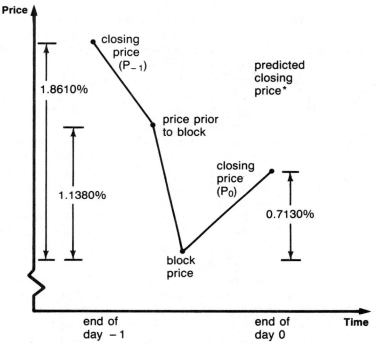

Source: A. Kraus and H. R. Stoll, "Price Impacts of Block Trading on the New York Stock Exchange," *The Journal of Finance*, 27, no. 3 (June 1972): 545.
Average percentage price differences between selected prices in the period from the close of trading on day −1 to the close of trading on day 0.

*Closing price if stock's price had changed by same percentage as market index.

sampled by Marsh (1981) suggests that in the United Kingdom the price effect on equity of making new issues of stock to existing shareholders is small.

These results are consistent with the hypothesis that shares in different companies can be viewed as though they were relatively uniform commodities distinguished only by price, expected return, and risk. That is, shares in different companies are good substitutes for one another. Thus an offering of a large block of shares in one company at a discount of, say, 1.5 percent on the current market price attracts funds that might have been spent on other financial securities currently not available at an obvious discount. The evidence suggests that the demand for a share becomes very elastic when its price falls relative to its worth. This evidence concerning the elasticity of demand for shares and the fairly rapid (fifteen minute) adjustment period for prices provides substantial support for the efficient markets hypothesis.

STRONG FORM TESTS OF MARKET EFFICIENCY

That the market discounts publicly available information is not a new notion. However, the relatively long periods of time by which public announcements of important information are anticipated is important. The professional analysts employed by brokers, securities firms, insurance companies, investment companies, and bank trust departments, who have come to dominate market trading, evidently are doing their job. Among them they somehow anticipate likely future developments of economic significance to the firm. The resulting buying and selling behavior of portfolio managers and other investors makes share prices discount the future in a manner that appears consistent with the efficient markets hypothesis.

The efficiency of professional analysis and portfolio management in this regard raises some interesting questions. Surely some professional portfolio managers are more skillful than the average individual investor. The portfolio manager has many advantages that would make him or her something of an insider. He or she has many sources of information not available generally to the public, with the resources to have this information analyzed adequately. Of course portfolio managers compete with many other professionals who have similar resources. The interesting question is: Can professional managers expect to outperform the general market index in a market that has been demonstrated to exhibit weak form and semistrong form efficiency? Can the private investor hope to improve investment performance by buying units in mutual funds of proven performance?

Each shareholding or unit in a mutual fund represents a proportion of the underlying assets, consisting of cash and a professionally managed portfolio of securities. The mutual fund agrees to buy back units whenever holders want to sell at a price representing the holder's proportion of the current market value of the underlying cash and securities.

Jensen (1969) measured the risk-adjusted performance of 115 mutual funds for the period 1955–1964 in comparison to both a general market index of equities and risk-free government securities. Jensen's main findings are summarized in Figure 12.5. The horizontal axis represents a measure of risk (beta). The vertical axis measures monthly (log) returns gross of expenses. The diagonal line represents a naive investment strategy of holding various combinations of a risk-free government security (at the intercept) and holding a portfolio of all securities in the market at point M. The points represent the returns and associated risks from investment in each of 115 mutual funds. As may be seen, many funds performed relatively poorly in comparison to the naive strategy. The number of funds performing significantly better was not more than would have been expected by the operation of chance.

The average mutual fund, given its level of risk, did not quite perform as well as an investor who held equivalent risk portfolios of government securities and equities. Jensen found that although the funds earned a gross positive abnormal return, any relative advantages of professional management appear to have been lost in management expenses and transactions costs. Jensen also found that mutual funds selected on the basis of past

Figure 12.5   *Evidence on mutual fund performance: scatter diagram of risk and (gross) return for 115 open-end mutual funds in the period 1945–1964*

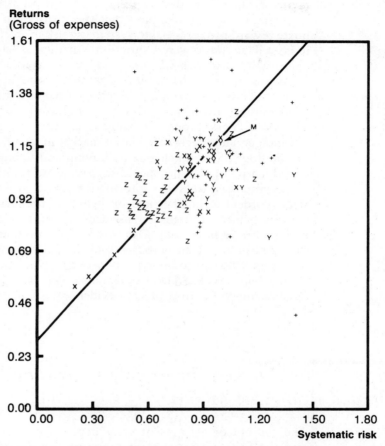

Source: M. C. Jensen, "Risk, the Pricing of Capital Assets and the Evaluation of Investment Portfolios," *Journal of Business,* 62, no. 2 (April 1969): 229.

performance could not be expected to perform significantly differently from average subsequently.

One implication of Jensen's evidence is that portfolio managers should not make numerous portfolio changes by trading actively unless they have insider information or superior forecasting ability. Otherwise, the costs of making the transactions are wasted when a buy and hold policy would prove more profitable. Companies that have some influence on the management of their pension funds will want to ensure that any costs incurred in trading the securities in the pension fund portfolios are offset by extra returns in excess of those that could be obtained by means of a buy and hold policy.

Although one might expect that financial analysts and their clients could obtain superior returns by, for example, investing in innovative companies or industries that show promise of increased future earnings, the evidence in favor of superior returns is scanty. The capital asset pricing model that we discussed earlier does suggest that speculators can expect to obtain an adequate reward proportional to systematic risk in an efficient market. However, it is still an unanswered question whether speculators are able to make abnormally large risk-adjusted returns after transactions costs and taxes.

All this may be disappointing to those who hope to make their fortune in the stock market without soiling their hands in industry. To be sure, some insiders must profit from advantages not available even to the professionals. The New York Stock Exchange specialist is a good example of insider advantage. The specialist makes a market in the shares of various companies on the floor of the Exchange by buying and selling shares in the companies on which he or she is a specialist, paying no transactions costs. In this role a specialist has access to information about various kinds of buying and selling orders to be executed on behalf of brokers. These orders have first priority before any transactions made on the specialist's own behalf. Nevertheless, Niederhoffer and Osborne (1973) have found that NYSE specialists earn a positive return on 82 percent of transactions for their own accounts. Investors who pay transactions costs and who cannot afford to buy a seat on the New York Stock Exchange to gain such privileged information do not find much comfort in such evidence.

Efficient Capital Markets, Imperfectly Competitive Product, Labor, and Real Asset Markets

The concept of net present value depends upon a number of assumptions: that the firm has investment opportunities in imperfect product markets, that the financial market's valuation of information concerning the firm's investment decisions is efficient, and that management provides sufficient information to the financial market to ensure that the value of the firm's securities fully reflects the economic value of its investments. Let us consider each of these assumptions.

HOW POSITIVE NET PRESENT VALUE IS CREATED

The evidence that competitive capital markets are efficient informationally may not apply to other markets in which firms operate that are less competitive (product, labor, or real asset markets). Companies that obtain capital at fair and competitive rates in an efficient capital market have opportunities to use the capital to invest in assets in less competitive real asset markets. If a company enjoys a monopoly position in a product market, or if it can maintain a unique cost advantage, it can charge prices that provide positive net present value. That is, a company with a sustainable advantage over its competitors can charge a price to earn a rate of return from real assets that exceeds the rate obtainable from financial securities of equivalent risk.

The critical issue, of course, is the sustainability of a competitive advantage once it has been obtained. Wherever there are economic rents or positive net present values, there is an incentive for competitors to enter the market. Competitors can be expected to enter the market until prices are bid down to the break-even level where the rate of return on real assets equals the cost of capital, that is, until the net present value for the last potential market entrant would be zero. At this point the value of any remaining economic rents to existing market participants will depend upon the technology and economies of scale available to the last potential market entrant. For any capital investment, management must include in cash flow forecasts the expected effects of price attrition due to increasing competition over time. Response by competitors is not instantaneous; there are delays in receipt of information about the intended actions of other companies and further delays in recognition of the need to alter strategy. In this sense we can say that product (or output), labor, and real asset markets are in varying degrees informationally inefficient.

As the essence of net present value lies in arbitrage between efficient capital markets and inefficient product and labor markets, managers should make it a policy to search out market segments that they are equipped uniquely to supply and where there are barriers to entry for potential competitors. Costly research and development, trade secrets, patents, and particularly close customer relationships are some of the elements that managers can exploit successfully to produce net present value for shareholders.

SIGNIFICANCE OF MARKET EFFICIENCY FOR PRESENT VALUE RULES

If the financial or stock market were not efficient compared with product markets, the arbitrage that we have described between efficient sources of capital and inefficient product markets could not take place. As a result there could be no objective assessment of the value of management action in the marketplace, and NPV calculations would lose much of their economic meaning.

Suppose, for example, a company invests in a new capital project with an expected net present value of $1 million. If the financial market is efficient, the total value of the company's securities will increase by $1 million as soon as the relevant information reaches the market. The total wealth of the holders of the company's securities will thereby be increased immediately, as the prices of the securities adjust to the new information. However, if the financial markets are inefficient, and market prices reflect the new information with a significant delay (or never reflect it), the full effect of the capital project's net present value on the wealth of security holders is not realized. Thus, in a capital market that is not efficient, we would have to alter the discounted present value methods that we use in project appraisal to take account of delays in the changes in shareholder wealth.

THE VALUE OF INFORMATION

Of course, the stock market can only value information that it knows, anticipates, or expects. The market cannot anticipate all that is known to the management about future plans that could affect the value of the shares. Actually, it is not in the interests of the company or its shareholders for management to reveal all that it knows, for much of the information of interest to shareholders is of vital importance to competitors also. Free dissemination of company information would tend to increase competition, thereby making product markets more efficient and dissipating positive net present values. The incentive to invest would be reduced, and neither the shareholder, the employee, nor the consumer would benefit. While individual investors and investment firms have every incentive to anticipate what is going to happen, management must try to preserve the division between efficient capital markets and inefficient product markets by withholding information that would be of value to competitors.

Shareholders who appoint managers as agents to create value for them have to give managers the freedom to make decisions in secrecy without prior shareholder scrutiny or approval. Of course, to be effective, management action eventually must be reflected in stock market prices; and in an efficient stock market the economic benefit of such action will be reflected rapidly in returns to shareholders as soon as sufficient information emerges to feed investor expectation. One of the indirect ways managers provide information to the stock market (and hence to the owners) without revealing the source of the value is through dividend changes, as we will discuss in Chapter 15. For example, an increase in dividends may be used to signal that management expects an increase in the level of the firm's earnings. Informing the market of important developments so as to ensure that stock prices reflect the value of the firm's assets is an important function for financial management, provided it can be achieved without giving too much information to competitors.

Some Unexplained Results

Not all tests of efficiency have provided such comforting results as those we have mentioned. While most tests of stock market efficiency have been consistent with the efficient markets hypothesis, some have not. For example, abnormally high returns appear to have been obtained from investments in small firms. Also, advice of at least one investment analyst has produced significantly positive abnormal returns for clients.

THE SMALL FIRM EFFECT

Work by Basu (1977) suggests that stocks with low price-to-earnings (PE) ratios appear to outperform stocks with high PE ratios and that abnormal returns can be made by buying low PE stocks and selling high PE stocks. Reinganum (1981) tested Basu's model using the capital asset pricing model. Analyzing common stock data from 1976 and 1977, he found that PE ratios could be used as the basis for selecting portfolios that systematically earned abnormal returns of 6 to 7 percent. Reinganum then examined the relationship between the size of the firm and the PE ratio. He found that small firms experienced average rates of return greater than those of large firms that were of equivalent systematic risk. He found that it was not the PE ratio that was the important discriminator, but that it was size. Small firms seemed to produce far greater returns than could be explained by their risks, as measured by the capital asset pricing model.

These results were confirmed in a separate test by Banz (1981), who examined stock returns over the much longer period of 1936–1975, finding that stocks of small firms earned higher risk-adjusted abnormal returns than those of large firms.

Roll (1981) suggested that the small-firm effect might be attributed to an incorrect estimate of the risks (betas) of the common stocks. Roll found that small stocks were traded much less frequently than large stocks, which makes it more difficult to obtain accurate estimates of their betas. Reinganum (1982) examined Roll's proposition and found that it explained only about one-third of the abnormal returns attributed to small size, with around two-thirds of the abnormal returns remaining unexplained.

More recent work by Blume and Stambaugh (1982) demonstrates that excess returns on small firm stocks are concentrated in January. And Carleton and Lakonishok (1983) found that the size effect had occurred systematically within industries, not simply for the stock market as a whole.

A possible explanation for the small-firm effect may be that the securities of many small companies are less marketable than those of similar companies that are larger. Evidence found by Silvers (1973) suggests that the marketability of corporate bonds affects their prices and thus their yields. (Marketability refers to the ease with which a security can be sold in large quantities without depressing its price.) It is also widely believed on Wall Street that the prices of the stocks of small firms that do not have active markets are affected similarly by their lack of marketability, although we have little evidence as yet on this point. If it is true that the stock prices of many small firms are lower because of a lack of marketability, one can expect correspondingly higher returns from them.

One indication that stocks of small firms may be less marketable than those of larger firms is a requirement of one mutual fund that specializes in small firms limiting the amount of money that individual investors can cash in from their investment in the fund each day. If an investor wants the fund to repurchase his units in excess of $250,000 in one day, the fund will not guarantee to repurchase with cash. Instead, the investor may have to accept payment in securities for amounts beyond the limit. This restriction may reflect a concern by the fund's management that it might not be able to raise enough cash by selling its investments in small firms without depressing their prices.

EARNINGS ANNOUNCEMENTS AND ABNORMAL RETURNS

Latané and Jones (1977) appear to have found a relationship between unexpected quarterly earnings and subsequent excess returns for common stocks, with unexpected earnings defined as the difference between actual reported earnings and expected earnings. As an estimate of expected earnings they used an extrapolation for one-quarter of the ordinary least squares trend line for the previous twenty quarters' earnings. They standardized unexpected earnings by dividing them by their standard deviation, calling the resulting ratio Standardized Unexpected Earnings (SUE). Results showed that modest but significant excess returns still could be realized after earnings were announced by buying the stocks of companies with the largest (positive) SUE and selling those with the most negative SUE.

Rendleman, Jones, and Latané (1982) obtained similar results for a large number of companies with more recent data (third quarter of 1971 through second quarter of 1980). For each quarter they placed each company in one of ten portfolios, depending upon the value of SUE for the company in that quarter. Portfolio 1 contained the stocks with the largest negative SUE, Portfolio 10 the stocks with the largest positive SUE in each quarter. In Table 12.5 we show the average (for thirty-six quarters) of the excess returns during a 120-day period around the earnings announcement date. Row 1 of the table shows that during the 110 days beginning 20 days before the announcement, the portfolio of shares with SUE in category 1 (the most negative) had an average return of −8.7 percent while those in category 10 (the most positive SUE) enjoyed excess returns of +8.0 percent. The excess returns on the other portfolios were also highly correlated with their SUE

Table 12.5   *Analysis of cumulative excess returns over 36 quarters 1971–1980*

	SUE category									
	1	2	3	4	5	6	7	8	9	10
Cumulative excess returns										
Days −20 to 90	−8.70	−7.30	−5.60	−3.60	−1.10	1.20	2.80	3.90	6.90	8.00
Days 1 to 90	−4.00	−3.20	−3.30	−1.80	−0.80	0.50	1.20	1.60	3.40	4.30
Days −20 to −1	−3.30	−3.10	−1.70	−1.40	−0.40	0.40	0.90	1.50	2.20	2.40
Day 0	−1.40	−1.00	−0.70	−0.20	0.10	0.30	0.60	0.80	1.30	1.30
Average beta	1.02	1.00	0.97	1.00	1.03	1.03	1.01	1.02	1.02	1.02
Maximum beta	1.30	1.65	1.25	1.19	1.16	1.16	1.15	1.20	1.49	1.36
Minimum beta	0.67	0.37	0.71	0.85	0.89	0.94	0.89	0.76	0.65	0.64

Source: R. J. Rendleman, C. P. Jones, and H. A. Latané, "Empirical Anomalies Based on Unexpected Earnings and the Importance of Risk Adjustments," *Journal of Financial Economics,* 10, no. 3 (November 1982): 283.

categories. In row 2 of the table we see that roughly half these excess returns occurred after the earnings announcement date and thus offered opportunities for modest profits, even after transactions costs, for portfolios in the lowest and highest SUE categories. For example, it still was worth selling the average stock in category 1 as it was about to lose 4.0 percent and worth buying the average stock in category 10 before it gained 4.3 percent. Row 3 gives the excess returns during the period before the announcement date, and row 4 shows the excess returns on the announcement date. The remaining rows give estimates of the beta value for each SUE category, showing that the systematic risks are very nearly the same for all categories.

These results appear to suggest that the stock market is not quick to reflect public information about unexpected earnings and that therefore the market is not semistrong-form efficient. As the results corroborate the earlier work by Latané and Jones, we cannot say that findings of a SUE effect are new. One can take either of two views concerning these results: that the stock market is inefficient, or that the SUE studies have uncovered effects that remain to be explained within the context of an efficient market. One explanation may be the small-firm effect, that small firms are for some reason more concentrated in the extreme SUE categories, thereby accounting for the larger returns.

ABNORMAL RETURNS FROM ANALYSTS' FORECASTS

Bjerring, Lakonishok, and Vermaelen (1983) evaluated the investment advice of a leading Canadian brokerage firm, whose recommendations included both United States and Canadian stocks. The data included all stocks recommended during the period from September 1977 to February 1981. During the period there were 221 new recommendations involving 93 different stocks, with each stock recommended on average 2.4 times. Bjerring et al. suggest that an investor following the brokerage firm's recommendations would have achieved significantly positive abnormal returns amounting to 9.3 percent per year even after allowing for transactions costs. Furthermore, the information content of the recommendations was not reflected immediately in market prices. Such evidence is not consistent with the semistrong test of market efficiency.

These results are consistent with the view that some financial analysts make the market more efficient by passing on valuable information to their customers. This particular broker's Canadian recommendations were concentrated in only a few industries (oil and gas, forest products, and mining). Thus an industry effect similar to the small-firm effect may be operating here. In addition, the brokerage firm was the only national brokerage house with headquarters in the same area as many of the recommended companies. Still, why was the new information reflected only slowly in market prices? It may be that the buying power of the brokerage firm's limited number of customers did not change prices significantly and that only when the information reached a wider public did prices move.

Summary

We have reported only selected highlights of the vast body of research that has developed in the last two decades concerning the efficiency of financial markets. The results are consistent for the most part, and most of the evidence that has emerged supports the hypothesis that the financial markets are competitive and efficient. In fact, evidence has highlighted the ability of the market to alter valuations of shares relative to other shares before public announcements of the relevant information. Although some individuals with inside information may gain an advantage from this knowledge, there appears to be no recognizable group (other than the market makers who must buy a seat on an exchange) profiting in any systematic way from such information.

There are two important exceptions to the efficient market hypothesis. First, investors in small companies have earned excess returns on average. No explanation has as yet been found for these abnormal returns. Second, there is some evidence that buying shares just after unexpectedly large earnings have been announced will produce abnormal gains. These results are still unexplained. It appears possible, however, that misspecification of the statistical model relating return and risk, rather than capital market inefficiency, is responsible for such apparent anomalies.

In general, the evidence supports the view that the major capital markets are at least reasonably efficient. As an efficient market, the stock market provides rapid valuation of corporate stocks by discounting forecasts of expected cash flows. Managers who communicate timely and reliable information to the market about significant company developments may be reasonably confident that equity prices will reflect and usually anticipate the present value of the future cash flows that are expected to result from capital projects and related commercial activities. Because the capital market appears to be relatively efficient, managers themselves cannot expect to make large systematic profits by engaging in stock market transactions. Instead, they should use the financial markets as a source of capital and invest the funds in less competitive product markets. In imperfect product markets, management can hope to exploit any competitive advantages that it may possess in order to earn the economic rents that generate net present value and increase the price of the company's stock in the financial market.

Review Questions

1. What is the expected net present value of an investment in financial securities?
2. Why is the efficiency of the capital market of interest to financial managers?
3. What are the characteristics of an efficient capital market? What is the difference between a perfect and an efficient financial market?
4. Describe the extent to which market price movements resemble the workings of a roulette wheel.
5. "Stock market price changes follow a random walk." Explain.
6. If the price of a common stock rose 5 percent yesterday to $50, what would be your best estimate of tomorrow's price? Explain your answer.
7. Describe three tests of efficiency, each one relating to the weak, semi-strong, and strong form tests of market efficiency.
8. Ignoring tax considerations, what are the implications of efficiency for the following financial decisions?
   The decision on when to issue new common stock.
   The impact of a large secondary offering on the price of the stock.
9. Why might managers expect to make positive NPVs in product markets?
10. If capital markets are so efficient, why is there a thriving securities analysis industry?
11. Do you believe that the small-firm effect disproves market efficiency? What might explain the small-firm effect, and could such an explanation be consistent with market efficiency?

Problems

*1. If you were told that the serial correlation coefficient for weekly returns on a security is 0.2, and statistically significant, what would this imply about trading this security? Would your conclusion change if the serial correlation coefficient were negative 0.2?

2. Is it possible for the serial correlation coefficient for a security's prices to be 0.8 while the serial correlation coefficient for the same security's price changes is equal to -0.1? Explain.

*3. A stock with a beta value of 1.5 has increased in price from $12.00 to $13.80 while the market has gone up only 10 percent in a week. Is there an incentive to buy or sell the stock?

4. Two securities appear to be identical at month 0, when they are priced equally. After twelve months, security A's price has gone down by 5 percent, while security B's has risen by 5 percent. Would there be an incentive to buy one security and sell the other, and why?

*5. (a) A coin is flipped 500 times and the score so far is $+50$ heads (i.e., there were $275 - 225 = 50$ more heads than tails). If the same coin were flipped another 500 times, what is the expected total score for the 1,000 trials?

(b) What characteristics in common do flipping a coin and forecasting stock price changes have?

6. A stock has an expected return of 1 percent per month. If the stock is held for ten years:

(a) Would the expected arithmetic average return for the period be equivalent to more, less than, or equal to 1 percent per month compounded?

(b) Would you expect the divergence of the realized ten-year return from the mean to be more or less than the divergence of the realized one-year return from the mean?

7. A stock with a beta equal to 1.50 is bought by a portfolio manager who expects to hold the stock for ten years, anticipating the annual rate of inflation to be 5 percent for the period. What arithmetic average rate of return should the portfolio manager expect from holding the stock during this period? Should the mean compound rate of return for the ten-year period be more or less than this average? State your assumptions.

References

Alexander, S. S., "Price Movements in Speculative Markets: Trends or Random Walks," *Industrial Management Review,* 2, no. 2 (May 1961): 7–26.

Banz, R. W., "The Relationship between Return and Market Value of Common Stock," *Journal of Financial Economics,* 9, no.1 (March 1981): 3–18.

Basu, S., "Investment Performance of Common Stocks in Relation to Their Price Earnings Ratio: A Test of Market Efficiency," *Journal of Finance,* 32, no. 3 (June 1977): 663–82.

Basu, S., "The Relationship between Earnings Yield, Market Value and Return for NYSE Common Stocks: Further Evidence," *Journal of Financial Economics,* 12, no.1 (June 1983): 124–56.

Bjerring, J. H., J. Lakonishok, and T. Vermaelen, "Stock Prices and Financial Analysts' Recommendations," *Journal of Finance,* 38, no. 1 (March 1983): 187–204.

Blume, M. E., and R. E. Stambaugh, "The 'Size Effect:' Results with Terrible Portfolios," unpublished paper, 1982.

Brealey, R. A., *An Introduction to Risk and Return from Common Stocks,* 2nd ed., Cambridge, Mass.: MIT Press, 1983.

Carleton, W. T., and J. Lakonishok, "A Note on the Relationship of Industry to the Firm Size Effect," University of North Carolina (December 1983).

Cootner, P. H., ed., *The Random Character of Stock Market Prices,* Cambridge, Mass.: MIT Press, 1964.

Copeland, T., and D. Mayers, "The Value Line Enigma (1965–1978): A Case Study of Performance Evaluation Issues," *Journal of Financial Economics,* 10, no. 3 (November 1982): 289–321.

Dann, L., D. Mayers, and R. Raab, "Trading Rules, Large Blocks, and the Speed of Adjustment," *Journal of Financial Economics,* 4, no. 1 (January 1977): 3–22.

Fama, E. F., "The Behavior of Stock Market Prices," *Journal of Business,* 38, no. 1 (January 1965): 34–105.

Fama, E. F., "Efficient Capital Markets: A Review of Theory and Empirical Work," *Journal of Finance,* 25, no. 2 (May 1970): 383–417.

Fama, E. F., and M. E. Blume, "Filter Rules and Stock Market Trading," *Journal of Business,* 39, no. 1 (January 1966): 226–41.

Fama, E. F., L. Fisher, M. C. Jensen, and R. Roll, "The Adjustment of Stock Prices to New Information," *International Economic Review,* 10, no. 1 (February 1969): 1–21.

Franks, J. R., "Insider Information and the Efficiency of the Acquisitions' Market," *Journal of Banking and Finance,* 2, no. 4 (December 1978): 379–93.

Franks, J. R., J. E. Broyles, and M. Hecht, "An Industry Study of Mergers in the United Kingdom," *Journal of Finance,* 32, no. 4 (December 1977): 1513–25.

Grossman S. J., and Schiller, R. J., "The Determinants of the Variability of Stock Market Prices," *American Economic Review,* 71, no. 2 (May 1981): 222–34.

Grossman, S. J., and J. Stiglitz, "The Impossibility of Informationally Efficient Markets," *American Economic Review,* 70, no. 3 (June 1980): 393–408.

Grossman, S., and J. Stiglitz, "Information and Competitive Price Systems," *American Economic Review,* 66, no. 2 (May 1976): 246–53.

Jensen, M. C., "Risk, the Pricing of Capital Assets, and the Evaluation of Investment Portfolios," *Journal of Business,* 42, no. 2 (April 1969): 167–247.

Kendall, M. G., "The Analysis of Economic Time Series, Part 1," *Journal of the Royal Statistical Society,* Series A, 116 (Part I 1953): 11–25.

Kraus, A., and H. Stoll, "Price Impacts of Block Trading on the New York Stock Exchange," *Journal of Finance,* 27, no. 3 (June 1972): 569–88.

Latané, H. A., and C. P. Jones, "Standardized Unexpected Earnings—A Progress Report," *Journal of Finance,* 32, no. 5 (December 1977): 457–65.

Mains, N. E., "Risk, the Pricing of Capital Assets, and the Evaluation of Investment Performance: Comment," *Journal of Business,* 50, no. 3 (July 1977): 371–84.

Mandelbrot, B., "Forecasts of Future Prices, Unbiased Markets, and Martingale Models," *Journal of Business,* 39, no. 1 (January 1966): 242–55.

Mandelker, G., "Risk and Return: The Case of Merging Firms," *Journal of Financial Economics,* 1, no. 4 (December 1974): 303–35.

Marsh, P. R., "Equity Rights Issues and the Efficiency of the U.K. Stock Market," *Journal of Finance,* 34, no. 4 (December 1979): 839–62.

Neiderhoffer, V., and V. Osborne, "Market Making and Reversal on the Stock Exchange," *American Statistical Association Journal,* 61, no. 4 (December 1973): 897–916.

Reinganum, M. R., "A Direct Test of Roll's Conjecture on the Firm Size Effect," *Journal of Finance,* 37, no. 1 (March 1982): 27–35.

Reinganum, M. R., "Misspecification of Capital Asset Pricing: Empirical Anomalies Based on Earnings, Yields and Market Values," *Journal of Financial Economics,* 9, no. 1 (March 1981): 19–46.

Rendleman, R. J., C. P. Jones, and H. A. Latané, "Empirical Anomalies Based on Unexpected Earnings and the Importance of Risk Adjustments," *Journal of Financial Economics,* 10, no. 3 (November 1982): 269–87.

Roberts, H. V., "Statistical Versus Clinical Prediction of the Stock Market," paper presented to the Seminar on the Analysis of Security Prices, University of Chicago (May 1967).

Samuelson, P. A., "Proof that Properly Anticipated Prices Fluctuate Randomly," *Industrial Management Review,* 6, no. 1 (Spring 1965): 41–49.

Scholes, M., "The Market for Securities: Substitution vs. Price Pressure and the Effects of Information on Share Prices," *Journal of Business,* 45, no. 2 (April 1972): 179–211.

Silvers, J. B., "An Alternative Analysis to the Yield Spread as a Measure of Risk," *Journal of Finance,* 28, no. 4 (September 1973): 933–55.

Solnik, B. H., "Note on the Validity of the Random Walk for European Stock Prices," *Journal of Finance,* 28, no. 5 (December 1973): 1151–59.

13

Valuation of Companies

In many situations it is important to be able to estimate what a company is worth. The most obvious example is when the management of a company wants to take over another company and must decide what price to bid for its stock. Also, when the stock of a company is to be sold to the public for the first time, the investment bankers who buy the stock from the company and resell it to the public must determine the price at which the stock can be sold. Another time one would want to price stock is if the major stockholders in a closely held concern decide to sell the company, in order to pay inheritance taxes, for example. The valuation of a company and its stock is an important task that arises frequently in financial management.

There are two main approaches to valuing companies that we shall discuss in this chapter. The first approach is to value a company's equity and liabilities. If all the company's securities are traded in the financial market, valuation of its stock and other liabilities is an easy task, for the securities are already priced in the market. Even if the company's stock is not traded in the stock market, an estimate of its value may be obtained by using the price-to-earnings (PE) ratios of comparable companies whose stock is traded.

The second approach is to value the company's assets. The value of the company's stock can be obtained by subtracting the value of the company's liabilities from the value of the assets. The value of the company's assets and liabilities can be estimated by means of the discounted cash flow method. This second approach may be necessary when the company's securities are not traded in the financial market and when there are no other sufficiently comparable traded companies whose PE ratios can be used. Whichever method is used, valuation is a difficult task, and estimates are usually subject to a large degree of error.

When one company is purchased by another, the price that is paid for the equity or common stock may be higher than the value obtained by the methods discussed in this chapter. Existing stockholders will usually interpret a takeover bid as evidence that the company is worth more than had been thought. Actually, a premium may be necessary in order to induce a sufficiently large number of stockholders to sell their stock. In order to justify this premium, the bidder must have a strategy in mind to improve the existing company's prospects or to put its assets to better use, which we will discuss in the next chapter.

Valuing Companies with Traded Securities

If a company's securities are actively traded in the financial market, valuing the company is a relatively easy matter. We can value the equity in the company by multiplying the market price per share by the number of shares outstanding. The resulting total value of the equity is the minimum that we would expect to pay if we tried to purchase all the common stock. We can also easily value some of the company's liabilities, such as bonds and preferred stock, if these liabilities are represented by securities whose prices are available in the financial market. Other liabilities, such as short-term bank borrowing, privately placed long-term debt, and accounts payable that are not traded, must be valued by other means. In many cases balance sheet values may be adequate for short-term liabilities. However, if there is a nontraded, long-term fixed-interest loan outstanding, and interest rates have changed since the loan was issued, we must discount the loan payments at the new interest rate in order to obtain the present value of the loan.

Let us consider some examples. Whitney Corporation and Woodstock Manufacturing Company are important suppliers to Bristol Corporation. Bristol Corporation is considering buying one or more of its major suppliers in order to obtain manufacturing economies and to improve quality control. Bristol Corporation's management wishes to know how much they might have to pay to buy either company, and they have asked us to value the two companies. Whitney Corporation's securities are traded in the financial market, but most of Woodstock's equity is held by a family trust and is not traded. Let us begin with the easier task, valuing the Whitney Corporation, whose securities are traded and therefore priced in the financial market.

In Table 13.1 we estimate the market value of Whitney Corporation's equity and liabilities. The table lists the company's securities, the number that is issued and outstanding, and the most recent market prices. The company's common stock represents a large proportion of the claims and is

Table 13.1   *Market value of Whitney Corporation's equity and liabilities*

Security	Number outstanding	Price	Value (dollars)
Common stock	2,000,000	9⅛	$18,250,000
Preferred stock	10,000	95	950,000
Debentures	40,000	96	3,840,000
Market value of securities			23,040,000
Bank borrowing (balance sheet value)			1,000,000
Accounts payable (present value)			2,525,000
Total value of equity and liabilities			$26,565,000

worth $18,250,000 (2,000,000 shares × 9⅛ per share). The total market value of the securities including common stock, preferred stock, and debentures represents claims worth $23,040,000. Some of the claims on the company are not traded, but we do have their balance sheet values. Whitney Corporation's balance sheet (not shown) lists $1,000,000 for bank borrowing and accounts payable of $2,576,000.[1] As the bank borrowing is short-term, and the interest rates payable should approximate market rates, the book value of this debt should be a sufficiently good approximation to its present value. As Whitney takes two months to pay its bills, however, the $2,576,000 in the balance sheet for accounts payable overstates the present value slightly. If we discount the accounts payable at 1 percent per month, the present value is $2,576,000/(1.01)^2 = $2,525,243. Thus the total value of Whitney's equity and liabilities is estimated to be $26,565,000 (rounded to the nearest $1,000) as indicated in Table 13.1.

If Bristol Corporation wishes to buy control of Whitney it does not have to pay $26,565,000. The owners' interest in the company is the value of the common stock, worth only $18,250,000. By purchasing a majority of the stock, Bristol Corporation can appoint Whitney's board of directors and thereby control the company. If it makes a successful bid to buy all (or nearly all) the shares from existing shareholders, Whitney Corporation effectively becomes a division of Bristol, and the balance sheets of the two companies can be consolidated in Bristol Corporation's accounts.

Bristol Corporation also is considering buying Woodstock Manufacturing Company, whose securities are not traded in the market. Other methods are required to value this sort of company.

---

[1]As Appendix 13.1 shows, the balance sheet value generally exceeds the discounted value of items of working capital other than cash.

Use of Price-to-Earnings Ratios to Value Nontraded Equity

Probably the most common method of valuing a company's nontraded equity involves the use of the **price-to-earnings ratio.** The method is simple, but it cannot be applied intelligently unless the characteristics and the limitations of the PE ratio are well understood. The PE ratio is defined as:

$$\text{PE} = \frac{\text{Market Price per Share}}{\text{Earnings per Share After Tax}} = \frac{\text{Market Value of Equity}}{\text{Earnings After Tax}}$$

Multiplying a company's current earnings by the PE of a comparable company or an average of the PE's of comparable companies, we obtain an estimate of what the total market value of the company's stock would be if it were traded.[2] If the company's stock is not traded, a downward revision should be made by subtracting the cost of obtaining a public quotation.

VALUING AN UNTRADED COMPANY: WOODSTOCK CORPORATION

Bristol Corporation's management is interested in buying the owners' interest in the Woodstock Manufacturing Company through negotiations with a family trust that owns most of Woodstock's shares. Woodstock Manufacturing is similar to Whitney Corporation in most respects, except that its stock is not traded in the capital market. Bristol's management has asked us to estimate a fair value for Woodstock as a going concern and to determine the worth of its outstanding stock. Woodstock's balance sheet is given in Table 13.2 and its income statement in Table 13.3.

The balance sheet gives a value of $22 million for the company's total assets, with the book value, of equity given as $14 million. Because the accounting values of assets are based upon historic cost, they are frequently out-of-date for reasons of inflation. In addition, accounting methods of depreciating assets usually do not reflect changes in the economic value of assets. For these reasons Bristol Corporation's management wishes to value Woodstock by other means.

Because Woodstock's securities are not traded in the financial market, we must value its liabilities and equity using the securities of similar companies that are traded in the market. First, let us estimate the value that the equity or owners' interest in the Woodstock Company would have if the company continued to operate independently.

---

[2]The earnings may have to be adjusted if they involve large extraordinary items.

Table 13.2 *Balance sheet for Woodstock Manufacturing Company (millions of dollars)*

ASSETS	
Current assets:	
Cash	0.97
Accounts receivable	3.50
Inventories	4.50
Total current assets	8.97
Fixed assets:	
Land and buildings	7.00
Net machinery and equipment	5.03
Patents and other intangibles	1.00
Total assets	22.00
LIABILITIES AND STOCKHOLDERS' EQUITY	
Current liabilities	
Accounts payable	2.00
Notes payable	1.00
Total current liabilities	3.00
Long-term liabilities	
Debentures payable	5.00
Total liabilities	8.00
Stockholders' equity	
Common stock	0.05
Paid-in capital	2.45
Retained earnings	11.50
Total equity	14.00
Total liabilities and equity	22.00

Table 13.3 *Income statement for Woodstock Manufacturing Company (millions of dollars)*

Net sales	20.00
Less cost of goods sold	10.00
Gross profit on sales	10.00
Less selling and administrative expense and interest charges	4.00
Profit before income taxes	6.00
Provision for income taxes	2.76
Net income	3.24

Whitney Corporation is Woodstock's nearest competitor; it is of roughly the same size and has the same growth prospects. Because of this, we may be able to use Whitney's PE ratio to value Woodstock's equity. Woodstock Manufacturing Company's annual earnings after taxes given in Table 13.3 are equal to $3,240,000. In order to value the company's equity, we could ask ourselves, what value would investors in the financial marketplace on Woodstock's $3,240,000 of annual earnings at this time? The PE ratio for a company is the price per share for its stock divided by the earnings per share. Whitney's PE ratio is calculated in the following way:

Price per share $9.125
Earnings $3,520,000
Number of shares   2,000,000

EPS = Earnings/(Number of Shares)

   = $3,520,000/(2,000,000)

   = $1.76

PE = Price per Share/EPS

   = $9.125/$1.76

   = 5.185

Multiplying Woodstock's earnings of $3,240,000 by Whitney's PE ratio, we obtain

5.185 × $3,240,000 = $16,799,400

as an estimate of the total value that Woodstock's equity would have if it were traded in the financial market.

The value of nearly $17 million obtained by the PE ratio method compares with only $14 million for Woodstock's equity that shows on the balance sheet (Table 13.2). One reason for this difference is that balance sheets attempt to value existing assets and not the net present value of future investment opportunities. The PE ratio reflects both the expected growth in earnings from existing assets and future assets. Of course, we have made the important assumption that Whitney's earnings are comparable to Woodstock's and consequently that Whitney's PE ratio can be used to estimate the value of Woodstock's earnings.

Comparability of Companies

An important assumption behind the PE ratio method is that traded companies can be found that are sufficiently comparable to the untraded company you want to value. A number of factors affect comparability.

COMPARABILITY OF GROWTH AND RISK

The specific contribution of growth and risk to the value of the PE ratio can be captured by deriving the PE ratio in terms of dividends and earnings. The present value of a share can be expressed as the present value of the dividends that are paid on the share. Suppose that the current annual dividends D_0 per share are expected to grow at the rate g for the indefinite future. The value of the share can be represented as the present value of a perpetuity with growth, and the required equation was derived in Chapter 3:

$$P = \frac{D_0(1 + g)}{R - g} \qquad R > g$$

where R is the discount rate reflecting the cost of the equity given its risk. We obtain the PE ratio by dividing both sides of the equation by the current annual earnings per share:

$$PE = \frac{d(1 + g)}{R - g} \qquad R > g$$

where d equals the current dividend payout ratio D_0/E_0. This equation should not be taken to imply that increasing the payout ratio d increases the PE ratio, for increasing d merely reduces the growth rate g, all other things being equal. The equation shows that a quoted company's PE ratio can be used to value the equity of an unquoted company only if the two companies are comparable in terms of dividend growth and risk.

COMPARABILITY OF EARNINGS

Companies in the same industry may not be comparable if their accounting earnings conceal differences in their economic income. If a company owns land or securities that can be expected to increase in value, its accounting earnings may understate its economic earnings. The reason for this is that accounting earnings do not reflect expected capital gains on residual values that are expected to be different from depreciated book values.

Another problem affecting comparability is that accountants in different companies calculate earnings in different ways, even in the same industry. For example, one company may use FIFO, another LIFO for valuing the cost of goods sold in calculating earnings. While two companies with the same dividends per share, the same expected growth in dividends, and the same risk should have the same price per share, if the same share price is divided by earnings per share that are different—because they are computed on the basis of different accounting conventions—the resulting PE ratios will not be the same.

Also, using an average of the PE ratios for a large number of comparison companies may help to reduce the effect of individual differences in growth, risk, and accounting methods among comparison companies, but a problem remains if the company being valued is very different from the average of the comparison companies. A worse problem arises when the earnings per share of the comparison companies are nearly zero or are negative, in which case the PE ratios may be easily misused.

For example, assume three almost identical companies A, B, and C in the same industry have virtually the same assets, pay the same dividend per share, and have the same risk. The price per share is $1.00 for each company. The earnings of all three companies are very nearly zero as they are in an industry in temporary recession that has had a bad year. The EPS of the three companies are $0.01, $0.02, and $0.03, respectively. At such a low level of earnings, small differences make large differences in their PE ratios, as may be seen below.

Company	Price per share	÷ EPS =	PE
A	$1.00	÷ $0.01 =	100
B	$1.00	÷ $0.02 =	50
C	$1.00	÷ $0.03 =	33.3

Which of these PE ratios can we use to value a company's stock?

Because the PE ratios of the three companies are very different, we would obtain correspondingly different results if we were to use any one of them to try to value the equity of another company. It might make more sense to use the average PE ratio for the three, which is $(100 + 50 + 33.3)/3 = 61.1$. Using this average PE ratio to obtain the value per share of each of the three companies, we obtain very different results:

A $61.1 \times \$0.01 = \$0.61$

B $61.1 \times \$0.02 = \$1.22$

C $61.1 \times \$0.03 = \$1.83$

We know, however, that each stock is worth $1.00 per share. The PE ratio method has given us an average value of $1.22 and a range of plus or minus $0.61. The variation is due to the differences in the earnings, which, although small in absolute terms, are large compared with the small average earnings. The average value of $1.22 is greater than $1.00 because the average of the PE ratios, 61.1, is greater than the PE ratio of 50 for the average company (B). The PE ratio of 100 for company A has had a disproportionate effect on the average for the three companies. If A's PE ratio had been larger, this bias would have been even greater.

We can remove the bias by using a weighted average of the PE ratios. We simply weight each PE ratio by a proportion. The proportion is the company's earnings as a fraction of the total earnings of all the companies that are used in the average. Assuming our companies have the same number of shares,

$$\text{Weighted Average PE} = (\text{Weight for A} \times \text{PE of A})$$
$$+ (\text{Weight for B} \times \text{PE of B}) + (\text{Weight for C} \times \text{PE of C})$$

where Weight = Earnings/(Total Earnings)

$$\text{Weighted Average} = \left(\frac{0.01}{0.06} \times 100\right) + \left(\frac{0.02}{0.06} \times 50\right) + \left(\frac{0.03}{0.06} \times 33.3\right)$$

$$= 50$$

Using this weighted average PE of 50 for the three companies we obtain:

A $50 \times \$0.01 = \$0.50$

B $50 \times \$0.02 = \$1.00$

C $50 \times \$0.03 = \$1.50$

By using the weighted average PE ratio we now obtain the correct average stock value of $1.00. The variation in the stock valuations around the average has been reduced from plus or minus $0.61 to plus or minus $0.50. A variation in value of 50 percent is still large, because we cannot escape the fact that if earnings are very small, a few cents' difference in earnings per share can have a large effect on the valuation that is obtained by means of the PE ratio method. The source of this misvaluation lies in the fact that very different PE ratios may imply very different growth prospects, especially for companies with low earnings.

When earnings in an industry are low, we frequently encounter companies that are making losses. If the company that we are trying to value has negative earnings per share, we cannot use the PE ratio method to value it.

Suppose that company D has an EPS equal to $-\$0.01$, and we use the average PE ratio of 50 for companies A, B, and C in the same industry to value it. The result would be $50 \times (-\$0.01) = -\$0.50$ per share. This is an absurd result, for stockholders enjoy limited liability and thus the stock cannot have a negative value. Suppose instead we tried using a negative PE ratio to value the company.

Company E in the same industry has a negative PE ratio equal to $\$1.00/(-\$0.03) = -33.3$. If we were to use this negative PE ratio to value company D, we would get a positive result of $-33.3 \times (-\$0.01) = \$0.33$. You can see that this result is still meaningless if you apply the same PE ratio to the EPS of a company with larger losses, for example an EPS of $-\$0.02$. Now we obtain the value $-33.3 \times (-\$0.02) = \$0.67$. In other words, we obtain the absurd result that the larger the losses, the more valuable the company, if we use a negative PE ratio to value a company that is making losses. This explains why the PE ratios of companies with negative EPS are not generally reported in the financial press.

These examples show that when a PE ratio is very high (current earnings are low in comparison to future earnings), it is difficult to obtain comparability and the PE ratio may be an unreliable yardstick for the valuation of the equity of other companies. Even a correctly weighted average of such PE ratios can produce a wide variance, if it is used to value companies that currently have low earnings. Finally, we cannot use the PE ratio method to value the equity of companies that are making losses.

The Present Value of a Company's Existing Assets and Goodwill

An alternative way of valuing the equity of a company whose stock is not traded in the financial market is to obtain the present value of the company's cash flow and subtract the present value of its liabilities:

Equity = PV of Assets − PV of Liabilities

This difference represents an estimate of the total market value that the company's common stock would have if it were traded in the stock market. Obtaining the present value for an ongoing company's cash flow is different from obtaining the present value of the cash flows for a capital project. The difference is that the present value of a company is attributable not only to existing investment but also to the potential to make profitable future investments. That is,

PV of Assets = PV of Existing Investments + NPV of Future Investments

In a manufacturing company the present value of existing investments can be divided into two parts, the present value of cash flows from existing products plus the present value of assets such as land, buildings, and machinery that could be sold when they are no longer needed. The net present value of future investments includes the various opportunities that the company may have to invest in new products and growth. More explicitly,

$$\text{PV of Assets} = \text{PV of Existing Products} + \text{NPV of New Products and Growth}$$
$$+ \text{PV of Residual Values of Assets}$$

In other words, if we wish to estimate the market value of a company's equity, we can do so by estimating the sum of these three principal sources of asset value and then subtracting from that an estimate of the present value of the company's liabilities.

ESTIMATING WOODSTOCK'S CURRENT FREE CASH FLOW

The first step in estimating the future cash flows for Woodstock Manufacturing Company is to determine a value for the free cash flow currently being generated by the business. The **free cash flow** for the existing business is defined as the after-tax cash flow that is generated from operations net of replacement expenditures and less increases in net working capital. Woodstock's free cash flow for the past year (in millions of dollars) is estimated as follows:

Earnings after tax	3.240
+ Depreciation and other noncash charges	1.039
+ Interest after-tax	0.324
− Replacement expenditure	− 0.703
− Change in net working capital	− 0
Free cash flow for existing business	3.900

The earnings of $3,240,000 were obtained from Woodstock's income statement in Table 13.3. The $1,039,000 depreciation was estimated by assuming a seven-year life for the machinery and equipment in the balance sheet in Table 13.2 and a twenty-year depreciable life for the buildings.

In valuing the total assets of the company, we must use total after-tax operating cash flows in the calculation. For this reason we have added back to the cash flow the $324,000 of after-tax interest payments that is estimated to have been subtracted in after-tax earnings. As the company owes $6 million, the after-tax interest charges were $(1 − 0.46) \times 0.10 \times \$6,000,000 = \$324,000$, assuming that the interest rate paid was 10 percent and that the corporate income tax rate was 46 percent.[3] There was no significant change in net working capital in the balance sheet during the year.

Combining these figures we obtained the estimate of $3,900,000 for Woodstock's free cash flow from existing business in the preceding year. We are told that the earnings on which this figure is based are net of $100,000 of after-tax research and development expenditure for new products. As we wish to distinguish between existing products and new products in our analysis, we shall add back this $100,000 to the $3,900,000 of free cash flow from the existing business in order to obtain the total free cash flow from existing products. (We shall take account of R & D expenditure when we value new products.) Thus the total free cash flow from existing products (in millions of dollars) currently is,

Free cash flow from existing business	$3.900
R & D expense after tax	0.100
Free cash flow from existing products	$4.000

We shall use this figure as the starting point or basis of our forecast of the future free cash flow that will be generated by existing products.

WOODSTOCK'S FUTURE FREE CASH FLOWS FROM EXISTING PRODUCTS

To use a free cash flow figure as the basis of our forecast of future free cash flows, the first question that we must ask is whether business conditions in the industry will change. If last year happened to be an unusually bad year in the industry, and Woodstock's earnings and cash flow were adversely affected, the $4,000,000 estimate of the free cash flow for that year may be atypical of the cash flow that would have occurred if business had been normal. For example, if business is becoming more buoyant, and if such business conditions would have produced 20 percent higher earnings had they prevailed last year, we should recompute the free cash flow using adjusted earnings. For the subsequent discussion, however, we shall assume that business conditions will not have changed and that we can use $4,000,000 as the basis of our free cash flow forecast.

Even if general business conditions remain the same, we will have to reduce the free cash flow from existing products for the combined effects of increasing competition and product obsolescence. Bristol Corporation's financial analysts (ignoring inflation) estimate that within a year Woodstock's income from existing products already will have declined by one-fifth and will be zero by the fifth year. If we assume that replacement expenditure

---

[3]We wish to exclude the tax benefits of interest so we add back interest net of taxes. If we wished to include the tax benefits of interest we would have added back the gross interest charges. This subject will be discussed in Chapters 21 and 22.

necessary to support existing business declines in the same proportion, the implied net cash flow in the first year is one-fifth less than $4,000,000, or $3,200,000, and the subsequent cash flows are approximately as follows (in millions of dollars):

End of year	1	2	3	4	5
Cash flow	3.200	2.400	1.600	0.800	0

At the same time that Woodstock's existing business declines at this rate, less working capital in each year will be required for the existing products. Assuming that the company's existing business will drop in five equal steps, working capital worth $1,100,000 will be released in each of the five years. (See Appendix 13.1 to see why the total of 5 × $1,100,000 = $5,500,000 is slightly less than the balance sheet figure for net working capital.) Therefore, the total free cash flow from existing products is given by the following totals (in millions of dollars):

End of year	1	2	3	4	5
Net cash flow after replacement expenditure	3.200	2.400	1.600	0.800	0
Reduction in net working capital	1.100	1.100	1.100	1.100	1.100
Free cash flow	4.300	3.500	2.700	1.900	1.100

Suppose we have used the methods of Chapter 9 to estimate that the discount rate for Woodstock's existing products is 8 percent assuming zero inflation. The present value of the above free cash flows discounted at 8 percent is $11,270,713. Note that the discount rate should be based upon the unlevered risk of the assets, since we are discounting cash flows after tax but without the deduction of interest charges. In Chapter 22 we show how to value the cash flows accruing to equity holders after deducting interest payments to lenders.

We have assumed that Woodstock's free cash flow from existing business will have disappeared after year 5. In other situations different assumptions may be appropriate. Some products have very long lives and will not be abandoned until it pays a company to do so. For example, a company enjoys rental income from a commercial property. As the property grows old and obsolete, the rental income net of expenses can be expected to decline. The company can be expected to keep the building as long as the discounted present value of the cash flow income from the building exceeds its market value in alternative uses. However, the buyer of the building must be able to put it to a better use. Similarly, the income from an existing product can be expected to continue until the assets that are required to produce the product can be put to a better use. For this reason a product-by-product analysis is required to determine how quickly free cash flow from a company's existing products will diminish.

NET PRESENT VALUE OF WOODSTOCK'S FUTURE INVESTMENT OPPORTUNITIES

In order to obtain the total economic value of the company, we also must add the net present value of the company's future investments in new products. As described earlier the company is spending $100,000 annually on research and development. This budget is relatively fixed in real terms and therefore its risk as measured by beta is low. Let us assume that the discount rate would be only 5 percent (in real terms with zero inflation). The present value of the annuity representing research expenditure, assuming that it continues for twenty years is,

$$\$100,000 \times A_{20,0.05} = \$100,000 \times 12.46221$$

$$= \$1,246,221$$

The present value of the expected research budget for the next twenty years is $1,246,221. This cost provides a benefit, the expectation of profitable investment in new products.

We have learned that the Woodstock Manufacturing Company is expecting to continue investing in new products at the rate of $2,700,000 annually (ignoring inflation) for the foreseeable future. This capital budget includes investment in machinery and equipment and working capital. It has been estimated that the profitability of this investment when measured in terms of net present value per dollar of investment will be equal to NPV/I = 0.25. In real terms the total net present value that is expected to be generated in each future year would be equal to:

$$I \times (NPV/I) = \$2,700,000 \times 0.25$$

$$= \$675,000$$

In each future year NPV worth a total of $675,000 is expected to be generated as a result of investment in new products. How much more should we be willing to pay for the equity of the Woodstock Manufacturing Company because we expect these future NPVs from investments in new products?

We can treat a constant stream of net present values generated by investment in new products as an annuity. Because the net present values on future investment can be relatively risky, the rate at which they should be discounted may be large; and in a subsequent section we show how such a discount rate can be estimated. Let us assume that the appropriate discount rate for this stream of future net present values from the investments in new products equals 20 percent in real terms. Let us assume further that this stream of positive net present values from new products can be maintained for twenty years. The present value of Woodstock's opportunities to invest in new products is given by

$$\frac{675,000}{1.20} + \frac{675,000}{(1.20)^2} + \cdots + \frac{675,000}{(1.20)^{20}} = \$675,000 \times A_{20,0.20}$$

$$= \$675,000 \times 4.86958$$

$$\cdot = \$3,286,967$$

The present value of the stream of future net present values worth \$675,000 annually from new products is \$3,286,967 when discounted at 20 percent. This represents the economic value of the company's goodwill, that is the company's expected ability to generate profitable investment opportunities in the future. Because the future net present values of investments in new products and growth have been discounted at a relatively high discount rate, the resulting goodwill represents only a small proportion of the total economic value of Woodstock's assets.

We should ask the question whether Woodstock really can sustain profitable new product development for the assumed twenty years. As the industry matures and new product possibilities begin to become exhausted, research and development become more expensive and breakthroughs are less frequent. Eventually relatively few new products may generate positive net present values. In Woodstock's case, if we had assumed a ten-year annuity, the present value attributable to new products would have been

$$\$675,000 \times A_{10,0.20} = \$2,829,919$$

As you can see the difference in this case is not large because we are using a high discount rate; consequently the NPV is comparatively insensitive to the length of the annuity.

PRESENT VALUE OF WOODSTOCK'S LAND AND BUILDINGS

As a final step we must estimate the present value of the company's land and buildings. The balance sheet shows land and buildings at a book value of \$7,000,000. This figure, however, is the depreciated historic cost of these assets and is not the assets' economic value. We have to estimate the present value of the after-tax cash flow that will be realized when the land and buildings are expected to be sold twenty years hence. At that time the buildings will be thirty years old. We have consulted realtors who tell us that such industrial buildings thirty years old on this site would sell today for only $10,000,000. In a competitive and efficient market, current market prices should equal the forecast after-tax discounted present values. In an active industrial property market it would be reasonable to assume that this relationship holds. Therefore the after-tax discounted present value of the land and buildings to a buyer would be the current market value of such assets at $10,000,000. (It is important to include appropriate maintenance costs in Woodstock's free cash flow, since we are assuming the building will be in the same physical state as comparable buildings that are used for valuation.)

Providing the buyers of such assets are in the same tax position as Woodstock, the current market price of the land and buildings will reflect any expected taxes to be paid on the realization of the assets. There are two circumstances under which Woodstock may wish to adjust the market prices for taxes: first, if Woodstock's tax position is different from the potential tax position of the buyers of the property. For example, if buyers were generally tax-exempt then Woodstock would not obtain a price that would compensate for the taxes it would have to pay. It would then be necessary to estimate the present value of the taxes payable and deduct this amount from the value of the land and buildings. Alternatively, if the company intended to hold the assets for a different period than that implied in current market prices, then a tax adjustment would also have to be made.

We shall assume in this example that Woodstock expects to have a capital gain on its property of $3,000,000 at the end of twenty years when the property will be sold. We shall assume that buyers of property are tax-exempt and therefore the present value of the taxes payable must be deducted from the value of the property. The capital gains tax in twenty years' time will be $0.28 \times \$3,000,000 = \$840,000$ assuming a capital gains tax rate of 28 percent. Assuming a discount rate of 10 percent for the taxes payable, the present value is $\$840,000/(1.10)^{20} = \$124,861$. As a result, the value of the land and buildings to Woodstock is equal to the current market value of $10,000,000 minus the present value of the capital gains tax of $124,861 to give a net present value of $9,875,139.

ESTIMATED VALUE OF WOODSTOCK'S EQUITY

We can obtain the estimated value of Woodstock's equity by subtracting the present value of its long-term liabilities from the total present value of the company's cash flow. We do not subtract short-term liabilities at this stage as these were included earlier in net working capital. The company's long-term liabilities consist of $5 million of debentures bearing an annual coupon of 10 percent and repayable in one balloon payment after eight years. Suppose that interest rates on such debentures have fallen to 7 percent. The current present value of the debentures is given by

$$P = \frac{500,000}{1.07} + \frac{500,000}{(1.07)^2} + \cdots + \frac{500,000}{(1.07)^8} + \frac{5,000,000}{(1.07)^8}$$

$$= \$500,000 \times A_{8,0.07} + \$5,000,000/(1.07)^8$$

$$= \$5,895,695$$

Because interest rates have come down since the debenture was issued, the present value of this liability has increased to $5,895,695 compared with $5,000,000 shown in the balance sheet.

Thus the net value of Woodstock's equity is obtained as follows (in millions of dollars):

Land and buildings	9.875
Existing products	11.271
New products	3.287
Research and development	−1.246
Net assets	23.187
Long-term liabilities	−5.896
Equity	17.291

On a discounted cash flow basis Woodstock's equity is estimated to be worth $17,291,000 compared with the balance sheet value of $14,000,000.

Why Net Present Values for Expected Future Investments Are Risky

One of the most common errors that is made in the valuation of unquoted companies when the discounted cash flow method is used is that too much value is attributed to growth or future investment opportunities. Because these future opportunities require further investment, only their net present values can contribute anything to the price that we might be willing to pay for the company now. Also, as these net present values can be highly risky, it is easy to make the error of discounting them at too low a rate.

The net present values on possible future investments may be highly levered in the sense that the net present value represents the difference between a risky present value of future cash flows and the present value of a fixed investment cost:

$$NPV = PV - PV(I)$$

Suppose, for example, that the present value equals 125 and the investment equals 100. In this case the NPV equals $125 - 100 = 25$. However, if the present value drops 20 percent to 100 while the investment remains fixed, the NPV drops to $100 - 100 = 0$. While the present value has dropped by only 20 percent, the net present value has dropped by 100 percent, demonstrating how the net present value of a project can be more volatile or riskier than its present value.

Table 13.4 illustrates in more detail why the net present value of future investments can be relatively risky. The table shows two possible outcomes for an investment of $100,000 in a new product that might take place one year from now. While the cost of the investment is expected to be fixed, the present value is different for each outcome with corresponding differences in the net present value.

For instance, there is a probability equal to 0.50 that in one year from now the present value of the project will be $125,000 and therefore that the net present value will be equal to $25,000. However, there is also a 0.50 probability that the present value of the project will be only $75,000, in which case the net present value would be negative. (In this event, with a present value less than the investment cost, the option to invest in the project would not be exercised; therefore, the net present value will be zero.) Thus while the present value can vary $125,000 - $75,000 = $50,000 the net present value varies only $25,000. When we express the range as a proportion of the mean expected cash flow, we find that the ratio for the NPV is 25,000/12,500 = 2, and the ratio for the PV is 50,000/100,000 = ½. In this case, also the value of beta for the project's net present value would be much larger than the beta for the project's present value and thus the risk premium would be larger.

This can be demonstrated in an approximate way by treating the project's present value as a portfolio consisting of the net present value plus the present value of investment cost.

$$NPV = PV - PV(I)$$

then

$$PV = PV(I) + NPV$$

The beta of the present value can be expressed as a weighted average of the betas of the investment and the net present value:

$$\frac{\text{Beta of}}{\text{Present Value}} = \left(\frac{PV(I)}{PV(I) + NPV}\right) \frac{\text{Beta of}}{\text{Investment}}$$

$$+ \left(\frac{NPV}{PV(I) + NPV}\right) \frac{\text{Beta of}}{\text{Net Present Value}}$$

Table 13.4   *Two outcomes for the net present value of a future investment (thousands of dollars)*

Probability	PV − I	=	NPV*
0.50	125 − 100		25
0.50	75 − 100		0
1.00			

*If PV − I ≤ 0 then NPV = 0

In our example the beta of the investment was assumed to be equal to zero (as it remained fixed). Rearranging the equation above:

$$\text{Beta of Net Present Value} = \left(\frac{PV(I) + NPV}{NPV} \right) \times \text{Beta of Present Value}$$

This equation exaggerates the relationship between the two betas, because the portfolio formulas that we have used assume that the option to invest will be exercised. In fact, the lower the probability of investment, the lower the resulting average beta for the NPV. If we adjust the equation for the probability of investment we obtain

$$\begin{matrix}\text{Beta of} \\ \text{Net Present Value}\end{matrix} = \left(\frac{PV(I) + NPV}{NPV} \right) \times \begin{matrix}\text{Beta of} \\ \text{Present Value}\end{matrix} \times \begin{matrix}\text{Probability of} \\ \text{Investment}\end{matrix}$$

In our example of Table 13.4 the value of the NPV (conditional on investment) is 25 and the investment is 100. The probability that the investment will be made is 0.50. Therefore

$$\text{Beta of Net Present Value} = \frac{125}{25} \times \text{Beta of Present Value} \times 0.50$$

$$= 2.50 \times \text{Beta of Present Value}$$

This shows that the risk associated with net present values of future investments can be relatively large, and when this is the case correspondingly high discount rates are required to obtain the contribution that they make to the present value of the firm.

Other Methods of Valuing Existing Assets

Company accounts are one of the primary sources of information that can be used to value a company. We used the income statement for information required in the PE ratio method and the income statement in the discounted cash flow method to value the Woodstock Manufacturing Company. We also used Woodstock's balance sheet to obtain information about the company's assets and liabilities, which we adjusted to obtain present values. The balance sheet represents the most readily accessible source of information concerning the cost and depreciation of a company's existing assets, although it does have some severe limitations.

HISTORIC COST BOOK VALUES

An analyst valuing a company uses the company's balance sheet and income statement as a primary source of information. The values of assets and liabilities in the balance sheet, however, are based upon accounting conventions. For example, most assets, such as plant and equipment, are valued using the purchase price (historic cost) of the asset after writing-down (or depreciating) the cost at the end of each accounting period to reflect wear and tear. There are a number of reasons why depreciated costs may not provide good estimates of the economic value of the assets.

The first problem is that the method of writing-down or depreciating the asset probably will not reflect the economic loss of value suffered by the asset. This problem is inevitable, because the accountant must choose a particular depreciation policy for a group of assets. The accountant may choose, for example, straight-line depreciation, whereby a constant proportion of the asset's original cost is deducted each year from the balance sheet value. Of course, the exact proportion will depend upon the accountant's forecast of the economic life of the asset, which inevitably can be estimated only in an approximate way. Alternatively, the accountant can choose faster methods of depreciating the asset. Accelerated methods of depreciation, such as the ACRS system that is used for calculating taxable income and described in Chapter 4, provide for larger amounts to be written off in the earlier years of an asset's life.

However, an accountant interested in producing realistic balance sheet values must use the depreciation schedule that best approximates the decline in the economic value of the asset. For example, in the case of automobiles there is a very active secondhand market, so one can easily determine an accounting depreciation schedule that would approximate economic depreciation. In many other classes of assets, however, active secondhand markets do not exist, so somewhat arbitrary accounting depreciation conventions must be used.

A second reason why asset values based upon historic cost usually do not reflect the asset's worth is that an asset should not have been acquired in the first place if its present value did not exceed its cost. Also, as the asset is used, economic conditions will change relative to what management expected, and the resulting change in the present value of the asset's remaining cash flows will not be reflected in historic cost-based measures of asset values.

Finally, a large fraction of a company's total assets may be found in the company's inventories and accounts receivable. As some of the inventories may be unsaleable, slow-moving, or obsolete, and the accounts receivable may include slow payers and bad debts, the balance sheet values for these often significant assets may be unreliable.

Unless assets have been frequently revalued to reflect the effects of inflation, and depreciation is based on the current rather than the historic value of assets, a company's balance sheet is unlikely to provide an up-to-date guide to the current value of the company. The accounting profession is considering changes in cost accounting methods that may result in more realistic balance sheet values and more realistic income statements.

WRITTEN-DOWN REPLACEMENT VALUES

The written-down replacement cost (WDRC) method has been increasingly discussed as an alternative to historic cost accounting. The method is based upon the following formula:

$$\text{WDRC} = \text{Current Cost of Asset} \times (1 - \text{Depreciation})$$

where current cost represents the cost of an equivalent asset if it were purchased at today's prices, and depreciation is the depreciation to date expressed as a fraction of cost.

Replacement cost accounting is an improvement on historic cost accounting for two reasons. First, in an inflationary period asset values are constantly rising; replacement cost accounting captures this increase in price. Second, if specific assets are being used in a highly profitable way, it is likely that the primary producers of the assets will be able to charge higher prices as a consequence. Similarly, if the industry using the capital assets is finding business difficult, and profits are low, asset values are likely to be weak (otherwise asset replacement will not take place). Thus replacement cost accounting can capture some of the changes in economic values that result from changing business conditions.

There are still a number of limitations to the replacement cost method. First, the depreciation methods used in the written-down replacement cost method may be no less arbitrary, and the economic life of the asset still must be estimated. Second, current prices of new assets charged by primary producers still will be below their economic values if firms are replacing assets (at positive net present values); or replacement even may not take place if replacement costs are above economic values. Finally, it may be difficult to obtain the prices of new assets that are similar to existing ones. When there is rapid technological change, prices of new (replacement) assets will reflect different levels of operating efficiency compared to similar assets in existing use.

In summary, replacement costs should be expected to provide superior estimates of asset values compared with historic costs. Such numbers provide useful estimates of value for managers who are comparing the cost of acquiring a company with the alternative of buying new assets from primary producers. The analyst always needs to be aware of the limitations of the written-down replacement method when valuing existing assets.

TRADED VALUES OF ASSETS

Accounting methods are used most frequently for valuing assets that are not frequently traded in secondhand markets. When assets such as cars or real estate are frequently traded, the accountant usually will use secondhand values for the traded value of a similar asset. Clearly, traded values are superior to book values reflecting accounting adjustments. Market prices capture economic values when they reflect how much buyers currently are willing to pay for a future set of cash flows. If unique or superior managerial abilities are involved in the management of the asset, though, the economic value will exceed the market value; and the resulting net present value will differ from one firm to another.

VALUATION OF EXISTING ASSETS: A SUMMARY

So far we have discussed four possible valuation approaches:

economic value in existing use

secondhand market value

written-down replacement cost

written-down historic cost

In many instances the values obtained would rank in the order above, with economic value in existing use highest and historic cost the lowest.

To the extent that managers are guided by profit motives the total value of assets in existing use will be greater than or equal to that of any alternative use (of which they are aware). This is an important distinction, particularly in a takeover where the intention of acquiring management may be to alter the use of existing assets of the acquired company. If secondhand market value were to exceed economic value in existing or intended use, the assets should be sold and put to better use elsewhere. Only by selling such unprofitable assets can managers capture the greatest value for shareholders.

Written-down replacement cost of comparable assets usually will be lower still than market values, primarily because of the conservatism of most depreciation methods. Under depressed economic conditions, however, it is possible for written-down replacement cost to exceed secondhand market values for assets that nobody wants. The implication is that companies do not find it profitable to replace their assets. If they wished to acquire further assets, they would prefer to buy secondhand assets rather than new assets from primary producers.

Usually lowest on the list of values would be book values based upon historic cost, particularly in an inflationary environment. The predominant use of fiscal methods of accelerated depreciation tends to make balance sheet values of assets even more conservative compared with market values.

PE Ratios and the Earnings per Share Game

Now that we have explored the principles and problems connected with valuing companies, we can take a break and play the "Earnings per Share Game."

Some financial managers believe that the name of the game in managerial finance is to maximize earnings per share on their companies' stocks. It should be clear to you by now that while accounting earnings are highly correlated with cash flow, the connection between earnings per share and shareholder wealth maximization can be very tenuous indeed. Earnings per share (EPS) depend not only on total earnings but also upon the number of pieces of paper, that is, the number of shares of stock that has been issued. By changing the company's financial structure through a takeover or by altering financial leverage, management can manipulate a company's earnings per share. As the resulting possibilities dawned on managers the earnings per share game was born.

In the 1960s the earnings per share game typically took the form of the conglomerate merger. The idea was that if you took over a company with a lower PE ratio than that of your own company, you could pay a premium for the company and still increase the earnings per share of the combined companies. Stockholders would benefit providing the stock market priced the acquisition's earnings on the same PE multiple as the acquiring company's earnings. By embarking upon a series of such takeovers, management could increase earnings per share indefinitely—almost. Predictably, the game has an ending, for paying premiums for companies is a cost borne by the existing shareholders of the acquiring company.

Because many managers still think that earnings per share manipulation can add value to the firm, we should examine the rules of the game a little more closely. Table 13.5 summarizes the essential data necessary to play the game for two companies A and Z. Company A intends to bid for company Z by offering stock in the ratio of two shares of A's stock for every three shares of Z's stock.

In the first three lines of the table the earnings per share are calculated for A and for Z. In the final three lines of the table are the market price per share, the PE ratio, and the expected annual growth rate in earnings (in the absence of mergers) for A and for Z. The higher PE ratio of A in comparison to Z may be explained in part by A's expected growth in earnings at 15 percent per year in comparison to zero growth expected for Z.

If A purchases Z on the terms of two shares of A for every three shares of Z, a bid premium of 28 percent on the value of Z is being paid at the current market prices for A's and Z's stock. Would you pay a premium for lower growth?

Now, how do the earnings of the combined company AZ look before and after the merger? Table 13.6 gives the answer. Look at the first column representing year 0. In the first three lines one can see the data from the last table giving the earnings of A and of Z. The earnings of the joint company are merely the sum $3.41 million of the earnings of A and the earnings of Z. In the purest form of the game one doesn't bother improving the operations of either company by means of the merger. However, in the next

Table 13.5   The earnings per share game

	Company A	Company Z
Current earnings after tax (millions)	1.0	2.41
Number of shares outstanding	10 million	18.5 million
Earnings per share (dollars)	0.10	0.13
Market price per share (dollars)	2.50	1.30
Price-to-earnings ratio	25	10
Expected annual growth rate in earnings in the absence of a merger (percent)	15	0

Bid terms: A purchases Z
2 shares of A for 3 shares of Z
Bid premium is 28%

Table 13.6   *Earnings of A and Z before and after the merger*

	Years						
	0	1	2	3	4	5	6
(a) Earnings ($m)							
A at 15 percent	1.0	1.15	1.32	1.52	1.75	2.01	2.31
Z at 0 percent	2.41	2.41	2.41	2.41	2.41	2.41	2.41
AZ	3.41	3.56	3.73	3.93	4.16	4.42	4.72
(b) Earnings per share (cents)							
A at 15 percent	10	11.5	13.2	15.2	17.5	20.1	23.1
Z at 0 percent	13	13	13	13	13	13	13
AZ	15.3	16.0	16.7	17.6	18.7	19.8	21.2

Number of shares outstanding: A, before merger, 10 million; Z, before merger, 18.5 million; AZ, after merger, 22.3 million

three lines we see that something quite magical happens to earnings per share. Where separately EPS of A was $0.10 and EPS of Z $0.13, the EPS of the combined company has leapt to $0.153. While the total earnings for the two companies is unchanged, the total number of shares has been reduced from 28.5 million to 22.3 million shares, thereby increasing the total earnings per share. The number of shares is lower because A is exchanging two shares of its own for three shares of Z.

Of course, we are just playing a game with the money of A's shareholders. The economics of the two businesses remain unchanged. The only real transaction here is a transfer of wealth from A's original shareholders to Z's in the form of the 28 percent premium paid. This premium dilutes A's shareholders' holdings in the combined company.

A further consequence of the merger may be seen by examining the subsequent periods in Table 13.6. While A's portion of the business is expected to grow at a rate of 15 percent annually, Z's business will remain static. As a result, the combined company AZ will have lower EPS growth than A would. In fact, after year 5, the EPS of A on its own would be greater than the EPS of AZ combined.

Actually, nothing of economic value is gained by manipulating the earnings per share of two companies in this way. We can show this by examining what happens to the PE ratios of the two companies when they merge. The PE ratio of the combined company AZ will be a weighted average of the two individual PE ratios:

$$(W_A \times PE \text{ of } A) + (W_Z \times PE \text{ of } Z) = PE \text{ of } AZ \qquad (13.1)$$

The weights are proportional to the respective earnings of the two companies:

$$W_A = \frac{\text{Earnings of A}}{\text{Earnings of A and Z}}$$

$$W_Z = \frac{\text{Earnings of Z}}{\text{Earnings of A and Z}}$$

We can now rewrite equation (13.1):

PE of AZ =

$$\frac{(\text{Earnings of A} \times \text{PE of A}) + (\text{Earnings of Z} \times \text{PE of Z})}{\text{Earnings of A and Z}} \tag{13.2}$$

Recall that earlier in the chapter we valued the equity of companies using the equation

$$\text{Equity} = \text{Earnings} \times \text{PE} \tag{13.3}$$

Substituting this into equation (13.2) above, we obtain the expression for the PE ratio of the combined company:

$$\text{PE of AZ} = \frac{\text{Equity of A} + \text{Equity of Z}}{\text{Earnings of AZ}} \tag{13.4}$$

This PE ratio for the combined company is exactly what we would expect for any company. Using equation (13.3) for AZ:

$$\text{Equity of AZ} = \text{Earnings of AZ} \times \text{PE of AZ}$$

$$= \text{Equity of A} + \text{Equity of Z} \tag{13.5}$$

The relative values of the PE ratios of A and Z do not change this result. The total value of the equity of the two companies is unchanged even if the takeover of a company with a small PE ratio by a company with a large PE ratio can temporarily increase the earnings per share of the acquiring company.

The important principle which underlies our arguments is that of value additivity. This principle suggests that the value of two firms combined is simply equal to the value of the two firms on a stand-alone basis assuming the after-tax operating cash flows of the assets are unaffected by the merger. If this was not the case we could not value individual assets or individual firms on a stand-alone basis.

The conglomerate takeover movement of the 1960s may have been encouraged by the earnings per share game. Needless to say, investors have long since become aware that the resulting increases in EPS could not be maintained in the long run and that they certainly were not worth the bid premiums being paid. Predictably, many conglomerates now are being dismantled as conglomerate managers try to recapture premiums for their shareholders by selling off less profitable assets. Sales can be made at a premium to other companies that either have better uses for the assets or managements who think that they too would like to play the EPS game.

Summary

An asset's value in existing use depends upon management's ability to deploy it in its most productive use and to operate it efficiently. The market value of a company depends in part upon the economic value of the expected cash flows from existing assets in their intended uses. At the same time, the value of a company is more than the value of its existing business. The market value also includes goodwill, representing the value that may be placed on management's ability to exploit its competitive advantage to generate future investment opportunities that will have positive net present values.

We have discussed the major methods employed in practice to value companies and have illustrated the advantages and limitations of each. We have stressed the importance of determining economic values and we have illustrated the pitfalls encountered in the practice of maximizing other financial variables, such as earnings per share, when negotiating purchases and sales of companies. Unless value can be added to the merged assets, the EPS game is merely a financial illusion.

In the following chapter we examine more closely the valuation of the economic benefits that may arise when one company acquires another, and why a company should expect to have to pay a premium over the market value of equity in order to acquire control of another company.

Appendix 13.1 The Present Value of Woodstock's Working Capital

The balance sheet in Table 13.2 lists the items of working capital under current assets and current liabilities. In Table A13.1 we compare Woodstock's

Table A13.1   *Present value of working capital for Woodstock
Manufacturing Company (millions of dollars)*

	Book value	Present value
Current assets		
Cash	0.97	0.970
Accounts receivable	3.50	3.431
Inventories	4.50	4.000
	8.97	8.401
Current liabilities		
Accounts payable	2.00	1.961
Notes payable	1.00	0.942
	3.00	2.903
Net working capital	5.97	5.498

balance sheet values with the present values of each component of working capital. Let us consider each item in turn.

The book value of Woodstock's cash is $970,000, which we have accepted as the present value of the company's cash. The present value of the accounts receivable is less than the book value of $3.5 million, because accounts receivable take months to collect. Assuming that the average collection period is two months and using a discount rate of 1 percent per month for receivables, the present value would be $3.5 million/$(1.01)^2$ = $3.431 million.

Woodstock's inventories are valued on the first in, first out (FIFO) basis in the balance sheet, so the figure of $4.5 million is relatively up-to-date (see Chapter 7 for a discussion of FIFO versus LIFO). However, we have reduced this figure to $4 million in the present value column because we have reason to believe that $500,000 worth of the inventory is unsalable.

The book value of accounts payable of $2 million has been reduced to a present value of $1.961 million in the same way as was done for accounts receivable. Assuming that payables are paid on average two months after invoices are received and by discounting at 1 percent per month we have $2 million/$(1.01)^2$ = $1.961 million.

Finally, we estimate the present value of notes payable. If the face value of the notes is $1 million, and they do not have to be paid for another six months, their present value is $1 million/$(1.01)^6$ = $942,045. The total present value of the current assets is $8.401 million and of the liabilities is $2.903 million. The net working capital is currently worth $8.401 million − $2.903 million = $5.498 million. This net working capital is not realized as a cash flow until it is no longer needed to support the existing business.

Review Questions

1. Why would you expect the book value of a company's equity to be different from its market value?
2. How would you calculate the PE ratio of a traded company?
3. An analyst intends to use the PE ratio of a comparable company to value the earnings of an untraded company. Define carefully what should be meant by comparable company.
4. When using comparable PE ratios to value a company, do you use earnings before interest (but after taxes) or earnings after interest and taxes? Justify your answer.
5. Why is it important to separate the expected cash flows of a company being valued into those coming from the existing business and those from growth opportunities?
6. When should the beta of growth opportunities be greater than the beta of assets in place? Are there situations when this would not be the case?
7. What important source of information does the PE ratio exploit that is not so easily incorporated into the discounted cash flow approach to valuing companies?
8. What are the alternative methods of valuing a company's existing assets?
9. "The name of the game in mergers is maximizing earnings per share." Comment on this statement.

Problems

*1. Swanning, Inc., is considering a takeover of X, Inc., a company traded on the NYSE. X, Inc., has 10 million common shares outstanding at $16.50 per share, and 1 million preferred shares with a market price of $5.50 per share. It also has 1.5 million units of debentures (each unit has a par value of $100) quoted at $97.00. The present value of X's accounts payable is $18.2 million, and the company has no other liabilities. What is the total value of X's equity and liabilities, and what offer should Swanning make in order to take over the whole company?

2. Swanning has identified another candidate for takeover: Y, Inc., which is not publicly traded. The book value of Y's common stock is $58 million (including retained earnings). The company has just reported annual earnings of $12,820,000. A Swanning analyst has identified the price-to-earning ratios of four companies similar in activities and size to Y, Inc., as 5.4, 6.2, 5.8, and 6.5. What value would you place on the common stock of Y, Inc.? Explain the discrepancy between the value you calculate and the book value.

*3. Given the following information from a balance sheet and income statement, calculate the earnings per share and the price-to-earnings ratio when the market price is $19.50 per share.

STATEMENT OF FINANCIAL POSITION		Dollars
Preferred stock issued, $5.00 par value		25,000
Authorized common stock capital		500,000
Common stock issued, $5.00 par value		300,000
Other capital		230,000
Retained earnings		430,000
STATEMENT OF EARNINGS		
Earnings before tax		185,000
Taxation		70,000
Earnings after tax		115,000
Minority interests		5,000
		110,000
Retained earnings brought forward		340,500
Earnings available for distribution		450,500
Preferred dividends	2,500	
Common dividends	18,000	20,500
Retained earnings carried forward		430,000

4. The required rate of return for FBC, Inc., as determined by the capital asset pricing model is 15 percent. The dividend payout ratio is expected to be 50 percent and the PE ratio is equal to 12. What expected growth rate in dividends is implied?

*5. A company has the following information for the year ending December 31:

Sales	$20,000
Cost of goods sold	$17,000

At the beginning of the period the company purchased fixed assets for $10,000 to be depreciated over ten years. The purchase does not qualify for the investment tax credit. The corporate tax rate is 46 percent. The company uses straight-line depreciation. Prepare an income statement, and with that information prepare an analysis of free cash flow for the year. Assume taxes are paid at the end of the year during which profits are earned.

6. The S.A. Company projects the following net cash flows for existing and new activities (in thousands of dollars) for a company that it wishes to purchase. The risk-free rate of interest is 5 percent. The risk premium on existing activities is 6 percent, and the new activities are three times as risky as existing activities. After year 5, the net cash flow of new

activities is expected to grow at a rate of 5 percent per year in perpetuity, and net cash flow in year 6 is expected to be $105,000.

End of year	0	1	2	3	4	5
Existing	100	80	60	40	20	0
New	0	20	40	60	80	100

(a) Value the existing activities,
(b) Value the new activities,
(c) Estimate the value of the company.

*7. Jarvis Retail Company owns a building in an area where property prices have been increasing at 8 percent annually. This increase is expected to continue for the next five years. The company has just received from a pension fund an offer of $10 million for the building, which now has a written-down value of $3.5 million. The vice president for finance has asked you to calculate the present value of the building, which will no longer be needed in five years' time. The real discount rate is 5 percent per year. Assume a capital gains tax rate of 28 percent. The company takes straight-line depreciation of $250,000 for the building each year. The corporate tax rate is 46 percent.

8. Company XYZ, Inc., has a ten-year $1,000 loan (with nine years remaining), at a fixed interest rate of 10 percent annually, and assets with a book value of $4,000. The company estimates the market value of its assets to be $6,500. Calculate (a) the market value of the loan (given that the current and expected future interest rate is 13 percent), and (b) the market value of the equity of XYZ, Inc.

*9. Value the assets of Jims Company, which has annual earnings of $100,000 after taxes. The book value of the assets is $500,000, and annual depreciation is $100,000. Annual capital expenditures have been $100,000 after investment tax credits have been taken. The rate of corporate tax is 46 percent. The risk-free rate of interest is 10 percent, the market's risk premium is 8.3 percent, and the value of the beta coefficient for the company's existing assets is 0.8. Sales of existing products are expected to continue their same pattern indefinitely. At the same time, the company expects some exceptional new investment opportunities over the next three years. The risk of the resulting new assets will be the same as for existing assets but not until the new assets are in place. Capital expenditures for the new opportunities (providing that they materialize) would be as follows (in thousands of dollars):

End of year	1	2	3
Investment	100	150	100

The probabilities that the three new investments will materialize are estimated to be 0.75, 0.50, and 0.25, respectively. The profitability index on these investments (if and when they take place) would average 1.33. In addition to the above investments in new activities, the company also plans replacement expenditures equal to depreciation for existing projects. Stating your assumptions, value the company.

10. Jims Company in Problem 9 has debt with a book value of $200,000. It consists of a 5 percent fixed interest, ten-year term loan negotiated five years ago. Interest and principal repayment on the loan are in the form of an annuity, with a remaining life of five years. Assuming that interest rates on equivalent five-year loans have increased to 10 percent, what is the economic value of the debt? (Ignore any benefit that might accrue from the tax deductibility of interest payments.) How does this value affect the sum of money that an acquirer would pay for the company?

*11. Leak Filters, Inc., is negotiating to buy Dregs Company, Inc., an untraded company. Dregs operates from a rented building. Its total assets consist of $100,000 worth of inventory and accounts receivable and an automatic metal bashing machine. The machine has a ten-year life and is now seven years old. It originally cost $200,000, and its remaining book value is $50,000. A similar machine sells new for $300,000. Dregs has liabilities consisting of accounts payable of $50,000 and a bank loan with an unpaid balance of $23,000. In the absence of further information, estimate how much Leak Filters should be willing to pay for Dregs. Show your methods and state your assumptions.

12. An untraded company has after-tax earnings of $10 million and is expected to grow at 8 percent annually for the foreseeable future. It operates in the same industry as three other companies that are about the same size in terms of turnover and net assets. Given the information for the untraded company alone, how would you value it? Suppose you were unsure as to the accuracy of your data, how would you use the information on companies A, B, and C to verify your previous estimate?

	Company A	Company B	Company C	Unquoted Company
PE ratio	9.08	11.37	8.46	—
Dividend payout ratio	0.50	0.31	0.47	0.40
Required rate of return (%)	15	13	14	14
Estimated annual growth rates (%)	9	10	8	8

References

Black, Fischer, "Corporate Investment and Discounting Rules," unpublished paper, Sloan School of Management, MIT, February 1983.

Durand, D., "Growth Stocks and the Petersburg Paradox," *Journal of Finance,* 12 (September 1957): 348–63.

Galai, D., and R. Masulis, "The Option Pricing Model and the Risk Factor of Stock," *The Journal of Financial Economics* (January–March 1976): 53–82.

Gordon, M. J., "Dividends, Earnings and Stock Prices," *Review of Economics and Statistics,* 41 (May 1959): 99–105.

Higgins, R. C., "Growth, Dividend Policy and Capital Costs in the Electric Utility Industry," *Journal of Finance,* 29 (September 1974): 1189–1201.

Kaplan, R. S., and R. Roll, "Investor Evaluation of Accounting Information: Some Empirical Evidence," *Journal of Business,* 43 (April 1972): 225–57.

Lintner, J., "Optimal Dividends and Corporate Growth Under Uncertainty," *Quarterly Journal of Economics,* 88 (February 1964): 49–95.

Malkiel, B. G., "Equity Yields, Growth and the Structure of Share Prices," *American Economic Review,* 53 (December 1963): 1004–1031.

Miller, M. H., and F. Modigliani, "Dividend Policy, Growth and the Valuation of Shares," *Journal of Business,* 34 (1961): 411–33.

Myers, S. C., "Determinants of Corporate Borrowing," *Journal of Financial Economics,* 5 (2) (November 1977): 147–75.

Ross, Stephen A., "A Simple Approach to the Valuation of Risky Streams," *Journal of Business,* 51 (July 1978): 453–75.

Williams, J. B., *The Theory of Investment Value,* Cambridge, MA.: Harvard University Press, 1938.

Acquisitions and Mergers

Every year large numbers of companies combine into new corporate organizations. A corporate combination is called a **merger** when it is the result of a friendly arrangement between the managements of companies that are of roughly equal size or strength. A holding company may be set up, and the stockholders of both companies may be offered an exchange of the holding company's securities for their existing stock. Alternatively, one of the two merging companies may play the role of a holding company and offer the stockholders of the other company an exchange of common stock, cash, or a combination of securities and cash for their stock. The shareholding in the combined enterprise will be divided among the shareholders of the merging companies.

Companies may also combine by means of an acquisition or takeover. A **takeover** occurs when one company acquires a sufficient proportion of another company's shares to control its decisions. The shares may be purchased in the stock market, or they may be acquired through a tender offer made directly to the shareholders of the company to be acquired. Often this is described as a **takeover bid.** The acquiring company offers a price for each share that invariably is higher than the market price that prevailed before the bid announcement or before rumors about the bid affected the price of the corporation's shares. The bid premium that is offered is made large enough so that enough of the acquired company's shareholders will accept it. To make matters simple, we shall use the word "merger" to refer to either type of corporate combination.

Why, one may ask, should companies merge in a competitive economy?

Why might it be worth one company paying a bid price in excess of stock market prices to acquire the common stock of another company? If financial markets are efficient, share prices already must reflect the market's view of what companies are worth. Consequently, if the management of one company is willing to pay a premium above the stock market price for the shares in another company, it must believe that the market value of the combined company will be greater than the market value of the two separate companies. For example, the merger might save corporate taxes; in this case, the discounted present value of such savings could justify the payment of a premium. This is an example of a *financial rationale* for a merger. Mergers also can provide opportunities to strengthen the commercial viability of the combined business and to introduce efficiencies, thus providing a possible *economic rationale* for merging. In this chapter we examine both economic and financial rationales for merging. We also describe some evidence relating to the past profitability of acquisitions in the United States and in Europe.

Types of Mergers

Economists traditionally have categorized mergers as

Horizontal. The merging firms are in the same industry, that is, their products are identical or close substitutes that are sold in the same markets. A merger between two computer manufacturers would be considered a horizontal merger. Horizontal mergers have been the principal object of antitrust laws and their enforcement ever since the Sherman Act of 1890. Consequently, such mergers do not occur with great frequency.

Vertical. The merging firms are involved in different stages of the production process for some final product. The acquisition by a steel firm or an electric utility of a coal producer would be considered a vertical merger, as both industries use coal to produce their final product.

Conglomerate. The merging firms are in different industries altogether. A food products company (General Mills) acquisition of a toys and games company (Parker Brothers) would be considered a conglomerate merger. Most recent acquisitions by large firms have been of this kind.

Economic Benefits of Merging

Why should there be any advantage in combining two companies into one? Throughout most of this book we have assumed value additivity holds; that is, the present value of the whole is the sum of the present values of the parts. If the value additivity principle holds for mergers, the mere act of combining firms would not create value. There is even some evidence that assets lose market value when combined. For example, closed-end funds appear to sell at a discount on the market value of their holdings of securities, after allowing for the present value of the costs of fund management. This underlines the argument that mergers are unlikely to increase the market value of the merged firms unless the earning power of one or both of them can be increased as a result of a merger. In the remainder of the chapter we shall discuss how the earning power of companies' assets can be increased by means of acquisitions and mergers.

One should be clear about the difference between a merger and a capital investment. A merger does not directly increase the productive capacity of the economy but simply records the transfer of title or ownership of a set of assets from one group of shareholders to another, while a capital investment actually adds real assets to the productive capacity of the industry as well as the firm. A merger on its own is simply a financial transaction, and it is this aspect that leads many managers to be skeptical about the profitability of merging. The payment of a bid premium for an acquisition cannot be justified from a stockholder's standpoint unless the acquirer has some means of increasing the expected profitability of the acquiree's assets (or its own) as a result of the merger. If a merger is to be successful, the acquiring firm must have a plan for adding value to the acquired or acquiring firm as a result of the merger.

CHANGES IN ECONOMIES OF SCALE

One of the more obvious incentives to merge is to take advantage of the economies of scale that might arise from a merger. In the case of a horizontal merger, economies of scale typically would arise in production. In conglomerate mergers, such economies are more often found in marketing and distribution or in research and development. It may be that General Mills could justify the acquisition of Parker Brothers on the basis that its well-developed sales distribution network would improve the sales of Parker's toys.

Consider now a horizontal merger in the brewing industry. Let us assume that a new brewing process has been developed that will reduce the unit costs of making a barrel of beer by 20 percent. The first question is: Should we replace the existing process with the new one? The change will be worthwhile only if the reduction in operating costs (discounted to present value) is greater than the capital investment required for the new plant that the process requires. Even if it is profitable to scrap the existing plant, the market share of the firm may not be sufficiently large to provide the minimum volume necessary to make the new plant break even. Thus a merger may be necessary to capture the extra market share that is required to obtain the new economies of scale. Mergers of small breweries in the United Kingdom and Germany in the 1960s frequently were justified on this basis.

When the market for a product is growing, firms with the largest market share benefit more rapidly from the economies of scale that come from additional new plant. Companies with a smaller share of the market may find it necessary to combine their market shares in order to justify the new plant that would provide comparable economies of scale. The simple diagram in Figure 14.1 illustrates how this incentive to merge may arise. Three firms, A, B, and C are in the same industry. For historical reasons, firm C has a much larger share of the market, with sales totaling fifty units. A potentially more efficient new plant is available, but such a new investment would not break even below fifty units of production per period.

Figure 14.1   *Growth and the incentive to merge*

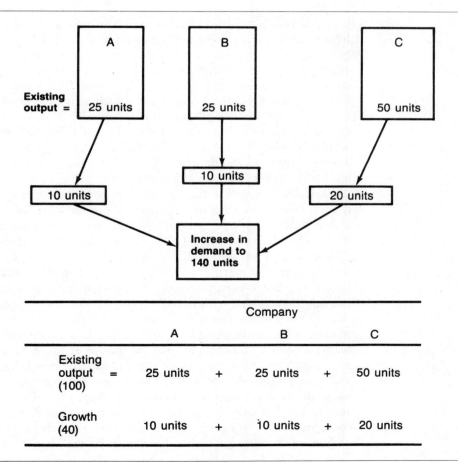

	Company		
	A	B	C
Existing output = (100)	25 units +	25 units +	50 units
Growth (40)	10 units +	10 units +	20 units

Table 14.1   *Break-even analysis for new production process*

	Units per period			
	25	35	50	70
Revenue ($1,000/unit)	$25,000	$35,000	$50,000	$70,000
Cost				
Variable cost ($500/unit)	12,500	17,500	25,000	35,000
Fixed cost	25,000	25,000	25,000	25,000
Total cost	37,500	42,500	50,000	60,000
Profit (Loss)	($12,500)	($7,500)	$ 0	$10,000

Table 14.1 provides a break-even analysis for the new production process. In column 1 it is apparent that companies A and B separately could not break even under the new process at their existing volumes of only twenty-five units per period. The price per unit is $1,000 and the revenue for each company at twenty-five units is only $25,000. The variable cost would be $500 per unit for a total of $12,500. With a fixed cost of $25,000, the total cost is $37,500, which exceeds the revenue by $12,500. In column 3 we see that if company C has a volume of sales of fifty units per period, revenue would be $50,000, variable cost would be $25,000, and total cost $50,000. Thus company C would just break even on the new process at their existing level of business, fifty units per period.

Now let us suppose that the market is expected to grow by 40 percent. If each company were to maintain its present market share, companies A and B will increase the volume of their respective sales by ten units (from twenty-five units to thirty-five units as indicated in Figure 14.1). Company C will increase its volume of business to seventy units. In column 4 of Table 14.1 we see that with a volume of seventy units company C would now exceed the break-even point, which would justify (eventually) replacing the existing investment with the new process. However, companies A and B at sales of only thirty-five units would not break even, even at the higher level of sales. Companies A and B must either build small, high-cost replacement plants or lose market share. An alternative is for A and B to enter into a joint venture or to merge, when they could achieve combined sales of seventy units per period. At this level of sales they could compete with company C using the new production process. The third possibility is for companies A and B to persuade company C to acquire them both, and together the combined three companies could achieve the greater economies of scale. Of course, such a merger would be subject to challenge by the Justice Department or the Federal Trade Commission on antitrust grounds.

INCREASED MARKET POWER

One company may acquire its competitors in order to reduce competition and thereby increase prices and profit margins. Such mergers also may improve the way that production or distribution facilities are employed in joint business activities. Although maintaining or increasing one's hold over the market could justify a merger, there are other factors to consider. First, the merger may be challenged by the Justice Department or the Federal Trade Commission. A legal objection can prevent or at least delay a merger. Second, high profits resulting from the merger might attract new entrants into the industry and encourage the development of close substitutes; thus the market protection afforded by a merger might be temporary only.

THE PURCHASE OF MANAGERIAL AND TECHNICAL SKILLS

Acquirers sometimes make a bid because they may wish to acquire unique managerial and technical skills in the acquired company that they can use to improve their own profitability. Before undertaking an expensive takeover campaign for this purpose, management first must consider alternative means to the same end. A less costly alternative may be to make attractive job offers to key individuals either in the company to be acquired or in other companies. The premium paid to individuals with unique skills might be less than the premium that would need to be paid for the common stock of the company that employs the required talent. For example, we do not observe baseball teams buying other teams in order to obtain a highly skilled player. It is more feasible to buy the player rather than buy the whole team.

The alternative to hiring individuals may not always be practical, however, when the unique managerial or technical skills are attributable to a large team or organization. The acquiring company may have no way of determining from the outside what subtle combination of elements within the management team makes it effective. Access to enough members of the team to be assured of a critical mass may not be possible without acquiring the company.

While a friendly merger could provide a rapid means of obtaining an excellent managerial or technical team intact, in a contested takeover a management team hostile to the merger may not be interested in maintaining its effectiveness. Many members may resign and take their talents elsewhere.

EXPLOITING A NEW PRODUCT RAPIDLY

In Chapter 6 we discussed why it is very important for management to exploit a new product's competitive advantages very quickly. A new product can often generate high cash flows during its early years before other companies can react with competing products. However, if the new product needs new production or distribution facilities that require a long time to be put into place, there will be less time for the company to exploit its competitive advantage. Competitors will have more time to adapt their existing products or to produce new ones, thereby reducing the innovation's competitive advantage and its net present value. The acquisition of another company's facilities may permit more rapid exploitation of a new product's competitive advantage. Need for a factory or a sales force thereby could justify a merger.

A firm with a new product may not have established a brand name for such products in the marketplace. Frequently, products lacking established brand names sell at a lower price and obtain a smaller market share than established products (at least in the short run). Consumers may not be convinced of the quality of the new product and may demand a lower price before they can be persuaded to change their purchasing habits. The lower price compensates the consumer for the possibility that the product guarantees (or warranties) might prove costly to exercise. For example, the consumer may have to spend time in exchanging defective products for new ones. The costs of establishing a brand name and the resulting delay in exploiting the new product can make it worthwhile to acquire another company's brand name by means of a merger.

ACQUIRING UNDERVALUED ASSETS

Some mergers have been justified because the acquiring management believes that the assets of the potential acquisition are currently undervalued in the stock market. Belief in market undervaluation has been based mainly on three assumptions:

1. The stock market as a whole is currently undervalued, and the acquiring company knows better than everybody else that the market is too low. Such an attitude is not convincing justification for an acquisition, for shareholders should be just as capable of perceiving an undervalued market as managers. If managers did have the unique ability to recognize an undervalued market, they could spend their time more productively speculating in the stock market, rather than by paying the additional costs involved in gaining control of other companies.
2. The potential acquisition's stock is really a good buy at the current price. Unless management has insider information about the potential acquisition's earnings prospects, actually there is no reason to believe that management has better forecasting ability than the rest of the market. If management does have insider information, it should buy shares in the potential acquisition. Presumably, the information will be revealed even-

tually, and management will make a profit on its investment. It is not always necessary to make a full-scale takeover bid for another company in order to profit from insider information.

3. The assets of the potential acquisition are priced below their replacement costs in the stock market. In this case it is clearly better to acquire the assets of another firm than to purchase assets from primary producers. Of course, acquiring the assets of another company still can only be justified if the assets can be used to generate positive net present value. This means that the acquiring firm must be more profitable than the companies that are to be acquired. For example, in 1978, secondhand values of ships were substantially below their replacement cost because prices reflected the low profitability of operating the ships. When a firm can operate ships more profitably than another company it would be profitable to buy the other company's ships. As more and more companies find it profitable to buy ships in the secondhand market, secondhand prices will rise until the alternative of buying new ships becomes equally attractive. An active market in acquisitions will tend to bring stock prices into line with the underlying replacement values of a company's assets.

Because markets for products, materials, and labor are imperfect, the value of a firm depends upon the way in which investors expect it to be managed. Given imperfect information, stock prices may not always fully reflect the value of assets in more profitable alternative uses. Because there are costs to obtaining information, neither the stock market nor the management of the acquired company may be aware of the more profitable alternative use of the assets envisioned by the management of an acquiring company. To take advantage of its insider information, the acquiring company could buy up some of the potential acquisition's shares quietly, and then reveal what it knows to the company and to the stock market before reselling the shares at a higher price in the market. However, if it is unlikely that the existing management would be willing or able to make effective economic decisions on the basis of the new information, a takeover may be necessary to realize the merger benefits.

While partial acquisitions of shares (toe-hold acquisitions) can be announced informally, SEC regulations require any company acquiring more than 5 percent of a class of another's common stock, to register the acquisition formally within ten days of the purchase (Schedule 13D). Evidence suggests that such purchases precede corporate takeovers. Halpern (1973) found that in a sample of seventy-seven companies twenty-three acquirers owned some of the seller's shares prior to merging. Similarly, Franks (1978) found in his sample of seventy-two mergers that thirty-five acquirers held shares before the merger. The average pre-merger stockholdings were 38.1 percent and 30 percent of the outstanding shares, respectively, in the two studies. It also appears that pre-merger purchases of shares lead to higher share prices. In a study of eighty-six firms that were subject to partial acquisition over the twenty-two months around the announcement month of the acquisition, Madden (1981) found that share prices of the partially acquired company rose during the announcement month and during the three months preceding the announcement. In the latter case, such abnormal returns may be a result of either buying pressure exerted by the acquiring company or information associated with the increased volume of trading. Abnormal returns in the announcement month may be due to anticipation of a full-scale merger and a possible bid premium.

Financial Benefits of Merging

A number of financial reasons have been put forward to justify acquisitions and mergers. These include: diversification to reduce risk; lower borrowing costs as a result of diversification and risk reduction; exploitation of unused debt capacity; and acquisition of tax losses that the acquirer can use to reduce its taxes. Let us examine each of these reasons in more detail.

MERGING AND DIVERSIFICATION

As we have described in Chapter 9, corporate diversification for the purpose of risk reduction can increase shareholder wealth if the costs of financial distress or default can be reduced. In the absence of such an advantage, the argument would be that company diversification is unnecessary if shareholders can achieve risk reduction for themselves by investing in a diversified portfolio of stocks on their own account, or by investing in mutual funds.

Let us assume that there are costs to financial distress and default. Suppose that either company A or B might default under different circumstances and that company earnings are perfectly negatively correlated. The probability that either company will default is, say, 0.05, or 5 percent. If a company defaults, the costs of default are, say, 20 percent of asset values. Thus, the expected costs of default for each company are 0.05 × 20, or 1 percent of the company's value. Suppose that the two companies merge. Because company earnings happen to be perfectly negatively correlated, the probability of default falls to zero for the combined company. How profitable is the merger? In fact, the merger has increased the combined value of the assets of the merged company by 1 percent. A 1 percent increase in value, however, is small compared with the bid premiums of 20 percent or more that usually are required to gain control. If a company were already in financial distress and definitely would default without a merger, anticipated costs of financial distress might be large enough to justify a merger.

What is the evidence on the size of default costs? The direct costs of default include the legal and administrative costs of reorganization: payments to lawyers and accountants. These costs appear to be relatively low in comparison with the value of the assets, if we can accept the evidence of Warner (1977) who examined the reorganization of eleven United States railroads. Other costs to default are less direct. A default may deprive managers of their jobs. Further, the stigma of default may reduce the manager's chances of getting another job. It was probably not just to protect stockholder interests that the management of Chrysler made such strenuous efforts to avoid default and ultimate liquidation in the late 1970s. Because complete information is not always available, any bankruptcy may reflect unfairly on the abilities of individual employees. This risk cannot be diversified easily by managers whose main wealth is in their own human capital, that is, in their ability to earn high wages in the future. In these circumstances, a manager may reject some risky projects that might be profitable to diversified stockholders. And note the resulting information problem: Investors never know about the profitable projects that have been rejected.

One should not imagine that the self-interest of managers necessarily is inconsistent with the interests of shareholders. Managers and other employees in risky, undiversified companies will tend to demand higher salaries or other benefits in compensation for the risks entailed in working for such companies. Such higher labor costs must be borne by the owners or shareholders. Furthermore, managers whose job security is at risk may bias investment decisions toward safe projects. If diversification can reduce such costs and encourage unbiased investment decisions, shareholder interests as well as employee interests may be served by some degree of company diversification. Putting the matter differently, in a going concern workers and managers are paid less than the value of their marginal contributions, leaving a net contribution (net present value) for the owners. Protecting some of this net present value for the owners (stockholders) may require "spending" some of the net present value on measures such as mergers that increase the security of the employees.

RISK REDUCTION AND LOWER BORROWING COSTS

When the earnings streams of two firms are imperfectly positively correlated (or, alternatively, negatively correlated), the risk of their combined earnings stream can be reduced by means of a merger. While this reduction of risk affects the costs of borrowing, it is not clear that these effects benefit shareholders, as we shall see.

In Table 14.2 we show a simple example of the way in which diversifying mergers can reduce the risk of the combined earnings stream for merging companies whose operating earnings are perfectly negatively correlated. At the end of the period we assume there can be only two outcomes, state 1 or state 2. In state 1 the operating earnings of company A will be $150 while the operating earnings of company B will fall to −$30. In state 2 the operating

Table 14.2   *Merging companies with perfectly*
negatively correlated earnings

	Earnings at end of period one (dollars)
Company A	
State 1	150
State 2	−50
Company B	
State 1	−30
State 2	170
Company A+B	
State 1	120
State 2	120

earnings of company A will be −$50 while the operating earnings of company B will rise to $170. Obviously, the expected earnings streams of the individual companies are risky and move in different directions. In either state one company will default on its loan. If the interest rate charged by banks on borrowed funds depends on the risk of the borrower's earnings, higher risk means higher borrowing costs. Because operating earnings are perfectly negatively correlated, the combined company A + B would have the same $120 earnings in both outcomes and therefore would be risk free.

It follows that the merged A + B company could borrow at lower interest rates than company A or company B individually. Normally, of course, the operating earnings streams of two companies that are involved in a merger will not be perfectly negatively correlated. Earnings, however, will almost certainly be imperfectly correlated; therefore, at least some of the benefits of the diversification effects that we have illustrated in Table 14.2 will be present in virtually every merger.

Our example shows that a merger can reduce the risk of a company's earnings stream and lead to lower borrowing costs. However, do such lower costs mean that the merged company is worth more than the total assets of the two companies valued separately? To answer the question we must distinguish carefully between the effect of a merger when there is outstanding debt prior to merging and the effect of a merger on the terms for raising new debt.

We shall discuss new debt first. If a merger of two companies reduces the risk of the combined earnings stream below the risk of the earnings streams of the individual companies before the merger, the merged firms are able to borrow at a lower interest rate. The risk of the debt has been reduced because if one of the firms defaults on its debt obligations, the surplus of the other firm is applied to the deficiencies of the first. This is known as the **coinsur-**

ance effect; each firm insures the deficiencies of the other. The merger of the two firms reduces the risk of default only because the shareholders are giving up some of the protection of limited liability; in the absence of a merger the shareholders of each firm are not required to make good the debts of the other should a default occur.

It is easier to understand this problem by considering an individual who controls an incorporated business. The owner is a wealthy person owning a large house and securities in addition to stock in the company. Let us assume that the corporation is borrowing from a bank at 3 percent over the prime interest rate. The bank suggests that the owner guarantee the loans of his company personally, and it will reduce its interest rate on the outstanding loans. In other words, the bank is asking for a merger of the owner's personal assets and those of the firm. Is the bank being generous? Certainly not. It is asking the owner to permit personal assets to be applied to any deficiencies of the company should default occur. Thus, it is asking the owner to give up the protection of limited liability that incorporation allows. The lower borrowing costs result from a smaller probability of default.

What about the effects of a merger when there is existing fixed interest long-term debt outstanding? If two companies whose earning streams are imperfectly correlated merge, the merged company will be less likely to default. If the probability of default is lower, the debt is less risky than it was before the merger, and the loan becomes more valuable to the lenders. If the value of the debt to the lenders has increased, someone must have paid for it. Who is worse off as a result? As the total of the debt and equity claims on the assets must be equal in value to the value of the assets, an increase in the value of the debt must be matched by a corresponding decrease in the value of the equity if the total value of the assets is assumed to be unchanged by the merger.

In general, even though a merger reduces the risk of the earnings stream and the cost of borrowing, the merger will not of itself increase the value of a firm's stock. Indeed, if there is fixed-interest debt, outstanding debtholders may gain at the expense of stockholders.

UNUSED DEBT CAPACITY

A number of authors, including Stapleton (1974), have claimed that a firm will prove attractive to a would-be acquirer if it does not use all its debt capacity. However, we shall show in chapters 21 and 22 that the advantages to debt financing usually are not very large and in any case are not by themselves sufficient to justify the typical bid premiums of 15 to 20 percent plus the costs of carrying out an acquisition. Also, the acquiring firm actually need not acquire control over the assets of the underlevered company in order to obtain an advantage from the unused debt capacity. The acquiring firm needs only to buy the shares of the inadequately levered company and to borrow, using the purchased shares as collateral for the loan.[1] Thus, the opportunity to exploit unused debt capacity is not by itself much incentive for a merger.

TAX LOSSES AND THE INCENTIVE TO MERGE

It may be argued that companies that anticipate the possibility of making tax losses should consider mergers as a way of absorbing the benefits of tax losses as and when they arise. Consider an example based on the data in Table 14.2.

In Table 14.3 we show the before-tax earnings of two companies, A and B. In the top panel we assume that the two companies are operating separately. The before-tax earnings and taxes payable are shown under two outcomes, referred to as state 1 and state 2. In state 1 company A pays tax of $69, but company B has a losing year and pays no taxes. Under current tax laws, a company with a tax loss does not necessarily receive a tax rebate. It must carry the tax loss forward until it can offset the loss against (or shelter) future taxable profits. The present value of the tax effect thereby is reduced. As a result, total taxes paid by A and B are $69.00 in state 1 and $78.20 in state 2.

The second panel of Table 14.3 shows what would have been the combined before-tax earnings and taxes payable of companies A and B if they had merged. The total taxes payable on the merged entity are $55.2 in both states 1 and 2.

Table 14.3   *Tax incentives to merge*

	Before-tax earnings		Taxes payable (46%)		Total taxes payable A + B
	A	B	A	B	
COMPANIES A AND B SEPARATELY					
State 1	150	−30	69	0	69
State 2	−50	170	0	78.2	78.2
COMPANIES A AND B MERGED					
State 1	120		55.2		
State 2	120		55.2		

[1]This point is discussed in detail by J. R. Franks and J. J. Pringle (1983).

It should be clear that companies A and B in their merged state pay less tax than they would have done if they had not merged. The student who remembers the analysis in Chapter 4 will not be surprised at this result. That chapter demonstrates how two projects may shelter each other's taxable profits and tax losses in different periods. What applies to projects also applies to merged companies.[2]

There is one other important implication of this analysis. In a previous section, we suggested that corporate diversification is not beneficial, as shareholders can diversify their own assets. Our findings here qualify that proposition, because a corporate diversification that reduces taxes may increase firm value. Indeed, the more diversified the merger, the greater the opportunity to obtain tax benefits. So there is one financial reason in favor of conglomerate mergers: The present value of taxes can be reduced by tax-motivated diversification.

The Principles of Acquisition Valuation

In any acquisition valuation there are four important questions to answer.

1. What is the value of the company in its present form? If it is traded, we must examine the market value of the company's securities and deduct some fraction due to rumors of a merger and a possible bid premium. If the company's securities are not traded, we must estimate value by other means, as we discussed in Chapter 13.
2. What is the source and value of the merger benefits? So far we have outlined some of the benefits to merging, both economic and financial. The present value of the expected merger benefits establishes the maximum premium that should be paid over the value of the acquisition as managed currently. It is important to deduct from these merger benefits the professional and administrative costs of acquiring the company, including some charge for managerial time.
3. What are the alternatives to merging? The potential acquirer should ascertain whether there are any other methods for capturing the benefits from the merger. The net present value of the best alternative reduces the maximum bid premium that must be paid to the acquiree's shareholders.
4. What price will be adequate to gain control of the potential acquisition? The answer to the first of the three questions above defines the minimum price that the acquiree's shareholders could possibly accept, but if the bid is to succeed, a higher price must be offered. The answers to questions 2 and 3 define the maximum price that the acquirer should consider offering.

[2]How to value the tax diversification effect is analyzed in detail by Green and Talmor (1983), who treat tax liabilities as a call option.

A higher bid would mean paying more for the acquiree than it is worth to the acquirer. It is important to establish a range of prices within which a bid might be acceptable to both acquiree and acquirer, because an aborted bid is expensive both in management time and indirect costs and in legal fees.

WHY PAY A BID PREMIUM?

Why do we find that acquirers usually have to pay a bid premium? That is, why do they have to pay more than the current market price of a company in order to purchase a sufficiently large block of shares to gain control? There are a number of possible reasons. First, if the merger creates new business opportunities that increase the earning power of the assets, part of the discounted present value of those gains may have to be paid over to the shareholders of the acquired company. For example, if the benefits of the merger can be obtained by many potential acquirers, while there is only one acquiree, competitive bidding may increase the bid premium enough so that a large proportion of (if not all) the value of the benefits of the merger is paid to the acquired company's stockholders as a part of the bid price.

When there are no other bidders for a company, it is possible that a successful bid can be pitched more closely to prevailing stock market prices, and the corresponding bid premium will be smaller. This does not imply that no bid premium need be paid. If the bid premium were zero, many shareholders would still believe there were merger benefits and would hope for a better future bid from either the current bidder or another.

Furthermore, Grossman and Hart (1980) suggest that some shareholders may refuse to sell their shares even when a bid premium is offered because they wish to remain as minority shareholders in the merged company, thereby enjoying any additional gains that may accrue to them as a result of the merger benefits. Let us examine an example of Grossman and Hart's theory. Let us assume that a company wishes to acquire another company whose shares stand at $1.00 per share in the stock market. The acquiring company bids $1.20 per share, even though it estimates that the present value of the expected merger benefits would be worth $0.50 (for a total potential value per share of $1.50). The bid still may not succeed even if the merger benefits can be obtained only by the one company making the bid. The reason lies in different shareholder expectations. Shareholders who suspect that the value of the merger benefits exceeds $.20 per share may prefer to keep their shares and participate in all the merger benefits as minority shareholders on the basis that remaining shareholders will accept the bid. If a sufficient number of individual shareholders believe that the value of the merger benefits exceeds the bid premium and behave in this way, the bid will fail at that price. Grossman and Hart call this a free-rider problem because some stockholders hope to gain on the backs of other stockholders.

An alternative strategy for a company that wishes to acquire only a part of the existing assets of another company is to consider negotiating for the purchase of the required assets rather than making a bid for the entire company. Negotiation with the management of the company instead of with its numerous individual shareholders allows the acquirer to sidestep the problem of minority shareholder holdouts. For this reason the acquisition of spin-offs (parts of companies) may be a more attractive vehicle for an acquisitive company than a full-scale acquisition.

THE MINIMUM AND MAXIMUM BID PRICE

The minimum price that the seller's shareholders could accept is the existing value of the company without bid prospects. On the other hand, the maximum price that the buyer should pay is the existing value of the company without bid prospects plus the net present value of the merger benefits to the acquirer. This net present value will be reduced by the net present value of suitable alternatives to the merger. Somewhere within this range of values is a price that may be attractive to both parties. Let us examine a specific example.

A company is about to announce a bid for another company. The stock price of the company to be acquired is currently $97. The management has estimated that the present value of the merger benefits would be $25 per share. What is the maximum price that the acquirer should pay? If the stock market has anticipated the bid, and if the share price already reflects part of the premium to be paid, this premium must be taken into account in deciding the maximum bid terms. Table 14.4 provides price data for the acquisition over the six months prior to the announcement date. The share price of the acquisition has risen over 20 percent from $80 to $97, while the market as measured by the Standard & Poor's index has risen only 5 percent. How much of the $17 price rise can be attributed to the anticipation of the bid?

We would have expected the security to rise only 10 percent, or twice as fast as the market, because its beta value is equal to 2.0. The difference between what we would have expected, given the movement of the market, and the actual return constitutes the abnormal return. The stock price rose over the six months by $17 instead of the $8 that we would have expected; consequently the abnormal return is $17 − $8 = $9 per share.

If the merger is to be profitable for the acquirer's shareholders, the bid price must not exceed the current price of $97 plus the difference between the expected merger benefits of $25 per share and the past abnormal gain of $9 per share. The maximum bid price is therefore $113 [97 + (25 − 9)]. Of course, abnormal gain in a period may reflect circumstances other than

Table 14.4   *Estimate of acquisition's abnormal gains from share price movements*

	Dates relative to announcement date		
	−6 Months	−3 Months	0 Months
Standard & Poor's index	500	512	525
Actual price of potential acquisition (dollars)	80	88	97
Expected price of acquisition (dollars)	80	84	88
Abnormal return (dollars)	0	4	9

Risk, or beta, of acquisition = 2.0

rumors of a bid, unexpectedly good earnings results, for example. A thorough review of recent news clippings and stockbroker reports concerning the company may reveal whether there have been other factors affecting the share price. Judgement must therefore be exercised in adjusting market prices to their value without bid prospect.

When the benefits can be obtained by several potential acquirers, and there is only one potential acquiree, the acquiree will gain a greater share of the benefits than if the benefits can be obtained only by one bidder. Stapleton (1971) suggested that merger analysis should include consideration of investment projects that provide alternatives to merging for the acquiring company. If the acquiring company can obtain part of the benefits (the net present value of merging) by investing directly in new capital equipment, this alternative net present value reduces the maximum premium that the acquirer should pay for the acquisition. For example, an acquisition whose equity currently is worth $10 million in the capital market is expected to generate merger benefits that have a present value of $3 million. If the management of the acquirer estimates that the same or equivalent benefits could be achieved by investing in a capital project that has a net present value of $1 million, the merger would still be the best alternative as long as the premium that is paid for the equity of the acquired company does not exceed $3 − $1 = $2 million. In this case, the most that the company should be willing to pay for the equity of the acquisition would be $10 + $2 = $12 million.

In some cases the alternatives to merging may not be obvious; for example, the merger benefits may derive from closing down the acquisition's production facilities and increasing the capacity utilization of the facilities of the acquiring company. However, the spare capacity of the acquiring company has an opportunity cost. First, the company may be growing internally, and that growth may use (gradually) the spare capacity. The merger benefits will therefore be confined to the present value of accelerating the utilization of the spare capacity. Second, the spare capacity could be used by acting as a subcontractor for the potential acquisition instead of a direct takeover.

It is essential that the acquirer examine the profitability of alternatives to merging, not only because they may prove to be preferred solutions, but also because their cost will affect the acquisition price.

Profitability of Past Mergers

We have described a number of conditions that could produce a profitable merger. An interesting empirical question is: How profitable have actual mergers been? In this section, we review the evidence from some of the many studies relating to United States and European mergers that attempt to answer four questions that relate to profitability.

1. Do stock markets anticipate mergers before they are announced by the merging companies?
2. Is it possible to make abnormal returns by trading in the common stocks of merging companies after the announcement has been made?
3. Are mergers profitable to the stockholders of the acquiring and acquired companies?
4. How are merger gains divided between the two sets of stockholders? What determines which group gains?

We shall review five studies that have provided evidence concerning these questions.

KITCHING'S STUDY

Kitching surveyed the acquiring managers involved in over 400 mergers that took place in Europe in the 1960s. The mergers were divided into five categories: (1) horizontal mergers, where one company acquired another in a similar type of business; (2) vertical mergers, where the acquisition was in the same industry but at a different stage in the production or distribution process (e.g., oil producer buys an oil refining company); (3) mergers based on new technology, but with common customers; (4) mergers based on the acquisition of new customers; and (5) conglomerate mergers, where the companies were in unrelated fields.

Figure 14.2 provides a summary of Kitching's results. The figure shows that 59 percent of managers thought their horizontal mergers were successful,

Figure 14.2   *Profitability of mergers as perceived by managers*

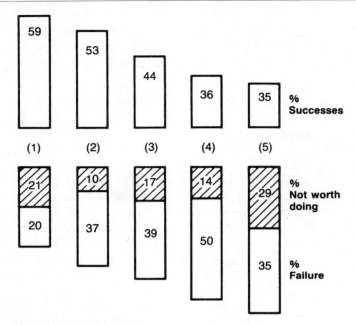

Acquisition type
(1) Horizontal (264 cases)
(2) Vertical (30 cases)
(3) Common customers: new technology (37 cases)
(4) Common technology: new customers (23 cases)
(5) Conglomerate (49 cases)

Adapted from *Acquisitions in Europe: Causes of Corporate Successes and Failures,* prepared by J. Kitching.

while 20 percent considered them a failure, and 21 percent were neutral (the merger was not worth doing). The criteria used by management to judge success were subjective perceptions of the gains from the merger, which is an important qualification of the results.

Two interesting conclusions may be drawn from this survey. First, the more diversified the merger, the less successful it is perceived to be by the acquiring management. To many managers this conclusion would seem sensible. After all, an acquiring management that is more familiar with businesses in the same industry may be in a better position to obtain merger benefits. A second observation is that managers considered that about 52 percent of the mergers were successful, while the remainder were either not worth doing (i.e., resulted in neither gains nor losses) or were unsuccessful.

MANDELKER'S STUDY

Other authors have tried to isolate the financial consequences of a merger. Mandelker (1974) examined 252 mergers in the United States and estimated the resulting changes in shareholder returns. He calculated the incremental returns or losses for companies involved in mergers by subtracting from the returns of each company that portion estimated to be attributable to movements in the market rather than to the merger. He calculated incremental returns or losses over a period of forty months prior to the merger and added them cumulatively. As may be seen in Figure 14.3, Mandelker found that small losses were made by the acquired companies' shareholders during the period between forty months and thirty months before the merger announcement. Subsequently, up to eight months prior to acquisition, the share prices of the companies moved with the market. At the end of that period, the share price started to move up relative to the market, with abnormal gains of about 18 percent up to the announcement date (month 0). Similarly, the acquirers' share prices improved relative to the market before the merger, but by a smaller margin of 3.5 percent. (This last result is not significantly different from zero in statistical terms.)

Figure 14.3   *Cumulative average abnormal returns for 252 acquisitions*

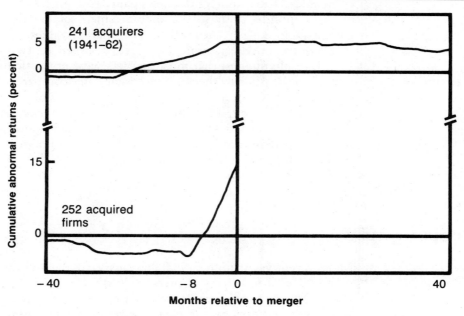

Source: B. Mandelker, "Risk and Return: The Case of Merging Firms," *Journal of Financial Economics,* 1, no. 4 (December 1974): 303–35.

Well, what can we say from Mandelker's study? There appear to be net gains to mergers, because acquirees' shareholders have gained substantially and the acquirers' shareholders have either gained or at least not lost, on average. "Not lost" suggests that the acquirers have obtained the risk-adjusted required rate of return on their investment in acquisitions, for Mandelker removed market movement and adjusted for the effects of any differences in systematic risk between the acquirer and the market. A second conclusion is that the market does appear to anticipate mergers prior to formal announcement. Finally, at least for part of the period of forty months prior to merging, the stockholders of acquired companies incurred losses on their investment and stockholders of acquiring companies gained; one possible conclusion is that acquiring companies were more profitable than acquired companies.

FRANKS, BROYLES, AND HECHT'S STUDY

In Britain, Franks, Broyles, and Hecht (1977), using a similar method to Mandelker's, estimated the gains to shareholders arising from seventy-one mergers in the breweries and distilleries industry during the period 1955–1972. Again, substantial net gains to merging were found for a majority of companies. The acquirees obtained gains averaging 26 percent over a period of three months prior to the announcement of the merger, and acquirers gained about 2.5 percent on their own market values.

There are, however, some differences between the two sets of results. The British results suggest that most mergers were not anticipated until less than three months prior to the announcement date, compared with eight months in the Mandelker results. The difference may simply have been due to the use of different sources of information, and different definitions of critical dates, about the bid. The British acquirees had abnormal losses prior to merging, perhaps indicating that weaker companies were being acquired. A further difference is that the abnormal gains of the acquirers disappeared subsequent to the takeover.

ASQUITH'S STUDY

More recently, Asquith (1983) has analyzed the returns obtained for 587 successful and unsuccessful mergers in the United States during the period 1962–1976. Asquith's results, which are summarized in Table 14.5, evidence a complex reaction by the capital market to the bidding process. Asquith divided his sample of companies into the four groups shown in Table 14.5. The first two groups are the target firms (the acquired companies), and the second two the bidding firms (the acquirers). Target firms and bidding firms

Table 14.5   *Abnormal returns for firms engaged in merger bids (%)*

	Pre-press period[a]	Press date[b]	Interim period[c]	Outcome date[d]	Post-outcome period[e]
211 Successful target firms	−14.1[f]	+6.2[f]	+8.0[f]	+1.3[f]	Not available
91 Unsuccessful target firms	−10.5[f]	+7.0[f]	−8.1[f]	−6.4[f]	−8.7[f]
196 Successful bidding firms	+14.3[f]	+0.2	−0.5	+0.2	−7.2[f]
89 Unsuccessful bidding firms	+2.2	+0.5	−6.2[f]	−0.2	−9.6[f]

[a]The pre-press period is the period from 480 days before the announcement of a merger bid until 21 days before. The abnormal returns given are for the entire period.
[b]Press date is the day that news of the merger bid first appears in the *Wall Street Journal.*
[c]Interim period is the period from 1 day after the press day until 2 days before the outcome date. The abnormal returns given are for the entire period.
[d]Outcome day is the day that the outcome of a merger bid is reported in the *Wall Street Journal.*
[e]The post-outcome period is the period from 1 day after the outcome date until 240 days after the outcome date. The abnormal returns given are for the entire period.
[f]The abnormal return is significantly different from 0 at the 1 percent level.

Source: P. Asquith, "Merger Bids, Uncertainty and Stockholder Returns," *Journal of Financial Economics,* 11, nos. 1–4 (1983): 81.

are divided further into mergers or bids on the basis of success and failure. The table shows abnormal returns for each group for five periods around the date of mergers, calculated in the same way as Mandelker's results.

The first or earliest period is the pre-press period, which begins 480 days before the announcement of a merger bid and ends 21 days before. The table shows that in the pre-press period the abnormal returns were significantly negative for the two groups of target firms and were significantly positive for the group of successful bidding firms. This evidence lends further support to the view that it is the strong firms that take over the weak.

On the press date, the day that news of the merger bid first appears in the *Wall Street Journal,* all four groups showed positive abnormal returns, but only the two groups of target firms showed significantly positive abnormal returns, approximately 6 to 7 percent more than could be attributable to general movements in the market.

The next period, the interim period, begins one day after the press day and finishes two days before the "outcome date," when the outcome of the merger is reported in the *Wall Street Journal.* In the interim period the abnormal returns continue to be significantly positive only for the group of successful target firms, while they are significantly negative for the two groups of firms involved in unsuccessful mergers. It is possible that the bid talks during the interim period revealed further information about poor profit prospects and reduced the chances of the bid being pursued successfully.

On the outcome date large significant negative abnormal returns continued for the group of unsuccessful target firms. Finally, in the post-outcome period, beginning one day after the outcome date until 240 days after the outcome date, all groups except for the successful target firms showed significantly negative abnormal returns. The results in the last column are surprising, because they would seem to indicate that all the parties to a merger (except for successfully acquired companies) lose money after the outcome of a merger is announced. These results are not easy to explain. For if they were repeated in the future, they would suggest that investors should sell the shares of acquiring companies on the announcement of a merger. Such a conclusion is not consistent with the concept of an efficient stock market described in Chapter 12.

Results of all three share price studies suggest that successful target firms experience substantial abnormal returns as a result of the bid. Successful acquiring firms, before the outcome of the bid, may make small gains as a result of the merger. On this evidence, one reasonably may conclude that there have been net gains to mergers for stockholders. After all, the stockholders of acquired firms gain, and the stockholders of acquiring firms either gain or do not lose. The only disturbing note in these rather neat conclusions is Asquith's result that stockholders of acquiring firms experience substantial abnormal losses after the outcome of the bid is known. One possible explanation is that these mergers were expected to be profitable when they were announced. However, the anticipated merger benefits were not fully realized and therefore led to abnormal losses.

BRADLEY, DESAI, AND KIM'S STUDY

So far we have examined studies that tried to estimate the gains or losses to shareholders from mergers. In a study by Bradley, Desai, and Kim (1983), an attempt was made to measure how the gains from mergers are distributed between the acquired and the acquiring company. The study examined a sample of 183 tender offers successfully completed between 1962 and 1980 in order to identify factors that determine how the gains from corporate combinations are divided over the stockholder groups of the merging firms.

If there is only one bidding firm, it may have managerial skills that are uniquely fitted to produce merger benefits. When there are many bidders, such skills are less likely to be unique. The more bidding firms there are, the less specialized the managerial talent of the individual acquiring company is apt to be. If the bidding firm is unique in possessing particular managerial skills, all the gains from the merger may accrue to the bidding firm.

Bradley et al. found that stockholders of target firms sought by multiple bidders earned significantly greater abnormal returns than stockholders of target firms that were sought by only one bidder. The cumulative abnormal return earned by the acquisition's stockholders was 40 percent during the fifty days surrounding date of the tender offer in the case of multiple bidders, and only 26 percent in the single bidder case. Either mergers sought by multiple bidders were more profitable or a greater proportion of the gains went to the target's stockholders. The authors found abnormal returns of 4.6 percent were earned by the stockholders of the acquiring firm in the case of multiple bidders and 0.8 percent in the single bidder case. If the authors' proposition is to be supported, we would have expected multiple bidders to have earned less than single bidders. It does seem that mergers involving multiple bidders have been more profitable than the single bidder case.

A Case Study: The Occidental–Cities Service Merger

Up to this point we have described the merger process dispassionately, as a bloodless activity. In fact, many mergers are contested by groups of the target firm's directors or owners. Frequently such contests involve takeover bids by more than one company including "friendly" takeover bids by "white knights." Gains and losses in friendly takeovers are distributed among owners of more than two companies, which may raise the question whether the directors of any of the companies acted in the best interest of their shareholders.

The merger between Occidental Petroleum and Cities Service is instructive. It began with an announcement by Cities Service on May 28, 1982, that Mesa Petroleum intended to bid for it and ended on August 26, 1982, with acceptance by Cities Service of a bid from Occidental Petroleum. The entire sequence of events as recorded by Ruback (1983) included a friendly and a subsequent hostile bid for Cities Services by Mesa Petroleum; a friendly and two hostile bids for Mesa Petroleum by Cities Service; a merger agreement between Gulf Oil and Cities Service; Cities Service's repurchase of stock held by Mesa and a standstill agreement between Mesa and Cities Service; Gulf Oil's termination of its merger agreement with Cities Service; and two friendly bids and one hostile bid by Occidental Petroleum for Cities Service.

Ruback's summary of the abnormal returns to the owners of each of the four firms involved is given in Table 14.6. The results are consistent with those of other studies. Cities Service (the successful target) shareholders realized an abnormal return of 12.45 percent, Occidental (the successful bidder) shareholders earned an abnormal return of almost zero, and Mesa and Gulf Oil shareholders (the unsuccessful bidders) large negative abnormal returns of -5.90 percent and -17.56 percent, respectively. These results are consistent with those of Asquith.

Table 14.6   *Summary of abnormal returns for firms involved in the Cities Service takeover*

Firm	Holding period	Cumulative abnormal return (percent)	Cumulative abnormal change in equity value (millions of dollars)
Cities Service	May 28–August 26	12.45	$352
Mesa Petroleum	May 28–June 21	−5.90	−64
Gulf Oil	June 17–August 26	−17.56	−1,131
Occidental Petroleum	August 13–August 26	−0.25	−4

The holding period is from the firm's first indication of its involvement in the Cities Service takeover through the day of the merger agreement between Cities Service and Occidental Petroleum, except in the case of Mesa, whose involvement ended on June 21 when Mesa agreed not to bid for Cities Service.

Source: Ruback, R. S., "The Cities Service Takeover: A Case Study," *Journal of Finance*, 38, no. 2 (May 1983): 328.

In the presence of such an outcome, it is natural to ask whether the merger activity that we observe is consistent with shareholder wealth maximization. After all, for Occidental the Cities Service acquisition appears to have been a zero NPV decision, and for Gulf an extremely costly one. Unfortunately, from the outside we cannot always tell why one loses and why the other gains. It is possible that part of the abnormal loss incurred by Gulf's shareholders was caused by market reflection of substantial lawsuits brought against the company as a result of the bid. However, the study does raise the issue that entering a bid battle may be a costly business.

Summary

In this chapter, we have stressed the need to justify mergers in terms of potential economic and financial benefits. When examining these benefits one should compare them with the alternatives to acquisition or mergers. The bid price must reflect alternative ways of obtaining the benefits of the merger. A merger is frequently costly, both in terms of legal costs and management time, and in terms of the bid premium that is paid by the acquirer to the acquiree's shareholders. Benefits thought to be associated with a merger might be obtained at a lower cost, for example, by direct investment in real assets. We have described in some detail the financial advantages to merging for shareholders. Some seem minor, exploitation of unused debt capacity and the coinsurance effect, for example. Finally, we have examined some of the evidence concerning the profitability of mergers that suggests there have been some net benefits to merging, although most of the value of the benefits appears to have been paid over to the acquired company's shareholders in bid premiums. The amount of the benefit may depend upon how unique the skills of the acquiring management are and how many bidders are competing.

Review Questions

1. Why is it frequently so difficult to value a fast growing, unlisted company?
2. Acquisitions that allow firm diversification can reduce the variability of earnings and therefore benefit managers and shareholders. Evaluate this statement.
3. A listed company is totally financed by equity. As a consequence, a potential acquirer is willing to purchase the company at a premium on its current market value. The acquirer justifies the bid premium on the basis of the tax benefits of borrowing that would accrue after purchase. Can such tax benefits justify the bid premium?
4. Why would takeover activity be more concentrated in some industries rather than others?
5. Company X wishes to acquire company Y. The required rates of return on the equity of the two companies are 12 percent and 15 percent, respectively. Which rate would you use to calculate the present value of any merger benefits that X forecasts? Provide detailed reasoning with your answer.
6. A merger between two firms whose earnings are imperfectly correlated will reduce the company's borrowing rate and increase the value of the firm. Evaluate this statement.
7. Why do you think mergers come in waves? Why do those waves appear to be correlated with rising stock markets?

Problems

*1. Two companies of equal size have plants of the same efficiency. They have an equal share of the market for product X. New technological developments can be taken advantage of in a new plant, but it would have to operate at twice the individual capacity of each company. The two companies are contemplating a merger that would allow them to exploit this possibility. The operating costs would be lowered from an equivalent annual cost of $1.20 per unit to $0.96 per unit, assuming combined total production remains the same at 2 million units.

Estimate the potential merger benefits. How should the benefits be distributed between the companies? (See Chapter 6 for discussion of equivalent annual costs.)

*2. Company X's management believes that acquiring the production facilities of Y, instead of building and equipping their own, will save the company $50 million in capital costs and at the same time enable it to meet the increased demand for its products. The present value of the merger benefits from increased production and sales is estimated at $15 million. It is estimated that $3.5 million will be obtained from the disposal of some other machinery but $18 million will be used to close some operations. What is the maximum premium that can be paid on Y's share price, given that there are 5 million shares outstanding, and the current price is $50 per share?

3. Sailmaker, Inc., is operating at full capacity and wishes to meet an increased demand for windsurfer sails. One of its main competitors, who has spare operating capacity, has approached Sailmaker for a merger at a cost of $6 million to Sailmaker. Given the projected revenues and costs, the net present value of the increase in sales of the merged company is estimated at $22 million. This NPV will be divided between the two companies on the basis of their market values. The competitor is valued on the stock market at $28 million, while Sailmaker's market value is $49 million. The alternative to the merger is to buy the manufacturing facilities of a bankrupt company for $11.5 million. However, this purchase option will increase costs of transportation, the present value of which would be $1.5 million. Assuming both options have about the same operating capacity and the same time lag to the start of operations, which option should Sailmaker accept? The other competitors are all operating at full capacity and cannot meet the increased demand.

*4. A company has identified a new product and is considering whether to buy new facilities from another company for $2,250,000 or to build the facilities to manufacture it. It would cost the company $850,000 in the first year, and $420,000 and $350,000, respectively, in the second and third years to build. The incremental cash flows from the new product, which are expected to decline with time because of increasing competition, in the first three years would be $480,000, $360,000, and $240,000, respectively.

If the company's cost of capital is 15 percent, should it buy or build? Assume that the facilities can be purchased immediately and the building would be completed in three years.

5. Company P has accumulated tax losses over the last five years that amount to $4.8 million. As the company anticipates profits in the future,

it expects to absorb the accumulated losses over four years. The forecast taxable profits are shown below (in millions of dollars).

End of year	0	1	2	3	4
Taxable profits	0.0	0.86	1.18	1.32	1.44

The company has been approached by a conglomerate about the possibility of a merger. The conglomerate can use the accumulated tax losses immediately. Company P will continue its operations unchanged. If the only reason for merging lies in the tax losses, what is the most that should be paid for company P? (Corporate tax rate is 46 percent.) Company P uses a discount rate of 10 percent.

What other ways than merging are there to obtain tax benefits?

*6. An investment banking firm is about to announce a takeover bid for company X at a price of $100 per share. The current share price is $90. Over the past six months the share price has risen from $50 to its current level. The market index has risen from 1,000, six months ago, to its current level of 1,250. Assuming the beta coefficient for the company is 1.25, estimate the bid premium being paid by the acquiring firm. What qualifications, if any, would you put on your conclusions?

7. An acquirer has purchased 10 percent of a potential acquisition three months prior to the launch of a bid. The shares were purchased at a price of $90 when the market index was 1,000. At the time of the bid, the share price was $110 and the market index was at 1,100. The bid price was $115 and there were 900,000 shares to be acquired.

Assuming that the acquiree's beta coefficient equals 1, what is the expected bid premium? Compute the profit on the pre-merger equity interest.

*8. Company A has made a takeover bid for company B, which is a small company engaged in food manufacturing. The offer price is $100 in cash for every share in B. Prior to the bid announcement, the market price of B's shares was $90. Company B's management has strongly recommended that its shareholders reject this offer on the grounds that the company's shares are worth more than $100. In particular, they have argued that, as B's earnings per share for the past year were $25, A's offer values B on a price-to-earnings ratio of only 4.0. Because the average price-to-earnings ratio for companies engaged in food manufacturing is currently 7.0, B's management argues that the company shares must be worth at least $175 and that an offer of $200 would be more realistic when the company's growth opportunities are taken into account. Company B's shareholders seem convinced, and as B's shares currently stand at $115 in the market, there seems little chance of A's bid succeeding.

Company A is considering whether to make an increased offer, and if so, at what price. As an adviser to company A, you have been asked to write a brief report explaining the principles of acquisition valuation and how company A should establish the maximum bid price.

*9. Two companies, K, Inc., and P, Inc., are considering merging in order to undertake a new project. Both companies are totally equity financed, and the new project will also be equity financed. What will be the market value of the combined company, KP, Inc., and its new beta value, given the following information?

	K, Inc.	P, Inc.
Market value (millions of dollars)	6.54	14.23
Beta (without project)	1.1	0.9
Net present value of project		3.60
Beta of project		1.3

References

Appleyard, A. R., and G. K. Yarrow, "The Relationship Between Take-over Activity and Share Valuation," *Journal of Finance,* 30, no. 5 (December 1975): 1239–50.

Asquith, P., "Merger Bids, Uncertainty and Stockholder Returns," *Journal of Financial Economics,* 11, nos. 1–4 (April 1983): 51–83.

Asquith, P., R. F. Bruner, and D. W. Mullens, "The Gains to Bidding Firms from Mergers," *Journal of Financial Economics,* 11, nos. 1–4 (April 1983): 121–39.

Bradley, M., A. Desai, and E. H. Kim, "Determination of the Wealth Effects of Corporate Acquisition via Tender Offer: Theory and Evidence," University of Michigan, Ann Arbor (September 1983).

Cooper, I. A., and J. R. Franks, "The Interaction of Corporate Financing and Investment Decisions," *Journal of Finance,* 38, no. 2 (May 1983): 571–83.

Firth, M., "The Profitability of Takeovers and Mergers," *Economic Journal,* 89, no. 354 (June 1979): 316–28.

Firth, M., "Takeovers, Shareholder Returns and the Theory of the Firm," *Quarterly Journal of Economics,* 94, no. 2 (March 1980): 235–60.

Franks, J. R., "Insider Information and the Efficiency of the Acquisitions Market," *Journal of Banking and Finance,* 2, no. 4 (December 1978): 379–93.

Franks, J. R., J. E. Broyles, and M. J. Hecht, "An Industry Study of the Profitability of Mergers in the U.K.," *Journal of Finance,* 32, no. 5 (December 1977): 1513–25.

Franks, J. R., and J. J. Pringle, "Debt Financing, Corporate Intermediaries and Firm Valuation," *Journal of Finance,* 37, no. 1 (June 1982): 751–62.

Green, R. C., and E. Talmor, "On the Structure and Incentive Effects of Tax Liabilities," University of Wisconsin at Madison (July 1983).

Grossman, S. J., and O. D. Hart, "Takeover Bids, the Free-Rider Problem and the Theory of the Corporation," *Bell Journal of Economics,* 11, no. 1 (Spring 1980): 42–64.

Halpern, P. J., "Corporate Acquisitions: A Theory of Special Cases? A Review of Event Studies Applied to Acquisitions," *Journal of Finance*, 38, no. 2 (May 1983): 297–317.

Halpern, P. J., "Empirical Estimates of the Amount of Distribution of Gains to Companies in Mergers," *Journal of Business*, 46, no. 4 (October 1973): 554–75.

Jensen, M. C., and R. Ruback, "The Market for Corporate Control: The Scientific Evidence," *Journal of Financial Economics*, 11, no. 5, 1–4 (1983): 5–50.

Kim, E. H., and J. L. McConnell, "Corporate Mergers and the Co-Insurance of Corporate Debt," *Journal of Finance*, 32, no. 2 (May 1977): 349–63.

Kitching, J., *Acquisitions in Europe: Causes of Corporate Successes and Failures*, Geneva: Business International (1973).

Lee, K. W., "Co-Insurance and Conglomerate Mergers," *Journal of Finance*, 32, no. 5 (December 1977): 36, no. 5, 1527–37.

Madden, G. P., "Potential Corporate Takeovers and Market Efficiency: A Note," *Journal of Finance*, 36, no. 5 (December 1981): 1191–98.

Mandelker, B., "Risk and Return: The Case of Merging Firms," *Journal of Financial Economics*, 1, no. 4 (December 1974): 303–35.

Meeks, G., "Disappointing Marriage: A Study of the Gains from Merger," Cambridge University Press, London, 1977. Occasional Paper 51.

Miles, J. A., and J. Rosenfeld, "An Empirical Analysis of the Effects of Voluntary Spinoff Announcements upon Shareholder Wealth," *Journal of Finance*, 38, no. 5 (December 1983): 1597–1606.

Mossin, J., "Merger Agreements: Some Game Theoretic Considerations," *Journal of Business*, 41, no. 4 (1968): 460–71.

Newbould, A., *Management and Merger Activity*, Liverpool: Guthstead Press, 1970.

Ruback, R. S., "The Cities Service Takeover: A Case Study," *Journal of Finance*, 38, no. 2 (May 1983): 319–30.

Singh, A., "Take-overs, Natural Selection and the Theory of the Firm," *Economic Journal*, 85, no. 339 (September 1975): 497–515.

Smiley, R., "Tender Offers, Transaction Costs and the Theory of the Firm," *Review of Economics and Statistics*, 58, no. 1 (February 1976): 22–39.

Stapleton, R. C., "The Acquisition Decision as a Capital Budgeting Problem," *Journal of Business Finance and Accounting*, 2, no. 2 (Summer 1975): 187–201.

Stapleton, R. C., "Merger Bargaining and Financing Strategy," *The Manchester School*, 39, no. 2 (June 1971): 131–44.

Stewart, J. F., R. S. Harris, and W. T. Carleton, "The Role of Market Structure in Merger Behaviour," *Journal of Industrial Economics*, 32, no. 3 (March 1984): 293–312.

Stiglitz, J. E., "On the Irrelevance of Corporate Financial Policy," *American Economic Review*, 64, no. 5 (December 1974): 851–66.

Warner, J. B., "Bankruptcy, Absolute Priority, and the Pricing of Risky Debt Claims," *Journal of Financial Economics*, 4, no. 3 (May 1977): 237–76.

V

Dividends, Taxes, and Financing Decisions

Raising capital is one of the principal functions of financial management. In the next nine chapters we show how companies obtain the funds that they need for replacement of assets and investment in new commercial activities, and how financing and investment decisions interact. Funds generated internally from ongoing operations provide the main source of equity finance for most companies. External sources of funds are usually employed only when internally generated funds are expected to be inadequate to meet the capital requirements of the company's investment program. Since dividends are also paid out of internally generated funds, however, the amount of dividends that are paid affects the external financing that may be required. In Chapter 15 on dividend policy we show how the company's dividend payment policy interrelates with its financing decisions. We also discuss the effect of differences in shareholder tax rates on dividends and capital gains on companies' dividend payout policies and how changes in dividends can be used to signal price-sensitive information to the stock market.

In the following three chapters we consider external sources of long-term finance. In Chapters 16 and 17 we discuss long-term debt and the economics of interest rates and bond prices, and in Chapter 18 we show how companies raise cash by issuing common stock. We then go on in Chapters 19 and 20 to explain the economics of financial options and how the concept of an option sheds light on many important issues in corporate finance.

In the following two chapters we discuss how the balance between debt and equity finance by a company affects its taxes and may affect its investment decisions. In Chapter 21 we discuss whether the tax deductibility of interest payments should affect the amount of a company's borrowing, and in Chapter 22 we show how to analyze the effect of a company's tax position on its investment decisions. Finally, in Chapter 23 we continue our discussion of tax effects by showing how differences in the tax-paying positions of different companies form the basis of lease financing decisions.

15

Dividend Policy

Most corporations make regular cash dividend payments to their stockholders. Corporate dividend policy is an important issue for at least two reasons. First, there may be conditions where a change in dividend policy can alter the market value of the firm. Second, if dividend policy can alter the market value of the firm or its assets, it might also affect the value of its new capital projects. If dividend policy does affect the value of capital projects, the net present value of a given capital project will be different for a company with one dividend policy than for a company with a different dividend policy.

Dividend policy might affect the value of the firm for two reasons. First, tax rates on capital gains are usually different from tax rates on dividends. If the company could reduce taxes by transforming dividends into capital gains (or vice versa), shareholders might value the firm at a correspondingly higher level. A second reason why dividend policy might affect the value of the firm is that it could provide valuable information to shareholders. For example, suppose that a firm has important information about the profitability of new investment opportunities that it wishes to convey to shareholders without disclosing details that might be useful to competitors. Changing the level of dividends might be an effective method of signaling favorable developments, helping to ensure that the market value of the firm reflects fully all the information that is available to management.

How Shareholders Benefit from Corporate Profits

Let us assume that a company starts life with $1,000 in assets. At the end of the first year, trading operations have produced a cash profit of $200. What are the different ways in which shareholders can benefit from these profits?

CASH DIVIDENDS

The most obvious way shareholders might benefit is if the company were to distribute the profits directly to shareholders in the form of a cash dividend. The directors of the company would decide to pay the dividend to all registered shareholders on a particular day, with the amount of each check depending upon the number of shares the stockholder owns.

RETENTIONS VERSUS CASH DIVIDENDS

Suppose that the profits of $200 earned by the company were not paid out as a cash dividend but instead retained within the firm. As a result, the worth of the company increases from $1,000 at the beginning of the year to $1,200 at the end. If a cash dividend of $200 had been paid out, the company would continue to be worth $1,000.

How do shareholders benefit from the profits of $200 if they are retained by the company rather than paid out as a cash dividend? The answer is that the price of each share of common stock will appreciate by the amount of the retained profits divided by the number of shares outstanding. With 100 shares outstanding, each share will rise in price by $2. Putting aside issues such as taxation and transactions costs, this means the shareholder can receive the benefit of the company's profits in the form either of a capital gain of $2 or of a cash dividend of $2 per share.

Most companies pay out only a proportion of the profits as a cash dividend, while retaining the remainder. As a result, shareholders receive part of their returns in the form of dividends and part as a capital gain.

STOCK DIVIDENDS

The company need not issue a cash dividend but instead may pay a stock dividend. A stock dividend provides shareholders with additional shares in the company in place of a cash dividend. Suppose that the company in our example issued 20 new shares to existing stockholders; how would they benefit? In fact, issuing stock dividends has essentially the same effect as retaining the profits and making no dividend payment at all. The company would still be worth $1,200 at the end of the year, but it would have 120 shares outstanding worth $10 each. If there had been no new issue of shares, there would be 100 shares outstanding worth $12 each. Shareholders should be indifferent between the two alternatives.

REPURCHASE OF SHARES BY THE COMPANY

A fourth way in which shareholders can benefit from profits earned by the company is by company repurchase of its own common stock in the stock market. In our example, the company's stock price is $12 per share at the end of the year, and there are 100 shares outstanding. If the company uses its profits of $200 to buy 16⅔ shares from investors, there will be only 83⅓ shares outstanding. The company will be worth 83⅓ × $12, or $1,000 again. Repurchasing shares has the same effect on the company as paying a cash dividend, but it gives the stockholder a capital gain of $12 − $10 = $2. We are, of course, ignoring taxes and transactions costs. Later in the chapter we shall provide some tax reasons why share repurchasing may be preferable to paying a cash dividend.

RESTRICTIONS ON MAKING CASH DIVIDENDS

We have assumed previously that a company can pay out as large a cash dividend as it likes. In fact, there will be legal restrictions on the amount of dividends that are permitted to be paid. First, the company may have entered into contractual agreements with lenders that stipulate limits on dividend payments. For example, it is quite usual for bond agreements to restrict the company's cash dividends to a particular proportion of current profits. Such restrictions are made because cash dividends reduce the firm's assets otherwise available to service the debt contract.

A second restriction may be imposed by state laws that prohibit companies from paying cash dividends if such payments would make the company insolvent. The object of these laws is to protect creditors who do not have specific loan agreements with the company. Further legal restrictions also may apply. The company may be prohibited from paying out its paid-in capital as a cash dividend. In our example, suppose that the company had issued 100 shares at $10 each to finance the purchase of the original assets. The laws would imply that the company could pay out only profits of $200 and not the original capital of $1,000. The constraints usually are only binding when a company either has just begun business or has incurred past losses and thus has not accumulated sufficient retained earnings from which to pay dividends.

A third restriction is imposed by the company's cash position. If the company's cash is less than the year's profit, it cannot pay out all its profit as dividends to stockholders without resorting to external financing to raise the required additional cash.

WHEN ARE DIVIDENDS PAID?

Companies usually pay cash dividends quarterly, although some companies pay dividends annually or semiannually. Dividends are payable to investors who are stockholders of the company on a specific date known as the **date of record,** and dividend checks are mailed about two weeks later. There are formal arrangements that allow investors who buy the stock near the record date to know for certain whether the shares they purchase are going to receive the dividend. Stock sold up to four days before the record date is sold with the dividend, or **cum-dividend.** (Four days are necessary to allow time for registration to take place.) Investors who buy stock subsequently are buying stock **ex-dividend,** which means that they do not receive the previously announced dividend.

Corporate Attitudes Toward Dividend Policy

We shall be concerned mainly with two aspects of dividend policy: the level of dividends that is paid by a company and the manner in which this level is changed in different circumstances. First we review some evidence as to how the average company relates dividends to the level of earnings and how it attempts to achieve a stable dividend policy when earnings are changing. We also describe how companies can make changes in dividends in order to convey valuable information to the market that cannot be conveyed as effectively by other means. In subsequent sections we shall show how tax effects have been used to try to explain differences in the level of dividends that companies pay.

STABILITY OF DIVIDEND POLICY

Lintner (1956) conducted a survey to determine the pattern of dividend payments adopted by financial managers. In general, he found that managers aimed to pay out some target proportion of earnings. However, since future earnings are changeable and uncertain, when earnings increased managers were willing to change dividends only partway toward the level implied by the target proportion of earnings in any one year. In a later empirical study, Fama and Babiak (1968) found that companies in their sample aimed to distribute about half of their net income in dividends. When earnings rose, these companies increased dividends about one-third of the way toward their target payout in the first year.

For example, suppose that management aimed to pay out 50 percent of earnings in the form of dividends but were willing to alter the existing dividend only one-third of the way each year towards the target. If earnings per share of $6.00 are to be announced, and the existing dividend has been $2.00 per share, what will be the new level of dividends? One would expect a dividend of $2.33 per share calculated as follows:

Earnings per share	$6.00
Target payment (0.50 × $6.00)	3.00
Existing dividend per share	2.00
Potential change in dividend	1.00
Actual change in dividend (0.33 × $1.00)	0.33
Existing dividend	2.00
New dividend per share	$2.33

The example shows a target payment of 50 percent of earnings, with an adjustment factor of 33 percent. If the company were operating in a more risky environment, it might choose to pay out a smaller proportion of earnings and to make smaller adjustments to dividends when earnings increase in order to ensure its ability to maintain a dividend level. Lintner found that most managers wish to avoid increasing dividends if increases later have to be reversed.

INFORMATIONAL CONTENT OF DIVIDENDS

Management often has information that it would like to convey to the company's stockholders. An obvious and direct way to do this is by an announcement to the press, or by a comment included with the company's quarterly earnings statement. A less direct method of conveying information is through the company's dividend policy. There are two possible reasons why management might prefer to signal information by changes in dividends. The first has to do with credibility. Management's favorable statements on company prospects might not be believed completely unless there is concrete evidence to support them. By paying higher dividends than the level expected by stockholders, management can signal in a material way that future prospects are better than previously expected. Such signals actually may not be credible if they did not have a cost because of the possibility of deceit. If we assume like Bhattacharya (1979) that increased dividends incur more taxes (because of higher stockholder marginal tax rates on dividends than on capital gains), increasing the dividend has such a cost.

A second reason to use dividend policy as an indirect means of conveying information to stockholders may be that management does not wish to make public the specific nature of the information in its possession. For example, suppose that a pharmaceutical company has developed a new drug it does not want its competitors to know about. At the same time, the company wishes to raise funds by means of an issue of stock to be sold to new stockholders. If management believes that the current market price of the stock does not yet reflect the bright prospects for the new drug product, the issue of new stock will be underpriced; the new stockholders will get a bargain at the expense of existing stockholders. If the company increases the dividend as a signal to investors that the company's prospects have improved (for undisclosed reasons), management helps to ensure that the issue of new stock can be sold at something like its full value and that existing stockholders will have the benefit of the capital gain.

If changes in dividends do convey information to the market about company prospects, they should affect share prices. In a study of dividend changes for 135 firms, Pettit (1972) found abnormal price changes associated with announcements of dividend changes. Such price changes were in excess of those that could be explained by movements in the market index and by the relative risk of the individual securities. Most of the price adjustment was found to take place either on the day of the dividend announcement or by the following day, and the largest price changes were associated with the largest percentage dividend changes. Pettit concluded that dividend changes do convey new information to the market.

One limitation of Pettit's study concerns the possible effect of simultaneous earnings announcements. Because earnings and dividend announcements frequently are made jointly, the large abnormal price changes that were observed to be associated with changes in dividends might be explained by large changes in earnings announced at the same time. Pettit's study on its own does not prove that dividends rather than earnings were the source of the information that caused the observed abnormal price changes. Aharony and Swary (1980), however, were able to separate the dividends effect from the earnings effect by examining only the quarterly dividends that were announced on dates different from the dates of earnings announcements. This study strongly suggests that changes in cash dividends do provide new information that affects stock prices.

A study by Asquith and Mullins (1983) suggests that the information effect of dividends is much larger than previously calculated by Aharony and Swary. They contend that share prices already reflect expectations about future dividend changes. As a result, studies measuring the impact of dividend changes on stock prices capture only the difference between the actual change and the anticipated or forecast change that already is reflected in the share price. In order to examine the total effect of dividend changes on share prices (not just the unanticipated portion), Asquith and Mullins analyzed a sample of 160 firms that announced their first dividend after paying no dividends for at least ten years. They assumed that the whole of the first dividend was unexpected. Their results showed that statistically significant increases in shareholder wealth resulted from such "initiating" dividends. The abnormal returns over the two-day announcement period averaged +3.7 percent, compared to the 1 percent observed by Aharony and Swary. When the authors excluded from the sample firms that announced other important information (earnings, mergers, and spin-offs) within twenty-one days of the dividend announcement, the results were more pronounced. For eighty-eight firms with no other information announcements, the excess returns over the two-day period averaged +4.7 percent. These results strongly suggest that dividends do have information content, and that share prices are significantly affected by changes in dividend policy. These results would confirm the view of those analysts who believe that dividend policy is an important information signaling device.

If dividends are an important mechanism for signaling information, we can understand why firms may want to change the dividends that they pay. Signaling alone, however, does not explain the target dividend payouts that a firm chooses. Some firms pay out a large proportion of earnings as dividends, others a much smaller proportion. Much of the literature on dividend policy has sought to explain dividend payout in terms of tax effects.

Dividend Policy in a World Without Taxes

The best way to appreciate the impact that taxes may have on the target dividend payout ratio is first to understand valuation in a world without taxes. In their 1961 article on dividend policy, growth, and valuation of shares, Miller and Modigliani (hereafter referred to as MM) showed that in a world of perfect capital markets and without taxes, dividend policy is irrelevant to the value of the company. Under such conditions, shareholders are indifferent between returns in the form of cash dividends and returns in the form of capital gains. New investment can be financed by retained earnings or by new equity; it does not affect the current value of the firm.

Let us examine the cash flows of an all-equity financed firm that has no debt outstanding. Its sources and uses of funds must be equal:

Uses of Funds = Sources of Funds

As a result, we may say that,

Dividends   New   Net Cash Flow from   New Capital
Paid Out +Investment=Existing Investment +Raised

$$D \quad + \quad I \quad = \quad E \quad + \quad C$$

By rearranging the above equation we get,

$$D - C = E - I$$

If we hold investments (I) at some fixed level, earnings (E) will be fixed also. Hence, if we wish to raise the dividend (D), we must raise new capital (C). New equity capital can come from two sources: existing stockholders and new stockholders. Let us consider each in turn.

CASE 1: NEW EQUITY IS RAISED FROM EXISTING STOCKHOLDERS

If the dividend is to be increased, and an equivalent amount of money is raised from existing stockholders, the same people who receive the dividends use the dividends to buy the new shares. In this case, stockholders will be no worse or no better off because of a change in dividend policy (without transactions costs).

CASE 2: NEW EQUITY IS RAISED FROM NEW STOCKHOLDERS

Suppose that the new money to finance the increase in dividends comes from new stockholders. Providing that new common stock can be sold at the existing market price (and not below it), dividend policy is still irrelevant.

EXAMPLE OF DIVIDEND IRRELEVANCE

An example will illustrate this proposition. Table 15.1 shows that an all-equity financed company has $9,000 in fixed assets and $3,000 in cash earmarked for a project that has a net present value of zero. If the project is undertaken, the total assets in the balance sheet will still have a market value

Table 15.1   *Balance sheet example to show dividend irrelevance*

Balance sheet

Cash (for project)	$3,000	Equity (market	$12,000
Fixed assets	9,000	value of	
		1,000 shares	
		outstanding)	
Total assets	$12,000	Total Equity	$12,000

of $12,000. Thus, the 1,000 shares of equity also have a total market value of $12,000. If the firm distributes $3,000 as a dividend, funds must be raised for the project. Assuming no change in capital structure, additional stock must be issued to raise the cash. If the issue is sold to the existing shareholders (who have just received the dividend), funds which had been paid out in dividends are merely paid by the shareholders back to the firm in exchange for additional stock certificates. Therefore, in the absence of taxes and issue costs for the stock flotation, dividend policy is irrelevant to the value of the firm.

Suppose now that the capital is raised from new shareholders. What will the price of the new stock be? Prior to the dividend, existing shares sell for $12,000/1,000, or $12. However, after the dividend the assets have been reduced by $3,000 and the stock will sell for $9,000/1,000, or $9. The holder of one share formerly worth $12 now has a dividend worth $3 and a share worth $9, so he or she is no worse off. The fair price for the new stock is $9, and the required $3,000 can be raised by selling $3,000/9, or 333.3 shares at this price. If this new block of equity can be sold without depressing the price of the existing shares, the existing shareholder worth remains unchanged, and the dividend is still irrelevant to the total value of the firm.

In Chapter 12 we discussed the evidence of Scholes (1972), which showed that large blocks of equity could be sold without depressing the stock price significantly. Scholes's study dealt with sales of shares from the portfolios of institutional investors rather than with stock issues by corporations to raise new equity. Nevertheless, his evidence is consistent with the view that cash paid out as dividends can be raised by the sale of stock without affecting the company's stock price significantly.

We have made some simplifying assumptions in this discussion: first, that there are no flotation or other costs associated with the issue of new shares or with the payment of dividends; second, that information can be disseminated perfectly and without cost; and third, that there are no taxes. The relaxation of any of these assumptions may weaken or overturn the irrelevance proposition.

Dividend Policy and Taxes

We have seen that if we lived in a world without taxes, the target level of dividend payments that a company chooses to make would be irrelevant (in the absence of information costs and of flotation costs for new issues of stock). However, when we introduce the reality of taxes, a number of important issues emerge.

MILLER AND MODIGLIANI

Of course we do not live in a world without taxes, and the possible effect that taxes might have on dividend policy is what the dividend controversy mostly centers on. Miller and Modigliani (1961) described the likely impact of these effects. Their principal concern was with the more favorable treatment accorded to capital gains over dividends. The lower tax rate on capital gains gives some weight to the view that earnings should be retained, or at least not paid out in the form of taxable dividends. MM point out, however, that the tax effect is somewhat diminished by the fact that a substantial (and growing) proportion of total shares outstanding currently is held by investors for whom there are either no taxes, and thus no tax differential between capital gains and dividends (charitable and educational institutions, foundations, pension funds, and low-income retired individuals), or for whom the tax advantage is, if anything, in favor of dividends (taxable corporations generally pay corporate tax on only 15 percent of their dividends).[1] Furthermore, many charitable institutions and trusts are not allowed to spend capital, thus they require dividends for the necessary cash to provide their services.

Actually, the dividend preferences of stockholders are very diverse. MM expect that companies will adopt a similarly diverse range of dividend policies to meet the particular tax positions and income needs of different stockholder groups.

FARRAR AND SELWYN

Farrar and Selwyn (1967) analyzed the position of an individual shareholder attempting to maximize after-tax income. If an individual investor pays a lower tax rate on capital gains than on dividend income, how does a company's dividend policy affect him or her? Suppose a firm adopts the policy

---

[1] Corporations pay corporate taxes on 15 percent of dividends received and 15 percent of capital gains, if the latter are realized in less than one year. If the capital gain is realized over more than one year, the capital gains tax is the same as the corporate tax rate on the total gain.

that all corporate earnings are to be paid out entirely as dividends and thereby taxed as personal income. If we assume that corporate and personal debt are held constant, we can analyze what one additional dollar of net operating income generates in terms of after-tax income for the shareholder. We shall assume a corporate tax rate of 46 percent and a marginal tax rate on income for the investor of 30 percent:

Before-tax income to the corporation	$1.00
Corporate taxes (46%)	0.46
After-tax corporate income	0.54
Gross dividend	0.54
Personal taxes (30%)	0.16
Net dividend	$0.38

If the after-tax proceeds from the additional dollar of before-tax income are distributed as a dividend, the shareholder will receive only $0.38. The total tax paid is $0.46 + $0.16, or $0.62. The government in fact is taking two bites at the apple, once with corporate tax and again with personal tax.

The corporation does have the choice not to pay the dividend and to retain the earnings. Under this alternative, the amount of taxes paid to the federal government would decrease by $0.16 on each dollar of before-tax income. For each dollar that the company earns before taxes it would have $1.00 − $0.46 = $0.54 to retain and reinvest, and the stock price would appreciate by a corresponding amount. If the effective marginal capital gains tax rate paid by shareholders is less than the marginal rate of tax that would be paid on income from dividends (30 percent in our example), Farrar and Selwyn would argue that the shareholder is better off with zero dividends.

The implications of Farrar and Selwyn's analysis for dividend policy would seem to be that companies should not distribute any more cash than they can help. If companies were to retain all their earnings indefinitely, a shareholder's tax obligation would be limited to capital gains taxes payable upon selling stock. Of course, the Internal Revenue Service in due course would challenge 100 percent earnings retention if it appeared that the only purpose of such a policy was the avoidance of taxes.

MODEL 1: BRENNAN

Brennan (1970) extended Farrar and Selwyn's results by considering how the prices of stocks might be affected by different dividend policies. He assumed that the market prices of stocks would adjust in such a way that the after-tax rate of return received by holders of a company's stock would be the same no matter what dividend policy the company adopted. This is a plausible assumption, because shareholders spend after-tax dollars for consumption, not before-tax dollars. In Brennan's model, buyers and sellers of the stock would require the same after-tax return from the stock even if the company adopts a different dividend policy. This means that if a firm adopts a high dividend payout policy, and if the shareholders have to pay higher taxes as a result, the firm's stock will have a lower price. The price will have to be lower in order to maintain the same after-tax rate of return that the shareholders require.

Table 15.2 provides an example illustrating Brennan's proposition. The table compares two dividend policies. Under policy A the company pays no dividends; the shareholder enjoys a capital gain instead. Under policy B the company pays out all earnings as dividends, and there is no capital gain. The earnings per share for the company are, of course, unaffected by the two dividend policies at $11.90 per share (expected to be constant in perpetuity). The company currently operates under dividend policy A, paying no dividends; its share price is $100. What would the share price (P_B) be if the company changed to policy B and paid out all its earnings in dividends?

If the company retains all its earnings under policy A, the price per share is expected to grow from $100 to $111.90 after one year, while under policy B the unknown share price P_B remains unchanged, because all the earnings per share of $11.90 are paid out in dividends. Brennan assumes that the effective marginal rates of income tax paid by shareholders would be the same under the two policies (40 percent), and we assume that the marginal capital gains tax rate is only 16 percent.[2] Using these tax rates, we obtain

Table 15.2   *Example of difference in share prices as a result of low and high dividend payout policies under Brennan's proposition*

	Policy A (no payout)	Policy B (100% payout)
Earnings per share	$ 11.90	$11.90
Current share price	$100.00	P_B
Next year's share price	$111.90	P_B
Dividend	0	$11.90
Tax on dividend at 40%	0	$ 4.76
Capital gain	$ 11.90	0
Tax on capital gain at 16%	$ 1.90	0
After-tax income	$ 10.00	$ 7.14
After-tax required rate of return	10%	10%
Current share price	P_A = $100.00	P_B = $71.40

[2]The capital gains tax (on net long-term gains) is 40 percent of the investor's marginal income tax rate (marginal tax rate $0.4 \times 0.4 = 0.16$).

the after-tax returns to shareholders of $10.00 per share from the capital gain under policy A (assuming that the shareholder realizes the gain at the end of the year) and only $7.14 per share from the dividend under policy B.

From these after-tax returns to shareholders, we can obtain the implied current share price under each policy. In Brennan's model, the shareholder's after-tax required rate of return is assumed to be the same regardless of which dividend policy is adopted by the company. In our example, the shareholder's after-tax required rate of return is 10 percent. Thus, an after-tax income to shareholders equal to $10.00 from capital gains under policy A must imply a share price of $100 (0.10 × $100 = $10.00). Similarly, under policy B the implied share price is $71.40 (0.10 × $71.40 = $7.14). At the price of $71.40 the shareholder's after-tax return of $7.14 under policy B provides the shareholder with an after-tax rate of return of 10 percent. Because the shareholder's required rate of return is the same under both dividend policies in Brennan's model, the policy that generates the largest tax payments will result in the lowest share price. If the company were to change from dividend policy A to policy B, its share price would fall from $100 to $71.40.

We can reconcile the difference between the share prices for policies A and B in the example of Table 15.2 by discounting the difference in tax payments under the two policies. Under dividend policy B the tax per share is $4.76 per year, and for policy A it is only $1.90 per year. The savings of tax under policy A would repeat every year in perpetuity (assuming a constant earnings per share). We obtain the present value of a perpetuity by dividing the annual incremental cash flow by the discount rate.

$$\frac{\$4.76 - \$1.90}{0.10} = \$28.60$$

The present value of the annual tax savings under policy A is equal to $28.60, which explains the difference between P_A and P_B ($100.00 − $71.40 = $28.60). It should now be clear that, in Brennan's model, if an increase in dividends increases the taxes paid, the company's share price is lower as a result.

An implication of Brennan's model is that a firm can change its value by changing its dividend policy. In our example, a firm that had been following dividend policy B could increase its stock price from $71.40 to $100.00 simply by reducing dividends to zero. What would be relevant for the firm would be just as relevant for a project. A firm that pays out a constant proportion of its earnings as dividends also pays out some proportion of the earnings of each new project. Under Brennan's model a project's net present value can be altered by the simple device of the target dividend payout ratio. The same project would have different values after tax to firms with different dividend policies.

This means that a firm with a lower target dividend payout ratio, leading to lower shareholder taxes, would find it profitable to buy the assets of firms with high dividend payout ratios. In reality, as project profitability often is the result of the unique ability of the management of a single firm, transfers of assets between firms with different dividend policies may be impractical and expensive; it would be easier for firms to alter their dividend policies than to transfer assets.

If the taxes on dividends are greater than the taxes on capital gains, a firm ought to pay zero dividends. Actually, we know that some firms pay very large dividends while others pay very small ones. In the face of such observation, it is difficult to explain actual payout ratios using only Brennan's model of dividends and taxes.

One way of testing Brennan's proposition is to determine whether differences in dividend payout ratios are accompanied by differences in before-tax rates of return. If dividend policy does not affect the effective rates of taxes being paid, and if the after-tax market rates of return are unaffected by dividend policy as Brennan assumed, before-tax rates of return must be different for companies with different dividend payout policies. There have been a number of studies on Brennan's model that it will be useful to review.

EMPIRICAL TESTS OF BRENNAN'S MODEL

Black and Scholes (1974) tested the proposition that before-tax returns on companies with high dividend yields would be significantly greater than those for comparable companies with low dividend yields. Using a modification of the capital asset pricing model (see Chapters 8 and 9), they suggested that, if dividends and taxes are important, before-tax returns on shares would depend not only on the risk-free rate plus a premium for systematic risk but also on a dividend term. Black and Scholes's modification to the CAPM can be written as follows:

$$\text{Expected Return} = \frac{\text{Risk-free}}{\text{Rate}} + \frac{\text{Premium for}}{\text{Systematic Risk}} + \frac{\text{Premium for}}{\text{Dividend Yield}}$$

The first two terms on the right-hand side are the familiar capital asset pricing model, where the premium for systematic risk equals the risk premium on the market portfolio multiplied by the beta coefficient. The third term, the premium for dividend yield, was defined by Black and Scholes as

$$\text{Premium for Dividend Yield} = \text{Dividend Impact Coefficient}$$

$$\times \frac{\text{Yield on Stock} - \text{Yield on Market Portfolio}}{\text{Yield on Market Portfolio}}$$

The premium for dividend yield is proportional to the percentage difference between the dividend yield on a particular common stock and the dividend yield on the market portfolio. If the dividend impact coefficient turns out to be significantly positive, this would indicate that investors expect higher before-tax returns from companies that pay higher dividend yields than average. Black and Scholes tested this model on portfolio annual returns and dividend yield data for the years 1936 to 1966, failing to find a significantly positive value for the dividend impact coefficient. Their evidence was not enough to reject the hypothesis that dividend yield is irrelevant.

Litzenberger and Ramaswamy (1979) tested a similar model using individual stocks instead of portfolios and monthly data instead of annual data. They found a statistically significant relationship between before-tax excess returns on stocks and excess yields on a large sample of individual stocks. However, when Miller and Scholes (1982) replicated Litzenberger and Ramaswamy's results, they found that their own results could be explained by dividend information effects rather than by dividend tax effects. As we have discussed, announcements of increased dividends convey favorable information to investors, resulting in increased share prices. Miller and Scholes adjusted the test procedure to eliminate possible information effects. When they dropped all firms from the sample that paid a dividend in the same month that the dividend was announced, the dividend yield coefficient became insignificantly different from zero. While Litzenberger and Ramaswamy's results confirmed Brennan's hypothesis that dividends are undesirable, Miller and Scholes's 1982 results suggest that such a conclusion is not supported when dividend tax effects are separated from dividend information effects.

While the preponderance of published evidence does not support the undesirability of dividends, Long's (1978) results provide strong evidence that dividends actually were preferable to capital gains in the case of stockholders investing in two classes of shares issued by the Citizens Utilities Company in 1956. This company's Series A stock pays only stock dividends that are not taxed as ordinary income (by virtue of a special IRS ruling), while Series B stock pays only cash dividends. Historically, the dividends on Series A have been 8 to 10 percent greater than the corresponding cash dividends on Series B. If investors were indifferent between capital gains and dividends, the price of the Series A shares would have averaged 8 to 10 percent above the price of the Series B shares, fully reflecting the difference in level between the higher stock dividends and the cash dividends. However, Long observed that the price of the Series A stock dividend paying shares was somewhat below this level relative to the corresponding price of the Series B cash dividend paying shares. Long concluded that in this case cash dividends commanded a slight price premium in the market over equal amounts (before taxes) of capital gains.

Previous studies have paid little attention to the fact that investors pay different tax rates depending upon income and tax status. For example, some institutional investors are virtually tax-exempt, while some private investors pay taxes at the rate of 50 percent. The fact that investors have different tax rates suggests that investors may hold some stocks in preference to others. This preference for particular stocks depending upon an investor's marginal tax rate is known as the **tax clientele** effect.

Stockholders who pay higher income tax rates on dividends compared with capital gains will prefer low payout stocks. In contrast, those stockholders who pay relatively lower tax rates on dividends compared with capital gains will prefer high payout stocks. If high dividend payout companies attract low tax rate stockholders, and low dividend payout companies attract high tax rate stockholders, the clientele effect implies that the required before-tax returns under different dividend policies need not be very different, even if both types of stockholders require the same after-tax returns as Brennan suggests.

ELTON AND GRUBER'S EVIDENCE ON TAX CLIENTELES

Elton and Gruber (1970) provided evidence for the proposition that companies with different payout ratios attract different stockholder clienteles. They examined the price performance of stocks around the time of the dividend payment, measuring the average price decline when stocks went ex-dividend. For example, if a stock is priced currently at $10, and a dividend of $1 per share is announced, what happens to the share price when the dividend is paid? Before the ex-dividend date shareholders are entitled to the dividend. After the ex-dividend date, a new purchaser is not entitled to receive it. On the ex-dividend date the security falls in price, because the buyer must wait for the next dividend. If taxes were zero, we would expect the price decrease to be equal to the lost dividend, or exactly $1 per share. However, if the new shareholder would have had to pay taxes on the dividend, the net after-tax loss of not receiving the dividend would be less than $1. Therefore the fall in the price of the stock on the ex-dividend date should be less than the gross amount of the dividend paid.

Elton and Gruber derived a relationship whereby the drop in stock price, after it goes ex-dividend, must equal the dividends paid out, after adjusting for any personal taxes. They called the drop in price $(P_B - P_A)$, where P_B is the price of the stock with the dividend and P_A is the price of the stock without the dividend. Because this price drop represents a capital loss, it can offset any capital gains for tax purposes. If the capital gains tax rate is T_G, the after-tax price drop is

$$(P_B - P_A)(1 - T_G)$$

This price drop must equal the dividends received after personal taxes, that is $D(1 - T_P)$, where D is the dividend and T_P is the stockholder's personal tax rate on the dividend. In order that the individual stockholder should be indifferent between selling the stock before or after the ex-dividend date, the after-tax capital loss must equal the after-tax dividend

$$(P_B - P_A)(1 - T_G) = D(1 - T_P)$$

Rearranging the equation above, Elton and Gruber obtained

$$\frac{P_B - P_A}{D} = \frac{1 - T_P}{1 - T_G}$$

By measuring the ratio on the left-hand side of the equation for a large sample of companies declaring dividends, Elton and Gruber were able to obtain implied tax rates on the right-hand side. They had to assume some fixed relationship between the tax rate on dividends (T_P) and the tax rate on capital gains (T_G), so they assumed that the capital gains tax rate was half the personal income tax rate ($T_G = 0.50\ T_P$).

Elton and Gruber's results are summarized in Table 15.3. They ranked their sample of stocks according to ten dividend yield (D/P) groups. Group 4 in the table, for example, has a mean dividend yield of 3.28 percent (column 1). The price drop on the ex-dividend date as a proportion of the dividend is 62.46 percent. That is, for \$1 of dividend paid the price drop was \$0.6246.

Table 15.3 *Elton and Gruber's evidence for dividend yield statistics ranked by deciles*

Group	Mean dividend yield	Price drop as a proportion of dividend*	Implied tax bracket**
1	0.0124	0.6690	0.4974
2	0.0216	0.4873	0.6145
3	0.0276	0.5447	0.5915
4	0.0328	0.6246	0.5315
5	0.0376	0.7953	0.3398
6	0.0416	0.8679	0.2334
7	0.0452	0.9209	0.1465
8	0.0496	0.9054	0.1747
9	0.0552	1.0123	—
10	0.0708	1.1755	—

*$(P_B - P_A)/D$
**Assuming that the capital gains tax rate is half the personal tax rate.

Source: E. J. Elton and M. J. Gruber, "Marginal Stockholders' Tax Rates and the Clientele Effect," *Review of Economics and Statistics*, 52, no. 1 (1970): 72.

To obtain the stockholder's implied marginal tax rate:

$$\frac{P_B - P_A}{D} = \frac{1 - T_P}{1 - 0.5T_P}$$

As we know, the left-hand side is 62.46 percent for group 4. To solve for T_P

$$0.6246 = \frac{1 - T_P}{1 - 0.5T_P}$$

Solving, $T_P = 0.5459$

According to this equation, then, the stockholder's marginal tax rate T_P for group 4 is 54.59 percent, which is slightly different from Elton and Gruber's figure of 53.15 percent as some of Elton and Gruber's table entries appear to have been calculated slightly differently.

It is noticeable in the table that the ratio of ex-dividend price changes to dividends tends to increase with the dividend yield, which implies lower stockholder tax rates for stocks with higher dividend yields. This evidence suggests that tax clienteles exist, for share prices do behave around dividend dates as though the shareholders of high-yield stocks pay taxes at a different rate from that of shareholders of low-yield stocks.

Elton and Gruber's results have generated considerable discussion. For example, Miller and Scholes (1982) in a review of the empirical work cast doubt on Elton and Gruber's results, because they would imply profitable trading opportunities for investors. Let us examine an example. Assume that market prices are set by investors with a 30 percent marginal tax rate. The price of a particular stock is $100.00 just before a dividend is paid; this would fall by $8.75 to $91.25 after a dividend of $12.50 is paid. What would be the reaction of two individual shareholders with marginal income tax rates of 30 percent and 0, respectively? (Assume that the high-rate taxpayer pays capital gains taxes at a rate of only 15 percent and that there are no transactions costs.)

The high-rate taxpayer would sell the stock for $100.00 per share immediately before the dividend is paid in order to avoid the high tax on the dividend, buying the shares back for $91.25 immediately after the dividend is paid when the shares go ex-dividend. The shares will have dropped $12.50 × (1 − 0.30) = $8.75, as that is the value of the dividend after taxes to the dominant group of shareholders at a tax rate of 30 percent. The high-rate taxpayer would make an after-tax capital gain of $8.75 × (1 − 0.15) = $7.44. In contrast our zero rate taxpayer would buy the stock for $100.00 just before the dividend is paid, collect the dividend of $12.50 (paying zero taxes), and sell the stock for $91.25. Such an investor would make −$100 + 91.25 + 12.50 = $3.75 per share.

Such arbitrage possibilities can arise if trading in securities is dominated by a group of investors who have the same tax rate. Shareholders with tax rates above or below the tax rate of the dominant group can make money by trading around the dividend date. In reality, if such arbitrage trading continued without limit, nobody would pay taxes above the capital gains rate. Such trading usually is restrained either by rules laid down by the Internal Revenue Service or by the transactions costs of buying and selling shares. For example, the IRS might revoke the tax-exempt status of an institutional investor caught engaging in such obvious forms of tax arbitrage. The implication is that Elton and Gruber's conclusions would be valid only if restrictions by the IRS restricted tax arbitrage.

MODEL 2: MILLER AND SCHOLES

Miller and Scholes (1978) discuss ways in which shareholders can transform cash dividends into capital gains by exploiting two seemingly unrelated provisions of the Internal Revenue Code. The first provision allows deductions of interest payments on borrowed funds from taxable income. Individual borrowers can avoid or decrease income tax on dividends by setting interest charges against taxable dividend income. The second provision allows the stockholder to invest in an insurance policy or pension plan where the income is virtually tax free. Miller and Scholes show that shareholders can use these provisions to avoid paying different rates of tax on dividends and capital gains. If they are correct, taxes have no effect on dividend policy.

Miller and Scholes give an example of an investor who owns $100,000 worth of shares from which he or she expects dividend income of $5,000 plus a capital gain of $4,500. The gain will not be taxed until the shares are sold. The dividends will be taxed immediately unless the investor can offset the dividend income against interest payable on personal loans. In fact, the investor has borrowed $50,000 at 10 percent and pays $5,000 in interest. The position is summarized as follows.

Shares	$100,000		
Capital gains		$4,500	
Dividends			$5,000
Borrowings	50,000		
Interest at 10%			−5,000
Capital gains		$4,500	
Taxable income			0

The shareholder has no taxable income arising from the dividends because dividend income can be set against the interest charges on personal borrowing. What can the investor do with the proceeds of the $50,000 loan? It can be invested in a tax-free insurance policy or pension program. The insurance company or pension fund invests the $50,000 in bonds returning 10 percent. (We assume the bonds are of the same risk as the individual's borrowing so that the two interest rates will be equal.) The bond income of $5,000 is not taxed because savings programs of this type are tax-exempt. Only when the funds are distributed to the saver by the pension fund or insurance company is tax due, and then it is at the lower capital gains tax rate. This device allows the investor effectively to transform taxable dividend income into capital gains. Although the capital gains tax eventually must be paid, in the meantime the investor enjoys the benefits of (compounded) tax-free accumulation of wealth.

Miller and Scholes have shown there may be ways that investors can reduce personal taxes on dividends to the capital gains rate by appropriate tax planning. If this is so, the effect of the difference between tax rates on dividends and on capital gains may be much less than had been supposed by Farrar and Selwyn and by Brennan. If Miller and Scholes are correct, the world of asset valuation and taxes is very simple. Firms with the same risks will use exactly the same discount rate to value capital projects, and the same capital projects will have the same value, irrespective of which firms own them, and irrespective of differences in firms' dividend payout ratios. From a tax point of view, dividend policy becomes irrelevant to a company's valuation.

Actually, according to Feenberg (1981), not many investors have taken advantage of the method described by Miller and Scholes. This could be because the transactions costs of such schemes are excessive for some investors. Alternatively, the complexity of the tax code and uncertainty about future legislation may have made it too difficult for many investors to take advantage of the opportunity.

Even if one cannot use the Miller and Scholes model, it may be that there are other mechanisms by which the investor can avoid higher taxes on dividends. One such vehicle would be **dual purpose funds,** which provide dividend paying shares for those investors who like dividend income and capital shares for those investors who like capital gains. Such funds provide all the services of a mutual fund, but in addition they are able to channel dividends to investors with low tax rates and capital gains to investors with high tax rates.

Dividend Policy and Flotation Costs

In the absence of taxes or any informational content to dividends, it is clear from Miller and Modigliani's argument that, from a shareholder's perspective, retained earnings and new equity are perfect substitutes. That is, no extra costs are incurred when a company increases its dividend payments by $1 (thereby reducing retained earnings by $1), and then replaces the $1 by selling $1 of new equity if these transactions do not involve any leakage of cash to other parties such as the Internal Revenue Service. Clearly, however, the sale of new shares does involve such leakages: flotation expenses. In Chapter 18 we discuss the manner in which new equity is purchased from corporations by investment banking firms and sold to investors. This activity generates flotation expenses, which range from 4 percent of an issue's gross proceeds in the case of large stock offerings ($100 million to $500 million) to around 14 percent for small offerings ($0.5 million to $2 million). These flotation expenses make dividends less desirable (hence retained earnings more desirable).

To illustrate, let us assume that a company plans to increase its dividends by $1, then to replace the funds by issue of new stock. If the flotation expense is 10 percent of gross proceeds, the company must offer enough shares to produce a gross amount of $1 \div (1 - 0.1) = \$1.11$. In effect, this raises the cost of the dividend of $1 per share up to $1.11. The existence of flotation expenses means that companies may resist increasing cash dividends when increased dividends would require them to issue otherwise unnecessary new securities to raise cash for investment.

Alternatives to Dividends

If a company generates more cash than it needs for current investment in capital projects, it can use the cash to pay dividends. Alternatively, the company can invest the cash in securities to hold on behalf of its shareholders. Eventually, the shareholders will expect to receive the earnings from these securities either in the form of increased dividends or in the form of capital gains. Whether it is practical for the company to hold securities in this way is determined in part by tax considerations. The three types of securities that companies frequently purchase include their own stock, government securities, and stocks of other companies.

REPURCHASING THE COMPANY'S OWN STOCK

Some United States companies use surplus cash to repurchase their own stock. Share repurchase is the most direct way for the company to put cash into the hands of shareholders in a form that is not taxable as dividend income but instead as capital gains. For example, Table 15.2 illustrated a company paying out all its earnings in the form of dividends (policy B). At earnings per share of $11.90, the shareholder paid taxes on the dividend amounting to $4.76. After-tax income therefore was equal to $11.90 − $4.76 = $7.14. Assuming that the shareholder's after-tax required rate of return is 10 percent, this policy results in a share price equal to $71.40.

Now suppose that the company adopts policy C, which involves using all earnings to repurchase its own stock. Under this policy the company's share price will be $100 as it was under policy A (where the company paid no dividends). The price will be $100 because the repurchase of shares will create a taxable capital gain that is the same as that under policy A (if the shareholder should sell the balance of his shares at the end of the first year).

The (simplified) details of the repurchase transaction are as follows. Let us assume that the shares initially are worth $100. There are 1,000 shares, so the all-equity financed company is worth $100,000. The company then earns $11,900, or $11.90 per share. The additional earnings prior to payout make the company worth $111,900 and the shares worth $111.90 each. The additional earnings represent a proportion of 11,900/111,900 = 10.6344 percent of the value of the outstanding shares. Therefore, if the company uses all its earnings to buy its own stock, it will have to repurchase 10.6344 percent of the outstanding stock. As there are 1,000 shares, after the repurchase there will be 10.6344 percent fewer, or 893.655 shares. While the company had $111,900 worth of assets prior to repurchase of the stock, it has only $100,000 worth of assets after repurchase, having used the difference to finance the repurchase. With 893.655 shares outstanding, the remaining shares are worth $100,000/893.655 = $111.90 per share. When the company repurchases stock, the shareholder realizes a capital gain of $11.90 for each share sold back to the company. When the remaining stock is sold at the end of the year, the shareholder will be taxed on the $11.90 capital gain on each of these shares as well. Assuming a capital gains tax rate of 16 percent, the after-tax gain is $10.00. Therefore, the original value of the shares is $100 if the shareholder's required rate of return is 10 percent.

Compare the $100 value for the shares under policy C to repurchase with the $71.40 value under policy B to pay out all earnings as dividends and to the $100 value under policy A to pay no dividends at all. Given our assumptions that shareholders pay a higher marginal rate of tax on dividends than on capital gains, that all capital gains are realized at the end of one year, and that the shareholders' after-tax required rate of return remains unaltered, a policy of share repurchase could be as favorable as a policy of zero dividends. Both policies appear superior to the payment of cash dividends. Unfortunately, only in the case of tender offers involving redemption of more than 20 percent of outstanding corporate stock is the repurchase sure of being taxed as a capital gain (according to Section 302 of the U.S. Internal Revenue Code).

Vermaelen (1981) published a study of stock repurchases made by cash tender offers in which he found that the average increase in stockholder wealth around the time of the announcement of the share repurchase was 15.7 percent. Such a large gain cannot be explained completely by the tax advantages of stock repurchase compared with dividend payments. Vermaelen made the point that stock repurchases evidently convey information to shareholders. His evidence confirms the signaling hypothesis that stock repurchase can be used as a device to convey favorable information to stockholders, and that this information adds additional value to the shares that cannot be explained merely by different tax treatment of dividends and capital gains.

INVESTING IN TREASURY BILLS

Let us consider investment by the company in Treasury bills and compare the resulting after-tax returns with the alternative of letting the company's shareholders invest the same funds in Treasury bills for themselves. If the company invests in a Treasury bill yielding 10 percent, it must pay corporate taxes on the income. When the income eventually is paid out as a dividend, the shareholder will have to pay personal taxes on the dividend at that time. If instead the dividend is paid immediately, the shareholder pays personal taxes on the dividend now rather than later and can then purchase Treasury bills with the net-of-tax dividend. In both cases the present value of the personal taxes on the dividends is the same. The difference between the two alternatives lies solely in the comparison between taxes paid by the company with taxes paid by shareholder on the income from the Treasury bill. If the company holds the Treasury bill, it must pay taxes on the income at the corporate tax rate, currently 46 percent. If the shareholder holds the Treasury bill during the same period, the tax would be less assuming the effective personal tax rate on income from such securities is lower than the federal corporate income tax rate of 46 percent. Consequently, unless the company is currently in a nontaxpaying position, accumulating Treasury bills is unlikely to be a good alternative either to paying dividends or repurchasing the company's own stock.

INVESTING IN THE STOCKS OF OTHER COMPANIES

An alternative way to use the firm's idle cash is to invest in the stock of other companies. Eighty-five percent of the dividends received by the investing company are exempt from corporate taxes. Similarly, any capital gains, if they are realized by the investing company in less than one year, also enjoy the 85 percent exemption. Beyond a one-year holding period all gains are taxed at the corporate tax rate. Clearly, the 85 percent exemption makes short-term investment in the stocks of other companies more attractive than investment in Treasury bills from a tax point of view. However, does this fact affect dividend policy?

If the company reduces its target dividend payout ratio in order to invest in stocks in other companies, its effective rate of tax on the income becomes $(1 - 0.85) \times 46 = 6.9$ percent if its marginal corporate tax rate is 46 percent. Note that income from holdings in other corporations has already borne corporate taxes paid by the originating firm. Thus, the tax of 6.9 percent paid by the investing corporation is a tax that would not have been paid if the shares were held by individuals rather than corporations.

If the firm has spare cash only temporarily, paying it out in dividends and having it returned via a new stock issue is too expensive because of flotation costs. The cash would be better invested in marketable securities. From a tax point of view, it would seem that purchasing other companies' securities is preferable to buying Treasury bills (although the latter are less risky and involve lower transactions costs).

There are other reasons why firms purchase common stock in other companies. The most obvious motive is a prelude to a merger. Even without a merger, an equity stake may be a useful way of influencing competition, although such purchases may arouse the interest of the antitrust division of the Justice Department.

Summary

Evidence suggests that companies tend to follow predictable patterns of dividend payment. Companies appear to choose a target dividend payout ratio and to move toward this target dividend payout each year. Temporary deviations from the usual pattern of dividend adjustments to new earnings will not be interpreted immediately as a change in policy. Significant deviations from the pattern are interpreted by investors as new information with implications about future earnings prospects.

The question arises as to how a company should choose its target dividend payout ratio. Current theory and evidence do not provide much support for the view that the difference in dividend and capital gains tax rates affects the choice of dividend payout. This may be partly because high dividend payout policies seem to attract low-taxpaying shareholders, and low dividend payout policies attract high-taxpaying shareholders (the tax clientele effect). The amount of taxes actually paid under each policy may not be very different.

If taxes do not determine the dividend payout ratio, what does? Because flotation costs are high for new issues of securities, and reductions of regular cash dividends signal unfavorable information to investors, a company can be expected to set the level of regular cash dividends low enough so that it can maintain the level, given the expected variability of the company's earnings. If the target payout ratio is set too high and earnings fall, maintaining the dividend may require frequent outside financing and unnecessary flotation costs. The greater the variability of earnings, the lower the dividend target payout ratio should be, and the slower the adjustment of regular cash dividends to increases in earnings that may be only temporary. As a conservative payout ratio for the regular dividend frequently results in the accumulation of surplus cash, companies distribute the excess funds to stockholders in the form of "extra" dividends or "special" dividends. Investors who understand that these additional dividends may not be repeated are less likely to interpret the loss of such additional dividends as unfavorable information about the company's future.

Review Questions

1. Why do companies use dividend policy to convey information indirectly to shareholders? Why not give the shareholders the information by means of a specific public announcement?
2. Why might a company provide stockholders with the choice of receiving either a cash or a stock dividend?
3. "Shareholders prefer the certainty of cash dividends now rather than the prospect of future capital gains." Analyze this statement, assuming a world without taxes.
4. What are the important assumptions behind Modigliani and Miller's view of dividend policy in the absence of taxes? Assume that, if a dividend is paid, new capital must be raised to finance profitable capital investment.
5. In the example given in Table 15.2, how could a company adopting policy B increase its share price?
6. Why would the existence of tax clienteles create arbitrage opportunities around dividend announcement dates? Give an example different from that used in the chapter.
7. Why might dividend policy be relevant to the valuation of new capital projects?
8. How might the capital asset pricing model be altered if dividend yields affect the market values of companies' stocks?
9. Summarize your own view as to the relevance of dividend policy to the market valuation of companies' securities.

Problems

*1. If Brennan's model applies in the stock market, what would be the before-tax rates of return for companies X and Y, given they both have the same after-tax rates of return of 12 percent and that the dividend yields are 5 percent and 20 percent, respectively? Assume the tax on dividends to be 30 percent and the tax on capital gains 15 percent.

2. From the information in Problem 1, show how, in Brennan's world, the value of company Y would change if it reduced its dividend yields to (a) 5 percent, and (b) 0 percent. The initial share price for Y is $100. Show your calculations.

*3. If a company's share price is $100 with-dividend and the dividend is $10, what does Elton and Gruber's model say happens to its price when it goes ex-dividend? Assume the personal tax rate is 40 percent and the capital gains tax rate is 40 percent of the personal tax rate.

4. Assuming that Elton and Gruber's model is correct, what should (a) an investor with a personal tax rate of 60 percent do, and (b) an institutional investor with a low tax rate of 15 percent do around the ex-dividend dates? What are the limitations to your answers?

*5. If a stock is priced at $50.00 with dividend, and its price falls to $46.50 when a dividend of $5.00 is paid, what is the implied marginal rate of personal tax for its shareholders? Assume that the tax on capital gains is 40 percent of the rate of personal income tax.

*6. A company is deciding whether to invest some of its cash in Treasury bills or to return it to shareholders as dividends. The company pays corporate tax at 46 percent and estimates that the average marginal tax rate of its shareholders is 30 percent. What should the company do? How does the situation alter if its shareholders pay tax at an average marginal rate of 50 percent? Use an example to illustrate your answer.

7. A company has identified some stocks in which it could invest cash in the short term. The most feasible alternative is to pay the cash as increased dividends to its shareholders, rather than to repurchase its own shares.
   (a) If the majority of its shareholders are tax-exempt charities and institutions, and low income pensioners, what should it do?
   (b) What should the company do if it estimates that its shareholders, on average, pay tax at a marginal rate of 40 percent?

*8. A company has 500,000 shares outstanding at $90 per share. Its earnings for the last year were $3 million. Assuming that the price-to-earnings ratio remains the same, what will be the new share price after it repurchases 100,000 shares at $90 per share? The company has spare cash for this repurchase. What other assumptions are made in your analysis?

9. If a company has forecast its future earnings to be $100 million and its financing needs to be $40 million, what would be its dividend payout ratio if its forecast investment is (a) $135 million, or (b) $115 million?
   What would the company have to do if it wished to have a target dividend payout ratio of 20 percent and it wishes to invest $135 million?

10. A company normally has declared dividends in a predictable pattern. Its target dividend payout appears to be 55 percent of annual earnings. When earnings change, however, the company usually changes its dividend only half way toward the level that the target dividend payout ratio would imply. The last dividend was $1.00 per share, and the company has just announced annual earnings of $3.00 per share.

(a) What level of dividend per share would the market now expect?
(b) The company announces that total dividends for the year will be $2.00 per share. How will the market react to this announcement and why?

References

Aharony, J., and I. Swary, "Quarterly Dividend and Earnings Announcements and Stockholders' Returns: An Empirical Analysis," *Journal of Finance,* 35, no. 1 (March 1980): 1–12.

Asquith, P., and D. W. Mullins, Jr., "The Impact of Initiating Dividend Payments on Shareholders' Wealth," *Journal of Business,* 56, no. 1 (January 1983): 77–96.

Bhattacharya, S., "Imperfect Information, Dividend Policy, and 'The Bird in the Hand' Fallacy," *Bell Journal of Economics,* 10, no. 1 (Spring 1979): 259–70.

Black, F., and M. Scholes, "The Effects of Dividend Yield and Dividend Policy on Common Stock Prices and Returns," *Journal of Financial Economics,* 1, no. 1 (May 1974): 1–22.

Brennan, M., "Taxes, Market Valuation and Corporate Financial Policy," *National Tax Journal,* 33, no. 4 (December 1970): 417–27.

Eades, K. M., P. J. Hess, and E. Han Kim, "On Interpreting Security Returns During the Ex-dividend Period," *Journal of Financial Economics,* 13, no. 1 (March 1984): 3–35.

Elton, E. J., and M. J. Gruber, "The Effect of Share Repurchase on the Value of the Firm," *Journal of Finance,* 35, no. 1 (March 1980): 135–49.

Elton, E. J., and M. J. Gruber, "Marginal Stockholders' Tax Rates and the Clientele Effect," *Review of Economics and Statistics,* 52, no. 1 (February 1970): 68–74.

Fama, E., and H. Babiak, "Dividend Policy: An Empirical Analysis," *Journal of the American Statistical Association,* 63, no. 4 (December 1968): 1132–61.

Farrar, D., and L. Selwyn, "Taxes, Corporate Financial Policy and Returns to Investors," *National Tax Journal,* 30, no. 4 (December 1967): 444–54.

Feenberg, D., "Does the Investment Interest Limitation Explain the Existence of Dividends," *Journal of Financial Economics,* 9, no. 3 (September 1981): 265–70.

Hess, P., "The Ex-dividend Behavior of Stock Returns: Further Evidence on Tax Effect," *Journal of Finance,* 37, no. 2 (May 1982): 445–56.

Khoury, N., and K. Smith, "Dividend Policy and the Capital Gains Tax in Canada," *Journal of Business Administration,* 8, no. 2 (Spring 1977): 19–37.

Kim, E. H., W. Lewellen, and J. McConnell, "Financial Leverage Clienteles: Theory and Evidence," *Journal of Financial Economics,* 7, no. 1 (March 1979): 83–110.

Long, J. B., Jr., "The Market Valuation of Cash Dividends: A Case to Consider," *Journal of Financial Economics,* 6, nos. 2–3 (June/September 1983): 235–64.

Lintner, J., "Distribution of Incomes of Corporations Among Dividends, Retained Earnings and Taxes," *American Economic Review,* 46, no. 2 (May 1956): 97–113.

Lintner, J., "Optimal Dividends and Corporate Growth Under Uncertainty," *Quarterly Journal of Economics,* 78, no. 1 (February 1964): 49–95.

Litzenberger, R., and K. Ramaswamy, "Dividends, Short Selling Restrictions, Tax-Induced Investor Clienteles and Market Equilibrium," *Journal of Finance,* 35, no. 2 (May 1980): 469–82.

Litzenberger, R., and K. Ramaswamy, "The Effect of Personal Income Taxes and Dividends on Capital Asset Prices: Theory and Empirical Evidence," *Journal of Financial Economics,* 7, no. 2 (June 1979): 163–96.

Miller, M., and F. Modigliani, "Dividend Policy, Growth and the Valuation of Shares," *Journal of Business,* 34, no. 4 (October 1961): 411–33.

Miller, M., and K. Rock, "Dividend Policy Under Asymmetric Information: Part I," University of Chicago, March 1982.

Miller, M., and M. Scholes, "Dividends and Taxes," *Journal of Financial Economics,* 6, no. 4 (December 1978): 333–64.

Miller, M., and M. Scholes, "Dividends and Taxes: Some Empirical Evidence," *Journal of Political Economy,* 90, no. 6 (December 1982): 1118–41.

Pettit, R. R., "Dividend Announcements, Security Performance, and Capital Market Efficiency," *Journal of Finance,* 37, no. 5 (December 1972): 993–1007.

Ross, S. A., "The Determination of Financial Structures: The Incentive Signalling Approach," *Bell Journal of Economics,* 8, no. 1 (Spring 1977): 23–40.

Vermaelen, T., "Common Stock Repurchases and Market Signalling," *Journal of Financial Economics,* 9, no. 2 (June 1981): 139–83.

Government and Corporate Debt

Borrowing represents an important source of finance both for federal, state, and local governments and for corporations. Because governments have lower credit risk than business firms, their interest costs are lower; still they must compete directly for funds in the capital market. For this reason, it is important to understand the patterns of both government and corporate borrowing and the most important kinds of government debt instruments. This chapter also describes the more important types of intermediate to long-term fixed interest corporate securities and how these securities are traded and quoted in the financial press. Finally, we describe the credit quality of corporate debt: how aggregate financial ratios for U.S. corporations have been changing in recent years, the credit rating services offered by Moody's and Standard & Poor's, and some key financial ratios that they and other financial analysts use to assess the financial health of companies.

In the next chapter we shall discuss in more detail the economics of bond prices and interest rates.

Patterns of Corporate and Government Finance

A major fact of life for financial officers of American corporations is that in recent years business and government both have made heavy demands on funds from the financial market. Conventional economic thinking suggests that government deficits are inevitable, and even desirable, during recessions. Government surpluses, however, should be realized during periods of economic expansion so that reduced pressure on capital markets allows the demands of the expanding business sector for debt financing to be met. As Table 16.1 shows, federal, state, and local governments have not conformed to this model over the past decade. They raised $207.1 billion in 1982, compared with $31.5 billion a decade earlier. And in mid-1983, federal deficits of over $200 billion per year over the next several years were being forecast.

At the same time, corporate demand for funds also has grown rapidly. As Table 16.2 shows, external sources of corporate funds have varied within a range of 24 to 55 percent of total sources. While the dollar amount of new corporate debt and equity issues more than doubled from 1973 to 1982 (Table 16.3), government financing required a large and growing percentage of the total funds raised in the capital markets, rising to 71 percent in 1982.

The pattern we are describing is one in which business and government competed for funds supplied by individual savers. If the government has to finance a deficit, such financing can be accommodated only if

Corporate demand for funds goes down, which may reduce investment and economic growth

Household saving rates go up

Capital flows to the United States from other countries rise

Interest rates rise

The Federal Reserve tries to reduce the competition for funds by increasing the rate of growth of the money supply. With some lag, this tends to increase the inflation rate and, subsequently, interest rates. (Chapter 7 discusses the relationship between interest rates and inflation.)

Each of these adjustments to accommodate increased government financing has occurred during the 1980–1983 period. From the perspective of corporate financial management, however, the increase in interest rates has been the most visible: interest rate yields on twenty-year United States government bonds averaged 7 to 9 percent until the late 1970s. From 1980 to 1982 they ranged from 11.4 to 13.7 percent.

Government needs, of course, are dictated largely by expenditure programs and income from taxation rather than by profitability criteria. Nevertheless, the government's power to tax and its almost unlimited borrowing power give government bonds the highest credit standing and hence the lowest interest rates. Consequently, any action by federal and local governments or agencies that affects interest rates on their own debt also will tend to have a similar effect on the interest rates on corporate debt. For example, we would expect an increase in the yield on twenty-year government bonds to produce an equivalent rise in the yield on twenty-year corporate bonds.

Table 16.1
Funds raised by government units in the United States capital market (billions of dollars)

	1970	1971	1972	1973	1974	1975	1976	1977	1978	1979	1980	1981	1982
United States Treasury and agencies	12.8	25.5	17.3	9.7	11.8	85.4	69.0	56.8	53.7	37.4	79.2	87.4	161.3
State and local governments	11.3	17.8	14.2	12.3	15.5	13.7	15.2	15.4	19.1	20.2	27.3	22.3	45.8
Total	24.1	43.3	31.5	22.0	27.3	99.1	84.2	72.2	72.8	57.6	106.5	109.7	207.1

Source: Various Federal Reserve *Bulletins*.

Table 16.2
Nonfarm nonfinancial corporations' sources and uses of funds (billions of dollars)

	1972	1973	1974	1975	1976	1977	1978	1979	1980	1981
USES										
Expenditure on physical assets	99.0	121.5	137.9	109.7	148.3	175.1	202.2	219.8	220.5	260.9
Investment in financial assets	50.1	70.5	52.2	41.2	53.5	62.5	92.0	127.3	97.4	53.9
Total Uses	149.1	192.0	190.1	150.9	201.8	237.6	294.2	347.1	317.9	314.8
SOURCES										
Internally generated funds	85.0	91.7	85.6	119.7	134.2	157.4	175.7	188.8	197.5	231.1
Externally raised funds	66.6	100.7	104.4	37.2	76.6	94.9	139.7	157.5	136.2	121.1
Total sources	151.6	192.4	190.0	156.9	210.8	252.3	315.4	346.3	333.7	352.2
External sources as % of total sources	44	52	55	24	36	38	44	45	41	34
Statistical discrepancy	2.4	0.4	0.0	6.0	9.0	14.7	21.2	−0.8	15.8	37.4

Source: *Economic Report of the President*, February 1983.

Table 16.3
Corporate financing compared with government financing (billions of dollars)

	1973	1974	1975	1976	1977	1978	1979	1980	1981	1982
New corporate issues										
Bonds	22.3	32.1	42.8	42.4	42.0	36.9	40.1	53.2	44.6	53.2
Preferred stock	3.4	2.3	3.5	2.8	3.9	2.8	3.6	3.6	1.8	5.1
Common stock	7.8	4.0	7.4	8.3	7.9	7.5	7.8	16.9	23.6	25.4
Total	33.5	38.4	53.7	53.5	53.8	47.2	51.5	73.7	70.0	83.7
Federal, state and local governments	22.0	27.3	99.1	84.2	72.2	72.8	57.6	106.5	109.7	207.1
Total	55.5	65.7	152.8	137.7	126.0	120.0	109.1	180.2	179.7	290.8
Governments as % of total	40	42	65	61	57	61	53	59	61	71
Average yields on 20-year United States government bonds	0.069	0.081	0.082	0.078	0.077	0.085	0.093	0.114	0.137	0.129

Source: Various Federal Reserve *Bulletins*.

The United States Treasury is the largest single issuer of debt securities. As its credit standing is the highest in the world, the interest rates it pays are sometimes described as risk-free, because the probability of default is zero. On the other hand, because future inflation rates and real interest rates are not known with certainty, the real returns on Treasury bonds (in terms of purchasing power) are risky. If you buy a government security maturing next year, you can be certain about what your proceeds will be, but you cannot be certain about their purchasing power. Although the nominal or money rate of return is certain, the real return is uncertain. This point was illustrated in Chapter 7. Moreover, if you purchase a fixed interest government bond and plan to sell it before it matures, you do not know for sure what price you can sell it at or how much the proceeds actually will buy. Consequently, both nominal and real returns are uncertain. Fixed interest corporate bonds present investors with the same risks as well as the additional risk of nonpayment. For this reason, their expected yields have to be higher than those on government bonds in order to attract investors. Our starting point for discussion of interest rates and debt instruments is with the lowest risk obligations: those issued by the Treasury.

Treasury Debt Obligations

There are three types of Treasury obligations: Treasury bills, notes, and bonds.

TREASURY BILLS

Treasury bills are quoted in terms of a $100 denomination and issued in denominations of from $10,000 to $1,000,000 with maturities of up to one year, although most are issued with three- or six-month maturities. The bills pay no interest, and so the return to investors must be in the form of a capital gain. The investor buys the bills at a discount on the notional $100 face value and then receives $100 on maturity. An initial purchase of Treasury bills must be for a minimum of $10,000, with further amounts available in lots of $5,000. The effective interest rate depends upon the size of the discount and the time remaining to maturity.

Treasury bill discounts are quoted in the *Wall Street Journal* in the form shown at the bottom of Table 16.4, which gives quotations for various government securities at midafternoon on July 14, 1983. The bill maturing

Table 16.4   *Treasury bills and bonds*

Treasury Issues

* * *

Bonds, Notes & Bills

Thursday, July 14, 1983
Mid-afternoon Over-the-Counter quotations supplied by the Federal Reserve Bank of New York City.
Decimals in bid-and-asked and bid changes represent 32nds; 101.1 means 101 1/32. a-Plus 1/64. b-Yield to call date. d-Minus 1/64. n-Treasury notes.

Treasury Bonds and Notes

Rate	Mat. Date	Bid	Asked	Bid Chg.	Yld.
15⅞s,	1983 Jul n	100.8	100.10	....	6.66
9¼s,	1983 Aug n	99.31	100.3	....	7.73
11⅞s,	1983 Aug n	100.6	100.10	— .1	7.44
16¼s,	1983 Aug n	100.27	100.29	— .1	8.10
9¾s,	1983 Sep n	100	100.4	....	8.86
16s,	1983 Sep n	101.9	101.13	....	8.53
15½s,	1983 Oct n	101.20	101.24	....	9.09
7s,	1983 Nov n	99.6	99.10	....	9.06
9⅞s,	1983 Nov n	100	100.4	— .1	9.32
12⅝s,	1983 Nov n	100.26	100.30	....	9.35
10½s,	1983 Dec n	100.10	100.14	....	9.44
13s,	1983 Dec n	101.9	101.13	— .1	9.68
15s,	1984 Jan n	102.18	102.22	— .1	9.74
7⅞s,	1984 Feb n	98.17	98.21	+ .1	9.69
15¼s,	1984 Mar n	102.29	103.1	— .1	9.98
14¼s,	1984 Mar n	102.21	102.25	+ .1	9.94
14¼s,	1984 Mar n	102.23	102.27	....	9.97
13⅞s,	1984 Apr n	102.21	102.29	— .1	9.95
9¼s,	1984 May n	99.12	99.20	....	9.73
13¼s,	1984 May n	102.11	102.19	— .1	9.91
13¾s,	1984 May n	102.26	102.30	+ .1	10.14
15¾s,	1984 May n	104.9	104.13	— .1	10.08
8⅞s,	1984 Jun n	98.28	99.4	....	9.86
14¾s,	1984 Jun n	103.21	103.25	— .1	10.11
13⅛s,	1984 Jul n	102.22	102.26	....	10.20
6⅜s,	1984 Aug n	96.18	97.2	+ .2	9.30
7¼s,	1984 Aug n	97.6	97.14	+ .1	9.81
11⅝s,	1984 Aug n	101.6	101.10	— .1	10.36
13¼s,	1984 Aug n	102.24	103	+ .1	10.24
12⅛s,	1984 Sep n	101.23	101.27	+ .1	10.46
9¾s,	1984 Oct n	99.3	99.7	....	10.41
9⅞s,	1984 Nov n	99.6	99.10	— .1	10.43
14¾s,	1984 Nov n	104.20	104.24	....	10.45
16s,	1984 Nov n	106.20	106.24	....	10.43
9⅝s,	1984 Dec n	98.15	98.19	....	10.44
14s,	1984 Dec n	104.16	104.24	— .1	10.49
8s,	1985 Jan n	96.18	96.26	....	10.24
9¼s,	1985 Feb n	98.4	98.12	+ .1	10.42
9⅜s,	1985 Feb n	98.16	98.20	....	10.57
14⅜s,	1985 Feb n	105.18	105.26	— .2	10.53
9¾s,	1985 Mar n	98.14	98.18	....	10.57
13⅜s,	1985 Mar n	104.2	104.10	+ .2	10.55
9½s,	1985 Apr n	98.6	98.10	+ .2	10.56
3¼s,	1985 May	93.3	94.3	+ .3	6.74
4¼s,	1975-85 May	93.26	94.26	+ .4	7.34
9⅞s,	1985 May n	98.20	98.22	+ .1	10.67
10⅜s,	1985 May n	99.19	99.27	— .3	10.47
14⅛s,	1985 May n	105.13	105.17	— .1	10.71
14⅜s,	1985 May n	105.24	106	— .2	10.68
14s,	1985 Jun n	105.20	105.24	— .4	10.66
10s,	1985 Jun n	98.24	98.26	— .1	10.68
8¼s,	1985 Aug n	95.20	95.28	....	10.51
9⅜s,	1985 Aug n	97.27	98.3	— .1	10.67
13⅛s,	1985 Aug n	104	104.8	....	10.78
15⅞s,	1985 Sep n	109.18	109.26	....	10.76
9¾s,	1985 Nov n	97.26	97.30	....	10.76
11¾s,	1985 Nov n	101.21	101.25	....	10.86
14⅛s,	1985 Dec n	106.23	106.31	— .1	10.81
13½s,	1986 Feb n	105.14	105.22	— .2	10.91
9⅞s,	1986 Feb n	97.26	97.30	....	10.81
14s,	1986 Mar n	106.20	106.28	— .2	10.99
7⅞s,	1986 May n	92.25	93.1	— .1	10.80
9⅜s,	1986 May n	96.14	96.18	+ .1	10.81
13¾s,	1986 May n	106.12	106.20	....	10.96
14⅞s,	1986 Jun n	109.12	109.16	— .2	11.02
8s,	1986 Aug n	92.15	92.23	— .1	10.85
12¼s,	1986 Sep n	103.2	103.6	....	11.04
6⅛s,	1986 Nov	90.23	92.23	+ .4	8.69
13⅞s,	1986 Nov n	107.18	107.22	+ .1	11.05
16⅛s,	1986 Nov n	113.15	113.23	— .2	11.08
10s,	1986 Dec n	97.6	97.10	— .1	10.96
9s,	1987 Feb n	94.4	94.12	— .2	10.94
12¾s,	1987 Feb n	104.12	104.16	— .1	11.19
10¼s,	1987 Mar n	97.14	97.18	....	11.07
12s,	1987 May n	102.17	102.25	+ .9	11.09
14s,	1987 May n	108.7	108.15	+ .3	11.22
10½s,	1987 Jun n	98.2	98.4	— .2	11.10
13¾s,	1987 Aug n	107.26	108.2	....	11.23

Rate	Mat. Date	Bid	Asked	Bid Chg.	Yld.
7⅝s,	1987 Nov n	88.27	89.3	+ .1	10.85
12⅝s,	1987 Nov n	104.12	104.20	+ .2	11.25
12¾s,	1988 Jan n	103.22	103.30	+ .2	11.24
10⅛s,	1988 Feb n	96.5	96.13	+ .1	11.14
13¼s,	1988 Apr n	106.27	107.3	+ .1	11.28
8¼s,	1988 May n	89.20	89.28	+ .6	11.01
9⅞s,	1988 May n	95.6	95.10	+ .2	11.16
14s,	1988 Jul n	109.20	109.30	— .1	11.33
10½s,	1988 Aug n	97.7	97.11	....	11.20
15⅜s,	1988 Oct n	115.8	115.16	— .2	11.37
8¾s,	1988 Nov n	90.21	90.29	+ .4	11.05
14⅜s,	1989 Jan n	112.15	112.23	— .1	11.44
14⅜s,	1989 Apr n	111.22	111.30	+ .2	11.48
9¼s,	1989 May n	92	92.8	— .24	11.09
14½s,	1989 Jul	112.19	112.27	....	11.48
11⅞s,	1989 Oct n	101.25	102.1	+ .2	11.41
10¾s,	1989 Nov n	97.14	97.22	+ .1	11.27
10½s,	1990 Jan n	96	96.4	+ .11	11.36
3½s,	1990 Feb	90.22	91.22	+ .4	4.99
10½s,	1990 Apr n	96.2	96.6	+ .3	11.33
8¼s,	1990 May n	86.24	87	+ .3	11.01
10¾s,	1990 Jul n	97.7	97.9	+ .5	11.33
10¾s,	1990 Aug n	97.3	97.11	— .2	11.31
13s,	1990 Nov n	107	107.8	+ .4	11.51
14½s,	1991 May n	114.1	114.9	....	11.67
14⅞s,	1991 Aug n	116.8	116.16	....	11.67
14¼s,	1991 Nov n	113.8	113.16	+ .1	11.67
14⅝s,	1992 Feb n	115.15	115.23	....	11.68
13¾s,	1992 May n	111.4	111.12	+ .4	11.65
4¼s,	1987-92 Aug	90.2	91.2	+ .1	5.52
7¼s,	1992 Aug n	77.10	78.10	— .2	11.10
10½s,	1992 Nov n	94.20	94.28	+ .2	11.41
4s,	1988-93 Feb	90.14	91.14	+ .1	5.14
6¾s,	1993 Feb	73.18	74.18	+ .7	11.13
7⅞s,	1993 Feb	80.5	80.21	+ .7	11.23
10⅞s,	1993 Feb n	96.20	96.28	— .1	11.42
10⅛s,	1993 May n	92.24	92.28	+ .3	11.35
7½s,	1988-93 Aug	77.17	78.1	+ .5	11.18
8⅜s,	1993 Aug	83.23	83.31	+ .6	11.33
8⅜s,	1993 Nov	83.16	83.24	+ .4	11.34
9s,	1994 Feb	85.15	85.23	+ .7	11.35
4⅛s,	1989-94 May	90.20	91.20	+ .8	5.15
8¾s,	1994 Aug	83.17	83.25	+ .5	11.36
10⅛s,	1994 Nov	92.4	92.12	+ .8	11.34
3s,	1995 Feb	90.16	91.16	+ .10	3.92
10⅜s,	1995 May n	93.30	94.6	+ .4	11.42
10⅜s,	1995 May	93.1	93.9	+ .9	11.44
12⅝s,	1995 May	106.20	106.28	+ .14	11.55
11½s,	1995 Nov	99.23	99.31	+ .9	11.51
7s,	1993-98 May	69.28	70.12	+ .10	11.13
3½s,	1998 Nov	90.10	91.10	+ .3	4.28
8½s,	1994-99 May	78.26	79.26	+ .9	11.26
7⅞s,	1995-00 Feb	73.30	74.6	+ .10	11.37
8⅜s,	1995-00 Aug	77.7	77.15	+ .6	11.40
11¾s,	2001 Feb	100.20	100.28	+ .12	11.63
13⅛s,	2001 May	110.20	110.28	+ .14	11.67
8s,	1996-01 Aug	74.2	74.10	+ .11	11.38
13¾s,	2001 Aug	112.20	112.28	+ .10	11.66
15¾s,	2001 Nov	130.27	131.3	+ .11	11.61
14¼s,	2002 Feb	119.10	119.18	+ .6	11.65
11⅝s,	2002 Nov	99.23	99.31	+ .10	11.62
10¾s,	2003 Feb	93.16	93.24	+ .10	11.56
10¾s,	2003 May	93.18	93.26	+ .9	11.55
11⅛s,	2003	96.10	96.14	+ .9	11.58
8¼s,	2000-05 May	75.24	76	+ .16	11.22
7⅝s,	2002-07 Feb	70.12	70.20	+ .11	11.18
7⅞s,	2002-07 Nov	72.10	72.18	+ .9	11.18
8⅜s,	2003-08 Aug	75.14	75.22	+ .11	11.31
8¾s,	2003-08 Nov	78.8	78.16	+ .10	11.35
9⅛s,	2004-09 May	81.6	81.14	+ .10	11.37
10⅜s,	2004-09 Nov	91.4	91.12	+ .10	11.42
11¾s,	2005-10 Feb	101.2	101.10	+ .15	11.59
10s,	2005-10 May	88.10	88.18	+ .11	11.37
12¾s,	2005-10 Nov	108.13	108.21	+ .11	11.65
13⅞s,	2006-11 May	117.7	117.15	+ .11	11.68
14s,	2006-11 Nov	118.16	118.24	+ .11	11.66
10⅜s,	2007-12 Nov	91.14	91.18	+ .9	11.37

U.S. Treas. Bills

Mat. date	Bid	Asked	Yield Discount	Mat. date	Bid	Asked	Yield Discount
-1983-				**-1983-**			
7-21	8.58	8.46	8.61	11-17	9.18	9.12	9.57
7-28	8.38	8.26	8.42	11-25	9.19	9.11	9.58
8- 4	8.76	8.68	8.86	12- 1	9.21	9.13	9.61
8-11	8.76	8.68	8.88	12- 8	9.22	9.14	9.64
8-18	8.74	8.66	8.87	12-15	9.22	9.14	9.66
8-25	8.70	8.60	8.82	12-23	9.24	9.16	9.70
9- 1	8.82	8.74	8.98	12-29	9.24	9.16	9.72
9- 8	8.85	8.77	9.03	**-1984-**			
9-15	8.86	8.78	9.06	1- 5	9.25	9.17	9.75
9-22	8.85	8.77	9.06	1-12	9.27	9.23	9.83
9-29	8.90	8.82	9.13	1-26	9.28	9.22	9.84
10- 6	9.06	8.98	9.32	2-23	9.31	9.23	9.86
10-13	9.08	9.04	9.40	3-22	9.33	9.25	9.92
10-20	9.11	9.03	9.40	4-19	9.40	9.32	10.04
10-27	9.08	9.00	9.39	5-17	9.34	9.26	10.01
11- 3	9.17	9.09	9.50	6-14	9.40	9.32	10.14
11-10	9.18	9.10	9.53	7-12	9.38	9.34	10.22

Source: *Wall Street Journal*, July 15, 1983.

in 28 calendar days on August 11, 1983 is quoted as follows:

Maturity date	Bid	Asked discount	Yield
8–11	8.76	8.68	8.88%

The bid and asked quotations here are on a **banker's discount** basis. The banker's discount is a way of expressing the dollar return from the bill as an annual return that would be earned over 360 days if the bill were reinvested at simple interest (not compounded). Note that the price of the bill is by convention not shown. However, we can describe the relationship between banker's discount, face value, maturity, and price. The actual asked bill price, *P,* equals $100 (the notional face value) less the actual discount, expressed as a proportion of the 27 days remaining to the bill's maturity (based on 30-day months). That is,

$$P = \$100 - \$8.68 \times \frac{27}{360}$$

$$= \$100 - \$.651$$

$$= \$99.349$$

The final figure of 8.88 percent in the yield column is the **bond equivalent yield.** Unlike the banker's discount, which is in dollars, the bond equivalent yield is expressed as a percentage. The yield is the actual dollar discount ($100.00 − $99.349 = $0.651) on the bill, expressed as a percentage of the bill's price and annualized on the basis of a 365-day year. Thus

$$\text{Yield} = \frac{365}{27} \times \frac{\$0.651}{\$99.349} \times 100$$

$$= 8.86\%$$

The small discrepancy of 0.02 percent between the calculated bond equivalent yield of 8.86 percent and the quoted yield of 8.88 percent may be due to typographical error.

The bond equivalent yield that is quoted in the *Wall Street Journal* is not the same as the annual compound rate of interest. The compound interest rate on the bond may be calculated on a 30-day month basis as follows:

$$R = \left(1 + \frac{0.651}{99.349}\right)^{360/27} - 1$$

$$= 0.0910$$

$$= 9.10\%$$

The annual compound yield on the bill would be 9.10 percent. This yield is based on the assumption that the bill's proceeds can be reinvested for the remainder of the year at the same interest rate to get an annual compound rate of return equal to 9.10 percent. In practice, reinvestment at exactly the same rate is usually not possible.

TREASURY NOTES AND BONDS

Unlike Treasury bills, Treasury notes and bonds pay interest (semiannually). **Notes** are issued with maturities of up to seven years; **bonds** can have any maturity but generally they have had original maturities of more than five years. The longest period bond outstanding on July 14, 1983, was issued as a thirty-year bond that matures in twenty-nine years in November 2012. The interest payment on a note or a bond is called the **coupon.** It is expressed as a proportion of the bond's face value (otherwise known as the **par value**).

Treasury bills, notes, and bonds are traded in the over-the-counter market, rather than on an organized stock exchange such as the New York Stock Exchange. The over-the-counter market is a market in securities conducted by dealers from their own offices. A dealer keeps an inventory of a security in which to deal, quoting a bid price at which he or she is willing to buy the security and an asked price at which he or she is willing to sell it. We can explain several features of these quotations using the 11⅛ percent bond maturing in the year 2003 that is quoted in Table 16.4.

Rate	Maturity	Date	Bid	Asked	Change	Yield
11⅛	2003	Aug	96.10	96.14	+.9	11.58

The bond's coupon is 11.125 percent of face value payable in semiannual installments. The bond will be repaid when it matures in August 2003. The final coupon is paid, by convention, in the month the bond matures. For a bond maturing in August, coupon payments are made semiannually in February and August (on or about the fifteenth day). The bid price of 96.10 means that dealers were paying $96 and ¹⁰/₃₂ of a dollar or $96.3125, not $96.10. Similarly the asked price of 96.14 means that dealers were selling at $96 and ¹⁴/₃₂ or $96.4375. The bid–ask spread of $96.4375 − $96.3125 or $0.125 is the amount that provides for the dealer's expenses and profits. On this bond there was a change of .9 or ⁹/₃₂ = $0.28125 from the previous day's bid price. The bond's yield is an annual return, which is based upon both the coupon payments and any capital gain or capital loss expected on redemption. In this example, the bond will be redeemed at face value, which is $100. Therefore a capital gain will be obtained on redemption. The actual calculations used to obtain these yield numbers are quite complex.[1] In the

[1]For the exact method of calculation, see *Standard Securities Calculation Methods,* by B. M. Spence, J. Y. Graudenz, and J. J. Lynch, Jr., New York: Securities Industry Association (1973): 28–29.

next chapter, we explain in greater detail the yield computation and its economic meaning.

Some bonds do not mature on a single date. Take for example the 10s 2005–2010 quoted in Table 16.4. The two dates 2005 and 2010 indicate that, although the bond finally matures in May 2010, it can be repaid at the Treasury's discretion at a specified **call price** at any time during the period from May 2005. The Treasury is said to call the bond if it exercises its option to repay or redeem the bond prior to May 2010. If the bond currently is selling below its call price (as the 10s are), the yield in the *Wall Street Journal* is calculated on the assumption that the bond will not be repaid until the final date, which in our example is May 2010. If the bond currently were selling at a price above the call price, however, the yield is based upon repayment at the first date (May 2005). The assumption behind this convention is that the Treasury will repay a bond at the call price if, and only if, the bond's market price exceeds the call price.

Intermediate-Term Corporate Debt

Intermediate-term corporate debt usually is defined as corporate borrowing that must be repaid within one to seven years. Corporate borrowing can take a wide variety of forms. Companies can borrow directly from banks, insurance companies, and individuals. They can take out mortgages secured by real estate, or they can issue intermediate- and long-term corporate bonds. Intermediate-term corporate debt usually takes the form of commercial bank term loans, leasing, and revolving credit agreements.

COMMERCIAL BANK TERM LOANS

The most important source of intermediate-term financing for the majority of firms is the commercial bank term loan, which generally has a maturity of one to seven years. A loan's interest rate may be fixed throughout the term of the loan, but more often it may vary with the prevailing market interest rates, usually the prime interest rate. The **prime rate** is a short-term lending rate available to the bank's lowest-risk customers. The prime rate is fixed by each bank on the basis of market interest rates, for example, in the Treasury bill or federal funds market. The loan contract includes the interest rate plus a mix of other conditions that the borrower must meet. These may include:

A repayment schedule, which will involve regular periodic payments
Security, with the pledging of specified assets as collateral for the loan

Information, with regular reporting to the bank of the borrower's financial position

Specific provisions, such as insurance policies on key individuals in the borrowing firm and/or

Restrictions, which typically include minimum working capital ratios and maximum dividend payments. The contract may also include maintenance of a minimum ratio of earnings to interest payments and a maximum debt-to-equity ratio. There may also be restrictions on capital spending and occasionally some constraints on additional financing.

OTHER SOURCES AND TYPES OF INTERMEDIATE-TERM DEBT

Two other major kinds of intermediate-term debt include leasing and revolving credit. Lease financing often is used when a company wishes to finance a specific asset such as an aircraft or a computer. Rather than borrow the money and purchase the asset directly, the company may choose to obtain the use of the asset by purchasing it indirectly through a lease. Under a leasing arrangement the leasing company retains ownership of the asset and charges rent to the lessee who actually uses the asset. In certain circumstances, there can be a number of advantages (including taxes) from leasing an asset rather than owning it. Because leasing is so specialized, Chapter 23 is devoted completely to the leasing decision.

Revolving credit agreements are loan contracts in which a lender allows the firm to borrow at any time any amount up to some dollar limit specified in the agreement. As the actual borrowing under such agreements usually matures in ninety days, revolving credit loans resemble short-term borrowing. However, because most revolving credit agreements are good for more than one year, it is appropriate to consider them as intermediate-term arrangements. The flexibility that such arrangements permit the borrower is obvious; the borrower need not borrow until the funds actually are needed. At the same time, the contractual obligation of the bank to provide funds if and when the need arises shifts the firm's risk of being illiquid to the bank. In a competitive financial market, this risk has a price. In most cases, the price for this particular risk will take the form of a higher interest rate, and possibly a onetime lump sum payment to the bank, a **commitment fee** related to the unused portion of the credit limit.

Long-Term Corporate Debt

While commercial banks prefer to make term loans with maturities of less than ten years, life insurance companies prefer to make loans for longer maturities. Consequently, firms frequently do their long-term borrowing from life insurance companies. A loan package often will be put together in which the shorter-term part of the loan is provided by a bank and the longer-term part by an insurance company. Aside from its longer maturity, long-term corporate debt can be distinguished in several other respects from short- or intermediate-term debt.

SECURITY

Long-term **mortgage bonds** typically are issued with maturities of between twenty and forty years. They give the lenders a first claim on some of or all the firm's assets if default occurs. The long-term debt of most utilities is in this form, while in recent years relatively few other corporations have issued mortgage bonds.

Debenture bonds normally are issued with maturities of up to twenty-five years.[2] They are not secured by specific assets as is the case with mortgage bonds. Thus, the holder becomes a general creditor in liquidation proceedings. Both debentures and mortgage bonds carry protective covenants of the kind mentioned earlier in connection with term loans. **Subordinated debentures** rank behind both mortgage bonds and debentures in their claim on the firm's assets, should default occur. When the firm is liquidated, the holders of mortgage bonds are repaid first (after any tax obligations). If any funds remain, debenture holders are repaid next, then subordinated debenture holders.

NATURE OF THE INTEREST PAYMENT

Debentures provide for semiannual interest payments over the life of the security. The interest payment is tax-deductible to the borrower and is taxable to the recipient.

HOW SOLD: PRIVATE VERSUS PUBLIC PLACEMENT

Long-term debt can be sold (or placed) privately to one or more investors, or it can be sold through a public offering. A **public offering** is made to the public on behalf of the borrower by a group of investment bankers known as the underwriters or **underwriting syndicate**. The underwriters

---

[2]It is conventional to describe debentures of less than fifteen years maturity as notes.

are responsible for finding buyers for the issue and for legal, accounting, and administrative aspects connected with the issue. Although utility holding companies can only give their underwriting business to the lowest bidder, most companies negotiate the terms of their underwriting agreements with the investment bankers with whom they normally do business.

While there are advantages and disadvantages to both private placements and public offers, there are economies of scale in both situations, as can be seen in Cohan's sample in Table 16.5. **Private placements** can be tailored more easily to the firm's circumstances than can public offerings, because there are relatively few lenders with whom to negotiate. Also, the transaction can be completed immediately once the terms have been worked out. Subsequently, if a company is in financial distress, it can negotiate modifications to the contract more easily with privately placed debt. Private lenders are more likely to impose more restrictive conditions than those on publicly issued debt. The more restrictive conditions compensate the lender for the fact that there are no public disclosure requirements for private placements, making it easier for a borrower to conceal information that could be relevant to the riskiness of the loan.

The direct costs of private placement are slightly lower than for an equivalent public issue, but interest costs are higher. In Cohan's sample in Table 16.5, issuing costs for privately placed issues of over $25 million were 0.4 percent, compared with 1.1 percent for public offerings of comparable size. Privately placed debt, which is not registered with the Securities and Exchange Commission (thereby avoiding registration costs), cannot be traded in public markets. Sales of the security therefore must be negotiated privately.

Table 16.5   *Issuing costs for corporate debt 1947–1950*

Issue size (millions of dollars)	Private placements Expenses as % of issue size			Public issues Expenses as % of issue size		
	Underwriting expenses	Other expenses	Total	Underwriting expenses	Other expenses	Total
Under 0.50	1.7	1.1	2.8	7.3	2.9	10.2
0.50 to 0.99	1.4	0.9	2.3	5.5	3.2	8.7
1.00 to 2.99	0.9	0.5	1.4	3.5	2.1	5.6
3.00 to 4.99	0.6	0.4	1.0	1.4	1.3	2.7
5.00 to 9.99	0.6	0.3	0.9	0.9	1.0	1.9
10.00 to 24.99	0.3	0.3	0.6	1.0	0.7	1.7
25.00 and above	0.2	0.2	0.4	0.7	0.4	1.1

Source: A. B. Cohan, *Yields on Corporate Debt Directly Placed,* Washington: National Bureau of Economic Research, 1967: 127.

Life insurance companies that have limited need for liquidity and do not need to trade the securities in their portfolios frequently tend to be the major purchasers of privately placed corporate debt. The amount and market share of private placements rose rapidly during the 1970s, as Kalotay has described in Table 16.6.

Clearly, from the borrower's standpoint, public and private debt issues should be close substitutes, once differences in registration costs, issuing costs, credit risks, and maturity are accounted for. Some research on corporate debt offerings from 1952 to 1971 has indicated that, even after such corrections, slightly higher yields may be found in private placements (Hays, 1977).

On the other hand, Kalotay has described in Table 16.7 a somewhat different pattern of costs for the years 1974 to 1979: Issuers of lower-rated securities (Baa/BBB) tended to pay a higher interest rate in private issues than public issues, whereas A-rated borrowers tended to pay more in public issues. It may be that the portfolio preferences of institutions that buy the private placements are an important factor in determining yield differentials.

SINKING FUNDS AND CALLABILITY

In a private placement, the principal repayment schedule is specified. For public debt issues, such repayments are in the form of a **sinking fund,** which

Table 16.6   *New corporate public and private financings (millions of dollars)*

	Public	Private	Total new financings	Private as % of total
1979	36,584	22,545	59,129	38
1978	31,150	32,456	63,606	51
1977	36,693	25,749	62,442	41
1976	42,352	21,240	63,592	33
1975	46,828	13,515	60,343	22
1974	31,799	10,674	42,473	25
1973	22,701	12,183	34,884	35
1972	34,241	11,825	46,066	26
1971	39,148	9,067	48,215	19
1970	31,130	6,373	37,503	17

Source: A. J. Kalotay, "Long-Term Debt and Equity Markets and Instruments," in *Financial Handbook,* 5th edition, edited by E. I. Altman, New York: Wiley (1981): Ch. 4, p. 22.

Table 16.7 *Spread relationship for private versus public markets of similar quality (basis points)*

	A quality		Baa/BBB quality	
	Average spread public vs. private	Range	Average spread public vs. private	Range
1979	+28	+17 to +41	−20	+29 to −48
1978	+12	−3 to +43	−33	−5 to −48
1977	+6	−17 to +22	−36	−18 to −60
1976	+11	−9 to +42	−33	+14 to −89
1975	+16	−15 to +44	−69	−25 to −100
1974	+28	+21 to +59	−27	+25 to −68
3-year average	+15		−30	
6-year average	+17		−36	
Widest positive spread over 6 years		+59, November 1974		+29, June 1979
Widest negative spread over 6 years		−17, March 1977		−100, November 1975

Source: A. J. Kalotay, "Long-Term Debt and Equity Markets and Instruments," in *Financial Handbook*, 5th edition, edited by E. I. Altman, New York: Wiley (1981): Ch. 4, p. 25.

is an account administered by independent trustees for the purposes of re-paying the bonds. Not all bonds have sinking funds, and those that do frequently provide for optional payments beyond those specified in the sinking fund schedule. Payments by the company to the sinking fund can be made either in cash or in bonds purchased by the company in the open market, or redeemed directly from debtholders at call prices specified in the debt contract (indenture), whichever is least costly to the borrower. If pay-ment is made in cash, the trustee can use the cash either to repurchase the bonds in the market or to redeem directly (again at preset prices) from bondholders. The trustee chooses the bonds to be redeemed by lottery in which each bond is identified by a serial number.

When the market price of the bonds is below their call value, it is cheaper for the firm to purchase the bonds in the open market than to redeem them by lottery. For example, suppose a bond's call price is $105 (i.e., 105 percent of the face value of $100) and that the bond is selling for $96. Clearly, sinking fund payments should be made with bonds purchased in the market at $96, not with bonds redeemed directly from bondholders at $105.

Obviously, the option to call a bond (redeem it at the call price) is valuable to the borrower and costly to the lender. In a competitive capital market, securities would be priced such that there should be no net advantage to issuing a callable versus a noncallable security. Therefore, we would expect new bond issues with call options to offer higher interest rates to compensate lenders for the call provisions.

The widespread practice of including a call provision in a bond issue may reflect management's preference for flexibility in financing. For example, if interest rates fall below the rate at which an existing bond was issued, management would be paying a relatively high rate of interest on its existing debt. The higher rate of interest could make the company less profitable than other companies borrowing at the lower rates of interest. To avoid this problem, a call provision in the loan agreement enables the firm to limit its losses by calling bonds when interest rates fall. The company then can issue new notes or bonds at the current lower rates of interest.

A typical bond offers call protection to investors in two forms: (a) a five- or ten-year prohibition against calling at any price for purposes of refunding at an interest rate below the issue cost; and (2) a schedule of minimum call prices that only gradually is reduced to the bond's par value.

EXAMPLE: A COMPARISON OF TWO THIRTY-YEAR BONDS

As the prior discussion suggests, the many dimensions of a long-term debt contract mean that it is difficult to make simple comparisons between bonds on the basis of yield alone. The following data describe two thirty-year bonds issued by Capital Cities Communications, Inc., and Niagara Mohawk Power Corporation.

Capital Cities Communications is engaged in television and radio broad-

	Capital Cities Communications, Inc.	Niagara Mohawk Power Corp.
Amount of issue	$200 million	$50 million
Date of issue	6/21/83	6/16/83
Maturity	6/15/2013	6/15/2013
Annual coupon	11.75	12.50
Offer price	99½	100
Yield to maturity	11.81%	12.5%
Dates of interest payments	6/15 and 12/15	6/15 and 12/15
Security	None (a debenture)	First mortgage bonds (secured by assets)
Sinking fund	Annual, beginning 6/15/94 sufficient to retire 76% of principal by maturity	None
Call features	Not redeemable prior to 6/15/93 through refunding at an interest rate of less than 11.81%	Not redeemable prior to 6/15/88 through refunding at an interest rate of less than 12.50%
Call prices	6/15/83 at 111.25	6/15/83 through 6/15/84 at 112.50
	Thereafter, declining 0.5625 annually to 100 on or after 6/15/2003	6/16/84 through 6/15/85 at 111.98
		Thereafter, declining 0.52 annually to 100 on 6/15/2008
Ratings by Moody's	Aa3	A3

casting, cable television franchising, and newspaper publishing in various locations throughout the country. Niagara Mohawk is an electric utility in upstate New York. These companies' offers of thirty-year bonds came to the market within a few days of one another, yet with different coupons and yields. Technically, the Capital Cities Communications issue was a debenture with a sinking fund requirement, while Niagara Mohawk's issue was a first mortgage bond with no sinking fund. However, the Capital Cities Communications bond provides greater call protection for investors and this would be one reason why it is rated higher by Moody's (Aa3 against A3).

PRICES AND YIELDS ON PUBLICLY TRADED CORPORATE BONDS

Although most trading in corporate bonds is in the over-the-counter market, some issues are listed and traded on organized exchanges as well. Commonwealth Edison's 16¾ first mortgage bond, for example, is listed on the New York Stock Exchange. Closing quotations for July 14, 1983, were reported in the *Wall Street Journal* on July 15, 1983, as

Bonds	Current yield	Volume	High	Low	Close	Net change
CmwE 16¾ 11	14.	70	118	118	118	−⅝

Prices are quoted in terms of eighths of a point. The bond will mature in the year 2011 (only the last two digits are quoted). The current yield is the annual coupon divided by the closing price and is quoted at 14 percent based on a price of 118.[3] Volume of trading of the Commonwealth Edison bond on this exchange was 70 bonds on July 14.

The Credit Quality of Corporate Debt and the Role of Financial Ratios

The credit quality of corporate debt is as important to lenders and equity-holders as callability, maturity, and sinking fund. Before analyzing the quality of any one firm's financial health, it would be useful for us to describe what has been happening over recent years to United States corporate debt in general.

THE DECLINE IN AGGREGATE CREDIT QUALITY IN THE UNITED STATES

Balance sheet ratios taken from corporate financial statements are used widely to gain some insight as to the credit risk of firms. While a financial manager is interested in the market value of the debt and equity claims on his firm, creditors for the most part employ book values in their analyses. Indeed, loan covenants usually are stated in terms of book value ratios and give the precise accounting definitions to be employed. One reason financial ratios are expressed in book value rather than market value is that much corporate debt is not traded regularly, so market values are not available. Even if corporate bonds were traded, the traded value of the equity claims (stocks) reflects the discounted value of the future cash flows of the firm, including those attributable to growth. Lenders typically prefer not to lend against that part of the firm's value that reflects these growth opportunities (see Myers,

---

[3]In fact, the quotations reported in the *Wall Street Journal* contained a typographical error. The current yield based on a price of 118 actually is 14.2 percent.

1977). In contrast, book values do not include the value or cost of these growth opportunities. We discuss this point in greater detail in Chapter 21. Even though there are inherent problems in interpreting historic cost-based financial statements, lenders believe that they can tell how well a firm is doing by analyzing corporate accounts.

Figure 16.1 depicts what has happened to corporate balance sheets over the past two decades: (1) The ratio of equity to total assets has fallen; (2) the ratio of short-term debt to total assets has risen; and (3) the ratio of liquid assets (cash and marketable securities) to total assets has fallen. This is a picture of increasing corporate reliance on debt (especially short-term debt) financing. A reasonable interpretation of Figure 16.1 is that the credit risk, or credit quality, of United States corporations has deteriorated since 1960.

MEASUREMENT OF CREDIT QUALITY BY RATING AGENCIES

The two major bond rating agencies, Moody's and Standard & Poor's, assign corporate bonds to credit quality classes on the basis of their assessment of

Figure 16.1   *Historic value of liquid assets, liabilities, and equity as a fraction of the historic value of assets*

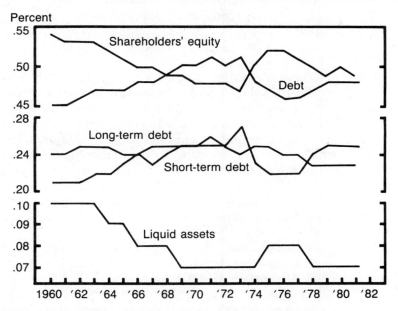

Source: Board of Governors of the Federal Reserve System as reported in Karlyn Mitchell, "Trends in Corporation Finance," *Economic Review*, Federal Reserve Bank of Kansas City (March 1983): 6.

the borrowing company's risks. These risks are judged in part on an analysis of financial ratios. Moody's rating definitions are presented in Appendix 16.1. The four top bond ratings (Aaa, Aa, A, and Baa) make a bond eligible to be included in particular investment portfolios. For example, bonds rated at least Baa by Moody's would be considered to qualify for purchase by financial institutions (e.g., a pension fund portfolio managed by a commercial bank trust department), which are prevented legally from holding speculative securities. In recent years, rating agencies have added gradations to the categories described in the appendix; 1, 2, and 3 have been added by Moody's and plus and minus by Standard & Poor's. For example, in the two-bond example given earlier in this chapter, Moody's has rated the Capital Cities Communications bond at the lower end of the Aa range, Aa3, and Niagara Mohawk's bond at the lower end of the A range, A3.

The rating agencies assess industry risk, the firm's business risk, and the quality of the firm's accounting records. In addition, they analyze the firm's financial statements extensively and evaluate key financial statement ratios relative to industry norms.

In the past, such ratios were analyzed and compared on a somewhat ad hoc basis in conjunction with other, subjective factors affecting a company's credit. In recent years, some analysts have used discriminant analysis techniques to help select the most useful ratios and to combine them in the most effective way in credit ratings.

Discriminant analysis is used to select the values of the weights a_i in the following discriminant function equation where the X_i ($i = 1, 2, \ldots, N$) represent accounting ratios.

$$Z = a_1 X_1 + a_2 X_2 + \cdots + a_N X_N$$

The values of the weights a_i ($i = 1, 2, \ldots, N$) are selected in such a way that the value of Z (the Z score) can be used to discriminate among companies in a large sample of firms with different credit ratings. Different ranges of value for Z can be made to correspond to different credit ratings.

For example, Pinches and Mingo (1973) used such a model together with the following six variables to predict Moody's bond ratings for samples of corporate bonds:

1. Subordination status of the bonds to other debt claims
2. Years of consecutive dividends
3. Issue size
4. Net income plus interest-to-interest ratio
5. Long-term debt-to-total assets ratio
6. Net income-to-total assets ratio

Pinches and Mingo used one sample to obtain estimates of the weights and another sample to test the model. Their total sample consisted of all 180 newly issued industrial corporate bonds that were rated between Aa and B by Moody's for the two-year period January 1967 through December 1968. From these bonds, 132 were randomly selected for the estimation sample, with the remainder of 48 bonds assigned to the validation sample. In the estimation sample, 92 out of 132 bonds (70%) were classified "correctly" (the same as Moody's). In the validation sample of 48 bonds, 65 percent of the ratings were predicted correctly. All but one of the bonds were predicted within one classification of the actual Moody's rating.

FINANCIAL RATIOS AS PREDICTORS OF DEFAULT

Debt contracts specify compliance with minimum conditions stated in terms of balance sheet ratios, so it should not be too surprising to find that financial ratios have also been found to be useful predictors of financial distress and bankruptcy. In 1966, Beaver found evidence of the usefulness of individual ratios as predictors of financial distress. Five of the most useful ratios were:

1. Cash flow to total debt
2. Net income to total assets
3. Total debt to total assets
4. Working capital to total assets
5. Current ratio

In a sample of seventy-nine failed and seventy-nine paired nonfailed companies, he found that the values of these ratios deteriorated significantly for the failed companies in comparison to the nonfailed companies up to five years prior to failure. The cash flow-to-total debt and net income-to-total assets ratios each incorrectly classified only 13 percent of the firms one year before failure and only 22 and 28 percent, respectively, of the firms five years before failure.

Altman (1968) used discriminant analysis to predict bankruptcy among a sample of thirty-three bankrupt firms paired with thirty-three nonbankrupt firms. The resulting discriminant function was

$$Z = 0.012X_1 + 0.014X_2 + 0.033X_3 + 0.006X_4 + 0.010X_5$$

where the X variables are

X_1 = Working capital to total assets

X_2 = Retained earnings to total assets

X_3 = Earnings before interest and taxes to total assets

X_4 = Market value of equity to book value of total debt

X_5 = Sales to total assets

Companies with high values of Z (or Z scores) were nearly all nonbankrupt, while those with low Z scores were nearly all bankrupt within one year. Altman determined the value of Z that divided the bankrupt from the nonbankrupt companies with the least error.

For the estimation sample of sixty-six firms, the misclassification rate was only 5 percent. Altman tested the resulting model with two validation samples. The first sample consisted of twenty-five bankrupt firms with the same range of asset sizes as for the estimation sample. Twenty-four of the twenty-five firms in this validation sample were correctly predicted to be bankrupt. Altman's second validation sample consisted of sixty-six nonbankrupt firms that had "suffered temporary profitability difficulties" but did not become bankrupt. In this case, the discriminant function identified fifty-two of the sixty-six firms as nonbankrupt.

As there is now a large amount of such evidence showing the usefulness of financial ratios in predicting the creditworthiness of companies, let us examine some of the most commonly used ratios more closely.

KEY FINANCIAL RATIOS

The key financial ratios that bond rating agencies (as well as banks, insurance companies, and trade credit suppliers) use in credit quality analysis are grouped typically into four categories:

1. Profitability
2. Activity
3. Liquidity
4. Leverage

We shall illustrate how these are measured using financial statements taken from the 1982 annual report of UMC Industries, Inc., a diversified manufacturing firm shown in Appendix 16.2. We should note at the outset that there are many different ways of constructing ratios from financial statements. If you are interested in more detail or in the overlapping nature of alternative financial ratios, you may want to read Foster (1978) and Chen and Shimerda (1981).

PROFITABILITY. Table 16.8 shows profitability ratios. UMC Industries did not enjoy a good year in 1982, a recession year, as its income statement in Appendix 16.2 clearly shows: net sales (in thousands of dollars) fell from $335,604 to $321,322, while expenses fell less rapidly. Consequently, UMC's net income-to-sales ratio dropped from 0.027 to 0.013. Net income is calculated after the deduction of interest charges on debt, so changes in the net income-to-sales ratio may reflect variation in operating performance or interest charges. In order to isolate the variations in operating performance,

Table 16.8   *Profitability ratios for UMC Industries*

Ratio	1981		1982	
Net income to sales	$\dfrac{9{,}127}{335{,}604}$	= 0.027	$\dfrac{4{,}223}{321{,}322}$	= 0.013
Earnings of operations to sales	$\dfrac{20{,}743}{335{,}604}$	= 0.062	$\dfrac{11{,}836}{321{,}322}$	= 0.037
Return on equity (1982)			$\dfrac{4{,}223}{0.5(104{,}998\ +\ 105{,}426)}$	= 0.040

interest charges and taxes are excluded to obtain the ratio of earnings from operations-to-sales. UMC's earnings from operations was $11,836 in 1982. Its earnings from operations-to-sales ratio fell from 0.062 in 1981 to 0.037 in 1982, as shown.

Management is also interested in relating its profitability to the value of equity employed, so it uses the return on capital equity ratio. UMC Industries' return on equity (ROE) in 1982 was 4 percent as the table shows. An average value of equity for the year is obtained in the denominator of the ratio by adding the equity at the beginning of the year to the year-end value and dividing by two.

ACTIVITY. Creditors and owners are interested in how well a company's management uses the assets that it has at its disposal. Activity ratios express the firm's sales per dollar of average investment for particular asset categories. For example, UMC Industries' receivables turnover ratio was 6.10 in 1982 as shown in Table 16.9.

The company's inventory turnover ratio in the same year was 4.99. There is a potential problem, however, in how this ratio is calculated. UMC Industries values its inventories at historic cost using LIFO procedures. Inasmuch as net sales include profit markups, a more appropriate inventory turnover ratio to measure inventory productivity might use cost of goods sold as the numerator. UMC Industries' inventory turnover ratio measured at cost was:

$$\frac{259{,}166}{0.5(56{,}801\ +\ 71{,}925)} = 4.03$$

Total asset turnover is the ratio of sales to the firm's average total assets. In 1982, UMC Industries' total asset turnover ratio was 1.38 as shown in Table 16.9.

LIQUIDITY. Liquidity ratios estimate the ability of a company to generate cash from assets in order to meet obligations. There are three liquidity ratios

Table 16.9   *Activity ratios for UMC Industries*

Ratio		1982
Receivables turnover	$\dfrac{321{,}322}{0.5(48{,}796 + 56{,}563)}$	= 6.10
Inventory turnover	$\dfrac{321{,}322}{0.5(56{,}801 + 71{,}925)}$	= 4.99
Total asset turnover	$\dfrac{321{,}322}{0.5(228{,}290 + 238{,}462)}$	= 1.38

commonly used. The acid test ratio consists of the sum of cash, marketable securities, and short-term notes and receivables divided by current liabilities. UMC Industries' 1982 acid test ratio rose somewhat from 1.09 in 1981 to 1.38 in 1982 as shown in Table 16.10. Somewhat less stringent is the current ratio, defined as current assets divided by current liabilities. The company's current ratio was 2.41 in 1981 and 2.75 in 1982 as is shown. Finally, a more inclusive measure that includes the effect of accounting depreciation, taxes, and replacement expenditure on the cash flow available from a going concern's operation is the cash flow-to-total debt ratio. The numerator is net earnings plus depreciation charges plus additions to deferred taxes. The total debt in the denominator is the sum of total current liabilities, deferred income taxes, and long-term debt in the UMC balance sheet. The company's cash flow-to-total debt ratio was 0.12 for 1982 as indicated in the table.

LEVERAGE. Leverage ratios provide measures of the degree to which company earnings are levered up. The basic notion is straightforward, as we indicate with a small amount of balance sheet and income statement algebra. We can define net income, *NI*, as

$$NI = (1 - T) \times (rA - iL)$$

Table 16.10   *Liquidity ratios for UMC Industries*

Ratio	1981		1982	
Acid test	$\dfrac{63{,}862}{58{,}844}$	= 1.09	$\dfrac{63{,}668}{46{,}270}$	= 1.38
Current ratio	$\dfrac{141{,}784}{58{,}844}$	= 2.41	$\dfrac{127{,}465}{46{,}270}$	= 2.75
Cash flow to total debt (1982)		$\dfrac{4{,}223 + 8{,}675 + 1{,}598}{(46{,}270 + 5{,}922 + 71{,}100)}$		= 0.12

where T = corporate tax rate

          r = ratio of income to assets, i.e., the pretax accounting rate of return

          A = book value of total assets

          i = interest rate on book value of debt

          L = book value of debt

Expanding terms and dividing by book value of equity E:

$$ROE = \frac{NI}{E} = \frac{(1 - T)[r(L + E) - iL]}{E}$$

$$= (1 - T)\,[r + (r - i)L/E]$$

That is, the company's ROE increases with the amount of leverage, as measured by the debt-to-equity ratio L/E, so long as $r > i$. UMC Industries' total debt-to-equity ratio was 1.17 at the end of 1982 as Table 16.11 shows. On the other hand, to the extent that fluctuations in short-term debt reflect short-term operations unrelated to long-term capital planning (including seasonal operating cycles or timing of tax payments), the long-term debt-to-equity ratio may be a more useful measure of financial leverage. UMC Industries' long-term debt-to-equity ratio was 0.68 at the end of 1982 as may be seen in the table. Finally, some analysts would include in the debt figure any off-the-balance sheet liability, such as the capitalized value of noncancellable leases and the amount by which the present value of the company's pension fund obligations is estimated to exceed pension fund assets. A ratio that captures this is the total balance sheet and off-balance sheet debt-to-

Table 16.11   *Leverage ratios for UMC Industries*

Ratio	1982	
Total debt to equity	$\dfrac{46{,}270 + 5{,}922 + 71{,}100}{104{,}998}$	= 1.17
Long-term debt to equity	$\dfrac{71{,}100}{104{,}998}$	= 0.68
Total balance sheet and off-balance sheet debt to equity	$\dfrac{46{,}270 + 5{,}922 + 71{,}100 + 4{,}923 + 9{,}711}{104{,}998}$	= 1.31
Net income to net interest payments coverage	$\dfrac{4{,}223}{(7{,}519 - 2{,}490)}$	= 0.84
EBIT to net interest payments	$\dfrac{6{,}757 + 7{,}519 - 2{,}490}{(7{,}519 - 2{,}490)}$	= 2.34

equity ratio. UMC Industries' net capitalized leases at the end of 1982 amounted to $8,119 - $3,196 = $4,923. And net pension fund liabilities were estimated to be $35,218 - $25,507 = $9,711. Thus, the company's total balance sheet and off-balance sheet debt-to-equity ratio was 1.31.

It may be obvious to you that capacity to repay debt is measured incompletely by the balance sheet. In our algebraic formulation above, debt contributes to ROE only insofar as r is greater than i. That is, when the before-tax return on assets exceeds the interest rate on the book value of debt. The degree to which this is so can be measured by various coverage ratios. One of these is the net income-to-interest payments coverage ratio. For UMC Industries in 1982, this ratio was 0.84 as shown in Table 16.11. Note that we have netted interest income against interest expense in calculating the ratio. Alternatively, because taxes are paid only after net interest payments have been made, a more useful index may be the ratio of earnings before interest and taxes (EBIT) to net interest payments, 2.34 in 1982. We should mention that some analysts use more elaborate coverage ratios in which the numerator reflects only cash flows from operations available to service obligations, and in which the denominator includes interest payments, noncancellable lease payments, and debt principal payments, that is, all fixed charges.

As we have shown, financial ratio analysis is useful in estimating the quality of bonds and in predicting financial distress for industrial companies. While statistical techniques such as multiple discriminant analysis can be used to improve the accuracy and effectiveness of financial ratio analysis for estimating the creditworthiness of companies, much work is left to be done before such financial statement analysis can be put on a sound footing. The problem is that we do not yet have an economic model of corporate creditworthiness and financial distress upon which to base such analysis. If and when an adequate theoretical model can be developed, we may be able to put credit analysis on a more scientific basis. We shall also be able to see more clearly why certain combinations of financial ratios appear to be better than others for measuring creditworthiness and predicting financial distress.

Summary

The corporate sector competes with federal, state, and municipal governments for debt financing in the financial market. Because governments have almost unlimited access to other sources of funds, the possibility of their default on obligations is remote; government securities are regarded as risk-free in monetary (if not purchasing power) terms. Thus, interest rates on such securities set the standards for minimum-risk rates. Individual companies, on the other hand, might default on interest and principal repayment, so they must pay premiums over the minimum-risk rates of interest to compensate lenders for the additional risk.

Corporate borrowing arrangements can take on a large variety of forms to meet the various requirements of individual companies. Borrowing requirements may range from the short term to the very long term. Commercial banks prefer to make term loans of less than ten years, while insurance companies will lend for somewhat longer periods. Companies also issue long-term bonds, with maturities ranging from fifteen to forty years. Bonds secured by specific assets are called mortgage bonds, and bonds not secured by specific assets are called debentures. They may be placed privately with a limited number of investors or sold to the public through underwriters.

Bond quality and bank credit ratings typically are stated in terms of key financial ratios dealing with profitability, activity, liquidity, and leverage. Such ratios turn out also to be useful predictors of corporate bankruptcy.

Appendix 16.1 Moody's Corporate Bond Rating Definitions

Aaa

Bonds which are rated Aaa are judged to be of the best quality. They carry the smallest degree of investment risk and are generally referred to as "gilt-edged." Interest payments are protected by a large or by an exceptionally stable margin and principal is secure. While the various protective elements are likely to change, such changes as can be visualized are most unlikely to impair the fundamentally strong position of such issues.

Aa

Bonds which are rated Aa are judged to be of high quality by all standards. Together with the Aaa group they comprise what are generally known as high-grade bonds. They are rated lower than the best bonds because margins of protection may not be as large as in the Aaa securities or fluctuation of protective elements may be of greater amplitude or there may be other elements present which make the long-term risks appear somewhat larger than in Aaa securities.

A

Bonds which are rated A possess many favorable investment attributes and are to be considered as upper medium-grade obligations. Factors giving security to principal and interest are considered adequate, but elements may be present which suggest a susceptibility to impairment sometime in the future.

Baa

Bonds which are rated Baa are considered as medium-grade obligations, i.e., they are neither highly protected nor poorly secured. Interest payments and principal security appear adequate for the present but certain protective elements may be lacking or may be characteristically unreliable over any great length of time. Such bonds lack outstanding investment characteristics and in fact have speculative characteristics as well.

Ba

Bonds which are rated Ba are judged to have speculative elements, their future cannot be considered as well-assured. Often the protection of interest and principal payments may be very moderate, and thereby not well safeguarded during both good and bad times over the future. Uncertainty of position characterizes bonds in this class.

B

Bonds which are rated B generally lack characteristics of the desirable investment. Assurance of interest and principal payments or of maintenance of other terms of the contract over any long period of time may be small.

Caa

Bonds which are rated Caa are of poor standing. Such issues may be in default or there may be present elements of danger with respect to principal or interest.

Ca

Bonds which are rated Ca represent obligations which are speculative in a high degree. Such issues are often in default or have other market shortcomings.

C

Bonds which are rated C are the lowest-rated class of bonds, and issues so rated can be regarded as having extremely poor prospects of ever attaining any real investment standing.

Source: Moody's Investors Service, New York.

Appendix 16.2 UMC Industries

Consolidated Balance Sheet

Consolidated Statement of Operations

Consolidated Statement of Retained Earnings

Consolidated Statement of Changes in Financial Position

Extract from Notes to Financial Statements

CONSOLIDATED BALANCE SHEET

	December 31	
In thousands	**1981**	**1982**
ASSETS		
CURRENT ASSETS		
Cash	$ 4,851	$ 2,246
Short-term investments, at cost (approximates market)	2,358	12,626
Notes and accounts receivable, less allowances of $1,334 in 1982 and $1,180 in 1981	56,653	48,796
Inventories	71,925	56,801
Prepaid expenses, including deferred income taxes	5,997	6,996
Total current assets	141,784	127,465
PROPERTY, PLANT AND EQUIPMENT		
Land	4,380	4,651
Buildings	44,426	50,881
Machinery and equipment	71,536	75,580
Construction in progress (including $6,373 in 1982 and $5,999 in 1981 of construction funds held by trustees)	8,149	8,579
Other	11,492	11,777
	139,983	151,468
Less accumulated depreciation and amortization	61,574	68,154
Net property, plant and equipment	78,409	83,314
OTHER ASSETS		
Patents, trademarks and licenses, net	1,599	1,507
Cost in excess of net assets of purchased businesses, net	11,227	10,893
Long-term notes receivable	3,912	3,338
Other	1,531	1,773
	18,269	17,511
TOTAL ASSETS	$238,462	$228,290
LIABILITIES AND SHAREHOLDERS' EQUITY		
CURRENT LIABILITIES		
Notes and loans payable to banks	$ 10,956	$ 3,274
Accounts payable	23,683	17,255
Wages, salaries and commissions	7,017	6,204
Accrued pension expense	2,504	2,718
Other accrued liabilities	7,523	9,894
Income taxes	3,995	1,022

Consolidated Balance Sheet continued

	December 31	
In thousands	**1981**	**1982**
Current maturities of long-term debt	3,166	5,903
Total current liabilities	58,844	46,270
DEFERRED INCOME TAXES	4,324	5,922
LONG-TERM DEBT	69,868	71,100
CONTINGENT LIABILITIES	—	—
SHAREHOLDERS' EQUITY		
Preferred stock, $100 par value; 200,000 shares authorized; none issued	—	—
Common stock, $2.50 par value; 10,000,000 shares authorized; 7,076,170 shares issued	17,690	17,690
Capital in excess of par value	21,064	21,029
Retained earnings	83,632	84,182
Equity adjustment from foreign currency translation	(559)	(1,652)
	121,827	121,249
Less cost of treasury shares: 1982—951,448 shares; 1981—960,214 shares	16,401	16,251
Total shareholders' equity	105,426	104,998
TOTAL LIABILITIES AND SHAREHOLDERS' EQUITY	$238,462	$228,290

CONSOLIDATED STATEMENT OF OPERATIONS

In thousands except per-share amounts	Years ended December 31	
	1981	1982
Net sales	$335,604	$321,322
Cost of goods sold	263,602	259,166
	72,002	62,156
Operating expenses		
Selling and distribution	24,046	21,895
General and administrative	27,213	28,425
	51,259	50,320
Earnings from operations	20,743	11,836
Other income (deductions)		
Interest expense	(7,926)	(7,519)
Interest income	2,443	2,490
Miscellaneous	1,028	(50)
	(4,455)	(5,079)
Earnings from continuing operations before income taxes	16,288	6,757
Provision for income taxes		
Current	6,933	1,516
Deferred	543	1,018
	7,476	2,534
Earnings from continuing operations	8,812	4,223
Discontinued operations		
Operating earnings, net of income taxes	70	—
Gain on sales, net of income taxes	245	—
Earnings from discontinued operations	315	—
Net earnings	$ 9,127	$ 4,223
Earnings per share of common stock		
Continuing operations	$ 1.44	$ .69
Discontinued operations		
Operating earnings	.01	—
Gain on sales	.04	—
Net earnings	$ 1.49	$ .69

CONSOLIDATED STATEMENT OF RETAINED EARNINGS

	Years ended December 31	
In thousands	1981	1982
Balance at beginning of year	$81,834	$83,632
Net earnings	9,127	4,223
	90,961	87,855
Dividends paid (per share: $.60 in 1982 and $1.20 in 1981)	(7,329)	(3,673)
Balance at end of year	$83,632	$84,182

CONSOLIDATED STATEMENT OF CHANGES IN FINANCIAL POSITION

	Years ended December 31	
In thousands	1981	1982
CASH PROVIDED BY		
Net earnings	$ 8,812	$ 4,223
Depreciation and amortization	8,125	8,675
Deferred income taxes	838	1,598
Net earnings from discontinued operations (including gains on sales and items not requiring the use of cash)	248	—
Cash provided by operations	18,023	14,496
Decrease (increase) in working capital (see below)	2,685	8,676
Proceeds from dispositions of property, plant and equipment	1,902	200
Proceeds from long-term borrowings	5,707	7,213
Proceeds from exercise of stock options	215	—
Decrease (increase) in long-term notes receivable	573	574
Total cash provided	29,105	31,159

Consolidated Statement of Changes in Financial Position continued

In thousands	Years ended December 31	
	1981	1982
CASH USED FOR		
Additions to property, plant and equipment	16,213	13,873
Dividends paid	7,329	3,673
Reduction in long-term debt	5,570	5,804
Other	124	146
Total cash used	29,236	23,496
Increase (decrease) in cash and short-term investments	$ (131)	$ 7,663
CASH PROVIDED BY (USED FOR) CHANGES IN WORKING CAPITAL		
Notes and accounts receivable	$ (829)	$ 7,857
Inventories	(3,099)	15,124
Prepaid expenses, including deferred income taxes	(533)	(999)
Notes and loans payable to banks	2,022	(7,682)
Accounts payable	5,705	(6,428)
Wages, salaries and commissions	49	(813)
Accrued pension expense	(1,804)	214
Other accrued liabilities	(201)	2,371
Income taxes	(629)	(2,973)
Current maturities of long-term debt	2,762	2,737
Changes in working capital	3,443	9,408
Foreign currency translation adjustments	(758)	(732)
Cash provided by (used for) decrease (increase) in working capital	$ 2,685	$ 8,676

EXTRACT FROM NOTES TO FINANCIAL STATEMENTS

PENSION PLANS. Charges to earnings with respect to Company–sponsored pension plans, which generally cover employees not included in union-sponsored plans, aggregated $2,474,000 in 1982, $2,266,000 in 1981 and $2,625,000 in 1980. In 1981 the Company changed several actuarial assumptions used in calculating pension expense. The more significant changes were to increase the assumed rate of return on investments from 6% to 8% and to increase the composite average of salary increases from 4.2% to 6.7%.

The net effect of these changes was to reduce pension expense by $1,178,000 and to increase net earnings by $638,000 ($.10 per share) in 1981.

At January 1, 1982 and 1981 Company-sponsored defined benefit plans' accumulated benefits (as estimated by consulting actuaries) and net assets, on an aggregate basis, were:

In thousands	1981	1982
Actuarial present value of accumulated plan benefits		
Vested	$23,106	$24,640
Nonvested	782	867
Total	$23,888	$25,507
Net assets available for benefits	$34,091	$35,218

In addition the Company contributed $822,000 in 1982, $989,000 in 1981 and $1,048,000 in 1980 to union-sponsored pension plans financed by industry employers.

LEASES. The Company leases various assets used in its operations, primarily building space. Certain leases contain renewal options and require the Company to pay utilities, insurance, taxes and maintenance. Leased capital assets, primarily buildings, included in property, plant and equipment have a capitalized value of $8,119,000 in both 1982 and 1981 and accumulated depreciation of $3,196,000 and $2,938,000 at December 31, 1982 and 1981, respectively.

Future minimum lease payments for leased capital assets and future minimum rental payments for all noncancellable operating leases at December 31, 1982 are:

In thousands	Leased capital assets	Noncancellable operating leases
1983	$ 524	$2,429
1984	267	1,612
1985	268	1,190
1986	269	753
1987	268	317
Later years	3,484	386
Total minimum lease payments	5,080	$6,687
Less amount representing interest	1,988	
Present value of net minimum lease payments	$3,092	

Total minimum rental payments on noncancellable operating leases have not been reduced by minimum sublease rentals of $125,000 due in the future under noncancellable subleases.

Rental expense on operating leases for the years 1982, 1981 and 1980 was $3,562,000, $3,591,000 and $3,809,000, respectively, after deducting rentals from subleases of $125,000 in 1982 and 1981 and $275,000 in 1980.

Review Questions

1. In what ways are government and corporate borrowing interrelated?
2. What are the characteristics of the securities used by the United States government for short-term debt financing?
3. Briefly describe the sources and types of intermediate-term borrowing available to corporations.
4. What forms of long-term debt are used by corporations, and how are they issued?
5. Explain the purpose and operation of a bond sinking fund.
6. What has happened to the quality of corporate credit in the decades after 1960? Why?
7. Moody's description of corporate bond ratings in Appendix 16.1 is rather vague. What do you think the descriptions for the Aa and the B ratings really mean?

Problems

*1. Look up the table of United States Treasury bills in a recent copy of the *Wall Street Journal*. Explain what is meant by the terms bid and asked discount, and the yield for a three-month Treasury bill.
 2. If a six-month Treasury bill has an asked discount of $9.23, what is its price on the issue date? Use your result to find the bond equivalent yield and the annual compound rate of interest.
*3. The *Wall Street Journal*, August 11, 1983, quotes an asked discount of 9.49 for a Treasury bill maturing on November 10, 1983, and a yield of 9.86. Use the asked discount to calculate the bond equivalent yield. Compare this to the yield given in the *Wall Street Journal*.

*4. You are given the following information from the *Wall Street Journal* of July 15, 1983, for two Treasury notes:

Coupon	Maturity	Bid	Change	Yield
9⅞	1985 May 15	98²⁰⁄₃₂	—	10.67
14⅜	1985 May 15	105²⁴⁄₃₂	−⁴⁄₃₂	10.68

(a) Explain why two notes of the same maturity are selling at two different prices.

(b) For each bond, draw up the schedule of interest and capital payments until maturity that an investor would receive if he or she bought the bond on July 15, 1983.

5. The following information for IBM was shown in the *Wall Street Journal* of August 10, 1983:

Bonds	Current	Volume	High	Low	Close	Net
9½ 86	10	283	95⅛	94½	95	+⅜
9⅜ 04	12	895	80½	80¼	80⅜	+⅛

Explain how the current yield is obtained, and suggest reasons why the current yield on the 2004 9⅜ percent bond is higher than the 1986 9½ percent bond.

6. Altman's 1968 study came up with the following discriminant model:

$$Z = 0.012X_1 + 0.014X_2 + 0.033X_3 + 0.006X_4 + 0.010X_5$$

where X_1 = Working capital to total assets

X_2 = Retained earnings to total assets

X_3 = Earnings before interest and taxes to total assets

X_4 = Market value of equity to book value of total debt

X_5 = Sales to total assets

Companies A and B have the following ratios for 1981:

	X_1	X_2	X_3	X_4	X_5
A	0.134	0.110	0.068	0.452	10.84
B	0.158	0.004	0.011	0.091	0.20

Use Altman's Z-function to predict if the companies are bankrupt; the cutoff point for bankruptcy is a Z-score of 2.675 or less. The ratios have to be expressed in percentage terms. What factors may contribute to incorrect prediction of bankruptcy?

References

Altman, E. I., "Financial Ratios, Discriminant Analysis, and the Prediction of Corporate Failure, *Journal of Finance,* 23, no. 4 (September 1968): 589–609.

Beaver, W. H., "Financial Ratios and Predictions of Failure," *Empirical Research in Accounting: Selected Studies,* supplement to *Journal of Accounting Research,* 4 (1966): 71–111.

Chen, K. H., and Shimerda, T. A., "An Empirical Analysis of Useful Financial Ratios," *Financial Management,* 10, no. 1 (Spring 1981): 51–60.

Cohan, A. B., "Yields on Corporate Debt Directly Placed," Washington: National Bureau of Economic Research, 1967.

Foster, G., *Financial Statement Analysis,* Englewood Cliffs, N.J.: Prentice-Hall, 1978.

Hays, P. A., "Determinants of the Yield Spread Between Comparable Direct Placements and Public Offerings," Ph.D. dissertation, University of North Carolina, Chapel Hill, 1977.

Kalotay, A. J., "Long-Term Debt and Equity Markets and Instruments," in *Financial Handbook,* 5th ed., edited by E. I. Altman, New York: Wiley, 1981.

Mitchell, K., "Trends in Corporation Finance," Federal Reserve Bank of Kansas City *Economic-Review* (March 1983): 3–15.

Myers, S., "Determinants of Corporate Borrowing," *Journal of Financial Economics,* 5, no. 2 (November 1977): 147–75.

Pinches, G. E., and K. A. Mingo, "A Multivariate Analysis of Industrial Bond Ratings," *Journal of Finance* 28, no. 1 (March 1973): 1–18.

Spence, B. M., J. Y. Graudenz, and J. J. Lynch, Jr., *Standard Securities Calculation Methods,* New York: Securities Industry Association (1973): 28–29.

Standard & Poor's Corporation, *Credit Overview, Corporate and International Ratings,* New York: 1982.

The Economics of Interest Rates and Bond Prices

In the previous chapter we described the market for government and corporate borrowing. The sale of bonds plays an essential role in this market. When companies issue bonds with different lives or different maturities, they need to consider the effective rate of interest that is to be paid during the life of a bond and how market interest rates are likely to change before the bond matures. Clues concerning the market's view of changes in future rates of interest are contained in the term structure of interest rates. A corporate treasurer must understand the term structure of interest rates in order to make better decisions on the timing, prices, and maturities of bond issues.

In this chapter we discuss reasons why yields vary for bonds with different maturities. We shall make an important distinction between bond yields and interest rates and show how the relationship between bond yields and bond maturities reflects the term structure of interest rates. We shall describe the various theories that have been used to try to explain the term structure of interest rates and discuss the impact of taxes on the term structure. Finally, we explain why yields on corporate bonds are different from yields on government bonds.

Coupon Bonds and Discount Bonds

Most government and corporate bonds are **coupon bonds,** that is, they pay interest twice yearly. The interest payments are frequently referred to as coupon payments. The return to the bondholder is a combination of the interest that is received in the form of coupons and a possible capital gain (or loss) that may arise during the period in which the bond is held. For example, if the market price of the bond is below the amount to be repaid on the bond, a capital gain is expected to accrue. **Discount bonds,** on the other hand, are bonds that do not pay coupons. The return to the holder of a discount bond consists solely of the difference between the bond's face value, or the amount to be repaid, and the price that was paid for it. Treasury bills are the most important example of discount bonds that are traded in the financial market; they were described in detail in the previous chapter. Longer-term discount bonds also have been issued by some companies. In recent years the term *discount bond* has also been applied to those bonds issued with a small coupon and at a significant discount below their face values.

A Bond's Yield to Maturity

As discussed in Chapter 16, the price at which a bond is traded generally is different from its face value. The bond's **face value** is the amount to be repaid by the borrower at maturity (the face value is also referred to as the **par value**). For most bonds, the face value is $100. For example, a bond trader's bid quotation of 90 for a particular bond expresses a willingness to buy this bond (which has a $100 face value) for $90. Given this price and knowledge of what the bond's promised cash flows are for each year to its date of maturity, the bond's yield to maturity or internal rate of return can be calculated.

Let us examine a bond that pays two coupons each year, repaying the face value at the end of $N/2$ years. Between coupon payment dates, the buyer of a bond pays the bond's market price plus any accrued interest.[1] For simplicity's sake, we shall assume that the bond price is observed just after a coupon has been paid. As the interest payments occur every six months, the bond's internal rate of return equals its semiannual yield to maturity and is given by,

$$P = \frac{C}{(1 + Y)} + \frac{C}{(1 + Y)^2} + \cdots + \frac{C}{(1 + Y)^N} + \frac{S}{(1 + Y)^N} \tag{17.1}$$

where P is the bond price, C is the semiannual coupon, S is the bond's face value (the amount to be repaid), and N is the number of semiannual periods. The semiannual internal rate of return is found by solving for Y in equation

[1]The Wall Street conventions for calculating bond yields both on coupon dates and on noncoupon dates are described in Spence, Graudenz, and Lynch (1973).

(17.1). By Wall Street convention, the bond's annual **yield to maturity** is reported as $2Y$. This convention understates the true compound yield on the bond, because the semiannual coupons can be reinvested to produce additional income.[2] For the sake of simplicity, we shall assume in the discussion following that bond cash flows are received in single annual payments. Accordingly, equation (17.1) will be used to describe an annual yield, Y, for a bond with a life of N years. For example, if a bond with four years to maturity has an annual coupon of $10 and is priced at $90, its annual yield Y is the solution to the following equation:

$$90 = \frac{10}{(1 + Y)} + \frac{10}{(1 + Y)^2} + \frac{10}{(1 + Y)^3} + \frac{10}{(1 + Y)^4} + \frac{100}{(1 + Y)^4}$$

The yield to maturity or internal rate of return $Y = 0.1339$, or 13.39 percent. The **coupon rate** is the annual coupon divided by the face value. The **current yield** is the coupon divided by the current price or $10/90 = 11.11$ percent, which compares with the yield to maturity of 13.39 percent. The reason that the yield to maturity exceeds the current yield is that the bondholder enjoys a capital gain of $100 - $90 = 10 when the bond matures and is repaid.

Spot Rates of Interest and the Term Structure

If you pick up the *Wall Street Journal* on any day, it is likely that you will find that the yield quoted on long-term government bonds is different from the yields on short-term government bonds. Corresponding differences in yields also can be observed for corporate bonds. The reason is that the market discounts a bond's cash flows at different rates depending on the date of receipt. This set of discount rates is often referred to as the term structure of interest rates.

In order to analyze the term structure of interest rates, financial economists use the following representation of a bond's discounted present value:

$$P = \frac{C_1}{(1 + R_1)} + \frac{C_2}{(1 + R_2)^2} + \cdots + \frac{C_N}{(1 + R_N)^N} \qquad (17.2)$$

---

[2]For example, a semiannual yield of 5.5 percent, which is reported as an annual yield of 11 percent, is the equivalent of

$(1 + 0.055)^2 - 1 = 0.1130$

or 11.3 percent, with semiannual compounding.

This equation is different from equation (17.1) in that we now use the spot rates of interest R_t ($t = 1, 2, \ldots, N$) as the discount rates for the bond's cash flows C_t instead of a single discount rate Y for all periods. We have included both the face value and the final coupon in the final cash flow C_N. The set of spot rates R_t represents the **term structure of interest rates.** For example, R_2 is the discount rate that should be applied to a cash flow in period 2 to obtain its present value in period 0. R_2 is known as the **spot rate of interest** for the cash flow occurring at the end of period 2. Understanding spot interest rates helps us to understand how bonds are priced.

In order to understand how a bond is priced, it is useful to think of a bond that makes payments to bondholders for N periods as equivalent to a ready-made portfolio of discount bonds. Remember that a discount bond is a bond that makes no coupon payments. Each discount bond (or zero-coupon bond) provides for only one payment at maturity. Thus for an N–period coupon-paying bond there will be an equivalent portfolio of N discount bonds. We shall price a coupon-bearing bond using spot rates of interest derived from a set of discount bonds where the yield on a discount bond equals the spot rate of interest for the period to maturity of the bond. The price of the coupon bond in equation (17.2) can be described as the sum of the present values of an equivalent portfolio of discount bonds. Thus, each term on the right-hand side of equation (17.2) can be interpreted as representing the present value of a discount bond maturing at time t and having a face value totaling C_t.

For example, consider the bond in Table 17.1. The price is \$108.7717, and the annual coupon is \$15.00. The dollar cash flows are \$15.00, \$15.00 and \$115.00. The bond's price reflects the underlying term structure of interest rates, which we have assumed to be $R_1 = 0.10$, $R_2 = 0.11$, and $R_3 = 0.115$. (We shall describe in a later section how these may be calculated.) We can say that the first period's cash flow has a price

$$P_1 = \frac{\$15}{1 + R_1} = \frac{\$15}{1.10} = 0.90909 \times \$15 = \$13.6364$$

Table 17.1   *Pricing a bond using spot rates of interest*

End of year	Cash flow (Dollars)	Spot rate	Discount factor	Present value (Dollars)
1	15	0.10	0.90909	P_1 = 13.6364
2	15	0.11	0.81162	P_2 = 12.1743
3	115	0.115	0.72140	P_3 = 82.9610
				Bond price P = 108.7717

That is, a discount bond with a maturity value of $15.00 at the end of one period would be priced at $13.6364. The second period's cash flow also has a price

$$P_2 = \frac{\$15}{(1 + R_2)^2} = \frac{\$15}{(1.11)^2} = 0.81162 \times \$15 = \$12.1743$$

and the third period's cash flow has a price

$$P_3 = \frac{\$115}{(1 + R_3)^3} = \frac{\$115}{(1.115)^3} = 0.72140 \times \$115 = \$82.9610$$

The values in the portfolio of discount bonds that would give the same cash flow as the coupon bond add up to the price of $108.7717 for the coupon bond. This principle is important to understand when we wish to measure the term structure of interest rates, which is the subject of the next section.

Bond Prices and the Term Structure

Bond analysts can predict the selling price of a newly issued bond if they can estimate the rates that the bond market will use to discount the bond's cash flows. If they have sufficient information to estimate the term structure of spot interest rates, they can use these spot rates to discount the bond's cash flows and to estimate its price accurately. Many analysts do not use spot rates of interest, but rather the yield to maturity on a similar existing bond as the discount rate. The question is: Can we always use the yield to maturity rather than the spot rates for bond pricing?

PRICING A BOND USING SPOT INTEREST RATES AND THE YIELD TO MATURITY

In Table 17.1 we described a three-year bond paying an annual coupon of $15.00. That bond was priced in the market at $108.7717. Assume now that another bond is about to be issued by a corporation. This bond, as described in Table 17.2, has a maturity of three years and will pay an annual coupon of $1.00. At what price can this bond be sold?

Let us price the new bond in two ways, first, by using spot rates to discount the bond's cash flows and second, by using a similar traded bond's yield as the discount rate for the new bond's cash flows. The spot rates of interest for the three periods are $R_1 = 0.10$, $R_2 = 0.11$, and $R_3 = 0.115$.

Table 17.2   *Pricing a new bond using spot rates of interest*

End of year	Cash flow (Dollars)	Spot rate	Discount factor	Present value (Dollars)
1	1	0.10	0.90909	0.9091
2	1	0.11	0.81162	0.8116
3	101	0.115	0.72140	72.8614
			Bond price P =	74.5821

Table 17.2 shows that when the new bond's cash flows are discounted by these spot rates, we obtain the present value of $74.5821. How close would we come to this price if we use the yield on the traded bond described in Table 17.1 as the discount rate for the new bond's cash flows? The traded bond's yield is 11.3864 percent, which can be found by calculating the IRR on the cash flows of the bond in the second column of Table 17.1. Applying this yield as a discount rate to the cash flows for the bond described in Table 17.2:

$$\frac{1.00}{(1 + 0.113864)} + \frac{1.00}{(1 + 0.113864)^2} + \frac{101.00}{(1 + 0.113864)^3} = \$74.7882$$

The price of the bond based on the yield of a traded bond of similar maturity is $74.7882, compared to the $74.5821 we calculated using spot rates of interest. The difference of $0.2061 does not seem very large. If the corporation were selling $100 million worth (par value) of bonds the difference between the two pricing methods would be $20,610. This is not a large amount to a corporation issuing such a bond, but companies would be happy to arbitrage for such a profit by simultaneous borrowing and lending.[3] If the difference in spot rates from one period to another had been larger than in our example, the difference in bond prices obtained by the two approaches also would be larger. The lesson is that the yield approach to bond pricing is reliable only when spot interest rates for different periods are equal. You may wish to prove this statement by assuming $R_1 = R_2 = R_3$ in the previous example.

HOW TO ESTIMATE SPOT RATES OF INTEREST

The spot rate of interest R_t for each period t in equation (17.2) is the bond market's current discount rate for a bond's cash flow that is to be received

---

[3]The yield to maturity would prove an even better approximation if the coupons on the two bonds were less unequal.

in period t. If there exists a discount bond maturing in the period, we could obtain the spot rate of interest for the period from the yield on the discount bond. However, there are few discount bonds other than Treasury bills, and they have relatively short maturities. Thus, for most periods we cannot obtain spot rates of interest directly. Instead, we have to calculate spot rates by estimating the discount rates that are implied by the prices of coupon-paying bonds. If you examine equation (17.2), you can see that there are N different discount rates (spot rates of interest) used to discount the cash flows of a coupon-paying bond maturing N periods in the future. There are N unknown spot rates of interest in the equation, and therefore we need N such equations to solve for the N unknowns. In order to obtain the N equations we must use the prices, coupons, and redemption values on N different bonds; the first maturing in one period, the second maturing in two periods, and so on up to N periods.

Let us see how we can estimate the spot rates of interest that are implied by the prices of three coupon-paying bonds with maturities of one, two, and three years. If only one bond matures in each period, and if all the bonds have the same risk, the solution is straightforward. Table 17.3 illustrates the solution. At step 1 we use the one-year bond to calculate the first spot rate R_1.

Given the price of \$95.45 for the one-year bond, we can calculate R_1:

$$95.45 = \frac{105}{(1 + R_1)}$$

Rearranging,

$$R_1 = \frac{105}{95.45} - 1$$

$$= 0.10$$

Table 17.3   *Bond data for calculating the term structure of interest rates*

	Bond price	End of year cash flow		
		1	2	3
1-year bond	95.45	105	0	0
2-year bond	91.48	6	106	0
3-year bond	94.11	9	9	109

Step 2 is to calculate R_2 from the two-year bond that is described in Table 17.3:

$$91.48 = \frac{6}{(1 + R_1)} + \frac{106}{(1 + R_2)^2}$$

We know R_1 from the one-year bond; therefore we can solve for R_2:

$$91.48 = \frac{6}{(1 + 0.10)} + \frac{106}{(1 + R_2)^2}$$

Rearranging,

$$91.48 - 5.4545 = \frac{106}{(1 + R_2)^2}$$

$$(1 + R_2)^2 = \frac{106}{(91.48 - 5.4545)}$$

$$1 + R_2 = \left(\frac{106}{91.48 - 5.4545}\right)^{1/2}$$

The result is that R_2 equals 11 percent. At step 3 we calculate R_3 from the three-year bond, which is priced at \$94.11. The price of the bond can be found by discounting its cash flows in the equation

$$94.11 = \frac{9}{(1 + R_1)} + \frac{9}{(1 + R_2)^2} + \frac{109}{(1 + R_3)^3}$$

Substituting the values of R_1 and R_2 from the prior two steps, we obtain

$$94.11 = \frac{9}{(1.10)} + \frac{9}{(1.11)^2} + \frac{109}{(1 + R_3)^3}$$

The solution for R_3 is 11.5 percent.

While the method of estimating implied spot rates that we have just illustrated is straightforward, obtaining the required data is not always easy. In the case of government bonds that have no default risk, we may accept that the bonds of different maturities have the same (zero) risk. Consequently, we can in principle determine the spot rates that are implied by their prices and cash flows. For some future payment dates, though, there may be no bonds maturing. If we can estimate spot rates up to year t, but no bond exists that matures in year $t + 1$, we will be unable to determine the spot rate for period $t + 1$. In addition, there may be several bonds maturing on the same future payment date, that have different patterns of cash flows. Finally, different bonds are held by investors in different tax brackets, so choosing the correct set of bonds for the purpose of measuring spot rates is not simple. We shall discuss why when we introduce taxes later in the chapter.

The simpler alternative method that many financial analysts use for describing the term structure is the yield curve. The **yield curve** is simply the plot of yields to maturity for bonds of similar risk but with different periods to maturity. The yield curve is at times a somewhat imprecise indicator of the term structure, because the yield represents a constant discount rate [Y in equation (17.1)] for all payments up to a bond's maturity. That is, the yield is the same for all periods in the bond's life as it is defined to be equal to the internal rate of return on the bond's cash flows. However, the yield on a four-year bond, for example, would not necessarily equal the market spot rates of interest for years 1, 2, 3, and 4 unless these interest rates happened, by coincidence, to be equal to each other (called a flat term structure). The examples in Tables 17.1 and 17.2 demonstrate this point. In general, the term structure is not flat, and therefore the yield curve will not give a very precise picture of the underlying term structure of interest rates. Nonetheless, a comparison of sophisticated estimates of term structures with yield curves for the same dates provides some comfort to analysts who use yields as a proxy for spot rates of interest. The results in Figure 17.1, which is taken from a study by Chambers, Carleton, and Waldman, of United States Treasury notes during the years 1976–1980, provide us with some idea of the size of the problem. This period was one of substantial interest rate changes. As Figure 17.1 shows, yield curves for bonds with maturities of up to about nine years were reasonably close to the term structure of spot rates of interest. This good approximation held for all the dates studied, whether yield curves were upward or downward sloping. Of course, if the yield curves had been steeper, the results would have been different, and the yield to maturity would have proven a less reliable approximation.

How Can We Explain the Term Structure of Interest Rates?

As we have said, and as Figure 17.1 illustrates, the term structure of interest rates usually is not flat. Ordinarily, spot interest rates are higher for longer maturities. Sometimes, however, they rise for the shorter maturities and fall for the longer maturities (and vice versa). What explains such differences in spot interest rates (and yields) for different periods? We shall discuss four propositions that try to explain the term structure.

Figure 17.1   *A comparison of the term structure of interest rates based on estimated spot rates with calculated bond yields*

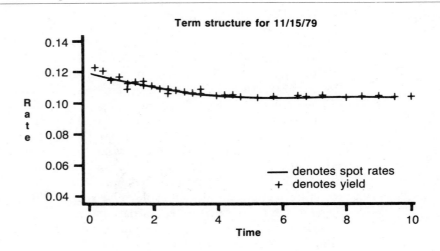

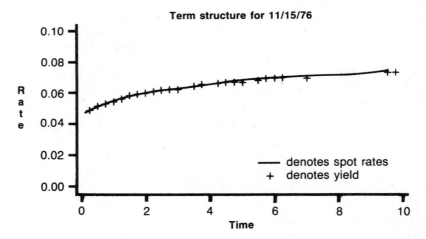

Source: D. R. Chambers, W. T. Carleton, and D. R. Waldman, "Estimation of the Term Structure of Interest Rates Using a Simple Polynomial," University of North Carolina at Chapel Hill, December 1983.

THE PURE EXPECTATIONS HYPOTHESIS

The **pure expectations hypothesis** is based upon the assumption that the term structure of interest rates reflects the bond market's expectation of how interest rates will change in the future. The theory is often used in reverse to estimate the bond market's expectation of future interest rates. Suppose that the spot rates of interest for one- and two-year bonds are known to be $R_1 = 0.05$ and $R_2 = 0.0747$, respectively. What does the pure expectations hypothesis tell us about the bond market's expectation of the one-year spot interest rate X that will prevail one year from now? The spot rate of interest R_2 must reflect both the spot rate of interest for year 1 and the spot rate of interest that is expected to prevail in year 2. Thus

$$(1 + R_2)^2 = (1 + 0.05)(1 + X)$$

$$1.155 = (1.05)(1 + X)$$

$$X = 0.10$$

The one-year interest rate that is expected to prevail when we arrive at the beginning of the second year is 10 percent under the pure expectations hypothesis.

When an implied one-period expected spot interest rate is derived in this way from the term structure of spot rates, it is called a one-period **forward interest rate.** In the example above, X is a forward rate. The pure expectations hypothesis is based on the principle that the forward rates equal the bond market's expectations of the corresponding spot interest rates that will prevail in the future. We can derive forward rates for different years from estimates of the term structure of spot rates of interest. The resulting forward rates then can be used as forecasts of spot interest rates for those periods.

What are the theoretical arguments that support the pure expectations hypothesis? If this hypothesis does not hold, bond speculators can make money through arbitrage transactions. For the previous example, the pure expectations hypothesis implies that investing in a sequence of two one-year bonds should be no more profitable than investing in one two-year bond and holding it for two years. Investing $1,000 in the two-year bond and holding it for two years will yield

$$\$1,000 \times (1 + 0.0747) \times (1 + 0.0747) = \$1,000 \times 1.155$$

$$= \$1,155$$

By investing the $1,000 in a sequence of two one-year bonds, we would expect to accumulate the same wealth. The interest rate on the one-year bond at the beginning of period 2 is expected to be 10 percent ($X = 0.10$).

Thus,

$$\$1,000 \times (1 + 0.05) \times (1 + 0.10) = \$1,000 \times 1.155$$

$$= \$1,155$$

The result of the two investment strategies is expected to be the same only if the 10 percent forward rate for the second year equals the expected one-year spot interest rate in the second year.

Suppose, however, that we expect the one-year spot interest rate in the second year to exceed the currently observed forward rate; say it is expected to be 12 percent. In this case, we could expect to make a profit by borrowing $1,000 for two years at 7.47 percent (compounded annually) and investing sequentially in two one-year bonds. At the end of the two years we must repay the loan (with interest), which will cost us $1,155. However, we expect to have earned from the investment in two one-year bonds:

$$\$1,000 \times (1 + 0.05) \times (1 + 0.12) = \$1,000 \times 1.176$$

$$= \$1,176$$

Simultaneous borrowing and lending will give us a profit of $1,176 − $1,155 = $21 in two years without investing any of our own money.

There must be a catch. Such profits do not come easily in competitive financial markets. Speculators will take advantage of them. The resulting forces of supply and demand will move bond prices to the point where it is no longer possible to make such easy profits. If there were no such opportunities left, and if there were no complicating factors such as taxes, transactions costs, or risk (to be discussed later), the expectations hypothesis would fully explain the term structure of interest rates.

In the pure expectations hypothesis world, what determines forward rates (and therefore spot rates)? To get some insight on this question, let us return to the discussion of inflation in Chapter 7. You will recall the Fisher effect, which is

$$(1 + \text{Nominal Rate of Interest}) = (1 + \text{Real Rate of Interest})$$
$$\times (1 + \text{Expected Rate of Inflation})$$

If we put this equation in terms of expected future interest rates, it becomes

$$\begin{bmatrix} 1 + \text{Expected Future} \\ \text{Rate of Interest} \end{bmatrix}_t = \begin{bmatrix} 1 + \text{Expected Future} \\ \text{Real Rate of Interest} \end{bmatrix}_t$$
$$\times \begin{bmatrix} 1 + \text{Expected Future} \\ \text{Rate of Inflation} \end{bmatrix}_t$$

This says that our expectations concerning the nominal rate of interest that will prevail in a future period t are determined by our expectations for the real rate of interest and for the rate of inflation in that future period. Under the expectations hypothesis, the forward rates equal the expected future spot rates of interest. Thus, in the expectations hypothesis, expected future real interest rates and inflation rates determine the forward rates; as a result they also determine the spot rates of interest. If we assume real rates of interest are constant, then differences in expected future interest rates are explained solely by differences in expected rates of inflation.

It is important to note that the expectations hypothesis assumes that investors must have a neutral attitude toward risk. They are assumed to be willing to trade only on the basis of expected values, even though, for example, the second year's rate of interest cannot be known with certainty until the beginning of the second year. There is always a risk that the actual interest rate in the future period will not equal the rate that had been expected. If investors are not risk-neutral, the pure expectations hypothesis may not fully explain the term structure of interest rates. An alternative hypothesis is needed.

LIQUIDITY PREFERENCE

Clearly the expectations hypothesis and the Fisher effect jointly give us insights as to why the term structure of interest rates may rise or fall for different maturities. However, as we have noted, the expectations model ignores the effects of uncertainty or it assumes that investors have a neutral attitude towards risk. Predictions of real interest rates and inflation rates are uncertain. Even if market forecasts about forward rates are unbiased or correct on average, usually they will turn out to be wrong in any given year. Chapter 7 on inflation and the investment decision demonstrated why long-term government bonds are risky in real terms when future rates of inflation are uncertain. The reason, of course, is that although the nominal coupon and redemption payments to be made by the government are known with certainty, the purchasing power of these payments is uncertain and therefore risky. If bond investors dislike risk, they will not buy risky long-term bonds unless they have relatively lower prices and higher yields.

Table 17.4 illustrates the effect of changes in spot rates of interest on the prices of discount bonds of different maturities. The price of a discount bond with a redemption value of $100 is equal to the discount factor (using the spot rate of interest as the discount rate) multiplied by $100. As is shown in the table, when the spot rate of interest rises from 8 percent to 12 percent on a twenty-year discount bond, the price of the bond falls from $21.45 to only $10.37. This represents a drop of more than 50 percent in the bond price. The table also shows that the prices of discount bonds of shorter

Table 17.4   *Effect of changes in spot interest rates on the prices of discount bonds of various maturities*

Maturity	($R_t = 0.08$)	($R_t = 0.10$)	($R_t = 0.12$)
1	92.59	90.91	89.29
10	46.32	38.55	32.20
20	21.45	14.86	10.37

maturities are less sensitive to changes in interest rates. For example, the price of the one-year discount bond changes only slightly from $92.59 to $89.29 when the spot interest rate for that maturity rises from 8 percent to 12 percent. The table illustrates the association that exists between the maturity of a discount bond and the sensitivity of its price to unexpected changes in interest rates. If investors dislike risk and find it costly or impossible to hedge against it, they will require a higher rate of interest on bonds of longer maturities.

Recognition of these effects has led to the **liquidity preference theory,** as a modification to the pure expectations hypothesis. If the capital market is dominated by risk-averse lenders, each forward rate will include a risk premium, or liquidity premium, and the spot rates R_t will tend to increase with maturity t. Figure 17.2 describes the result as it would affect the term structure.

As the years to maturity increase, the figure shows an increasing divergence between the term structure we observe (which includes liquidity premiums) and the term structure (as it would be without liquidity premiums), which we do not observe. This means that, when liquidity premiums are present, forward rates are higher than expected future rates, so the pure expectations hypothesis cannot be employed to estimate investors' forecasts of future interest rates.

SEGMENTED MARKETS

An extreme alternative view of the term structure, which acknowledges specialized investor preferences, is the **segmented markets** approach. It can be observed that financial institutions holding bonds tend to specialize in securities of particular maturities. Banks, for example, tend toward the shorter maturities, while life insurance companies and pension funds hold long maturities on balance. Under the segmented markets perspective, bond investors are seen as absolutely preferring specific maturity ranges independent of interest rate expectations. In contrast with the pure expectations

Figure 17.2   *Term structure of interest rates and liquidity premiums*

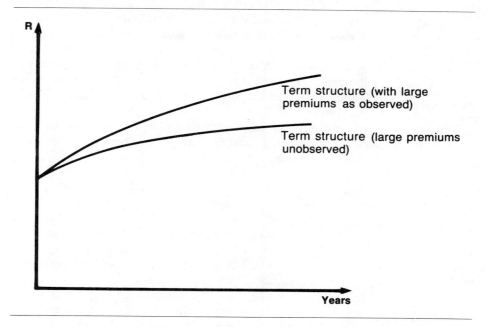

hypothesis, in which investors are viewed as risk-neutral profit seekers willing to shift assets and liabilities among all available maturities, the segmented markets viewpoint holds that investors are absolutely unwilling (because of risk aversion) or unable (because of regulatory restrictions) to shift maturities in order to earn expected profits. Extreme proponents of this view would agree that the term structure of interest rates can be observed (or estimated). But they would go on to say that the forward rates implied in the structure need not have any relationship to expected future spot rates of interest, because limitations on investors switching maturities by buying and selling bonds prevent the results of the pure expectations hypothesis from being fulfilled. Such an extreme view, however, appears to open up the opportunities for arbitrage that we have discussed already, so it is difficult to see how this view of the world could hold.

PREFERRED HABITAT

Intermediate between the liquidity preference and segmented markets theories is the **preferred habitat** approach. As in segmented markets, investors are observed to have bond maturity preferences (preferred habitats), but these are not absolute. If an investor invests in bonds in order to save for an expenditure that must be made at the end of N years, he or she takes a risk by holding bonds that mature either earlier or later than exactly N years. In this case the bond maturity preference or preferred habitat would be N years. This insight about risk exposure is illustrated easily. Consider the interest rate possibilities depicted in Table 17.5. The term structure is assumed to be flat now and in the future, and all spot rates currently are at 10 percent. At the end of year 1, spot rates could change to either 8, 10, or 12 percent, say, and at the end of year 2 they could range from 7 to 13 percent in the same fashion.

Assume an investor with a planning horizon, or a need for funds, at the end of year 2, is contemplating three possible investment strategies, all with two-year horizons:

Strategy 1: Buy a two-year bond and reinvest the first year's coupon in a one-year bond.

Strategy 2: Buy a one-year bond and reinvest the first year's coupon plus principal in another one-year bond, for the second year.

Strategy 3: Buy a three-year bond, reinvest the first year's coupon in a one-year bond, and sell the three-year bond at the end of the second year.

The range of payoffs from these alternative strategies, given the interest rates assumed in Table 17.5, appears in Tables 17.6, 17.7, and 17.8. The tables show that when future interest rates are uncertain the need to reinvest intermediate cash flows magnifies the risk of the final outcome of an investment strategy.

Let us first consider strategy 1, where the investor's 10 percent coupon bond matures at the end of year 2. The investor receives $110 (principal plus the year 2 coupon) plus the proceeds of the first year's coupon which has been reinvested for one year at a rate of 8, 10, or 12 percent. The total proceeds, as shown in column 4, will be either $120.80, $121.00, or $121.20.

Table 17.5   *Spot interest rate outcomes*

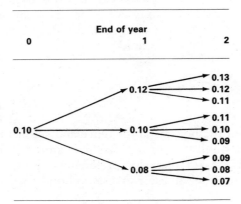

	End of year	
0	1	2

Table 17.6   *Payoffs from investment strategy one: (Buy a two-year bond and reinvest coupon)*

Spot rate year 1 (1)	Proceeds in year 2 from reinvesting first-year coupon (2)	Second-year coupon and principal (3)	Total proceeds (4)	Realized rate of return* (%) (5)
0.12	$11.20	$110.00	$121.20	10.09
0.10	11.00	110.00	121.00	10.00
0.08	10.80	110.00	120.80	9.91

$$* \text{ Rate of return} = \left(\frac{\text{Total proceeds}}{100}\right)^{1/2} - 1$$

As a result, the realized compound annual rate of return on the original $100 investment will turn out to be either 9.91, 10, or 10.09 percent. The reason for this range is that the coupon paid before the two-year horizon must be reinvested at an uncertain future interest rate. This source of risk could be eliminated only if we could invest in a zero-coupon bond maturing at the two-year horizon.

Strategy 2 analyzed in Table 17.7 is less conservative than strategy 1. At the end of year 1, the one-year bond matures, and the investor receives $110. This sum then will be reinvested at whichever one-year spot rate (8, 10, or 12 percent) is available then. As a result, the investor's proceeds available at the planning horizon will range from $118.80 to $123.20 (column 2), and the realized rate of return will range from 9 to 11 percent (column 3).

Strategy 3 analyzed in Table 17.8 produces a still wider range of possible payoffs. At the end of year 1, the investor reinvests the coupon received on the three-year 10 percent bond. This will produce either $10.80, $11.00, or $11.20 at the end of year 2 (column 2) depending on rates available at the

Table 17.7   *Payoffs from investment strategy two (buy two one-year bonds and reinvest coupon and principal)*

Spot rate year 1 (1)	Total proceeds (2)	Realized rate of return (%) (3)
0.12	$123.20	11.00
0.10	121.00	10.00
0.08	118.80	9.00

Table 17.8   *Payoffs from investment strategy three: (Buy one three-year bond, reinvest coupon, and sell at the end of year 2)*

Spot rate year 1 (1)	Proceeds from reinvesting first-year coupon in year 2 (2)	Spot rate year 2 (3)	Total proceeds* (4)	Realized rate of return** (%) (5)
		0.13	$118.55	8.88
0.12	$11.20	0.12	119.41	9.27
		0.11	120.30	9.68
		0.11	120.10	9.59
0.10	11.00	0.10	121.00	10.00
		0.09	121.92	10.42
		0.09	121.72	10.33
0.08	10.80	0.08	122.65	10.75
		0.07	123.60	11.18

* Total proceeds = \$10 (1 + Spot Rate, Year 1) + \$10 + \$110/(1 + Spot Rate, Year 2)

** Rate of return = $\left(\dfrac{\text{Final proceeds}}{100} \right)^{1/2} - 1$

end of year 1. At the end of year 2 the investor also receives another $10 coupon from the original bond plus the proceeds from selling the bond (which has one more year to maturity) at the then-prevailing interest rates. The sum of these proceeds can range from $118.55 to $123.60 (column 4) and the realized rate of return from 8.88 to 11.18 percent (column 5). If the investor wishes to consume at the end of the planning horizon, the strategy that minimizes risk is the first one. But even this strategy is not riskless.

Under the preferred habitat theory, the investor is willing to adopt a strategy where expected return is sufficient compensation for risk exposure. Trading among investors with different maturity preferences is acknowledged to take place, but one cannot tell how large the resulting risk premiums on bonds are or how they might be related to bond maturity.

As a final note, it requires no great stretch of the imagination to see that if investors face the preferred habitat problem, so can borrowers. For example, an investor making an investment now that has a certain single cash inflow in two years faces interest rate risk if he or she finances the investment with borrowings that mature either before or after two years.

Maturity, Interest Rates, and Duration Measures

In a previous section we showed that the relationship between maturity and risk is more complex for coupon-paying bonds than for discount bonds, because the effective maturity of a coupon bond depends on the timing and the amount of coupons paid as well as upon the date of redemption. Economists have developed a measure of a bond's effective maturity called **duration,** which reflects these factors. The duration D on a bond is measured as the weighted average payment to bondholders:

$$D = 1W_1 + 2W_2 + \cdots + NW_N \tag{17.3}$$

where N is the date of the final payment at maturity. Each weight W_t is the proportion of the total present value (price) of the bond that is contributed by each year's cash flow C_t

$$W_t = \frac{\text{Present Value of } C_t}{P} = \frac{C_t/(1 + R_t)^t}{P} \tag{17.4}$$

using the spot rates R_t as the discount rates, or

$$W_t = \frac{C_t/(1 + Y)^t}{P} \tag{17.5}$$

using the bond's yield Y as the discount rate.

To illustrate, consider a bond that has a maturity of four years, is priced at \$90 to yield 13.39 percent, and has a duration of 3.46 years calculated as follows:

$$\frac{1 \times 10/1.1339}{90} + \frac{2 \times 10/(1.1339)^2}{90} + \frac{3 \times 10/(1.1339)^3}{90} + \frac{4 \times 110/(1.1339)^4}{90}$$

$$= 3.46 \text{ years}$$

Contrast this result with that of another four-year bond that pays a coupon of 20 and is priced at \$119.50 to yield the same 13.39 percent. Its duration is

$$\frac{1 \times 20/1.1339}{119.50} + \frac{2 \times 20/(1.1339)^2}{119.50} + \frac{3 \times 20/(1.1339)^3}{119.50} + \frac{4 \times 120/(1.1339)^4}{119.50}$$

$$= 3.18 \text{ years}$$

The higher coupon bond returns cash to its owner earlier than the lower coupon bond; it has a duration of only 3.18 years compared to 3.46 years. It should be clear that if two bonds have the same maturity, the bond with the longer duration should have the higher yield when the slope of the term structure of spot rates of interest is rising and should have the lower yield when the slope is declining. One reason duration measures have come into wide use is that volatile interest rates have produced bonds of equivalent maturity with different coupons; therefore they trade at substantially different yields. In such circumstances, duration differences are used to express risk differences between bonds of equivalent maturity. Indeed, the percentage change in a coupon bond's price can be related directly to its duration and to (small) changes (ΔY) in the bond's yield by the following formula:

$$\frac{\Delta P}{P} = \frac{-D \times \Delta Y}{1 + Y} \tag{17.6}$$

where D is the bond's duration as calculated from equations (17.3) and (17.5), and Y is its yield as calculated in equation (17.1). Equation (17.6) says that, other things being equal, the longer a bond's duration, the greater the proportionate response of its price to changes in yield.[4]

Bond portfolio selection methods have been developed to minimize the kinds of risks suggested in our example of preferred habitat strategies. They are called immunization methods, and one popular one uses duration as its centerpiece. If a portfolio of bonds is constructed so that its duration, D, is set equal to the investor's planning horizon, the interest rate risk of his portfolio at that horizon will have been minimized (subject to some technical qualifications). [See Bierwag, Kaufman, and Toevs (1982) and Chambers, Carleton, and McEnally (1982).]

Financial Innovations and the Term Structure

While the term structure probably does reflect risk premiums that make forward interest rates higher than expected future spot rates, recent changes in the bond market may be reducing this effect. With the high interest rate volatility in the late 1970s, innovations were introduced that permitted lenders to minimize exposure to interest rate risks.

VARIABLE RATE BONDS AND LOANS

Variable rate bonds allow the borrower and lender to vary the interest rate on the loan according to prevailing market rates. Interest rates payable may be changed monthly, quarterly, or semiannually and related to the prime interest rate of a specific bank or to the average prime rate of a group of banks.

---

[4]Equation (17.6) can only be an approximation. It is strictly valid only when the term structure (hence the yield curve) is flat. When the term structure is not flat, it should be obvious that $\Delta P/P$ depends on D as measured by equation (17.4) and on the change in the entire structure of spot rates. As a result, many authors have criticized duration measures.

INTEREST RATE SWAPS

Interest rate swaps have developed as a consequence of the existence of variable rate contracts. In the typical swap, a corporate borrower would like to secure funds on a fixed rate debt contract. It borrows on a variable rate basis and arranges to swap interest payments with another firm (typically a bank), which concurrently has borrowed an equal amount of fixed rate funds. The bank's credit standing gives it access to fixed rate bonds, while its asset and liability structure permit it to absorb (at a price) the variable interest rate risk.

ORIGINAL ISSUE DISCOUNT BONDS (OIDs)

The deeper the discount from par that is reflected in a bond's price when it is issued, the more closely the duration measure approaches its maturity. The extreme case of this is the zero-coupon bond in which the borrower pays no coupons and repays the bond in one lump sum when it matures. An investor with, say, a five-year horizon who buys a five-year zero-coupon bond completely avoids the reinvestment risk associated with interest rate uncertainty.

COUPON STRIPPING

Even more fascinating is the development of coupon stripping, in which an intermediary (a trust set up by a securities firm) is created to buy coupon-bearing bonds and to sell claims on the coupons separately from claims on the principal repayments. The zero-coupon securities that are created in this way permit investors to match investment income more closely to their planning horizons.[5] The risks that we described in the preferred habitat approach would not be important if coupon stripping could be practiced without restrictions.

INTEREST RATE FUTURES

In recent years, active futures markets have arisen in several different kinds of financial instruments, notably Treasury bills, notes, and bonds. A financial futures contract is an agreement to buy or sell a standardized financial instrument with a price and yield that is fixed when the transaction takes place

---

[5]For a good discussion, see "The New World of Coupon Stripping," by T. E. Klaffky, Salomon Brothers, August 1982.

and with delivery to take place at a specified month in the future. With the yield determined ahead of time by a transaction in the futures market, it is possible for risk-averse borrowers and lenders to hedge away as much interest rate risk as possible.[6]

For example, suppose a corporate treasurer who is planning to issue $30 million in bonds six months from now fears that interest rates will be higher at that time. First, he or she can sell $30 million in Treasury bond futures for delivery six months hence. Six months later he or she will buy $30 million in Treasury bonds to close out the position at the same time as the issue of the $30 million in corporate bonds. If yields have risen in the six months, the sale of Treasury futures will produce a gain (the Treasury bonds closing out the position can be purchased at a lower price). This gain offsets the corporate bond's higher interest cost. If yields have fallen, the treasurer loses on the futures transaction, with the loss offset by the lower borrowing cost on the new bond.

To summarize, financial innovations that have developed in response to increased interest rate volatility have led to a more complete market, that is, a market that accommodates the diverse needs of borrowers and lenders more fully. In an efficient capital market, the availability at low cost of financial instruments for shifting or minimizing interest rate risk carries important implications. If interest rate risk does not have to be borne, no risk premium is required. To the degree that this is becoming reality, the term structure of interest rates may be coming closer to reflecting forward rates that equal expected future spot rates (as in the pure expectations hypothesis), undistorted by the presence of significant interest rate risk premiums related to the bond's maturity.

The Impact of Taxes on Interest Rates

Most analyses of the term structure of interest rates ignore tax effects. Obviously, though, the tax status of different bonds is of importance to the taxpaying investor. The tax status of income from any given bond to an investor depends upon several factors:

1. The type of bond. Coupon income from bonds issued by state and local governments (municipal bonds) is exempt from all federal and most state income taxes. Coupon income from all other bonds (United States government and government agencies, corporations, foreign governments) is fully taxable as ordinary income.

---

[6]For a descriptive treatment, see "A Guide to Financial Futures at the Chicago Board of Trade," Chicago Board of Trade.

2. Capital gains and losses from buying and selling bonds of any kind are subject to the tax treatment accorded capital transactions. As the capital gains tax rate is lower than the ordinary income tax rate, the value of bond income to a taxpaying investor depends on whether the income takes the form of coupons or capital gains.

3. Investors are subject to different tax requirements and are in different marginal tax brackets. For example, financial institutions are required to treat capital gains from bond transactions as ordinary income, while individuals treat them as capital gains, and pension funds pay no taxes on them at all.

The implications of taxes for bond markets suggest a **clientele effect**. That is, some investors will prefer specific types of bonds and certain maturities depending upon their individual tax status. For example, taxpaying institutions and high tax bracket individual investors who wish to avoid taxes tend to hold municipal bonds, whose coupons are tax-free. Also, where coupons are taxable, high rate taxpayers tend to hold low coupon-paying bonds, while high coupon-paying bonds tend to be held by low rate taxpayers.

What is less widely appreciated is that, in the presence of different tax rates, it may be impossible to find a single term structure of interest rates that results in the same after-tax rate of return for all investors. Schaefer (1981) provides the example given in Table 17.9, which looks at two one-period bonds of equal risk and two investors. One investor pays no taxes, while the other pays a 50 percent tax on coupons and zero taxes on capital gains (perhaps because of unused capital losses). In this example, there is no way for a common set of prices, P_1 and P_2, to make the net present value of the two bonds equal to zero for both investors. The direct consequence is that some investors may have profitmaking opportunities. For example, an investor may be able to go short in the bond that is overvalued in terms

Table 17.9   *Schaefer's example of bond market tax arbitrage*

	Bond 1 (Coupon = 4%)	Bond 2 (Coupon = 10%)
Investor 1 (tax-exempt)	$P_1 = \dfrac{104}{1+Y}$	$P_2 = \dfrac{110}{1+Y}$
Investor 2 (tax rate = 50%)	$P_1 = \dfrac{102}{1+0.10}$	$P_2 = \dfrac{105}{1+0.10}$
	$= \$92.73$	$= \$95.45$

Source: S. M. Schaefer, "Measuring a Tax-Specific Term Structure of Interest Rates in the Market for British Government Securities," *The Economic Journal,* 91, no. 2 (June 1981): 416–17.

of his or her own tax position and long in the bonds that are undervalued, thereby making a profit.

In Schaefer's example, if the bonds' prices satisfy the taxpaying investor at a yield of $Y = 0.1$,

$$P_1 = \frac{102}{1.1} = \$92.73 \text{ and } P_2 = \frac{105}{1.1} = \$95.45.$$

To the tax-exempt investor, however, the prices above imply a yield Y of

$$\frac{104}{92.73} - 1 = 12.15\% \text{ for the first bond, and } \frac{110}{95.45} - 1 = 15.24\%$$

for the second. An arbitrage opportunity exists in which the tax-exempt investor can sell the first bond short, purchase the second, and generate a riskless return $(0.1524 - 0.1215)$. Selling a bond short means that an investor sells a bond that he or she does not possess, but which must be purchased later before a prescribed date. Because people are not observed making such large arbitrage profits, Schaefer goes on to reason that there must be restrictions (transactions costs, or limits on short sales) that severely limit such tax arbitrage opportunities.

Finally, our discussion of taxes would not be complete if we failed to note that the bond market innovations we have mentioned were motivated by tax as well as by interest rate risk considerations. For example, zero-coupon corporate bonds were first issued by Martin Marietta in 1981. At that time the principal advantages were in eliminating reinvestment risk to the lender and in permitting the borrower a tax deduction for the difference between the bond's par value and its issue price prorated over the life of the bond. Tax legislation in 1982 eliminated this advantage.[7] The lesson to be drawn here is that the specific economic impact of taxes on interest rates (and on corporate financial management) is not engraved in stone. Tax treatments evolve as financing or investing strategies do.

Bond Quality and Interest Rates

Note that our analysis thus far applies to all bonds, corporate as well as government, although our examples have been drawn from prices on United States government securities. Given that government securities provide the

[7]An excellent treatment of this and related matters can be found in "Tax Aspects of Recent Innovative Financing—Strategies for Existing Discount Debt and for New Securities," by D. C. Walter, *Taxes—The Tax Magazine,* December 1982: 995–1009; and "Recent Innovative Financing Technologies—An Addendum," also by D. C. Walter, *Taxes—The Tax Magazine,* March 1983.

lowest risk for any given maturity, we can represent the yield on a corporate bond as the yield on a government bond of the same maturity plus a premium due to the risk characteristics or quality of the corporate bond. Let us consider what variables determine the quality of a corporate bond.

DEFAULT RISK

The simplest way to differentiate corporate bonds from government bonds is in terms of their default, or credit risk. When the government issues a claim promising to pay $110 one year hence, the promise is a good one. For all other borrowers, however, there is some probability, however small, that this promise will not be fulfilled, or will not be fulfilled on time. The expected value of the cash flow to bondholders therefore is less than the contracted amount. For example, if the discount rate is $R_1 = 0.10$ on the government promise, an investor is willing to pay

$$P = \frac{\$110}{1.1} = \$100$$

for the claim. If the investor's expectation (allowing for the probability of default) for a similar promise to pay $110 by a corporation is only $108, the price that we observe on the claim will be

$$P = \frac{\$108.00}{1.1} = \$98.18$$

Consequently, when we observe the price $P = \$98.18$ and calculate the required return, R, on the promised cash flow of $110, we get

$$R = \frac{\$110.00}{\$98.18} - 1 = 0.1204$$

The default or credit risk premium on the corporate bond is thus $0.1204 - 0.1000 = 0.0204$, or 2.04 percent.

Of course, the quality of corporate bonds varies substantially, both among firms and over time. As we discussed in the last chapter, both Moody's and Standard & Poor's assign corporate bonds to credit quality classes on the basis of an assessment of relative credit risks. Although ratings change, and the two agencies differ frequently in their evaluations, the yields of traded bonds do tend to agree with credit ratings.

The spread between the yields on a corporate bond and a government bond of the same maturity tends to go up for lower-rated bonds when interest rates rise. Thus, firms with greater credit risk face greater uncertainty about what their future bond borrowing costs will be. It is also worth noting that the bond market is dominated by financial institutions, which are restricted in their holdings of the lower-rated bonds either because of regulation or fiduciary responsibilities. Commercial banks, for example, are restricted in their municipal bond holdings to investment-grade issues, which include those rated Baa/BBB or higher. Consequently, the downgrading of a firm's bond rating implies the likelihood of a diminished demand for and higher cost on subsequent bond issues.

MARKETABILITY

As Silvers (1973) has documented, companies whose bonds enjoy a good secondary market pay lower interest rates than those whose bonds have a limited market.

SINKING FUND

Typical sinking fund provisions, as noted in the last chapter, permit the bond trustee the option of calling bonds that are selected by lottery to be redeemed prior to maturity, or of purchasing bonds in the open market at market prices. In addition, some bonds permit an increase in sinking fund payments. From the perspective of bondholders, the presence of sinking fund options on a bond issued during periods of high interest rates reduces the bond's value, or increases its yield, if subsequent interest rates should turn out to be lower. If the lower interest rates increase the bond's price above par, the price will be depressed slightly and the yield increased by the possibility that the trustee will call the bond by lottery and redeem it at the predetermined call prices.

CALL FEATURES

The option to call a bond becomes more valuable to the firm, other things being equal, when interest rates fall or become more volatile. For example, Southern Bell issued a 16 percent forty-year debenture in 1981, with no call permitted for five years. In June 1982, this bond traded at a yield of about 2 percent (referred to as 200 basis points) higher than twenty-year United States government bonds. By the end of September 1982 (after interest rates had fallen sharply) the Southern Bell issue was yielding about 250 basis points above twenty-year government bonds. Clearly the Southern Bell bond then was trading at a yield to maturity reflecting a non-zero probability that it would be called four years hence. The value to the company of the option to call the bond corresponded to a reduction in the bond's value (hence increase in yield) to the bondholder. Indeed, if it were certain that the bond would be called at a specific date, the bond would have a correspondingly shorter maturity, and the yield would be calculated on the basis of the call date and the call price.

INTERACTIVE EFFECTS

Companies that have greater credit risk not only pay a higher coupon rate on their bonds than do lower-risk firms, but typically they also have to protect investors by offering bonds that involve fewer provisions in favor of the borrower. Also, companies with greater credit risk must comply with stricter indenture provisions. To the extent that these features provide options to lenders, they imply greater borrowing costs that are not captured in the coupon rates on the debt. In addition, during periods of rising interest rates, weaker borrowers usually are not able to borrow for the longer maturities that are available to companies with stronger credit ratings.

Summary

The term structure of interest rates is best measured by spot rates of interest that can be derived from the prices and the payments to holders of bonds of different maturities. Spot rates of interest are the implied discount rates that can be used to discount payments to bondholders in order to obtain the prices of new bonds. The spot rates of interest can also be used to obtain forward rates of interest, which the pure expectations hypothesis claims should equal the market's expected spot rates of interest for corresponding future periods. Thus the term structure of interest rates that exists at one time may reflect the market's expectation of spot rates of interest that will prevail at later points in time.

As forward rates can be expressed in terms of expected real rates of interest and expected rates of inflation, the term structure of interest rates also may reflect the market's expectation of the future course of both real interest rates and inflation. However, other factors may affect this simple model, risk in particular. The prices of bonds of longer maturities are particularly sensitive to unexpected changes in interest rates, making them risky. Liquidity preference theory suggests that, because many investors do not like risk, their relative preferences for shorter-term bonds may reduce the prices and hence increase the yields on bonds of longer maturities. Recent innovations in the bond market have allowed investors to reduce if not eliminate such risks. The existence of taxes complicates our understanding of how interest rates are related to bond maturities but does not appear to undermine the basic underlying relationship between the term structure and market expectations about future interest rates.

Corporate bond yields are higher than government bond yields because of the possibility that companies may default. Corporate yields are also affected by special features of the bonds such as marketability, call protection, and indenture provisions. Such features can affect a corporate bond's price as well as its coupon yield.

Review Questions

1. Explain how a bond's yield to maturity can be calculated.
2. Why should a bond's yield be different from its coupon rate?
3. Describe the term structure of interest rates.
4. For what shape of term structure of interest rates will a bond's yield to maturity equal the market's spot rates of interest?
5. How would you go about pricing a new bond?
6. Describe the pure expectations theory and explain its importance in forecasting future interest rates.
7. What is the relationship between spot rates and forward rates?
8. Explain the difference between the pure expectations approach and the liquidity preference theory.
9. If financial markets were complete, why would you *not* expect to observe the risk premiums that are implied by liquidity preference?
10. Why might a five-year bond be riskier to hold than a three-year bond for a particular investor? Is it possible for a three-year bond to be riskier than a five-year bond for another investor?

Problems

*1. Calculate the semiannual yield on the 13⅛ 1984 July Treasury bond. The following information is from the *Wall Street Journal* of August 11, 1983:

Rate	Maturity	Bid	Asked	Bid change	Yield
13⅛	1984 July	102.2	102.6	−.2	10.57

Compare the semiannual yield with the yield quoted in the *Wall Street Journal*. By convention 102.6 means $102%/32.

2. (a) Calculate the current (coupon/price) yield and the yield to maturity for two Treasury notes quoted in the *Wall Street Journal* of July 16, 1983. Assume interest is paid annually.

Coupon	Maturity	Bid	Change	Yield
4¼	1985 May 15	94	—	7.83
14⅛	1985 May 15	105¹²/32	−⁴/32	10.78

(b) Explain why the coupon yield is so different when compared to the yield to maturity quoted in the *Wall Street Journal*.

*3. Calculate the value of a bond that pays a coupon of 12 percent annually for four years, with capital redemption in the fourth year. The spot rates of interest for the four years are 11.4, 12.2, 12.8, and 13.0 percent, respectively. Assume the first coupon is due in one year.

4. Estimate the spot rates of interest from the following information on four Treasury notes from the *Wall Street Journal* of August 10, 1983. Assume that the 1983 coupon has just been paid and that coupon payments are made annually. Note that for example 96.30 means $96³⁰/32.

Rate	Maturity	Bid	Asked	Bid change	Yield
7¼	1984 August	96.30	97.6	—	10.25
8¼	1985 August	94.27	95.3	−.2	11.04
11⅜	1986 August	99.17	99.21	+.4	11.51
13¾	1987 August	105.16	105.24	−.1	11.91

5. From the spot rates of interest calculated in Problem 4, estimate the forward rates of interest implicit in the term structure.

*6. Calculate the duration of a 10 percent bond with a maturity of three years, priced at $93⁹/32 to yield 12.84 percent. Another bond of the same maturity with a 12 percent coupon priced at $98 has the same yield. Which bond would you prefer if the term structure of spot interest rates is rising? Assume that the coupon payments on both bonds are made annually.

References

Bierwag, G. O., G. C. Kaufman, and A. Toevs, "Single Factor Duration Models in a Discrete General Equilibrium Framework," *Journal of Finance,* 32, no. 2 (May 1982): 325–38.

Carleton, W. T., and I. A. Cooper, "Estimation and Use of the Term Structure of Interest Rates," *Journal of Finance,* 31, no. 4 (September 1976): 1067–83.

Chambers, D. R., W. T. Carleton, and R. W. McEnally, "Immunizing Default-Free Bond Portfolios with a Duration Vector," University of North Carolina at Chapel Hill, October 1982.

Chambers, D. R., W. T. Carleton, and D. R. Waldman, "Estimation of the Term Structure of Interest Rates Using a Simple Polynomial," University of North Carolina at Chapel Hill, December 1983.

Chicago Board of Trade, "A Guide to Financial Futures at the Chicago Board of Trade."

Jordan, J. V., *Studies in Direct Estimation of the Term Structure,* Ph.D. dissertation, University of North Carolina at Chapel Hill, 1982.

Klaffky, T. E., "The New World of Coupon Stripping," New York: Salomon Brothers, August 1982.

McCulloch, H. M., "Measuring the Term Structure of Interest Rates," *Journal of Business,* 44, no. 1 (January 1971): 19–31.

Schaefer, S. M., "Measuring a Tax-Specific Term Structure of Interest Rates in the Market for British Government Securities," *The Economic Journal,* 91, no. 2 (June 1981): 415–38.

Schaefer, S. M., "Tax Induced Clientele Effects in the Market for British Government Securities: Placing Bounds on Security Values in an Incomplete Market," *Journal of Financial Economics,* 10, no. 2 (July 1982): 121–59.

Silvers, J. B., "An Alternative Analysis to the Yield Spread as a Measure of Risk," *Journal of Finance,* 28, no. 4 (September 1973): 933–55.

Spence, B. M., J. Y. Graudenz, and J. J. Lynch, Jr., "Standard Securities Calculation Methods," New York: Securities Industry Association, 1973.

Walter, D. C., "Recent Innovative Financing Techniques — An Addendum," *Taxes — The Tax Magazine,* 61, no. 1 (March 1983): xxx.

Walter, D. C., "Tax Aspects of Recent Innovative Financing — Strategies for Existing Discount Debt and for New Securities," *Taxes — The Tax Magazine,* 60, no. 4 (December 1982): 995–1009.

Preferred Stock, Common Stock, Warrants, and Convertible Securities

Corporations can raise capital by issuing a variety of different securities. In the last two chapters we discussed the various forms of debt financing including the issue of corporate bonds. Other securities that corporations issue to finance their operations include preferred stock, which has some of the fixed-interest features of debt; equity or common stock, which represents the shareholders' ownership of what is left of the firm's assets and earnings after all other claims have been paid; and warrants and convertible securities, which are claims that can be made on the firm's equity depending upon the price performance of its common stock. There are analytical questions and policy issues associated with each of these forms of financing that we consider in this chapter.

Preferred Stock

Preferred stock has characteristics both of debt and of common stock. For example, holders of preferred stock receive cash payments, usually in the form of a dividend at a fixed dollar amount expressed as an annual amount per $100 of par value (face value). Until recent years most preferred stock did not include a redemption feature and therefore was perpetual. Now, however, preferred stock issues typically carry sinking fund provisions, with the consequence that they are retired gradually. Preferred stock differs from long-term debt in that the firm is not legally bound to pay the dividend. The payment of preferred stock dividends does take priority over common stock dividends. Indeed, common stock dividends cannot be paid until the preferred stock dividends are made. As a result, preferred stock has a claim on corporate earnings that is said to be senior to the claims of common stockholders. An additional protection in most preferred stock contracts is that holders acquire voting power when dividends are in arrears.

The seniority of preferred stock makes it less risky to its holders than common stock. However, if the preferred dividend is fixed, preferred stockholders do not gain from any growth in earnings and dividends as common stockholders do. There are some exceptions, where preferred stock contracts include a participation clause, which provides for additional preferred dividends to be paid if the firm's performance is above a predetermined level.

TAX IMPLICATIONS OF PREFERRED STOCK FINANCING

Preferred stock is similar to debt in that the preferred stock contract normally imposes restrictions on the firm that are similar to the restrictions in a bond contract. But preferred stock is more like common stock than debt in one very important respect: The payment of dividends is not a tax-deductible expense to the corporation. This would appear to make preferred stock an inferior form of financing compared with debt were it not for the fact that the United States tax laws permit corporations that hold preferred stock to treat only 15 percent of the preferred dividends that they have received as taxable income. The low corporate taxes on preferred dividends enable preferred stock to be sold to corporate investors, such as insurance companies, at before-tax yields that are lower than the before-tax yields of comparable bonds of the same risk, making them less costly before-tax than borrowing. However, the after-tax advantages to the firm issuing preferred stock are not clear. Miller (1977) has argued, using a particular model of corporate and investor taxes, that the after-tax costs of debt and equity are equal. (See Chapter 21 for a more detailed discussion.) If Miller's proposition can be extended to preferred stock, the after-tax cost of preferred stock would be equal to the after-tax cost of both debt and equity.

Actually, almost all preferred stock is issued by public utilities. Therefore, it may be appropriate to look to the intricacies of utility regulation rather than to taxes to explain the industry choice of preferred stock financing over debt. Under current regulatory practice, public utilities can more easily pass the costs of preferred dividends on to their customers through the prices they charge than they can the cost of equity, which is estimated rather than observed. This is because regulatory commissions can miscalculate the cost of equity. It would be difficult to do the same with the cost of preferred stock, since the interest rate or yield can be observed. As a result, utilities may find preferred stock a useful financial instrument, as it will not threaten a company with default (like debt), but it provides a visible cost of finance to state regulators.

REPORTING OF PREFERRED STOCK PRICES

The preferred stock of large firms may be traded either on organized securities exchanges such as the New York Stock Exchange (NYSE), or in the over-the-counter market. The transactions are reported in the *Wall Street Journal* on the following day. Although the prices quoted in the *Wall Street Journal* are for securities listed on the NYSE, the prices shown are a composite of transactions that have taken place on several exchanges and in the over-the-counter market. Consider AT&T's $3.64 preferred stock as it appeared in the *Wall Street Journal* on August 12, 1983.

52 weeks										
High	Low	Stock	Div	Yield %	PE Ratio	Sales 100s	High	Low	Close	Net Chg
38½	31	ATT	pf 3.64	9.9	...	18	36⅞	36½	36⅝	−⅛

AT&T preferred stock had traded between a high of $38½ and a low of $31 over the prior fifty-two weeks. Its annual dividend per share is $3.64. Based on the August 11 closing price, its current yield was $3.64/$36.625 = 9.9 percent. The trading volume on August 11 was 18 × 100 = 1,800 shares. During the day the stock reached a high price of $36.875 and a low price of $36.50. The closing price was $36.625, or $0.125 lower than the prior day's closing price.

Common Stock

Common stockholders are the legal owners of the corporation. They enjoy **limited liability,** which means they cannot be held personally responsible for the corporation's debts. At the same time, their claim on the corporation's earnings and its assets is also limited. The claims of creditors, debtholders, and preferred stockholders must be met first. Since debt is repaid on an agreed schedule, the claims of debtholders on the firm have a limited maturity, while the residual claim of the stockholders continues as long as the corporation legally exists.

Under the terms specified in the corporate charter, stockholders elect a board of directors as their agents for employing managers, overseeing the operations of the firm, and authorizing dividend payments. In a closely held corporation (one with relatively few stockholders), the coordination of aims and objectives between common stockholders (or a controlling group of shareholders) and management can be quite close. Large United States corporations, however, have thousands of stockholders, so the relationship between owners and managers often is remote. Boards of directors rarely poll the owners for their views except occasionally at annual shareholder meetings and then only on broad policy matters. When challenged by dissident stockholder groups, the directors normally win any resulting dispute. For the most part, however, the owners' views are conveyed only indirectly, through changes in the price of the firm's common stock in the stock market, for example. Such market signals may not be very effective when they are obscured by other factors affecting the price of the firm's stock, such as changes in investors' expectations of the performance of the industry and of the economy.

Although the threat of takeover by another firm (which purchases its shares from existing stockholders) can be part of the financial market's discipline on a firm's management to work on behalf of shareholders, this threat may be reduced by a challenge by the antitrust division of the Department of Justice. A takeover also can be blocked by directors and management if they own or can influence a sufficient percentage of the outstanding common stock.

BOOK VALUES AND MARKET VALUES

Firms issue common stock under conditions specified in a corporate charter. For legal purposes common stock will carry a nominal value or par value (zero in the case of no par value shares), but this value has no economic significance. For example, as shown in Appendix 16.2, in the Consolidated Balance Sheet as of December 31, 1982, UMC Industries had been authorized by its shareholders to issue 10 million shares of $2.50 par stock, of which 7,076,170 shares already had been issued. About 951,448 shares had been repurchased as treasury shares at a cost of $16,251,000 for such uses as officer and employee stock option plans. The par value of all issued shares is $17,690,000. Additional capital in excess of par value, $21,029,000, represents the difference between the cash amount paid by investors for past issues of stock and their par value. Retained earnings amount to $84,182,000; and there is a small deduction, $1,652,000, to reflect changes in exchange rates of UMC Industries' foreign assets and liabilities.

It is usual to refer to the sum of the common stock, paid in capital, and retained earnings as the **book value** of the firm's common stock or equity. In the example in Appendix 16.2, the book value of the firm's common stock is $104,998,000. The **market value** of the equity is calculated by multiplying the current share price by the number of shares outstanding. For example, the market value of UMC Industries' common equity on August

11, 1983, was \$95,698,781, based on a stock price of \$15⅝ and 6,124,722 (i.e., 7,076,170 − 951,448) shares outstanding. It is important to appreciate that the market value of the firm's equity will not equal its book value except by coincidence. The market value of the firm's equity represents the present value of expected cash flows from both existing assets and potential growth opportunities minus the present value of the firm's existing and potential liabilities. In contrast, the book value of the equity reflects the history of money received from past equity issues less repurchases and the accumulation of retained earnings (earnings after tax minus dividends). The difference between the two sets of numbers reflects the differences between cash flows and accounting earnings, and historic versus future-based estimates of profitability.

Some firms issue different classes of equity, each with different ownership privileges. For example, a closely held firm may create two classes of common stock, A and B. Both share equally in dividends, but Class B shares have superior voting privileges to the A shares. Differences between classes of stock may be created when a firm has to secure equity funds during a period of financial distress. For example, one class of owners may be given a prior claim to dividends up to some specified amount, even though both share in voting rights.

COMMON STOCK DIVIDENDS

A corporation typically aims to pay some target proportion of its earnings to stockholders as dividends. The dividend is not tax-deductible for the corporation as interest payments on debt are. Dividends are paid with the approval of the Board of Directors, but outstanding bond or loan contracts may limit the amount of cash dividends. Sometimes companies pay stock dividends instead of cash dividends. A **stock dividend** is a free issue of additional shares to existing shareholders in proportion to the shares already held. As dividend policy is an important subject in its own right, we have devoted an entire chapter (Chapter 15) to its analysis.

REPORTING OF MARKET PRICES OF COMMON STOCK

To illustrate the manner in which common stock prices are quoted, we reproduce data from the *Wall Street Journal* for August 12, 1983, reflecting the previous day's trading for UMC Industries.

52 weeks										
High	**Low**	**Stock**	**Div**	**Yield %**	**PE Ratio**	**Sales 100s**	**High**	**Low**	**Close**	**Net Chg**
18½	8⅛	UMC	.60	3.8	28	80	15¾	15½	15⅝	−⅛

UMC Industries' per share price range for the prior fifty-two weeks was $8.125 to $18.50. The current annual dividend is $0.60 per share, representing four times the most recent quarterly dividend. Based on a closing price of $15.625, the current dividend yield is $0.60/$15.625 = 3.84 percent (rounded to 3.8). The price-to-earnings ratio (usually called the PE ratio) is equal to 28, based on the closing stock price and the most recent twelve months earnings (after taxes) per share. Turnover in the stock that day was 8,000 shares. The stock's high price on August 11 was $15.75, the low was $15.50, and the closing price was $15.625, or $0.125 lower than on the preceding day.

The Issue of New Shares

In general, existing common stockholders have a prior or **preemptive right** to anything of value distributed by the firm—including new shares. In practice, some firms specify in their articles of incorporation that new sales of equity have to be made by means of **rights issues,** meaning that the shares must be offered to each existing stockholder in proportion to the number that he or she already holds. Other articles of incorporation permit new sales of shares to be **public offerings** in which the shares may be offered to any investor at some predetermined price. In some instances, shareholders have been asked by boards of directors to relinquish their claim to rights issues. A major example is American Telephone and Telegraph Company, which until the mid-1970s always sold new stock via rights issues. More recently, the board of directors secured from the stockholders a waiver of their rights privilege. AT&T's common stock sales since then (other than through dividend reinvestment and employee stock purchase plans) have taken the form of public offerings.

PUBLIC OFFERINGS

In a public offering of debt or equity, the underwriter's role can be very important. The underwriter is usually an investment banker or, in the case of large issues, a group or **syndicate** of investment bankers and stockbrokers who purchase the issue of securities from the corporation and then resell the securities to individual investors or institutions. The issuing corporation compensates the underwriters with fees and a discount on the price at which the offering firm and the underwriters have agreed to try to sell the securities to the public. Fees are payable in the case of a **negotiated underwriting,** when the corporation seeks the advice of an investment banking firm and negotiates the timing, amount, and other features of the issue with them. The investment banking firm assists with registering the issue with the Securities and Exchange Commission and with gaining the SEC's approval for the issue. The investment banking firm will then organize a syndicate, if a substantial issue is involved, in order to spread the risk and to gain access to a broad range of institutional and individual investors. The investment bankers thus provide essential services in helping to organize the issue as well as participating in the underwriting.[1]

The most significant variable cost in an issue of stock is the discount that is offered to the underwriters. The underwriters require a discount for at least four reasons. First, in reselling the stock the underwriters incur costs that must be recovered. Second, underwriters must make a return on their capital. During the several weeks that it may take to resell the issue, they have a great deal of money invested in the issue that they could have invested elsewhere. A part of the discount that is given to underwriters represents a return on their investment equal to the return that could have been obtained at equivalent risk from alternative investments in the financial market. Third, the success of the issue may depend in part on the reputation of the underwriters who are reselling the stock. By agreeing to underwrite the stock the underwriters are, in effect, putting their stamp of approval on the issue. Because such approval is worth something in the financial market, particularly when there may be uncertainty concerning the reasons why the issuing company needs more money, underwriters are able to charge for it in the discount. Finally, unless the market for the underwriting is perfectly competitive, there also may be some element of additional profit included in the discount.

Consider the following example. Firm XYZ has outstanding 10,000 shares valued in the market at $100 per share. The total value of the firm is therefore $1 million.

	XYZ	
	Before issue	**After issue**
Number of shares outstanding	10,000	12,222
Price per share	$100	$98.18
Market value of XYZ	$1,000,000	$1,200,000

The firm decides upon an issue of $200,000 in new shares to finance capital projects that have zero NPVs so we suppose that the public announcement

---

[1]For a more extensive treatment of the underwriting function, see S. L. Hayes, A. M. Spence, and O. V. P. Marks, *Competition in the Investment Banking Industry*. Cambridge, Mass.: Harvard University Press, 1983.

of the stock offer does not by itself have any impact on XYZ's stock prices. Next, assume that the underwriters require a discount on the current stock price of $10 per share. That is, they purchase XYZ's new shares from the firm at $90 each. This means that $200,000 \div 90 = 2,222$ shares finance the capital projects. XYZ's new market value after the issue is $1,000,000 + $200,000 = $1,200,000. But the share price is now $1,200,000 \div 12,222 = $98.18. This price assumes that the existing shareholders receive no net financial benefit from the services of the underwriters.

The underwriters' costs and profit must be recovered from the difference between the price of $98.18 at which they expect to sell the issue and their purchase cost of $90. The underwriters receive ($98.18 − $90.00) × 2,222 = $18,176. As we have shown, this cost would result in a fall in the price of the currently outstanding stock from $100.00 to $98.18 if the existing shareholders did not receive any net benefit from the services of the underwriters. However, the underwriters provide services that do benefit shareholders and that would result in a smaller loss in the price of the currently outstanding shares. The company receives cash from the underwriters immediately instead of having to wait perhaps several days until the issue can be sold to investors. The company can invest the cash during these days and earn a return that benefits shareholders. Also, by agreeing to underwrite the issue, the underwriters are signaling to the financial market their confidence in the company and its securities, and this information is likely to have a favorable effect on the price of the currently outstanding stock. For these reasons, the cost of underwriting a stock issue may be somewhat lower than the size of the discount given to the underwriters would imply.

SEC RULES AND THE COST OF ISSUANCE

As some of the costs of a new issue effectively are fixed costs, there may be significant economies of scale achievable. For example, in order to ensure disclosure and prevent fraud, the SEC requires the preparation of an SEC registration statement. While the resulting disclosure of information does serve a useful purpose, it also adds to the fixed costs of the issue. For small issues (offered by firms issuing less than $1,500,000 of new securities per year) full registration with the SEC is not necessary. The SEC in recent years has reduced the costs of stock (as well as bond) issuance by permitting "shelf registration" in its Rule 415, under which a firm secures an advance blanket authorization to sell additional shares, in one or more issues, for up to two years under a single registration statement. Most issues now are under shelf registration, which permits companies to bring offerings to market quickly and in relatively small amounts. The costs associated with registration and approval can also be avoided by selling **letter stock** to small groups of private investors. Letter stock is stock that is not registered with the SEC and that cannot legally be resold in the secondary market by the purchaser for at least two years. Of course, purchasers of letter stock issues run the risk of not being able to resell their stock should they need to do so. Also, small or new venture corporations that issue stock may find it necessary to bear the underwriting risk themselves; that is, the investment bankers may only make a **best efforts distribution** on behalf of the firm without actually purchasing the issue.

Table 18.1 shows that the average cost of public stock offerings, as a percent of net proceeds, runs from around 15 percent for small issues (under $2 million) to 4 percent for issues in the $100 million to $500 million range.

RIGHTS OFFERINGS

In a rights offering the entire issue of new shares is offered to existing shareholders in proportion to the number of shares already held. Rights issues also involve investment bankers, but in a somewhat different role from the one they take for a public offering. Filing a registration statement with the Securities and Exchange Commission and complying with its rules is still required. However, at the time of filing, a warning letter must be sent to the shareholders notifying them of the impending issue. At this stage the stock begins trading on a **rights on** basis. If the stock is rights on, the present holder of the stock is entitled to purchase the new shares. When the SEC finally indicates that the registration is effective, shareholders are sent warrants together with information as to how many rights plus how many dollars enable them to purchase a new share of stock. The expiration date of the offer is also indicated. During the period from the offer to the expiration date, shareholders have the opportunity to exercise their rights to buy the new shares or, alternatively, to sell the rights to the new shares to other investors. The investment banker's underwriting role in a rights offer is a standby one: He buys the shares that remain unsold if some rights remain unexercised at the expiration date of the offer.

The most important thing to understand about rights issues is that, in contrast to the case of the public offer, existing shareholders are indifferent to the discount at which the new stock is sold. They are indifferent because the discount is effectively being offered by the shareholders to themselves and therefore cannot result in a loss of value. Whether an individual shareholder exercises the right to buy the shares or sells the right to someone else, his or her total wealth should be unaffected. The market value of the existing shareholder's shares plus cash before the rights issue should equal the total market value of the shares and cash after the issue. Let us consider an example that illustrates this principle.

An investor holds five shares in a company, and each share sells for $30 prior to the announcement of the rights offering. Subsequently, the company announces a rights offering that permits the shareholder to buy one new

Table 18.1
Issuing costs for common stock 1971–1975 as a percentage of size

Size of issue, (millions of dollars)	General underwritten cash offers			Underwritten rights issues			Nonunderwritten rights issues
	Underwriter compensation	Other expenses	Total cost*	Underwriter compensation	Other expenses	Total cost*	Total cost
Under 0.50							9.0
0.50 to 0.99	7.0	6.8	13.7	3.4	4.8	8.2	4.6
1.00 to 1.99	10.4	4.9	15.3	6.4	4.2	10.5	4.9
2.00 to 4.99	6.6	2.9	9.5	5.2	2.9	8.1	2.9
5.00 to 9.99	5.5	1.5	7.0	3.9	2.2	6.1	1.4
10.00 to 19.99	4.8	0.7	5.6	4.1	1.2	5.4	0.7
20.00 to 49.99	4.3	0.4	4.7	3.8	0.9	4.7	0.5
50.00 to 99.99	4.0	0.2	4.2	4.0	0.7	4.7	0.2
100.00 to 500.00	3.8	0.1	4.0	3.5	0.5	4.0	0.1
Weighted average	5.0	1.2	6.2	4.3	1.7	6.1	2.5

Source: C. W. Smith, Jr., "Alternative Methods for Raising Capital: Rights Versus Underwritten Offerings," *Journal of Financial Economics*, 5, no. 3 (December 1977): 277.

* Totals subject to rounding error.

share for every five shares held at a price of only $27. Thus, our shareholder is able to buy one new share at $27.

What price will the shares sell for after the rights offering? Let us assume for the sake of simplicity that the proceeds of the rights issue will be invested in projects with zero net present values. With this assumption, we may say that the shares should be priced in the market after the rights offering in such a way that the stockholder's wealth position is neither improved nor worsened as a result of the issue. Before the rights offering, the value of the stockholder's shares in the company is

$$5 \times \$30 = \$150$$

The stockholder who buys one new share at $27 will own six shares. If he or she is to be no worse off, the price of the stock after the rights offering, i.e., the **ex rights** price, must be

$$\frac{\$150.00 + \$27.00}{6} = \$29.50$$

Thus the ex rights price is $0.50 less than the rights on price. The next question is, what happens if the investor does not wish to exercise the right to buy one new share at $27.00? If the investor is to be no worse off, he or she must be able to sell the rights to the new share for $29.50 − $27.00 = $2.50. After the issue the five shares will be worth

$$5 \times \$29.50 = \$147.50$$

If we add the $2.50 value of the right, the stockholder's wealth position is restored to its previous level of $150.00.

So long as the shareholder does not let the rights expire by refusing either to exercise the rights or to sell them, he or she is neither better nor worse off by virtue of the terms of the offer. At a lower issue price, what the stockholder loses as a result of the lower ex rights price is exactly made up for in the value of the rights.

From the perspective of the underwriter, however, it is important that the issue or subscription price be set low enough to ensure the success of the issue. If the market price should fall below the exercise price during the time (approximately three weeks) given to shareholders to exercise their rights, the shareholders will not exercise their rights, and the underwriter would have to pay more for the shares than they actually are worth in the market. Thus the underwriters are providing a kind of insurance for the issue. The pricing of this insurance for rights issues is discussed in more depth in Chapter 19.

Finally, as you can see in Table 18.1, the costs of a rights issue also decline with size (whether or not the issue is underwritten), and the costs of a rights issue are less than the costs of public offer.

THE QUESTION OF BOOK VALUE

As we discussed earlier, the cost of the underwriting of a public offering of stock is borne by the existing stockholders in the form of a lower share price. Managers frequently confuse this market value effect with the effect of an offering on book values. It should be clear that changes in book value as a result of an offering rarely have direct bearing on stock prices and shareholder wealth. What is important in an offering is whether the offering gives too much away to the underwriters and whether the funds are to be put to a profitable use. In the hypothetical illustration of the XYZ public offering, we did not consider book value. If the book value per share prior to the offer had been $50.00, the offer would have increased this figure to $57.27 as indicated below:

	XYZ offering	
	Before offer	**After offer**
Number of shares	10,000	10,000 + 2,222 = 12,222
Book value of equity	$500,000	$500,000 + $200,000 = $700,000
Book value per share	$50	$700,000 ÷ 12,222 = $57.27

What is the relevance of this book value per share? It reflects the total accumulated historic values of past share offerings plus accumulated retained earnings divided by the total number of shares that has been issued. Thus, changes in book value per share resulting from an issue need not correspond in any consistent manner to changes in the market value per share. For example, shares sell at a *premium* on book value when the economic value of the firm's assets and growth opportunities exceeds the depreciated historic cost of its existing assets less the book value of its liabilities. In this situation an issue of shares increases the book value per share. If the shares are offered at a large discount to the underwriters, the market price per share of existing equity actually can be reduced by the issue while the book value per share is increased. Financial managers where possible should avoid letting accounting arithmetic obscure the true economic impact of their financing decisions on existing shareholders.

The real question is, why does the firm need the cash from a new issue in the first place? If the issue alerts the market to an unexpected deterioration in the firm's cash position, a drop in share value may result from this unfavorable information that has been conveyed to the market. In practice, common stock is issued more frequently for the purpose of new investment in capital projects. If the market believes that the new projects potentially are profitable, a change in the market value of the company's existing equity will reflect the difference between the net present value of the projects and the costs of the new issue.

Warrants and Convertible Securities

Warrants are securities giving the holders of the warrants the right to buy a company's common stock directly from the company at potentially advantageous prices. Each warrant specifies the number of shares that the warrant holder can buy and the price. Some warrants are perpetual warrants with no time limit to exercise. Most warrants, however, specify time limits within which the exercise price on the warrant holds good. **Convertible securities** such as convertible preferred stock or convertible bonds are conventional securities that give the holders privileges normally associated with warrants. One essential difference between warrants and convertibles is that the exercise of warrants increases the total capital of the firm with the sale of the new shares to the warrant holder, while conversion of a security such as convertible debt does not increase the total capital of the firm (if the conversion does not require additional cash for the new shares). In the latter case conversion merely changes the composition but not the amount of the corporation's capital. Let us examine warrants, convertible bonds, and convertible preferred stock a little more closely.

WARRANTS

Warrants usually are issued in combination with privately placed bonds as "equity kickers" intended to make the bonds more attractive. They also may be issued in connection with some public debt offers. For example, a newer, more risky enterprise might issue warrants to those who subscribe for its debt in order to give the debtholders an opportunity to participate in the growth of the enterprise through eventual exercise of the warrants. The conditions of each warrant specify the price or price schedule at which the holder can purchase a specified number of shares from the company (for example, two warrants might give the warrant holder the option to buy one share at $10 per share). Unless the warrant is perpetual, the warrant also specifies the expiration date by which time it must be exercised. If the warrant specifies a schedule of exercise prices, it also will specify the dates between which each price holds good. If the warrant is issued in connection with debt, it also will state whether the warrant is **detachable** from the debt. If a warrant is detachable, it can be sold by the holder and traded in the market as a separate security.

Normally a warrant is **protected** in the sense that if the company should pay out additional shares as dividends to shareholders (a stock dividend), or if it gives away new shares to existing shareholders (a stock split), thereby diluting the market value of the existing shares, the exercise price on the warrant is adjusted accordingly. For example, if the company has 1,000,000 shares outstanding before a stock split and 1,500,000 shares outstanding after the split, the exercise price would be multiplied by a factor of 1,000,000/ 1,500,000 = 0.667. Consequently, if the split is expected to reduce the market price of the common stock by one-third, the exercise price or prices on the warrant also are reduced by one-third if the warrant is protected. Also, the number of shares that can be purchased by a warrant must be increased proportionately—in the previous example by a factor of 1.00/0.667 = 1.5 if the market value of the warrant is to be protected fully.

In August 1982, NCNB Corporation, a large regional bank holding company headquartered in North Carolina, sold a $50 million debenture and stock warrant issue. The debentures carried a coupon of 7.34 percent, well below prevailing borrowing costs. However, the warrants permitted the holder to buy new shares at $18.18 when the common stock sold for $14.00. The prospect of gain on converting the warrants into common stock should the market price rise above $18.18 permitted a lower interest rate to be paid on the debenture.

The theoretical minimum value of a warrant is the number of shares that can be purchased with one warrant multiplied by the difference between the price of the company's shares and the exercise price on the warrant. If a company's warrants call for one share to be purchased with two warrants plus $25, and the company's stock price currently is $30, the warrant's minimum price is

$$0.5 \times (\$30.00 - \$25.00) = \$2.50$$

This value is actually a lower limit, because the option to wait and see if the share price goes higher before exercising the warrant adds further value. In the next chapter we show how such options can be valued.

Warrants have a role in corporate finance because they provide a means of redistributing risk among existing shareholders and other parties, such as bondholders. If warrants are attached to the loan, some of the upside risk is shifted from shareholders to debtholders. If the company should do well, the lenders receive not only the agreed interest and repayments on time, but they also can participate in the company's prosperity because the value of their warrants will increase if the market price of the company's stock rises. Warrants provide a means whereby the stockholders of a risky company can induce debtholders to subscribe to an issue of debt at a reasonable interest rate by giving the debtholders a chance to participate in future gains ordinarily available only to stockholders. Warrants also provide some protection against certain moral hazard problems. For example, owners may be tempted to direct management to undertake activities that increase the risk of the firm and thereby increase the default risk to debtholders. The potential gain to equityholders from these activities is shared with the debtholder if the debtholder also holds warrants.

CONVERTIBLE BONDS

The holder of a convertible bond has an option to exchange the bond for a specified number of shares of the company's stock at a predetermined price during a future period. The lower limit to the price of the convertible bond is the value of the convertible as a straight bond. When the company's share price is relatively low, there may be little or no incentive to convert. As the stock price rises, though, the value of conversion increases. Thus a convertible bond can be viewed as a combination of a conventional bond plus a warrant.

For example, consider the Virginia Electric and Power Company (VEPCO) 3.625 percent coupon convertible debenture, which matures in 1986. Fifty million dollars is outstanding in this Baa-rated issue, with no sinking fund requirements. The conversion price is $23.25 and the holder at conversion receives 43.01 shares per $1,000.00 par value of the debenture. If the stock price is sufficiently high relative to the convertible bond price, the bondholder will be tempted to convert.

Suppose the debentures having a par value of $1,000 currently sell in the market for $1,100. The $1,100 worth of debentures translates into a common stock value of $1,100 ÷ 43.01 = $25.58 per share. If the market price for the stock simultaneously stood at, say, $26.00, the convertible bondholder would profit by converting his bonds to stock. His profit would be ($26.00 − $25.58) × 43.01 = $18.06 for each $1,000 par value of bonds held. In an efficient market the benefits of conversion will be reflected in the price of the convertible security. That price will reflect conversion taking place at the optimum time.

In an efficient market the convertible bond price not only already reflects the potential value of conversion *now,* but it also reflects additional value for the possibility of conversion at even more advantageous stock prices in the *future,* as we shall see when we discuss options in the next chapter. Most convertible debt has a call feature, which means that the company can repay or redeem the convertible at specified prices (which are always above par).

CONVERTIBLE PREFERRED STOCK

Convertible preferred stock contains essentially the same features as convertible bonds, but, as you will recall, the dividends on the preferred stock are not tax-deductible to the company. For example, consider the Piedmont Aviation $2.375 cumulative preferred issue, sold in November 1980. The price to the public was $25.00, and the yield was 9.5 percent. The stock is redeemable by Piedmont at a price varying from $27.14 in 1982 to $25.00 after December 15, 1990. Each preferred share is convertible into common at the rate of 1.3514 shares of common stock per share of preferred. On the date of the offer, the common stock closed at a price of $15.50; thus the preferred's market value of $25.00 was greater than its immediate conversion value, $1.3514 \times \$15.50 = \$20.95$. Clearly holders should not convert at these market prices.

An interesting question concerns the role that convertible bonds and preferred stock should or do play in corporate financing. In an efficient capital market, the "no free lunch" rule should prevail. Many of the claims made for convertibles during the 1960s implied that something was available for nothing: that a firm could outguess the stock market and issue common stock early and cheaply with convertibles, or that the dilution impact of conversion (which, remember, raises no new capital but shifts the capital structure to a higher proportion of equity) was priced incorrectly in the stock market. There should be no net benefit from the use of convertibles, as debt and equity are merely alternative claims on the same assets of the firm. Shifts between one form of financial claim and another do not of themselves increase the value of the firm's cash flows. For the past decade, moreover, firms have been required to report per share earnings on both nondiluted (preconversion) and diluted (assuming conversion) bases.

The best interpretation that explains the use of convertible bonds may be that they contribute to making the capital market more complete in the sense that they provide investors with a greater variety of portfolio choices. To the extent that such variety is valuable to investors, it may result in a lower cost of funds to the firm. A second reason may be that convertibles reduce the conflicts of interest between various claimholders. For example, if management unexpectedly increased the risk of the firm, shareholders may be able to reduce the value of the debtholders' claims. By including a conversion feature in the debt contract, debtholders are able to recapture part of such wealth transfers. This is a subject we shall consider in more detail in Chapter 21.

Summary

Firms can issue a variety of securities in which some ownership attributes are involved. Common stock is the most basic. Common stockholders are the firm's legal owners who have the residual claim to the firm's assets and income after all the more senior claims have been settled. Common stock in a firm is sold either to the public (via public offerings) or to existing stockholders (via rights issues), depending upon the terms specified in its corporate charter. The role of underwriters is particularly important in a public offering.

Preferred stock typically pays a fixed dividend, when corporate earnings permit. Preferred dividends can only be paid after debtholders' claims have been met. Furthermore, common stock dividends can only be paid after preferred dividends have been paid. Most preferred stock financing is done by utilities, which can pass on the nontax-deductible dividend cost to its customers in the form of higher prices.

Warrants, convertible debentures, and convertible preferred stock give the holder a contingent claim on the firm in the form of an option to purchase its stock at prespecified prices. Warrants typically are used as "sweeteners" to increase the lender's expected payoff from loans to risky ventures. At one time, convertibles were analyzed primarily in terms of the effects of the timing of conversion on earnings and on earnings per share. More recently, however, theory and evidence that United States capital markets are highly efficient has suggested that the gains to the firm from the issue of convertible securities are likely to be small.

Review Questions

1. List six types of security that are issued by companies to finance their activities.
2. How do the characteristics of preferred stock differ from those of common stock?
3. Discuss the tax implications to a company of issuing preferred stock.
4. What are the implications of limited liability of the corporation for common stockholders?
5. How could changes in dividend policy cause conflicts of interest between different security holders?
6. What are the important differences between rights issues and public offerings of common stock?
7. How do existing stockholders benefit from the services of the underwriters in a public offering of stock?
8. How does the discount on the price of stock sold via a rights offering affect the wealth of the existing stockholders?
9. What is the significance to stockholders of the dilution of book value per share that may arise as a result of the issue of additional stock?
10. What is a warrant, and why do companies issue them?
11. What is a convertible? Compare two examples of convertibles.

Problems

*1. Look up the *Wall Street Journal*'s list of NYSE Composite Transactions, and note the following items for ITT Preferred Stock, Series K and O:

current price of stock

dividend yield

Explain why the dividend yield for series K is different from that of series O.

2. On the balance sheet of ITT at December 31, 1982, stockholders' equity is given as follows:

	Thousands of dollars
Common stockholders	5,681,877
Cumulative preferred stockholders	440,743
Total stockholders' equity	6,122,620

ITT had 133,171,836 common shares outstanding. Calculate the book value per share of common stock, and compare this with the 1982 average market price of $31.25. Give reasons for the differences observed.

*3. In the *Wall Street Journal*'s list of NYSE Composite Transactions, note the following items for ITT's common stock:

current price of stock

dividend yield

PE ratio

Calculate the earnings per share and the dividend per share.

4. Company X has 3 million shares outstanding at a market price of $46.80 per share. The finance vice president has suggested that a stock split would make the shares more marketable. The terms would be on the basis of three shares for every one share outstanding. What will be the price of the new shares? Is the stockholder better or worse off as a result of the split? Give reasons for your answer.

*5. The common stock of XYZ Corporation currently sells for $100 and there are 10 million shares outstanding. A one-for-two rights issue is announced granting existing shareholders the right to buy one share of stock within twenty-one days at a price of $85 for every two shares now held. What are the rights-on and ex-rights prices of the stock, and for what minimum price would each right sell?

6. A company has announced a two-for-one rights issue giving shareholders the right to buy new shares for $20. A stockholder who owns 2,000 shares in the company is convinced that the company is selling the new shares too far below the current market price of $60. He thinks that the exercise price on the rights should have been $40 per new share. You have been asked to explain to him why the terms of the offer do not affect his wealth. Use a numerical example to illustrate your argument.

*7. Fogley, Inc., is planning a private placement of 50,000 new shares to a new investor at a 10 percent discount on the present market price of $40. There are 200,000 shares outstanding. If the book value of stockholders' equity is $4,828,000, calculate the book value per share and market value per share after the private placement. Can you say whether existing shareholders are better off as a result of the new issue?

8. An investor has $10,000 of Clipper Board, Inc.'s, debenture at 10 percent, redeemable in 1990. Each $1,000 debenture carries one hundred warrants. The conditions provide that the holder of four warrants can buy a share for $25. What is the minimum value of the warrants to this investor if the current market price of one share is $27? Why would you expect the market price to be higher?

9. Megazone Manufacturers has issued $10 million worth of convertible debentures with a 7 percent coupon, which mature in three years. The $1,000 par value debentures are trading currently at $1,120. An investor who bought $10,000 worth of the debentures when they were issued has asked you whether she should convert the debentures to common stock, as this is the last day of the conversion period. The terms of conversion specify a conversion price of $25.00, and the stock sells currently for $28.50. Explain what the investor should do and why. State any necessary assumptions.

References

Green, Richard C., "Investment Incentives, Debt and Warrants," *Journal of Financial Economics*, 13, no. 1 (March 1984): 115–36.

Hayes, S. L., A. M. Spence, and D. V. P. Marks, *Competition in the Investment Banking Industry.* Cambridge, Mass.: Harvard University Press, 1983.

Logue, D. E., and R. A. Jarrow, "Negotiation vs. Competitive Bidding in the Sale of Securities by Public Utilities," *Financial Management,* 7, no. 3 (Autumn 1978): 31–39.

Miller, M. M., "Debt and Taxes," *Journal of Finance,* 32, no. 2 (May 1977): 261–76.

Smith, C. W., Jr., "Alternative Methods for Raising Capital: Rights Versus Underwritten Offerings," *Journal of Financial Economics,* 5, no. 3 (December 1977): 273–307.

19

Valuation of Options on Common Stocks

In this chapter we describe the characteristics of options on common stock. We explain what determines an option's value and how to price one using two valuation methods, the binomial model and the Black–Scholes model.

Options are big business. The volume of options trading on the Chicago Board Options Exchange (CBOE) has exceeded the turnover on the New York Stock Exchange, an indication of how important options have become as financial instruments. Understanding the concept of an option helps us to understand a large variety of problems in corporate finance. For example, risky corporate debt contains an "option" to default. The possibility to sell unnecessary equipment or other assets for a price may represent an option to abandon an activity. In this chapter, we confine ourselves to pricing options on common stock, while in the next chapter we shall discuss applications of the options concept to problems such as valuing the debtholder's option to default and management's option to abandon a business activity.

What Are Options?

Before we describe options on common stock, we shall examine a simpler type of option. Suppose you find a house you would like to buy that costs

$50,000. However, you need a month to arrange financing before you can contract to buy the house. In the meantime, the seller might dispose of the house at a higher price to another party unless you obtain an option from the seller ensuring that you can buy the house at $50,000. If you exercise the option subsequently and buy the house, you will have to pay only $50,000, regardless of how high the market value for the house goes in the meantime.

Of course, if you should fail to raise the $50,000, you would have to let the option lapse. Also, if for some reason the house should no longer be worth as much as $50,000, you would have the alternative of letting the option lapse and of renegotiating a lower price on the house. Clearly, such an option is a valuable financial instrument to the buyer, and the seller is unlikely to give it away for nothing. How do you determine how much an option is really worth?

The option on the house illustrates four important characteristics of options.

1. The option expires on a specific date. As a result, we know the option's **maturity,** or time to expiration.
2. Before it matures, the option can be exercised at a specific price that is agreed upon in advance. The exercise price is often called the **striking price.**
3. The decision to exercise the option will depend upon the difference between the market value of the asset (the house) and the exercise price of the option (purchase price of the house).
4. Issuing the option does not affect the value of the underlying asset (the house).

The example also illustrates why options are bought and sold. Just as insurance does, options allow risks to be shared in particular ways. For example, you as the purchaser of the option on the house were not able to buy the house immediately, nor did you wish to be compelled to buy it during the next month should the financing prove unavailable. At the same time, you wanted to make sure you had first call on the house and that the price would be fixed in advance. The option allows a buyer all these benefits, but the seller of the option is giving the buyer a valuable advantage and will want to charge a price for it.

For example, if house prices suddenly fell, you would not exercise your option, and the seller would lose (since the house could have been sold to another buyer for $50,000). In contrast, if house prices suddenly rose, you could exercise the option and pay the lower price that was fixed in advance. If the seller had not granted you as potential buyer an option, presumably the house could be sold immediately (at least in principle) for $50,000. Clearly, an option gives an advantage to the buyer. It has a value for which a price should be paid. This chapter will show how such options can be priced.

CALL OPTIONS ON COMMON STOCK

There are two important kinds of options, **call options** (calls) and **put options** (puts). A call option on a common stock permits the holder of the option to buy the stock at a fixed price during some future (prespecified) period. The option in our example of the house purchase was a call option. A put option on a common stock permits the holder of the put to sell a common stock at a fixed price during some future (prespecified) period. The holder of the call option hopes that the market price of the common stock will rise above the exercise price after the option has been purchased so that the stock can be bought for less than its market value. The holder of the put option hopes that the price will fall below the exercise price on the put, so the holder can buy the stock at the market price and sell it at a higher price by exercising the put.

The buyer of a call option on a common stock, for example, on American Telephone and Telegraph (AT&T), is permitted to purchase one share of common stock in AT&T at a predetermined price at any time during the remainder (maturity) of the option's life. Let us assume the buyer purchases a three-month call option (options on common stock are sold with maturities of up to nine months) at an exercise price of $10, while the current price of AT&T stock is $15. At any time in the next three months, the buyer of the call option is able to buy one AT&T share for $10, regardless of how the stock price moves before the option matures. What is the minimum value of the option? The option must sell for at least $5. To understand why, suppose that the option costs only $2. An investor would buy the option and immediately pay the exercise price of $10; the total cost of buying the stock via the option would be $12. He could then sell the stock for the current market price of $15 and make a nice profit of $3 per share. The price of the option must be $5 to stop such easy profits being made.

Actually, options (usually) are worth more than the difference between the current market stock price and the exercise price, if there is any time remaining before the option expires; we shall explain why in a subsequent section. We can also say that the option will not be exercised at all if the price of the common stock remains below the exercise price. For example, if the price of AT&T fell below the exercise price, to say $8, the holder of the call option would be better off letting the option lapse. Instead of exercising the option at $10 the holder of the call could buy AT&T stock directly for only $8. It should be apparent that the buyer of a call option wants the price of the common stock to rise, for the option will be exercised only when the market price is above the exercise price. In contrast, the seller of the call option wants to see the option lapse. The seller hopes that the price of the common stock will be below the exercise price when the option expires. If the seller of the call option created the option in the first place, he or she is called the writer of the option.

In Table 19.1 we have reproduced from the *Wall Street Journal* a list of option prices for AT&T. On March 19, 1984, AT&T's common stock traded

Table 19.1   *The prices of AT&T call options*

AT&T common stock price	Striking price (or exercise price)	Price of call option for different expiration dates		
		April	July	October
16¾	15	2	2⅛	2½
16¾	20	⅛	¼	½

Source: *Wall Street Journal,* March 20, 1984.

at a price of $16¾. It was possible on that day to buy six different call options on AT&T's stock, distinguished by differences in maturities and exercise prices. The option that expired in April (always on the first trading day of the month) had less than one month to go before maturity. For the April maturity it was possible to buy options with exercise prices of $15, or $20. As we explained before, if the option's exercise price is less than the market price of the common stock, the price of the call will sell for at least the difference between the option's exercise price and the price of the common stock. In the case of the option with an exercise price of $15, the option's price is $2, whereas the difference between the share price and the exercise price is only $16¾ − $15 = $1¾.

For the other April option the exercise price is above the current price of the common stock. Despite this, the option still is worth something, because there is some possibility that the common stock price might rise above the exercise price before the option expires on April 1. A second feature to notice is that the options that expire in October sell for a higher price than the options (with the same exercise price) that expire in July. This would appear to imply that options with a longer maturity sell for a higher price than those with a shorter maturity. We shall explain why this is so in a later section, but you might like to think about the reason now.

PUT OPTIONS ON COMMON STOCK

The holder of a put option has the right to sell the underlying stock at a fixed exercise price at any time during the period of the option. If the exercise price for one share of AT&T is $15 and the option runs for three months, the holder will exercise the option only if the price of the common stock falls below the exercise price. The buyer of the option will want to exercise his option to sell AT&T at $15 only if he can purchase the common stock below $15. Thus, the buyer of the put option hopes to see the price of the common stock fall. In contrast, the seller or writer of the put would like the common stock price to be above the $15 exercise price for that would ensure that the option would not be exercised.

In Table 19.2 we have reproduced prices of AT&T's put options from the *Wall Street Journal*. Let us examine the put option expiring in April that has an exercise price of $20. What should be the minimum price for the put option? Since the put option provides the holder with the option to sell AT&T's common stock at $20 compared with a current market price of $16¾, we would expect the option to sell for at least $3¼. In fact, the option is priced at $3½. The option's price is greater than the difference between the exercise price and the common stock price because there is some possibility that the common stock price will fall further, thereby increasing the profit to be gained from exercising the put. Also, we see in the table that the other put expiring in April has a lower exercise price of $15, and it sells for only $⅛ compared with $3½ for an exercise price of $20. We expect the price of a put to be smaller if it has a lower exercise price, because the possibility to sell a stock at a lower price must be less valuable. This is the opposite from a call option, which is more valuable when the exercise price is reduced.

Finally, we note that the October put with the exercise price of $20 is worth $3⅝ compared with the July put which is worth only $3½. In general, both put and call options are worth more for longer maturities. A longer maturity provides more time for the stock price to drift to a level where it would be profitable to exercise the option.

TRADED OPTIONS

Until the establishment in 1973 of the Chicago Board Options Exchange (often called the CBOE), there was no secondary market in options on common stock. That is, an investor purchasing a three-month call option in

Table 19.2   *The prices of AT&T put options*

AT&T common stock price	Striking price (or exercise price)	Price of put option for different expiration dates		
		April	July	October
16¾	15	⅛	5/16	7/16
16¾	20	3½	3½	3⅝

Source: *Wall Street Journal*, March 20, 1984.

AT&T could either exercise it or permit it to lapse, but could not sell the option to another party. The establishment of the CBOE allowed options to be traded. The holder of a three-month option can sell it at any time during the three-month period providing that trading is in progress on the Exchange. Of course, the price at which such options are traded depends upon a number of variables, including the time remaining to maturity or expiration.

The primary advantage of an options exchange is that it permits the investor to get in and out of options at any time before the option matures. For example, what would be the position of a holder of the three-month AT&T call option if the common stock rose from $15 to $20 after only six weeks? Since the minimum price of the option must be equal to the difference between the stock price and the $10 exercise price, it would rise from at least $15 − $10 = $5 to at least $20 − $10 = $10, after six weeks. Now the investor would have a profit on the purchase price of the option, and he or she might like to quit while still ahead. In a traded options market, the investor can sell the option (which still has six weeks to expiration) to another investor who would like to purchase a six-week call option. Before the establishment of the traded options exchange, getting out of an option before it expired meant exercising it prematurely and thereby losing the value attributable to the time remaining before expiration of the option.

A second advantage of a traded options exchange is lower transactions costs. Before the CBOE was established, buying options involved high transactions costs for a variety of reasons, including the number of middle-men involved. The CBOE set up a computerized low-cost operation (administered by the Options Clearing House) that allows the purchase and sale of options with standardized periods of maturity and exercise prices. The result is that trading in options has increased enormously.

Limits to the Value of a Call Option

In order to appreciate what variables determine the value of an option, it helps to think about the minimum and maximum price an option can have, given an exercise price. Let us consider an option on a common stock that does not pay dividends. The price of the common stock is $50, the exercise price is $40, and the time to maturity of the option is three months. Even without a valuation model, we should be able to determine limits within which the price of the option must move. The first limit that we can predict is that the option's price will never be negative.

The reason that an option's price is nonnegative is that the holder of the option is not obliged to exercise it; therefore, no additional liability arises. In fact, when the stock price is above the exercise price, the minimum price for the option will be greater than zero. For example, go back to the call option example of AT&T in Table 19.1. The common stock sold for $16¾ and the exercise price on the option maturing in October was $15. How much would you have paid for this option? You would have paid at least $1¾ because you could have exercised the option to buy the common stock for $15 and sold the stock immediately for the then current market price of $16¾.

Actually, the minimum price you would be willing to pay for the call option is greater than the difference between the current price of the stock and the exercise price on the option. The reason is that if the option is not going to be exercised immediately, you would really be interested in the present value of a future difference between the stock price and the exercise price. The present value of this difference is larger because the present value of the future stock price is equal to the current stock price, whereas the present value of the future exercise price is less than the exercise price. To obtain the present value we can use the riskless rate as the discount rate. As a result we can say that:

Price of Call Option > Current Price of Stock

— Present Value of Exercise Price

We have used the "greater than" (>) symbol because if the option has time left to maturity, then there is a chance that the option can be exercised to greater advantage. If the stock price should fall you do not have to exercise the option and the most that you can lose is the price that was paid for the option. On the other hand, if the stock price should rise, the option can be exercised and the potential gain is very large.

Suppose that you knew with certainty that the stock would pay a particular dividend before the option expires. Clearly, if you held the underlying stock, you would receive the dividend; whereas if you held the option, you would not receive it. Therefore, the minimum option price for a dividend paying stock can be expressed as follows:

$$\text{Price of Call Option} > \text{Price of Stock} - \text{Present Value of Dividend} - \text{Present Value of Exercise Price}$$

So far we have set a minimum price for the call option. What about the maximum price of the option? Let us assume the extreme case, that the exercise price or striking price of the option is zero. In this case, what would the option on the AT&T stock priced at $16¾ be worth? It could not be worth more than the prevailing market price of the common stock. If the option were priced at $18, investors would rush to sell the option and buy the common stock instead. Thus, the maximum price for the option is

Price of Call Option < Price of Common Stock

Our values for the maximum and minimum price of the option will be helpful when we try to understand what determines the exact price of an option.

What Determines the Value of an Option?

There are four variables that determine the value of an option on a nondividend paying stock: the risk of the underlying stock, the maturity of the option, the stock price relative to the exercise price, and the risk-free rate of interest.

THE RISK OF THE UNDERLYING STOCK

One characteristic of options is that the more volatile the underlying common stock, the more valuable the option. This result may surprise you, for you have become accustomed to the proposition that increased risk reduces an asset's value. However, this proposition does not apply to the relationship between the value of an option and the risk of the underlying common stock. Options are valuable precisely because of the risk of the underlying common stock.

Suppose that you owned a call option to purchase a completely riskless stock with an exercise price equal to the current market price. How much would you pay for such an option? The answer is nothing, because there is no possibility that the stock price will increase. Suppose, however, that the exercise price were $40 and the stock price $50, how much would you pay now for a three-month call option on a riskless stock? In fact, you would pay exactly $10, which is the difference between the exercise price and the stock price. You would not pay more because the stock price is not expected to increase.

Now let us make the stock risky, and let both the stock price and the exercise price be $50. You are told now that at the end of the three-month period the stock will be worth either $60 or $40 (there are no other possibilities). How much will you be willing to pay for the option? Clearly the option must be worth something, for if the price of the common stock rises to $60, you will make $10; if the price falls, you will lose nothing but the price of the option, because you will not exercise the option but let it lapse. Most people would give something for a chance to win $10; therefore the option must have some value.

Suppose now you are told that the common stock is more risky, and that two possible prices for the common stock are $30 and $70 (instead of $40 and $60). The exercise price for the call is still $50. The option still has value, because a chance to win $20 is worth something. However, what is interesting is that the option on the more risky common stock (the one with the greatest range of possible outcomes) is more valuable, because the chance of winning $20 is more valuable than the chance of winning $10.

In general, there is no upper limit on the price of a common stock. Once the investor has bought a call option, the option holder faces unlimited upside potential, but limited downside risk. The investor only exercises the option (and pays out more money) if there is a profit to be made; that is, when the market price is above the exercise price of the call option. As long as the investor cannot lose more than the price of the option, increased risk implies a greater potential for upside stock movements—and consequently greater possibility of profit.

The fact that we chose to make the exercise price equal to the initial stock price does not change the argument. If we had made the exercise price $40 when the current stock price was $50, the option would have been worth more than the $10 difference between the exercise price and the current market price of the stock. Increasing the risk of the common stock still would increase the value of the option.

MATURITY OF THE OPTION

The longer the maturity of the option, the more valuable it is. The reason is that the holder of the call option benefits when the stock price rises, and a longer maturity for the option provides more opportunities for the stock price to rise. You can compare this to being allowed to throw dice more than once and adding up the score; even if you don't win the first time, still you might accumulate a winning score. To take a more practical example, consider an option on a house currently worth $50,000, with an exercise price of $50,000. Would you pay more for a three-month option than a one-day option? Of course, you would. In one day you would expect the value of the house to change relatively little, if at all; in three months the value of the house might change significantly in your favor. Note that if the value of the house moves against you, you do not have to exercise the option and pay out any more money.

THE STOCK PRICE RELATIVE TO THE EXERCISE PRICE

It should be obvious now that the higher the stock price for a given exercise price, the greater the value of the call option. We showed earlier that the option is worth at least the positive difference between the stock price and the present value of the exercise price.

It is interesting to plot how the value of a call option changes with the share price, given a particular exercise price. In Figure 19.1 we have drawn this relationship. The solid line represents the lower limit to the value of a call option discussed earlier. The broken line illustrates how the value of the call option changes with the price of the common stock. At point 1, the stock price and the option price are both equal to zero. Moving toward point 2, where the share price is equal to the present value of the exercise price, the value of the call option rises. The reason for this rise in value is that as the stock price moves closer to the exercise price, the probability is increased that the share price will actually wander above the exercise price and that the option will be worth exercising. As the share price increases beyond the present value of the exercise price, the value of the call option approaches (but actually never reaches) the difference between the value of

Figure 19.1   *The relationship between the value of the call option and the stock price*

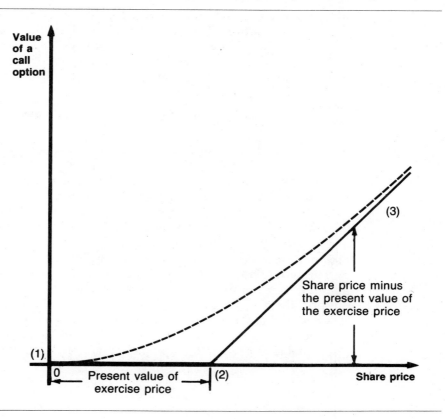

the share and the present value of the exercise price (point 3), as long as there is some possibility that the share price will rise.

THE RATE OF INTEREST

The final variable that affects the value of an option on common stock is the risk-free rate of interest. The higher the interest rate, the higher the value of the option. This may seem counter-intuitive at first, for higher interest rates tend to reduce the values of most other financial assets. A higher interest rate increases the value of an option because it reduces the present value of the exercise price (and the present value of the dividends on the underlying stock), as you can see from the following relation giving the lower limit on the value of a call option

$$\text{Price of Call Option} > \text{Price of Stock} - \text{Present Value of Dividend} - \text{Present Value of Exercise Price}$$

The exercise price can be viewed as the face value of a loan to the purchaser of the call option. The "loan" is repaid when the option is exercised. The present value of a loan decreases as the interest rate increases. Thus an increase in the interest rate reduces the present value of the effective liability and therefore increases the present value of the option.

WHEN SHOULD THE OPTION BE EXERCISED?

If the underlying stock pays no dividends, an option should not be exercised before the expiration date. As long as there is a chance that the stock price could go higher before the exercise date, the option is worth more alive than dead.[1] An option holder who no longer wants the option is better off selling the option rather than exercising it before maturity, because the remaining time before the option expires will be worth something to other investors. The need to trade options that still have some time remaining before maturity is the main reason the CBOE was established.

So far we have said little about dividends that are paid on the common stock during the remaining life of the option. Merton (1973) has shown that under certain circumstances, when a dividend is imminent, it may be more profitable to exercise the option prematurely, before its exercise date.

---

[1] Call options on common stocks are often referred to as either American or European. American calls can be exercised at any time, but European calls can be exercised only at the expiration date.

A Graphic Description of Options

Figure 19.2 is a graphic description of the possible returns to both buyer and seller of a call option immediately before expiration of the option. We have assumed, for the sake of simplicity, that the exercise price is equal to the current stock price. On the vertical axis is the change in the wealth of the investor that would arise from the impact of changes in the stock price.

First let us examine the returns to the buyer of a call option represented by the solid line. If the stock price does not change at all, the buyer merely loses C, the price that he paid for the call. Even if the stock price falls, the buyer of the call still loses only C, for the option will not be exercised. On the other hand, if the stock price rises, the buyer of the call will start to recover the cost of the option. The payoff of the option rises (or falls) in dollar terms by the same absolute amount as the common stock; this explains why the solid and dotted lines are both at an angle of 45 degrees to the horizontal line. However, the change in the price of the option as a proportion of its value will be much larger than the corresponding proportionate change in stock price, because the value of the option is less than the value of the stock. This leverage effect is greatest when the difference between the stock price and the exercise price is smallest, and therefore when the option price is smallest.

The seller or writer of the call option is in the mirror image position of the buyer. The returns to the seller are represented by the dotted line. If the

Figure 19.2   *Graphic representation of calls*

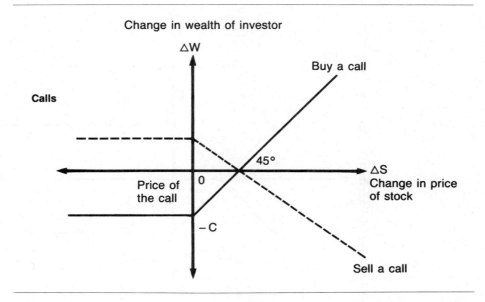

stock price declines, the seller keeps the price C that was paid for the option. If the stock price rises, the seller must be prepared to pay the difference between the striking price and the stock price. In this game the buyer's losses and the seller's gains are limited. Because the buyer's potential gains are almost unlimited, the seller's potential losses are also almost unlimited. This difference between the gains and losses accruing to each party would be unfair if the price of the option did not fully compensate the writer of the call for the risks taken. An analogy with insurance, although not exact, is a helpful one. The householder who wishes to insure a house pays a fixed amount; if the house burns down, the insured receives a much larger pre-determined amount. The insurer receives only the insurance premium, which limits the gain. If the cost of the insurance reflects the expected value of these unequal payoffs, the game is still a fair one.

Figure 19.3 is a graph depicting the returns arising from the purchase and sale of a put option. The buyer of the put (whose returns are represented by the solid lines) is betting that the stock price will decline; if it does not decline, the holder of the put loses the price P of the put. No matter how much the stock price rises, the buyer can lose only a maximum of P. If the stock price falls, the investor is able to buy the stock at the lower price and sell it profitably at the exercise price on the put option. The seller or writer of an option pays out (receives) what the buyer receives (pays out): Option trading is a zero–sum game.

Figure 19.3   *Graphic representation of puts*

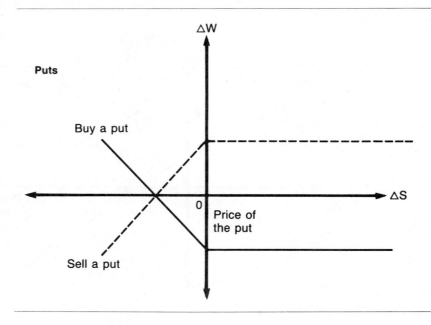

Why Should Anyone Want to Buy Options?

Gambling and speculation often are considered frivolous activities that are of very little use to society. At the same time, insurance is considered solid and respectable. In fact, fire insurance is a gamble, where the insurer is betting that your house will not burn down, and you are betting that it will. Such bets do not affect total wealth as long as the possession of insurance does not change the number of houses burned down. However, the benefits arising from insurance are of great value to society, because insurance allows people to shift risk to others who are willing to bear it. Options, like insurance, permit the redistribution or sharing of risks at a market-determined price.

Suppose an individual holding a portfolio of stocks learns suddenly that a single event of great importance will be announced that will have a dramatic effect on the price of one stock. An example might be the announcement of the outcome of an oil drilling report or the test marketing results of a new product. The temporary increase in risk prior to the announcement may not be acceptable to the stockholder. Of course, the investor could sell the stock before the outcome has been announced and buy it back afterward. In that case, though, transactions costs for buying and selling might be significant, and the transaction might also create an unwanted capital gains tax liability. The sale of the stock also would reduce the diversification of the investor's portfolio. An alternative would be to buy a put option on the stock before the announcement. If the news turns out to be unfavorable and the stock price drops, the put option will be profitable.

As a second example, the executors of an estate may wish to hedge the beneficiaries of the estate against stock market price changes for a limited period. This may be useful when the portfolio of securities cannot be sold or changed for limited periods because of pending inheritance taxes. The executors can purchase options (or advise the beneficiaries to do so) for a period up until the date when the portfolio might be changed.

Behind all these examples is one particular theme: Options provide additional financial instruments that permit investors to buy and sell risks in a more comprehensive way. The creation of an option makes for a more complete (or less incomplete) financial market.

How to Estimate the Price of an Option: The Binomial Model

In this section we shall show how the price of an option can be derived using the binomial model developed by Cox, Ross, and Rubinstein (1979). An expression for the price of an option can be formulated if one assumes that the options market is efficient and therefore that speculators cannot make abnormal returns by simultaneously buying or selling combinations of options and the underlying stock. We shall show that there is a unique price for an option of given maturity if we know the price and the risk of the underlying stock and the risk-free rate of interest. Let us examine the following example.

Assume that a stock pays no dividends, that the investor has an investment horizon of only one period, and that the outcomes are revealed at the end of the period. For the sake of simplicity, we shall assume also that the price at the end of the period can be one of only two different values. Suppose that there is a 0.80 probability that the stock price will rise by 25 percent and a 0.20 probability that it will fall by 25 percent. If the stock is priced at $100 at the beginning of the period, the end-of-period stock price will be either $125 or $75. The expected return $E(R)$ is, therefore, 15 percent.

$$E(R) = (0.8 \times 0.25) + (0.2 \times (-0.25))$$

$$= 0.15 = 15\%$$

We are offered a one-period call option with an exercise price of $100. Assuming that the riskless rate of interest is 6 percent per period, what is the fair (or equilibrium) price of the option that would make the holder of the option on the stock indifferent between the returns on the stock and the returns on the option?

CALCULATING THE HEDGE RATIO

Options and common stock can be combined in such a way as to create a riskless investment (or **hedge**). We know that the fair return on such a combined riskless investment must be the risk-free rate of interest. This fact allows us to obtain the value of an option. If we could determine how much stock to hold and how many options to buy (or sell) so that, whatever happened to the stock, our combination of stock plus options would give a safe return comparable to a loan, we could derive the price of the option. Let us assume that the riskless hedge is composed of one share of common stock with price S and a call option with price C written against the common stock. The payoffs on the common stock are as follows:

End-of-period payoff

$S = \$100$ → $125
        → $75

The payoffs corresponding to one call option with an unknown price C and an exercise price of $100 are

End-of-period payoff

$$C \begin{cases} \rightarrow \$25 \\ \rightarrow 0 \end{cases}$$

We can now construct a risk-free hedge composed of the purchase of one share of stock, and the sale of n call options. If the payoffs at the end of the period from the stock S and from the sale of the n options are equal, we have a riskless hedge.

End-of-period payoff

$$(S - nC) \begin{cases} \rightarrow \$125 - n\$25 \\ \rightarrow \$75 - 0 \end{cases}$$

We can now solve for the number of call options n that we must sell or write to obtain a riskless hedge (i.e., the same payoff irrespective of what happens to the common stock)

$$\$125 - n\$25 = \$75$$

$$n = 2$$

Thus, to create a riskless hedge in our example we must write two call options for every unit of common stock purchased.

The ratio of calls written to the number of shares of stock purchased is known as the hedge ratio. We can write the hedge ratio more generally as

$$\text{Hedge Ratio} = \frac{\text{Range of Possible End-of-period Common Stock Values}}{\text{Range of Possible End-of-period Option Values}}$$

In our example the range of possible end-of-period option values is $25, and the range of end-of-period common stock values is $50. Therefore

$$\text{Hedge Ratio} = \frac{50}{25} = 2$$

We can check that our hedge ratio provides us with a riskless hedge using the same calculation as before.

End-of-period payoff

$$(S - 2C) \begin{cases} \rightarrow \$125 - (2 \times \$25) = \$75 \\ \rightarrow \$75 \end{cases}$$

As a result, the payoff is $75 whether the stock price rises or falls, because for every share of stock purchased we have hedged by selling the number of call options that is determined by the hedge ratio.[2] We are now in a position to determine the price of the call option by comparing the hedged combination of common stock and call options with an investment in a riskless asset.

DETERMINING THE PRICE OF THE OPTION

Our initial investment was $100 less $2C$, where $2C$ is the amount received from selling two call options. This investment outlay ($100 − 2C$) plus the interest that could have been received for such an outlay on a riskless asset must equal the certain payoff of $75 to be received one period hence. Thus

$$(\$100 - 2C) \times (1 + r) = \$75$$

where r is the riskless rate of interest, which we shall assume is 6 percent for the period.

$$(100 - 2C)(1 + 0.06) = \$75$$

$$(100 - 2C) = \frac{75}{(1 + 0.06)}$$

$$2C = 100 - 75/1.06$$

$$C = \$14.6226$$

The price of the option must be $14.6226.

The value of $14.6226 for the call option assumes that there are to be no easy profits from arbitrage. For example, if the option actually were priced at $14, what would you do? You would sell the stock and buy options instead. Alternatively, what would you do if the option were priced at $15? A hedging strategy that involved buying a share of stock for every two call options sold would give a return greater than the riskless rate of interest, r. You might try to solve for the value r in our example with a call option price of $15. You will find that the actual return on this riskless investment is greater than 6 percent.

---

[2]Our example makes life simple by using a one-period horizon. If transactions could take place in two or more successive periods, the hedge ratio would have to be changed for each period.

WHY THE STOCK'S EXPECTED RETURN DOES NOT AFFECT THE OPTION'S PRICE

There are two further points to notice in this example. First, the fact that the return on the underlying stock was 15 percent per period was not required for estimating the value of the option. This omission is no accident, for it is an important implication of option theory that the value of the option is independent of the expected return on the underlying stock. Instead we use the riskless rate of interest to estimate the option's value, because the hedge ratio allows us to create a portfolio that provides a certain income, no matter what the future returns on the stock are expected to be. You must keep this fact in mind and note that in the following section another option valuation model also uses the riskless rate of interest, not the expected return on the stock.

The binomial method is very easy to use, as we have shown. One important drawback, however, is that only two discrete outcomes for the stock are permitted in each period. This is not so with the Black and Scholes model.

Black and Scholes's Option Pricing Model

If we subdivide an option's period to maturity into an infinite number of periods, we can have an infinite number of outcomes for the stock price, which is the continuous time approach to option valuation that was developed by Black and Scholes (1973). Their model of option valuation gives the correct expression for the value of an option for an infinite number of subperiods before expiration of the option, assuming continuous trading.

Although Black and Scholes's formula looks formidable, in practice it is not too difficult to use for calculating the value of a call option. The formula consists of one main equation and two subsidiary equations. The main equation is

$$C = S \times N(d_1) - \frac{E \times N(d_2)}{e^{rt}}$$

where

C	=	price of the option
S	=	current price of the stock
E	=	exercise price (or striking price)
t	=	time remaining before expiration of the option usually expressed as a proportion of a year

r = continuously compounded riskless rate of interest

e = base of the natural logarithm, or 2.71828

$N(d)$ = the probability that a normally distributed random variable with a mean of zero and a standard deviation equal to one will have a value less than or equal to d

$$d_1 = \frac{\ln(S/E) + (r + 0.5\sigma^2)t}{\sigma \times \sqrt{t}}$$

$$d_2 = d_1 - \sigma \times \sqrt{t}$$

where σ = standard deviation of the continuously compounded rate of return on the stock[3]

Notice that $\ln(S/E)$ means the *natural* logarithm of (S/E), and not log (base 10), which would give an entirely different answer. Once we have computed (d_1) and (d_2) from the two subsidiary equations, we can find the values of $N(d_1)$ and $N(d_2)$ from a table of the cumulative normal distribution function. You also might notice that the only variable that has to be estimated is the standard deviation (σ) of the stock's returns. A measure of the standard deviation can be obtained by using past returns data for the individual stock. Such returns data should be in natural log form before the standard deviation is computed.[4] (You should be warned, however, that the standard deviation of past returns may not be a good proxy for future variability, which may give rise to errors. The reason for a changing standard deviation may be due to changes in the risk of the company's underlying assets or due to alterations in capital structure.)

The best way to appreciate the application of this model is by using it, so we shall start with an example, assuming the following data.

S = \$2.36 (current price of the stock)

E = \$1.90 (exercise price)

e = 2.71828

t = 22 days, or 0.06027 of a year (maturity of the option)

σ = 0.40 (on a continuously compounded annual basis)

r = 9.25 percent, or 0.0925

Step 1
Calculate d_1 and d_2 rounding the answers to the fourth decimal place.

---

[3]The continuously compounded rate of return on the stock is defined as $\ln(P_t/P_{t-1})$ where P is the stock price and the time period is one year.
[4]Let monthly log returns be $\ln(P_t/P_{t-1})$. Then annual log returns are $12 \ln(P_t/P_{t-1})$.

$$d_1 = \frac{\ln (2.36/1.90) + (0.0925 + 0.5 \times 0.40^2)0.06027}{0.40 \times \sqrt{0.06027}}$$

$$= \frac{0.21681 + 0.01040}{0.09820}$$

$$= 2.3137$$

$$d_2 = d_1 - \sigma \sqrt{t}$$

$$d_2 = 2.3137 - 0.0982$$

$$= 2.2155$$

Step 2

Compute $N(d_1)$ and $N(d_2)$ using the table of values for the cumulative normal distribution function in Table 19.3. To use this table locate the number closest to the value of d in the d column. In the case of our example, $d_1 =$ 2.3137, and the closest value in the table is 2.30, which gives a value for $N(d_1)$ of 0.9893. This value is only an approximation, and we could be a little more accurate by interpolating between the values of d between 2.30 and 2.35.

$$N(d_1) = 0.9893 + \left(\frac{2.3137 - 2.30}{2.35 - 2.30}\right) \times (0.9906 - 0.9893)$$

$$= 0.9893 + 0.0004$$

$$= 0.9897$$

Thus, the revised value for $N(d_1)$ is very slightly changed to 0.9897.

The value for d_2 is 2.2155, and the closest value for $N(d_2)$ in the table is 0.9861. As before, this is only an approximation, and to obtain a more accurate value we can interpolate again.

$$N(d_2) = 0.9861 + \left(\frac{2.2155 - 2.20}{2.25 - 2.20}\right) \times (0.9878 - 0.9861)$$

$$= 0.9861 + 0.0005$$

$$= 0.9866$$

Step 3

We are now in a position to compute the value C of the option. We shall remind you of the main equation and then insert the numbers. The calculated

Table 19.3   *Cumulative normal distribution function*

d	N(d)	d	N(d)	d	N(d)
		−1.00	.1587	1.00	.8413
−2.95	.0016	−.95	.1711	1.05	.8531
−2.90	.0019	−.90	.1841	1.10	.8643
−2.85	.0022	−.85	.1977	1.15	.8749
−2.80	.0026	−.80	.2119	1.20	.8849
−2.75	.0030	−.75	.2266	1.25	.8944
−2.70	.0035	−.70	.2420	1.30	.9032
−2.65	.0040	−.65	.2578	1.35	.9115
−2.60	.0047	−.60	.2743	1.40	.9192
−2.55	.0054	−.55	.2912	1.45	.9265
−2.50	.0062	−.50	.3085	1.50	.9332
−2.45	.0071	−.45	.3264	1.55	.9394
−2.40	.0082	−.40	.3446	1.60	.9452
−2.35	.0094	−.35	.3632	1.65	.9505
−2.30	.0107	−.30	.3821	1.70	.9554
−2.25	.0122	−.25	.4013	1.75	.9599
−2.20	.0139	−.20	.4207	1.80	.9641
−2.15	.0158	−.15	.4404	1.85	.9678
−2.10	.0179	−.10	.4602	1.90	.9713
−2.05	.0202	−.05	.4801	1.95	.9744
−2.00	.0228	.00	.5000	2.00	.9772
−1.95	.0256	.05	.5199	2.05	.9798
−1.90	.0287	.10	.5398	2.10	.9821
−1.85	.0322	.15	.5596	2.15	.9842
−1.80	.0359	.20	.5793	2.20	.9861
−1.75	.0401	.25	.5987	2.25	.9878
−1.70	.0446	.30	.6179	2.30	.9893
−1.65	.0495	.35	.6368	2.35	.9906
−1.60	.0548	.40	.6554	2.40	.9918
−1.55	.0606	.45	.6736	2.45	.9929
−1.50	.0668	.50	.6915	2.50	.9938
−1.45	.0735	.55	.7088	2.55	.9946
−1.40	.0808	.60	.7257	2.60	.9953
−1.35	.0885	.65	.7422	2.65	.9960
−1.30	.0968	.70	.7580	2.70	.9965
−1.25	.1056	.75	.7734	2.75	.9970
−1.20	.1151	.80	.7881	2.80	.9974
−1.15	.1251	.85	.8023	2.85	.9978
−1.10	.1357	.90	.8159	2.90	.9981
−1.05	.1469	.95	.8289	2.95	.9984

values of the variables are

$$C = S \times N(d_1) - \frac{E \times N(d_2)}{e^{rt}}$$

$$= 2.36 \times 0.9897 - \left(\frac{1.90}{e^{0.0925 \times 0.06027}} \times 0.9866 \right)$$

$$= 2.3357 - \left(\frac{1.90}{1.00559} \times 0.9866 \right)$$

$$= 0.47157$$

The value of our call option with twenty-two days to expiration is $0.47157. You can easily check whether the answer is a reasonable one. After all, you know that the value of the option must be at least the difference between the stock price and the exercise price, which is $0.46. Because the option period is so short, you would not expect the option to be priced much above that figure, so our value of $0.47157 looks reasonable.

Black and Scholes made a number of assumptions in constructing their model:

there are no transactions costs and no taxes

the risk-free rate is constant for the life of the option

the market operates continuously (day and night)

the stock price is continuous, and there are no sudden jumps

the stock pays no cash dividends

the option can be exercised only at the expiration date

the underlying stock can be sold short without penalty

the distribution of returns on the underlying security (the common stock) are lognormal.

Some of these assumptions appear very restrictive, for example, continuous trading and no transactions costs. If you wish to construct a riskless hedge, you must change the hedge ratio as the price of the underlying stock alters; continuously adjusting the hedge may prove expensive in terms of transactions costs. In a later section we shall see that option values obtained using Black and Scholes's model approximate the option prices quoted on the CBOE.

Valuation of Put Options

We have mentioned already why some investors may prefer to buy put options. Certain problems in corporate finance also require an understanding of put options. There is an important relationship between call option values and put option values on the same security reflected in the put–call parity formula.

$$P = C - (S - Ee^{-rt})$$

where 　　P = value of the put option on a stock

　　　　　C = price of the call option on the same stock

　　　　　S = current price of the stock

　　　　　E = exercise price for both the put and call options

　　　　　e = 2.71828

　　　　　r = continuously compounded riskless rate of interest

　　　　　t = time remaining before expiration of both options expressed as a proportion of a year

The put-call parity formula describes how to find the value of the put option from the value of the call option with the same exercise price and the same maturity on the same security. Let us examine our previous example where we computed the value of the call option as being $0.47157. The formula tells us that the value of the put option can be calculated by combining the value of one call option ($C = 0.47157$), with selling one unit of stock ($-S = -\$2.36$) and borrowing an amount equivalent to the present value of the exercise price. Initially we calculate the present value of the exercise price,

$$Ee^{-rt} = 1.90 \times \frac{1}{1.00559}$$

$$= \$1.88944$$

Thus

$$P = 0.47157 - (2.36 - 1.88944)$$

$$= \$0.00101$$

Why is the put option value so much smaller than the call option value? Remember that the current share price is $2.36 and the exercise price is $1.90. The call option will be exercised even if the share price falls by anything up to $0.46; in this respect, the call option is said to be **in the money** and is relatively valuable. However, the put option will not be exercised unless the price drops by more than $0.46; in this case the put option is said to be **out of the money** and is not very valuable. Clearly, an option that is in the money is more valuable than one that is out of the money.

One more point that is worth noting about the put–call parity formula is that a put option may be obtained by constructing a combination of securities, consisting of buying the call option, selling the stock, and investing the present value of the exercise price in a risk-free security. As a consequence, put options do not always need to be sold as separate securities if a combination of existing securities can be used to construct the same payoffs.

The Black and Scholes model is difficult to understand intuitively, because it assumes continuously compounded returns. Earlier in the chapter we calculated the value of an option assuming one discrete time period rather than continuous trading. The binomial approach used to value the option also could have been used if there had been more than one period. Alternatively, we may note that if we divide the period into subperiods and increase the number of subperiods toward infinity, the discrete time model approaches the continuous time model. Copeland and Weston (1983) describe in greater detail the relationship between the discrete and the continuous time approaches.

Black and Scholes's model is widely used by financial analysts who value options on the Chicago Board Options Exchange, while the discrete time binomial model is becoming increasingly recognized as potentially useful in a wider variety of applications.

Empirical Evidence on the Black and Scholes Model and the Efficiency of the Options Market

A recent study by Whaley (1982) examined ninety-one dividend paying stocks and their respective options over the period January 1975 to February 1978. He valued the options using Black and Scholes's model, after adjusting the common stock price for the present value of dividends paid during the life of the option. The average quoted price of his sample of options was $4.1388 (standard deviation was 5.2400). Using the standard deviation implied by the price of the call option from a previous period, he calculated an average option price of $4.1071 (standard deviation was 5.1036) using Black and Scholes's model. The average of the model's prices was within approximately $.03 of the average of actual option prices. Whaley showed also that the profits from buying the individual apparently undervalued options and selling the individual apparently overvalued options were insufficient to cover the market maker's spread, let alone other transactions costs, such as commissions and transfer fees. This evidence suggests that the results obtained from Black and Scholes's model provide a good approximation to actual prices, and that it is not possible to make money by trading on the basis of any mispricing implied by the model.

Summary

In this chapter we have discussed the principles underlying the pricing of call options and put options on common stock. We saw that the price is determined by the risk of the underlying stock, the period remaining before the option matures, the current price of the underlying stock in relation to the exercise price, and the riskless rate of interest. We noted that the market value of an option that has not reached maturity is worth more than the value that can be realized from exercising it. We also saw that because options can be used to form a perfectly riskless hedge, the value of the option is independent of the expected return on the underlying stock. Instead, the value of the option depends upon the riskless rate of interest. We showed how to derive the option price using both a binomial approach and the Black–Scholes continuous time option valuation formula. The value of the corresponding put option can be determined from the value of the call.

Review Questions

1. Describe a put option and a call option on a common stock. What information do you need to value a put or a call option?
2. How would you describe the following in terms of options?
   insurance
   abandonment decision on a factory
   warrant
   call provision in a loan agreement
3. How would you construct a put option on a stock, assuming that a call option existed?
4. Why is the expected return on the underlying common stock not considered in either of the two models of option valuation given in the chapter?
5. Why did the establishment of a traded options market increase the volume of trading substantially?
6. Why can the option price not exceed the price of the underlying common stock?

7. Issuing options on common stocks does not affect the value of the underlying common stocks when the options are exercised. Is this true for warrants on common stocks? Explain.
8. Why are contemporary option models described as arbitrage models?

Problems

*1. On June 2, 1983, the *Wall Street Journal* listed the CBOE prices of ITT options as follows:

Option NY latest	Strike price	Calls-Last			Puts-Last		
		Jun	Sep	Dec	Jun	Sep	Dec
ITT							
38¾	35	4	5¼	5⅝	¹⁄₁₆	¾	r*
38¾	40	½	2⅛	3⅛	1⁵⁄₁₆	2⅞	r
38¾	45	¹⁄₁₆	⅞	1¾	r	r	r

*r = not traded

(a) Which call option is in the money?
(b) For the September series, explain why the price of the call option decreases as the exercise price or striking price increases.
(c) For the call option with a $40 exercise price, explain why the price of the call increases as the date of exercise increases. Should the same hold for the put option?
(d) For the September 1983 put series, explain why the price of the put increases as the strike price increases.
*2. If the price of the stock of ABC, Inc., is $100 and the exercise price of a three-month call option on the stock is $85, what is the minimum price of the option? Assume that no dividend will be paid in the three-month period and that the risk-free rate of interest is 12 percent annually.
3. Given the information in Problem 2, what would be the minimum price of the call option if a dividend of $10 per share is to be paid exactly two months after the option is valued?
*4. Fill in the boxes with the appropriate action, on the day of exercise of the option, of Ms. Buyer, the holder of an option. The price of the underlying stock on the day of exercise is shown on the next page. Also indicate in the boxes whether Ms. Buyer and Mr. Seller, who has written the option, have made a gain or loss on the transaction.

(a) Call option: Exercise price of $80.

Stock price at day of exercise	Ms. Buyer	Mr. Seller
$90		
$70		

(b) Put option: Exercise price of $70.

Stock price at day of exercise	Ms. Buyer	Mr. Seller
$85		
$60		

5. The exercise price of a three-month call option on ABC, Inc., is $85, and the annual rate of interest is 12 percent per year. Assuming no dividends are paid, what would be the minimum price of the option if the stock price ranges from $80 to $140? Plot the minimum value and the maximum value of the option against the share price.

6. Given the information in Problem 5 for ABC, Inc., what would be the minimum values of a put option if the potential stock price ranges from $0 to $100? Plot this minimum bound on a graph of option value against stock price.

*7. Stock X has a market price of $100 now. There is a one-period call option outstanding with an exercise price of $105. The probabilities of the market price rising or falling by 10 percent are 0.70 and 0.30, respectively.

   Stock Y has the same market price of $100 now and also has a one-period call option with an exercise price of $105; however, the probabilities of an increase or decrease of 10 percent in the market price are 60 percent and 40 percent respectively. The riskless rate of interest is 1 percent for the period.

   (a) Calculate the expected returns on stocks X and Y.
   (b) State what you would expect the call option price on Stock Y to be, and explain why.

*8. The call option for stock Y in Problem 7 is valued at $2.723.
   (a) What would you do if the call option were traded at $3? Show calculations to support your answer.
   (b) What would you expect to happen to the share and option prices if investors acted on this disequilibrium?

*9. Use the Black–Scholes formula to price a three-month call option on XYZ, Inc., stock, given the following information:

Stock price   = $100

Exercise price = $80

Time remaining before expiration of the option (in calendar days) is forty-four days. The continuously compounded riskless rate of interest is 10 percent per year, and the standard deviation of the stock's annual returns is 30 percent. Assume no dividends are to be paid in the three-month period.

(b) What value would you place on a put option of the same maturity?

(c) Why is the value of the put option so low when compared with the value of the call option?

10. Using the data in Problem 9, describe how the value of the call option would be affected by a dividend of $10 to be declared fourteen days before expiration of the option. Under what circumstances would the option be exercised prematurely?

References

Black, F., and M. Scholes, "The Pricing of Options and Corporate Liabilities," *Journal of Political Economy,* 81, no. 5 (May–June 1973): 637–54.

Boyle, P. P., and D. Emmanuel, "Discretely Adjusted Option Hedges," *Journal of Financial Economics,* 8, no. 3 (September 1980): 259–83.

Copeland, T. E., and J. F. Weston, *Financial Theory and Corporate Policy,* 2nd ed., Chapter 8, Reading, Mass.: Addison-Wesley, 1983.

Cox, J., and S. Ross, "The Pricing of Options for Jump Processes," Working Paper No. 2–75, University of Pennsylvania, April 1975.

Cox, J., S. Ross, and M. Rubinstein, "Option Pricing: A Simplified Approach," *Journal of Financial Economics,* 7, no. 3 (September 1979): 229–63.

Latané, H., and R. J. Rendleman, Jr., "Standard Deviations of Stock Price Returns Implied in Option Prices," *Journal of Finance,* 31, no. 2 (May 1976): 369–82.

Merton, R. C., "Option Pricing When Underlying Stock Returns Are Discontinuous," *Journal of Financial Economics,* 3, no. 1/2 (January–March 1976): 125–44.

Merton, R. C., "Theory of Rational Option Pricing," *Bell Journal of Economics and Management Science,* 4, no. 1 (Spring 1973): 141–83.

Rendleman, R. J., Jr., and B. J. Bartter, "Two-State Option Pricing," *Journal of Finance,* 34, no. 5 (December 1979): 1093–1110.

Rubinstein, M., and J. C. Cox, *Options Markets,* Englewood Cliffs, N.J.: Prentice-Hall, forthcoming.

Smith, C. W., Jr., "Option Pricing Review," *Journal of Financial Economics,* 3, no. 1/2 (January–March 1976): 1–51.

Whaley, R. E., "Valuation of American Call Options on Dividend Paying Stocks," *Journal of Financial Economics,* 10, no. 1 (March 1982): 29–58.

Options in Financing and Investment Decisions

In the previous chapter we described how to value options on common stocks. There are three reasons you want to understand how options are valued. First, the trading of stock options is a major activity of the securities markets. Second, options on other assets, such as currencies, are being traded. Third, options are present implicitly in many financing and investment decisions, and they must be valued if the assets and liabilities are to be priced correctly.

In this chapter we examine three options related to financing decisions: underwriting a common stock rights issue, valuing the option to default in a bond contract, and estimating the wealth transfers that arise from the effect of mergers on the prices of the two merging companies' bonds. Subsequently, we describe some option characteristics present in various investment projects. For example, we describe problems of valuing the option to postpone opening a mine and valuing the abandonment option in a capital project.

Underwriting a Common Stock Issue

Some corporations raise cash by offering additional shares to existing shareholders. Such new issues, which were described in detail in Chapter 18, are known as rights issues. A rights issue gives each stockholder the right to buy additional shares at a fixed exercise price. The number of shares offered to each shareholder is proportional to the number of shares already owned. The company must allow shareholders some time (three to four weeks) to consider whether they wish to purchase the new shares. The delay between the announcement of the new issue and the final date of purchase introduces an element of chance for the company, because stockholders may not exercise their right to purchase the new shares. In this respect, the company is giving stockholders call options on the new shares.

One reason why the new shares may not be purchased is because the exercise price at which the shares are to be sold must be fixed when the rights issue is first announced, and the market price for the stock may fall below the exercise price for each new share. If the market price remains below the exercise price until the final subscription date, shareholders will not exercise their right to purchase the new shares, and the company will fail to raise the necessary new capital. A failed issue may mean substantial delays in obtaining new funds, and delay may mean the postponement or cancellation of new projects. As rights issues also involve substantial costs of administration, the company will try to prevent the issue from failing.

The company has two means by which it can prevent the failure of the issue. The first is to price the new shares at a **deep discount,** so far below the current market price that there is almost no chance of the stock price falling below the exercise price for the new shares prior to the final subscription date. As we explained in Chapter 18, the price of the new shares in a rights issue is irrelevant to existing shareholders as long as it is below the current stock price. However, there may be a good reason why a firm might not be able to price the new shares at a deep discount if the current share price is close to its par value (the nominal price or face value of the shares). Many state laws prohibit the issue of new shares at prices below par value.

A second method of preventing the failure of a new issue is by having the issue insured by securities firms. Such insurance is known as **underwriting.** Underwriting means that if all or part of the new issue of the shares is not purchased by existing shareholders, the remainder will be taken up by the underwriter at the price fixed by the company for the new shares. The question that we wish to address is, how much should the underwriters be paid for the agreement to purchase the new shares at a fixed price?

You may have observed that a firm having a new stock issue underwritten effectively is buying a put option from the underwriters. Should the market price of the outstanding common stock fall below the fixed price of the new shares (the exercise price), shareholders will not purchase the new shares. If stockholders do not purchase the new shares because the market price has fallen below the exercise price, the firm will exercise the put option and put the unsold portion of the new stock issue onto the underwriters. The underwriters are obliged to buy unsold stock at the exercise price or issue price, irrespective of the current market price of the common stock. As a result the underwriters would have to pay more for the shares than their current market price. If, however, the shares are bought up by stockholders, the underwriters will not have to take up any shares; they simply will keep their fee. We can show by an example how much the call option given to shareholders is worth, and how much the put option purchased from underwriters is worth.

VALUING AN UNDERWRITING CONTRACT

A company plans to make an offer to its existing shareholders giving them the right to buy one additional share at $1.90 for every two shares now being held. An agreement is reached with an underwriter to take up any of the shares not sold to shareholders at the exercise price of $1.90 per share. Currently the shares are selling for $2.59. If the underwriting agreement were to be signed while the shares stood at this price, what would be a fair price to the corporation for the underwriting contract, expressed as a percentage of the $1.90 issue price on the new shares?

In order to answer this question, we must appreciate that shareholders are given a call option when they are given the right to buy new shares. If the new issue of shares is underwritten, the company also buys a put option from the underwriters. First, we must value the call option given to stockholders, then we can value the put option purchased by the company from the underwriters. The first piece of information that we need to know in addition to the $1.90 exercise price is the current price of the existing traded common stock after taking into account the new issue of shares.

Initially a shareholder who owns two shares has equity worth $2 \times \$2.59 = \$5.18$. If the shareholder exercises the right to buy, the company's assets are increased by $1.90 as a result of the share purchase. He or she will have equity worth $\$5.18 + \$1.90 = \$7.08$, but then have three shares rather than two, so the resulting value per share would be $7.08/3 = \$2.36$. The new equity capital together with the old is worth $2.36 per share, which is the expected price of the new shares after they have been issued.[1] This price is the estimated **ex-rights** price and is the one used when determining the value of the underwriting contract. In order to simplify calculation, we have used the data from the option example in Chapter 19 to describe the rights offering.

C = price of one right to each new share

S = $2.36 (ex-rights market value of the stock)

E = $1.90 (exercise price or striking price for the new shares)

e = 2.71828

t = 22 days (maturity of the option) or 0.06027 years

---

[1]This estimate of the ex-rights price is only a first approximation because the exercise price has not been discounted and the cost of underwriting is not included.

σ = 0.40 (annual standard deviation of continuously compounded stock returns)

r = 9.25 percent (continuous compounded risk-free interest rate)

The calculated value C is the value to shareholders of the call option represented by a right to buy one new share. We demonstrated in the previous chapter that the minimum value of such a call option would be the difference between the existing ex-rights value and the present value of the exercise or offer price for the new shares; that is,

$$\$2.36 - \$1.90e^{-(0.0925 \times 0.06027)} = \$0.47056$$

In fact, the right to each new share should sell for more than $0.47056, because the stockholder's option to wait for twenty-two days before deciding to exercise the option is valuable. We already know that C equals $0.47157 cents, as we calculated the value of a call option with identical data in Chapter 19.

The next question concerns the value of the underwriters' agreement to take up new shares at $1.90 if they are not bought by other stockholders. Management effectively purchases a put option from the underwriters to put the stock onto the underwriters if the shareholders fail to buy the new shares. The relationship between the value of a put option and the value of a call option on the same share with the same exercise price is expressed in the put-call parity formula described in the last chapter. We can use the put-call parity formula to value the equivalent put option. That is, from the value C of the right (the call option) we subtract the difference between the price of the share (S) and the present value of the exercise price (Ee^{-rt}) to obtain the value P of the effective put obtained from the underwriters:

$$P = C - (S - Ee^{-rt})$$

$$= 0.47157 - (2.36 - 1.90e^{-(0.0925 \times 0.06027)})$$

$$= 0.47157 - 0.47056$$

$$= 0.00101$$

The put option purchased by the company from the underwriters is worth one tenth of a cent, or about 0.05 percent of the exercise price (0.00101/ 1.90).

ARE UNDERWRITERS PAID TOO MUCH?

Although the value of the underwriting contract as insurance against a failed issue of stock is worth about 0.05 percent of the issue price in this case, the underwriters may charge a somewhat higher fee to compensate them for legal and administrative costs and to provide a larger profit. In a study by Marsh, it appeared that investment bankers who underwrite rights issues in the United Kingdom charged fees significantly in excess of those predicted by the Black–Scholes model. This finding is of interest since the particular group of underwriters studied incurred no significant legal or administrative costs in the underwriting. The administrative costs of the issues were borne by other investment bankers.

Why do underwriters, at least in the United Kingdom, appear to obtain a return greater than that predicted by the Black and Scholes model? One possible reason is that the underwriters are able as a group to fix prices and thereby are able to charge higher prices. However, high prices gradually should attract new entrants into the industry who would undermine such prices. Another explanation is that underwriters provide services that are not valued explicitly by the model. One possible "service," or benefit, is that the underwriters, by agreeing to underwrite the new issue at a particular price, are signaling to the market that the funds raised are being put to good use. Such validation by an independent party could be valuable, because stockholders often are uncertain as to whether a rights issue is a sign of good news (new profitable investment opportunities) or bad news (much lower cash flows than expected).

If the company finds the underwriting fees too high, it can try to negotiate either a lower fee or a higher price for the new shares. Increasing the exercise price of the new shares increases the value of the underwriting, for it increases the probability that the underwriters will have to buy the new shares for more than they will be worth on the final exercise date. If such negotiations prove to be unfruitful, the firm can try using a deep discount and avoid underwriting altogether.

IS THE UNDERWRITING FEE COSTLY TO THE COMPANY?

An underwriting fee certainly seems expensive to the stockholder, because the company pays a fee to the underwriters, cash leaves the company, and as a result the value of the company should be reduced. However, assuming a fair underwriting fee, the cost should be viewed as the price of a gamble or insurance. If the gamble is fairly priced, it has a zero net present value; as a result, the payment of an underwriting fee should not reduce the value of the firm. The company is gambling in that it is making a bet with the underwriter that the new issue will fail. If the issue fails, the underwriters must buy any remaining stock at the issue price. Their loss will be determined by the difference between the issue price and the prevailing market price. However, if the new issue is bought by existing stockholders, the company will have lost the bet, and the underwriters will be richer by the price of the bet.

Underwriting also can be described as insurance. The company is insuring that it raises the amount of funds required. Without insurance, the issue might fail, and the company would fail to raise the funds it needs. If the funds are required to finance new investment, failure to raise the cash might mean postponing new projects, with the consequent loss of net present value. In this respect, the effective put option that is provided by underwriters can be worth more than its cost and increase company value.

Valuing Risky Debt

If a firm wishes to issue debt, the interest rate that it will have to pay will depend not only on prevailing market rates, but also on the probability that the firm will default on its bond repayments. The difference between the price of a risky bond and a default-free bond with the same schedule of payments is often called the **default premium.** For example, if there existed a firm that could not default and it could sell for $1,000 a ten-year bond providing an interest rate (or coupon) of $100 per year, and another company could sell a bond with the same coupon payments and repayment terms for only $900, the default premium would be the $100 difference. One could also express this default premium as an interest rate differential between the risky and the riskless bond. How can one estimate the size of the default premium? In fact, the problem of pricing risky bonds is (in part) an option valuation problem.

DEBT AS A PUT OPTION

We can view the debt of a corporation as incorporating a put option. If the value of the assets of the firm falls below the value of the debt, the share-holders in effect can direct management to put the firm's assets onto the debtholders by defaulting on the loan payments. The right to do so is what is implied by limited liability for stockholders. A debtholder granting a loan to a limited liability corporation is selling a put option (that is, an option to default) to the shareholders as an implied part of the loan transaction. The value of the put affects the amount that can be borrowed against a given stream of interest and principal repayments. The more valuable the put (the more likely that the firm will default), the larger the interest payments. Thus the shareholders in a levered corporation hold a put as part of the value of their equity.

EQUITY AS A CALL OPTION

An alternative way of analyzing the problem is to view the total value of the equity as representing the value of a call option. The shareholders have a call on the value of the firm's assets, which they exercise by requiring the company to honor the interest and repayment obligations to debtholders. At the time of loan payments, if the value of the assets is in excess of the liabilities or debt obligations, the company will pay the debtholders and not default on the loans; if the assets are less than the debt obligations, the shareholders need not exercise their option, and debtholders will have the value of the remaining assets. Thus the amount of the loan to be repaid effectively serves as the exercise price to be paid by shareholders if they wish to exercise their equity (call) option to own the firm. One way to value risky debt is to value the equity as a call option and then to calculate the corresponding value of the debt with the familiar formula

Value of Assets = Value of Debt + Value of Equity, or

Value of Debt = Value of Assets − Value of Equity

The assumption here is that we know the market value of the underlying assets of the firm. Once we have found the value of the debt we can compute the default premium by comparing the price of the risky bond with the price of a riskless bond. Let us take an example for illustration.

VALUING A RISKY BOND

A company issues a zero-coupon bond with a ten-year maturity, promising to pay the holder $100 at the end of ten years. The company wishes to know what price the lender will pay for the bond, given the following data:

Value of the assets, S	= $200
Annual standard deviation of the assets, σ	= 0.50
Risk-free rate of interest, r (continuously compounded)	= 10 percent

The face value of the bond ($100) is in fact the effective exercise price (E) of the call option, for the equityholders will wish to own the firm (at the end of the ten-year term) only if its value is above the $100 required by the bondholders. The maturity (t) of the bond is the maturity of the option.

We can use the Black and Scholes formula explained in detail in Chapter 19 to value the call option. Remember that the model consists of one main equation with two subsidiary equations. The main equation is

$$C = S \times N(d_1) - \frac{E}{e^{rt}} \times N(d_2)$$

The two subsidiary equations determine the value of $N(d_1)$ and $N(d_2)$.

$$d_1 = \frac{\ln(S/E) + (r + 0.5\,\sigma^2)t}{\sigma \times \sqrt{t}}$$

$$d_2 = d_1 - \sigma \times \sqrt{t}$$

The values of $N(d_1)$ and $N(d_2)$ can be found by using the table of values for the cumulative normal probability distribution function (Table 19.3).

$$d_1 = \frac{\ln(200/100) + (0.10 + 0.50(0.50)^2)10}{0.50 \times \sqrt{10}}$$

$$= \frac{0.69315 + 2.25}{1.58114}$$

$$= 1.86141$$

$$d_2 = d_1 - \sigma \times \sqrt{t}$$

$$= 1.86141 - 1.58114$$

$$= 0.28027$$

The cumulative normal probability distribution function in Table 19.3 gives the closest values for $N(d_1)$ and $N(d_2)$ as

$$N(d_1) = 0.9678$$

$$N(d_2) = 0.6179$$

We have not interpolated to obtain a more accurate result since our example is only illustrative.

The value C of the call option can now be calculated using Black and Scholes's main equation:

$$C = S \times N(d_1) - \frac{E}{e^{rt}} \times N(d_2)$$

$$= 200 \times 0.9678 - \left(\frac{100}{e^{0.1 \times 10}} \times 0.6179\right)$$

$$= 193.56 - \left(\frac{100}{2.71828} \times 0.6179\right)$$

$$= 193.56 - 22.7313$$

$$= 170.8287$$

Given that the value of the firm is \$200 and the value of the equity is \$170.8287, the value of the debt must be the difference between the two because

Value of Assets = Value of Debt + Value of Equity

The value of the risky debt is therefore \$200 − \$170.8287 = \$29.1713.

The final question to answer is what is the default premium? For this we must know the price P_B of zero-coupon riskless debt with a ten-year maturity and repayment of \$100 at the end of ten years when the (continuously compounded) riskless rate of interest is 10 percent. Such a bond can be priced easily.

$$P_B = 100e^{-rt}$$

$$= \frac{100}{e^{0.1 \times 10}}$$

$$= \$36.7880$$

The default premium is

Default Premium = Price of Riskless Bond − Price of Risky Bond

$$= \$36.7880 - \$29.1713$$

$$= \$7.6167$$

In this example we have made a number of simplifying assumptions, for example, that the firm pays no dividends and could be declared in default only at the end of ten years. However, nearly all bond agreements have covenants that enable debtholders to intervene before the time comes for the repayment of the bond. Valuation of most real-life bonds would require a more complex formula. (Brennan and Schwartz (1982) have developed such models.) Finally, it is worth noting that companies frequently do not exercise the option to default even when the value of the assets is less than the face value of the bonds. One reason is, of course, that an option usually is worth more alive than dead. Additionally, there are bankruptcy costs, and managers and other employees have an obvious stake in the continuation of the firm. Given the imperfect relationship between ownership and management control in most corporations, such stakeholders (managers) may be able to prevent exercise of the default option.

Mergers and the Coinsurance Effect

In a previous chapter on mergers, we described the way in which two firms might combine in order to lessen financial risks and thereby reduce the cost of borrowing. We suggested that if two separate firms both have debt outstanding, a merger of the two can increase the value of the debt and thus reduce the value of the equity. We justified this conclusion by the following logic.

AN EXAMPLE

Two firms, A and B, each with assets of $200, merge. The risk or annual standard deviation of the value of A's assets is 50 percent or 0.50, and of B's is 30 percent or 0.30. Each company has a ten-year zero-coupon $100 bond outstanding prior to the merger. In the case of firm A, the price of the risky bond is $29.171; we calculated this value in the previous section. The price of the risky bond for firm B is $35.667 (calculated in the same way as firm A's risky bond, using a standard deviation of 0.30). Firm B's bond is more valuable, because the firm is less risky.

We shall assume that after the merger the bonds of A and B have equal priority claims on the combined firm's assets. In order to know how the value of the combined debt will change as a result of the merger, we must calculate the standard deviation of the value of the merged firm's assets. In Chapter 8 we demonstrated how to calculate the variance s^2 (the square of the standard deviation) of a portfolio of two securities using the formula

$$s_P^2 = (x_1 s_1)^2 + (x_2 s_2)^2 + 2r_{1,2}(x_1 s_1)(x_2 s_2)$$

where s_1 = standard deviation of returns on security 1

   x_1 = proportion of portfolio invested in security 1

   $r_{1,2}$ = coefficient of correlation between returns on securities 1 and 2

Assume that the two firms' earnings streams and therefore their asset values are uncorrelated; that is, $r_{1,2} = 0$. As a result

$$s_P^2 = (x_1 s_1)^2 + (x_2 s_2)^2 + 0$$

$$= (0.5 \times 0.5)^2 + (0.5 \times 0.3)^2$$

$$= 0.085$$

The variance of the merged firm's asset value is 0.085. If we take the square root of the variance, we obtain the standard deviation of the merged firm's asset value: 0.29155. Compare this value with the standard deviation of each firm's value before the merger. We can now compute the value of the merged firm's equity, remembering that the total value of the assets is now \$400 and that the face value of the debt is \$200. Using Black and Scholes's formula as before we obtain

$$d_1 = \frac{\ln(S/E) + (r + 0.5\sigma^2)t}{\sigma \times \sqrt{t}}$$

$$= \frac{\ln\left(\dfrac{400}{200}\right) + (0.1 + 0.5 \times 0.29155^2)10}{0.29155 \times \sqrt{10}}$$

$$= 2.29744$$

$$d_2 = d_1 - \sigma \times \sqrt{t}$$

$$= 2.29744 - 0.92196$$

$$= 1.37548$$

Using Table 19.3, we find that (without interpolation)

$$N(d_1) = 0.9893$$

$$N(d_2) = 0.9192$$

Substituting these values into Black and Scholes's main equation, we obtain

$$C = S \times N(d_1) - \frac{E}{e^{rt}} \times N(d_2)$$

$$C = 400 \times 0.9893 - \left(\frac{200}{e^{0.1 \times 10}}\right) \times 0.9192$$

$$= 395.72 - 67.6310$$

$$= 328.089$$

The value of the risky debt of the combined firm is

Debt = Assets − Equity

$$= 400 - 328.089$$

$$= 71.9110$$

Before the merger each company had liabilities in the form of a bond with a par value of $100. The debt of the combined company has a par value of $200. The $71.911 value of the combined debt must be divided by two if it is to be made comparable with the values of the pre-merger bonds in terms of the price per $100 of par value.

$$\frac{\$71.911}{2} = \$35.9555$$

Our results are summarized in the following table.

Value of pre-merger debt		Value of debt post-merger
Company A ($\sigma_A = 0.50$)	Company B ($\sigma_B = 0.30$)	
$29.171	$35.667	$35.9555

Two points should be obvious from the table. The price of the risky bonds of the merged firm is slightly more than the price of the risky bond of firm B. Bondholders in the aggregate have gained as a result of the merger, but virtually all the gains have accrued to the debtholders of firm A, which was the more risky firm in the first place. The second point is that the gains to debtholders must be at somebody's expense: the stockholders. Changes in the value of the common stock are summarized as follows:

Value of pre-merger common stock		Value of post-merger common stock of each firm
Company A	Company B	
170.829	164.333	164.0445

It is apparent that the stockholders of firm A, which had the largest increase in the value of its debt, have suffered an equal loss in the value of their equity. On a smaller scale the same has happened with firm B. The total value of the firm (equity + debt) post-merger is still $164.0445 + $35.9555 = 200. The coinsurance effect of mergers does not change the value of the assets; rather, it affects the way that the value is distributed between bondholders and stockholders.

Our previous example has assumed zero correlation between the earnings of firm A and firm B. If we had assumed positive correlation, the changes in the value of the debt and equity would have been less than those shown. Conversely, if we had assumed negative correlation between the earnings of firm A and firm B, there would have been even greater changes in value, because the effects of diversification on risk would have been greater.

How is it that the value of the stockholders' equity has been reduced? After all, the value of shareholders' equity depends upon the systematic risk (or beta) of the firm's earnings stream. In fact, the merger has increased the levered beta of the equity stream. Because the value of the debt has been increased (as a result of reduced default risk), the debt-to-equity ratio of the firm has also increased. As a higher debt-to-equity ratio implies a greater risk to the equityholders, the levered beta will rise. An increase in the levered beta will imply a higher discount rate for earnings in the capital asset pricing model, and if earnings remain unchanged, the value of the equity will be reduced.

SOME FURTHER OBSERVATIONS ON THE COINSURANCE EFFECT

It seems clear that mergers can benefit debtholders at the expense of equity-holders. However, the results need qualification. First, debt agreements often contain provisions allowing corporate borrowers to renegotiate the terms of bonds, or permitting them to call or repay the bonds at specified prices and dates. Call provisions may be valuable to a firm that is expecting to make major acquisitions and reduce its level of risk. Alternatively, the analysis may make it clear why some firms issue more short-term than long-term debt; short-term debt reduces the transfers of wealth between shareholders and bondholders when the risk of the firm is expected to change, because the firm can quickly renegotiate the terms of new loans when existing loans become due.

Second, we have assumed that the borrowing power of the merged firm is no greater than the sum of the pre-merger parts. As default risks actually have been reduced by the merger, the firm should be able to borrow more. If tax advantages or other benefits to borrowing add additional value to the firm, any incremental debt capacity resulting from a merger can increase the value of the stockholders' equity.

Third, as we demonstrated in Chapter 14 on acquisitions and mergers, two companies will have an incentive to merge if one firm has tax losses when the other has tax obligations. The rationale for such a merger lies in the unequal treatment of corporate profits and losses. If the company makes profits, it pays taxes; if it makes losses, the government does not necessarily provide a tax rebate. A merger may permit one company to use its tax losses to shelter the other company's taxable profits, thereby reducing the total amount (in present value terms) of taxes paid. The presence of taxes and the unequal treatment of tax losses and taxable profits may lead to a tax coinsurance effect that can increase the value of the equityholders' claims. These issues are explored in some detail by Green and Talmor (1983).

A fourth qualification concerns the costs of financial distress. If a merger reduces the risk of default, the expected costs of default and of financial distress also may be reduced.

Options and Loan Guarantees

In 1982 the aggregate value of outstanding loans guaranteed by the federal government was $331 billion. A small but increasing proportion of these guarantees were for loans to industrial and commercial corporations. Some of these loans were granted to firms in financial distress (Chrysler Corporation, for example), others as an incentive for firms to invest in particular locations, such as in areas of high unemployment. Two important questions arise concerning such guarantees. The first question, and the most obvious, is how to value them. The answer is important not only to the government, which is taking on a liability, but also to the company whose loan is being guaranteed. Second, what does the firm have to do to obtain the guarantee? Usually such guarantees do not come without cost, or at least they should not be given away free. In the case of corporations in financial distress, the loan may include conditions that prevent the firm from closing unprofitable factories for a specified period of time. In other cases, the guarantees may reward a firm establishing a factory in a particular location. Presumably, such locations entail higher capital costs or higher operating costs than other locations. In both examples, the value of the guarantee must be compared with the costs incurred in retaining unprofitable units or in relocation. Likewise, the government also will wish to ensure that the value of the guarantee is not too far in excess of the extra costs imposed on the firm because of the guarantee.

In most loan guarantees, the government guarantees future debt rather than existing debt. The reason should be obvious. If existing debt were to be guaranteed, the value of the guarantee would accrue primarily to existing debtholders. The example in the last section will illustrate this point. The value of the firm is $200, the value of a ten-year zero-coupon bond is $29.171, so the value of the equity is $170.829. The default premium on the debt instrument can be computed by comparing the value of the risky bond with the value of a riskless bond (which will pay $100 in ten years, with no coupon payments). When the continuously compounded riskless rate of interest is 10 percent, the value of the riskless bond is

$$\frac{\$100}{e^{0.1 \times 10}} = \$36.788$$

The default premium is therefore $36.788 - \$29.171 = \$7.617$. With the government guarantee, the bond's price would increase by this amount from $29.171 to $36.788. This price appreciation accrues to the holders of the bonds and not to the shareholders. The shareholders do not benefit from the guarantee on the existing debt unless the debt capacity of the firm is increased as a result of the guarantee. An increase in debt capacity could be of value to the firm, although we shall not try to value it here.

Obviously, the equityholders should insist that the guarantees be given for newly issued debt rather than for outstanding debt. Who gains from guarantees on new debt? The simplest answer is that most of the benefits (usually) will accrue to the current equityholders, for the company would be able to issue additional debt at a yield approximating the risk-free rate of interest. Without the guarantee, the company would have to issue debt at a much higher interest rate, one that reflects the firm's risk of default.

The equityholders benefit from the guarantee on new debt because it allows the corporation to sell debt for a much higher price than could have been possible without the guarantee. However, the story does not end here. Existing bondholders also benefit. Because the firm's value is increased by the guarantee, the probability of default is reduced, and therefore the existing debtholders' risk will be reduced. In this respect, existing debtholders also gain from the issuance of the new (guaranteed) debt. Any such increase in the price of outstanding bonds must be at the expense of equityholders. The company could prevent the bondholders obtaining this windfall gain by negotiating the redemption of existing debt at the bond's value prior to the issuance of the guarantee. When the Chrysler Corporation negotiated federal loan guarantees in 1980, it also arranged with its bankers to redeem a large proportion of existing debt at a large discount below the face value of the debt. This redemption was important, because the value of the guarantees appeared to be a substantial proportion of the value of the firm's assets.

What have we learned from our analysis?

Government loan guarantees are valuable. How valuable depends upon how risky the firm's debt is.

The guarantee (usually) is not given free. Presumably the firm will have to invest in projects that have a cost (a negative NPV). It is important for both the government and the firm to compare the costs and the benefits.

If the guarantee is for newly issued debt, most of the value of the guarantee usually will accrue to the equityholders, although some will accrue to existing debtholders.

The firm can reduce the windfall gains accruing to holders of existing debt by trying to negotiate the redemption of the debt at market prices that prevailed prior to the guarantee.

The previous analysis also gives us some insight into other financing problems. For example, we have mentioned the Chrysler Corporation and its financial problems in 1980 and 1981. One question that may puzzle some financial analysts is why Chrysler did not make an issue of new equity. At first sight such an issue could have been very profitable to the firm for two reasons. First, if Chrysler had gone into liquidation there would have been significant costs. The firm's assets might have been sold for less than their value as part of a going concern, while legal and professional fees would have been substantial. A second reason is that Chrysler had substantial unused tax benefits because of past tax losses. If the new equity issue had been invested in riskless and taxable bonds, the income would have been tax-free to investors because the interest income would be shielded by tax losses. Thus, taxpaying shareholders would have been able to hold bonds tax-free through the corporation.

Such an injection of equity, however, would have reduced the probability of default for existing bondholders, who would have obtained windfall gains at the expense of shareholders. These gains could be substantial, because some of Chrysler's bonds were extremely risky (they yielded a 20 percent return against 11 percent on equivalent riskless government securities). Thus, part of the value of the new equity would have accrued immediately to bondholders. These observations may demonstrate why firms in financial distress do not always try to raise new equity finance to relieve their financial difficulties.

Options in Capital Projects

Decisions made in most large capital projects are not totally irrevocable. Management usually has chances to change the nature of the project in the light of ensuing events after the project has been started. Each such change in the project has a cost, and the investment required for each additional change may be regarded as the exercise price of a **real option.** The most common real options in capital projects concern options to expand, modernize, replace, or abandon projects. Decisions to exercise such options are contingent upon changes in the present values of cash flows that would result if the options were exercised. A more general way of looking at the problem is to realize that when a capital investment is undertaken, usually it creates opportunities to make further capital investments in the future. Such options on the future often are called growth opportunities. They represent growth in the sense that they can confer additional net present value upon the firm.

MINERAL EXTRACTION PROJECT AS AN OPTION

A good example of the potential usefulness of option valuation can be found in the valuation of mineral extraction projects. A company decides it would like to invest in some coal reserves with the object of developing and selling the coal sometime in the future. The board of directors asks financial analysts to determine the profitability of the coal reserves and the price that should be paid for the coalfield. The analysts estimate today's development costs for the mine and forecast operating expenses, revenues, and taxes. Then they discount the net cash flows and come up with a net present value. Suppose that the present value turns out to be zero, indicating there would be no net gain or loss to developing the coal reserves now. When asked what price is reasonable to pay for the reserves, one analyst suggests "one cent." The directors are not happy with this answer, so they hire a consultant to provide an answer more to their liking. How would you respond?

In fact, this problem can be put into the form of an option. Although analysts have determined that it is unprofitable to mine the coal today, the company does not need to develop the reserves today; it simply can wait to see if the price of coal rises more than projected in current forecasts. If it does, then it can decide whether to exercise the option (effectively, a call option) to commit the development costs and exploit the field. In this case, the development costs constitute the exercise price of the option.

A factor that increases the value of this option is that it is perpetual; it never expires. In this respect, even if the coal reserves are unprofitable to mine today, as long as there is some probability that the development will become profitable in the future, the reserves have some value. Thus, the value of the reserves includes the value of the call option. This problem has been examined in some detail by Tourinho (1979).

Brennan and Schwartz (1982) have examined a similar option problem relating to the value of a gold mine. They assumed that after the development of a mine the owners had the option to close (and then reopen) the mine if the price of gold fell sufficiently. They wanted to know how much this option was worth, taking into account the costs of closing and reopening the mine. The value of such an option in the future could affect the initial decision to develop the mine.

A word of warning should be made concerning the valuation of real asset options. The Black and Scholes option pricing model was not derived with valuation of real asset options in mind. First, Black and Scholes assume a finite life for the option. For a natural resource option of infinite life, why would anyone exercise such an option if an option is worth more alive than dead? Second, the model assumes that exercising the option does not affect the value of the underlying asset. This latter assumption is appropriate in the case of, say, AT&T stock, as the holder of an option on AT&T stock is unlikely to affect the price of AT&T upon exercising the option. The decision to exercise a real asset option, on the other hand, may affect the value of the asset. For example, if a gold mine were large enough, exercising an option to develop the mine could change the price of gold, thereby affecting the value of the underlying asset. Such a result would not be consistent with the assumptions of Black and Scholes's option pricing model. Third, real asset options are not always marketable; therefore, you cannot always create a riskless hedge, which is a necessary assumption for the valuation model.

Even if producers compete freely and individually are unable to influence gold prices, they have an incentive to develop their reserves, for the first to exercise an option to develop would obtain the highest prices and the last the lowest prices, because the development of reserves by competitors will lower subsequent prices. (See Cox and Rubinstein for a discussion of this point with respect to the pricing of warrants.) The natural resource example illustrates that it can be difficult to apply the Black and Scholes model to the valuation of real asset options. This does not mean that more generally applicable models cannot or will not be derived. Nevertheless, even in the present state of the art, the options pricing framework is a useful means of understanding the characteristics of real asset options.

THE ABANDONMENT OPTION

There are many other types of real options in corporate finance, for example, the abandonment option. Different residual values or abandonment values of assets could influence the final choice between two mutually exclusive projects. Some financial analysts are surprised to find that conventional analysis often favors capital investment in relatively unattractive areas where building and land values are low compared with identical investment in areas where the land and building values are much higher. In fact, their analysis may be incomplete. Let us assume there is a significant probability that the investment in either place will be abandoned. Construction costs are the same in both places, but if the project fails, the land and buildings will have to be sold. The land and buildings in the high-priced area often can be resold more quickly and at a price that recovers a greater proportion of the cost than sale of holdings in a low-priced area. The option to terminate or abandon the project may be of greater value in one place than in another, and such factors must be acknowledged in the analysis, if only in a qualitative fashion.

In many companies, management has considerable scope to alter the shape of existing projects and to create new growth opportunities. The value of the resulting portfolio of real option possibilities may constitute a significant proportion of the value of the company. In the case of a new company that has developed new technologies or products, option possibilities may make up most of the company's value. This is a circumstance in which the firm's investment outlays are made sequentially and are dependent on information developed over time as to the final earnings prospects. The valuation (hence financing) of such options is made more complicated by virtue of the fact that the companies involved typically have no publicly traded securities. Venture capitalists, both individual and institutional investors, specialize in the evaluation and financing of the capital needs of such companies. Cooper and Carleton (1979) have analyzed the venture capital decision environment in this light.

Both Myers and Majd (1983) and Broyles and Cooper (1980) have analyzed how the value of the company and its equity is composed of two parts, the present value of assets in their existing form and the value of the growth opportunity options open to management. One implication of this research is that a positive net present value for a project does not imply necessarily that management should proceed to invest in the project immediately. If the investment is postponed, it becomes an option that may be exercised in the future. The option to postpone has a positive value. Management should not invest in a project until the net present value is greater than the value of the option to postpone investment. There are conditions under which postponement may be more valuable than immediate investment. Our coalfield is an example of the value of postponement.

Finally, the options valuation formula provides us with insights into the way some variables affect the value of real option growth opportunities. We know that, providing the value of the asset remains the same, an increase in either the interest rate, the risk of the underlying asset, or the maturity of the option will increase the value of an option. Option valuation suggests why, for example, many companies are willing to engage in long-term research and development into new products that have a highly uncertain future. They are right to do so as long as the present value of the research and development budget is less than the value of the options created by research and development activities. Although the precise way in which these real options should be valued is beyond the scope of the existing literature, the value of real options such as those generated by research and development still needs recognition in valuing conventional capital projects.

Summary

In this chapter we have provided some examples of how the option pricing model can be used to value corporate liabilities. These examples raise some interesting questions about the advantages and disadvantages of certain financial policies, such as merging for the purpose of reducing the costs of borrowing. Other applications of the option pricing model for the purposes of valuing real assets also were described. We suggested that many familiar types of capital project actually embody options that could affect the value of the asset. The value of such real options could alter the accept–reject decision, or simply alter the timing of the decision to develop a project. Although the current options models are not always robust enough to provide realistic values for real options, they do help us better understand the greater complexity of such projects.

Review Questions

1. Describe the two options in an underwritten rights issue.
2. A corporation intends to make an underwritten rights issue when its shares are trading at $5.
   (a) Does it matter from the underwriters' point of view at what price the new shares are sold?
   (b) Does the price of the new shares matter to the stockholders? Assume that the underwriters' fees are fair.
3. How would you use the option pricing framework to analyze the following statement: "As a firm borrows more, it must pay higher interest rates. Even in the absence of default costs, the higher interest rates reduce the attractions of borrowing."
4. Critically examine the following statement: "Firms whose earnings are imperfectly correlated can obtain an advantage from merging. A merger will reduce the future costs of borrowing."
   Is this statement correct in a taxless world? Are your conclusions altered when we introduce taxes?
5. What are the important differences between valuing an option on a common stock and valuing an option on a real asset?
6. Describe two additional options implied in capital projects that are not mentioned in this chapter.

Problems

*1. Griffin, Inc., is considering a rights issue to raise funds for further capital investment. Shares are trading currently at $120, and shareholders have been offered shares on a one-for-two basis at $90 per share. The continuously compounded risk-free rate is 15 percent per year, and the standard deviation on the annual returns of Griffin, Inc., common stock is 40 percent. There are thirty days within which to exercise the rights offer.
   (a) What price should each right to a new share sell for at the beginning of the first day of trading?
   (b) What would you expect the price of each right to be just before the rights offer lapses on day 30?

2. Martin Manufacturers has arranged for a rights issue to be underwritten for a fee of 4 percent of the funds raised. The company is offering rights of one share for every two held, at a price of $55 per share. The current market price is $62.50, while the risk-free rate of interest is 12½ percent per year. The stock price has been fairly volatile over the past year and has a standard deviation of 58 percent. The time period to the expiration

of the rights offer is twenty-two days. What is the value of the put option obtained from the underwriters? Compare this with the cost of underwriting.

*3. A company has $8 million in outstanding debt with zero coupon, which matures in eight years. The value of the company's assets is $12 million. The standard deviation of the assets is 40 percent per year. The continuously compounded riskless rate of interest is 10 percent per year. Calculate (a) the value of the debt, and (b) the default premium.

 4. Given the information in Problem 3, what happens to the values of equity and debt if unanticipated inflation increases the continuously compounded riskless rate of interest from 10 percent to 15 percent? Explain which group of security holders benefits from this increase in the riskless interest rate. Assume the unanticipated inflation has no effect on the value of the company's assets.

*5. Given the following information for two companies X and Y, calculate the value of the combined debt of the two companies, which have merged. The earnings streams of the two firms are positively correlated, and the estimated correlation coefficient is 0.3. The continuously compounded riskless rate of return is 10 percent, and debt for both X and Y is zero coupon and matures in 8 years.

	X	Y
Asset values ($)	12 million	12 million
Face value of debt ($)	8 million	8 million
Standard deviation of returns on assets	40%	60%

Compare the value of the combined debt with the values of the individual companies' debt before the merger, and explain why the values have changed.

 6. What do you think would happen to the value of equity and debt in Problem 5 when the correlation coefficient is (a) zero, and (b) −0.40 and why?

References

Black, F., and M. Scholes, "The Pricing of Options and Corporate Liabilities," *Journal of Political Economy,* 81, no. 3 (May–June 1973): 637–54.

Brennan, M. J., ed., *Option Pricing: Theory and Application,* Lexington, Mass.: Lexington Books, 1983.

Brennan, M. J., "The Pricing of Contingent Claims in Discrete Time Models," *Journal of Finance,* 34, no. 1 (March 1974): 53–68.

Brennan, M. J., and E. S. Schwartz, "An Equilibrium Model of Bond Pricing and a Test of Market Efficiency," *Journal of Financial and Quantitative Analysis,* 15, no. 3 (September 1982): 301–29.

Brennan, M. J., and E. S. Schwartz, "Evaluating New Resource Investments," University of British Columbia, May 1983, revised June 1983.

Broyles, J. E., and I. A. Cooper, "Real Asset Options and Capital Budgeting," *Nijenrode Studies in Business,* Boston: Martinus Nijoff, 1980.

Cooper, I. A., and W. T. Carleton, "Dynamics of Borrower-Lender Interaction: Partitioning Final Payoff in Venture Capital Finance," *Journal of Finance,* 34, no. 2 (May 1979): 517–28.

Cox, J. C., J. Ingersoll, and S. A. Ross, "A Theory of the Term Structure of Interest Rates," Graduate School of Business, Stanford University, 1978.

Cox, J. C., and M. Rubinstein, *Option Markets,* Englewood Cliffs, N.J.: Prentice-Hall. Forthcoming.

Galai, D., "Corporate Income Taxes and the Valuation of Claims on the Corporation," UCLA, July 1983.

Galai, D., and R. Masulis, "The Option Pricing Model and the Risk Factor of Stock," *Journal of Financial Economics,* 3, no. 1/2 (January–March 1976): 53–82.

Geske, R., "The Valuation of Compound Options," *Journal of Financial Economics,* 7, no. 1 (March 1979): 63–81.

Green, R. C., and E. Talmor, "On the Structure and Incentive Effects of Tax Liabilities," Working Paper, University of Wisconsin, July 1983.

Jarrow, R., and A. Rudd, "Approximate Option Valuation for Arbitrary Stochastic Processes," *Journal of Financial Economics,* 10, no. 3 (November 1982): 347–69.

Jones, E. P., and S. P. Mason, "Valuation of Loan Guarantees," *Journal of Banking and Finance,* 4, no. 1 (March 1980): 89–107.

Marsh, P. R., "Equity Rights Issues and the Efficiency of the UK Stock Market," *Journal of Finance,* 34 (September 1979): 839–62.

Merton, R. C., "An Analytic Derivation of the Cost of Deposit Insurance and Loan Guarantees: An Application of Modern Option Pricing Theory," *Journal of Banking and Finance,* 1, no. 1 (June 1977): 3–11.

Merton, R. C., "On the Pricing of Corporate Debt: The Risk Structure of Interest Rates," *Journal of Finance,* 29, no. 2 (May 1974): 449–70.

Merton, R. C., "Theory of Rational Option Pricing," *Bell Journal of Economics and Management Science,* 4, no. 1 (Spring 1973): 141–83.

Myers, S., and S. Majd, "Calculating Abandonment Value Using Option Pricing Theory," Working Paper 1462–63, Sloan School of Management, Massachusetts Institute of Technology, 1983.

Rendleman, R. J., and B. Bartter, "Two-State Option Pricing," *Journal of Finance,* 34, no. 5 (December 1979): 1093–1110.

Roll, R., "An Analytic Valuation Formula for Unprotected American Call Options on Stocks with Known Dividends," *Journal of Financial Economics,* 5, no. 2 (November 1977): 251–58.

Rubinstein, M., "The Valuation of Uncertain Income Streams and the Pricing of Options," *Bell Journal of Economics,* 7, no. 2 (Autumn 1976): 407–25.

Rubinstein, M., and H. Leland, "Replicating Options with Positions in Stock and Cash," *Financial Analysts Journal,* 37, no. 1 (May–June 1981): 63–72.

Smith, C., "Option Pricing Review," *Journal of Financial Economics,* 3, no. 1/2 (January–March 1976): 1–57.

Stapleton, R. C., "Mergers, Debt Capacity, and the Valuation of Corporate Loans," in *Mergers and Acquisitions,* edited by M. Keenan and L. J. White, Lexington, Mass.: Lexington Books, 1982.

Stoll, H. R., "The Relationship Between Put and and Call Option Prices," *Journal of Finance,* 34, no. 5 (December 1969): 802–24.

Tourinho, O. A. F., "The Valuation of Reserves and Natural Resources: An Option Pricing Approach," Ph.D. Dissertation, University of California at Berkeley, 1979.

Cost of Debt and Capital Structure

Most companies need more than one source of capital to finance their assets. For instance, many corporations use short- and long-term debt financing as well as common stock. Utilities use preferred stock in addition to debt and common equity. You might wonder whether one source of finance is less costly than another. For example, the interest on debt is a tax-deductible expense for the corporate borrower, while dividend payments to shareholders are not. As a result, some analysts believe that debt finance costs less than equity finance. If this is true, if one source of finance is less costly than another, it is important to understand in what proportions the corporation should use different financial instruments. Determining the best or optimum proportion is often described as determining the corporation's optimum capital structure.

The issue of how best to finance the assets of the corporation is an important one. If one source of finance is less costly than another, it is possible that the actual value of an asset can be changed by the method of financing that is used. In this respect, identifying the cost of different sources of finance is important not only for determining the best capital structure for the corporation but also for valuing the assets of the corporation, including new capital projects.

In this chapter, we shall describe two different models of capital structure. The first is based on the principle that the after-tax value of a corporation's assets cannot be altered by changing the way they are financed. In this model, the value of an asset is determined solely by the value of its operating cash flows. From this point of view, the different sources of finance used by the firm reflect only the different tastes of management. For example, some managers may be less risk averse than others and therefore may employ more debt. The crucial point to understand about this model, however, is that the values of assets from a shareholder's perspective cannot be altered by employing more or less debt.

We shall also describe a second model that suggests that one source of finance may be less costly than another, implying that the value of the assets of the firm can be increased if the firm employs this less costly source of finance. In other words, the after-tax value of an asset or a new project is affected not only by the value of the operating cash flows but also by advantages of specific sources of finance. The tax deductibility of interest payments is frequently used to suggest that debt is cheaper than equity. If debt finance is less expensive than equity, we must determine in what proportion it should be used to finance the corporation. In other words, we need to know what determines the corporation's optimum capital structure.

Capital Structure

Capital structure refers to the proportions of different financial instruments used to finance a company's assets. Capital structure is often measured in terms of a company's debt-to-equity ratio. This ratio is usually calculated on the basis of the values of the liabilities given in the company's balance sheet. Let us look at an example.

Table 21.1 illustrates a simplified balance sheet. As of the end of the accounting period, the company is shown to have assets and liabilities each totaling $100. The company owes $5 in short-term debt and $15 in long-term debt (including term loans and corporate bonds). As a result, the total assets of $100 are financed by $20 of debt and by $80 of equity (including retained earnings and issued common stock). This company's capital struc-

Table 21.1   *A simplified balance sheet (in dollars)*

Assets	Liabilities	
Fixed assets 100	Short-term debt	5
	Long-term debt	15
	Equity	80
100		100

ture can be represented by a debt-to-equity ratio equal to 20/80 = 0.25, or by a debt-to-debt plus equity ratio equal to 20/100 = 0.20.

Capital structure also can be stated in terms of the market values of the assets as well as their book values. Suppose the financial securities of the corporation described in Table 21.1 were traded publicly. If the equity were valued at $90 and the debt securities were traded at their book value of $20, what would the company's debt-to-equity ratio be? In fact, it would be equal to 20/90 = 0.222, and the debt-to-debt plus equity ratio would be 20/110 = 0.182. Lenders and borrowers typically describe the debt ratios in terms of book values. (In the next chapter we will suggest some reasons why lenders may use one form rather than another.)

How Borrowing Makes the Firm's Equity More Risky

We can illustrate the way in which debt financing increases the variability of earnings accruing to stockholders and, as a result, makes the common stock riskier. Changes in the debt ratio affect the risk of equity and thereby the cost of equity capital. If stockholders dislike the increased risk that debt financing implies, they will require a higher rate of return on their equity to compensate them for the extra risk. Thus the total cost of debt to stockholders includes not only interest payments that the corporation makes to bondholders but also the extra return that the stockholders themselves require in compensation for the increased risk to their earnings stream. Let us examine an example.

Suppose that the company's assets described in Table 21.1 are financed entirely by equity and that the balance sheet looks like Table 21.2. Let us also assume that the balance sheet values equal the market values of the company's assets and liabilities. The company is expected to produce annual earnings before interest of $10 in perpetuity. For the sake of simplicity, assume that the company is nontaxpaying. There are one hundred shares

Table 21.2   *Balance sheet with all-equity financing (in dollars)*

Assets	Liabilities	
Fixed assets 100	Debt	0
	Equity	100
100		100

outstanding, so the earnings per share (EPS) are equal to $10/100 = $0.10. With no debt outstanding, the market value of the one hundred shares equals the market value of $100 for the company's assets.

Now suppose exactly the same assets of the corporation described in Table 21.2 had been financed with $50 of debt and $50 of equity, instead of $100 of equity. We have described such a financing arrangement in Table 21.3. The assets have not changed; they are still worth $100. (We assume for this example that the interest rate i remains at 5 percent as leverage is increased. Issues surrounding risky debt are discussed later in this chapter.) The question that we wish to examine is how have the earnings per share (EPS) altered as a result of the new financing arrangements?

If the firm borrows, its earnings after interest are less than earnings from operations by the amount of the interest that is paid. If we let i represent the interest rate and B the book value of the debt, the earnings E_L (levered by debt) for the firm after interest are represented as follows:

$$E_L = E_O - iB$$

where E_O are the earnings from operations, and the earnings per share (EPS) are obtained by dividing by the number of shares N:

$$EPS = (E_O - iB)/N$$

This expression represents the company's EPS in a world without taxes. (We can introduce tax effects later.)

The first result of substituting the debt for equity would be that earnings after interest would drop from $10 to $7.50 as a result of the $2.50 interest payment. However, the EPS would rise from $0.10 to $0.15 because of the smaller number of shares (fifty instead of one hundred shares). That is,

$$EPS = (E_O - iB)/N$$

$$= (\$10.00 - 0.05 \times 50)/50 = \$7.50/50$$

$$= \$0.15$$

Table 21.3   *Balance sheet with 50 percent debt in the capital structure (in dollars)*

Assets		Liabilities	
Fixed assets	100	Debt	50
		Equity	50
	100		100

Now suppose earnings from operations E_O turn out to be different from $10. Table 21.4 summarizes the effects of different levels of earnings before interest on the EPS of the firm under two different financing assumptions: all equity, and half debt and half equity. From the earnings in the first row we subtract interest charges (entered in the second row) to obtain the earnings after interest shown in the third row. By dividing the earnings after interest by the fifty shares outstanding, we obtain the EPS in the fourth row. For comparison we show the EPS for all-equity financing in the fifth row, obtained simply by dividing earnings in the first row by one hundred shares.

The figures in Table 21.4 should suggest to you that debt financing adds to the riskiness of the firm's equity returns, because it increases the variability of earnings per share. The possible range of the EPS with debt financing is $0.30 (−0.05 to 0.25) compared with only $0.15 (0 to 0.15) under all-equity financing. In Table 21.4, the critical level of earnings (before interest) is $5.00. At this point, the earnings per share are the same with all-equity financing and with 50 percent debt financing. Below this level of earnings, the EPS are lower with debt financing than would have been the case with all-equity financing. The example of Table 21.4 demonstrates that although debt financing can increase the earnings per share on a company's common stock, the earnings per share become more risky from the standpoint of the stockholder.

A number of very important issues arise from such considerations. If debt financing makes a firm's equity riskier, what is its overall effect on the firm's cost of capital? An equivalent question is, how does the introduction of debt into a firm's capital structure affect the total market value of the firm? Also, if the market value of the firm is affected by debt financing, what proportion of debt in a firm's capital structure maximizes the firm's market value? These questions are among the most important in corporate finance. The optimum capital structure for a firm depends upon many factors, one of which may be corporate and personal taxes.

Table 21.4   *The effect on earnings per share of changing the financing mix (in dollars)*

	Earnings (E_0)			
	0.0	5.0	10.0	15.0
EPS WITH DEBT FINANCING				
Interest	−2.5	−2.5	−2.5	−2.5
Earnings after interest	−2.5	2.5	7.5	12.5
EPS	−0.05	0.05	0.15	0.25
EPS WITHOUT DEBT FINANCING				
EPS	0.0	0.05	0.10	0.15

Modigliani and Miller's Model: Debt and No Taxes

In 1958, Modigliani and Miller (MM) wrote an important article providing an ingenious and rigorous demonstration that, aside from the effect of taxes, alterations to capital structure do not change the value of the firm. They reasoned that in a competitive capital market the assets of a firm would sell for exactly the same price regardless of how they were financed. MM proposed that two firms having identical assets with the same earning power would sell for the same price, even if one is financed partly by debt and the other is financed entirely by equity.

In a world without taxes, the earnings E_U of the unlevered firm that has no debt equals earnings from operations:

$$E_U = E_O$$

However, for the levered firm, E_O is divided between the shareholders and the debtholders as follows:

Shareholders: $\qquad E_L = E_O - iB$

Debtholders: $\qquad\quad I = iB$

Total: $\qquad\qquad\overline{E_L + I = E_O}$

It is clear that whatever the amount of borrowing B that the firm undertakes, the combined income paid out to shareholders and debtholders is the same,

$$E_L + I = E_O$$

Modigliani and Miller used this fact to prove that the total market value of a firm's securities is unchanged by its borrowing. As the combined income paid out to the holders of the corporation's securities is unchanged irrespective of its capital structure, MM were led to the conclusion that the value of the corporation similarly is unchanged.

WHY FIRMS WITH IDENTICAL ASSETS MUST SELL AT IDENTICAL PRICES

Let us imagine that in the example of Table 21.3 the levered firm is overvalued at $55; therefore, the total value of the levered firm is $105. Which firm's common stock would the investor prefer to hold? Naturally, if both companies earn the same income, the investor will try to arrange matters to share in this income at the lowest possible price. By purchasing 10 percent of the unlevered company's outstanding securities (all equity) at a cost of

$10, an investor can buy 10 percent of the unlevered company's income, which provides annual income of $1.

The investor also can buy the same annual income of $1 by purchasing 10 percent of the levered company's securities, but it will cost more, as we show below.

10% of the equity	$ 5.50
10% of the bonds	$ 5.00
	$10.50

The total cost to the investor of buying 10 percent of the levered company's securities is $10.50 compared with only $10.00 for the unlevered company's securities. The income is exactly the same in the two cases.

Assuming that all earnings after interest charges are distributed in the form of dividends, the investor in the levered company would receive $1.00 (made up of $0.75 in dividends and $0.25 in interest income), but this $1.00 of annual income would cost $10.50 as against $10.00 for the unlevered firm.[1] As a consequence, investors will sell shares in the levered firm, and buy shares in the unlevered firm, until the value of the common stock of the levered firm falls to $50.00. Because the value of the debt is still equal to $50.00, the total value of the levered firm falls to $100.00, or exactly the same as that of the unlevered firm.

The investor will prefer to buy the unlevered firm's equity as long as the (equity) of the unlevered firm value is less than the total value (debt plus equity) of the levered firm. In general, investors will "buy cheap and sell dear" until identical streams of earnings are priced equally in the market. Thus a firm's leverage is irrelevant to the market value of its assets if there are no taxes or transactions costs. A formal proof of this arbitrage argument appears in Appendix 21.1.

An alternative strategy, which has the same results for an investor, would be to sell the shares of the levered firm, borrow on his or her own account, and buy the shares of the cheaper unlevered firm. In this way, by individual borrowing (often referred to as "homemade leverage") the investor obtains the same leverage (at a lower price) that could have been obtained by holding the levered company's shares.

MM argued that investors will not pay a premium for the equity of a company that borrows unless the company's borrowing creates an advantage that cannot be obtained by investors themselves. If the investor can borrow on the same terms as the company, individual borrowing is a perfect substitute for corporate borrowing. Therefore, there is no net advantage to a company's borrowing that would increase its value. The value of a company is determined by the operating cash flows, not by the way that the cash flows are distributed over various classes of securities. By simply packaging cash

---

[1]The investments in the levered and unlevered firms are of equivalent risk, for by buying the levered firm's bonds the investor is undoing the levered firm's borrowing position.

flows in a different way, i.e., by redistributing income and risk between equity and debt, you cannot increase the value of a company's assets.

This result should seem sensible. Suppose you were offered a house for $100,000. You intend to finance it with $50,000 of your own funds and a $50,000 mortgage at an interest rate of 2 percent above the prime interest rate. Now, if the seller already had a $50,000 mortgage on the house, repayable over twenty years at 2 percent above the prime interest rate, and she offered to sell the house with the mortgage, how much would you pay her for the house and mortgage? You should agree to pay no more than $50,000, because you are accepting an additional liability worth $50,000.

Suppose the seller asked a price of $55,000 for her equity in the house on the grounds that she was offering you an attractive financing deal for the remaining $50,000. How would you respond? As long as you are able to borrow on exactly the same terms as the seller, the asset value of the house is worth no more and no less than $100,000 with or without the loan. Only if you were offered a relatively favorable financing package that you could not obtain yourself, could it add value to the house. Clearly, financing an asset with debt does not lead automatically to an increase in the value of the asset.

MM'S ASSUMPTIONS

Modigliani and Miller made a number of important assumptions in their proof including that:

1. The shareholder can borrow on the same terms as a corporation.
2. There are no taxes.
3. There are no costs to bankruptcy and financial distress.
4. The capital market is highly competitive and efficient.
5. There are no transactions costs.

We shall briefly examine assumptions (1) and (4) and then examine in detail the remaining assumptions.

In assumption (1), MM assumed that individuals can borrow on the same terms as companies. In fact, individuals usually find borrowing more expensive than companies do. There are several reasons. First, companies usually borrow far larger sums, and, as a consequence, the costs (as a proportion of the loan) to the lender of processing the loan and of monitoring the borrower's performance are less for companies than for individuals. Second, individuals may be more risky borrowers than companies, and as a result they may pay higher rates of interest. In the latter case, greater risk leading to higher interest rates does not necessarily invalidate MM's first assumption. Their assumption means that individual borrowers can borrow on the same terms as companies of equivalent risk; by equivalent risk we mean where the probability of default is the same. Although we would expect many individuals to borrow at somewhat higher rates of interest than companies, we would not expect the differentials to be very large where the borrowers are of equivalent risk.

MM's assumption (4) that the capital market is competitive is crucial to their proof, for if the market does not value assets in a consistent way the prices of two identical assets actually may be different. In our discussion of the efficiency of the capital market in Chapter 12, we found that much of the evidence suggested the market appears highly competitive and efficient, although not all the evidence supported this conclusion.

Much of the controversy over MM's propositions about debt financing and firm valuation centers on their other assumptions, how taxes and the costs of financial distress affect firm value.

Modigliani and Miller's Model: Debt and Corporate Taxes

Using their original assumptions, Modigliani and Miller proved that, in the absence of tax, the value of a company would not be altered by changes in the company's capital structure. In a later (1963) article, however, they agreed that if interest payments by companies are tax-deductible, and if such a tax deduction cannot be obtained by shareholders borrowing on their own account, corporate borrowing enjoys a tax advantage that does increase the value of the company. For example, if a company borrows $50 and pays interest at the rate of 10 percent, the interest charges of $5 per year are tax-deductible. In this case, if the interest rate on debt to stockholders is equal to the cost of (comparable risk) common stock before taxes, the interest rate is lower after taxes by 4.6 percent, if the corporate tax rate is 46 percent. The discounted present value of this tax savings increases the value of the company by a corresponding amount. Let us derive the increase in value.

MM assumed that all companies pay taxes at the rate T_c. The after-tax income of the unlevered firm is given by:

$$E_U(1 - T_c) = \text{EBIT}(1 - T_c)$$

where EBIT is the earnings before interest and taxes. Now let us assume with MM that the levered firm pays interest at a rate i on its debt B and that the resulting interest payments $I = iB$ are deductible from taxable income. The resulting after-tax income to shareholders can be written as follows:

$$E_L(1 - T_c) = (\text{EBIT} - iB)(1 - T_c)$$

$$= \text{EBIT}(1 - T_c) - iB + iBT_c$$

The total after-tax income of the levered firm is divided between shareholders and debtholders in the following way:

Shareholders: $E_L(1 - T_c) = \text{EBIT}(1 - T_c) - iB + iBT_c$

Debtholders: $I = iB$

Total: $E_L(1 - T_c) + I = \text{EBIT}(1 - T_c) + iBT_c$

Thus we see that the total after-tax income to shareholders and debtholders for the levered firm is equal to the after-tax income $\text{EBIT}(1 - T_c)$ of the unlevered firm plus the tax savings iBT_c due to the deduction of interest payments on taxable income. The net increase in the income that the firm can distribute to its securityholders if it borrows is iBT_c.

Modigliani and Miller proposed that borrowing increases the value of the firm by an amount equal to the present value of the tax-saving stream iBT_c:

$$\text{Present Value of Taxes Saved} = \frac{iBT_c}{(1 + i)} + \frac{iBT_c}{(1 + i)^2} + \cdots + \frac{iBT_c}{(1 + i)^n} \quad (21.1)$$

Note that MM assumed (at least initially) that the investors' required rate of return is the same for both debt and equity because they assumed that the firm's earnings are risk-free and that investors pay no personal taxes: thus the interest rate i is the discount rate used to obtain the present value of taxes saved. If we assume that the debt is perpetual, the tax savings also are a perpetuity (see Chapter 3 if you have forgotten how to value a perpetuity), and equation (21.1) simplifies to:

$$\text{Present Value of Taxes Saved} = \frac{iBT_c}{i} = BT_c \quad (21.2)$$

If the life of the debt is finite, however, the tax benefit would have to be calculated each year and discounted to a value that would be less than for a perpetuity, as we show in Chapter 22.

If the all-equity financed company in our example of Table 21.2 had assets with a market value of $100, and it decided to substitute perpetual debt for half the equity, what would be the increase in the value of the firm? Using equation (21.2), we find that with a corporate tax rate of 46 percent, the increase in value would be $0.46 \times \$50 = \$23$. Thus, the firm's value would increase 23 percent from $100 to $123.

On the basis of the previous analysis, we can conclude that the value of any firm (or asset) that is partially debt-financed is simply the value of the firm as though it were all-equity financed plus the present value of the tax advantages of the debt.

One implication of the tax advantage described above is that the value of the firm increases as the proportion of debt financing in the company's capital structure is increased. As a consequence, management would be encouraged to increase debt to, say, 99.9 percent of the firm's capital structure, according to MM. Although no management would care to take this course of action because of its risk and the consequent costs of bankruptcy, it also is a fact that lenders would not permit such high levels of leverage.

At least two conditions must exist for there to be tax advantages to corporate borrowing. The first is, of course, that interest charges must be tax-deductible. The second condition is that the tax-deductibility of interest rates must not have the effect of increasing total corporate borrowing and market rates of interest.

Miller's Model: Debt and Both Corporate and Personal Taxes

In the preceding analysis, we implied that the government's tax subsidy on interest payments to corporate borrowers would encourage a corporation to borrow as much as possible. More recently, Merton Miller (1977) has argued that any tax subsidy on interest payments would lead to greater borrowing by corporations and result in an increase in the interest rates that must be paid by them. Interest rates would increase, he argued, to the level where the after-tax cost of debt to companies would be equal to the cost of equity. As a result, in effect there would be no tax benefit to corporate borrowing, and the tax subsidy on debt would accrue to lenders rather than to borrowers.

Miller assumed a world of certainty in which initially interest is not tax-deductible; that there are only two groups of investors, those that are tax-exempt (e.g., pension funds, and some individuals), and those that pay taxes; and that there are only two kinds of securities, common stocks and bonds. Taxable investors could avoid paying taxes on common stock dividends, but they could not avoid paying taxes on bond interest income. In such a world, taxable investors will prefer to hold common stocks and tax-exempt investors will hold the bonds. Thus no taxes would be paid by either class of investor (capital gains taxes are assumed to be negligible). The cost of debt could not be less than the cost of equity, otherwise tax-exempt bondholders would begin buying stocks instead.

Miller then asked how the situation would change in his world if the government were to introduce a tax subsidy on debt by making interest charges tax-deductible to a corporation. His answer was that companies then would find that debt is cheaper than equity, and, as a consequence, they would borrow more. However, in order to borrow more they must find investors who are willing to lend. The resources of tax-exempt investors are limited, and companies would find that they needed to attract into the bond market taxable investors who were previously holding only common stock. A taxable investor will not sell his common stock and lend unless the interest rate that he receives compensates him for the taxes that he would pay on the bond income; otherwise he would prefer to continue holding only common stock. Companies would continue to borrow until the after-tax interest rate on debt equals the cost of equity.

Let us examine Miller's analysis more closely. In a world of certainty, both debt and equity are risk-free. Any differences between the costs of debt and equity in a perfect market could be due only to differences in tax treatment. From the standpoint of the taxable investor, the minimum acceptable (demand) rate of interest (r_d) from corporate bonds would have to equal the tax-free rate of return the investor could enjoy on stocks. That is,

$$\text{Interest Rate After-Tax} = \frac{\text{Rate of Return on}}{\text{Riskless Common Stocks}}$$

$$r_d (1 - T_{pb}) = r_0$$

where T_{pb} represents the stockholders' rate of personal tax on marginal income from bonds and r_0 is the tax-free rate of return on (risk-free) equity. That is, the minimum acceptable pre-tax rate of interest to the marginal purchaser of bonds who pays tax on bond income at the rate T_{pb} is

$$r_d = \frac{r_0}{(1 - T_{pb})}$$

As demand for corporate borrowing rises, the interest rate offered by corporate borrowers will have to increase because the borrower will have to attract lenders with higher marginal personal tax rates T_{pb} who previously were holding common stock.

If $r_0 = 10$ percent, and the marginal investor's tax rate is 30 percent, the resulting (demand) rate of interest r_d will be

$$r_d = \frac{0.10}{1 - 0.30} = 0.1429$$

or 14.29 percent. To induce such an investor to hold bonds requires an interest rate of 14.29 percent to provide the after-tax return of 10 percent that is equal to the rate already enjoyed on holdings of common stock.

What is the maximum (supply) rate of interest r_s that the corporation would be willing to pay on bonds supplied to the market if the corporate tax rate is T_c? Corporations will continue to issue debt until the after-tax interest rate is equal to the cost of equity:

$$r_s (1 - T_c) = r_0$$

Rearranging the equation to solve for the maximum supply rate of interest, we obtain:

$$r_s = \frac{r_0}{(1 - T_c)}$$

If the interest rate paid on debt were higher than r_s, it would be cheaper after tax for a company to issue equity. If we assume that the tax rate is 46 percent, the maximum rate of interest that corporations will be willing to pay is

$$r_s = \frac{0.10}{(1 - 0.46)}$$

$$= 0.1852$$

or 18.52 percent. As corporations are willing to pay as much as 18.52 percent and can sell bonds at interest rates as low as 14.29 percent, corporations will go on issuing debt to progressively higher-rate taxpayers until the marginal investor is paying a personal tax rate equal to the corporate tax rate. Thus equilibrium is not reached until the before-tax interest rate i equals:

$$i = r_d = r_s = \frac{r_0}{(1 - T_{pb})} = \frac{r_0}{(1 - T_c)}$$

This equation implies that corporations will continue issuing bonds until $T_{pb} = T_c$; that is, until both marginal borrowers and marginal lenders are in the same tax brackets, and the market interest rate is 18.52 percent. As the federal corporate tax rate is the same for most corporations (currently 46 percent), Miller expects the interest rate to reflect this tax rate.

This process is presented graphically in Figure 21.1. This total dollar amount of bonds that will be issued will be B^*. At this point the demand rate of interest r_d for bonds held by taxable investors will be equal to the supply rate of interest r_s paid by corporations. If the actual amount of bonds issued is less than B^*, corporations will have an incentive to issue more bonds because they will be paying an interest rate less than $r_0/(1 - T_c)$.

The implications of Miller's argument are very important. First, the value of the taxpaying corporation is independent of its capital structure when interest payments are tax-deductible, for the after-tax cost of debt equals the cost of equity. You might well ask who reaps the reward from the government's tax subsidy on interest payments? The answer is that lenders who pay marginal tax rates below the corporate tax rate benefit considerably, and in fact, tax-exempt lenders gain the most. In our example they were willing to lend at 10 percent (r_0) before the tax subsidy was introduced, and yet they earn 18.52 percent after the introduction of the tax subsidy.

A second implication of Miller's argument is that, although the firm is indifferent to financing with debt or equity, there is an optimal debt-to-

Figure 21.1   *Demand and supply of debt in Miller's world*

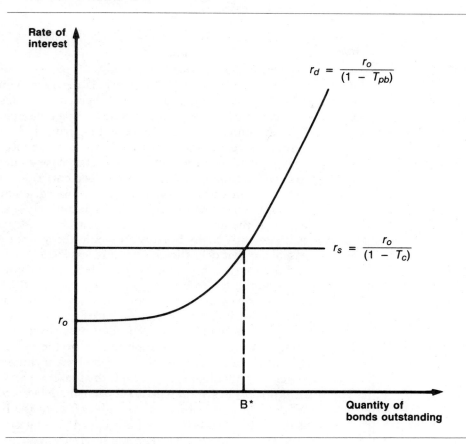

equity ratio for the economy. In fact, the higher the corporate tax rate, the more bonds will be issued. The optimal quantity B^* of bonds issued is reached when both borrowers and marginal lenders are paying the same marginal tax rates.

We have discussed Miller's proposition that the taxable corporation should be indifferent between debt and equity financing. If the corporation is tax-exempt, on the other hand, or temporarily is nontaxpaying because of past tax losses or tax credits associated with a large investment program, it should not borrow. After all, if the cost of debt equals the cost of equity after taxes, then debt must be more expensive than equity before taxes. A simple example will demonstrate this.

Suppose that before the tax subsidy is introduced the cost of debt is equal to the cost of equity: $i = r_0 = 10$ percent, say. If, subsequently, interest becomes tax-deductible, and the corporate tax rate is 46 percent, interest rates will rise to 18.52 percent. If the taxpaying corporation borrows, the after-tax cost of debt is

$$0.1852 \times (1 - 0.46) = 0.10$$

or 10 percent. As the cost of equity is also 10 percent, the after-tax cost of debt equals the cost of equity. However, if the firm is not taxpaying, the cost of debt is the before-tax rate of 18.52 percent, because the corporation will not be able to obtain the tax deduction. As a consequence, debt is more expensive than equity for the nontaxpaying firm, and such a firm should avoid borrowing. Even if the firm is only temporarily nontaxpaying, it would prefer not to borrow, for the after-tax cost of debt will be greater than 10 percent (although less than 18.52 percent) since tax deductions for interest payments must be delayed and, therefore, discounted.

You can appreciate Miller's argument intuitively by supposing what would happen if the government were to withdraw the current tax subsidy on interest payments. Many borrowers would recognize that the cost of debt had increased and that debt thereby became less attractive. As a consequence, they would reduce their borrowing. If the demand for borrowing decreased, interest rates would fall toward the cost of equity. If this logic is correct, it is also reasonable to suppose that interest rates are higher as a result of the tax-deductibility of interest payments.

While Miller has made some important assumptions in his model, you should find his main argument appealing: that the tax subsidy on interest payments should be at least partially capitalized in higher interest rates to the borrower, and that lenders will capture at least a part of the tax subsidy. The truth probably lies somewhere between the MM world and the Miller world. While there might be some tax advantage to the firm from borrowing, it also may be very much smaller than MM suggested.[2]

Interaction of Corporate and Personal Taxes: A General Formula

In the MM model of debt and taxes and in Miller's model, various assumptions were made about the corporate tax rate and the personal tax rates on bonds and common stock. Miller (1977) has provided a very useful expression that enables us to capture entirely the effect of personal and corporate

---

[2]Some empirical work by Skelton (1982) has examined Miller's proposition in relation to tax-exempt and taxable bonds bought and sold by banks. Results show that when banks were permitted to pay the market interest rate, the marginal tax rate implied in the interest rate on taxable bonds was 46 percent, which is what Miller's model would predict.

taxes on the value of the firm. The expression, given below, is derived in Appendix 21.2. It assumes that interest is tax-deductible.

$$L = B \left(1 - \frac{(1 - T_c)(1 - T_{ps})}{(1 - T_{pb})} \right)$$

where L = the gains from leverage

            B = amount borrowed

            T_c = corporate tax rate

            T_{ps} = personal tax rate on common stock income

            T_{pb} = personal tax rate on bond income

This equation embraces both the Modigliani and Miller model and the Miller model. For example, Modigliani and Miller assumed effectively that $T_{ps} = T_{pb}$. Substituting into the equation for L above we obtain

$$L = BT_c$$

which is the Modigliani and Miller result that the value of the firm increases with leverage at a rate equal to the amount of borrowing multiplied by the corporate tax rate.

In contrast, Miller assumed that shareholders can avoid taxes on share income so that $T_{ps} = 0$. Also, in equilibrium the tax rate that is paid by the marginal debtholder equals the corporate tax rate, that is $T_{pb} = T_c$. Substituting into the equation for L we obtain

$$L = B \left(1 - \frac{(1 - T_c)(1 - 0)}{(1 - T_c)} \right)$$

$$= 0$$

which is the Miller result, that the effect of leverage on the value of the firm is zero.

In Appendix 21.3 we examine how debt financing can affect the weighted average cost of capital of the firm assuming a Miller or a Modigliani and Miller world of debt and taxes.

Risky Debt and the Value of the Firm

The preceding analysis has totally ignored risk and the fact that, as the individual firm borrows more, at some point lenders may charge a higher interest rate. Superficially, this observation would seem to invalidate MM's proposition. In MM's world you might expect that higher interest charges (because of greater default risk) would increase the cost of debt compared with the cost of equity. However, the fact that debt is risky and that firms must pay higher interest rates on such risky debt compared with riskless debt would not invalidate MM's proposition, providing that there were no costs associated with default or financial distress. A formal proof that MM's propositions still hold is given in Appendix 21.4, but we shall provide a more intuitive argument here.

It is helpful to think of the price of a risky bond as consisting of two components:

Price of Risky Debt = Price of Riskless Debt − Discount for Risk

A firm that sells a bond receives the price of a riskless bond less a discount. The discount reduces the price that the borrower can obtain for the bond and forces the borrower to pay a higher effective interest rate on the amount borrowed.

The important point to understand is that, although limited liability borrowers such as corporations pay more interest on risky debt, they receive in exchange the benefit of being able to default on the loan if it should turn out to be in their interest to do so. Lenders, on the other hand, charge more interest, but accept a greater probability of loss through default if the borrower increases the debt in the firm's capital structure. As long as the increased probability of default is paid for by higher interest rates, neither party to the company's loans expects to lose or to gain on average from the transaction. Because selling risky debt is a zero–sum game for the borrower and the lender, the value of the firm remains unchanged. The existence of the possibility of default, as Appendix 21.4 proves, does not by itself invalidate MM's proposition that borrowing leaves the value of the firm unchanged in a tax-free world.

You may have noted that up to this point we have made two important assumptions: first, that the risk of the assets of the firm as a whole does not change as its debt ratio is altered; and second, that corporate borrowing requires merely a simple debt contract specifying only a promise to pay interest and principal. Although the risk of default by itself does not affect the value of the firm's underlying assets, it can give rise to various costs that lead in turn to a more complicated relationship between equityholders and debtholders. That is, without the existence of default-related costs, there is no inherent conflict between equityholders and debtholders, so that maximizing the value of the firm is equivalent to maximizing the value of the equity. As we shall see, however, existence of a conflict of interest between equityholders and debtholders complicates the question of what constitutes an optimum capital structure.

We have made a third assumption, that is the tax system is symmetrical.

The implication is that when firms make taxable profits, taxes are paid, but when the firm makes taxable losses, the IRS provides a tax rebate (or those tax losses can be sold to other companies). Talmor, Haugen, and Barnea (forthcoming) and DeAngelo and Masulis (1980) examine the implications for capital structure when taxable profits are uncertain and the tax system is asymmetrical. The main conclusion is that there may be an optimal capital structure in both an MM and Miller worlds.

COSTS OF LIQUIDATING THE FIRM'S ASSETS

The risk of default may impose real costs on the firm. For example, if the firm defaults, the lenders may have to sell the firm's assets to raise the cash that is owed to them. Liquidating assets costs money, including the costs of advertising, selling, and lawyers' and accountants' fees. When figuring a rate of interest, the lender will estimate what such costs might be, together with the probability that they will occur, and then incorporate the expected value of the costs into the interest rate charged.

For example, suppose a bank estimates that the cost of liquidating the firm would be 10 percent of the value of the assets. At the time the loan is negotiated, the probability of default is estimated to be 5 percent. The expected costs of default would be

$$0.05 \times 0.10 = 0.005$$

or only one-half of one percent of the value of the assets. In a study of the liquidation of eleven United States railroads, Warner (1977) found that the expected costs of default were less than one percent of the value of the assets as measured seven years before the bankruptcy petition was filed.

If the only additional costs associated with risky debt were the expected liquidation costs of the assets, the problem would seem small, if not trivial. However, there are other costs that lenders incur, which must be paid for by the borrower in the form of higher interest rates. Lenders are fearful not only of the possible deterioration of a business that might lead to default, but also of **moral hazard,** the possibility that the borrower might not abide by the terms of the loan contract.

THREE EXAMPLES OF MORAL HAZARD

We shall discuss three examples of moral hazards. First, the owners or managers of a company might change the risk of the business without informing the lender. For example, let us assume that the firm has only two investments each costing $10,000 and having the same systematic risk.

Outcome	Probability	Payoff	
		Project 1	Project 2
1	0.5	$11,000	$ 4,000
2	0.5	$13,000	$20,000

The firm reveals the first project to its bank and requests a loan for $10,000. The project appears riskless, because the payoffs in all possible outcomes exceed the initial loan. As a consequence, the bank agrees to charge a very low rate of interest that reflects a zero risk of default. After taking out the loan, the firm substitutes project 2 for project 1. The two projects have equal profitability (and the same systematic risk), but the risk to the bank has increased dramatically. In the event that project 2 pays off only $4,000, the bank will have lost the greater proportion of its investment.

To prevent such hazards the bank will try to protect itself by including in the loan agreement covenants of the kind we discussed in Chapter 16, which prevent the firm from altering the risk of its assets. However, the bank will still have to bear the costs of monitoring the firm in order to ensure that the covenants are honored. Because the bank cannot monitor all the firm's actions instantly, the bank will charge a higher rate of interest to compensate both for the monitoring costs and for the possibility that the firm still might be able to increase the risk of its assets without the knowledge of the bank.

A second moral hazard problem can arise if the firm gets into financial distress and then refuses to invest in profitable projects unless the bank agrees to renegotiate the loan. This problem is especially serious when the resale or secondhand values of the firm's assets are much lower than their value in existing uses. Let us examine an example.

A company has defaulted on payments on a $10,000 bank loan, and the bank must decide whether to liquidate the company. Because of a commercial setback, the company's expected future cash flows have been reduced, and the total present value of its assets has fallen from $15,000 to only $7,000 ($5,000 in plant and machinery and $2,000 in cash).

As the company's liabilities exceed its assets, the managers, who we will assume are also the stockholders, have little incentive to keep the company going. Their stock is worthless. If the bank liquidates the company, however, the plant and machinery will realize only $3,000 in the secondhand market, while it is worth $5,000 in its present use if the company is kept going. Also, if the company is not liquidated, it has an opportunity to invest its $2,000 cash in a project that has an additional present value of $3,000. Thus, if management can be persuaded to keep the company going, the present value of the company's assets will rise to $10,000 (consisting of $5,000 for the existing plant and equipment plus the new capital project worth $5,000). At that time the total present value of the company would equal the $10,000 liability of the loan, so the company would have the potential to repay the loan in full eventually. Consequently, the bank would like to keep the company in operation.

The managers, on the other hand, may have little incentive to invest in the project because the present value of the company's assets still would not exceed the liability of the loan, and their common stock in the company would have little if any value. As the bank's interest in the company is greater than that of the stockholders, the management might try to force the bank to restructure the company's balance sheet in favor of the stockholders. By reducing the value of the loan, the bank might be forced to transfer sufficient value to the equity stockholders to provide an incentive for them to keep the company going and invest in the new project, so that eventually the (reduced) loan can be repaid.

This example shows why banks often are willing to lend up to some proportion of the depreciated book value of the assets rather than to lend a proportion of the present value of the cash flows that the assets might generate. The depreciated cost of the assets may approximate their resale value more closely if the business has to be liquidated. If a bank lends more money than can be justified on the basis of the depreciated cost of the assets, it may demand a premium in the interest rate for moral hazard.

The example also demonstrates another point hinted at in many places throughout this book: that the NPV of a project to the firm as a whole may be different from the NPV of a project to the stockholders. Thus, maximizing the value of the firm may not lead to the same result as maximizing the value of the common stock.

A third moral hazard problem may arise when the firm is actually in financial distress. The management may conceal its financial problems in order to prevent the firm from being liquidated. Management may even continue with unprofitable projects or invest in additional ones with negative net present values, just to postpone default; after all, "something might turn up."

Although these moral hazard problems seem formidable, the costs should not be exaggerated. The managers of modern corporations usually are not the owners, and as a result, they have less incentive to deceive lenders. Also, managers have obligations to *all* the holders of financial claims on the corporation's assets. Each set of holders of securities has a contract with the corporation, and it is management's task to ensure the contracts are kept. Thus, management may not try to fool lenders, because this would put them in breach of the corporation's contract. Indeed, if lenders feel cheated, they might refuse to deal with the managers again. Managers may deceive a bank once, but after that they may not get a second chance.

COSTS INCURRED BY THE BORROWER AS A RESULT
OF FINANCIAL DISTRESS

So far, we have analyzed the cost of financial distress to the lenders. Borrowers also incur costs. For example, when a firm is having cash flow problems, a great deal of management time is spent talking to creditors, providing them with information, and monitoring the business. As a result, less time can be spent searching for new investment opportunities. Profitable investments even might be postponed if the financial risks to the firm were increased to an unacceptable level as a result of such investments.

A second cost to the firm can be customer fear that a default will make product guarantees worthless and increase the cost of spare parts. For example, Chrysler may have had to charge lower prices on its cars in 1980–1981 because of its well-known financial problems. The prices may have been lower than otherwise would have been possible to compensate customers for the risk that their service warranties could prove difficult to enforce and spare parts for the cars would be difficult or costly to obtain in the event the firm had to go into liquidation.

Finally, the income of most managers depends mainly on their jobs. Default and the resulting reorganization or liquidation of a firm not only may deprive some managers of their jobs (albeit temporarily) but also could cast doubt upon their abilities. It is often difficult to tell whether a firm has defaulted because of bad luck or because of bad management. Thus, the loss of a job as a result of default represents a risk to their employment that most managers would take pains to avoid.

Motives for Borrowing

If you are interested in business history, you may be puzzled by the fact that there was plenty of individual and corporate borrowing prior to the introduction of the tax-deductibility of interest charges. Would companies continue to borrow if the government withdrew the tax advantages to both corporate and personal borrowing? The answer is clearly yes. There are three reasons for borrowing in a world without tax benefits. The first and most obvious reason relates to transactions costs. It usually is cheaper to raise debt finance than to float an equity issue through the financial markets. Flotation costs for the issue of securities are especially high when the proposed investment is of a short duration. For example, British Petroleum financed a large part of a North Sea oil field investment with debt finance partly because the capital cost was expected to be repaid from the production and sale of the oil within three years. It would have been expensive if not impossible for British Petroleum to return the capital to shareholders only two or three years after floating a large equity issue.

A second reason why companies would borrow without tax advantages is related primarily to small businesses. If the owner has limited capital and wishes to expand, debt finance may be the only available source of finance that would enable the owner to expand without losing a controlling interest.

A third reason for using debt is when management believes that the net present value of an investment has not been reflected or fully reflected in the price of the corporation's common stock and other securities. For example, suppose a company wished to finance an investment costing $1 million, which is expected to produce a net present value of $0.5 millions. If the market price of the company's common stock does not reflect the net present value of the investment, then it may be better for the company if debt is issued rather than equity to finance the investment program. The equity is far more underpriced than the new debt.

Why might the market price of the common stock not reflect an investment's expected net present value? It is possible that management may not wish to make public information about the product that is generating the large positive net present values. Alternatively, the market may not believe the company's management. This problem frequently arises with new businesses that do not have much of a track record and are raising money for the first time. Under these conditions the company may have to employ more debt and less equity than they would otherwise wish.

In a world without taxes, lending transactions would still take place because of low transactions costs and because of differences in information, expectations, and risk preferences among borrowers and lenders.

Optimal Capital Structure

How do we operationalize the concept of an optimal capital structure in the presence of the costs just described? Because bondholders and equityholders do not have identical interests, it is not sufficient to say that managers simply trade off tax advantages and expected costs of financial distress so as to maximize the value of the firm (i.e., the value of the sum of debt and equity). After all, managers may consider themselves agents of the owners, not the creditors. Nonetheless, if the interests of creditors are protected sufficiently by the existence of loan covenants, management can seek debt levels, through time, that take maximum advantage of the tax benefits of borrowing, subject to staying within tolerable levels of risk, and can maximize the value of equity without impairing the value of the debt.

In Chapter 22 we will discuss ways in which the capital structure decision problem phrased in this fashion can be answered more analytically. At this point, we would note that it is difficult to find models that can determine, in an analytical way, the firm's optimum capital structure, but these things we do know about its characteristics:

1. The costs of distress that we have mentioned do explain, in part at least, why it is both in the lender's and the borrower's interests not to employ an excessive amount of debt financing even if there is some tax advantage to debt. As the firm increases the proportion of debt in its capital structure, any tax advantages accruing to debt gradually are offset by higher interest rates, which in part reflect greater monitoring costs by banks and higher expected costs of financial distress. The fact that at some point the incremental tax benefits would be offset entirely by these additional costs may explain the existence of an optimal capital structure for the firm.

2. You also can see why the optimal capital structure may differ from one company to another. If there are differences in the costs of monitoring, the resulting costs will vary across firms. When there is an active secondhand market for particular assets, the lender has an easier job calculating the value of a firm's assets to determine its borrowing capacity. Lower monitoring and moral hazard costs permit higher debt ratios for some companies. This concept of a liquid market in assets may be very important to determining a firm's debt capacity.

3. While we have been able to identify a number of advantages to debt finance, we also have shown that there are costs associated with too much debt. In fact, most companies try to maintain their borrowing at a relatively modest level that bears a stable relationship to total capitalization. Company treasurers and their bankers frequently use the average debt-to-equity ratio for the industry as a guideline, altering it according to the unique factors affecting the borrowing costs of the individual firm.

Summary

In the first part of this chapter we described a very simple concept in finance: that in a perfect capital market the value of an asset could not be altered by changing the way it is financed. In such a world without taxes capital structure is irrelevant to the value of the corporation. Similarly, one may say that capital structure cannot alter the corporation's cost of capital. This view of capital structure is often associated with Modigliani and Miller. In the presence of taxes, however, the picture can change. MM argued that the tax-deductibility of interest provided borrowing with important tax advantages, which made it less costly than equity finance. This argument requires that the level of interest rates is unaffected by the introduction of the tax subsidy on debt. Miller argued that the tax subsidy would lead to greater borrowing and, as a result, interest rates would rise until corporations became indifferent between equity and debt finance. The tax subsidy, instead of going to borrowers, would accrue to lenders.

Which model of debt and taxes you accept is quite important. In Miller's model the value of an asset (to a taxpaying company, at least) is unaffected by the way it is financed. In MM's model an asset may be unprofitable on the basis of its operating cash flows, but it can be made profitable if it is financed with debt. The empirical evidence is not sufficient to decide which view is correct. Our view inclines more toward Miller's view. We feel (intuitively if not intellectually) that, as debt finance is not a scarce resource, it is not likely to add positive net present value to an asset. As a consequence, new projects must justify their acceptance on the basis of their operating cash flows rather than by the way they are financed.

Neither Modigliani and Miller nor Miller alone could find any rationale for an optimal capital structure. MM suggest that the firm should use as much debt as possible, while Miller suggests that the firm would be no worse off if it used no debt at all. We have mentioned here some nontax reasons for using debt financing, suggesting some reasons why the firm might wish to limit the amount of debt financing that it uses and why the limit may vary from one firm to another.

Appendix 21.1 *Proof that the Value of the Firm Does Not Alter with Changes in the Debt-to-Equity Ratio If There Are No Taxes*

Modigliani and Miller's arbitrage proof that debt does not change the value of the firm in a world without taxes was contained in a reply to Heins and Sprenkle (Modigliani and Miller, 1969). We will outline the proof using the following notation:

S = value of equity

B = value of debt

$V_U = S_U$ value of the unlevered firm

$V_L = S_L + B_L$ value of the levered firm

X = stream of operating earnings generated by each firm

a = fraction of the firm owned

i = interest rate

Let us assume that the individual holds a fraction a of the shares in the unlevered firm. He obtains a return aX for a total investment of aS_U, and, in the case of the unlevered firm,

$$aS_U = aV_U$$

An identical return of aX also can be obtained for a total investment of aV_L in the levered firm by the following means:

	Investment required	Returns produced
Buy a fraction *a* of the shares in the unlevered firm	$aS_U = aV_U$	aX
Or		
Buy a fraction *a* of the shares in the levered firm, and	$aS_L = a(V_L - B_L)$	$a(X - iB_L)$
Buy a fraction *a* of the bonds in the levered firm	aB_L	aiB_L
Total for levered firm	aV_L	aX

Therefore, if $V_L > V_U$, the investor would not wish to invest aV_L in the levered firm, for that would yield only the same return aX as investing aV_U in the unlevered firm, which is a smaller investment by the amount $a(V_L - V_U)$.

Similar arbitrage arguments hold true for $V_U > V_L$.

Appendix 21.2 Interaction Between Corporate and Personal Taxes and the Effect of Debt on the Value of the Firm

We can derive a general expression for the net present value attributable to debt financing when interest payments are tax-deductible by corporations and when investors pay different rates of personal taxes on bond and share income.

The value of the firm is equal to the present value of the after-tax income to all the firm's securityholders. We shall assume that securityholders receive income only from equity shares (stock) and from bonds (debt). The after-tax income to shareholders in the levered firm is given by

$$(\text{EBIT} - iB)(1 - T_c)(1 - T_{ps}) \tag{A21.2.1}$$

where   EBIT = earnings before interest and taxes

i = interest rate on borrowing

B = amount borrowed

T_c = corporate tax rate

T_{ps} = personal tax rate on share income

The after-tax income to bondholders is given by

$$iB(1 - T_{pb}) \tag{A21.2.2}$$

where T_{pb} is the personal tax rate on bond income.

If the firm is all-equity financed (unlevered), the after-tax income to securityholders (only stockholders) is

$$\text{EBIT} \, (1 - T_c)(1 - T_{ps}) \tag{A21.2.3}$$

The net incremental after-tax income to all securityholders due to debt financing must be given by the sum of equations (A21.2.1) and (A21.2.2) minus equation (A21.2.3). Thus the net incremental after-tax income to securityholders that would be due to debt financing is given by

$$iB(1 - T_{pb}) - iB(1 - T_c)(1 - T_{ps})$$

The effect of debt financing on the value of the firm would equal the present value of the net incremental income due to the debt financing. If we assume perpetual debt, this additional income is a perpetuity. We obtain the present value of the perpetuity simply by dividing this additional income by the discount rate $i(1 - T_{pb})$. Thus, the net present value L due to debt financing is given by

$$L = \frac{iB(1 - T_{pb}) - iB(1 - T_c)(1 - T_{ps})}{i(1 - T_{pb})}$$

That is,

$$L = B \left(1 - \frac{(1 - T_c)(1 - T_{ps})}{(1 - T_{pb})} \right)$$

This is the general expression (given originally by Miller (1977)) for the combined effect of corporate and personal taxes on the value of the firm when debt is tax-deductible.

Appendix 21.3 WACC Using MM's and Miller's Models

In the chapter we have examined how the value of the firm may be altered by using debt financing as a substitute for common stock. Now we wish to examine how debt financing alters the firm's cost of capital. To keep matters simple, we shall analyze how the firm's weighted average cost of capital is affected by different models of debt and taxes. In the next chapter we describe alternative ways of incorporating debt financing into a company's (or project's) cost of capital.

The formula for the weighted average cost of capital is

$$\text{WACC} = i(1 - T_c) \frac{B}{B + E} + R_L \frac{E}{B + E}$$

where $B/(B + E)$ is the market value proportion of debt in the capital structure, $E/(B + E)$ is the proportion of equity, and R_L is the levered cost of equity capital.

WACC IN AN MM WORLD OF DEBT AND TAXES

Modigliani and Miller assumed that the before-tax cost of debt is equal to the cost of (risk-free) equity in a world of certainty and perfect capital markets:

$$i = r_0$$

The formula for the weighted average cost of capital under certainty thus becomes

$$\text{WACC} = r_0 (1 - T_c) \frac{B}{B + E} + r_0 \frac{E}{B + E}$$

By multiplying and rearranging terms MM obtain:[3]

$$\text{WACC} = r_0 \left(1 - T_c \frac{B}{B + E}\right)$$

---

[3]$\text{WACC} = r_0 (1 - T_c) \dfrac{B}{B + E} + r_0 \dfrac{E}{B + E}$

$\qquad = r_0 \dfrac{B}{B + E} + r_0 \dfrac{E}{B + E} - r_0 T_c \dfrac{B}{B + E}$

The term in the equation containing the proportion of debt $B/(B + E)$ is subtracted; therefore, as the proportion of debt in the capital structure is increased, the WACC declines. In our earlier example, the before-tax cost of debt and of (riskless) equity were both equal to 10 percent. With the preceding formula we can use the Modigliani and Miller model to obtain the WACC under certainty. If the firm is 50 percent financed by debt,

$$WACC = 0.10 \ (1 - 0.46 \times 0.50)$$

$$= 0.077$$

The weighted average cost of capital declines as the proportion of debt is increased because Modigliani and Miller assumed that the before-tax market interest rate on debt is unaffected by the tax subsidy on interest payments.

WACC IN MILLER'S WORLD OF DEBT AND TAXES

In Miller's world we encounter a very different picture, because Miller proposes that the before-tax cost of debt is forced up until the after-tax cost of debt equals the cost of equity. In a risk-free world we have

$$i(1 - T_c) = r_0$$

The weighted average cost of capital formula is,

$$WACC = i(1 - T_c) \ \frac{B}{B + E} + R_L \ \frac{E}{B + E}$$

In our example $i = 18.52$ percent for Miller compared with 10 percent for MM. Thus,

$$WACC = 0.1852 \ (1 - 0.46)(0.5) + 0.10(0.5)$$

$$= 0.10$$

We could have substituted r_0 for $i(1 - T_c)$ and have obtained the same answer of 10 percent.

In Miller's world the weighted average cost of capital equals the unlevered

---

Since $\dfrac{B}{B + E} + \dfrac{E}{B + E} = 1,$

then $WACC = r_0 \left[1 - T_c \dfrac{B}{B + E} \right]$

cost of equity. Thus, the rate at which the firm's income is capitalized is unchanged by increases in the proportion of debt in the capital structure, leaving the value of the firm unaffected. For this reason, companies in Miller's world are indifferent to the amount of debt financing that they use.

The weighted average cost of capital given by Miller's model in our example is 10 percent compared with only 7.7 percent according to the Modigliani and Miller model. If we had assumed a larger proportion of debt financing than 50 percent, the WACC would have been even less than 7.7 percent using the Modigliani and Miller assumptions. Obviously, it makes a great deal of difference which view one takes, Modigliani and Miller or the later Miller view. The contrasting implications of the two viewpoints are explored more fully in the next two chapters.

Appendix 21.4 Proof of MM's Proposition with Risky Debt (After-Tax)

This proof is an expanded version of that contained in Rubinstein (1973). An important assumption is that the tax system is symmetrical with regard to the IRS's treatment of taxable profits and losses. We shall show that Modigliani and Miller's proposition concerning debt and taxes is unaltered by risky debt: that the value V_L of a levered firm is given by

$$V_L = V_U + T_c B_L \qquad (A21.4.1)$$

if its value without debt is equal to V_U and it has risky debt in the amount B_L while paying tax at the rate T_c.

Proof

We shall derive Equation (A21.4.1) by obtaining an expression for the expected after-tax operating income $E(X)(1 - T_c)$ for the unlevered firm and setting it equal to the corresponding expression for the after-tax operating income of the same firm when it is levered.

UNLEVERED FIRM (*U*)

The expected return $E(\tilde{R}_U)$ on the unlevered firm with uncertain operating income $\tilde{X}$ is given by

$$E(\tilde{R}_U) = \frac{E(\tilde{X})(1 - T_c)}{V_U} \qquad (A21.4.2)$$

where the returns $\tilde{R}_U$ and the operating income $\tilde{X}$ are random variables. This expected return can be related by the capital asset pricing model to the risk-free rate of return R_f and to the covariance between R_U and the market rate of return $\tilde{R}_m$ as

$$E(\tilde{R}_U) = R_f + \lambda \ \text{Cov}(\tilde{R}_U, \tilde{R}_m) \qquad (A21.4.3)$$

where λ is the market price of risk. However, $\text{Cov}(\tilde{R}_U, \tilde{R}_m)$ can be put into terms of X by using equation (A21.4.2):

$$\text{Cov}(\tilde{R}_U, \tilde{R}_m) = (1 - T_c)\text{Cov}(\tilde{X}, \tilde{R}_m)/V_U \qquad (A21.4.4)$$

Equating equations (A21.4.2) and (A21.4.3), substituting equation (A21.4.4) for the covariance and multiplying through by V_U, we obtain an expression for the after-tax operating income for the unlevered firm:

$$E(\tilde{X})(1 - T_c) = R_f V_U + \lambda(1 - T_c)\text{Cov}(\tilde{X}, \tilde{R}_m) \qquad (A21.4.5)$$

We shall now obtain the corresponding expression for the same firm when it has risky debt.

LEVERED FIRM (*L*)

Suppose now that the firm has risky debt in the amount B_L on which it pays interest at the rate $\tilde{R}_{fL}$. The expected return $E(\tilde{R}_L)$ on the equity S_L for the firm when it is levered is given by

$$E(\tilde{R}_L) = \frac{[E(\tilde{X}) - E(\tilde{R}_{fL})B_L](1 - T_c)}{S_L} \qquad (A21.4.6)$$

The expected return is still related (using the capital asset pricing model) to the risk-free rate R_f and to the covariance between $\tilde{R}_L$ and the market rate of return $\tilde{R}_m$ as:

$$E(\tilde{R}_L) = R_f + \lambda \ \text{Cov}(\tilde{R}_L, \tilde{R}_m) \qquad (A21.4.7)$$

Combining equations (A21.4.6) and (A21.4.7) and multiplying through by S_L, we obtain an expression for the after-tax operating income for the levered firm L:

$$E(\tilde{X})(1 - T_c) = R_f S_L + E(\tilde{R}_{fL})B_L(1 - T_c) + \lambda \, \text{Cov}(\tilde{R}_L, \tilde{R}_m)S_L \quad \text{(A21.4.8)}$$

Equation (21.4.8) can be put into a more useful form if we substitute the following expressions for $\text{Cov}(\tilde{R}_L, \tilde{R}_m)$ and for $E(\tilde{R}_{fL})$. First we note from the definition of $\tilde{R}_L$ implicit in equation (A21.4.6) that

$$\text{Cov}(\tilde{R}_L, \tilde{R}_m) = [(1 - T_c)\text{Cov}(\tilde{X}, \tilde{R}_m) - B_L(1 - T_c)\text{Cov}(\tilde{R}_{fL}, \tilde{R}_m)]/S_L$$
$$\text{(A21.4.9)}$$

Furthermore, the expected interest rate $E(\tilde{R}_{fL})$ on the risky debt is also given in the capital asset pricing model as

$$E(\tilde{R}_{fL}) = R_f + \lambda \, \text{Cov}(\tilde{R}_{fL}, \tilde{R}_m) \quad \text{(A21.4.10)}$$

Substituting equations (A21.4.9) and (A21.4.10) into equation (A21.4.8), we obtain the desired expression for the after-tax operating income for the firm after it has been levered with debt:

$$E(\tilde{X})(1 - T_c) = R_f S_L + R_f B_L (1 - T_c) + \lambda(1 - T_c)\text{Cov}(\tilde{X}, \tilde{R}_m) \quad \text{(A21.4.11)}$$

TAX EFFECT OF LEVERAGE ON THE VALUE OF THE FIRM

We shall now see how the introduction of risky debt has affected the value of the firm. First we note that the expected after-tax *operating* income $E(\tilde{X})$ $(1 - T_c)$ of the firm is unchanged by debt, and thus the right-hand side of equation (A21.4.11) is equal to the right-hand side of equation (A21.4.5):

$$R_f S_L + R_f B_L (1 - T_c) = R_f V_U \quad \text{(A21.4.12)}$$

The same covariance term that appeared on both sides of the resulting equation has dropped out; thus risk is found to be of no effect in equation (A21.4.12). Now we note that the value of the levered firm is the sum of the values of its debt and equity:

$$V_L = B_L + S_L \quad \text{(A21.4.13)}$$

Consequently, by dividing equation (A21.4.12) through by R_f and substituting equation (A21.4.13) for $B_L + S_L$ we obtain the result that

$$V_L = V_U + T_c B_L \quad \text{(A21.4.14)}$$

which is MM's equation for the value of the levered firm after-tax. Thus we have shown that Modigliani and Miller's proposition is unaltered by risky debt.

The crucial assumption in the proof is that the higher interest rates on risky debt (compared with riskless debt) compensate only for the increased covariance risk of interest income to lenders due to possible risks of default or of financial distress. If higher interest rates are due in part to the expected costs of liquidation or agency costs incurred by banks, the value of the firm cannot be described by equation (A21.4.14). In this case, as the firm borrows more and the risks of default increase, separate negative sums would have to be incorporated into the formula such as

$$V_L{}^* = V_U + T_c B_L - \text{Present Value of Expected Costs of Liquidation}$$
$$- \text{Present Value of Expected Monitoring Costs}$$

We also should subtract terms for the costs of financial distress incurred by the firm, including management time spent dealing with creditors and the possible loss of profitable investment opportunities because of financial problems.

Review Questions

1. A company wishes to finance an investment program with debt capital. It is told that earnings per share (EPS) with debt financing are higher than with all equity financing. What qualifications should accompany such an EPS analysis?
2. What are the tax advantages to debt for the company? Is the size of these advantages exactly the same for the individual shareholder? If there were no tax advantages to corporate borrowing, would companies still borrow?
3. Describe in detail the arbitrage conditions that Modigliani and Miller use to prove that the cost of debt is the same as the cost of equity in a world without taxes.
4. How would the size of the tax benefits of debt financing affect a project's value?
5. Is it possible that a project can be unprofitable (have negative net present value) with all equity financing but be profitable with a combination of debt and equity financing? State your assumptions.
6. How does the presence of bankruptcy costs affect the amount of debt a company will wish to undertake? Why do you think these costs may be large or small?
7. Suppose only one investor is taxpaying and that the tax rate is equal to the corporate tax rate. Would you still expect Miller's world of debt and

taxes to prevail? Why might investors in common stocks wish to see such an investor leave the bond market?

8. If a corporation is temporarily nontaxpaying, which is the less costly source of finance, debt or equity? Give reasons for your answer.

Problems

*1. An all-equity financed company with volatile cash flows is contemplating borrowing $10 million at an annual rate of 12 percent or issuing another 5 million shares to expand its activities. Calculate the company's break-even point from a graph of earnings per share on earnings before interest, with and without the proposed debt. The expected operating cash flows range from −$500,000 to $2.5 million. The number of shares already issued is 10 million. Ignore taxes.

2. Geared, Inc., and Ungeared, Inc. are identical companies with identical business risk. Geared, Inc.'s debt has a market value of $175 million and provides a return of 8 percent on market value. It also has 3.5 million ordinary shares at $100 each, market value. Ungeared, Inc., has only 7 million ordinary shares at $84 each and no debt. Miss Petty has inherited a million shares in Ungeared, Inc., and has asked you, her financial adviser, what implications Modigliani and Miller's propositions have on her inheritance. Both companies earn $56 million per year in perpetuity. Assume all retained earnings are distributed.

*3. Stonemasons, Inc., is an all-equity financed company that is contemplating raising some perpetual debt. The corporate tax rate is 46 percent. The total market value of the equity is $15 million at present. What would be the increase in the value of the firm in Modigliani and Miller's world if the firm used the debt to repurchase:
(a) 30 percent of its equity
(b) 50 percent of its equity

4. Explain the differences in the value of the Stonemason firm if the company's three alternatives to raising $10 million debt were:
(a) one-year loan at 10 percent annually
(b) six-year loan at 9 percent annually, with the capital repaid at maturity
(c) perpetual debt at 8 percent annually
Assuming that all taxes are paid at the end of the year, and that the corporate tax rate is 46 percent, which alternative would be most beneficial to Stonemasons in Modigliani and Miller's world?

*5. Gearmore, Inc., is planning to finance a $125 million project next year with 80 percent debt at a cost of 15 percent per year. The project is expected to last five years, after which the debt will be repaid.

(a) Calculate the increase in the value of the firm in Modigliani and Miller's world, if the equity (before-tax) required rate of return is also 15 percent, and:

(i) The company pays taxes

(ii) The company does not pay taxes for the first two years but can carry the tax shelters into the future

The corporate tax rate is 46 percent.

(b) How are your results different in Miller's (1977) world?

6. The equilibrium interest rate in the economy is now 13 percent and the corporate tax rate is 46 percent. What would happen to debt levels and interest rates in Miller's world if the corporate tax rate:

(a) Increases to 60 percent

(b) Decreases to 35 percent

*7. A company uses the weighted average cost of capital as the discount rate for its capital projects. The prevailing corporate tax rate is 50 percent, and the company's WACC is 12 percent; the debt-to-equity ratio is 0.6. Assuming Miller's world holds, what will happen to the company's cost of debt if the corporate tax rate is reduced to 35 percent?

*8. A company that is all-equity financed is considering a project that needs $100 million investment. The finance vice president would like to use debt financing to obtain the tax benefits of interest deductibility. Calculate the NPV of debt financing if the corporate tax rate is 46 percent, and the personal tax rates on dividend income and bond income are 15 percent and 30 percent, respectively. Compare this to the NPV of the same proposal if the personal tax rates on dividend income and bond income are the same.

*9. How do default costs affect MM's propositions in a world without taxes and in a world with taxes? Illustrate your answer graphically.

10. An asset that costs $5 million is to be fully financed by a bank loan. The bank's basic annual lending rate is 15 percent. Calculate the extra interest rate payable for expected costs of default and monitoring, given that:

(a) The cost of default is 5 percent of the asset value of the company

(b) The probability of default is 2 percent

(c) The cost of monitoring the loan is 2 percent of asset value

References

Brealey, R., "A Note on Dividends and Debt Under the New Taxation," *Journal of Business Finance,* 5 (1973): 66–68.

Brennan, M. J., "Taxes, Market Valuation and Corporation Financial Policy," *National Tax Journal,* 23, no. 4 (December 1970): 417–27.

Cooper, I., and J. R. Franks, "The Interaction of Financial and Investment Decisions When the Firm Has Unused Tax Credits," *Journal of Finance,* 38, no. 2 (May 1983): 571–84.

Copeland, T. E., and J. F. Weston, *Financial Theory and Corporate Policy,* Second Ed., Reading, Mass.: Addison-Wesley Publishing Company, 1983.

DeAngelo, H., and P. W. Masulis, "Optimal Capital Structure Under Corporate and Personal Taxation," *Journal of Financial Economcs,* 8, no. 1 (March 1980): 3–29.

Franks, J. R., and J. Pringle, "Debt Financing, Corporate Financial Intermediaries, and the Value of the Firm," *Journal of Finance,* 37 (June 1982): 751–61.

Galai, D., "Corporate Income Taxes and the Valuation of Claims on the Corporation," Working Paper, July 1983.

Hamada, R. A., "The Effect of the Firm's Capital Structure on the Systematic Risk of Common Stocks," *Journal of Finance,* 27, no. 2 (May 1972): 435–52.

Jensen, M. C., and W. H. Meckling, "Theory of the Firm's Managerial Behavior, Agency Costs and Ownership Structure," *Journal of Financial Economics,* 3, no. 4 (October 1976): 305–60.

Levy, H., and M. Sarnat, *Investment Portfolio Analysis,* Chichester, England: John Wiley and Sons, 1972.

Majd, S., and S. C. Myers, "Valuing the Government's Tax Claim on Risky Assets," Working Paper, January 1984.

Miller, M. H., "Debt and Taxes," Presidential Address at the Annual Meeting of the American Finance Association, *Journal of Finance,* 32, no. 2 (May 1977): 261–75.

Modigliani, F., and M. H. Miller, "The Cost of Capital, Corporation Finance and the Theory of Investment," *American Economic Review,* 48, no. 3 (June 1958): 261–77.

Modigliani, F., and M. H. Miller, "Corporate Income Taxes and the Cost of Capital: A Correction," *American Economic Review,* 53, no. 3 (June 1963): 433–43.

Modigliani, F., and M. H. Miller, "Reply to Heins and Sprenkle," *American Economic Review,* 54, no. 4 (September 1969): 592–95.

Myers, S. C., "Determinants of Corporate Borrowing," *Journal of Financial Economics,* 5, no. 2 (November 1977): 147–75.

Myers, S. C., and N. S. Majluf, "Stock Issues and Investment Policy When Firms Have Information Investors Do Not Have," Working Paper, Sloan School of Management, MIT, Cambridge, MA, 1978.

Pitts, C. G. G., and J. R. Franks, "Asymmetric Taxes, Mergers and Risk-taking," Paper presented at European Finance Association, September 1984.

Rendleman, R. J., Jr., "The Effects of Default Risk on the Firm's Investment and Financing Decisions," *Financial Management,* 7, no. 1 (Spring 1978): 45–53.

Rendleman, R. J., "Information Asymmetries and Optimal Project Financing," Working Paper, Graduate School of Business, Duke University, Durham, NC, 1980.

Rubinstein, M., "Mean Variance Synthesis of Corporate Financial Theory," *Journal of Finance,* 28, no. 1 (March 1973): 167–81.

Skelton, J., "Banks, Firms and the Relative Pricing of Tax Exempt and Taxable Bonds," University of California at Berkeley, August 1982.

Stapleton, R. C., "Taxes, The Cost of Capital and the Theory of the Firm," *Economic Journal*

Talmor, E., R. Haugen, and A. Barnea, "The Value of the Tax Subsidy on Risky Debt," *Journal of Business,* forthcoming.

Trzcinka, C., "The Pricing of Tax Exempt Bonds and the Miller Hypothesis," *Journal of Finance,* 38, no. 4 (September 1981): 907–23.

Warner, G., "Bankruptcy Costs: Some Evidence," *Journal of Finance,* 32, no. 2 (May 1977): 337–48.

The Financing Mix and Investment Appraisal

In this chapter we examine three methods of appraising capital projects that are financed by both debt and equity: the weighted average cost of capital, the adjusted present value, and the equity residual income methods. The methods differ in their complexity, in the data that they require, and in the amount of information that they provide. Using an example, we show that the three methods provide the same net present value for a project only under a very special set of assumptions. A comparison of the three methods suggests the circumstances in which an analyst might prefer one over another.

Using the methods illustrated in this chapter, we show how the benefits attached to different kinds of financing, such as tax benefits or subsidized loans, can be valued. Finally, we consider the conditions under which investment decisions cannot be separated from financing decisions.

Corporate Debt Capacity

We would like to be able to estimate the net present value that would be attributable to the increase in borrowing that a company can undertake as a result of investing in a capital project. We shall call this increase in borrowing by the firm the project's **incremental borrowing capacity.** How would we determine a firm's capacity to borrow, and how does a project contribute to this capacity? Ordinarily, a company chooses a target proportion of debt for its capital structure. In Chapter 21 we described some of the determinants of a target capital structure, such as the tax-deductibility of interest payments and the expected costs of financial distress. However, such variables are not always easy to quantify, and corporate treasurers generally choose a target capital structure that keeps the firm's borrowing safely within prudent limits. In practice, the debt capacity of the firm is defined by a target capital structure that is adopted in consultation with commercial bankers, investment bankers, and other financial advisers.

CORPORATE VERSUS PROJECT DEBT CAPACITY

Usually, it is a company that borrows, not an individual project. At the same time, a large company can be thought of as a portfolio of projects or assets, with each asset having a different number of years remaining in its life. The way in which the different cash flow patterns for these assets add up helps to determine the company's anticipated financing needs over time. The risk of the total cash flow of the company determines the risk of loans to lenders and the rates of interest that are charged.

Occasionally, some form of project financing is arranged so that an individual project can be treated by lenders as though it were a stand-alone entity. However, such project financing can be expensive, and there are good reasons why the cost of borrowing should be lower when borrowing is done at the corporate level. As we discussed in Chapter 14, in diversified companies cash flows of successful projects can be set against possible losses from a failing project. Because the risk of a portfolio of assets generally is lower than the risk of an individual asset within the portfolio, loans to companies tend to be less risky than loans to stand-alone projects. As a consequence, the risk of financial distress is lower, and therefore so are the expected costs of financial distress. A second argument in favor of overall corporate financing rather than project-based financing is that a lender's monitoring costs are lower when it does not have to analyze financial data for individual projects. By the same token, separating out the cash flows of a project (which often involve joint costs) from the commercial activities of which it is a part is costly and often difficult.

ATTRIBUTING DEBT CAPACITY TO INDIVIDUAL PROJECTS

In this chapter, debt capacity refers to borrowing at the level of the corporation, and a project's incremental debt capacity is defined as the contribution that the project makes to the company's ability to borrow at the corporate level.[1]

If adding a project does not change the target capital structure of the company, the target capital structure of the project is the same as the target capital structure of the company. The borrowing capacity of the project can be defined as a target proportion of the market value of the project.

However, if the project is large and its characteristics sufficiently alter the risk of the company's portfolio of assets to cause a change in the target capital structure, the project's incremental debt capacity must be different from that of the corporation as a whole. Examples of risk-changing projects are an electric utility company that decides to build a nuclear power station, or a manufacturing firm that acquires a large investment in real estate. In such cases, estimation of a project's incremental debt capacity is more difficult. There are no precise methods of estimation but rough estimates can be made in two ways. First, one can try using an average of the capital structures of firms that specialize in businesses that are similar to that of the project. Second, the company's bankers can advise how much extra borrowing would be possible if the company were to invest in the project. The incremental debt capacity of the project is equal to the additional borrowing at the corporate level that is made possible by the project. This incremental debt capacity can be expressed as a proportion of the present value of the project's after-tax operating cash flows. In practice, debt capacity may be expressed in loan contracts as a proportion of book values of assets.

WHY DEBT CAPACITY IS USUALLY BASED ON BOOK VALUES

We shall assume in a large part of this chapter that debt capacity is based upon the asset's or the corporation's present value of future cash flows, otherwise known as its **economic value.** In fact, most loan contracts specify debt capacity as a proportion of the book values of assets rather than their economic values. If the corporation is not traded, the use of book values rather than economic values is not so surprising. After all, present values depend upon management's forecasts of cash flows, which may be biased. Book values are based upon the cost of assets, which are objective measures of value. A second reason for using book values is that, should the firm get into financial distress, the sale value of assets is more likely to be based on their costs than on their present value in a particular use. In other words, the banker bases debt capacity on the asset having a zero net present value,

---

[1]We make the assumption that the target capital structure is the optimum capital structure. See Franks and Pringle (1982) for a discussion of the implications of a firm operating at less than its optimum level of debt.

rather than the positive net present value expected by the corporation when it invests in the asset.

An important exception to this rule occurs when the asset's revenues are based on a product that is tradeable. For example, the owner of an oil field may often borrow on the basis of the oil field's net revenues rather than on investment, because the oil does not have different values in different uses or under different owners. Thus, loan contracts secured on extraction projects may not be based on book values.

Suppose a company's common stock is traded, however. Would the loan contract be based on the market value of the common stock? In fact, loan contracts are still specified in book values even when the corporation's common stock is traded. One reason has been given in Chapter 13. There we described how the value of the corporation reflects the value of assets already in place and the net present values of future assets not yet in place. Myers (1977) refers to the latter as growth opportunities. Lenders, he argues, will lend only on assets in place, because the value of growth opportunities usually is specific to the managerial skills of the individual company. As a result, lenders base debt capacity on book values, which reflect more closely the value of assets in place rather than a value that includes future asset opportunities. Should the corporation get into financial distress, such future asset opportunities would not be undertaken, nor could they probably be sold to other parties.

In our analysis of the three appraisal methods, we shall assume that a project's incremental debt capacity already has been estimated and that the only question remaining is: What is the net present value of the project including the value of any benefits that may be conferred by the incremental debt capacity of the project?

Three Methods of Valuing a Project

We referred at the outset to three methods of valuing projects financed by a mixture of debt and equity: the weighted average cost of capital (WACC), the adjusted present value (APV), and the equity residual income (ERI) methods. They differ in ways that can give different results. For example, the APV method explicitly separates the value of any benefits arising from the method of financing a project from the net present value of the project's operating cash flows, while the other two methods combine the two sets of cash flows into a single value. Separating out the value of the financing benefits from the value of the operating cash flows can be important, because it tells management to what extent a project's estimated profitability is attributable to the method of financing. Also, the APV and ERI methods are more complex than the WACC method, and the analyst must know how to decide when the additional complexity is necessary.

We shall use the capital asset pricing model to obtain the appropriate discount rates used in each of the three methods. We use the CAPM because it is well known, and because you have been exposed to the model in previous chapters. However, our conclusion that each of the three methods provides the same value for a project does not depend on the use of the CAPM. Any other model of risk and return should support the same proposition of equivalence, providing that consistent assumptions are used.

The Weighted Average Cost of Capital

A traditional approach to the choice of discount rates for a project is first to establish the cost of equity and the cost of debt to the firm, then to combine the two into a weighted average cost of capital (WACC) reflecting the relative proportions of debt and equity in the capital structure. The formula for the weighted average cost of capital is

WACC = Cost of Debt After-tax × (Proportion of Debt)
           + Levered Cost of Equity × (Proportion of Equity)

Let us consider an example. Suppose that the company pays interest on its debt (assumed to be riskless) at an average rate of 10 percent with interest tax-deductible at a tax rate of 46 percent. Then

After-tax Cost of Debt = Interest Rate × (1 − Tax Rate)

$$= 0.10 \times (1 - 0.46)$$

$$= 0.054$$

The after-tax cost of debt would be 5.4 percent under these assumptions.

Now we must calculate the company's cost of equity capital. The cost of equity capital must reflect the amount of debt in the firm's capital structure. To obtain an estimate of the cost of equity, let us use the capital asset pricing model in the manner described in Chapter 9. The cost of equity equals the risk-free rate plus a risk premium:

Cost of Equity = Risk-free Rate
           + (Beta of Equity × Risk Premium on the Market)

The cost of equity is a levered cost of equity, because the risk or beta of the company's common stock reflects the fact that the returns (dividends and capital gains) to stockholders will be made more volatile by the use of debt financing.

Let us assume that the beta of the common stock is 0.7530, that the risk-free rate of interest is 10 percent, and that the risk premium on the market index is 8.3 percent. Using the previous equation for the expected return on equity,

$$\text{Cost of Equity} = 0.10 + (0.7530 \times 0.0830)$$

$$= 0.1625$$

The cost of equity is therefore 16.25 percent. The overall cost of capital of the firm is a weighted average of the cost of debt (5.4 percent) and the cost of equity (16.25 percent). Note that in the formula for the cost of equity the risk-free rate of 10 percent is taken gross of taxes. The reason is that the firm must earn 10 percent after corporate taxes on its investments in order to provide the stockholder with a (before personal tax) risk-free return of 10 percent.[2]

Management must now decide what weights to apply to the cost of debt and the cost of equity in the weighted average cost of capital formula. Some financial analysts obtain the required weights from the balance sheet. In many cases this procedure may suffice to provide a good approximation to market values of debt and equity. In other cases, market values will be required. WACC really requires market values because a constant discount rate must imply a constant capital structure related to the present value (or market value) of the assets. A proof of this proposition is in Miles and Ezzell (1980).

As a consequence, the weights used in the WACC formula should be market value weights rather than book value weights. The value of the company's equity would be obtained by multiplying the price per share of common stock by the number of shares that has been issued. Likewise, the value of the debt would be equal to the market price of each bond multiplied by the number that has been issued. To the value of the traded bonds would be added the present value of interest and repayments on any nontraded debt liabilities, using current interest rates as the discount rate. The proportion of debt would be obtained by dividing the market value of the debt by the total market value of the debt and the equity. The proportion of equity is obtained in a similar manner.

Finally, the interest rate used as the cost of debt in the WACC represents the current cost of debt rather than an historical cost. If interest rates have risen since the debt was issued it is the current interest rate on the debt rather than the historical rate that should be used. This is consistent with the approach of using market interest rates to value the amount of debt for determining the weights in the WACC.

---

[2]Because corporate taxes represent a layer of taxes in addition to personal taxes, the implication is that a corporation must earn a higher rate of return than individuals holding the same assets.

Let us assume that by using market value we find that the debt to debt-plus-equity weighting is 20 percent and thus the equity to debt-plus-equity is 80 percent. Then the WACC is 14.08 percent, calculated as follows:

$$\text{WACC} = \left(\text{Cost of Debt After Taxes} \times \frac{B}{(B + E)}\right)$$

$$+ \left(\text{Levered Cost of Equity} \times \frac{E}{(B + E)}\right)$$

$$= (0.054 \times 0.20) + (0.1625 \times 0.8)$$

$$= 0.1408$$

Consider the project in Table 22.1, which is of average risk for the firm. Discounting the project's net cash flows at the weighted average cost of capital of 14.08 percent, we obtain a net present value of $218.8975.

So far we have assumed that a weighted average cost of capital applicable to the firm as a whole can be used as a discount rate or as a required rate of return for an individual project. Later in the chapter we will show how to adapt the weighted average cost of capital method for individual projects with different levels of risk that impart different incremental borrowing capacities to the firm.

The Adjusted Present Value Method

An alternative approach to the WACC is the adjusted present value method proposed by Myers (1974). Myers has suggested that it would be more appropriate to separate the value of the project's operating cash flows from

Table 22.1 *Cash flows and net present value for a project using the WACC as the discount rate (in dollars)*

		End of year			
	0	1	2	3	4
Net operating cash flows		350	351	350	350
Investment	−800				
	−800	350	351	350	350
Net present value at 14.08%	= 218.8975				

the benefits (or costs) of debt financing. If the tax benefits of debt financing are valued separately, the operating cash flows of the project must be valued using a discount rate that is based on all-equity finance and not on a weighted average cost of different financing methods. The net present value of the operating cash flows is then adjusted by adding the present value of any financing benefits attributable to the project:

$$\text{Adjusted Present Value} \atop \text{of the Project} = {\text{Net Present Value of Project's} \atop \text{Operating Cash Flows}} + {\text{Present Value of} \atop \text{Financing Benefits}}$$

Valuing a project using the weighted average cost of capital method we obtained a net present value of approximately \$218.90. Let us now compare the results that we obtain using the adjusted present value method to value the same project. We expect four annual after-tax net operating cash flows, one at the end of each of four years. To value the net operating cash flows, we require an unlevered cost of equity capital, that is, an all-equity cost of capital. Using the capital asset pricing model we have already obtained a levered cost of equity equal to 16.25 percent for the firm. Now we wish to convert the levered cost of equity to an unlevered cost. To accomplish this conversion we must first convert the levered beta to an unlevered beta (also called an asset beta) using the formula given in Chapter 9:

$$\text{Unlevered Beta} = \text{Levered Equity Beta} \times \frac{\text{Equity}}{\text{Debt} + \text{Equity}}$$

As before, we have assumed, for simplicity only, that the beta of debt is zero. We show in Chapter 10 how to obtain an unlevered beta if the beta of debt is not zero.

The levered equity beta is already known to be equal to 0.7530. The market value proportion of equity in the capital structure is 0.80, the same weight that we used for equity in the WACC. Therefore, the value of the unlevered beta for all-equity financing is

$$\text{Unlevered Beta} = 0.7530 \times 0.80$$

$$= 0.6024$$

It is now possible to calculate the unlevered cost of equity capital using the capital asset pricing model. We shall use the risk premium on the market index of 8.3 percent that was obtained in Chapter 9.

$$\text{Unlevered Cost of Equity} = \text{Risk-free Rate} + \text{Unlevered Beta} \atop \times (\text{Risk Premium on the Market})$$

$$= 0.10 + 0.6024 \, (0.083)$$

$$= 0.15$$

We can now use the unlevered cost of equity capital of 15 percent to value the project's operating cash flows.[3] Using the same project data as in Table 22.1:

Net Present Value of Project's Operating Cash Flows =

$$-800 + \frac{350}{(1+0.15)} + \frac{351}{(1+0.15)^2} + \frac{350}{(1+0.15)^3} + \frac{350}{(1+0.15)^4} = 200$$

Remaining to be ascertained is the value of the tax benefits of debt financing that should be added to the $200 net present value of the operating cash flow stream. To answer this question, first we must decide how much debt financing is attributable to the project. Earlier we assumed that the market value proportion of debt in the company's capital structure is 20 percent, and we used this proportion when we analyzed the project using the weighted average cost of capital method. To be consistent, we will use the same proportion in the adjusted present value method by assuming that the project can support additional borrowing by the firm up to an amount equal to 20 percent of its present value at all times during the project's life. It is important to note that if the project's present value declines during its life the borrowing attributable to the project also will decline. Thus, although the debt ratio stays at 20 percent of the present value throughout the project's life, the dollar amount of debt and the corresponding tax benefits will decline. In our example the present value of the project's operating cash flows is initially $1,000 calculated as follows:

$$1,000 = \frac{350}{(1.15)} + \frac{351}{(1.15)^2} + \frac{350}{(1.15)^3} + \frac{350}{(1.15)^4}$$

After one period, however, there are fewer cash flows left to discount, and the present value drops to $800:

$$800 = \frac{351}{(1.15)} + \frac{350}{(1.15)^2} + \frac{350}{(1.15)^3}$$

In subsequent periods the present value drops to $569, $304.35, and 0 as can be seen in row 2 of Table 22.2. In row 3 of the table we show the borrowing attributable to the project. Initially, 20 percent of $1,000, or $200, can be borrowed. After one year, the present value has dropped to $800 and 20 percent of $800, or $160, can be borrowed. Similarly, the borrowing attributable to the project declines in each succeeding year as in row 3 of the table.

Having determined the amount of borrowing capacity in each period of

---

[3]The unlevered cost of equity capital of 15 percent is actually higher than the weighted average cost of capital of 14.08 percent, because we have assumed a Modigliani and Miller world of debt and taxes. We show in Appendix 21.1 that in a Miller world the unlevered cost of equity is equal to the WACC.

Table 22.2   *Present value of the first layer of a project's tax benefits with 20 percent debt financing and APV (in dollars)*

	End of year				
	0	1	2	3	4
Operating cash flow after taxes		350	351	350	350
Present value at 15% of remaining cash flow	1,000.00	800.00	569.00	304.35	0
Borrowing at 20% of the present value of the project	200.00	160.00	113.80	60.87	0
Interest at 10%		20.00	16.00	11.38	6.09
Tax benefits at 46%*		9.20	7.36	5.23	2.80
Present value of tax benefits discounted at 15%	18.60				
APV of project 200 + 18.60 = 218.60					

*These benefits should be lagged if the company pays taxes after the period in which it incurs tax liabilities.

the project's life, now we can calculate the interest payments and the resulting net tax savings. In row 4 of Table 22.2, we see that borrowing $200 in period zero requires an interest payment of $20 at the end of period 1. In subsequent periods, interest payments decline as a result of reduced borrowing. The tax benefits depend upon the corporate tax rate. At 46 percent, the tax benefit is shown in the fifth row as 46 percent of the interest paid for the year. Miles and Ezzell suggest using the same discount rate on the tax benefits as is used on the firm's operating cash flows, so the present value of the benefits is $18.60, using the 15 percent discount rate.

We use the same rate to discount the tax benefits because the tax benefits of debt are related to company earnings. If earnings drop, the company's capacity to borrow lessens and the interest tax shields fall. In other words, the risk of the tax shields is similar to the risk of the operating cash flows. The crucial assumption that must be made is that the project's debt capacity is determined by the expected present value of the project's cash flows. In many loan contracts, debt capacity is determined by the book value of assets rather than the present value of the asset's cash flows. A second assumption is that the tax system is symmetrical; that is, when the firm makes taxable profits it pays taxes, and when it makes taxable losses a tax rebate is provided by the IRS.

To obtain an accurate value of the project's NPV, one more step is required. The present value of $18.60 attributable to the tax benefits of borrowing permits an additional layer of borrowing. Initially, the additional borrowing is 20 percent of $18.60, or only $3.72, and this small additional layer of borrowing declines during the life of the project. In Table 22.3 we show how the second layer of borrowing adds value to the project in Table 22.2. The additional net present value due to the tax benefits of the second layer of borrowing is $0.29, which increases the total net present value of the project to $218.89.

Thus, the adjusted present value of the project becomes:

$$\text{Adjusted Present Value} = \text{Net Present Value of Project's Operating Cash Flow} + \text{Present Value of Financing Benefits}$$

$$218.89 = 200 + 18.89$$

This result is virtually the same as the one obtained using the weighted average cost of capital method.

APV VERSUS WACC METHODS

Why would one undertake the considerable extra effort to use the APV method when in many cases (as in this example) the WACC gives the same

Table 22.3 *Present value of two layers of a project's tax benefits and APV (in dollars)*

			End of year		
	0	1	2	3	4
Net operating cash flow		350	351	350	350
Present value at 15% of remaining cash flow	1,000.00	800.00	569.00	304.35	0
Present value of first layer of tax benefits to borrowing	18.60	12.20	6.67	2.43	0
Total present value including value of first layer of tax benefits	1,018.60	812.20	575.67	306.78	0
Borrowing at 20% of total present value	203.72	162.44	115.13	61.36	0
Interest at 10%	0	20.37	16.24	11.51	6.14
Tax benefits at 46%	0	9.37	7.47	5.29	2.82
Present value of tax benefits discounted at 15%	18.89				
APV of project = 200 + 18.89 = 218.89					

result? It is tempting to say that an advantage of the APV method is that it separates the present value of the tax benefits of borrowing from the net present value of the project. However, we can use the WACC method to obtain a separate figure for the present value of the tax benefits. For the same example the present value of the tax benefits is obtained as follows:

Net present value of the project discounted at the WACC of 14.08%	$218.90
Less:	
Net present value of the project discounted at the unlevered equity required rate of return of 15.0% that excludes the tax benefits of debt	$200.00
Present value of the tax benefits of debt	$ 18.90

This value for the tax benefits is the same (allowing for rounding error) as that obtained in Table 22.3 using the APV method. The tax benefits due to borrowing assume the Modigliani and Miller world described in the last chapter. In a Miller world the benefits disappear as shown in Appendix 22.1.

The main advantage of the APV method is that it can be applied in situations where the WACC cannot be used easily. For example, suppose the company is not paying taxes temporarily (because of past tax losses) and that all tax allowances including deductions for interest payments must be carried forward as credits against future taxable income. In this situation a conventional application of the WACC method will not work, for the after-tax interest rate in the weighted average cost of capital will be different in each period, so no single discount rate or WACC can be used to discount the cash flows of a project in each and every period. In the APV method, however, tax benefits can be treated as cash flows in the taxpaying periods in which they occur, and all the cash flows then can be discounted at the same unlevered cost of equity capital.

A second reason for using the APV method is that a project's debt capacity may not be determined by the present value of its cash flows. For example, banks usually state a corporation's (or a project's) borrowing capacity in terms of its book values rather than in terms of its discounted present values. As a result, the WACC method as we have described it no longer provides an accurate result, because it assumes that a project's borrowing capacity is a constant proportion of the market value (or present value) of the project. The APV method, however, can accommodate a borrowing schedule based upon book values. The analyst simply figures the incremental borrowing that would be granted by banks in each period, calculates the related tax benefits, and then discounts them.

ADJUSTED PRESENT VALUE AND SUBSIDIZED LOANS

The APV approach is useful for valuing any type of financial advantage. One such advantage that arises frequently is that of a subsidized loan. Take the example of the project shown in Table 22.2. Say that a federal agency offers a four-year loan of $300 at a fixed interest rate of only 6 percent, on the condition that the company invest in this project. The loan's repayment schedule calls for repayment at the end of four years. How much is the cheap loan worth? We shall ignore the tax advantages of debt to keep the calculations simple.

The value of the loan subsidy can be obtained simply by calculating the present value of the interest payments and loan repayments using the company's usual market borrowing rate as the discount rate, and subtracting the value of the loan using the actual interest rate charged by the federal agency. First, the company must decide what market rate of interest it would have to pay on a $300 loan with a single loan repayment at the end of the fourth year. Let us assume that the market interest rate is 13 percent. The interest payments of $18 in each of the four years and the loan of $300 is repaid at the end of the fourth year. We discount the loan's expenses at the market interest rate (the rate at which we would have to borrow) to obtain the present value:[4]

$$\text{Present Value} = \frac{18}{(1 + 0.13)} + \frac{18}{(1 + 0.13)^2} + \frac{18}{(1 + 0.13)^3} + \frac{318}{(1 + 0.13)^4}$$

$$= 237.536$$

The value of the interest rate subsidy is $62.464, or the difference between the initial loan ($300) and the present value of the liabilities of the loan ($237.536). The adjusted present value of the project is the net present value of the project ($200), assuming that it was all–equity financed, plus the present value of the interest rate subsidy ($62.464), making a total of $262.464. The advantage of the APV method is that management knows exactly where the profits of the project are coming from. Would you be able to use the WACC method to value this subsidy? No, for you would not be able to calculate a single discount rate to value the project accurately. The reason is that the debt ratio is not a constant proportion of the project's present value through time.

ADJUSTED PRESENT VALUE AND PROJECT FINANCING

The adjusted present value method provides useful information for banks when they finance specific projects that are separated for the purposes of

---

[4]In this case we use the borrowing interest rate as the discount rate since the total amount that is to be borrowed is known with certainty, and the risk equals the risk of the loan.

default risk from the rest of the company's projects. In principle, a loan repayment schedule should be proportional to the decline in the present value of the project over time. Loan repayments should be scheduled at a rate that will ensure that the unpaid principal is less than the declining value of the asset. For banks financing oil fields, pipelines, or other mineral extraction projects, the APV approach can provide a useful way of estimating the minimum feasible repayment schedules. In the example in Table 22.3 the outstanding balance on the loan would be given by line 5, with the repayment schedule dictated by changes in the project's borrowing capacity each period.

Equity Residual Income Method

Both the WACC and APV methods value a project's cash flows that accrue to the corporation after taxes. Some analysts, however, prefer to calculate the cash flows that accrue to stockholders, that is, after the deduction of the project's loan payments and interest payments. Many real estate projects are analyzed in this way. In this section we shall show how such an analysis may be made with the equity residual income (ERI) method.

We can apply the ERI method to the example we have analyzed by the WACC and APV methods and show that, if we are consistent in our assumptions, we obtain the same result. Table 22.4 again shows the project's operating cash flows from Table 22.3, subtracting the cash flows associated

Table 22.4   *Project's net cash flows accruing to equityholders (in dollars)*

		End of year			
	0	1	2	3	4
Net operating cash flow		350	351	350	350
Investment	−800				
Loan	203.72				
Loan repayment		−41.28	−47.31	−53.77	−61.36
Interest at 10%		−20.37	−16.24	−11.51	−6.14
Tax benefits at 46%		9.37	7.47	5.29	2.82
Equity residual income	−596.28	297.72	294.92	290.01	285.32
Net present value at 16.25% = 218.88					

with borrowing in order to obtain the residual income that is attributable to the shareholders. Thus we add the income from the loan in row 3 and subtract the loan repayments in row 4. These repayments equal the changes in the borrowing shown on row 5 of Table 22.3. We also subtract interest payments in row 5 but add back the tax shields on the interest charges in row 6. The net figures in row 7 are the residual income from the project that belongs to the stockholders.

The question now arises: What discount rate should be used to discount the residual income? The answer is simple. As we have levered the cash flows associated with borrowing using the same leverage (20 percent of present value) as for the corporation, we can use the firm's 16.25 percent levered cost of equity capital as the discount rate for residual income. Discounting at 16.25 percent, we obtain a net present value of $218.88 for the project. Allowing for rounding error, this result is the same as we obtained using the WACC and the APV methods.

If the project's debt capacity is based upon its expected present value, we require the same loan schedule as was calculated in the APV method. As a result, calculating the ERI requires us to obtain the same data as for the APV approach. Why not put in the loan repayment schedule that is specific to the project's loan? If the risk of the default is borne by the corporation as well as by the project, the project's loan is part of the corporation's debt capacity. As a result, the specific loan used to finance the project may not provide a reliable guide as to the contribution of the project to the corporation's debt capacity. Only if the loan and the project stand alone would it be appropriate to use the specific loan's interest and repayment schedule as representing the project's debt capacity.

Adjusting for the Risk of the Individual Project

Up to this point in the chapter, we have assumed that the project has the same risk characteristics as the company. In other words, we suppose that the project's operating risk and its debt capacity are the same as for the corporation as a whole. In Chapter 10, however, we explained why projects within a company may have risks different from the average. In addition, we showed how we might obtain an estimate of the project's systematic risk. In this chapter we reviewed the method of obtaining an estimate of the systematic risk of the unlevered equity of the corporation, and how to calculate the unlevered cost of equity for average projects, using the CAPM. The question that we wish to answer here is how to adjust that rate in order to value projects of differing risk using each of the three appraisal methods.

WEIGHTED AVERAGE COST OF CAPITAL
FOR THE INDIVIDUAL PROJECT

Although analysts usually compute the WACC for a firm rather than for a project, there is no reason a WACC cannot be computed for a project. Let us show how the data would be obtained. The equation for the WACC is

Weighted Average Cost of Capital = (Interest Rate on Debt After-tax) × (Proportion of Debt) + (Levered Cost of Equity × Proportion of Equity)

Estimation of the WACC for a project requires us to know the debt capacity of the project. In this case, the debt and equity ratios in the WACC formula must be based on the present value of the project rather than on the value of the firm. Management either can assume that the project supports the same debt capacity as the firm or estimate a different debt capacity for the project. The next information that we require for the WACC is the project's levered cost of equity. It is probable that we cannot observe from stock market data a project's levered cost of equity. Therefore, we must use a less direct means of obtaining the project's risk.

In Chapter 10 we showed various methods by which we could estimate a project's unlevered cost of equity. If the unlevered systematic risk of the project is estimated to be, say, twice that of the average for the firm, then the unlevered beta for the project will be double the unlevered beta of the firm. The levered beta of the project can be estimated from the same equation rearranged in the following way:

Levered Beta = Unlevered Beta/Proportion of Equity

where the proportion of equity is equal to one minus the proportion of borrowing that can be supported by the individual project. Once we have a value for the levered beta of the project, we can use the CAPM to calculate the levered cost of equity capital for the project that is required in the formula for the project's weighted average cost of capital. The WACC method can give an accurate result only if the incremental borrowing capacity contributed by the project is proportional to the project's discounted present value through time and if the firm is not in a temporary nontaxpaying position.

ADJUSTED PRESENT VALUE

A project's APV may be calculated in two stages. First, calculate the NPV of the project's net operating cash flows using the project's unlevered cost of equity as the discount rate. The second step is to discount the tax benefits of debt, after specifying the project's incremental debt capacity using the same discount rate.

EQUITY RESIDUAL INCOME METHOD

In this method we discount the net cash flows of the project, including the cash flows of the loan, at the levered cost of equity capital for the project. The levered cost of equity for the individual project given its risk is estimated in the way described above for the WACC method if the debt is a constant proportion of the present value of the remaining cash flows.

Comparison of the Weighted Average Cost of Capital, Adjusted Present Value, and Equity Residual Methods

Our numerical example demonstrated the underlying equivalence of the three methods. Provided that consistent assumptions are used, the WACC, the APV, and the equity residual income methods yield the same net present value.[5] The choice of method depends upon the data available and the output required. If the company is either permanently taxpaying or nontaxpaying, and if debt capacity is a constant proportion of the project's present value, the weighted average cost of capital method is the simplest to use. In a company where financial analysis is carried out in the divisions rather than at corporate headquarters, the simplicity of the WACC makes it a very attractive method for managers who are not skilled financial analysts. Yet the conventional application of a single weighted average cost of capital discount rate is not adequate to cope with the problem of temporary non-taxpaying where the tax shields on interest charges must be carried forward to a future date. Such complicated tax lags can be handled more directly and effectively using the APV method, because the timing of the tax payments can be treated explicitly in the cash flows rather than implicitly in the discount rate.

The ERI method provides the greatest possibility for confusion because analysts incorporate into the cash flows a loan schedule that may not reflect the project's true contribution to the firm's debt capacity. Also, analysts often do not use the correct value of the levered cost of equity that is appropriate for the level of borrowing. It is probably fair to say that most companies use the WACC because it is simple to use and because the calculations are less complex than in other methods. For evaluation of major projects, however, we would recommend use of the APV method.

---

[5]The net present value is the same because we assume that the debt ratio for the project is maintained at a constant proportion of the project's market (or present) value. See Myers (1974) and Miles and Ezzell (1980) for a discussion of this point.

Interaction Between Investment and Financing Decisions

Our analysis has assumed that the financing decision is relevant to the investment decision only insofar as the tax subsidy on debt adds to the value of a project. However, the decision to finance a project or a set of projects with debt or equity will be affected by a number of other factors. The first, as we have already mentioned in Chapter 21, is default risk. The default risk of the firm may be altered by the business risk of individual investments as well as by the financial risk inherent in the leverage effects of debt finance. Even if a project is profitable and can be financed by debt, its business risk combined with the extra default risk introduced by further debt may discourage management from using that particular source of finance. The costs of default are not simply the administrative costs of liquidation or bankruptcy; they are the possible costs of having to sell assets rapidly, of rejecting profitable projects because of lack of liquidity, and finally the cost of management time spent staving off liquidation. In this sense, the value of a single project is dependent not only on how it is financed, but also on the business risk and financial risk of other projects in the firm.

A second factor affecting the choice of projects relates to their individual financing needs. If a specific group of projects requires equity finance, but the equity cannot be generated from internal sources, an issue of shares must be necessary, perhaps at a point when management may believe that a stock issue is not timely. Directors and officers may feel that they do not wish to disclose the information about new investments (and new products) that would be required for the issue prospectus. In addition, the lack of information may cause the common stock to be underpriced and therefore make a new equity issue more costly. As a consequence, an investment program may be altered to fit in with what management believes is a sensible financing program, both in terms of the amount of money raised and in the ratio of debt to equity finance. There is some evidence—in the United States from Jalilvand and Harris (1984) and in the United Kingdom from Marsh (1982) —that corporations attempt to time new issues of common stock and long-term debt. For example, at times of historically high stock prices, new equity issues are made more frequently (and debt issues less frequently). Such results would suggest that management may not always accept that projects with positive NPVs always can be financed in the capital market (without detrimentally affecting stock prices). Whether such beliefs have a good basis has yet to be proven.

A third factor that can contribute to the interaction of investment and financing decisions is the availability of subsidized financing at a rate of interest below the market rate for specific kinds of projects. For some types of exports, for instance, federal agencies offer subsidized debt finance. Projects located in particular regions of the United States or in particular industries may qualify for low-cost debt or for debt guarantees that insure the lender against default.

Fourth, we have assumed that the firm is in a taxpaying position and therefore is able to acquire tax benefits from depreciation as well as from debt financing. You might assume that, for a company in a nontaxpaying position, tax benefits are delayed or eliminated in the project evaluation. This is not always true if there are other means of capturing the tax benefits. For example, leasing is a common method of financing an investment when the firm is not paying taxes. Leasing, as Chapter 23 will describe, permits another company, a bank, for example, to buy equipment and to borrow in order to capture the tax benefits. The bank then leases the asset to the nontaxpaying company and shares with it a proportion of the tax benefits by reducing the lease payments. Thus, a decision to lease can affect the net present value of a project if tax benefits can be obtained at an earlier date by means of leasing. One result is that under some conditions the value of a project with lease finance affects that of other projects (and their leases). Such conditions require the value of the portfolio of projects to be found before one can determine the value of individual projects, as we will show in the next chapter.

Summary

This chapter has described three different methods for valuing a project financed with a mixture of equity and debt. All three methods, WACC, APV, and ERI, can provide the same NPV for a project under a specific and somewhat restrictive set of assumptions. Which method is used depends upon making appropriate assumptions on the company's tax position, how debt capacity is defined, and how the analyst wishes to present the information. It is important to be aware of the conditions under which investment decisions interact with financing decisions.

Appendix 22.1 The Relationship Between the Unlevered Cost of Equity and the Weighted Average Cost of Capital in Miller's World

The question arises as to what would be the relation between the WACC and the unlevered cost of equity in a Miller world of debt and taxes compared with Modigliani and Miller's world of debt and taxes. Note, that in a Miller world the cost of debt after taxes equals the cost of (risk-free) equity, that is, there is no advantage to debt financing when interest charges are tax-deductible. If this is so, then the WACC should be equal to the unlevered cost of equity. The implication is that the firm's overall cost of capital cannot be reduced by increasing the proportion of debt financing. We shall show how the example in the text would be altered by the assumptions of a Miller world of debt and taxes.

If the before-tax interest rate on debt is 10 percent in a Modigliani and Miller world, the before-tax interest rate will be greater than 10 percent in a Miller world. We showed in Chapter 21 that the interest rate in a Miller world will be the rate in an MM world grossed up by the investor's marginal tax rate, which at the margin (in equilibrium) must equal the corporate tax rate. As a result, the interest rate on debt in a Miller world will be 18.5185 percent assuming a corporate tax rate of 46 percent.

$$i = \frac{0.10}{1 - T_c} = \frac{0.10}{1 - 0.46}$$

$$= 0.18519$$

In Miller's world the after-tax cost of debt $i(1 - T_c)$ equals the riskless cost of equity R_f,

$$R_f = i(1 - T_c)$$

$$= 0.18519 \ (1 - 0.46)$$

$$= 0.10$$

The first term on the right-hand side of the capital asset pricing model is the risk-free rate which in Miller's world is equal to the after-tax cost of borrowing:

$$\begin{aligned} \text{Levered Cost} \atop \text{of Equity} &= {\text{Risk-free} \atop \text{Rate}} + {\text{Levered Beta} \atop \text{for Equity}} \times {\text{Risk Premium on} \atop \text{Market Portfolio}} \\[2mm] &= i(1 - T_c) + {\text{Levered Beta} \atop \text{for Equity}} \times {\text{Risk Premium on} \atop \text{Market Portfolio}} \end{aligned}$$

The change that we have made in this equation reflects the fact that the cost of riskless equity R_f is equal to the after-tax interest rate $i(1 - T_c)$ on bonds.

Using the data from Table 22.1, the corporate tax rate T_c is 46 percent, the levered equity beta of the firm is 0.7530, and the risk premium on the market index is 8.3 percent. For the levered cost of equity,

$$R_E = i(1 - T_c) + \text{Levered Beta for Equity}$$
$$\times \text{Risk Premium on Market Portfolio}$$

$$R_E = 0.10 \quad + (0.7530 \times 0.083)$$

$$= 0.1625$$

The levered cost of equity is therefore 16.25 percent. The weighted average cost of capital was calculated assuming a debt ratio of 20 percent and an equity ratio of 80 percent. If the cost of debt is 18.519 percent before taxes, the WACC is:

$$\text{WACC} = i(1 - T_c) \left(\frac{B}{B + E} \right) + R_E \left(\frac{E}{B + E} \right)$$

$$\text{WACC} = 0.18519 \times (1 - 0.46)(0.20) + 0.1625 \times (0.8)$$

$$= 0.15$$

If the WACC is 15 percent in a Miller world, we also should expect to find the unlevered cost of equity to be 15 percent. To show this is the case, we must initially compute the unlevered equity beta β_A.

$$\text{Unlevered Beta for Equity} = \text{Levered Beta} \times \text{Proportion of Equity}$$
$$\text{for Equity}$$

$$\beta_A = \beta_E \left(\frac{E}{E + B} \right)$$

$$= 0.7530 \times 0.8$$

$$= 0.6024$$

Substituting the unlevered equity beta into the CAPM:

$$\frac{\text{Unlevered Cost}}{\text{of Equity}} = \frac{\text{Risk-free}}{\text{Rate}} + \frac{\text{Unlevered Beta}}{\text{for Equity}} \times \frac{\text{Risk Premium on}}{\text{Market Portfolio}}$$

$$= 0.10 + (0.6024 \times 0.083)$$

$$= 0.15$$

Thus, we have shown that the unlevered cost of equity is equal to the WACC in a Miller world.

Review Questions

1. Define a project's debt capacity.
2. What determines a corporation's target capital structure?
3. How would you go about determining a project's debt capacity?
4. Why do banks usually specify a corporation's debt capacity in terms of the book values of assets rather than their market values? Under what conditions might the lender use market values?
5. Under what conditions will the APV and WACC methods provide the same value for a project?
6. If a company is temporarily incurring tax losses, why is it difficult to use the WACC method to value a project that contributes debt capacity to the corporation?
7. "Because the unlevered cost of equity is unobservable, the WACC method is preferable to the APV approach." Comment on the validity of this statement.
8. "The WACC is equal to the unlevered cost of equity capital." Is this statement true in a world without taxes? How is your answer affected by the existence of taxes?
9. "The WACC requires an estimate of the levered cost of equity capital, which is observable. As a result, if the analyst uses the WACC no assumption has to be made about an MM or a Miller world of debt and taxes. This cannot be said about the APV approach." Are these statements true? Justify your answer.

Problems

*1. Calculate the weighted average cost of capital for Kingston, Inc., which has equal amounts of debt and equity (book value terms). The cost of debt is 12 percent before-tax, and the cost of levered equity is 16 percent. How is the WACC changed if the market values of debt and equity are 35 percent and 65 percent, respectively, of the total value of the firm? Assume that interest is tax-deductible at a corporate tax rate of 46 percent.

2. A firm's capital structure consists of 40 percent debt and 60 percent equity. The interest rate on the debt is 10 percent before-tax, and the (levered) beta value is 1.27. Given that the risk premium on the market is expected to be 9 percent and the risk-free rate is 10 percent, what is the value of the weighted average cost of capital?

   Assume the corporate tax rate to be 46 percent and that all interest payments are tax-deductible.

*3. W.E.T., Inc., is considering a project costing $500 with after-tax operating cash flows of $250 per year for five years. The risk of the project is the same as the risk of the firm. Given the following information, calculate the WACC and the NPV of the project.

Cost of debt	= 0.10 (before-tax)
Risk-free rate	= 0.10 (before-tax)
Risk premium	= 0.10
Debt-to-equity ratio	= 0.4/0.6
Beta of W.E.T.'s common stock	= 1.27

Assume a corporate tax rate of 46 percent and no personal taxes.

4. Given the information in Problem 3, calculate the adjusted present value for the project. Assume the project increases the incremental debt of the firm by an amount equivalent to 40 percent of the project's present value.

Compare this to the NPV calculated in Problem 3, and explain the difference.

*5. A project's operating cash flows are $350 per year for five years for a capital outlay of $1,000. The unlevered cost of equity for the project is 15 percent after taxes, and the firm's borrowing rate is 7 percent before taxes.

(a) Calculate the adjusted present value for the project.

(b) What percentage does the present value of the tax benefits represent of (i) the present value of the project, and (ii) the net present value of the project?

Assume that the corporate tax rate is 46 percent and that the project increases the incremental debt of the firm by an amount equivalent to 25 percent of the project's present value.

6. Given the same project in Problem 5, what would be the adjusted present value for the project if the levered cost of equity capital was observed to be 15 percent after taxes? The firm's borrowing rate is 7 percent before taxes, the same rate as the risk-free rate of interest. The after-tax risk premium in the market is expected to be 10 percent. The debt-to-equity ratio is 0.25/0.75. Compare the APV with that calculated in Problem 5, and explain the difference.

*7. (a) Use the information below to calculate the WACC and the NPV of the project whose cash flows are given on page 628.

Cost of borrowing (before-tax)	= 12 percent
Risk-free rate	= 9 percent
Risk premium on market	= 10 percent
Levered beta of stock	= 1.2
Corporate tax rate	= 46 percent
Debt-to-equity ratio	= 0.3/0.7

End of year	0	1	2	3	4
Cash flow (after-tax)	−1,000	250	350	450	550

(b) Calculate the unlevered cost of equity (using the information above) and the NPV of the project. Then estimate the present value of the tax benefits.

*8. (a) A government agency has offered a firm a subsidized loan of $2 million at a fixed rate of 5 percent per year for a special defense project. Interest on the loan is to be paid annually with the repayment of the capital at the end of the project in four years' time. The prevailing market interest rate is 12 percent for unsubsidized loans on such projects. Calculate the value of the loan subsidy.

(b) What would happen to the value of the loan subsidy if prevailing market interest rates increased suddenly?

9. The government has agreed to lend $1 million to a company for five years at a fixed annual rate of 8 percent for a specific project; the market rate of interest for a similar loan is 12 percent per year. The capital cost of the project is $2 million, and the after-tax operating cash flows are $600,000 for each of the five years.

(a) Assuming that the corporate tax rate is 46 percent, what is the value of the project if the unlevered cost of equity is 15 percent?

(b) What is the value of the government's loan subsidy? Assume that capital is repaid at the end of the fifth year.

(c) What is the value of the tax advantage on the subsidized debt?

(d) What is the adjusted present value of the project?

(e) How would your answer be affected if there were no subsidized loan?

*10. Using the information for W.E.T., Inc., in Problems 3 and 4, use the equity residual income method to obtain the NPV of the project.

References

Arditti, F. D., and H. Levy, "The Weighted Average Cost of Capital as a Cutoff Rate: A Critical Analysis of the Classical Textbook Weighted Average," *Financial Management,* 6, no. 3 (Fall 1977): 24–34.

Boudreaux, K. G., and H. W. Long, "The Weighted Average Cost of Capital as a Cutoff Rate: A Further Analysis," *Financial Management,* 8, no. 2 (Summer 1979): 7–14.

Chambers, D. R., R. S. Harris, and J. J. Pringle, "Treatment of Financing Mix in Analyzing Investment Opportunities," *Financial Management,* 11 (Summer 1982): 24–41.

Franks, J. R., and J. J. Pringle, "Debt Financing, Corporate Financial Intermediaries and the Value of the Firm," *Journal of Finance,* 37, no. 3 (June 1982): 751–61.

Jalilvand, A., and R. S. Harris, "Corporate Behavior in Adjusting to Capital Structure and Dividend Targets: An Econometric Study," *Journal of Finance,* 39, no. 1 (March 1984): 127–45.

King, M. A., "Taxation and the Cost of Capital," *Review of Economic Studies,* 41 (January 1974): 21–35.

Marsh, P., "The Choice Between Equity and Debt: An Empirical Study," *Journal of Finance,* 37, no. 1 (March 1982): 121–44.

Miles, J. A., and J. R. Ezzell, "The Weighted Average Cost of Capital Markets and Project Life: A Clarification," *Journal of Financial and Quantitative Analysis,* 15, no. 3 (September 1980): 719–30.

Modigliani, F., and M. H. Miller, "Corporate Income Taxes and the Cost of Capital," *American Economic Review,* 53, no. 2 (June 1963): 433–42.

Myers, S. C., "Determinants of Corporate Borrowing," *Journal of Financial Economics,* 5, no. 2 (November 1977): 147–75.

Myers, S. C., "Interactions of Corporate Financing and Investment Decisions— Implications for Capital Budgeting," *Journal of Finance,* 29, no. 1 (March 1974): 1–25.

Myers, S. C., and G. A. Pogue, "A Programming Approach to Corporate Financial Management," *Journal of Finance,* 29, no. 2 (May 1974): 579–99.

Scott, J. H., "A Theory of Optimal Capital Structure," *Bell Journal of Economics and Management Science,* 7, no. 1 (Spring 1976): 33–54.

Stapleton, R. C., and C. M. Burke, "Taxes, the Cost of Capital and the Theory of Investment: A Generalization to the Imputation System of Dividend Taxation," *Economic Journal,* 85 (December 1975): 888–90.

Warner, G., "Bankruptcy Costs: Some Evidence," *Journal of Finance,* 32, no. 2 (May 1977): 337–48.

Wrightsman, D., "Tax Shield Valuation and the Capital Structure Decision," *Journal of Finance,* 32, no. 2 (May 1977): 371–88.

Lease Valuation

Lease financing, a growth industry for many years, now has assumed a major importance in the financing of United States corporations. Obviously, leasing must have advantages that make it competitive with other forms of financing. In this chapter we explain how to value some of these advantages and how to determine when a lease is more profitable than the alternative of outright purchase financed by borrowing. We shall examine two methods of lease evaluation and discuss the strengths and weaknesses of each method, as well as examine the economics of leasing.

Leasing and Ownership

Table 23.1 illustrates the variety of ways that a company can obtain the use of an asset, ranging from outright purchase and ownership at one extreme to short-term rental at another. A lease is a contract between two parties for the rental of a specific asset. The user of the asset, the **lessee,** decides what kind of asset is needed and for how long. The other party, the **lessor,** pays for the purchase of the asset and remains the legal owner, although never intending to use it. Of course, the user of the asset must pay a rental to the owner in compensation for the capital cost, for the time value of money, and for risk. The rental includes a premium for risk because of the possibility

Table 23.1   *Methods of obtaining the use of an asset*

Outright purchase	**Purchase with the firm's own funds**
Unsecured loan	**Purchase with borrowed funds not secured by the equipment**
Mortgage	**Purchase with funds borrowed on the security of the equipment**
Conditional sale	**Purchase with title passing on completion of installment payments**
Rent with an option to purchase	**Rent with option to purchase title at a nominal price**
Financial lease	**Rent for the economic life of the asset—non-cancellable**
Operating lease	**Rent for some term—which is cancellable**
Rental	**Short-term rental**

that the lessee might default on rental payments. If the lessee should default, the lessor would have to incur additional expense. For example, the lessor might have to sell the used asset prematurely and at a loss. Alternatively, he or she might have to find someone willing to lease a used asset and might have to accept lower rental payments than the original lessee was paying.

Leases may be grouped into two main categories—financial leases and operating leases. A **financial lease** is a contract in which the lessee is committed to make sufficient payments to repay the lessor for the entire purchase cost of the asset and all the associated (after-tax) financing costs, such as interest payments. In comparison, an **operating lease** does not compensate the lessor for the full costs because the lessor normally expects to take possession of the asset before the end of its useful life in order to re-lease the asset or to sell it. The rentals for an operating lease normally will be higher than the rentals for a financial lease, as the lessor is more exposed to changes in lease rental rates and resale values because of the necessity either to release or to sell the asset when the first lease expires.

Table 23.2 shows the total dollar volume of domestic lease contracts for the years 1978 and 1979. The data include three categories of leases: direct financing, leveraged leases, and operating leases. With **direct financing,** the lessor pays for the asset from its own funds, while under **leveraged leasing** the lessor raises part of the funds for the purchase of the asset by borrowing (leveraging) from other lending institutions or from individual investors. With a leveraged lease the lessor may put up, for example, only 20 percent of the funds and still be able to depreciate the full value of the asset for tax purposes. The table shows the relative importance of the three sorts of leases, as well as the enormous growth that occurred over the two years. Leased assets comprised about 17 percent of all capital assets used by American industry at the end of the period, which makes leasing a significant factor in the financing of American business activity.

Table 23.2   *Value of lease contracts (millions of dollars)*

| | Equipment cost | | |
Lease type	1978	1979	Increase over previous period
Direct financing	3,949	5,677	+44%
Leveraged leases	2,046	3,170	+55%
Operating leases	484	729	+51%

Source: Responses by 224 members of the American Equipment Leasing Association to a survey (1979) conducted by Deloitte Haskins and Sells, San Francisco.

Table 23.3 shows the value of leases broken down into nine categories of assets. The table shows that a wide variety of assets are being leased in different industries. The large concentration in transportation equipment is accounted for mainly by railroads and airlines, which have an enormous requirement for new capital equipment combined with periods of low earnings. When earnings are low, companies requiring capital equipment may find it difficult to take full advantage of the tax shields from depreciation; as we shall show, these conditions generally are favorable to lease financing.

Why Lease?

What is making lease financing so attractive for so many kinds of assets? There are at least three reasons for the growth of lease financing in the United States and elsewhere.

CONVENIENCE

The first reason is convenience. If a company wishes to use an asset for a relatively short period of time, it will often lease the asset. For example, consider a construction company that needs the use of a crane for only one day. Clearly, the company would not waste the effort and incur the expense of buying the crane and then reselling it a short time later. In this respect, the lessor acts as an intermediary able to reduce the costs of transactions by dealing in many cranes and with numerous customers. A company intending to use an asset for a period that is appreciably shorter than the length of the asset's useful life may find that leasing the asset is more convenient and less costly than buying it.

Table 23.3   *Assets leased by type of equipment (percent)*

	Financed directly	Leveraged leases	Operating leases
Office machinery and equipment	15.8	—	17.3
Computers	16.1	15.5	25.3
Transportation equipment	15.6	59.1	29.0
Construction machinery	6.6	—	2.4
Production machinery	16.2	15.3	8.1
Agricultural machinery	6.0	—	4.0
Medical equipment	7.3	—	8.3
Nonproduction machinery	8.1	—	1.6
Other	8.3	10.1	4.0
	100.0	100.0	100.0

Source: Responses by 224 members of the American Equipment Leasing Association to a survey (1979) conducted by Deloitte Haskins and Sells, San Francisco.

RISK SHARING

The second reason for leasing lies in risk. By leasing instead of owning assets, the lessee can insure against the risks of large unexpected changes in the asset's value (e.g., those caused by technological obsolescence). If the lessee intends to use the asset for a period appreciably shorter than the asset's life and then sell it, uncertainty about the future market value of the used asset becomes an important consideration. A lessee obtaining use of the asset by means of an operating lease can transfer such risks to the lessor. As the lessor owns the asset, he or she is the one who must sell or re-lease the asset for whatever price it is possible to get at the end of the term of the initial lease. For this reason, many companies prefer to lease computers rather than to buy them, because the prices of secondhand computers are particularly sensitive to the risks of technological obsolescence. While lessees can protect themselves against the risk of technological obsolescence by means of operating leases, the rental payments charged by the lessors will be higher to reflect the additional risks that they bear on behalf of the lessee.

TAXES

The third reason for the increasingly widespread use of lease financing stems from the tax system. Financial leases provide an effective means of obtaining tax advantages in certain circumstances. When a company purchases an asset, it obtains an investment tax credit and tax shields owing to depreciation. The investment tax credit is a proportion of the original cost of the asset that can be subtracted from the taxes payable by the corporation. The depreciation tax shield is a deduction from taxable profits which saves taxes. If the company does not have taxable profits in the current year, the benefits from the investment tax credit and the depreciation tax shields may have to be carried forward until the time when the company resumes paying taxes. If tax benefits must be postponed in this way, their discounted present value is reduced.

If the company leases the asset, however, and if the lessor currently is paying taxes, the lessor can obtain the tax benefits of purchase without delay. In a competitive leasing market, a lessee can negotiate a rental stream that reflects these tax advantages enjoyed by the lessor. Thus leasing provides a means whereby a taxpaying lessor can transfer some of the tax advantages of purchase to a (currently) nontaxpaying lessee through lower rentals. It is perhaps not so surprising that many leasing companies are subsidiaries of banks, which have the necessary taxable profits to obtain an immediate benefit from the tax credits and depreciation tax shields arising from the purchase of assets.

Issues in Leasing

In this section we shall focus our attention on issues concerning financial leases, although the conclusions will also be applicable to long-term operating leases. One of the advantages most often attributed to leasing is that the lessee is permitted to acquire the use of the asset without recourse to its own funds. Actually this claim is misleading, as lease payments themselves represent a legal obligation (similar to interest charges on debt). The lessee is in an analogous position to an individual who purchases a house with a mortgage provided by a savings and loan association and repays the lender by regular installments. Each installment consists of part repayment of the loan and interest on the outstanding balance. Because a lease, like a home mortgage, requires a deposit or some form of advance payment, the lessee usually contributes to the initial cost of the equipment. In fact, the covenants in a lease agreement often will stipulate that the company maintain a minimum level of equity and liquid assets in the business. In this respect the lease contract is similar to any other secured loan agreement. While it is true that leasing provides an *alternative* means of obtaining the use of outside funds to finance capital equipment, leasing is not fundamentally different from borrowing.

It should be clear that financial leasing is a form of debt financing that effectively allows the company to acquire the asset as though it had purchased it. The Financial Accounting Standards Board (FASB) recognizes this reality, and FASB standard number 13 requires that all financial leases should be capitalized, that is, the present value of all future lease payments should be shown as a liability on the lessee's balance sheet. The depreciated value of the asset itself must also be shown on the balance sheet as an asset as if it were owned by the lessee. In addition, future lease rentals, both in aggregate and for each of the five succeeding years, must be shown in notes to the financial statements.

Even if leases were not capitalized, intelligent bankers would attempt to obtain information about any such contractual obligations entered into by the company. Also, investors and their financial advisers would try to estimate all the fixed costs of the business, including lease rentals, that contribute to the sensitivity of the company's earnings to changes in revenues.

A further advantage claimed by some lessors is that clauses in lease agreements are thought to be less restrictive than corresponding covenants in loan agreements. Lease agreements may contain fewer clauses, but only because the lessor retains title or ownership of the asset, while in a secured loan agreement the asset belongs to the user. A lessee in financial distress cannot sell the leased asset because he or she does not own it. As a result, it may be easier for a lessor to repossess a leased asset if the lessee defaults.

While many virtues have been attributed (sometimes falsely) to leasing, the main advantages continue to be convenience, insurance against risk, and tax advantages when a company is currently nontaxpaying. These advantages are sufficiently important to give leasing a significant role in corporate finance.

Leasing and Capital Investment

In a world of perfect capital markets, the value of an asset would be independent of the way it was financed. This irrelevance proposition was described in some detail in Chapter 21 in relation to debt finance. It is the imperfections, including transactions costs and taxes, that may make one form of finance less costly than another. We can apply these same principles to lease finance. In a perfect capital market, a leasing decision would have a zero net present value just like any other financial instrument. It is the imperfections that may make leasing a less costly source of finance in some situations.

We have already discussed how operating leases permit the user of an asset to shift the risk of changing residual values to the lessor, for some price. In this respect the lessor is providing residual value insurance. Such insurance may be valuable if, for example, the lessor finds risk less costly to bear than the lessee.

A second imperfection discussed previously is one relating to taxes. We have described how lease financing may be profitable if the user of the asset is unable (temporarily or permanently) to obtain the depreciation tax shields and the investment tax credit. In this case the lessor buys the asset, takes advantage of the tax shields at the earliest opportunity, and passes them through to the user or lessee by lower rentals. The tax asymmetry between the two parties creates a tax advantage to the lease. How much of the gain goes to either party depends upon the demand for tax-motivated leasing transactions and the supply of taxable earnings to shelter the tax shields. The question arises as to how the gains in leasing should be allowed to influence the decision to purchase an asset.

Let us make the simplifying assumption that a corporation has sufficiently large tax losses from the past that it does not expect ever to resume taxpaying. We shall later relax this assumption. The company is valuing a new project and wants to know how leasing should influence the capital investment decision. In this respect, leasing may be viewed as a financing decision that is dependent on the investment decision, as corporations cannot lease without using the assets. The financial analyst must answer two questions:

Is leasing profitable compared with direct purchase?

Is the project profitable when financed by the lease?

An asset should be leased only when the answer to both questions is positive. It should be noticed that an asset may have a negative net present value based on purchase, but a positive net present value when combined with a lease. Of course, we shall wish to qualify these statements later in the chapter. However, the important point is that leasing under some circumstances can change the decision on new capital projects. In the case of one lease by the Anaconda Company (which we discuss in detail in Appendix 23.1), the leasing decision could have been worth up to $35 million to the company. In that case the asset cost $110 million. It is not difficult to see that leasing can be a valuable source of finance.

How to Value a Financial Lease

There are three reasons why company analysts should undertake detailed valuations of lease contracts. First, unless the circumstances are favorable and the terms of the lease are right, outright purchase may be cheaper than leasing an asset. Second, because the precise terms of the lease (such as its length and the timing of rental payments) can materially affect its present value, a valuation method is required so that alternative terms can be compared. Finally, it is important to know the size of the "cake" (net present value) obtained from the lease, and how the cake is to be shared between lessor and lessee. Let us examine an example using a simple lease.

A SIMPLE LEASE

In order to fulfill a particular contract, Smith, Inc., needs a specialized machine tool. The contract is profitable, and management is satisfied that the machine tool would represent an attractive project with a positive net present value. Management is contemplating lease financing for the machine tool, and a leasing company has offered a financial lease for the length of the machine's economic life, four years. The purchase price of the machine tool is $1 million. The lease contract stipulates five payments of $210,000 per year, with each payment to be made in advance. As Smith, Inc., is fully taxpaying, it can obtain the investment tax credit,[1] and tax shields from depreciation.

An analysis of the proposed lease is given in Table 23.4. The lease payments are shown in column 1, with the corresponding tax savings of $96,600 based on a corporate tax rate of 46 percent shown in column 2. If Smith, Inc., leases the machine tool, it will save paying the $1 million purchase price in column 3, but it will lose the tax benefits related to purchase shown in columns 4 and 5. These tax benefits, based upon straight-line depreciation, total $115,000 each year (250,000 × 0.46). A more accelerated form of depreciation usually is used (Chapter 4), but we have chosen the straight-line method to make the calculations easier to follow.

The difference between the cash flows associated with the lease and the cash flows associated with purchase is given in column 6 of the table. These net incremental cash flows have been discounted at the after-tax borrowing rate of Smith, Inc., because interest charges are tax-deductible. Given the current corporate tax rate of 46 percent and interest at 10 percent, the after-tax interest rate is simply $0.10 \times (1 - 0.46) = 0.054$ or 5.4 percent. It is important to appreciate that the after-tax interest rate used in the analysis should be the rate that Smith, Inc., would have to pay if it took out a secured loan on the asset repayable on the terms that are implicit in the lease rental schedule. In effect, we compare lease financing with debt financing for the asset by discounting at the after-tax interest rate on the equivalent loan.

After discounting the net cash flows (column 8), we find that the net present value of the lease is −$15,827. This negative NPV means that leasing

---

[1]We have included the tax credit for illustration, although the entire tax credit is not ordinarily available for assets with lives of less than five years (see Chapter 4).

Table 23.4
Analysis of a financial lease from the standpoint of a taxpaying lessee (thousands of dollars)

End of year	Lease payment (1)	Tax shield for lease payments (210 × 46%) (2)	Purchase cost (3)	Investment tax credit (10%) (4)	Tax shield from depreciation (250 × 46%) (5)	Total cash flow (6)	Discount factor at 5.4% (7)	Present value (8)
0	−210	96.6	1,000	−100		786.6	1.0000	786.600
1	−210	96.6			−115	−228.4	.94877	−216.699
2	−210	96.6			−115	−228.4	.90016	−205.597
3	−210	96.6			−115	−228.4	.85404	−195.063
4	−210	96.6			−115	−228.4	.81028	−185.068

Net present value of leasing versus purchase = −15.827

is more expensive than borrowing the funds from the bank to purchase the machine tool. However, it is possible that Smith, Inc., still may wish to lease the asset because of some intangible benefits. For example, the leasing company may offer quick delivery or a speedy repair and maintenance service, while taking care of insurance premiums. The value of such convenience to Smith, Inc., can be compared with the NPV of the lease.

We have seen that the lease being proposed to Smith, Inc., is unprofitable from Smith's point of view. How much is the lessor making on this particular lease? The figures from the point of view of the lessor are shown in Table

Table 23.5
Analysis of a financial lease from the standpoint of a taxpaying lessor (thousands of dollars)

End of year	Lease payment (1)	Tax payment (2)	Purchase cost (3)	Investment tax credit (4)	Tax shield from depreciation (5)	Total cash flow (6)	Discount factor at 5.4% (7)	Present value (8)
0	210	−96.6	−1,000	100		−786.6	1.0000	−786.600
1	210	−96.6			115	228.4	.94877	216.699
2	210	−96.6			115	228.4	.90016	205.597
3	210	−96.6			115	228.4	.85404	195.063
4	210	−96.6			115	228.4	.81028	185.068

Net present value of leasing versus lending = 15.827

23.5. Note that the numbers in this table are exactly the same as the numbers in Table 23.4 except that the signs have been reversed. This really should not be surprising, for the lessee's payment is the lessor's receipt, and both are paying taxes. Thus, the lessor is making a positive net present value totaling $15,827, the same as the lessee's loss. We have discounted the lessor's cash flows at the same 5.4 percent rate as we did for the lessee's cash flows as this is the after-tax lending rate that the lessor's banking parent company would have charged the lessee if the funds had been lent directly in the form of a loan. From the lessor's point of view, the lease is comparable to a direct loan to Smith, Inc.

In our simple example leasing is a zero–sum game, unless the lessor can perform services for the lessee at a cheaper rate than the lessee (or its agent) could perform for itself. The picture would change radically, however, if the lessee were not paying taxes.

A NONTAXPAYING LESSEE

Let us suppose now that Smith, Inc., will not be paying taxes in the foreseeable future; what is the value of the lease now? Table 23.6 provides the answer, and the analysis is remarkably simple. Notice that the lease payments and the purchase cost of the asset are exactly the same as in the previous example, but there is now no investment tax credit, nor are there any tax shields from depreciation. Smith, Inc., cannot capture these tax shields because the firm is not expected to pay taxes in the foreseeable future. Similarly, the net cash flows have been discounted at the firm's 10 percent before-tax

Table 23.6
Analysis of a financial lease from the standpoint of a nontaxpaying lessee (thousands of dollars)

End of year	Lease payment (1)	Tax shield from lease payments (2)	Purchase cost (3)	Investment tax credit (4)	Tax shield from depreciation (5)	Total cash flow (6)	Discount factor at 10% (7)	Present value (8)
0	−210	0	1,000	0		790	1.000	790.000
1	−210	0			0	−210	.90909	−190.909
2	−210	0			0	−210	.82645	−173.555
3	−210	0			0	−210	.75131	−157.775
4	−210	0			0	−210	.68301	−143.432

Net present value of leasing versus purchase = 124.329

borrowing rate. Although interest payments are an allowable tax deduction, the firm cannot claim the deduction unless it has taxable income.

When Smith, Inc., is nontaxpaying, leasing has become substantially more profitable, and the value of the lease compared with purchase and borrowing is $124,329 now. Leasing has become more attractive because the lessor is still able to claim the tax benefits of purchase even if the lessee cannot. The lessor must have given some of the benefits to the lessee through the lease payments, or the NPV would not be positive.

Note that we have made a number of simplifying assumptions regarding taxes. The first is that the tax deduction on the lease rentals is obtained simultaneously with their payment. In fact, because corporate taxes are paid quarterly, a delay of up to three months could occur in the receipt of the tax deduction. Secondly, the investment tax credit is assumed to be obtained at the same time that the purchase is made, while the tax shields from depreciation are delayed by one year. We have made the latter assumption because depreciation can be claimed only after the asset is ready for use, and as we are using annual discounting, the first tax shield from depreciation is assumed to occur at the end of the first year. In reality, a smaller tax shield would accrue every quarter. We would stress that with a real lease the exact timing of payments and tax benefits is very important, and monthly or quarterly discounting often will be necessary.

Two comments should be made about the tax advantages of leasing. First, only a limited number of companies are in a nontaxpaying position. The largest in this group are charities, which are tax-exempt and therefore unable to obtain tax shields arising from the assets that they buy. Companies in some industries, such as the airlines and shipping industries, frequently are temporary nontaxpayers because of the accumulation of generous tax incentives associated with their investment programs or because of a poor earnings record.

Second, the lessor's before-tax interest rate is the same as the lessee's before-tax interest rate. This may seem surprising, as you might think the lessor should be able to borrow at a cheaper rate than the lessee. This is beside the point. The lessor is comparing the lease to an equivalent loan that may be granted to the lessee secured on the same asset. Similarly, the lessee is comparing the lease with effectively the same loan that it might obtain directly from a bank or some other lender. Therefore, both parties assume the same before-tax interest rate, although their after-tax interest rates will be different if they are in different taxpaying positions. The particular lending rate will reflect the creditworthiness of the borrower, the duration of the effective loan, the repayment schedule, and the risks to the lessor.

The discounted cash flow method of lease valuation that we have used was proven to be correct by Myers, Dill, and Bautista (1976) who examined companies that were either taxpaying or permanently nontaxpaying. Franks and Hodges (1978) adapted that method to situations where a company is in a temporary nontaxpaying position.

TEMPORARY NONTAXPAYING LESSEES

Most companies currently not paying taxes expect to do so eventually when they start earning taxable income again. If a company's current profits are insufficient to absorb past losses, or if they are insufficient to absorb all the tax shields (investment tax credits and depreciation) generated by newly purchased assets, the company is in a nontaxpaying position. However, if it expects that future profits eventually can absorb the tax shields being generated and can absorb the losses being carried forward, its nontaxpaying position is temporary. In order to calculate the net present value of a lease, it is necessary to estimate the future date when the company will return to taxpaying.

The question is, how should a lease be valued when the tax position is expected to change? In Table 23.7 we have assumed that Smith, Inc., is expected to be in a nontaxpaying position for exactly two years, and in the third year it will resume paying taxes. Although the lease rental payments are the same as in previous examples, the tax shields from the lease payments will not be available to Smith, Inc., until the third year. In the third year the company is able to obtain tax shields of 4 × $96,600 = $386,400, as it is allowed to carry forward the unused tax shields from the three previous payments. Likewise, if the company had purchased the asset, it would have obtained the investment tax credit in the third year and also would have obtained the tax shields from depreciation. As the table shows, the value of the lease to Smith, Inc., has been reduced significantly compared with the permanent nontaxpaying position, from $124,329 to −$7,844.

Table 23.7
Analysis of a financial lease from the standpoint of a temporary nontaxpaying lessee (nontaxpaying for two years) (thousands of dollars)

End of year	Lease payment (1)	Tax shield from lease payments (2)	Purchase cost (3)	Investment tax credit (4)	Tax shield from depreciation (5)	Total cash flow (6)	Discount factor* (7)	Present value (8)
0	−210	0	1,000			790	1.0000	790.000
1	−210	0				−210	0.94457	−198.360
2	−210	0				−210	0.89417	−187.776
3	−210	386.4		−100	−345	−268.6	0.84836	−227.869
4	−210	96.6			−115	−228.4	0.80490	−183.839
					Net present value of leasing versus purchase =			−7.844

*Derived in Appendix 23.1

When valuing leases we first obtain the net incremental cash flow for the difference between leasing and purchase. The net incremental cash flow must reflect the timing of any tax effects, which will depend on whether the company is in a taxpaying, a permanently nontaxpaying, or a temporarily nontaxpaying position. In each case, the after-tax borrowing rate must be used as the discount rate in order to obtain the required comparison between leasing and debt finance. If the company is taxpaying, the after-tax borrowing rate is used as the discount rate, and if the company is permanently nontaxpaying, its after-tax rate becomes equal to the before-tax borrowing rate. However, when a company is temporarily nontaxpaying, the tax adjustment to the discount rate changes with time. The problem is that for some periods the company is nontaxpaying and therefore unable to take immediate advantage of the tax shields on interest payments.

You might suggest that we simply use a before-tax discount rate for the nontaxpaying periods and an after-tax discount rate for the taxpaying periods. Such a simple solution is incorrect, however, because unused tax credits can be carried forward from one period to another. For example, at Smith, Inc., the tax shields from the interest payments that cannot be deducted in the first two nontaxpaying periods can be carried forward and deducted when Smith, Inc., is expecting to have taxable income. A simple example will illustrate the problem of obtaining an after-tax interest rate when a company is in a temporary nontaxpaying position.

Suppose that a nontaxpaying company borrows $100 for one year at 10 percent, with cash flows as follows:

	Year 0	Year 1
Principal	+100	−100
Interest		−10
	+100	−110

The effective rate of interest on the loan is obviously 10 percent. You can check this by calculating an internal rate of return on the loan. If the borrower is taxpaying at a rate of 46 percent, what would be the effective after-tax interest rate being paid? The cash flows are still quite simple:

	Year 0	Year 1
Principal	+100	−100
Interest		−10
Tax saving		+4.6
	+100	−105.4

It is just as obvious that the after-tax interest rate is now 5.4 percent $[0.10 \times (1 - 0.46)]$. Of course, we have assumed that the tax saving on the interest income is enjoyed immediately, when the interest is paid by the borrower. If the tax savings are always delayed by one year, how would the after-tax interest rate change? Would it go up or down? The answer is it would go up, because if tax savings are delayed, their present value is reduced. The cash flows in the example would now appear as follows:

	Year 0	Year 1	Year 2
Principal	+100	−100	
Interest		−10	
Tax			+4.6
	+100	−110	+4.6

The effective after-tax interest rate for the loan is not quite so obvious now, but it can be calculated by discounting the delayed tax savings in year 2 back to year 1 as shown below. The after-tax discount rate that should be used to discount the tax savings in year 2 for this purpose is the after-tax interest rate for that year. In this case, the year 2 after-tax interest rate is $10 \times (1 - 0.46) = 5.4$ percent, as by year 2 the company is taxpaying and can take deductions against taxable income immediately. The present value in year 1 for the tax saving of \$4.60 in year 2 is $4.6/(1.054) = \$4.3643$. As a result, the effective after-tax interest rate applicable to year 1 is $10 \times (1 - 0.43643) = 5.6357$ percent as can be seen below:

	Year 0	Year 1	Year 2
Principal	+100	−100.0000	
Interest		−10.0000	
Discounted tax savings		+4.3643	0
	+100	−105.6357	0

We use similar principles to compute the after-tax discount rate when tax savings are postponed even longer than one year, as in the example of Table 23.7. In Appendix 23.1 we show how the discount rates used in the table were derived. The most important point to understand is that the after-tax discount rate must reflect the *timing* of the tax savings on interest expense (or for lenders, the timing of the tax payments on interest income). Tax delays are most important when a company is in a temporary nontaxpaying position. Such delays occur in everyday situations whenever tax payments or savings are delayed. It has been estimated that recently 27 percent of United States companies were not paying corporate taxes.

Loan Balance Method

In all the examples so far, leases have been valued using an after-tax discount rate. When the lessee is in a temporary nontaxpaying position, the calculation of the after-tax rates can be complex, as Appendix 23.1 shows. In this section we demonstrate an alternative method of obtaining the net present value of a lease that is entirely consistent with the after-tax discount rate approach. The alternative is called the **loan balance method.** The object of the loan balance method is to determine the sum of money that, if placed in a bank today, would be just sufficient (together with interest from the bank) to pay the after-tax lease cash flows, with nothing left over at the end of the lease. This initial sum in the bank is equal to the present value of the lease. Therefore, the difference between the purchase cost of the asset and the initial sum in the bank is equal to the net present value of the lease. If the bank deposit that would be required to pay the lease rentals is less than the cost of the asset, the net present value is positive, and the lease is profitable. This method of calculating net present value was described in Chapter 3.

An advantage of the loan balance method is that it does not require explicit calculation of the period-by-period after-tax discount rate. We can use the same procedure for a company in any tax- or nontaxpaying position. The interest received in the loan balance method is equal to the interest that would have been paid had the company borrowed to purchase the asset and then repaid the loan on the schedule implicit in the lease rentals. Because the absolute amount of money that would be paid as interest is revealed by the loan balance method, the corresponding tax savings can be calculated and shown where they actually occur in the correct taxpaying period.

The loan balance method is not difficult to use when the lessee is in a temporary nontaxpaying position. In Table 23.8 we have constructed the equivalent loan balance for the example analyzed earlier in Table 23.7, in

Table 23.8   *Loan balance method: first try (thousands of dollars)*

End of year	Lease obligation (1)	Interest income (at 10%) (2)	Tax on interest income (3)	Net change in bank balance (4)	New bank balance (5)
0					1100.000
0	−210.0			−210.000	890.000
1	−210.0	89.00		−121.000	769.000
2	−210.0	76.90		−133.100	635.900
3	−268.6	63.59	−105.565	−310.575	325.325
4	−228.4	32.533	−14.965	−210.832	114.493

which the company was assumed to be nontaxpaying for just two years. Column 1 provides the cash flow obligations of the lease, taken from the total cash flow column in Table 23.7 except for year 0. We have removed the purchase cost of $1 million from the cash flow in year 0 because we wish to estimate the initial bank deposit that will provide for the cost of the lease and to compare this deposit with the $1 million purchase cost of the machine. Column 2 of Table 23.8 shows interest income on each new bank balance. Column 3 shows the tax payments on the interest income (the first tax payments on the interest income are not paid until year three as the firm is nontaxpaying for the first two years). Column 4, headed "Net change in bank balance," is the sum of all the cash flows in columns 1, 2, and 3. The final column is the bank balance, which is the sum of the previous year's bank balance less the net cash flows of the current year.

In the table we have arbitrarily chosen an initial loan balance of $1,100,000. We pay off the first lease rental (which is in advance) immediately, and the new loan balance is $890,000. We receive interest income of $89,000 on the outstanding loan balance at the end of year 1 and make the second lease payment of $210,000; the bank balance is reduced by $210,000 − $89,000 = $121,000 to $769,000 at the end of the first year. As we continue this process through the second, third, and fourth years, we find that after paying off all obligations of the lease there is still a positive balance in the bank of more than $114,000.

It should be clear that the initial amount of $1,100,000 in the bank is more than sufficient to pay off the obligations of the lease. What amount then should the initial balance be? Obviously, an amount smaller than $1,100,000. If we try $1 million, we would find this to be too small an amount, for a negative balance would be left at the end of year 4; you might like to check this for yourself. We could continue by trial and error until we arrive at the unique initial loan balance that exactly pays off the after-tax cash flows associated with the lease and leaves a zero bank balance at the end of year 4, (or we could obtain a final solution more quickly with the interpolation method that we use to find the internal rate of return for a capital project).

Table 23.9 shows that the unique bank deposit that would be sufficient to pay all the lease cash flows with nothing left over is $1,007,844. The net present value of the lease is obtained by subtracting from the $1 million purchase cost of the asset the initial loan balance of $1,007,844 leaving an NPV of −$7,844. This result is identical to the result in Table 23.7, which was obtained by the discounted cash flow method.

This example demonstrates a number of important points. First, the loan balance method can provide the NPV of a lease without requiring the calculation of after-tax discount rates. Second, the loan balance method is equivalent to the after-tax discount rate approach. Third, the loan balance method is easier than discounting when there are complex lags in tax payments. Fourth, both methods have assumed that lease finance is exactly equivalent to debt finance and that lease finance displaces debt on a dollar-for-dollar basis. This assumption is explicit in the loan balance method where

Table 23.9   Loan balance method: solution (thousands of dollars)

End of year	Lease obligation	Interest income	Tax on interest income	Net change in bank balance	New bank balance
0					1,007.844
0	−210.0			−210.000	797.844
1	−210.0	79.784		−130.216	667.628
2	−210.0	66.763		−143.237	524.391
3	−268.6	52.439	−91.534	−307.695	216.696
4	−228.4	21.670	−9.968	−216.698	0.0*

*Because of rounding error the loan balance is in fact 0.002, rather than 0.000.

the lease is compared directly with an equivalent loan interest and repayment schedule. Finally, the two methods can be used by both lessors and lessees.

The discounted cash flow and the loan balance methods are only two ways of obtaining the net present value of leasing versus purchase. Many companies, however, prefer to obtain the internal rate of return for a lease.

Net Present Value Versus Internal Rate of Return

We have used net present value (obtained by two methods) to compare leasing versus purchase. A survey conducted by Paul Anderson and John Martin (1977) disclosed that out of forty-eight major United States companies, twenty-four companies used the internal rate of return method to evaluate a lease, and only eleven used the net present value method; the two methods together were used by over 70 percent of the sample. Two questions arise from this survey. Why is the IRR method so popular; and, are there any advantages to using one method over another?

The IRR method is popular because it provides a percentage return from a lease that can be compared with the equivalent loan interest rate. Thus, the lessee is able to compare directly whether a lease is cheaper or more expensive than borrowing, and the lessor is able to compare whether a lease is more or less profitable than lending. Although the NPV method does use the equivalent borrowing (or lending) rate to evaluate a lease, the resulting profit or loss (i.e., the NPV) cannot be compared directly with market interest rates. For this reason analysts who like to think like bankers find rates of return a more appealing measure than dollar profits.

You may remember that in Chapter 5 we showed that the IRR method generally is unsuited for comparisons between mutually exclusive alternatives. We found that the IRR can be larger for one of two alternative investments even though the NPV is smaller. Frequently, it may be necessary to compare bids submitted by different lessors or even to compare different leases with different lives. The IRR method may suggest that one lease provides a greater rate of return than another lease, even though the NPV is smaller. Thus the IRR method can lead to wrong decisions in some circumstances. (If you do not understand how this can arise, review Chapter 5; there is also an exercise at the end of Chapter 5 that demonstrates the point.)

A second objection to the use of the IRR method in leasing concerns the choice of the after-tax interest rate with which the IRR should be compared. This objection may best be understood by studying the example in Table 23.7. The IRR calculated on the net cash flows shown in column 6 of the table is 6.078 percent. To decide whether the lease is profitable using the IRR, we must compare it with the after-tax borrowing rate of the lessee. However, we have shown that there is no single after-tax borrowing rate for this particular lease. In Appendix 23.1 we show that the after-tax interest rate varies from one period to another for a temporarily nontaxpaying company. The after-tax interest rate for each year is shown below:

Period	After-tax interest rate (%)
0–1	5.869
1–2	5.636
2–3	5.400
3–4	5.400

The after-tax interest rates vary from one period to another because the remaining nontaxpaying period is being reduced as we approach the end of the lease. In our example, an IRR of over 6 percent suggests that the lease is profitable because the after-tax cost of money is always less than 6 percent. However, to use the IRR method we had to calculate the after-tax interest rates in order to make this comparison. If the after-tax interest rates in some years had been higher than 6 percent, it would have been difficult to know whether the lease is profitable. As in this situation, the IRR method appears to have a distinct disadvantage. Although we are not suggesting that analysts should never use the IRR method, one should be wary of the pitfalls in the IRR method and should obtain the NPV of leases as a safeguard.

Residual Values

In all examples, we have assumed that the value of a leased asset at the end of the term of the lease is zero. In general, the value of the asset at the end of the lease is not zero. In most lease contracts the lessee receives the benefit of only a stipulated proportion of the residual value of the asset when it is resold. The remaining proportion will be lost to the lessee if the equipment is leased but will not be lost if the equipment is purchased. Thus the portion of the residual value of the equipment that goes to the lessors when the lease is terminated will be a negative cash flow in the lessee's analysis of the lease. In the extreme case of an operating lease, the entire residual value of the equipment may go to the lessor; in this case the residual value of the leased asset is an important part of the cash flow.

Frequently, the estimation of the residual value is a difficult exercise. For example, suppose that Smith, Inc., wishes to lease a car for two years and that at the end of the two-year period the car will be returned to the lessor. The lessee wishes to know what residual value it should use in the cash flow at the end of the two-year period when comparing leasing with purchase. The value can be estimated by using the ratio of the current secondhand price for a two-year-old car to the value that it had when it was new. This ratio when multiplied by the price of the new car that is to be leased will give an estimate of the possible residual value two years hence. The estimated value that is obtained in this way would have to be altered if there has been a change in the rate of inflation. Because the estimate of the residual value involves risk, the discount rate that is used for the residual value in the lease analysis should include a premium for systematic risk. For this purpose it would be necessary to estimate the value of beta for secondhand car prices.

Another approach that can be employed to obtain the residual value of some assets is to use the certainty equivalent residual values that can be obtained from residual value insurance contracts that are offered by some insurers, e.g., Lloyds of London. If the residual value of the asset is insured, the minimum residual value is certain and can be discounted at the risk-free rate. However, the cost of insurance premiums must also be included as a cash flow in the analysis of the lease.

A more difficult example would be a two-year computer lease. The decline in a computer's value during two years can be related to its original cost in exactly the same way as with used cars, but we may not be able to assume that the same rate of decline in secondhand value will hold in the future, unless we believe that the past rate of technological obsolescence will be sustained during the life of the lease. If the rate of inflation is reduced, or if the rate of obsolescence is expected to increase, for example because of the introduction of a new generation of computers during the life of the lease, the ratio of the residual value of the two-year-old computer to its value when new would require downward adjustment. Alternatively, the insured value under a residual value insurance contract may be used as a certainty equivalent value, if such insurance is available.[2]

---

[2]An alternative approach to residual values would be to use an option valuation model. See J. J. McConnell and J. S. Schallheim (1983) for a description of such an approach.

Implications of Modigliani and Miller's versus Miller's Model of Debt and Taxes for Leasing

An important assumption made thus far in our analysis of leasing is that the alternative to a lease is the purchase of the asset financed by debt. The debt finance alternative has determined the discount rates that we have used to analyze leases so far. This assumption that the alternative to a lease is debt finance is based upon the proposition by Modigliani and Miller (1963) discussed in Chapters 21 and 22 that the before-tax cost of debt equals the cost of equity. Therefore, debt financing is always cheaper than equity financing if the borrower can deduct the interest payments from his taxable income. When debt is cheaper than equity, debt financing becomes the logical alternative to lease financing. A further implication of the Modigliani and Miller model is that if a lessee is only temporarily nontaxpaying, debt is still cheaper than equity, and the discount rate that a temporarily nontaxpaying lessee should use as its own after-tax cost of borrowing obtained in the manner that we have discussed in this chapter.

In Chapters 21 and 22 we also discussed an alternative model suggested by Miller (1977) that has somewhat different implications for the discount rate used in leasing. In Miller's model of debt and taxes, it is the after-tax cost of debt that equals the cost of equity. This means that if the borrower is either nontaxpaying or temporarily nontaxpaying, the after-tax cost of debt is greater than the cost of equity, for the borrower does not enjoy the full benefit of the tax-deductibility of interest payments. Consequently, the alternative to lease financing would be purchase of the asset financed by new equity.

Accordingly, a lessee that is either nontaxpaying or temporarily nontaxpaying should discount the cash flows for a lease using the (risk-free) cost of equity, which is equal to the after-tax cost of debt that would be paid by a fully taxpaying company. Therefore the discount rates calculated for the example in Table 23.7 no longer apply in Miller's world. As the Miller view of the world implies smaller after-tax discount rates for temporarily nontaxpaying lessees, the attractiveness of leasing for them is diminished, if the Miller view is correct.

The Modigliani and Miller and the Miller views of the world of debt and taxes are at two extremes. If the truth lies somewhere between, we at least know how to obtain the range of net present values corresponding to the two models. A more complete analysis of leasing based on Miller's model of debt and taxes is given in Appendix 23.2.

Interactions Between Leasing and Investment Decisions

Leasing may be viewed as a financing decision that depends upon an investment decision. It may be that for some companies in temporary nontaxpaying positions a project will appear unprofitable until financed by a lease or until combined with some other means of capturing unused tax shields.

To analyze a lease, the analyst must forecast the dates when tax payments actually will be made. The resumption of taxpaying may be difficult to forecast. Not only would projects currently under consideration alter the tax allowance position and change the nontaxpaying period, but future (possibly unknown) projects may do so as well. The question is, what incremental difference does the current project (with a lease) make to the forecast nontaxpaying period and to the after-tax value of the firm? This is a difficult comparison to make, because future projects must be defined, and their cash flows must be forecast. There is a second implication of this analysis, which is that the net present value of a capital project with or without a lease cannot be separated from the corporation's portfolio of other projects. This problem was examined in Chapter 4, when we analyzed how the tax flows of two projects interacted with each other when one project had a tax loss at the same time as the other project had a taxable profit. The value of one project can be calculated only by initially valuing the entire portfolio of projects. This problem is analyzed in some detail by Cooper and Franks (1983).

In our analysis, it should be remembered that leasing is only one method of taking advantage of unused tax benefits. The firm could acquire taxpaying companies and combine the taxable income of the acquired company with its own tax-deductible losses. Clearly, there are costs and benefits associated with acquisitions. Whether a company chooses leasing, or acquisition, or some other route to obtaining the tax benefit from unused tax credits depends upon the costs of each of these financial transactions and the resulting benefits.

Another point that should concern lessees is the leasing "package" that is offered. A lessor who does not do a sufficiently thorough credit analysis prior to offering the leasing package may overestimate the customer's credit risk. The creditworthy lessee should ensure that the lessor is aware of the lessee's credit rating and that the interest implicit in the lease reflects a fair estimate of the lessee's credit risk.

Lease Rates and Competition in the Leasing Market

We already have described how the profitability of leasing will be affected if one party to the transaction is currently nontaxpaying or is in a temporary nontaxpaying position. We did not say what factors affect the division of the tax benefits from a lease between the lessor and the lessee. If we assume that the amount of taxable profits available as a tax shelter to lessors is greater than the demand for it by lessees, we would expect lease rental rates to be lower and most of the tax gains from leasing to accrue to lessees. Conversely, if large numbers of firms are in nontaxpaying positions, and there is a shortage of taxable profits among lessors, lease rates will be driven up and lessees will obtain a smaller proportion of the gains. Lessors can only make positive NPVs from leasing if there is a scarce resource. In this case, the potential scarce resource is the taxable profits made available to shelter the unused tax benefits of nontaxpaying corporations.

The exact size of the tax benefits to leasing depends upon two important factors other than the tax positions of the parties involved. The first is the level and the timing of the tax benefits that the federal government allows industry for capital investment. The higher the tax credits and allowances and the earlier they are received, the more valuable leasing will be if one party is nontaxpaying. The second factor is high interest rates. If interest rates were zero, the acceleration of tax benefits would be worthless, as the present value would be unaltered. Because high interest rates mean a high discount rate, bringing forward or accelerating the tax benefits of a project through leasing increases the net present value of the project. Thus high interest rates favor leasing.

You might well ask why the government permits leasing. If a lease is profitable for tax reasons, it provides tax incentives for an investment that might otherwise not occur if the firm is nontaxpaying. Corporate leasing enables the firm to recapture part of the tax benefits even though the firm is not currently paying taxes. Leasing cannot result in tax losses to the Internal Revenue Service greater than those that would have been lost had the firm been taxpaying and been able to obtain the tax benefits on its own account. However, if the IRS does believe that a leasing arrangement is purely a tax avoidance exercise, it has the right to invalidate the contract.

Summary

In this chapter we have described different types of leasing and how a lease can be valued under different tax positions. We have shown how the lease's value can change dramatically with different assumptions about the forecast taxpaying position of the lessee. We calculated the NPV of a lease using the discounted cash flow approach and the loan balance method. We also compared the NPV and the IRR measures for a lease, noting that although IRR is the more popular method, it can give incorrect signals under some circumstances. Finally, we have discussed the economics of leasing, isolating some factors that determine the profitability of leasing and the distribution of gains between lessees and lessors.

Appendix 23.1 Temporary Nontaxpaying Periods and the After-tax Discount Rate

The calculation of discount factors when there is a temporary nontaxpaying period is complex. Consider the example in the text (Table 23.7) where the firm is nontaxpaying for two years; the first tax payment is therefore in year three.

In our example there are three different tax periods. The cash flows that accrue at the end of periods 3 and 4 are subject to no delays in taxes, as they fall within the taxpaying period. The cash flow that occurs at the end of period 2, however, is subject to a one-year tax lag; that is, tax benefits are received only in year 3 on year 2's cash flows. Finally, the tax effects associated with the cash flow occurring at the end of period 1 are not felt until period 3.

We shall now calculate the after-tax interest rate for each period. It is quite easy to determine the rate for period 4 in the absence of a tax lag. The after-tax interest rate r_4 for the period is simply 5.4 percent

$$10 \times (1 - 0.46) = 5.4\%$$

if 10 percent is the before-tax borrowing rate of the firm. Similarly, the after tax rate of interest r_3 for period 3 is also 5.4 percent, as cash flows occurring at the end of period 3 are not subject to any tax lag. The single-period discount factor for both these periods is 1/1.054. Cash flows received in period 2 are subject to a tax lag of one year; for interest payments made in period 2 tax benefits are not received until period 3. We obtain the after-tax interest r_2 for period 2 using the following procedure. For interest charges occurring in period 2, tax benefits accrue to period 3, as outlined below:

	Period 2	Period 3
Interest	10	
Tax		−4.6

As the before-tax interest rate is 10 percent, we can calculate the after-tax interest rate for period 2 by discounting the tax benefits back one year using period 3's discount factor (calculated previously as 1.054):

$$r_2 = 10 - \frac{4.6}{1.054}$$

$$= 5.6357$$

The discount factor for period 2 therefore will be 1/1.056357. We use exactly the same procedure to calculate the after-tax interest rate r_1 for period 1, except that we must recognize that the tax benefits occur with a lag of *two* years.

	Period 1	Period 2	Period 3
Interest	10		
Tax			−4.6

We discount the tax benefits in period 3 to period 1 using the discount factors calculated for periods 2 (1/1.056357) and 3 (1/1.054):

$$r_1 = 10 - \frac{4.6}{1.056357 \times 1.054}$$

$$= 5.868512$$

The discount factor for period 1 is therefore 1/1.05868511.

The after-tax interest rates and discount rates for each period are as follows:

Period	After-tax interest rate (r)
0–1	5.868512
1–2	5.6357
2–3	5.4
3–4	5.4

We must now calculate the discount factors that will carry the cash flow of any period back to period zero as follows:

Cash flow at end of year		Discount factor
1	$\dfrac{1}{(1.05868512)}$	= 0.94457
2	$\dfrac{1}{(1.05868512)(1.056357)}$	= 0.89417
3	$\dfrac{1}{(1.05868512)(1.056357)(1.054)}$	= 0.84836
4	$\dfrac{1}{(1.05868512)(1.056357)(1.054)(1.054)}$	= 0.80490

The cash flow occurring at the end of year 4 is discounted back to the end of year 3 at 5.4 percent, then back to the end of year 2 again at 5.4 percent, then to the end of year 1 at 5.6357 percent, and finally back to period 0 at 5.868512 percent. Of course, such discounting can be done in one step by multiplying year 4's cash flow by that year's discount factor, once the discount factors have been obtained in the way that we have shown. These are the discount factors that have been used to value the lease in Table 23.7.

Franks and Hodges (1978) applied this method of valuation to a leveraged lease transaction that financed an Anaconda Company aluminum reduction mill at Sebree, Kentucky. They showed how the value of the lease versus purchase decision depended critically on when Anaconda expected to resume paying taxes. In Table A23.1 we show the value of the lease under different assumptions about Anaconda's taxpaying resumption date. The aluminum reduction mill costs $110.7 million, and the value of the lease versus purchase decision could have been up to $35.56 million, if Anaconda's nontaxpaying period turned out to be fifteen years. The decline in the value of the lease for nontaxpaying periods beyond year 15 is in part due to the fact that the investment tax credit and the depreciation tax shield could be carried forward for only seven and five years, respectively.

Appendix 23.2 Leasing in Miller's World of Debt and Taxes

Brealey and Young (1980) have described the implications of Miller's (1977) model of debt and taxes. Brealey and Young's argument may be summarized as follows. Because leasing involves a series of obligatory payments, it is usual to compare the cash flows of the lease with those of the equivalent buy and borrow decision. This comparison is made because borrowing is never a more costly source of finance than equity in a Modigliani and Miller world (see Chapters 21 and 22). However, in Miller's model, the cost of debt after taxes is equal to the cost of (risk-free) equity finance. On a before-tax basis, the cost of debt is actually higher than the cost of equity, according to Miller's analysis. Thus, for firms that are tax-exempt (charities or local governments) or firms that are temporarily nontaxpaying, equity would be a cheaper source of finance than debt. It would be incorrect to compare leasing to buy and borrow when equity is cheaper than debt; leasing should be compared rather to buying and equity financing.

Consequently, Brealey and Young show that in Miller's model firms that are in a permanently nontaxpaying position usually should use equity financing rather than lease (for tax reasons). The only exception, from a tax point of view, is when the present value of the tax savings from allowances (and investment tax credits) exceeds the present value of the taxes on lease rental receipts. This result is contrary to that obtained when we assumed an

Table A23.1   *Value of the Anaconda lease with different taxpaying commencement dates*

Taxpaying commencement period (years)	Value of the lease to Anaconda (millions of dollars)
0	−3.03
1	−2.67
2	−1.93
3	−0.90
4	0.38
5	1.85
6	5.70
7	13.07
8	23.64
9	27.97
10	31.17
.	.
.	.
.	.
15	35.56
.	.
.	.
.	.
20	30.31
.	.
.	.
.	.
∞	25.17

1. Tax rate is 50 percent.
2. Present value of salvage value is $0.847 million.
3. Tax depreciation shield assumes an eleven-year depreciable life and a 5 percent book salvage value. A double declining balance was used for the first two years. In the third year, a switch was made to sum-of-the years' digits.
4. Discount rate is 8.926 percent pre-tax (compounded semiannually).

Source: J. R. Franks and S. D. Hodges, "Valuation of Financial Lease Contracts: A Note," *Journal of Finance,* 30, no. 2 (May 1978): 667.

MM world where debt was cheaper than equity after taxes. For firms that are in a temporary nontaxpaying position, however, leasing is likely to be the preferred source of finance even in a Miller world.

We can determine the conditions under which leasing is the preferred way of financing an asset in a Miller world by setting out an expression for the present value of the cash flows accruing to both the lessor (designated by subscript "o") and the lessee (designated by the subscript "e"). The net total benefits to a lease are given by the sum of the net present value to the lessor and the net present value to the lessee,

$$NPV = NPV_o + NPV_e \tag{A23.1}$$

The net present value NPV_o to the lessor is given by the payment A that it makes for the asset, the present value L of the lease rental payments that it receives less the present value LT_o of the taxes it pays on the lease rental receipts plus the tax savings ITC_o due to the investment tax credit for the asset plus the present value BT_o of the depreciation tax shield:

$$NPV_o = -A + L - LT_o + ITC_o + BT_o \tag{A23.2}$$

The net present value NPV_e of the lease to the lessee is similar but with opposite signs:

$$NPV_e = A - L + LT_e - ITC_e - BT_e \tag{A23.3}$$

If we add equation (A23.2) to equation (A23.3) and substitute the sum into equation (A23.1), we obtain an expression for the total net present value of the lease. We find that A and L cancel out leaving us with,

$$NPV = -LT_o + LT_e + ITC_o - ITC_e + BT_o - BT_e \tag{A23.4}$$

This equation provides a general expression for the combined net present value for the lessor and lessee who are parties to a lease contract. We shall analyze whether leasing can be profitable to corporations in particular tax-paying positions.

PERMANENTLY NONTAXPAYING LESSEE

If the lessee is permanently nontaxpaying, the present value of all tax effects for the lessee are equal to zero. Thus Equation (A23.4) simplifies to,

$$NPV = ITC_o + BT_o - LT_o \tag{A23.5}$$

Equation (A23.5) provides the combined net advantage to leasing in a Miller world when the lessee is permanently nontaxpaying. For such a lessee leasing can only be advantageous if the investment tax credit to the lessor plus the present value of the lessor's depreciation tax shield exceeds the present value of the lessor's taxes on the lease rental receipts.

Brealey and Young imply that leasing is not profitable for permanently nontaxpaying firms, but they ignored the investment tax credit. Equation (A23.5) shows that with the investment tax credit this need not be the case.

TEMPORARILY NONTAXPAYING LESSEE

Suppose now that the lessor is fully taxpaying at the corporate tax rate T_c, and that the lessee is temporarily nontaxpaying (its effective marginal tax rate increases with time). We can rewrite equation (A23.4) in the following form. The net present value from leasing will be greater than zero if

$$BT_o - LT_o + ITC_o > BT_e - LT_e + ITC_e \qquad \text{(A23.6)}$$

The left-hand side of this relation is the same as the right-hand side of equation (A23.5), which told us that if the lessee is in a permanently non-taxpaying position in a Miller world, leasing is profitable as long as this sum is greater than zero. In comparison, equation (A23.6) tells us that even if the lessee is in a temporary nontaxpaying position, leasing still is profitable so long as the right-hand side of equation (A23.6) does not exceed this sum (the left-hand side).

Under what circumstances would this condition hold? We can see the required conditions more clearly if we write out the two sides of the relation. We shall assume there are H lease payments, where the first starts in period zero:

$$BT_o - LT_o + ITC_o = \sum_{t=0}^{H} \frac{(B_t - L_t)T_o}{(1 + r_E)^t} + ITC_o \qquad \text{(A23.7)}$$

$$BT_e - LT_e + ITC_e = \sum_{t=0}^{H} \frac{(B_t - L_t)T_e(t)}{(1 + r_E)^t} + ITC_e \qquad \text{(A23.8)}$$

where $T_e(t)$ is the lessee's effective tax rate as a function of time and where r_E is the cost of equity $[r_E = r_D(1 - T_c)]$ and r_D is the before-tax cost of debt. Equity is preferred to debt in Miller's world if the company is not fully taxpaying. Under what conditions would the sum in equation (A23.7) be larger than the sum in equation (A23.8)? As the lessor is in a fully taxpaying position, its tax rate is constant and equal to T_c in equation (A23.7).

In contrast, for the lessee in a temporary nontaxpaying position, the effective marginal rate of tax $T_e(t)$ is an increasing function of time t. For leasing to be preferred to equity financing, $(B_t - L_t)$ must be positive in the early years when the effective marginal tax rate $T_e(t)$ for the lessee is small, and negative in the later years as the effective marginal tax rate rises. With any form of accelerated depreciation combined with a flat or rising schedule of lease payments, this is likely to be the case. Thus, it is likely that leasing still is profitable, even in Miller's model, when one party is in a temporary non-taxpaying position.

Review Questions

1. Define an operating lease and a financial lease.
2. Under what circumstances can leasing be a less costly form of finance than debt?
3. Why might you expect the value of a lease to a lessee to increase as the period of nontaxpaying increases?
4. Would you expect higher interest rates to make tax-motivated leasing transactions more or less profitable? Why?
5. Describe a leveraged lease. Why are such leases so popular?
6. Would you expect lease finance to be equivalent to debt finance? Justify your answer.
7. Does it matter to leasing analysis whether you believe in an MM world of debt and taxes or a Miller world? Why or why not?
8. Why should long-term leases be capitalized and appear on the lessee's balance sheet? Who would find such information useful and why?
9. Under what circumstances should the leasing decision be permitted to change the accept-reject decision on a capital project?
10. "If a company is temporarily nontaxpaying, it is not possible to analyze a project or a lease in isolation from other investment decisions." Comment on this statement.

Problems

*1. Hammond Manufacturers, Inc., needs a computer costing $600,000 that has an economic life of five years. A lessor has offered Hammond a financial lease for the computer that consists of six payments of $125,000 per year for five years, with each payment to be made in advance. The alternative is for Hammond to borrow from the bank (using a secured five-year loan) at a cost of 12 percent per year. Both Hammond and the lessor pay corporate taxes at 46 percent and can recover the investment tax credit and depreciation tax shields.

    (a) Which alternative is beneficial to Hammond? Use ACRS depreciation.

    (b) What would be the NPV of the lease to the lessor?

2. What would happen to your answer if Hammond Manufacturers, Inc., expected to be in a temporary nontaxpaying position indefinitely owing to very large accumulated tax losses? Show workings to support your answer.

3. How would the decision to lease be affected if the accumulated tax losses are absorbed earlier, and Hammond is expected to start paying tax at the end of year 3? Assume that tax is paid annually and that ACRS depreciation is used.

*4. Calculate the appropriate after-tax discount factors for a five-year lease if a company is in a nontaxpaying position for the first four years. The rate at which it can borrow is 15 percent per year, and the corporate tax rate is 46 percent.

5. A company in a temporary nontaxpaying position is contemplating leasing an asset for its manufacturing operations. The asset costs $1,200,000 and would qualify for ITC and ACRS depreciation. Its economic life is three years. A leasing company has offered a financial lease calling for an advance payment immediately and three succeeding annual payments of $335,000 each.

    Assume both companies pay corporate tax at a rate of 46 percent and that the effective borrowing rate is 10 percent. Calculate the financial implications of leasing the asset if the company starts paying corporate tax in (a) year 1, or (b) year 3.

*6. Use the loan balance method to compute the value of a lease from the following information:

Cost of asset   = $600,000
Economic life = 5 years

Six financial lease payments for 5 years = $125,000 per year with each payment in advance.

Cost of borrowing = 12% annually
Corporate tax rate   = 46%

The company will start paying taxes at the end of year 3 and will take the ITC and begin using the ACRS depreciation tax shield in that year.

References

Anderson, P. F., and J. D. Martin, "Lease vs. Purchase Decisions: A Survey of Current Practice," *Financial Management,* 6, no. 1 (Spring 1977): 41–47.

Brealey, R. A., and C. Young, "Debt and Taxes: The Leasing Decision," *Journal of Finance,* 35, no. 5 (December 1980): 1245–1250.

Clark, T. M., *Leasing,* London: McGraw-Hill, 1978.

Cooper, I., and J. R. Franks, "The Interaction of Financial and Investment Decisions When the Firm Has Unused Tax Credits," *Journal of Finance,* 38, no. 2 (May 1983): 571–84.

Fabozzi, F. J., *Equipment Leasing: A Comprehensive Guide for Executives,* Homewood, Ill.: Dow Jones-Irwin, 1981.

Franks, J. R., and S. D. Hodges, "The Role of Leasing in Capital Investment," *National Westminster Bank Review* (1979).

Franks, J. R., and S. D. Hodges, "Valuation of Financial Leases: A Note," *Journal of Finance,* 30, no. 2 (May 1978): 657–69.

Hodges, S. D., "The Valuation of Variable Rate Leases," London Business School, Working Paper IFA No. 79.

McConnell, J. J., and J. S. Schallheim, "Valuation of Asset Leasing Contracts," *Journal of Financial Economics,* 12 (August 1983): 237–61.

Miller, M. H., "Debt and Taxes," *Journal of Finance,* 32, no. 2 (May 1977): 261–75.

Miller, M. H., and C. W. Upton, "Leasing, Buying and the Cost of Capital Services," *Journal of Finance,* 31, no. 36 (June 1976): 761–86.

Myers, S. C., D. Dill, and A. Bautista, "Valuation of Financial Lease Contracts," *Journal of Finance,* 31, no. 3 (June 1976): 799–819.

VI

Financial Planning

One of the primary responsibilities of financial management is to keep the company solvent. Solvency means that there are liquid assets in the company that can be turned into sufficient cash to pay its bills on time. Maintaining solvency requires efficient working capital management and the planning of timely flotations of long-term debt and equity financing. In the next two chapters we introduce working capital management, focusing on the management of accounts receivable in Chapter 24 and on the management of inventories in Chapter 25. Finally, in Chapter 26 concerning financial planning and forecasting, we show how the forecasts of a company's expected operating cash flows, working capital, dividends, capital investment, and financing decisions are brought together into its financial plan. We also consider how combinations of uncertain future events can impact on these forecasts and can affect both long-term and short-term financing requirements.

Working Capital Management and Investment in Receivables

Working capital management has two major components: management of accounts receivable and inventory management. This chapter discusses accounts receivable; Chapter 25 treats inventories. A company needs to develop a financial plan integrating working capital management with its other financial decisions. Consequently in Chapter 26 we shall bring together the components of working capital and show how they impinge on cash (or liquidity) management and financial planning.

What Is Working Capital Management?

Until now we have focused on the corporation's major financial decisions: capital expenditures, dividends, long-term debt and equity financing. Such decisions are made periodically rather than continually. Typically, they are based on forecasts of the firm's external environment and its business opportunities over several years into the future. But decisions concerning working capital management occur constantly. They can occupy far more management time than most other financial decisions.

Working capital is made up of cash and other current assets that can be converted into cash fairly quickly. For example, marketable securities can be sold and converted into cash within minutes, and accounts receivable and inventories can be converted into cash within months, depending on the firm's normal production and sales operating cycle. **Net working capital** is the excess of such current assets over current liabilities. Current liabilities arise either from operations (accounts payable, accrued wages and taxes) or from management choice (short-term debt). Working capital management involves planning and controlling these assets and liabilities so that the net of the two is kept at minimum levels consistent with not exposing the firm to an undue risk of defaulting on its short-term financial obligations.

Figure 24.1 illustrates how working capital management fits into the overall financial management of the corporation. The most important ingredients are:

production plans and sales forecasts

corporate policies with respect to credit sales, inventory levels, cash payment schedules, and limits on short-term debt

forecasts of the impact on current assets and liabilities of major investment and financing decisions

standby arrangements with the company's banks for cash and collection disbursement and for lines of credit

The assets and liabilities that make up working capital arise from a myriad of individual investment, financing, and operating decisions. The natural focus of working capital management is on how the sum of such decisions produces changes in the aggregate amount and composition of working capital. In contrast, our NPV rules have been developed for assessing one decision at a time.

Two criteria for a firmwide approach to working capital management are efficiency (not investing excessively in net working capital) traded off against **liquidity risk** (not being able to pay creditors on time). Contemporary finance theory does not define the role of liquidity formally. As a result, our net present value rules do not reflect a decision's impact on the liquidity of the corporation.

Some liquidity is stored, in the sense that marketable securities and other assets (such as accounts receivable and inventory) can be turned into cash (given sufficient time) to make cash payments. Some liquidity, such as unused bank credit lines, is of a standby nature that does not appear on the balance sheet.

The interrelated effects of the firm's activities on working capital require the firm's investment, financing, and operating decisions to be analyzed jointly, typically in the framework of an integrated set of forecasts, or financial plan.

Figure 24.1   *Schematic diagram of a firm's cash flow*

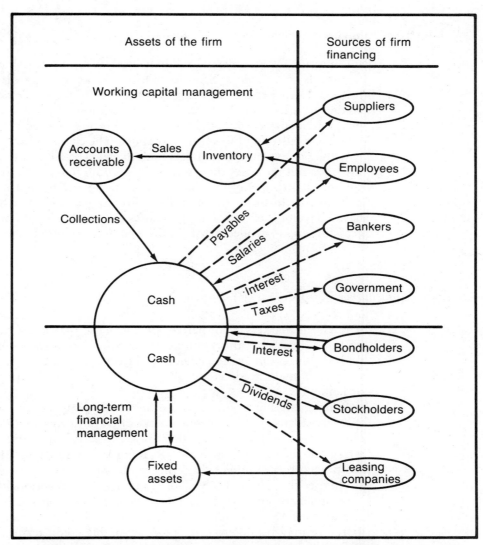

Source: Smith, K., *Guide to Working Capital Management,* New York: McGraw–Hill, 1979, p. 8

Accounts Receivable Management: An Overview

THE IMPORTANCE OF CREDIT SALES

It is unusual for commercial and industrial customers to pay cash immediately for goods and services. Sales include an extension of credit to the customer for an agreed period. The same is true, of course, for retail sales made on credit. In effect, credit terms are a dimension of the overall price for the buyer to consider. In other words, the terms of credit offered can affect whether a customer buys from a supplier. The choice of to whom the supplier is willing to extend credit affects both the level of sales and their risk. Because giving credit increases the company's ongoing investment in receivables, the supplier has to make sure that an appropriate rate of return is earned on the investment. In order to control the investment in receivables, the supplier has to develop cost-efficient procedures for monitoring the status of customer accounts and for collecting from the customers whose payments are overdue.

MARKET IMPERFECTIONS AND TRADE CREDIT

If financial markets were perfect (in the sense that loans could be arranged without incurring information, transactions, or other noninterest costs), trade credit could be considered a perfect substitute for a loan. However, such costs make trade credit more complex than ordinary bank borrowing or lending.

Since gathering information on the credit quality of individual customers is costly, firms typically offer one set of credit terms to all acceptable credit customers. Some customers thereby receive trade credit at an effective interest rate below that available to them on conventional loans. For other customers, these same credit terms represent effective rates of interest which are higher than the rates available to them on conventional loans.

Suppliers often have more information about their customers than banks do (or they may be able to secure such information more cheaply), and therefore may be able to offer more favorable credit terms.

For the borrower trade credit is a very flexible source of financing, something similar to a checking account overdraft. That is, the amount outstanding can be varied very quickly, and without incurring setup costs.

The current United States payment system involves delays while payments are in the mail, so there is constantly a large amount of accounts receivable outstanding in the economy as a whole—even without a deliberate delay of payments by credit customers.

In summary, imperfections in financial markets explain the continuing existence of trade credit in the economy as more than a simple substitute for bank loans. Many customers who borrow from their suppliers would find bank borrowing more expensive or even unavailable.

RECEIVABLES IN THE CORPORATE BALANCE SHEET

Table 24.1 illustrates the overall significance of customer receivables in current corporate assets from 1975 through 1982. Three features stand out. First, because receivables arise naturally as part of the sales-to-cash receipts cycle, corporations must make a significant continuing overall investment in customer receivables. Second, since early 1975 receivables have fluctuated in a fairly narrow range of 35.5 to 38.4 percent of total current assets. Third, there was some trend upward from 1978 through 1981, at the same time as short-term interest rates rose toward historically high levels. During this period, United States firms were financing an increasing share of customer credit needs.

CREDIT TERMS AND OPPORTUNITY COSTS

Credit can be extended most liberally with the least cost and risk if the variable cost of production is small in relation to price. In such circumstances the incremental amount invested in each sale is small compared with the amount billed. Nonetheless, it is important that credit extended to customers be related to their credit risk. For example, suppose that a supplier is a lower-risk borrower than its own customers. If it does not charge a higher effective interest rate on credit to its customers than it pays for borrowed funds, it may be subsidizing customers, unless, of course, it can justify this practice by extra sales revenues.

Charges for credit to retail customers who are billed monthly typically are built into the price for the goods. This policy may be unfair and costly to those retail customers who pay promptly. Given the high level of interest rates in recent years, it is common practice for companies to charge retail customers a substantial interest charge on unpaid balances after one month. A typical rate is 1.5 percent per month, or an annual rate of $(1.015)^{12} - 1 = 19.6$ percent.

The traditional practice in selling goods to business customers, however, is to offer a discount on goods that are paid for within a specified period. The billing expression of "2/10, net 30" specifies that a 2 percent discount may be taken by the purchaser if the invoice is paid within ten days; if it is not paid by that time, the net price is due within thirty days. A variant on this kind of credit extension is to charge interest on any unpaid balance remaining after thirty days.

Table 24.1   *Current assets of nonfinancial corporations (as percent of total current assets)*

Period	Cash	United States government securities	Receivables	Inventories	Other current assets
1975 I	9.7	1.7	35.7	44.2	8.8
II	10.3	1.7	35.9	42.9	9.2
III	10.2	2.0	36.5	42.2	9.2
IV	10.5	2.6	36.0	41.6	9.2
1976 I	10.1	2.8	36.1	41.6	9.4
II	10.1	2.9	36.2	41.6	9.2
III	9.7	2.9	36.4	41.9	9.0
IV	10.5	3.2	35.5	41.5	9.3
1977 I	9.6	3.2	36.1	41.8	9.3
II	9.7	2.6	36.5	41.9	9.2
III	9.5	2.5	37.1	41.7	9.2
IV	10.5	2.3	36.2	41.7	9.4
1978 I	9.6	2.3	36.6	42.2	9.4
II	9.6	1.8	37.3	41.8	9.5
III	9.2	1.6	37.9	41.9	9.4
IV	10.1	1.7	37.1	41.7	9.4
1979 I	9.5	1.8	37.6	42.0	9.2
II	9.0	1.9	37.7	42.2	9.1
III	8.9	1.5	38.3	42.1	9.1
IV	9.7	1.5	37.6	42.0	9.2
1980 I	8.9	1.2	38.1	42.1	9.7
II	9.0	1.1	37.6	42.6	9.6
III	9.0	1.3	38.1	41.8	9.7
IV	9.4	1.3	38.3	41.0	9.9
1981 I	9.1	1.3	38.4	41.1	10.1
II	9.1	1.4	38.4	40.7	10.4
III	8.9	1.3	38.4	40.9	10.5
IV	9.2	1.3	37.6	41.1	10.8
1982 I	8.6	1.2	37.6	41.7	10.9
II	8.8	1.2	37.5	41.5	11.1
III	8.8	1.3	37.0	41.4	11.5
IV	10.1	1.6	35.8	40.4	12.1

Rows do not sum to 100 owing to rounding errors
Source: *Federal Reserve Bulletin*.

Table 24.2 provides the details for a simplified analysis of a company's overall credit policy. The firm's annual sales are $12 million. As the average receivables balance is $1 million, we can see that the receivables turnover rate is twelve times per year. That is, every dollar invested in receivables generates $12 in annual sales revenue. Results of a study indicate that a shift from present credit terms, which include no discount, to terms of 2/10, net 30, would speed up collections substantially, reducing average investment in receivables from $1 million to $500,000. The study also estimates that customers would take $120,000 per year in discounts. Is the proposed discount worthwhile?

Because the simplifying assumption used to construct Table 24.2 is that the contemplated policy will not change sales volume, cost, or risk, the trade-off clearly is between reduced investment in accounts receivable and the cost of offering discounts. In essence, the company is contemplating reducing its "lending" to customers by $500,000. In doing so, it will lose what amounts to interest when customers take the discount. If the effective rate of interest is higher than the rate of return on alternative uses of the funds at equivalent risk, the company should not offer the discount. In our example, the contemplated policy generates a positive cash flow (i.e., reduced investment in receivables) in the first year of $500,000, with costs of $120,000 per year in discounts compared with the current policy. To compare two permanent policy alternatives, we treat the cash flow as a perpetuity:

$$NPV = \$500,000 - \frac{\$120,000}{1 + k} - \frac{\$120,000}{(1 + k)^2} - \cdots$$

The second and successive terms on the right-hand side represent a perpetuity. The value of a perpetuity is simply the annual amount divided by the discount rate. Therefore,

$$NPV = \$500,000 - \frac{\$120,000}{k}$$

Table 24.2   *Analysis of credit terms*

	Terms		
	0, net 30 (1)	2/10, net 30 (2)	Difference (1)—(2)
Annual sales	$12,000,000	$12,000,000	—
Average accounts receivable	$1,000,000	$500,000	$500,000
Annual receivables turnover	12	24	
Discounts taken	0	$120,000	−$120,000

We can solve for the break-even interest rate k that produces a zero net present value:

$$k = \frac{\$120,000}{\$500,000}$$

$$= 0.24$$

Thus, if the required rate of return is less than 24 percent, the firm should not offer discounts, because the present value of the future incremental cash outflows represented by the discounts taken would exceed the reduction in accounts receivable.

There are some additional points to take into account in analyzing a proposed credit policy. When analyzing a credit policy, one should be concerned with its long-term effects on the firm as opposed to its impact on individual customers. Thus, the relevant required rate of return is the (often long-term) rate that would reflect the risk of the accounts receivable. It should be noted that whenever the discounts and the sales that generate the receivables are expressed in before-tax terms, the required rate of return must also be before-tax.

Two final cautions: The analysis of credit policy alternatives is only as valid as the forecasted cash flow inputs. Changes in credit policy can cause changes in sales volume, which should be considered in the analysis. In fact, industry practices and the threat of competitive retaliation tend to dictate the ranges of credit terms that are customary or acceptable in each industry.

Accounts Receivable Management as an Integrated Set of Decisions

A complete company policy on trade credit and collections will include at least the following elements:

rules for determining the quality of credit that can be accepted

credit terms (as we have discussed)

rules and procedures for monitoring accounts and for collecting those over-due

Standards for each element will affect the timing, volume, and riskiness of operating cash flows and corporate investment in accounts receivable and inventory. As Figure 24.2 illustrates, a company can follow a sequential decision process for each customer credit request. NPV analysis helps us to evaluate alternative credit policies and can be used to evaluate specific customer credit requests in an internally consistent fashion. In practice, the task of developing general rules for managing credit and collections in an optimal manner is often complex.

Customer Credit Evaluation

At the outset, when a company's credit department spells out rules for accepting or rejecting new credit customers, it must balance many variables. The more customers the company extends credit to, the greater the sales volume and the greater the investment in working capital, other things being equal. More customers mean an increasing number of slow payers. Collection expenses increase, and required investment in accounts receivable increases. If the firm already is operating at full capacity, higher sales volume may require greater investment in production facilities and other fixed capital assets. On the other hand, when credit standards are raised, while these direct and observable costs fall, and the number of customers who pay late is reduced, sales volume falls also.

The credit department may base its decision to extend credit on information from a variety of sources, including the customer's financial statements, business references, bank references, credit bureau reports, sales people's opinions, and published information. Information on payment practices of existing customers also exists in the company's own records.

Credit bureau reports include Dun and Bradstreet publications that give financial details and credit ratings for a large number of companies. Figure 24.3 provides an example. Dun and Bradstreet also prepares special reports on individual companies.

Companies that turn their accounts receivable over to collection agencies (or factors) often can obtain information from the factor on the payment habits of potential customers if the factor is managing the accounts receivable of a number of companies who deal with that same customer.

In order of increasing cost, the firm's credit department typically would evaluate its own records and data provided by the customer first, then refer to Dun and Bradstreet lists, and then request special reports from Dun and Bradstreet or other credit bureaus and banks. The goal of this sequential exercise is to classify the creditworthiness of each customer in an efficient fashion—to reject credit to customers whose likelihood of slow payment or nonpayment exceeds some threshold, and to classify the acceptable credit customers for purposes of setting appropriate credit terms. For example, repeat customers with the most favorable paying characteristics may be

Figure 24.2   *Sequential credit analysis*

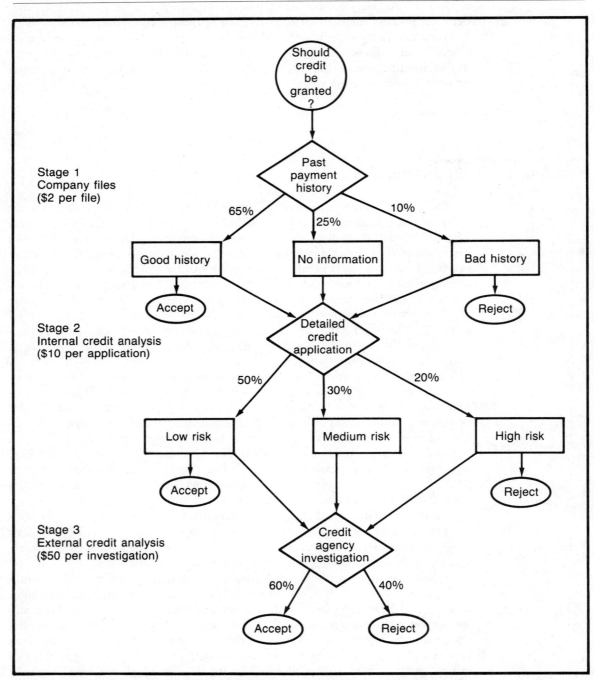

Stage 1
Company files
($2 per file)

Stage 2
Internal credit analysis
($10 per application)

Stage 3
External credit analysis
($50 per investigation)

Source: Smith, K., *Guide to Working Capital Management,* New York: McGraw-Hill, 1979, p. 125

Figure 24.3   *Dun & Bradstreet Report*

Dun & Bradstreet, Inc.

| BE SURE NAME, BUSINESS AND ADDRESS MATCH YOUR FILE | ANSWERING INQUIRY | This report has been prepared for:
SUBSCRIBER: 008-001042 |

THIS REPORT MAY NOT BE REPRODUCED IN WHOLE OR IN PART IN ANY MANNER WHATEVER

FULL REVISION - RATING CHANGE

DUNS: 06-647-3261
RETTINGER PAINT CORP

727 WHITMAN WAY
BENSON, MI 48232
TEL: 313 961-0720

CARL RETTINGER, PRES

DATE PRINTED
AUG 13, 198-
WHOL PAINTS &
VARNISHES

SIC NO.
51 98

SUMMARY
RATING CC2

STARTED	1950
PAYMENTS	SEE BELOW
SALES	$424,612
WORTH F	$101,867
EMPLOYS	5
HISTORY	CLEAR
CONDITION	GOOD
TREND	STEADY

SPECIAL EVENTS
07/10/8-   Business burglarized Jul 3 but $18,000 loss is fully insured.

PAYMENTS (Amounts may be rounded to nearest figure in prescribed ranges)

REPORTED	PAYING RECORD	HIGH CREDIT	NOW OWES	PAST DUE	SELLING TERMS	LAST SALE WITHIN
07/8-	Disc	30000	15000	-0-	2 10 N30	1 Mo
	Disc	30000	15000	-0-	1 10 N30	2-3 Mos
	Disc-Ppt	10000	5000	250	2 10 N30	1 Mo
	Ppt	10000	7500	-0-	30	1 Mo
06/8-	Disc	15000	7500	-0-	2 10 N30	2-3 Mos
05/8-	Disc	10000	5000	-0-	2 10 N30	1 Mo
	Ppt	1000	-0-	-0-	30	1 Mo

FINANCE
06/25/8-

Fiscal statement dated May 31 198-:

Cash	$	20,623	Accts Pay	$	47,246
Accts Rec		55,777	Bank Loans		34,000
Inventory		92,103	Notes Pay (Trucks)		7,020
Current		168,503	Current		88,266
Fixt & Equip		13,630	COMMON STOCK		35,000
Trucks		8,000	EARNED SURPLUS		66,867
Total Assets		190,133	Total		190,133

Annual sales $424,612; Net profit $17,105. Monthly rent $3,500. Fire insurance on mdse & fixt $95,000; Equipment $20,000.
Prepared from statement(s) by Accountant: Steige Co., CPA's, Detroit, MI. Extent of audit, if any, not indicated.

    --0--

On Jun 22 198-, John J Lawson defined monthly payments: $3,000 to bank, $400 on notes. Admitted collections slow but losses insignificant. Said inventory will drop to $60,000 by December. Expects 5% sales increase this year.

PUBLIC FILINGS
03/25/8-   On Mar 17 198-, a suit in the amount of $200 was entered against subject by Henry Associates, Atlanta, GA (Docket #H27519). Involves merchandise which Lawson says was defective.
05/28/8-   On May 21 198-, a financing statement (#H741170) was filed listing subject as debtor and NCR Corp., Dayton, OH as secured party. Collateral consists of equipment.

BANKING
06/25/8-   Account long maintained, carries average balance low to moderate five figures. Unsecured loans to moderate five extended and now open.

HISTORY
06/22/8-   CARL RETTINGER, PRES   JOHN J LAWSON, V PRES
DIRECTOR(S): THE OFFICER(S)
    Incorporated Michigan Feb 2 1950. Authorized capital consists of 3,500 shares common stock, no par value. Paid in capital $35,000. Officers own capital stock equally.
    CARL RETTINGER born 1920 married. Employed by E-Z Paints, Detroit, MI, 12 years; five as manager until starting subject early 1950.
    JOHN J LAWSON born 1925 married. Obtained accounting degree 1946 and then employed by Union Carbide, Chicago, Ill, until joining Rettinger at inception.

OPERATION
    Wholesales paints and varnishes (85%), wallpaper and supplies. 500 local accounts include retailers (75%) and contractors. Terms are 2 10 net 30 days. Peak season spring through summer.
    EMPLOYEES: 5, including the officers.
    FACILITIES: Rents 7,500 sq. ft. one-story block structure, good repair.

THIS REPORT FURNISHED PURSUANT TO CONTRACT FOR THE EXCLUSIVE USE OF THE SUBSCRIBER AS ONE FACTOR TO CONSIDER IN CONNECTION WITH CREDIT INSURANCE MARKETING OR OTHER BUSINESS DECISIONS CONTAINS INFORMATION COMPILED FROM SOURCES WHICH DUN & BRADSTREET INC DOES NOT CONTROL AND WHOSE INFORMATION UNLESS OTHERWISE INDICATED IN THE REPORT HAS NOT BEEN VERIFIED IN FURNISHING THIS REPORT DUN & BRADSTREET INC IN NO WAY ASSUMES ANY PART OF THE USER'S BUSINESS RISK DOES NOT GUARANTEE THE ACCURACY COMPLETENESS OR TIMELINESS OF THE INFORMATION PROVIDED AND SHALL NOT BE LIABLE FOR ANY LOSS OR INJURY WHATEVER RESULTING FROM CONTINGENCIES BEYOND ITS CONTROL OR FROM NEGLIGENCE granted open accounts with substantially higher credit limits than other customers.

Clearly, judgment is required in setting credit department standards and the evaluation of customers. Beyond standard financial statement analysis of the kind described in Chapter 16, a measure of subjectivity remains. Management science modeling techniques can be brought to bear on credit customer analysis. Such models usually involve a credit-scoring function combined with an opportunity cost model. The credit-scoring function is quite straightforward, although the statistical techniques used to derive the weights can be quite complex. Table 24.3 presents an abbreviated set of the questions that might be asked of a prospective retail credit customer and shows how the responses might be converted into numerical scores by a credit department. The credit-scoring function would provide the weights applied to numerically coded answers to these questions in order to give each customer an overall index rating.

For example, assume that

$$I = 5X_1 + 1X_2 + 3X_3 + 2X_4 + 0.1X_5$$

where $X_1 \ldots X_5$ are the numerical answers to questions one through five, and I is the index number. If you have a telephone in your home ($X_1 = 1$), have been two years in your present job ($X_2 = 2$), have rented your home ($X_3 = 0$) for two years ($X_4 = 2$) and have an income of \$25,000 ($X_5 = 25$), your score would be:

$$I = (5 \times 1) + (1 \times 2) + (3 \times 0) + (2 \times 2) + (0.1 \times 25)$$

$$= 13.5$$

The determination of the weights given to each answer and the rules for classifying results reflect the attempt to balance two costs. The first is the cost of accepting the credit of customers who turn out to be slow payers. The second is the opportunity cost of lost sales to customers rejected by the

Table 24.3   *Credit questionnaire*

1. Do you have a telephone at your place of residence? (1 = yes, 0 = no)	_____
2. How many years have you been working for your present employer?	_____
3. Do you own (1) or lease (0) your residence?	_____
4. How many years have you lived in your present residence?	_____
5. What is your annual income?	_____

Figure 24.4   *Probability distributions of I scores*

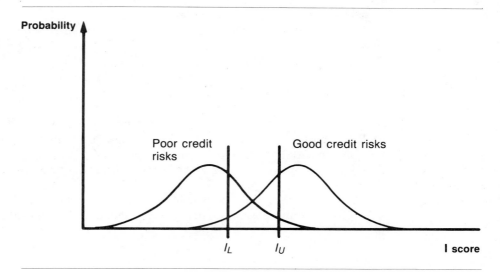

credit evaluation system who would have paid their accounts promptly. The basic problem is represented in Figure 24.4.

The challenge is to predict on the basis of an index score, I, whether a customer falls into the good risk or poor risk population. Although it is known that the mean score for good risks is larger than for poor risks, the two probability distributions overlap. Given estimates of the relative frequency of good versus poor risks in the overall credit customer population, a company can develop cutoff scores. For example, I_U represents the score above which the customer is given credit; I_L the score below which the customer's credit application is denied; customers with scores between I_L and I_U are assessed subjectively and, if accepted, may be subject to more stringent credit terms. If I_U were set at 11.5, for example, the credit application with a score of 13.5 would be accepted without further ado.

Credit–scoring decision models have their best role when there are large numbers of customers and a relatively small variation in the amount of credit requested. In such a situation the characteristics of the large sample that is used to produce the weights and cutoff scores can be relied upon. Obviously, a firm dealing with a relatively small number of heterogeneous corporate customers cannot construct its credit procedures with the same statistical precision. However, the elements of the problem and the criteria are the same: Judgment must be used to balance the cost of accepting poor credit risks against the opportunity cost of rejecting good credit risks.

Credit Terms

The terms of credit are a part of the terms of sale. As credit terms need not be accepted by the customer unless they are favorable, the granting of credit can be viewed as a price concession. The greater the credit risk, the greater the effective price concession granted. In this pricing decision, three questions are paramount:

1. Will the customer's buying decision be influenced by the terms of credit?
2. Is the supplier or the customer suffering from a shortage of funds; is either in a position of capital rationing?
3. Is the supplier working at or below full productive capacity?

Answers to these questions will determine whether the decision to lend is purely a credit decision or has some elements of an investment decision.

TRADE CREDIT AS A LENDING DECISION

The credit decision is a lending decision when the net effect of the decision is merely to change the size of the accounts receivable. If the refusal of credit would not result in the loss of business, and if the customer is able to turn to alternative sources of funds, the extending of trade credit is equivalent to the granting of a loan. Usually the implicit interest payment may be hidden in a fixed trade discount for early payment, and the effective interest rate will be determined by the time it actually takes the customer to pay the bill. When the credit decision can be treated as a lending decision, three questions arise:

1. What are the principal and the term of the loan?
2. Given the creditworthiness of the customer, what effective rate of interest would be required?
3. Taking into account the industry's customary terms of trade, how much credit should be extended to a customer given the risk of default?

When the credit decision does not affect total sales volume, the incremental investment arising from the extension of credit is the increase in accounts receivable net of discounts for early payment. The effective rate of interest charged to the customer will have to cover the prevailing risk-free rate of interest for the term of the loan, plus a premium to cover the probability of a default and the costs of administration, including collection.

Interest charged for credit can be charged explicitly to the customer's account, or it may be implicit in the price of the goods. More usually, the charge for credit is reflected in the discount for early payment. For example, consider the terms of the sale offered on the basis of 5/10, net 30. The supplier's charge for credit is 5 percent of the sales price. The expected income from customers who forego the discount must be sufficient to cover the supplier's cost of financing the customer's account.

A number of problems arise in actually trying to calculate the cost of credit. The first is estimating the period of the loan provided by the supplier. If the supplier offers payment terms that demand full payment within thirty days, one might get the impression that the credit period is one month. However, if the supplier offers a credit limit equal to one month's sales for as long as the customer continues in business, the loan may approach a perpetuity. Therefore, the appropriate interest rate to charge is that available on long-term interest-bearing securities of equivalent risk. The term of the effective loan is determined by how frequently the supplier is able to change the terms of credit for an existing customer.

EXAMPLES INVOLVING RISK-FREE CREDIT

A customer applies for credit in an industry where it is customary to offer a discount of 5 percent for immediate payment. Let us assume initially that the customer is risk-free and will continue making monthly purchases of $1,000 at list price indefinitely. How much credit can be extended?

If the customer uses the credit granted, he or she will save having to pay $950 immediately for each month's purchases, but will have to pay later $50 more because the discount for cash purchase will have been forgone. The amount of this principal will depend on the number of months' credit granted to the customer. If the customer is allowed two months' credit, the amount of credit taken, otherwise known as the principal, is $2 \times \$950 = \$1,900$.

For a customer purchasing $1,000 worth of goods per month, interest received on the effective loan is $50 per month. Although the dollar interest income is fixed by discounts on expected sales, the principal and effective interest rate depends upon the amount of credit that is granted to the customer. If the customer takes two months' credit, the interest rate is $50/(2 \times 950) = 2.63$ percent per month, or 36.6 percent per year. If the customer takes three months' credit, the interest is only $50/(3 \times 950) = 1.75$ percent per month, or 23.1 percent per year. The longer the customer takes to pay, the lower the effective interest rate that is received by the supplier. The equation is

$$\text{Interest Received} = \frac{\text{Discount} \times \text{Monthly Sales}}{\text{Cash Value of Credit Granted}}$$

$$= \frac{0.05 \times \$1,000}{3 \times \$950} = 0.0175$$

or 1.75 percent per month, where the cash value of credit granted is valued net of the discount for cash purchase. If the customer were really risk-free, the credit decision would consist in choosing that value of credit granted (in the denominator of the fraction) that would make the interest received at least equal to that obtainable on an equivalent conventional loan.

Example:

Monthly sales = \$2,500

Discount = 3%

Interest on equivalent loan = 1.5% per month

Interest received = $0.015 = (0.03 \times 2,500)/(N \times 0.97 \times 2,500)$

N = 2.06 months' credit (maximum)

RISKY CREDIT

If the customer's credit is risky, the analysis must be altered in several ways. First, the customer may default with some probability p in any month. Second, the credit department must incur increased administrative costs, including debtor monitoring, collection, and legal expenses. Given this risk, the expected interest rate received becomes

$$\frac{(\text{Discount} \times \text{Monthly Sales} - \text{Service Cost})(1 - p) - p \times \text{Cash Value of Credit Granted}}{\text{Cash Value of Credit Granted}}$$

where the service cost covers the average monthly incremental administrative expenses incurred in the credit department for each such risky credit account accepted.

In our previous example the customer bought \$1,000 worth of goods monthly. That would have cost only \$950 if the 5 percent discount for early payment was taken. Instead, the customer is delaying payment for three months and paying the additional \$50. Assuming that payment was certain to be received, the effective rate of interest was 1.75 percent per month or 23.1 percent per year. Suppose, however, that payment is not certain, that the probability that the customer will default (and never pay) in any one month is $p = 0.01$. Let us also assume the administrative cost of servicing the account is \$5.00 per month. The effective rate of interest becomes

$$\frac{(0.05 \times 1000 - 5)(1 - 0.01) - 0.01 \times (3 \times 950)}{(3 \times 950)}$$

$$= 0.005632$$

Thus the effective rate of interest when payment is uncertain is 0.5632 percent per month or only 6.97 percent per year compared with 23.2 percent under certainty. Since the nonpayment of several months' bills would be very costly to the supplier, small increases in the probability of default can greatly reduce the effective interest on trade credit.

It may be customary in the trade that one month's credit is granted to all credit customers. However, unless the credit department is prepared to administer very strict credit controls, some customers will actually take more credit when it suits them to do so. When customers delay payment for a longer period, they can reduce the effective rate of interest paid. More importantly, the customer may create credit in this way at any time it is needed, should other sources of funds be closed. It may be that the customer will create this credit just at the time when the lending corporation itself is also under some credit pressure.

The credit decision must reflect the degree of control that the credit department feels is feasible in a changing economic environment. The amount of credit actually granted will depend upon the ability of the credit department to enforce collections. In cases where little effective control can be exercised, the essence of the decision becomes in each case whether credit should be granted at all. If it is felt that the customer will take more credit than the credit department would be willing to grant, the firm has the option of refusing to grant credit.

Trade credit ordinarily represents a risky loan, so a suitable interest rate must be found that reflects the risk of default. Consider the fact that trade credit is always unsecured. In the case of liquidation, secured loans are ranked in front of claims of unsecured creditors. This fact alone would suggest that a higher interest rate incorporating a larger risk premium should be sought on trade credit than on secured loans of equivalent risk and maturity.

On the other hand, a purchaser may be wary of not paying the bills of suppliers because of the effect on supplier relationships. In addition, the supplier should be among the first to know if the customer is getting into financial difficulties. We do not wish to minimize the risks taken by suppliers, but merely to point out that the supplier may be in a better position to anticipate default or bankruptcy than a bank and to obtain the information at a lower cost; as a consequence, it is possible to take action for at least part repayment at an earlier stage. This means that the risk premium that a supplier actually requires may be lower in many cases than that required by other lenders.

TRADE CREDIT AS AN INVESTMENT DECISION

In some circumstances, the credit decision can no longer be considered a loan. In such cases the credit decision can usually be treated as an investment decision.

Frequently, credit decisions have important effects that extend beyond the account receivable. For some customers, the use of trade credit is vital for survival. Many companies face a shortage of capital at times, particularly those with limited access to capital markets. Their assets may be difficult to sell and may provide poor security for bank loans. Such companies, if they have to forego profitable projects because of lack of funds, are likely to favor those suppliers who are most generous in providing trade credit. For these reasons, credit policy may have an impact on the sales of the supplier as well as on the ability of the customer to operate effectively in conditions where the cost of credit from alternative sources is prohibitively high.

The form of credit analysis may change somewhat when the supplier is operating below capacity and the customer does not have a viable alternative source of funds. When the supplier does not expect to be operating at capacity, credit decisions actually may affect the volume of business that can be put through its facilities. If some customers are short of funds, and if there are competing suppliers operating below capacity, it may be necessary to extend credit in order not to lose sales to competitors. In this position, the credit decision becomes an investment decision. That is, an investment in working capital is required to secure the subsequent benefits of cash flow from sales.

If a new customer is accepted, a substantial investment of capital may be required to service the account. This investment may include cash, raw materials, work-in-progress, and finished goods inventories, as well as an investment in a receivables balance. More precisely, the lag between the payment of expenses associated with the new business and receipt of payments for goods and services provided to the customer requires an investment of funds. In return, the supplier must expect a return after taxes commensurate with the (systematic) risk of the resulting net cash flow stream.

Table 24.4 includes some of, but by no means all, the expenses that may be relevant: investment in cash and inventory (including raw materials, work-in-progress, and finished goods), variable expense, additional sales and administration (including collection), and taxes. Not shown is any charge for incremental capital expenditures on plant or machinery that may be required if the new business should require more capacity. In the case of additional capital investment, the credit-granting decision requires a full capital project appraisal. Also not shown as a separate item are incremental handling and warehousing expenses. If such significant incremental expenditures are required, they should be shown separately in the months in which payments are expected to be made.

The appropriate monthly discount rate should reflect the systematic risk of the net incremental cash flow resulting from extending credit to customers. A positive net present value would indicate that the incremental business is profitable and that the credit terms assumed in the analysis can be extended. However, one must take care that the analysis reflects an unbiased estimate

Table 24.4   *Cash flow associated with the extension of credit to a new customer*

End of month	0	1	2	3	4
Cash and inventory	−200				
Revenue		1200	1200	1200	1200
Variable expense		−1000	−1000	−1000	−1000
Sales and administration		−100	−100	−100	−100
Taxes*		−50	−50	−50	−50
After-tax cash flow	−200	50	50	50	50

*Assuming a combined federal and state tax rate of 50 percent.

of the timing of the cash flows associated with supplying the type of product to the appropriate category of customer credit risk and that all the likely incremental working capital and other net expenditures are included.

In order to avoid analyzing every new customer in such detail, a company can use a credit classification by customer type and product. Then it would perform a monthly cash flow analysis from time to time for each combination of credit class and product. The advantage of undertaking a detailed monthly analysis of credit and cash flow is that a company may find that there are classes of customers or credit risks who would be profitable when less precise and more conventional rules of thumb, which treat the extension of trade credit as a lending decision, would turn the business down.

Just as we used a formula governing the interest rate received when the extension of credit approximated a lending decision, there is a corresponding formula for the rate of return received when extending credit is an investment decision (that is, when the granting of credit will affect sales volume). The expected rate of return is given by

$$\frac{\left(\begin{array}{ccc}\text{Net Cash} & \text{Service} & \text{Inventory} \\ \text{Flow} & - \text{Cost} & - \text{Carrying Cost}\end{array}\right)(1 - p) - p \times \begin{array}{c}\text{Cash Value} \\ \text{of Credit}\end{array}}{\text{Net Investment in Working Capital}}$$

The net cash flow is incremental monthly sales minus cash costs of sales and taxes. The term p represents the probability of default in one period. The service cost covers monthly after-tax incremental administrative costs, including monitoring, collection, and legal expenses of the credit department. The inventory carrying cost includes such items as storage, handling, insurance, and obsolescence expenses after taxes, but excludes costs of finance in this case. The net investment in working capital includes cash, receivables, and inventory marginal cost, and is net of payables. The cash value of credit is the cost of goods sold for the receivable that is lost if the customer defaults with probability p.

The rule is similar to that adopted for the lending form of the credit decision, except that the incremental cash benefits and expenses included are more extensive when the granting of credit actually increases sales (or prevents the loss of them). If the after-tax rate of return calculated on this basis exceeds the after-tax risk-adjusted required rate of return for this type of investment (converted to a monthly rate), credit can be extended profitably to the customer.

What rate of return is required for such an investment in increased sales? First, we note that an increase in sales revenue involves a degree of systematic risk. Thus a risk premium will be required. How does the risk compare with that of the business of the division? If the incremental benefit arising from the marginal increase in sales involves no change in fixed operating expenditure, it is very likely that the risk of the resulting net revenues will be less than average for the division. The reader may wish to review Chapter 10 for an analysis of how to estimate such risk.

If the supplier suffers from capital rationing and wishes to compare the credit decision with other investments, it may do so with the help of the profitability index or the integer programming model discussed in Chapter 5. The value of the index can be obtained by dividing the monthly return received in the formula above by the required rate of return. This value can be compared with the index for an alternative project by dividing the sum of the net present value and the investment for the alternative project by the present value of the investment in the project.

Monitoring and Collecting Receivables

Trade credit is a useful and flexible source of finance used by most companies. Simply by delaying payment to creditors, companies can increase their liabilities without having to turn to their bankers for further loan financing. Advantages to users of trade credit represent corresponding disadvantages to its providers. Thus a company requires some form of control to protect against unanticipated financing requirements and associated costs from increases in accounts receivable and bad debts. The most common summary information report used to develop the size and composition of accounts receivable is an analysis of the aging of the accounts. Table 24.5 provides an example for a firm that makes all its sales on a one-month net basis.

An aging report can be broken down by type of customer and updated monthly to reveal seasonal or other patterns in customer payment schedules. Unanticipated shifts in the age distribution of receivables then can be spotted

Table 24.5   *Aging of accounts receivables*

	Amount	Percentage
Less than one month outstanding	$5,000	61.3
One month overdue	2,000	24.5
Two months overdue	750	9.2
Three months overdue	300	3.7
More than three months overdue	100	1.2
	$8,150	99.9

in a timely fashion, and management response (collection, planning for different company financing, changing credit terms) can be taken as necessary.

Collection policies typically follow a set pattern, with expected benefits at each stage at least equal to the cost. The sequence usually begins with mailed reminders for accounts just overdue. These are followed by telephone calls, then personal visits, and finally assignment of the overdue account to a collection agency or undertaking legal proceedings. These latter measures can be costly. Collection agencies, for example, may ask for as much as 50 percent of the proceeds of collected bills for their efforts. Nonetheless, occasionally it may be necessary to pursue overdue accounts, regardless of expense, in order to protect the firm's reputation. Perceived slackness may invite an increase in nonpayment by customers who know that the firm will ultimately give up on them.

Summary

The setting of trade credit terms is part of the pricing decision, because credit is valuable to the customer and it increases the costs of the supplier. The costs of trade credit include the cost of financing increased working capital, an increase in clerical and collection costs, and the potential costs of bad debts. However, a liberal credit policy may be the source of benefits through increased sales. Benefits can be made to outweigh the costs if adequate controls are exercised. The amount of credit extended to marginal customers must be strictly limited. The sales ledger must be monitored regularly to determine if customers significantly alter their expected patterns of payment.

A systematic reminder system should be operated, if only to make the customer aware that he or she is dealing with an efficient credit department that is likely to apply pressure should credit limits be exceeded.

Appendix 24.1 Sequential Evaluation of a Specific Customer Credit Request

Figure 24.2 showed the sequential nature of the information gathering and decision process involved in dealing with customer credit applications. The text described separate pieces of the credit policy analysis. We now join these pieces to illustrate a sequential evaluation model.[1]

Norcar, a specialty furniture maker, receives an order for ten of its wine racks. The order includes a request for credit, without which the sale will not materialize. The list price for each wine rack is $50; for credit sales, Norcar's terms are 2/30, net 60. Variable cost per wine rack is $35. Norcar's credit manager knows from experience that the average collection period on credit sales is sixty days, that average collection costs amount to $25, and that the probability of a bad credit loss is 15 percent. The credit manager wishes to minimize the expected costs of an immediate credit decision. The following equation helps:[2]

Expected Acceptance Cost = (Probability of a Bad Debt Loss)

× [(Variable Cost)

+ (Required Annual Rate of Return) ×

$\dfrac{\text{(Expected Collection Period)}}{365}$ (Variable Cost) + Average Collection Cost]

That is, acceptance cost is made up of the sum of three terms reflecting the consequences of a credit sale gone bad, loss of investment (variable cost), opportunity cost on investment before it goes bad (annual rate of return converted to a rate of return for the period during which the investment is outstanding and collectible), and average collection cost. This sum is

---

[1]This example is adapted from material in Chapter 14 of *Management of Corporate Liquidity: An Introduction to Working Capital Management,* by James H. Vander Weide and Steven F. Maier, New York: John Wiley, forthcoming.
[2]This example uses variable cost as the investment. In addition, it assumes that the decision to extend credit generates incremental business and is therefore an investment rather than a lending decision.

weighted by the probability that loss occurs in order to obtain the expected acceptance cost.

Expected rejection cost is simply the lost profit (net of the discount taken) on the sale multiplied by the probability that the credit would not have gone bad. If we assume that the required rate of return in this situation is 15 percent:

$$\text{Acceptance Cost} = (0.15)\left(\$350 + (0.15)\frac{60}{365}(\$350) + \$25\right) = \$57.54$$

$$\text{Rejection Cost} = (1 - 0.15)[\$150 - (0.02)(\$500)] = \$119.00$$

The obvious decision is to accept the credit sale.

On the other hand, the credit manager of Norcar has the opportunity to gather information (albeit at some cost) in two separate stages prior to making a final decision. He or she can examine the customer's credit file for prior payments history and make a decision, or proceed to an in-depth investigation, perhaps involving the use of a credit-scoring model. The first investigative stage costs $5, and the second costs $25.

A customer's payments history will be classifiable as good (G), poor (P), or new customer (N). The expected outcome of a credit sale varies substantially in these classes, as summarized in Table A24.1.

Having examined the customer's payments history, the credit manager can either make an accept/reject decision or proceed to a credit investigation. The result of this analysis will be a classification of the customer's financial position as either sound (S) or unsound (U), with a more detailed set of estimates of the credit outcome. Table A24.2 contains these estimates, and the structure of the credit manager's decision process is illustrated in the decision tree in Figure A24.1.

Analysis of the decision tree begins at the last stage, stage 3, at which six decision possibilities have to be evaluated, one for each possible combination of credit history (G,N,P) and credit investigation finding (S,U). The costs of acceptance (A) or rejection (R) in each one of these possible situations are

Table A24.1   *Norcar's estimates of credit sales outcomes if customer's payments history were to be examined*

Classification	Probability of classification	Required annual rate of return	Average collection period (days)	Average collection cost	Probability of bad debt loss
G	0.4	0.16	63	24	0.04
N	0.2	0.17	69	25	0.09
P	0.4	0.24	114	50	0.29

Table A24.2   *Norcar's estimates of credit sales outcomes if customer's payments history were to be examined and a credit investigation undertaken*

Classification	Probability of classification	Required annual rate of return	Average collection period (days)	Average collection cost	Probability of bad debt loss
Good past experience (G)					
S	0.8	0.160	60	20	0.01
U	0.2	0.180	75	40	0.15
New customer (N)					
S	0.7	0.165	60	20	0.05
U	0.3	0.185	90	35	0.18
Poor past experience (P)					
S	0.1	0.180	60	20	0.15
U	0.9	0.250	120	40	0.30

described in Table A24.3, and are based on information contained in Table A24.2.

Stage 2 decisions involve three situations, reflecting the possible outcomes of an initial investigation of Norcar's payments history. In each one of these situations the credit manager has three choices: accept, reject, or make a credit investigation. Acceptance and rejection costs are calculated as before, using the information in Table A24.1. Enumeration of the costs of further investigation is a subtler matter. The basic principle is to add the costs of investigation at stage 2 to the expected values of the outcomes at stage 3 of the investigation and to make an optimal decision in each possible situation. For example, in decision situation 2, the credit manager knows that there is a 0.8 probability that the customer will be classified S at stage 3 and the credit sale made at an acceptance cost of $3.79; there is a 0.2 probability that the customer will be classified as U, but still accepted with a cost of $60.31. So the cost of further investigation if the customer is found to have a good payments history is:

$$\$25 \; + \; (0.8)(3.79) \; + \; (0.2)(60.31) = \$40.09$$

Stage 2 decision evaluations are presented in Table A24.4, stage 1 in Table A24.5.

In stage 1, acceptance and rejection costs have already been computed to be $57.54 and $119.00, respectively. The cost of further investigation (examining the customer's payments history) is $5 plus the expected cost as-

Figure A24.1   *Complete numerical analysis of credit-granting decision*

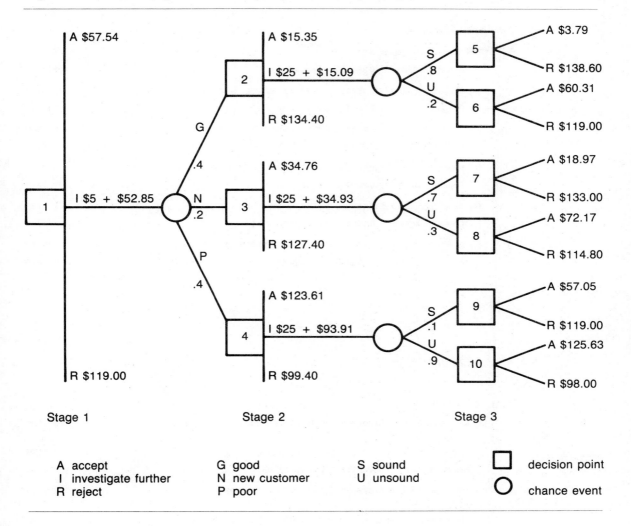

A accept
I investigate further
R reject

G good
N new customer
P poor

S sound
U unsound

☐ decision point
◯ chance event

sociated with an optimal decision under each possible outcome (G, N, or P). In Table A24.5 this cost is computed to be $57.85. The optimal decision (by a narrow margin), therefore, is for the credit manager to accept the credit sale in this case, and not to make any further investigation.

While our example might have been more elaborate (and perhaps more realistic), it does illustrate several features of real credit evaluation:

Credit granting can reflect the costs and benefits of a sequence of decisions.

Each decision entails a cost and a possible benefit (information).

Table A24.3   *Evaluation of stage 3 decisions*

Decision situation

[5] Acceptance cost = (0.01)[350 + (0.16)(60/365)(350) + 20]   = $ 3.79
    Rejection cost   = (0.99)[150 − (0.02)(500)]   = $138.60

[6] Acceptance cost = (0.15)[350 + (0.18)(70/365)(350) + 40]   = $ 60.31
    Rejection cost   = (0.85)[150 − (0.02)(500)]   = $119.00

[7] Acceptance cost = (0.05)[350 + (0.165)(60/365)(350) + 20]   = $ 18.97
    Rejection cost   = (0.95)[150 − (0.02)(500)]   = $133.00

[8] Acceptance cost = (0.18)[350 + (0.185)(90/365)(350) + 35]   = $ 72.17
    Rejection cost   = (0.82)[150 − (0.02)(500)]   = $114.80

[9] Acceptance cost = (0.15)[350 + (0.18)(60/365)(350) + 20]   = $ 57.05
    Rejection cost   = (0.85)[150 − (0.02)(500)]   = $119.00

[10] Acceptance cost = (0.30)[350 + (0.25)(120/365)(350) + 40]   = $125.63
    Rejection cost   = (0.70)[150 − (0.02)(500)]   = $ 98.00

Table A24.4   *Evaluation of stage 2 decisions*

Decision situation

[2] Acceptance cost = (0.04)[350 + (0.16)(63/365)(350) + 24]   = $ 15.35
    Investigate:
    further cost   = 25 + (0.8)(3.79) + (0.2)(60.31)   = $ 40.09
    Rejection cost   = (0.96)[150 − (0.02)(500)]   = $134.40

[3] Acceptance cost = (0.09)[350 + (0.17)(69/365)(350) + 25]   = $ 34.76
    Investigate:
    further cost   = 25 + (0.7)(18.97) + (0.3)(72.17)   = $ 59.93
    Rejection cost   = (0.91)[150 − (0.02)(500)]   = $127.40

[4] Acceptance cost = (0.29)[350 + (0.24)(114/365)(350) + 50]   = $123.61
    Investigate:
    further cost   = 25 + (0.1)(57.05) + (0.9)(98.00)   = $118.91
    Rejection cost   = (0.71)[150 − (0.02)(500)]   = $ 99.40

Table A24.5   *Evaluation of stage 1 decisions*

[1] Decision situation

Acceptance cost = (0.15)[350 + (0.15)(60/365)(350) + 25]	= $ 57.54
Investigate:	
further cost = 5 + (0.4)(15.35) + (0.2)(34.76) + (0.4)(99.40)	= $ 57.85
Rejection cost = (0.85)[150 − (0.02)(500)]	= $119.00

A least-cost choice at each decision stage has to incorporate the least-cost decisions and probable outcomes of all later decisions.

If the prospective size of credit sales and benefits of sequential investigative steps are large enough, it will be appropriate to develop a dynamic framework for customer credit analysis.

The example shows how optimum credit granting procedures can be developed.

Review Questions

1. A furniture shop sells its goods on credit. How should it go about estimating the cost of offering credit to its customers?
2. Under what circumstances is the decision to provide credit to a customer solely a financing decision?
3. Why is it difficult to define precisely the period of credit implicit in a receivable?
4. Under what circumstances should a purchasing firm accept a period of credit and pass up the discount for early payment?
5. Under what circumstances is it possible for the provision of trade credit to be profitable to both parties?

Problems

*1. Compute the average collection period for a company with annual sales of $132,000 and receivables of $14,000. If the maximum credit period granted by the company is thirty days, what might explain the difference between the average collection period and the maximum credit period?

*2. A company offers a 1 percent discount for payment within seven days. The maximum credit period is twenty-eight days, although some customers take longer to pay. Assuming that a customer's annual borrowing rate is 15 percent, should the customer accept the discount for early payment? What difference does it make to your calculations and conclusions if the customer takes forty-five days to pay?

*3. A firm that currently gives twenty-eight days' credit for all sales has found that its receivables are collected on the schedule listed in column 1 below (in thousands of dollars). The company decides to offer a 1 percent discount for payment within seven days. The resulting forecast of collections (gross of discounts) is given in column 2. The company's borrowing rate is 9 percent per year, and the average borrowing rate for the customers is 12 percent per year. Is the new credit policy profitable from the company's point of view?

Period	Without discount (1)	With trade discount (2)
Within 7 days	0	150
1 month	400	280
2 months	100	70
3 months	50	50
4 months	10	10
5 months	10	10
	570	570

*4. Customer X purchases $10,000 of goods each month from company Y with the usual two months' credit period. Although Y offers a 10 percent discount for immediate payment, Y is aware that X is a risky customer and considers that there is a 3.5 percent probability of default in any one month. Assume that X borrows at 20 percent per year and that Y can borrow at 10 percent per year. Is the discount a good idea from the seller's point of view? Show your computations.

*5. Both a supplier and its customers are very short of funds in a severe credit squeeze. In order to attract customers, however, the supplier believes it must offer one month's credit rather than the existing terms of cash on delivery. Existing sales are $10,000 per month, and the supplier anticipates an increase in sales to $12,000 per month as a result of the new credit policy. The gross margin on all sales is 50 percent of the sales price. The supplier forecasts that a third of all future sales will be on credit, with half of that total on one month's credit and the other half on two months' credit. The probability of an individual customer becoming a bad debt in any one month is 0.01.

In the past the company has borrowed funds at 10 percent. At this time funds can be obtained only by foregoing profitable projects that all have an internal rate of return of 20 percent and a required rate of return of 15 percent. The risk associated with the new credit policy is similar to that of the other projects.

The incremental administrative costs of the new credit policy total $100 per month. Payables are expected to equal one-half of receivables. Two months' inventory is carried, and the inventory carrying cost is 2 percent per month. Do you expect the new policy to be profitable?

References

Elton, E. J., and M. J. Gruber, *Finance as a Dynamic Process,* Englewood Cliffs, N.J.: Prentice-Hall, Inc., 1975.

Mehta, D. R., *Working Capital Management,* Englewood Cliffs, N.H.: Prentice-Hall, 1974.

Smith, K. J., *Guide to Working Capital Management,* New York: McGraw-Hill, Inc., 1979.

Vander Weide, J. H., and S. F. Maier, *Management of Corporate Liquidity: An Introduction to Working Capital Management,* New York: John Wiley, forthcoming.

25

Working Capital Management: Inventory

Investment in inventory has accounted for around 42 percent of total current assets for United States nonfinancial corporations in recent years. Some investment in inventory is essential to the smooth functioning of the business. Finished goods inventory acts as a buffer against the effects of fluctuating sales on production, and raw materials inventory provides insurance against shortages during long and uncertain delivery times from suppliers. An inadequate inventory control system will result in the wrong balance of inventory and will produce shortages, thereby reducing efficiency and profitability. Because the costs of carrying inventory are very high, the inventory control system deserves the attention of financial management.

Although the day-to-day operation of inventory control is administered by specialists, financial managers exercise an influence on inventory investment at two key stages. First, inventory reporting and other data processing associated with the inventory control system are usually the ultimate responsibility of a company controller. As a result, the responsibility for an inadequate system must rest with the controller and ultimately with the financial vice president. Second, the operation of the system requires periodic monitoring and control.

Working capital targets and priorities can change quickly, and the role of

This chapter is adapted with permission from J. R. Franks and J. E. Broyles, *Modern Managerial Finance,* New York: John Wiley, 1979: 253–68.

inventory must be evaluated in the context of changing corporate plans. If the inventory investment is significant, the vice president cannot advise the board adequately about current and future liquidity unless he or she is aware of trends in the company's investment in inventory and in its marketability.

In this chapter, we shall discuss how broad controls on inventory investment can be exercised by financial management. We shall then describe the kinds of stock control systems that can be installed by financial staff to help inventory managers operate more successfully. Finally, we shall consider the problems of operating detailed inventory controls when responsibility is shared among operating departments with conflicting interests—which is the usual situation.

Planning and Monitoring Inventory

The expected total investment in inventory is a consequence of planned production in relation to the sales forecast. Inventory (measured in physical units) at the end of any period will be determined by initial inventory plus purchasing and production during the period, less unit sales. Unexpected changes in inventory will be caused by deviations from planned purchases, production, or sales, or by a combination of the three.

Each production center usually requires an operating plan based on existing orders, sales forecasts, and planned changes in inventory investment. Actual production and sales then should be monitored and compared with plans and forecasts so that timely adjustments can be made as market conditions change.

Figure 25.1 is an example of a cumulative production, sales, and inventory chart. This chart provides an effective means of monitoring total inventory by profit center or by product. The solid line is the cumulative forecast. The circled points are cumulative sales to date (through June). The first uncircled point (on the vertical axis) is finished inventory at the beginning of the year, and the subsequent points represent cumulative production. The dashed line represents the cumulative production plan, and the vertical distance between the cumulative sales forecast and the cumulative production plan represents the planned levels of finished goods inventory at each point in time.

A similar chart can be used for raw materials. In this case, the circled points would represent usage in production and the solid line the forecast usage. The points that are not circled and the dashed line would represent cumulative purchases and planned purchases, respectively.

Concentrating as it does on an aggregate view, such cumulative production, sales (or purchasing), and inventory charts provide financial managers with a useful visual monitor of trends in requirements for investment in

Figure 25.1   *Production, sales, and inventory chart*

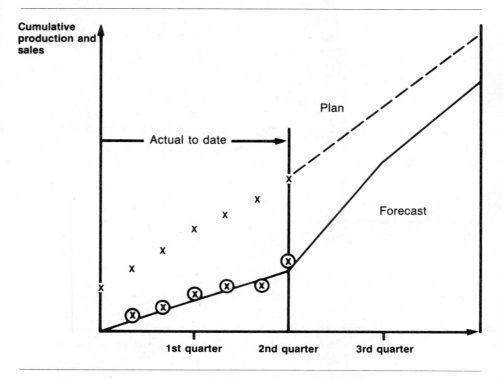

inventory. The charts show the relationship between inventory, planned production levels, and seasonal changes in sales. This overview helps to counteract the tendency to maintain a constant number of weeks' stock in every item, which would require changing production levels unnecessarily with temporary fluctuations in sales activity.

While the financial manager's primary interest should be in trends in the total investment in inventory, he or she also should be aware of their composition. Figure 25.2 illustrates the way in which the composition of inventories usually relates to the total volume of usage. The figure shows an inventory turnover profile, which emerges as a natural consequence of rates of usage varying for different items. As little as 25 percent of all items may constitute 60 to 75 percent of the total dollar volume. The reason is that the most popular items normally account for a large proportion of total sales. These A category stocks are the most important items, deserving individual attention. The next 25 percent of items, the B category, may only account for 15 to 20 percent of the volume of inventory usage, and the C category made up of the remaining 50 percent of the items may account for as little as 5 percent of the volume of usage.

Figure 25.2   *ABC analysis*

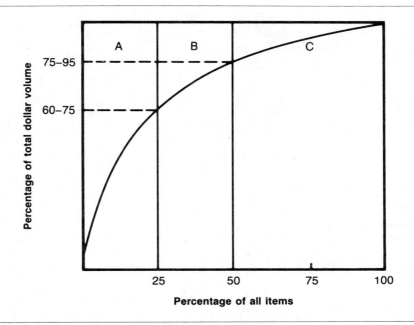

Cost of Carrying Inventory

The costs of carrying inventory are somewhat greater than the financing costs alone. There are at least four items of cost that need to be considered:

1. *Storage costs, handling, insurance.* Where there is a surplus of warehouse space with no alternative uses, and when marginal costing is appropriate, only such incremental items as handling and insurance would be included.
2. *Obsolescence, deterioration, and theft.* The costs arising from these causes are highly dependent on the nature of the item in storage.
3. *Clerical costs.* Stocks must be recorded and controlled. Costs of operating control systems for additional stocks can be significant.
4. *Financing costs.* Investment in inventory (as in any other capital investment) is risky and requires a rate of return that includes the risk-free rate of interest plus a risk premium.

Taking all such costs into account, annual carrying costs for inventory can range between 15 and 40 percent of the value of the goods in stock.

Investment in inventory can be viewed as a capital project. The problem is to determine the level of investment that maximizes the net present value.

Consider, for example, finished goods inventory. Carrying finished goods enables the company to provide faster service to customers than is possible when goods are made to order. When goods can be shipped and invoiced immediately upon receipt of an order, the financial benefits are obvious. By providing better service, companies can expect an increased volume of sales and possibly a higher price. Finished goods inventory also acts as a buffer between production and sales, enabling production in economical batch sizes independent of the sizes of orders received from customers. By this means production ordering costs and machine setup costs can be minimized. Thus, it is important that the investment in inventory should be maintained at levels consistent with efficient operations that tend to maximize the associated revenue benefits net of expenses after-tax.

Designing the Inventory Control System

Inventory control systems have been implemented in various ways to obtain a reasonable balance between the costs of inventory and the very considerable benefits that accrue from carrying inventory. Inventory plays an important role in cushioning the various stages of production from short-term changes in supply and in reducing delivery lead times to customers. The inventory system is crucial to the ability of the firm to provide service to customers and to do so efficiently at minimum cost. Inventories can be categorized as follows:

raw materials

component stocks

work in progress

finished goods

distribution stocks

Within each category, the inventory system often must provide:

inventories in anticipation of seasonal changes in demand

inventories arising from quantity ordering and batch production

safety stock to cover unexpected increases in demand

logistical inventories required to fill the pipeline between stages of production and the distribution system

The availability of inventory items at critical points in the production system can greatly shorten delivery lead times to customers and thus improve the competitive position of the company, while at the same time reducing manufacturing costs. The inventory control system should be designed so as to seek a reasonable if not optimum balance between these advantages and the very considerable costs of carrying stocks within the physical limitations of available space.

Elements of an Inventory Control System

An inventory control system can be described in terms of the method used to replenish stocks. The method chosen depends on the degree of uncertainty associated with the demands made on inventory and on the degree of monitoring that can be justified in each case. There are five basic stock replenishment systems commonly in use:

1. reorder level policy
2. reorder level policy subject to periodic review
3. reorder cycle policy
4. (s, S) policy
5. materials requirements planning (MRP)

These various systems are adapted for different degrees of uncertainty of demand and for varying degrees of monitoring.

REORDER LEVEL POLICY

The **reorder level policy** is adapted to continuous or real-time monitoring of inventories where the arrivals of orders follow no predictable pattern. One tends to find variations of the reorder level policy operating in retail and wholesale outlets, or in other parts of the system where many customers can make demands on inventories.

A forecast of the average rate of sales is required, as well as an estimate of the **lead time** required between the time a replenishment order is placed and the receipt of the goods in stock. For each item in stock, a **reorder level** must be calculated. When stock falls to the reorder level or below, a replenishment order is placed immediately. The reorder level is set high enough so that, if sales during the lead time are as forecast, the replenishment stock will arrive before the inventory is exhausted entirely. A margin for error is provided by the provision of **safety stock** in case sales exceed the forecast during the lead time.

The amount of safety stock required can be determined in terms of the statistical distribution of demand during the lead time. From the mean and variance of lead-time demand there are routine computer methods for determining the probability that a **stockout** will occur (inventory will be exhausted) before the stocks are replenished. The greater the safety stock, the lower the probability of a stockout, and the less average waiting time required for supply.

Also to be determined is the quantity that should be ordered when replenishment is required. The act of reordering requires clerical time; and the opportunity cost of setting up any machinery required to satisfy the order can be costly. If stock items were to be ordered in larger quantities, fewer replenishment orders would be required, and reordering costs would be reduced. However, the size of each batch or lot received in stock influences the size of the lot-size inventory that must be held while the batch is being exhausted. There are formulas for calculating an **economic order quantity** intended to minimize the sum of reordering and stockholding costs.

ECONOMIC ORDER QUANTITIES

The **economic order quantity** (EOQ) provides a basis for obtaining reordering quantities to be used in the stock control systems described in the chapter. The purpose of the EOQ is to minimize the sum of ordering costs and holding costs for inventory.

ORDERING COSTS. Annual ordering costs equal the number of orders multiplied by the cost D per order (typically administrative costs and any machinery setup costs). The estimated number of orders is obtained by dividing the forecast annual usage S by the order quantity Q. Therefore,

Annual Ordering Cost $= SD/Q$

The cost can be reduced by increasing Q in the ratio, as illustrated by the solid curved line in Figure 25.3. At the same time, increasing the order size Q increases the stock and stock holding costs.

STOCKHOLDING COSTS. Receipt of a stock replenishment in the amount Q increases stock initially by Q. This increase diminishes to zero on average by the time that the next replenishment arrives. Thus the lot-size inventory due to discrete replenishments of stock averages between Q and zero or about $Q/2$. If the cost per unit in stock is V, and the annual inventory holding charge is I per unit of value in stock, the cost of carrying lot-size inventory is given by

Stock Holding Cost $= IVQ/2$

Figure 25.3   *Ordering costs, holding costs, and total costs*

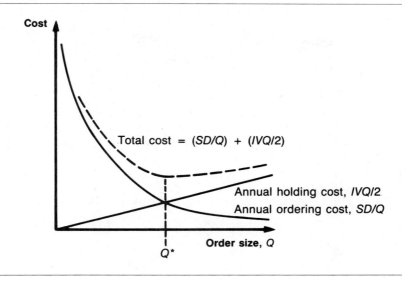

Consequently, stock holding cost increases with the value of Q, as illustrated by the straight line in Figure 25.3.

MINIMUM TOTAL HOLDING AND ORDERING COSTS. The objective of the EOQ is to minimize the total of holding and ordering costs:

$$T = (SD/Q) + (IVQ/2).$$

As you can see in Figure 25.3, the minimum occurs at the value of Q where the holding and ordering costs are equal. Thus we can solve for the value of Q* for which these two terms are the same:

$$SD/Q^* = IVQ^*/2$$

Solving for Q* we obtain the economic order quantity

$$Q^* = \sqrt{2SD/IV}$$

where S = Forecast annual usage
         D = Ordering cost per order
         I = Annual inventory holding charge as a proportion of V
         V = Cost per unit in stock

This result is known as the economic order quantity formula. Variations on this formula may be found in the standard textbooks on production and inventory control.

As an example suppose that a company orders 12,000 of a particular product each year. Each time that it places an order there is an administrative cost of 52 dollars. The product costs 5 dollars each, and the annual inventory carrying charge is 25 percent. That is,

$S = 12,000$

$D = \$52.00$

$I = 0.25$

$V = \$5.00$

The economic ordering quantity for the product is,

$Q^* = \sqrt{2SD/IV}$

$\quad = \sqrt{(2 \times 12{,}000 \times 52)/(0.25 \times 5)}$

$\quad = 999.2$

Thus the economic order quantity for the product is 999.2 units, which happens to be approximately one month's supply at a time.

In summary, the reorder level system requires forecasts of the reordering lead time, the mean and variance of usage during the lead time, reordering and machine setup costs, and the incremental costs of holding inventory items for one period. All this information can be derived from the management information system.

The reorder level policy suffers from two quite serious drawbacks. First, the usual assumption of random arrivals for orders against stock is inappropriate in a large number of cases, which means that the system does not take advantage of the anticipated timing of individual demands when replenishment orders are placed. Another drawback, which the use of computers has helped to counteract, is that the reorder level policy requires costly, continuous, real-time monitoring of every item of inventory. However, this is a system of control that is frequently encountered in industry.

REORDER LEVEL POLICY SUBJECT TO PERIODIC REVIEW

The **reorder level policy subject to periodic review** is designed to operate without the continuous monitoring required by the policy described above. The periodic review policy operates much in the same way as the continuous review policy, except that the status of each item of inventory is reviewed only once each reorder cycle (e.g., each week or month). When the stock is found to be below the reorder level, a replenishment order is issued in the same manner and in the same quantity as for the reorder level policy with continuous review. Since review is not continuous, the reorder level must be set higher in order to allow for expected demand during one-half of the reorder cycle in addition to the expected demand during the lead time. Also, safety stocks must be increased to allow for deviations from expected demand over the additional time period.

Although periodic review with the reorder level policy reduces the clerical and data processing costs of operating the inventory control system, there are offsetting holding costs for the additional stock. Formulas are available for determining the optimum reorder cycle time. However, the normal working cycle for control department personnel may not conform easily to a theoretically optimum review period.

REORDER CYCLE POLICY

The reorder cycle policy is another periodic review system that provides direct control on the stock that is to be carried, but no reorder level is used. In every cycle, a replenishment order is placed for the quantity that would bring the total amount of goods in stock and already on order up to a predetermined limit. This limit must be sufficient to cover forecast demand for one full cycle period plus the lead time. An additional amount for safety stock is included to allow for the variability of demand during this period.

A reorder cycle period is then chosen that minimizes the total of reordering costs and average lot-size stockholding cost.

THE (s, S) POLICY

The (s,S) policy is a hybrid between the reorder level policy (with periodic review) and the reorder cycle policy. Under the (s,S) procedure the stock is reviewed periodically but not replenished unless the stock has fallen below the reorder level s. In this respect, the (s,S) policy is exactly like the reorder level policy with periodic review. At the same time, a standard economic order quantity is not used. Instead, the replenishment order is issued for that quantity that makes the total of goods in stock and goods on order equal to the quantity S. In this latter respect, the method operates much like a reorder cycle system.

A difficulty with the (s,S) method is that the calculation of the best combination of s, S, and the review period for minimum total cost represents a rather complex mathematical problem. A reasonable approach is to make the difference (S − s) equal to the economic order quantity used for the reorder level policy, to make s equal to the safety stock in the reorder level policy with periodic review, and the review period the same as would operate under the reorder cycle policy.

MATERIALS REQUIREMENTS PLANNING

The four inventory control policies described so far all have one assumption in common, that individual demands on inventory items are unpredictable. As demand becomes more predictable, these policies become less efficient. To take a common example, suppose that a stock of finished goods is held for one customer who orders the same quantity at the same time virtually every month. No policy would be optimal that did not take advantage of this sort of demand information. If a replenishment order equal to the customer's monthly demand were placed just over one month's lead time before the expected receipt of the monthly order, virtually no finished goods inventory need be carried, for replenishment would occur almost simultaneously with demand. The replenishment stock should be timed to arrive just before receipt of the next monthly customer order. How many months' sales should be included in the replenishment order? Here we have a capital investment decision. The manager must determine the reordering policy that minimizes the present value of the resulting sequence of setup costs and holding costs.

In other words, when there are predictable, dependent relationships in the pattern of demand, an ordering policy can take advantage of this additional information. Operation of such a system, however, requires close attention to the demand characteristics of each such item of stock and it may be too costly to operate for the less important items.

To the extent that the firm is manufacturing to fill a backlog of orders, the demand pattern becomes relatively predictable in the short term. In this situation as well, the four reordering policies discussed earlier are no longer appropriate. The known demand in this case can be used to generate orders for the required parts and materials and components right back through the operating system. The resulting **materials requirements planning** system relies on lists of parts and numbers required to generate factory requirements from customer orders. These requirements are translated manually or by computer into schedules that take into consideration the demand for common components, existing stock levels, production and procurement lead time, and production batching policy.

Because most manufacturing companies produce to order and for inventory, their inventory control policies combine elements of the materials requirements planning and one or more of the stock replenishment policies. It is an art for the skilled operations manager to make such a blend of the required systems actually work.

Operating the Inventory Control System

Financial management is concerned primarily that the investment in total inventory yields the largest possible net present value. This goal cannot be achieved unless the system of individual item control results in the optimum total inventory. Individual stock control formulas typically are suboptimal in the sense that they do not consider the costs of changes in the overall level of production. Management must judge how quickly the overall level of production can be changed to meet seasonal or other changes in demand, while letting individual items of stock play their proper role as a buffer between production and the more short-term changes in demand. Broad production-level plans should be established on the basis of a target for the total inventory of items that are included in the production, sales, and inventory chart in Figure 25.1

In the course of time, the combination of the starting inventory, the sales forecast, and the production plan will dictate planned changes in inventory. If you look at Figure 25.1 for the end of the second quarter, you see that inventory, the difference represented by the vertical distance between the dashed line (cumulative planned production) and the solid line (cumulative forecast sales) is planned to reach a maximum and then to fall to a minimum three months later.

These planned patterns constrain total inventory to be different from the target that would be implied by the sum of all the individual economic order quantities and safety stocks. A stock control system will not operate optimally under these conditions unless replenishment order quantities are scaled up proportionally when the planned total inventory is to be above this theoretical target and scaled down proportionally when the planned total inventory is below this target.

Responsibility for the Investment in Inventory

Inventories are controlled by a variety of departments, each with its own interests in maintaining inventory at a substantial level. It often falls to financial management to ensure that conflicting interests are kept in balance.

Finished goods inventories are a necessary requirement for distribution and good customer service. It is natural for the marketing (or sales) department to take an active interest in finished goods, often trying to control stocks by item for each major customer. Marketing personnel often prefer to err on the side of having too much inventory in order to ensure against shortages and to maximize sales.

Finished goods inventory, providing a buffer between the market and the production process, also facilitates long production runs and minimizes short-term layoffs of production workers. For this reason, production management often plays a critical role in determining the volume of investment in inventory. Production managers may be less interested in maintaining the right balance of items in stock than in keeping operating units and production processes running efficiently. Often they will produce an excess of an easily manufactured item in order to keep a particular process going at a minimum cost per unit—perhaps at the expense of other items, which then may fall into short supply. Production managers may have an interest in maintaining substantial inventories in excess of what is required.

Raw materials inventories are necessary for continuity of operations. The responsibility for stocking raw materials lies with the purchasing department. The purchasing department is interested in supplying sufficient raw materials item by item and may work to stock-level limits that may be inappropriate in comparison to currently anticipated levels of production.

In manufacturing companies, a production planning and control department normally will be given the responsibility for balancing the interests of the various departments and for minimizing the costs of carrying inventory. Production planning and control departments usually report to a production manager and are frequently located within operating companies of the group. Because a production manager normally does not report even indirectly to financial management, his or her control may not always be consistent with the strategy and policies inherent in the company's financial plans.

Summary

Inventories normally comprise a significant proportion of corporate assets. For this reason they require the close attention of financial management. Inventories also are one of the more volatile elements of working capital, and an accumulating excess of potentially unmarketable inventory has led to the bankruptcy of a number of companies. The management of inventories is usually divided among a number of departments, most of which are often beyond the direct influence of financial management. Nevertheless, financial managers should have all the necessary information to influence the control of inventory in the management information system. The financial manager has the ultimate responsibility to see that the aggregate of inventory investment reflects a sound relationship between forecast sales and the cost of production and warehousing. Inventory control systems have been devised to assist management to achieve such a relationship.

Review Questions

1. What factors make inventory control an important part of the financial planning and control system?
2. Describe an effective means of planning and monitoring aggregate investment in inventories.
3. What are the main costs of carrying inventory? How significant are they in total?
4. What are the principal categories of inventory carried by companies, and what types of inventory must be provided for within each category?
5. What are the characteristics of the four basic stock replenishment systems in use? In what circumstances is the use of each most appropriate?
6. Describe some of the problems arising in the operation of inventory control systems.

Problems

1. LMN Company manufactures product line A at the rate of 30,000 units per month. The quarterly sales forecast is given below:

Quarter	Forecast
1	75,000
2	125,000
3	75,000
4	125,000

   Total inventory for product line A at the beginning of the year is 200,000 units. If the target inventory for the end of the year is equal to 66,500 units, when should the normal level of production be planned to resume? Plot the cumulative production, sales, and inventory chart.
2. Assuming ordering lead time is nil, identify and label the following on the diagram below: (a) order quantity, (b) reorder level, and (c) safety stock.
3. For the (s, S) stock control system, identify s and S on the diagram in Problem 2. How can appropriate values of s and S be estimated?
4. A product is manufactured for one industrial customer, who orders 35 units worth $30 each (at marginal cost) at the end of each month.

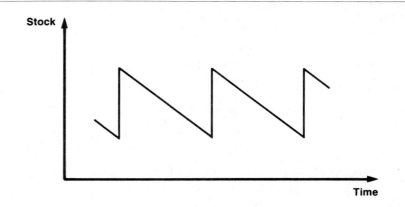

Assuming the inventory carrying cost is 30 percent per year and the reordering cost $100, how many months' stock should be in each batch?

5. Quagmire Distributors, Inc., operates a reorder point ordering system for replacing stock items that are supplied to a large number of retailers. The item costs $10, and Quagmire expects to order $120,000 worth of the item from the manufacturer during the year. Each order that Quagmire places with the manufacturer costs the company $50, including clerical costs of processing the order, paying the invoice, and handling the shipment when it arrives at the warehouse. The company estimates that the annual inventory holding costs amount to 20 percent of the value (at cost) of the goods in inventory.

(a) What is the economic order quantity for this item?

(b) If the manufacturer always delivers six weeks after the order is placed and if during this lead time the demand for the item should fluctuate no more than 50 percent from average, what is the most safety stock Quagmire should carry?

(c) What reorder level should the company use to trigger each replenishment order?

6. Quagmire Distributors, Inc., is considering changing its reordering system from a reorder level to an (s, S) policy. The company does not feel that it can implement the optimum cycle, for in practice it would be able to review each inventory item only once a month. Using the data in Problem 5, and making an appropriate assumption concerning the variation in demand for the relevant cycle and lead time, estimate values for s and S.

References

Bierman, H., Jr., C. P. Bonini, and W. H. Hausman, *Quantitative Analysis for Business Decisions,* 5th ed., Homewood, Ill.: Richard D. Irwin, 1977.

Franks, J. R., and J. E. Broyles, *Modern Managerial Finance,* New York: John Wiley, 1979: 253–68.

Kallberg, J. G., and K. Parkinson, *Current Asset Management: Cash, Credit, and Inventory,* New York: John Wiley and Sons, 1984.

Mehta, D. R., *Working Capital Management,* Englewood Cliffs, N.J.: Prentice-Hall, 1974.

Wagner, H. M., *Principles of Operations Research,* 2nd ed., Englewood Cliffs, N.J.: Prentice-Hall, 1975.

26

Financial Planning

Most of the financial tools discussed so far in this book have separated financial analysis into manageable parts: evaluation of individual capital projects, the dividend decision, one-period capital structure analysis, and the like. Although such separation simplifies financial decisions, and indeed the procedure has considerable support in modern finance theory, we know that it is artificial and imperfect. In fact, financial decisions, like grapes, grow in clusters rather than one at a time. Effective financial planning, which fits the pieces of the financial management puzzle together, is not only in the interests of management and employees, whose jobs may be at stake in the event of financial distress, but also in the interests of shareholders, banks, and others who finance the company.

In this chapter we explain why financial planning is important as an operational device that helps increase shareholders' wealth. We discuss the principal tools of financial planning and the difficulties inherent in making financial forecasts. We show how the assumptions underlying the forecasts can be organized and how the analysis of alternative possible future events and decisions can be simplified with the aid of scenario building. These points are illustrated with the two types of financial plans. The first is the cash budget, which provides the framework of short-term cash management. The second is the long-term financial plan, which is concerned with how the firm's economic environment affects its financial decisions for several years into the future. In the context of both kinds of planning frameworks, we show how to plan for contingencies arising from possible changes in the company, the industry, and the economy. Finally, we discuss extensions of these planning models to incorporate optimization of shareholder wealth under uncertainty and why the "ideal" financial plan is impossible to achieve.

The Practical Importance of Financial Planning

The criteria for financial decisions discussed in previous chapters were based on value maximization principles. One such criterion states that if a project's expected cash flows produce a positive net present value the project should be accepted. The assumption here is that projects can be financed if they have positive NPVs. There are a variety of reasons why this assumption must be qualified.

For example, an investment may seem profitable, but its acceptance still could expose the company to the risk of financial distress, or even bankruptcy. Significant costs can result from accepting such a project while a company is being reorganized or otherwise restored to financial health. These costs include not only legal and other fees associated with negotiations with creditors, but also losses from postponement or rejection of profitable investment opportunities while management is preoccupied with financial problems. Also, the personal wealth of management or employees usually does not represent a well-diversified portfolio. An individual's job usually represents his or her single most important investment, one that is not willingly exposed to much risk. Consequently, even the possibility of the company's encountering financial distress may discourage management from investing in profitable projects if they are too risky. Financial planning enables management to assess the implications of investment and financing decisions for the future viability of the firm in adverse circumstances and to take measures that reduce the likelihood of financial distress.

Even if management is more concerned than the shareholders about financial distress, one cannot conclude that managers necessarily behave in a manner contrary to the interests of shareholders. If the firm's ability to generate net present values from its projects depends on the quality of its existing management, the job security of managers is of valid concern to shareholders. Also, financial planning enables management to assess financial risks and, if appropriate, protect against them. By sharing the risks with other partners, by entering into contracts incorporating escalation clauses, or by negotiating long-term financing, management may be able to shift or to sell some of the risks to other parties. If, by means of the application of foresight in planning, management can forestall unnecessary financial risks or constraints imposed by creditors, shareholders can benefit from a more aggressive investment program made possible by the company's relative freedom from excessive financial risk.

Finally, because financial planning reduces frequent unanticipated demands for additional funds that result in unnecessarily high transactions costs, it reduces costs to shareholders and reduces both costs and risks to lenders.

Cash Management

Throughout this textbook we have evaluated financial decisions in terms of their impact on cash flows. Cash itself is an asset that needs to be managed efficiently. Cash (or liquidity) management often is described as the residual task facing the corporate treasurer. The task is residual because the treasurer must forecast the cash flow implications of decisions largely made by others within the firm, including:

major financing and/or debt retirements

scheduled investments in new projects

operating plans

credit and collection policies

policies affecting payments to suppliers

investment in inventories

The first two items are more easily forecast because they occur infrequently. The last four produce cash flows that are uncertain and can fluctuate widely, often with seasonal effects. The treasurer's job includes forecasting the combined effects on corporate liquidity of decisions in all six areas. First, however, the treasurer has to ensure that the firm's procedures for collecting, maintaining, and disbursing cash, and for managing cash excesses or deficiencies are as efficient as possible.

If bank demand deposits pay little or no interest, too much cash in the bank is wasteful, but too little cash can mean financial distress resulting from an inability to pay interest and other financial obligations on time. Corporate liquidity is defined as the ability to meet cash flow requirements promptly. Liquidity is provided through effective management of cash and money market assets and of bank credit lines and other sources of short-term funds.

THE CORPORATE CASH MANAGEMENT PROBLEM

Corporate cash revenues arise from payments by customers. Such cash is not available until the customers' checks actually are deposited in the company's account at the bank. This takes time, because a check may spend several days in the mail, and then it must be cleared by the banks involved. When the check is finally cleared, the firm gets credit for dollars in its account, and the customer loses dollars from its account. A mirror image of this process is involved when a company pays its suppliers; some time after mailing a check to a supplier, the firm's bank balance is debited for the amount involved. Meanwhile, the firm must keep some buffer stock of cash in its demand deposit account to allow for uncertainties and delays and also to ensure that all the checks it has written will be honored when presented by the payees' banks.

Collection float is defined as the average number of dollars collected each day multiplied by the average number of days taken up in the collection process described above. Because the money tied up in collection float could be invested in interest-bearing short-term securities, corporate treasurers have an obvious incentive to speed up the collection process.

Disbursement float is the opposite side of the coin. Subject to the costs associated with displeasing suppliers, corporate treasurers have an incentive to maximize disbursement float, that is, to earn interest on cash that has not reached suppliers' bank accounts.

MOVEMENT OF FUNDS IN THE UNITED STATES BANKING SYSTEM

Consider the case of Tar Heel Cookery in Chapel Hill, North Carolina, which has just received a $1,000 shipment of Chinese kitchen utensils with an invoice from SF Importers, Inc., in San Francisco. Tar Heel Cookery writes a $1,000 check on its account with North Carolina National Bank (NCNB) and mails the check and invoice to SF Importers. Several days later, SF Importers receives the check and deposits it for collection in its account with the Wells Fargo National Bank. In turn, Wells Fargo sends Tar Heel Cookery's check to the Federal Reserve Bank of San Francisco for clearing. Under Federal Reserve rules, Wells Fargo is entitled to consider the check collected two days later (although in fact it could take longer for the check to cross the country, be presented to NCNB, and the funds moved from NCNB's account with the Federal Reserve System to Wells Fargo's account). Therefore, SF Importers will be considered to have $1,000 available as **collected funds** two days after it makes its deposit at Wells Fargo. The total time between the dates when Tar Heel Cookery's check is written and when SF Importers obtains usable funds could be as much as eight days: three to five days for mailing time, one day for processing by SF Importers, and two days in the Federal Reserve collection process.

If eight days could be cut to, say, four, the value of this time saving to SF Importers would be (approximately)

$$\frac{4}{365} \times \$1,000 \times 0.10 = \$1.096$$

assuming simple interest at an annual rate of 10 percent. Small change, you say, and hardly worth the bother, but what if SF Importers receives 100 similar remittances each day, in an average amount of $5,000 per check? The saving of four days in the collection process would be worth

$$4 \times 100 \times \$5,000 \times 0.10 = \$200,000$$

per year. Under such circumstances it could be worthwhile to invest in some means of speeding up collection.

Enter the **lock box.** Wells Fargo, under current banking laws, cannot operate a branch office in North Carolina, nor NCNB one in California. But they can keep deposit balances in each other's bank, can transfer funds electronically between one another immediately, and can perform services in their home states for the other bank. This structure has made possible the development of lock box arrangements to reduce mail float for firms such as SF Importers. A corporation making deliveries to a distant part of the country specifies that remittances be made to a mail box number close to the location of the customers, thus reducing the mail float. The mail box is under the control of a local bank, which picks up the checks daily (or more frequently) and puts them into the collection process (at the same time handling the paperwork and depositing funds to the corporation's local account). Collected balances in such local banks can be transferred electronically for use elsewhere.

Lock box collection systems are widespread. Large banks with substantial corporate banking business design and implement lock box systems and use sophisticated models to determine the optimum number and location of the lock boxes around the country. The design of a lock box system requires information about the geographic pattern and volume of remittances to the corporation, as well as estimates of mail times from various customers' locations to alternative lock box city locations.

The next step in the cash management process is to gather the collected funds in **concentration accounts** to facilitate short-term investments and disbursements to suppliers. The reason for concentrating deposits in a few accounts is to obtain economies of scale, for transactions costs involved in the purchase and sale of short-term money market securities decrease relatively as the size of each such investment increases. Electronic funds transfer facilitates the sweeping of excess balances from many collection accounts to a few more easily managed concentration accounts.

For those making payments, the float is an advantage, for while a check remains uncashed in the float, the dollar amount of the check can be invested in the money market. Large banks offer modeling and consulting services to help their corporate customers select the number and location of **disbursement banks** with a view to increasing the float. The corporation can arrange to have funds in its disbursement accounts above some agreed-upon minimum level (perhaps as low as zero) automatically invested overnight in the financial market. Banks and large corporations frequently borrow for such short periods. The **repurchase agreement,** or repo, is one such mechanism. The bank sells the corporation United States government securities, simultaneously arranging to repurchase them the next day at a price that produces a return to the corporation. The Federal Reserve Board has been trying to cut the float to a minimum, publicly chastising securities firms for taking maximum advantage of disbursement float by, for example, remitting payments to New York customers with checks written on West Coast bank accounts. Undue delays in making funds available to vendors as a result of remote disbursement is bound to cause ill will, however, so the potential for increasing the float in this way is limited.

Cash Forecasting

While the corporate cash management system involves the investment of temporarily excess funds in money market assets, such as Treasury bills, certificates of deposit, and commercial paper, it also involves the setting up of credit lines with banks to meet both forecasted and unexpected cash needs. The technical requirements for successful cash management include good seasonal cash flow forecasts reflecting the firm's overall financial plan. A smoothly functioning relationship between the corporate treasurer and the firm's banks depends on the design and operation of an effective financial reporting and forecasting system.

The cash budget (sometimes referred to as a short-term pro forma financial statement) is one of the most important tools available for determining likely financing requirements or cash surpluses in the short to intermediate term (say, up to eighteen months). The cash budget is a forecast of cash receipts and expenditures for each future period. The choice of period, whether weeks or months, will depend on the nature and variability of the firm's cash flows. Net receipts or expenditures in each period are then used to make cumulative adjustments to the beginning cash balance in each subsequent period. Cash buildups or depletions projected in this manner may indicate either requirements for additional financing or the temporary investment of funds in money market securities.

The frequency with which forecasts are updated depends upon the nature of the business and the speed with which new developments are likely to alter the basis of the forecasts. Normally, cash budgets are recomputed no less than once a quarter. In some companies, weekly and even daily computerized forecasts are required to facilitate money market transactions.

AN EXAMPLE—THE CASH BUDGET AND MANAGEMENT
OF SHORT-TERM LIQUIDITY

Table 26.1 illustrates a simplified example of a monthly schedule of cash receipts based in part on an updated sales forecast and an assumed schedule of payments from credit customers. The problem of credit sales is the lag between sales and actual receipt of payment. Management is forecasting that 10 percent of credit sales will be paid with a delay of only one month and 90 percent will be paid with a delay of only two months. Thus, forecast total receipts in a given month represent collections for credit sales in several preceding months as well as cash sales for that month. Other cash receipts, such as dividends from investments in other companies' stocks and sales of fixed assets, also must be included. The resulting total cash receipts are then entered in the cash budget in Table 26.3.

Also to be entered in the cash budget in Table 26.3 are total cash payments from Table 26.2. The data in Table 26.2 are based on an operating plan. Purchases of raw material and subcontracted components in the early months may represent existing commitments based upon an earlier operating plan. In subsequent months, purchases will reflect current planning and any necessary adjustments to inventories of raw material and subcontracted components. Wages paid and other operating expenditures also will depend upon the operating plan, which affects such items as manpower levels, salary increases, and payments for overtime work. Nonoperating expenditures, such as expected payment of taxes, dividends and interest, and capital expenditures, also should be included.

The net cash increase or reduction in each period resulting from expected

Table 26.1   *Projected sales and cash receipts (thousands of dollars)*

	May	June	July	Aug.	Sept.	Oct.	Nov.
Total sales	83.0	85.0	88.0	101.0	111.0	103.0	109.0
Credit sales	74.7	76.5	79.2	90.9	99.9	92.7	98.1
Collections:							
1 month (10%)		7.5	7.7	7.9	9.1	10.0	9.3
2 months (90%)			67.2	68.8	71.3	81.8	89.9
Total collections			74.9	76.7	80.4	91.8	99.2
Cash sales			8.8	10.1	11.1	10.3	10.9
Other cash receipts:							
Money market investments			20.0	0	0	0	0
Sales of fixed assets			0	0	0	0	40.0
Other			1.0	2.0	1.0	1.0	1.0
Total cash receipts			104.7	88.8	92.5	103.1	151.1

Table 26.2   *Projected expenditures (thousands of dollars)*

	June	July	Aug.	Sept.	Oct.	Nov.	Dec.
Purchases:							
Raw material	45	45	45	45	50	50	50
Subcontracted components	20	25	25	25	15	15	15
	65	70	70	70	65	65	65
Cash payments for purchases		65	70	70	70	65	65
Wages paid		20	22	22	22	18	18
Other operating expenditures		10	13	13	13	7	7
Total operating expenditures		95	105	105	105	90	90
Other cash payments:							
Taxes		0	0	0	14	0	0
Dividends and interest		0	40	0	0	0	0
Capital expenditures		0	0	0	0	50	0
Total cash payments		95	145	105	119	140	90

receipts and payments is shown in Table 26.3. For example, at the end of July management expects to have $89,700 in cash when it has a credit line with a bank that requires a minimum or compensating cash balance of $20,000. Thus the safety margin or excess is $69,700 as indicated. Note that a shortfall emerges in October that continues through November.

The cash budget is a device for reflecting the impact of financial and operating decisions that have already been made on the projected cash position. The cash budget's operating significance is that it indicates to the treasurer when and to what degree cash excesses or deficiencies should be anticipated. Within agreed-upon limits, the treasurer's responsibility is to manage any discrepancies via short-term investment and borrowing. Should cash budget projections indicate that limits on anticipated cash excesses or deficiencies are likely to be breached, top management should reconsider one or more of the financial and operating decisions on which the cash budget projections are based.

UNCERTAINTY IN CASH FORECASTS

Such a procedure, however, often proves to be inadequate, as nothing so far indicates whether the minimum cash balance or the line of credit arranged

Table 26.3   *Net cash increase/reduction (thousands of dollars)*

	July	Aug.	Sept.	Oct.	Nov.	Dec.
Total receipts	104.7	88.8	92.5	103.1	151.1	104.0
Total payments	95.0	145.0	105.0	119.0	140.0	90.0
Net cash flow	9.7	(56.2)	(12.5)	(15.9)	11.1	14.0
Initial cash balance	80.0	89.7	33.5	21.0	5.1	16.2
Ending cash balance	89.7	33.5	21.0	5.1	16.2	30.2
Minimum balance	20.0	20.0	20.0	20.0	20.0	20.0
Excess (shortfall)	69.7	13.5	1.0	(14.9)	(3.8)	10.2

with bankers is sufficient to meet possible deviations from the forecast. There are several sources of uncertainty. The sales forecast usually is the least reliable data in the budget. Not only may the sales forecast prove to be wrong, but it also may turn out to be systematically too high or too low on average.

A second source of uncertainty is the promptness with which customers pay their bills. When business conditions are unfavorable for a company, they are likely to be adverse for customers as well. This may cause customers to delay payments at the very time when the cash is most required by the company. Of course, the company may also be able to stretch its own payments to suppliers. Frequently, however, adjustments to purchases and payments to suppliers cannot be large enough or made sufficiently rapidly to neutralize the effects of unanticipated changes in cash receipts.

Sensitivity analysis (described in Chapter 10) can be used to measure the possible effects of the uncertainty. Cash budgets based upon several alternative sets of assumptions about future events help to determine how robust the firm's cash position is and how adequate the standby liquidity arrangements are to deal with unanticipated situations.[1] For most firms, however, the capacity to respond quickly to contingencies is the key variable. The larger the potential deviations from plan induced by uncertainty, and the farther into the future they can arise, the more appropriate it is to have contingency plans that involve revisions of initial major capital investment and financing decisions.

---

[1]Computerized financial statement compilers nowadays make this task relatively simple for assistant treasurers, bankers, and MBA students.

Longer-term Financial Planning

The focus of long-term financial planning (up to five years or more) is on major items such as expected earnings and the acquisition and disposal of fixed assets. The plan provides for the timely issue of company securities and long-term debt. For this purpose, projections of sources and uses of funds are employed in pro forma funds flow statements that summarize the plan. Typically, such statements can be less detailed than a seasonal cash budget.

MODELING FRAMEWORKS

There are many different modeling frameworks for financial planning, all of which produce pro forma funds flow and other financial statements. These frameworks can be classified in terms of how they treat financial variables and in terms of the planning model's structure.

In general, a financial planning model's variables will fall into one of three categories:

1. *Forecast.* Corporate sales may be forecast directly, or may be forecast indirectly as a function of forecast gross national product (GNP). Plant and equipment outlays may be forecast directly from planned and actual capital project acceptances, or they may be forecast indirectly from the plant and equipment base that would be needed to support forecast sales.

2. *"Known" decision variables.* These are variables implied by predetermined decisions or policies that are taken as given. Future dividends, for example, may be included at current or planned levels.

3. *"Unknown" decision variables.* These are future variables that may be changed according to rules that have been incorporated in the model framework. For example, the planning model automatically may alter the assumed level of borrowing to satisfy forecast funds needs, up to the amount that will keep the firm's interest coverage ratio (earnings divided by interest payments) above a specified level. In an optimizing model, "unknown" decision variables will be changed so as to achieve the corporate financial plan's objectives (such as shareholder wealth maximization), subject to complying with such constraints as the minimum interest coverage ratio.

Planning models fall into three categories:

1. *Deterministic "what if" simulations.* The models trace out the consequences over time of sets of forecasted and/or predetermined economic and financial variables. Strictly speaking, these simulation models have no finance

content, because they merely add up the forecasted consequences of decisions already made or assumed to have been made rather than produce indicated future decisions that balance returns against risks.

2. *Deterministic optimizing simulations.* The models produce the best financial decisions subject to legal and management policy constraints (such as minimum acceptable interest coverage ratios) for each assumed set of future economic and business conditions. The implied pro forma financial statements are based upon mathematical programming solutions, which were discussed in Chapter 5.

3. *Probabilistic optimizing simulations.* The models incorporate probabilities of the possible future economic events in each future period and produce decision rules (e.g., optimum level of borrowing if bond yields fall in 1987) as part of the pro forma financial statements.

AN EXAMPLE OF A DETERMINISTIC "WHAT IF" SIMULATION

Tables 26.4 and 26.5 represent the 1984 financial statements of a hypothetical firm, Post Mills Controls, Inc. A financial plan is to be constructed that reflects the following forecasts, predetermined financial decisions, and man-

Table 26.4   *Balance sheet for Post Mills Controls, Inc., December 31, 1984 (millions of dollars)*

ASSETS		
Cash		2.0
Accounts receivable		6.0
Inventory		5.0
Plant and equipment		
Gross plant	20.7	
Less: Depreciation	−4.0	
Equals: Net plant		16.7
Other assets		4.0
Total assets		33.7
LIABILITIES AND EQUITY		
Current liabilities (accruals)		9.0
Short-term borrowing		3.2
Long-term debt		7.0
Equity capital		14.5
Total liabilities and equity		33.7

Table 26.5   Income statement for Post Mills Controls, Inc. for 1984 (millions of dollars)

Sales	50.000
Cost of goods sold	28.300
Selling expense	3.500
General and administrative expense	10.000
Depreciation	3.000
Operating income	5.200
Other income	0.400
Earnings before interest and taxes	5.600
Interest expense	0.892
Earnings before taxes	4.708
Corporate income taxes	2.307
Net income	2.401

agement decision rules. The forecasted variables are given in Tables 26.6, 26.7, and 26.8.

1. Sales are forecast to rise from $50 million in 1984 to $54.7, $66.0, $74.7, $86.0, and $94.8 million in the next five years.
2. Cost of goods sold is forecast directly at $30.0, $35.4, $40.5, $45.5, and $50.6 million for the next five years.
3. Selling expense is forecast directly at $4.1, $4.9, $5.6, $6.3, and $7 million for the next five years.
4. General and administrative expenses are forecast at levels of $12.8, $14.0, $16.0, $18.0, and $20.0 million for the next five years.
5. Plant additions and depreciation charges result in net plant growing to $33.8 million by the end of 1989. These figures (and the sales and operating expenses) summarize the projections from capital projects accepted as of year-end 1984.
6. Accounts receivable, inventory, and current liabilities are forecast as functions of future sales and average (as a percentage of sales) about 12.8, 10.6, and 19.0 percent, respectively.
7. Principal repayments on long-term debt are $1 million per year. Interest payments are 10 percent of the previous year's closing balance of unpaid long-term debt.
8. Dividend payments are planned at $600,000 per year.
9. Cash balances are to be maintained at no less than $2 million to support Post Mills Controls' credit line with its banks.
10. Funds shortfalls are to be made up by short-term borrowing at a forecast interest rate of 12 percent (paid on year-end balances).
11. Federal and state corporate income taxes total 49 percent.

Table 26.6
Pro forma balance sheets for Post Mills Controls, Inc. (millions of dollars)

	1984	1985	1986	1987	1988	1989
ASSETS	(actual)					
Cash	2.000	2.000	2.000	2.000	2.000	2.511
Accounts receivable	6.000	7.000	8.400	9.600	11.000	12.100
Inventory	5.000	5.800	7.000	8.000	9.000	10.000
Plant and equipment						
Gross plant	20.700	26.700	31.500	36.700	43.500	46.300
Less: Depreciation	−4.000	−6.000	−8.000	−10.500	−11.500	−12.500
Equals: Net plant	16.700	20.700	23.500	26.200	32.000	33.800
Other assets	4.000	4.000	2.000	2.000	0	0
Total assets	33.700	39.500	42.900	47.800	54.000	58.411
LIABILITIES AND EQUITY						
Accounts payable	9.000	10.400	12.600	14.400	16.200	18.000
Short-term borrowing	3.200	6.812	5.186	5.207	3.898	0
Long-term debt	7.000	6.000	5.000	4.000	3.000	2.000
Equity capital	14.500	16.288	20.114	24.193	30.902	38.411
Total liabilities and equity	33.700	39.500	42.900	47.800	54.000	58.411

The solution to the planning model requires allocating fund excesses to cash and fund deficiencies to short-term borrowing (STB). Consider 1985. The predetermined asset side of the balance sheet (Table 26.6) adds up to $39.5 million inclusive of the minimum cash balance ($2 million). The liabilities side also must add up to $39.5 million, or

$$39.5 = \text{Accounts Payable} + \text{Short-term Borrowing} + \text{Long-term Debt} + \text{Equity}$$

$$39.5 = 10.4 + \text{STB}(1985) + 6.0 + E(1985)$$

Rearranging,

$$\text{STB}(1985) + E(1985) = 23.1 \tag{26.1}$$

Simultaneously, equity for 1985 must be equal to E(1984) + retained earnings for 1985. That is:

$$E(1985) = E(1984) + [\text{EBIT}(1985) - I(1985)] \times (1 - \text{Tax Rate}) - \text{Dividends}(1985)$$

Table 26.7
Pro forma income statement for Post Mills Controls, Inc. (millions of dollars)

	1984	1985	1986	1987	1988	1989
	(actual)					
Sales	50.000	54.700	66.000	74.700	86.000	94.800
Cost of goods sold	28.300	30.000	35.400	40.500	45.500	50.600
Selling expense	3.500	4.100	4.900	5.600	6.300	7.000
General and administration expense	10.000	12.800	14.000	16.000	18.000	20.000
Depreciation	3.000	2.000	2.000	2.500	1.000	1.000
Operating income	5.200	5.800	9.700	10.100	15.200	16.200
Other income	.400	.400	.200	.200	0	0
Earnings before interest and taxes	5.600	6.200	9.900	10.300	15.200	16.200
Interest expense	.892	1.517	1.222	1.150	.857	.301
Earnings before taxes	4.708	4.683	8.678	9.150	14.343	15.899
Corporate income taxes	2.307	2.295	4.252	4.484	7.028	7.791
Net income	2.401	2.388	4.426	4.667	7.315	8.108

where EBIT(1985) is earnings before interest and taxes 1985 and I(1985) is total interest payments in 1985. Using the corresponding figures from the pro forma income statement in Table 26.7:

$$E(1985) = 14.5 + [6.2 - (0.1 \times 7) - (0.12 \times STB[1985])](1 - 0.49) - 0.6$$

where interest on the $7 million of long-term debt is 10 percent, interest on short-term borrowing for 1985 is 12 percent, and the total federal and state tax is 49 percent. Rearranging:

$$0.0612 \; STB(1985) + E(1985) = 16.705 \tag{26.2}$$

Solving equations (26.1) and (26.2) simultaneously gives values of STB(1985) = 6.812 and E(1985) = 16.288, which appear in Table 26.6, from which the 1985 income and funds flow statements for Post Mills Controls can be completed (Tables 26.7 and 26.8). Obtaining algebraic solutions one year at a time gives the complete statements of Tables 26.6, 26.7, and 26.8.

For the first four years, 1985 through 1988, Post Mills Controls' financial plan required a significant level of short-term borrowing, as Table 26.6 shows, rising at once to $6.812 million, then gradually falling to $3.805 million in 1988. In 1989, the firm pays off its short-term borrowing and increases its cash balance to $2.511 million.

Table 26.8

Pro forma funds flow projections for Post Mills Controls, Inc. (millions of dollars)

	1985	1986	1987	1988	1989
USES					
(Increases in):					
Cash	0	0	0	0	.511
Accounts receivable	1.000	1.400	1.200	1.400	1.100
Inventory	.800	1.200	1.000	1.000	1.000
Gross plant	6.000	4.800	5.200	6.800	2.800
Other assets	0	−2.000	0	−2.000	0
Dividends	.600	.600	.600	.600	.600
Total uses	8.400	6.000	8.000	7.800	6.011
SOURCES					
(Increases in):					
Accounts payable	1.400	2.200	1.600	2.100	1.700
Short-term borrowing	3.612	−1.626	.234	−1.615	−3.798
Long-term debt	−1.000	−1.000	−1.000	−1.000	−1.000
Net income	2.388	4.426	4.667	7.315	8.108
Funds represented by noncash charges	2.000	2.000	2.500	1.000	1.000
Total sources	8.400	6.000	8.000	7.800	6.011

How can such a model be used, when in practice almost all forecast inputs to the model will probably prove wrong since those forecasts are means based on a set of probabilities? To be useful, forecasts must also be calculated on alternative sets of assumptions about future events.

Difficulties of Financial Forecasting

It would be easier to forecast the inputs to financial planning models if one knew what assumptions to make about future developments. All other things being equal, business conditions may continue in the same direction, but recent trends might not continue for a variety of reasons. Events intervene: strikes, new competition, even changes in the weather.

There are basically two types of uncertain elements in a forecast. First, there are expectations. Second, there are discrete events that may occur and alter expectations. Trends or rates of growth in sales altered within each year for historical seasonal effects are examples of expectations. Government actions, strikes, and international incidents are examples of discrete events.

Although it may be reasonable to extrapolate or to alter expectations or trends on the basis of economic or business knowledge and judgment, it is the foreseeable but ignored discrete event that may ruin an otherwise good forecast. "Tell me what is going to be in the next federal budget and whether we are going to have a strike, and I can give you a good forecast," is the legitimate retort of the manager who has been asked for a better forecast but has been allowed no formal means of dealing with alternative sets of assumptions about future events. What the forecaster is telling us is that the forecasting problem divides itself into two parts: first, forecasts stating the alternative underlying assumptions about future political, economic, industry, and company developments, and second, forecasts of sales, costs, and other cash flows that such assumptions about future events imply.

Where there are many such events that affect company planning, and when these events can occur in various combinations over time, the complexity of the forecaster's problem appears to increase geometrically with the number of such eventualities. The usual recourse in the face of this complexity is to base forecasts on only the most likely set of future events and to ignore alternative possibilities. The dangers of ignoring possible developments that may significantly affect financial plans are self-evident.

Virtually every forecast must be made conditional on a whole series of possible events leading up to each future period. Who is to say which of the many combinations of events that could affect the forecast actually will occur? Scenario writing is one way of analyzing the alternative sequences of future events upon which financial plans depend.

Scenarios of the Future

When you are preparing a plan for the purpose of arranging finance to meet possible contingencies, you should ask which plausible sequences of events would cause you to require the most outside funding. For each such sequence of events or scenario, you then ask what actions should be taken now, given these possibilities, and how quickly management could respond if such events come to pass? Only when these questions have been considered can you reasonably be certain that sufficient funding is available to meet plausible eventualities.

Scenarios can be constructed routinely by following three steps.

1. List any plausible future developments or events for the economy, the industry, and the company that could affect the forecast significantly.

2. Relist these events in order of likely importance for each future period in the forecast.
3. Select from the most important events in each period those that are to be included in the scenario, and describe their relationships through time.

The criterion for selecting events in the scenario depends upon the purpose of the plan. If the purpose is to determine the kind and the amount of finance that is required to meet possible contingencies, the most important events for the scenario are those that are likely to increase the need for cash.

A comprehensive list of economic circumstances that are the raw material for scenarios can be maintained and updated on a routine basis as an integral part of planning and forecasting. The events to be considered at step (1) above may be classified into several categories, for example:

(a) Macroeconomic events and changes

(b) Government interventions

(c) Industry events and changes

(d) Events affecting the relationships between the company and other firms, such as customers, competitors, and suppliers

(e) Events relating specifically to the company, such as strikes

Possible events to include in such categories appear in Table 26.9.

How many scenarios should management construct? The number depends upon how risky the firm's environment is, and on the level of risk that management is prepared to accept. Management that is unwilling to accept any significant probability of default must try to consider as many events as possible that could impair the company's cash position.

The Use of Scenarios in Sensitivity Analysis

Using scenarios in financial planning is the right way to go about sensitivity analysis, or to follow the "what if" approach. A common problem in using sensitivity analysis is that the interrelationships between or among input variables are not specified adequately; they may even be ignored altogether. For example, in a sensitivity analysis, one might assume that wage rates will rise 10 percent in order to measure the effects on cash flows, while ignoring the fact that wage forecasts are related to general economic factors, such as the rate of inflation, growth prospects, and corporate profits, which also may affect the financial plan. This is not to say that wage rates are not determined also by contract termination dates, the strength of particular

Table 26.9   Raw material for scenarios: A partial listing

(a) **Macroeconomic events and changes**

Inflation	**Recession/recovery**
Exchange rates	**Credit squeeze**
Interest rates	**Birth rates/demography**
GNP growth	**Oil prices**
Capital investment	**Bank failures**
Consumer spending/saving	**Defense policies**

(b) **Government interventions**

Federal budget	**Investment tax credits**
Government spending	**Taxation of foreign earnings**
Conservation/ecology	**Import/export restrictions**
Antitrust rulings	**Product standards/safety**
Tax rates/fiscal measures	**Political instability, wars**

(c) **Industry and regional events and changes**

Market growth	**Labor costs**
Consumer preferences	**Transport costs**
Foreign competition	**Changes in credit terms**
Technology	**Weather, floods**
Energy costs	**Infrastructure**
Commodity prices	

(d) **Events and changes affecting relationships between companies**

New competitor/product	**Market share**
New customer	**Takeovers and mergers**
Loss of monopoly/patent protection	**Loss of supplier**
Security of information	**Sources of finance**

(e) **Events and changes relating to the company**

New product	**Labor supply**
Loss of management	**Local strikes**
Reorganization	**Large negligence claim**
New plant	**Accidents, fire**
Cost overruns	**Water, electricity supply**

unions, and the attitudes of management. However, to ignore the interrelationships between expected outcomes of wage bargaining and the economic context in the financial plan would constitute an important omission. The scenario approach enables the forecaster to test the effects on the financial plan of variables changing in combination, rather than one at a time.

Planning for Contingencies

Management should forecast the effect of changes in both the world and national economies on the industry and on the costs and revenues of the firm. In addition, estimates should be made of the value of the company's assets in both existing and alternative uses for each scenario. Table 26.10 gives an example of the sensitivity of industry and company revenues and fixed asset values to changes in the gross national product (which is in part determined by inflation rates). A deterioration in revenues and cash flow may require the sale of assets to raise cash. Therefore we need to know the likely resale values of assets that might be sold so that these can be included in the financial plans that are based on adverse scenarios.

Business adversity can materialize in many forms, each having its own implications for the resale value of the company's assets and the speed with which they can be sold. The most important circumstances to be considered are:

company business deteriorates in relation to the industry

industry declines in relation to the economy

economy deteriorates

If the company should suffer in relation to the industry, selling assets to more successful companies in the industry at favorable prices may be possible. However, if the industry is also in decline (but not the economy), the most liquid assets may be those with alternative uses in other industries. If the economy should be deteriorating as well, alternative uses for assets may be difficult to find, and some assets could realize little more than scrap value. In the best of circumstances, some fixed assets take a very long time to sell, and the time lag between the emerging need for cash in an unfolding crisis and their actual realization may become a critical factor that should be taken into account in financial projections based on adverse scenarios.

Thus, the amount of financing required to meet contingencies depends very much upon the nature of the contingencies that may arise and the company's likely response to them. How quickly can the company change its strategy and operating plans in response to events? What would operating management's response be to developments that could spell adversity, and

Table 26.10   *Relating planning model input variables to general economic changes*

Inflation rate (percent)	Changes in gross national product (percent)	Changes in industry demand (percent)	Net revenues of the company (millions of dollars)	Value of fixed assets (millions of dollars)
5	4	8	90	20
8	2	4	18	15
10	0	−2	−9	10

what would the cash flow implications of such changed strategies and plans be? These considerations must be built into a cash budget and funds flow projection if it is to be adequate for contingency planning.

There are, therefore, five basic steps in the financial planning and forecasting process:

1. Determine by means of funds flow forecasts and cash budgets the financial requirements implied by the corporate strategy and the operating plan. This provides the basic plan but does not provide for contingencies. Hence the following steps are also required.
2. Identify those alternative scenarios for the economy, the industry, and the company that could plausibly affect future plans and increase requirements for funds.
3. Assess the liquidity position of company assets under adverse scenarios.
4. Assess the likely adjustments that management will make to operating plans in response to unfolding events in each scenario.
5. Determine by means of funds flow forecasts and cash budgets the financing implications of alternative adverse scenarios.

These five steps enable financial management to determine how much financing is required to meet the requirements of operating plans and how much additional financing is required as a precaution against possible adverse developments. Until these steps are accomplished, management cannot know how fundamentally sound the company's financial position is in an uncertain world. How aggressive can a corporate strategy be, given the company's underlying financial strength in a variety of plausible circumstances? Financial management has an important role to play both in ensuring the provision of funds for operations and contingencies and in making the control of financial risk an integral part of the strategic planning process.

Extensions of "What If" Models and the Limitations of Financial Planning

You will recognize that the planning framework that we have described contains no analytical apparatus for making optimal sequential financial decisions under uncertainty, which is what financial management ideally is supposed to accomplish. In fact, the simulation model can be converted in a very limited way into an optimizing structure. Requirements arising from management policies (e.g., that dividends in any year be at least equal to the prior year's, or that debt capacity equals, say, 50 percent of the net book value of assets) or loan agreements (e.g., that earnings before tax be at least four times interest payments) can be imposed as constraints. By introducing an objective function, such as maximizing the present value of cash flows to shareholders over the planning horizon, we obtain a mathematical programming model such as the one described in Chapter 5. Major financial decisions become an output of the model and not merely an input. In the absence of any formal acknowledgment of uncertainty, the mathematical programming model is still a "what if" simulation, even if it is one that selects from among the possible outputs.

A more serious extension incorporating uncertainty is to build into the planning model a decision tree similar to the one we used in the credit-granting model described in Chapter 24. While appealing because of its completeness, the decision tree model unfortunately is rarely used in practice because of its complexity—all of which brings us to recognize why such an "ideal" financial plan is impractical.

THE "IDEAL" FINANCIAL PLAN

Throughout this book we have maintained that the most appropriate ultimate objective for the management of a corporation is to maximize the value of its common shareholders' investment. This objective provides one of the most basic reasons for the corporate form of business organization, in which management as the agent for owners performs a function for them that they cannot perform for themselves. Thus the role of *financial* management is seen as providing (for owners) *optimal* management of assets, investment opportunities, and financing. From this "ideal" perspective, a financial plan would provide a complete description of present and future project and financing decisions in each set of circumstances.

The functions served by such a financial plan include:

conversion of the implications of optimal corporate strategy and management policies into their cash flow representations

a benchmark for performance appraisals

an internal communication, motivation, and coordination mechanism for people in the organization

WHY THIS "IDEAL" IS UNATTAINABLE

Of course the "ideal" financial plan is unattainable. Thoughtful students of economics, psychology, and accounting can identify several reasons for this state of affairs. As long as the focus of this book is on implementing theory, it may be useful to give reasons why complete, optimal financial plans may never be developed.

1. The future is fundamentally uncertain. Successful management of the corporate enterprise requires the accumulation and transmission of information about the uncertain future of the firm to the capital market. The value of the shareholders' equity is determined by the market price of the stock. If the market price of the stock is to reflect management decisions correctly, it is necessary that investors have the same well-defined probability beliefs about future cash flows as management, and that management's decisions contingent on future economic events also are known to investors.

Clearly there is a dilemma here, for revealing corporate plans may not be in the stockholders' interests. This is because the unveiling of corporate strategies to competitors can undermine the competitive advantages upon which positive net present value depends. On the other hand, enough of this information has to be transmitted so that it can be capitalized in stock prices. Otherwise, some existing stockholders may sell out when their stock is under priced. In practice, the required information is conveyed indirectly in the form of financial statements, capital structure policies, and dividend changes. These signals comprise much of the information upon which investors' perceptions about the firm's future are based, but estimates of the impact of plans on shareholder wealth are imprecise.

2. Inside the firm it rarely is economic to develop an "ideal" plan both because of the costs involved and the quality of the information. Ultimately, in a world of uncertainty, virtually all specific forecasts turn out to be wrong, and the forecaster's probability beliefs are not really verifiable. The great cost of developing an "ideal" plan explains why managers try to maintain flexibility, with the ability to alter investment and financing decisions as the future unfolds, but not to the point of working out the details of every contingency, as the "ideal" plan would require.

3. The modern firm exists to develop organizational capabilities for creating and exploiting projects with positive expected net present values. Consequently, specific capital projects are to some degree unique to the firm. That is, they could not in principle be packaged and sold to other firms or to individual investors. This implies that the assumption of "value additivity," whereby specific projects and their financing are treated on a stand-alone basis and their separate values added together, is suspect. Nonetheless, at a practical level, the need to break the analysis of financial alternatives into manageable small components usually dictates some kind of additivity assumption. Indeed, much of this book's development is based on value additivity. Most financial planning models reflect some additivity assumptions when they take some important decisions of the firm as already given. Indeed, if, as is frequently the case, these models merely integrate the consequences of choices already made under alternative economic scenarios, they

cannot even be said to have any finance content, because no formal evaluation of decision alternatives is involved. Even if a formal optimization model is used, it stops short of the "ideal" if it takes as given any major choices—such as capital structure. A plan that merely integrates the cash flow consequences of project and financing decisions that have been evaluated one-at-a-time clearly is less than ideal.

4. A financial plan has behavioral implications for personnel within the firm. Completion of an "ideal" financial plan presupposes that management specifies unambiguously an NPV-maximizing model. Yet the overwhelming evidence is that corporate financial managers avoid taking this step overtly. Organizational realities may be partly responsible. There is a tendency among line managers to regard the output of an optimizing model as having some degree of authority by virtue of its logical structure. The model may be feared and resisted because it is perceived to shift decision-making influence toward those who are closest to the design and the running of the model.

Finance theory recently has given some attention to the division of power and authority in an organization, principally from the standpoint of separation between ownership and corporate management. In reality corporate management is not a monolithic entity but is itself subject to divisions that require a sensitive political accommodation to maintain an effective balance. Consequently, many effective managements tend to avoid explicit and detailed goal statements in their financial plans, because the ramifications of doing so may include poorer financial performance.

Summary

Financial planning enables management to assess the implications of investment and financing decisions for the future viability of the firm in adverse circumstances, and to take measures that reduce the likelihood of financial distress. If unnecessary risks can be reduced or avoided, the shareholders can benefit when the company can undertake a more aggressive investment program made possible by relative freedom from financial risk. Also, financial planning can help to reduce the high transactions costs resulting from frequent unanticipated demands for additional funds.

We have shown how cash management can be improved with the aid of cash budget forecasts and how to anticipate needs for long-term financing with long-term funds flow projections. Sensitivity analysis can be used with such models to predict the additional financing that would be required to protect the firm from financial distress under adverse future scenarios. Finally we have recognized the limitations of financial planning and seen why the ideal financial plan is unattainable in corporate organizations where decisions are taken one at a time, and, inevitably, power and authority are divided.

Review Questions

1. Why is the management of corporate liquidity important to shareholders?
2. What is the determining factor in the setting of cash balance targets by most large firms?
3. What are the costs associated with maximizing disbursement float and not minimizing collection float?
4. Define the treasurer's function in cash budgeting and forecasting.
5. Discuss the reasons why long-term financial planning is important to shareholders.
6. What are the differences between "what if" simulations and optimizing models in financial planning? Discuss the circumstances under which each of these models is more appropriately employed.
7. Why is scenario building rather than optimizing frequently adopted for practical use in financial planning?
8. "Financial planning models cannot, in the final analysis, make corporate decisions." Discuss.
9. Are multiyear financial planning horizons inconsistent with one-period equity valuation models such as the CAPM? Discuss.
10. To what extent is the usual definition of value additivity inconsistent with the purposes of financial planning?

Problems

*1. Construct Post Mills Controls' pro forma balance sheet and income statement for 1985 through 1989 assuming that the company's minimum cash balance is $3 million rather than $2 million. Is this increase in liquidity costly in terms of lost income?
2. Construct Post Mills Controls' pro forma balance sheet and income statement for 1984 through 1989 under the assumptions given in the chapter, except with dividends projected to be $1,500,000 per year. An-

alyze the impact of this policy change in terms of the company's financial position. Is the change a desirable one?

3. Suppose that 1985 works out as projected in the text for Post Mills Controls, but that for 1986 through 1989 a different, equally likely, forecast is now projected (in millions of dollars).

	1986	**1987**	**1988**	**1989**
Sales	60.000	65.000	65.000	65.000
Cost of goods sold	35.400	38.000	40.500	40.500
Selling expense	4.500	4.650	4.875	4.875
General and administrative expenses	14.000	16.000	16.000	16.000
Accounts receivable	7.680	8.320	8.320	8.320
Inventory	6.360	6.890	6.890	6.890
Current liabilities	11.400	12.350	12.350	12.350

All other forecasts and policies remain as originally stated. Construct the company's pro forma balance sheet and income statement for 1986 through 1989. What policy alternatives should Post Mills Controls consider in the light of this possible forecast?

*4. Now assume that Post Mills Controls' management has determined that future cash balances should be at least $2 million and its annual dividend at least $600,000. Furthermore, the company's bank insists that earnings before interest and taxes must be at least five times the annual interest expense. Are management's policies and the bank's requirements consistent with the company's original forecasts for 1985? (Note: We used two equations to make up the pro forma in the text, one equating the right- and left-hand sides as prior year's equity plus current income less current dividends. These equations contain four unknowns: current cash, current short-term borrowing, current equity, and current dividends. Setting any two of the constraints at their minimum values increases the number of equations to four. Then one can see if the third constraint is violated.) Discuss the policy alternatives available to Post Mills Controls.

5. Assume the same circumstances as in Problem 4, except that now the bank insists on an interest coverage ratio of only three times for 1985. Is this requirement consistent with management policies? Discuss whether there is enough information available to make optimal decisions for 1985.

6. Construct a scenario for a well-known company, or one with which you are relatively familiar, using the following steps:

(a) Draw up a list of events and changes that you think could materially affect the company's need for cash or financing in the next five or ten years (as appropriate). You can select your list from Table 26.9 and add any other items that you think may be important.

(b) Relist the items in a table like the one below. Put each item in the time period (or periods) in which it is likely to have the greatest impact on planning. List the most important items near the top of the table and the least important ones near the bottom.

Event or change	Time period				

(c) Select a scenario from the table, and say why your scenario provides an appropriate set of assumptions for inputs to a financial plan to be used for estimating the greatest plausible funding requirements for the company.

References

Carleton, W. T., "An Analytical Model for Long Range Financial Planning," *Journal of Finance,* 25, no. 2 (May 1970): 291–15.

Carleton, W. T., C. L. Dick, Jr., and D. H. Downes, "Financial Policy Models: Theory and Practice," *Journal of Financial and Quantitative Analysis,* 8, no. 5 (December 1973): 691–710.

Francis, J. C., and D. R. Rowell, "A Simultaneous Equation Model of the Firm for Financial Analysis and Planning," *Financial Management,* 7, no. 1 (Spring 1978): 29–44.

Franks, J. R., C. J. Bunton, and J. E. Broyles, "A Decision Analysis Approach to Cash Flow Management," *Operational Research Quarterly,* 25 (1974): 573–85.

McInnes, J. Morris, and W. T. Carleton, "Theory, Models and Implementation in Financial Management," *Management Science,* 28, no. 9 (September 1982): 957–78.

Sinkey, J. F., Jr., *Commercial Bank Financial Management,* New York: Macmillan, 1983.

Vander Weide, J. H., and S. F. Maier, *Managing Corporate Liquidity: An Introduction to Working Capital Decisions.* Forthcoming.

Warren, J., and J. Shelton, "A Simultaneous Equation Approach to Financial Planning," *Journal of Finance,* 26, no. 5 (December 1971): 1123–42.

International Capital Projects

27. *International Capital Projects*

A significant proportion of large United States corporations have invested in operations overseas. In Chapter 27 we discuss the main theories that try to explain movements in foreign exchange rates and show how companies can reduce their exposure to risk that arises from changes in these rates. Having provided this background, we are then able to show how to calculate the net present value for capital projects that involve cash flows in one or more foreign currencies. We also show how to analyze the interaction between foreign taxes and domestic tax credits and how to treat unremitted foreign income in project appraisals.

27

International Capital Projects

This chapter discusses the economic relationships that are believed to govern the foreign exchange markets. We show how inflation and interest rates in different countries affect the exchange rates between their currencies. In particular, we describe four hypotheses concerning foreign exchange: pure expectations, interest rate parity, purchasing power parity, and the Fisher open proposition. We then compare two methods of analyzing international capital projects. Finally we show how international companies can reduce the risk caused by unexpected changes in foreign exchange rates.

Spot and Forward Exchange Rates

The currencies of most of the major developed importing and exporting countries are traded relatively freely today in the foreign exchange markets. Foreign currency can be purchased immediately in the **spot market,** or it can be purchased for delivery at a specified future date in the **forward market.** If an American exporter bills a customer in a foreign currency, sterling, say, the exporter is taking a risk that the exchange rate may change before the bill is paid. Most of this risk can be hedged in the forward market. That is, an exporter who expects to be paid in sterling in three months' time can sell the sterling forward three months at a price agreed upon now. By contractually fixing the rate now at which sterling will be sold for dollars, the exporter eliminates the risk from an unexpected change in the exchange rate during the next three months.

Consider a simple example. Suppose the three-month forward rate of exchange between sterling and dollars is $1.3333 for each pound. An exporter in the United States who expects receipt of £75,000 sterling three months from now can contract now to exchange the £75,000 three months later for £75,000 × $1.3333/£1.00 = $99,998; that is, he or she can contract at the three-month forward rate prevailing today. Once the rate is fixed in this way, the exchange risk of the transaction is said to be **covered.** The exporter no longer stands to lose or gain as a result of subsequent changes in the foreign exchange rate. If the exporter does not cover the risk, he or she is said to have an **open** (or uncovered) position in the foreign currency. Covering risk also is referred to as **hedging.**

Of course, perfect hedges are not always obtainable if there is some element of uncertainty about the receipt of the money. If the customer pays late, the exporter is exposed to movements in the spot market in sterling during the interval between the end of the forward contract and the actual time when the customer's payment is received.

The difference between the forward and spot rates of exchange is called the **forward premium** or **forward discount** depending on whether the forward rate measured in dollars per unit of foreign currency is greater than or less than the spot rate. What determines the relationship between spot and forward rates of exchange? Why are they usually different? The difference between the spot and forward rates of exchange is related to expected changes in the spot rate and to the difference in interest rates between the two currencies.

PURE EXPECTATIONS HYPOTHESIS

The **forward rate of exchange** is the rate contracted now for the exchange of two currencies at a future date. The expected future spot rate is the rate of exchange expected (as of now) to prevail at a future date. We can show that there must be a relationship between forward rates of exchange and expected future spot rates of exchange. The **pure expectations hypothesis** suggests that the expected future spot rate of exchange between two currencies equals the currently quoted forward rate (for delivery on the same future date). We shall illustrate with an example why the pure expectations hypothesis should describe the relationship between expected future spot rates and the corresponding forward rates in efficient foreign exchange markets.

Let us suppose for a moment that the pure expectations hypothesis did not hold. Table 27.1 summarizes such an example. Column 1 shows that the three-month forward rate of exchange for sterling is quoted currently at $1.3333/£1.00 but that the current spot rate is $1.3400/£1.00. Column 2

Table 27.1   *Calculation of speculative profits when the pure expectations hypothesis does not hold*

	Exchange rate ($/£)	
	Now	**Expected in three months**
Forward	1.3333	1.3333
Spot	1.3400	1.3233
Speculative profit		0.0100

shows what is expected to happen in three months' time. The rate for delivery three months from now stays at \$1.3333/£1.00, if it is fixed by a forward contract. Suppose, though, that the market expects the spot rate of exchange to move from \$1.3400/£1.00 to only \$1.3233/£1.00 in three months. This would violate the pure expectations hypothesis, as it is less than the forward rate. The difference between the three-month forward rate and the expected future spot rate offers a speculative profit of \$0.0100/£1.00 or ten cents per pound. Speculators would sell sterling in the forward market at \$1.3333/£1.00 for delivery in three months. They would then wait until sterling fell to \$1.3233/£1.00 in the intervening period and buy the sterling in the spot market at this lower expected price. Having obtained the sterling at a lower price in the spot market, they then could deliver it at the higher price agreed upon in the forward contract.

This describes the kind of easy profit that one does not expect to find very often in efficient markets. What spot rate really should be expected if the market is efficient? Table 27.2 summarizes the situation if the pure

Table 27.2   *Calculation of speculative profits when the pure expectations hypothesis holds*

	Exchange rate ($/£)	
	Now	**Expected in three months**
Forward	1.3333	1.3333
Spot	1.3400	1.3333
Speculative profit		0
Expected change in spot rate	−0.0077	

expectations hypothesis holds in an efficient foreign exchange market. The data in Table 27.2 are the same as in Table 27.1 except that the expected future spot rate that is expected to prevail at the end of three months is equal to the three-month forward rate ($1.3333/£1.00). In this case, the expected speculative profit is zero as we would expect if the market is efficient. Thus the spot rate is expected to change by only −$0.0077/£1.00 under the pure expectations hypothesis, as indicated. In fact, empirical evidence suggests that the pure expectations hypothesis provides the best available predictor (although not always a very accurate one) of future spot rates of exchange.

You may have noted that speculators participating in the above transactions have open positions in sterling that are uncovered for exchange risk. Wouldn't speculators require a premium for such risks? Would such a premium introduce a bias altering the pure expectations relationship between forward rates and future spot rates of exchange? Not necessarily, for as there are two sides to every transaction in foreign exchange, a premium to the buyer of a currency would mean a discount for the seller. British participants in the market also would want a premium for open positions in dollars. As a premium cannot be paid to both, the premium may be canceled out.

Now let us turn to the related proposition that the difference between the forward and spot rates of exchange is explained by differences in nominal interest rates in the two currencies.

INTEREST RATE PARITY

The most reliable principle operating in the foreign exchange markets is called **interest rate parity.** The principle is that an investor should not be able to get different risk-free rates of interest in different countries once proceeds of an investment are converted into the home currency. If this were not so, risk-free profits could be made simply by lending in currencies where interest rates are high, borrowing where they are low, and covering the exchange risk in the forward exchange market. Let us look at an example. Suppose that a one-year British government bond pays 10 percent when United States government bonds maturing in one year pay 12 percent. One might be forgiven for supposing that the American rate of 12 percent is more attractive than the British rate of 10 percent. Certainly most everyone would be selling United Kingdom bonds and buying United States bonds if there were not more to this than meets the eye. What is wrong?

Consider the example in Table 27.3. If a United States investor buys a government bond (at par) for $100,000, he or she knows that the nominal value of the bond will still be $100,000 at maturity and will have earned $12,000 in interest at 12 percent. Now suppose the investor had invested $100,000 (at par) in one-year United Kingdom government bonds instead. At a spot rate of $1.3333 per pound the investor can buy £75,002 worth of bonds. If the United Kingdom government bonds yield 10 percent, the value

Table 27.3   *Comparison of covered sterling bond with dollar bond*

	Dollar bond	Sterling bond
Spot rate of exchange ($/£)		1.3333
Value of the bond	$100,000	£75,002
Current rate of interest	12%	10%
Future value of the bond	$112,000	£82,502
One-year forward rate of exchange ($/£)		1.3575
Future value of the bond in dollars		$111,997

of the bond plus interest totals £82,502. The investor, however, will wish to exchange sterling for dollars at the end of one year, and the future exchange rate is uncertain. It would be possible to contract to sell the proceeds of the sterling bond one year hence at today's one-year forward exchange rate, $1.3575/£1.00. Converting the sterling proceeds at that rate of exchange would yield $111,997. Disregarding transactions costs, this sum is almost exactly the same amount that the United States investor would receive by investing in the United States bond.

The example shows how differences in interest rates for comparable risk-free assets denominated in different currencies are reflected already in differences in the spot and forward exchange rates. In the same example, if interest rates rose above 10 percent in the United Kingdom, but the forward exchange rate remained at $1.3575/£1.00, what would speculators do? They would sell United States government bonds and purchase United Kingdom bonds, using the spot exchange market. At the same time they would sell sterling in the forward market, matching the maturity dates on the forward contracts with those on the United Kingdom bond. Such transactions are called **covered interest arbitrage.** In this way speculators would be protected from exchange rate losses and would make greater returns on United Kingdom bonds than on similar United States bonds. The pressure of such demand, however, would bring the forward exchange rate quickly into line with interest rates. Thus interest rate parity would be maintained.

Interest rate parity ensures that there are no easy profits from lending in currencies where interest rates are higher than in one's own country. By the same token, there are no bargains to be obtained by borrowing in currencies where interest rates are lower, because the cost of covering for the risk of changes in exchange rates in the forward exchange market eliminates the apparent gain. The interest rate parity theory states that comparable risk-free transactions in all currencies will yield the same rate of interest when expressed in the same currency and covered for exchange risk.

Interest rate parity is one of the most reliable of the various theories of foreign exchange. In fact, dealers in the Eurocurrency markets use interest rate parity to quote forward rates of exchange. **Eurocurrency** is mostly nonsterling currency deposited in London banks. Foreign exchange transactions between these banks and with multinational companies and foreign governments constitute the Eurocurrency market. Exceptions to interest rate parity are more likely to appear in markets where trading of the currency is infrequent, or where currency controls by local governments are in force. Apparent deviations from interest rate parity also may be caused by political risks and by the possibility that a foreign government might expropriate the assets of overseas investors. If United States investors felt such risks existed, they would demand a higher interest rate differential than would be accounted for by a simple comparison between forward and spot rates of exchange between the two currencies.

PURCHASING POWER PARITY THEOREM

We shall now see how arbitrage in foreign trade tends to produce changes in spot rates of exchange that preserve purchasing power when there are different rates of inflation for two currencies.

The **purchasing power parity** (PPP) proposition states that the rate of change in the spot exchange rate is proportional to the difference between the rates of inflation in the two countries. The basis of the PPP proposition is the law of one price, which simply states that identical assets must sell for the same price. In a world where goods and financial assets can be traded freely, we would expect that differences in price for the same good in different places would be accounted for by transport costs. Thus, a barrel of a particular grade of oil will sell at the same price (allowing for transportation costs) in London as in Houston. While the law of one price deals with individual commodities, purchasing power parity involves bundles of traded goods and services. Purchasing power parity can be used as a basis for making long-term forecasts of future spot rates of exchange with the following formula:

Expected Future Spot Rate at Time t = Current Spot Rate
$$\times \left(\frac{1 + \text{Domestic Inflation Rate}}{1 + \text{Foreign Inflation Rate}} \right)^t$$

This equation relating expected spot rates to rates of inflation assumes that the spot rate is a **direct quote,** that is, in terms of dollars per unit of foreign currency rather than an indirect quote (units of foreign currency per dollar). If the foreign rate of inflation exceeds the domestic rate of inflation, the foreign currency will weaken and fewer dollars will be required to buy each unit of the foreign currency. Importers must be able to buy more and more of the foreign currency for each dollar in order to be able to purchase the more rapidly inflating foreign goods. If the exchange rate changes in the manner suggested by the formula, importers can still sell the foreign goods at dollar prices that can allow them to maintain their competitive relationship with other prices in the domestic economy. If, on the other hand, the rate of change in the exchange rate is higher than that implied by the formula, the foreign goods become too expensive in terms of the dollar, and the resulting fall in demand for the foreign currency would tend to increase the exchange rate in favor of the domestic currency.

Clearly, if PPP were to hold at every moment, the problem of exchange rate risk would be small and rather trivial. Even the casual observer can appreciate that differences in the inflation rates of the United Kingdom and the United States did not account for all or even a large part of recent changes in the \$/£ exchange rate. During 1978–1979, sterling appreciated against the dollar by about 30 percent, even though the United Kingdom inflation rate was similar if not higher than the United States inflation rate. A higher rate of inflation would suggest that sterling should have depreciated against the dollar. Economists suggest that the appreciation of sterling was due in part to the fact that the value of Britain's substantial oil reserves increased rapidly as the real price of oil increased. However, by the end of 1979, many British goods appeared overpriced compared with similar goods in the United States. PPP would tell us that this situation could not persist indefinitely. Either the United States would cease to import the goods that became more expensive than those produced at home or the pound would depreciate. We know which happened: Sterling depreciated against the dollar when oil prices began to weaken in 1981 to the level that prevailed before 1978.

FISHER OPEN PROPOSITION

In Chapter 7 we briefly described the Fisher effect, which related nominal interest rates to inflation. Aliber (1978) calls this the "Fisher Closed Proposition." The nominal rate of interest is supposed to be roughly equal to a real rate of interest plus the expected rate of inflation for the same period of time. The reason for this relationship is that investors can borrow in order to purchase goods or commodities. If prices are expected to rise at a rate that exceeds the nominal interest rate (less the real rate of interest), it would pay investors to borrow, stockpile commodities, and bring forward in time purchases of finished products (of course, such transactions would have to cover storage costs).

The Fisher open proposition suggests that the difference between the interest rates on similar bonds in two countries equals the expected difference between the inflation rates in the two countries for the same period (the term of the bonds). In order for the Fisher open proposition to hold strictly, it would be necessary for real interest rates to be the same in both countries.

In the long run, differences in real rates of interest between countries would not be expected to persist, because funds would be attracted to those national money markets offering the highest real rates of interest. In fact the evidence in Table 7.1 suggests that for the period 1967–1978 the mean real rates of interest for nine major trading nations fell within the narrow range of −0.90 percent to +1.63 percent. These estimates of real interest rates are averages over a period of twelve years, so the actual differences in real rates between countries at one point in time can be greater than those implied by a simple comparison of averages. Of course when there are large differences in real rates of interest between two countries, and when they are expected to persist because of exchange controls or other reasons, these facts should be recognized in analyzing international capital projects.

International Capital Project Appraisal Methods

We shall consider two related methods of valuing the cash flows of an international capital project. We can compare the methods in their simplest form and show that under appropriate assumptions both give the same result. The comparison reveals how we can obtain the net present value of an international capital project without introducing distortions due to foreign exchange gains or losses. Initially, we assume that all a project's net cash flows are remitted (paid to) the parent company.

METHOD 1

Forecast net incremental cash flows of the project in the foreign currencies. Discount the foreign and home currency cash flows using the appropriate nominal discount rates for each currency, given the expected rate of inflation for the currency and the project's risk. Then translate the resulting foreign currency present values to the home currency using the current spot rates of exchange between the foreign currencies and the home currency. The net of the different present values, translated into the home currency, gives the home currency NPV of the project.

In Table 27.4 we demonstrate the application of method 1 to cash flows in a foreign currency subject to inflation at the rate of 50 percent. For the sake of simplicity, we assume initially that there are no taxes. The appropriate real discount rate for the project is 8 percent, and we will assume that expected future one-period risk-free rates of interest will equal the expected

Table 27.4   *Valuation of expected incremental cash flow from foreign project with zero taxes. Method 1 (in thousands)*

	End of year			
	0	1	2	3
CURRENCY B (50% INFLATION)				
Net incremental cash flow	−300	300	450	675
Net present value at 62%	215.4194			
Spot foreign exchange rate (A/B)	× 2.00			
CURRENCY A				
Net present value	430.8388			

rate of inflation (the real rate of interest is zero). Thus the expected nominal discount rate R is given according to Fisher's proposition (see Chapter 7):

(1 + Real Discount Rate)(1 + Inflation Rate) =

(1 + Nominal Discount Rate)

(1 + 0.08)(1 + 0.50) = (1 + R)

R = 0.62

The net incremental cash flow in row 1 of the table discounted at 62 percent gives a net present value of $215,4194 denominated in currency B. For the purpose of comparison, we must translate foreign currency present values into the home currency A (dollars). If the present spot rate of exchange is two units of A for each unit of B as indicated in the table, the present value of the foreign currency cash flow translated to currency A is

(A2.00/B1.00) × B215,4194 = A430,8388

In method 1 we simply translate present values denominated in foreign currencies to present values in the home currency using the current spot rate of exchange between the currencies. If a project involves cash flows in several different currencies, we can translate the present value of each foreign currency cash flow into the home currency and then compute the net of all the translated present values.

A variation on method 1 is to deflate the nominal foreign currency cash flows by using the appropriate foreign rate of inflation as the discount rate. The deflated cash flows are then discounted again using the sum of the real rate of interest and the project's real risk premium as the discount rate.

The two versions of method 1 are mathematically equivalent. They will give the same answer if the discount rates reflect the same assumed real rates of interest and the same expected rates of inflation.

METHOD 2

Forecast the foreign currency net incremental cash flows for the project. Translate each expected future cash flow into the home currency using forecast spot rates of exchange. Discount the resulting home currency cash flows at the appropriate home currency nominal required rate of return reflecting the project's risk. Alternatively, deflate the project's nominal home currency cash flows and then discount at the corresponding required real rate of return reflecting the sum of the real rate of interest plus the project's risk premium.

In Table 27.5 we show the application of method 2 to the foreign currency cash flows of the project. The rate of inflation in currency B is 50 percent, in currency A it is 20 percent, and we shall assume that the real rate of interest is zero. We assume initially that all the project's foreign currency cash flows will be remitted to the home country at the forecast exchange rates shown in line 3 of the table. If we use purchasing power parity as the basis of these forecast exchange rates, we obtain the same result as was obtained by method 1. Under purchasing power parity a future exchange rate at time t is given by:

$$S_t = S_0 \left(\frac{1 + G_A}{1 + G_B}\right)^t$$

where S is measured in units of A per unit of B and G_A and G_B are the rates of inflation in currencies A and B, respectively. For example, the expected exchange rate of 1.28 at the end of year 2 in Table 27.5 is obtained from,

$$S_2 = 2.00 \times \left(\frac{1.20}{1.50}\right)^2$$

$$= 1.28$$

The remitted cash flows are translated into currency A at the resulting forecast spot rates and then discounted at 29.6 percent. This discount rate was obtained from the Fisher effect by multiplying one plus the real discount rate $(1 + 0.08)$ by one plus the rate of inflation $(1 + 0.20)$ to obtain one plus the nominal discount rate $(1 + 0.296)$. The net present value of \$430,8388 in currency A is exactly the same as the value obtained under method 1.

The fact that the two methods give the same answer has some useful

Table 27.5   *Valuation of expected incremental cash flow from foreign project with zero taxes. Method 2 (in thousands)*

	End of year			
	0	**1**	**2**	**3**
CURRENCY B (50% INFLATION)				
Net incremental cash flow	−300	300	450	675
Cash flow remitted to parent company	−300	300	450	675
Foreign exchange rate	× 2.0	× 1.6	× 1.28	× 1.024
CURRENCY A (20% INFLATION)				
Remittances received in home currency	−600	480	576	691.2
Present value at 29.6% = 430.8388				

implications. In method 1 we did not have to forecast changes in future spot exchange rates, so the net present value obtained using that method did not reflect the effects of possible foreign exchange gains or losses. In method 2 we used purchasing power parity to forecast future spot rates of exchange. Method 2 gives the same answer and is, therefore, equivalent to method 1. It follows that the net present value obtained using method 2 does not reflect any net effects of possible foreign exchange gains or losses either. This is a very desirable property, for we want to be able to analyze an international capital project on the basis of its commercial merits without having its net present value distorted by the effects of possible foreign exchange gains or losses. The question as to whether the project exposes the company to foreign exchange risk and whether such risk should be hedged can be treated as a separate issue.

If the two methods give the same result, which should be used? In our example there were no taxes, and taxes may be payable in both the host country and the parent company's home country. If you look again at method 1 in Table 27.4, you will see that although it would be possible to use an after-tax cash flow in row 1, there is no way you can include home country taxes without altering the method. The alterations that are required are already included in method 2. That is, you need forecasts of future exchange rates in order to be able to translate taxable income into the home currency so that expected home country tax liabilities and foreign tax credits can be estimated in each future period.

In Table 27.6 we introduce taxes into our example using method 2. In row 2 we now show the estimated taxable income for each period, and in

Table 27.6   *Valuation of incremental cash flows for foreign project with differential inflation and remittance of all after-tax cash flows (in thousands)*

	End of year			
	0	1	2	3
CURRENCY B (50% INFLATION)				
1. Net incremental cash flow	−300.0	300.0	450.0	675.0
2. Estimated taxable income		200.0	350.0	575.0
3. Country B corporate taxes at 30%		−60.0	−105.0	−172.5
4. Cash flows remitted to parent company		240.0	345.0	502.5
5. Withholding taxes at 10%		−24.0	−34.5	−50.3
6. Remittance after-tax		216.0	310.5	452.2
7. Foreign exchange rate	× 2.0	× 1.60	× 1.28	× 1.024
CURRENCY A (20% INFLATION)				
8. Remittances received	−600.0	345.6	397.4	463.1
9. Estimated taxable income		320.0	448.0	588.8
10. Corporate tax at 50%		−160.0	−224.0	−294.4
11. Foreign tax credit		134.4	178.6	228.1
12. After-tax cash flow	−600.0	320.0	352.0	396.8
Net present value at 29.6% = 38.760				

row 3 we show the estimated foreign income taxes at a 30 percent tax rate for country B. Thus we obtain the after-tax cash flow in row 4, which we assume (for simplicity) is remitted to the parent company. However, country B withholds taxes at 10 percent on all remittances abroad, leaving the after-tax remittances in row 6. The expected after-tax remittances then must be translated at the expected foreign exchange rates shown in row 7. These exchange rates are based upon the purchasing power parity formula given earlier.

The home country A levies tax on all remittances of foreign taxable income but allows tax credits on foreign taxes paid. The estimated taxable income in row 9 was obtained by translating the currency B taxable income in row 2 into currency A taxable income using the foreign exchange rates in row 7. The resulting taxable income in row 9 is taxed in country A at 50 percent as indicated in row 10. However, tax credits for foreign taxes are allowed to be offset against these home country tax liabilities. The estimated foreign taxes paid are given in rows 3 and 5. The total foreign taxes paid in currency B have been translated at the rates given in row 7 and entered in row 11 as tax credits. Thus we can now obtain the net after-tax cash flow in row 12. The net present value at a discount rate of 29.6 percent is $38,760 (rounded) in the home currency after all taxes.

The distinction between estimated taxes in the foreign and home countries emphasized in method 2 can be important, if taxes payable in the home country on project earnings do not match the tax credits allowable on the project's foreign taxes. If taxes incurred in the home country on a project's foreign earnings exceed the available tax credits for foreign taxes paid, the after-tax incremental cash flow of the project must reflect the additional tax payable in the home country. On the other hand, if tax credits exceed home country taxes payable on the project and if the parent company is already in a nontaxpaying position, additional unused tax credits (if they are permitted to be carried forward) may extend the nontaxpaying period. In any such cases we require the framework of method 2 in order to evaluate the net incremental impact of the foreign project on the parent company's taxes.

UNREMITTED FUNDS

So far we have assumed that all after-tax incremental cash flows from the project are remitted to the parent company. It may be, though, that the parent company wants to retain cash in the foreign country for further investment. Also, many foreign countries restrict remittances to some proportion of reported profits earned in the country. If unremitted funds cannot be reinvested profitably abroad, or if they are in danger of being expropriated, the profitability of a foreign project could be affected adversely by nonremittance.

Table 27.7 shows how to analyze a project's unremitted cash flows. The method is similar to that of the preceding table, except that some of the after-tax cash flow is not remitted until the end of year 3. For example, note that in year 1 the after-tax cash flow in row 4 is 240,000 but that only 140,000 is remitted in row 5. The remaining 100,000 of unremitted cash flow in row 6 is assumed to be reinvested at a rate of return equivalent to the project's 62 percent required rate of return (equal to 8 percent real) in currency B. Similarly, 100,000 of unremitted cash flow is retained and reinvested at the end of year 2. By the end of year 3, the reinvested unremitted cash from years 1 and 2 will have accumulated to 424,400 in row 7. If the cash is remitted at that time, a 10 percent withholding tax would be payable (row 8), and the after-tax remittance would then be translated at the year 3 exchange rate (1.024). In rows 12 and 13, the taxable income is the same as in the preceding table, but the foreign tax credits are less for years 1 and 2 (row 14) because foreign withholding taxes are lower owing to the smaller remittances in those years. In year 3, withholding taxes and tax credits are correspondingly higher when the postponed remittances eventually are paid. The net present value of 38,760 (rounded) in this example with deferred

Table 27.7   *Valuation of incremental cash flow for foreign project with deferred remittances (in thousands)*

	End of year			
	0	**1**	**2**	**3**
CURRENCY B (50% INFLATION)				
1. Net incremental cash flow	−300.0	300.0	450.0	675.0
2. Estimated taxable income		200.0	350.0	575.0
3. Country B corporate taxes at 30%		−60.0	−105.0	−172.5
4. After-tax cash flow		240.0	345.0	502.5
5. Remitted cash flows		140.0	245.0	502.5
6. Postponed remittances		100.0	100.0	
7. Future value of postponed cash flows (when remitted)				424.4
8. Withholding taxes at 10%		−14.0	−24.5	−92.7
9. Remittances after-tax		126.0	220.5	834.2
10. Foreign exchange rate	× 2.0	× 1.60	× 1.28	× 1.024
CURRENCY A (20% INFLATION)				
11. Remittances received	−600.0	201.6	282.2	854.2
12. Estimated taxable income		320.0	448.0	588.8
13. Corporate tax at 50%		−160.0	−224.0	−294.4
14. Foreign tax credit		118.4	165.8	271.6
15. After-tax cash flow	−600.0	160.0	224.0	831.4
Net present value at 29.6% = 38.760				

remittances is exactly the same (allowing for rounding errors) as in Table 27.6 where we assumed that all after-tax foreign cash flows were remitted immediately.

The reason the net present value is unchanged is that we did not introduce any penalties for delayed remittances.[1] We assumed that unremitted cash flows were reinvested at the after-tax required rate of return until finally being remitted at the end of year 3. The compounded future value of the deferred remittances was then discounted, leaving the net present value unchanged. When the unremitted funds cannot be reinvested in the foreign country at the required rate of return for the risk involved, this reduces their discounted value. The longer remittances are deferred and the longer unremitted funds are committed to unprofitable investments, the lower the resulting present value.

[1]There may be tax advantages to a particular remittance policy.

Even if unremitted funds are invested profitably abroad, they may risk being frozen, indefinitely blocked, or expropriated. Unless expected returns from the reinvestment of unremitted funds compensate for the probability that some portion of the funds may never be remitted, the present value is reduced. In any analysis, you can adjust the future value downward to reflect such adverse possibilities. For example, you can multiply the 424,440 future value in the example above by one minus the probability of expropriation.

A conservative way of analyzing foreign projects is to include only those cash flows that can be remitted through normal channels. The benefits of possible circumvention of restrictions (e.g., via prices that are charged in transactions between divisions that are in different countries) or offsetting of excess foreign tax credits then can be discounted separately. Other items that may merit separate treatment include the ability to reduce or defer taxes by combining profits from operations in countries with relatively low and high taxes, or to move expenses and revenues from one affiliated company to another and reinvest profits in low-tax countries. The adjusted present value method given in Chapter 22 may be used for discounting such adjustments separately.

Our examples have assumed that the real rate of interest remains constant and equal for currencies A and B, and we used a real discount rate of 8 percent throughout. However, we easily could have incorporated changes in real rates of interest and differences in real rates of interest for different currencies. This can be done by adjusting the 8 percent real discount rate for different real rates of interest in the way that we described in Chapter 7, where we showed how to obtain nominal discount rates from the real rate of interest, the real risk premium, and the rate of inflation.

Required Rates of Return for International Projects

Since international projects involve a degree of diversification for shareholders which would not be possible to achieve through investment within their own country, we must question whether risk and therefore the risk premium in the discount rate for a foreign project should be different from that for a similar project in the home country.[2] The answer to this question depends upon whether stockholders' portfolios are already internationally diversified. If they are, then there would be no net advantage to company diversification abroad for the purposes of risk reduction. Therefore, the required rate of return for a project would not be altered by the fact that the project is to be located in a different country. Since there may be financial, informational,

---

[2]Another way of viewing this question is whether the required rate of return for a project should be the same for the domestic investor as for the overseas investor.

and sometimes legal barriers to individuals investing in foreign securities, the question as to whether company diversification overseas affects the discount rate is important.

The asset betas that we have used until now to obtain the risk premium for risky projects have been estimated using national stock market indexes such as the Standard & Poor's 500 Index in the United States or the Financial Times Actuaries 500 Index in the United Kingdom. The betas measured using these indexes reflect the systematic risks of domestic projects from the viewpoint, respectively, of United States and United Kingdom domestic investors. When it comes to estimating asset betas and risk premiums for overseas projects, a number of difficult issues arise. For example, if investors are sufficiently internationally diversified and the capital markets of the world can be viewed as one integrated financial market, then betas should be measured relative to a world market index (comprising all the national stock market indexes). Thus the estimation of asset betas and the resulting risk premiums for overseas projects may depend upon the degree to which the financial markets of the world have become integrated rather than segmented.

A useful way of discussing the relevance of market integration is to compare the implications of two extreme assumptions: first, that the financial markets of the world are completely segmented and, second, that they are perfectly integrated. We shall discuss these in turn.

If we assume that effective barriers exist preventing investors from holding foreign securities, then the financial markets of different countries would be segmented. In this situation a company that is not subject to such barriers to investment abroad or which can circumvent the barriers can reap the benefits of international diversification on behalf of its stockholders. All else being equal, this could lead to the lowering of the risk premium on international projects since the asset beta for an overseas project measured relative to the domestic market index would tend to be lower than the asset beta for a similar domestic project measured against the same domestic index. Consequently, the segmented markets assumption would represent the most favorable environment for international diversification by companies.

On the other hand, if we assume that there are no barriers preventing investors from holding foreign securities and shareholders can obtain the benefits of international diversification for themselves, the financial markets of the world would become fully integrated, and international diversification by companies would not reduce the risk premiums required on their foreign projects. The company's stockholders would measure beta for both domestic and foreign assets relative to the same world market index.

The truth almost certainly lies somewhere between these two extreme assumptions. While there are some barriers to international diversification by stockholders, they generally can and many do hold some foreign securities in their portfolios. Since the gains to international diversification in terms of reduced risk are considerable, one would expect the portfolios of both United States and United Kingdom investors (who currently face no obvious barriers to buying foreign securities) to include larger holdings of foreign securities.

In general their portfolios do not appear to be optimally diversified from an international perspective. Costs to holding foreign securities include differential taxes, possible expropriation, and costs of obtaining information. Cooper and Lessard (1981) have described this problem and have estimated that the observed compositions of actual portfolios are consistent with the existence of minimum additional costs to international investment is three percent annually. The existence of such costs would explain why international financial markets appear to be partially segmented. If such costs are lower for a company investing overseas than for its stockholders, then there would be a net advantage to international diversification by companies, which should be reflected in a lower required rate of return for foreign projects compared with the rate for similar domestic projects.

Short-term Hedging of Foreign Exchange Risk

Foreign exchange risk is a real issue for any company engaged in transactions involving foreign currencies. We showed at the beginning of the chapter how an exporter can use a forward exchange contract to protect against the possibility that the value of a foreign currency receivable may change if the exchange rate changes before the account is paid by the foreign customer. However, it is relatively difficult to obtain forward exchange contracts for delivery beyond a year. This is only one of several methods that can be used to hedge short-term foreign exchange risk exposure.

INVOICE IN THE HOME CURRENCY

An easy way for a United States exporter to hedge is to denominate invoices in dollars. This simple device assures that the actual dollar sum will be received regardless of subsequent exchange rate fluctuations or the timing of actual payment. However, the shifting of exchange risk to the foreign customer may not be acceptable to the customer in the absence of price concessions. This may be so particularly in the case of customers not accustomed to hedging in the forward market.

SALE OF RECEIVABLES

An alternative in many instances is for the exporter to bill customers in their own home currency, then to sell the (foreign) accounts receivable to an international commercial factor. A **factor** is a company, often the subsidiary of a bank, that will purchase (or lend against) the accounts receivable and collect the accounts receivable on behalf of the exporter. The factor pays a price under the face value of the receivables; the difference compensates the factor for the cost of borrowing, collection costs, and the risk of nonpayment. Receiving immediate cash in the home currency from the factor protects the exporter from changes in exchange rates that would affect the value of foreign accounts receivable. Additionally, an international factor may find it easier than an exporter to collect receivables from foreign customers through its foreign offices. The cost of the factor's discount on the accounts receivable may be worth the combined benefits of collection, reduced accounts receivable, lower foreign exchange risk exposure, and lower default risk.

An alternative to selling the receivable to a commercial factor is for the exporter to sell the receivable in the form of the customer's bill of exchange in the discount market where such bills are traded in the foreign country. The exporter then can exchange the proceeds for the home currency at the current spot rate. In this case, the seller (the exporter) would have to repay the purchaser of the receivable (the bill) if default occurred, whereas the international factor would accept the default risk for some agreed-upon fee.

MATCHING A LOAN WITH THE RECEIVABLE

Another way an exporter can hedge a receivable denominated in a foreign currency is to take out a loan with the same maturity and face value as the receivable. The proceeds of the loan are converted at the current spot rate into the domestic currency of the firm. Afterward the exporter uses the proceeds of the receivable to repay the loan. For example, suppose a United States firm exports goods valued at £75,000 ($100,000) to the United Kingdom, granting the United Kingdom importer three months' credit. The exporter can hedge the foreign exchange risk by taking out a three-month loan totaling £75,000 less interest and converting the proceeds immediately into dollars. The loan is repaid with interest when the United Kingdom importing firm pays the receivable at the end of three months.

CENTRALIZING A COMPANY'S FOREIGN EXCHANGE RISK EXPOSURE MANAGEMENT

It should be appreciated that a company operating in several countries may have open currency positions in different foreign subsidiaries that match positions in other subsidiaries. For example, the United Kingdom subsidiary of an American parent company may have sterling accounts payable at the same time that the parent company has sterling accounts receivable. The foreign currency positions of all subsidiaries (in an ideal world) should be combined with that of the parent in order to determine the net companywide open position in each currency. Only when the net position in each currency is known can one ascertain the degree of hedging that may be required. An exporter who has an open position in many currencies reduces exposure to foreign exchange risk because of the portfolio effects of diversification. The variability in the exchange rate between the home currency and a bundle of foreign currencies is likely to be less than the variability in the exchange rate between the home currency and only one of the foreign currencies.

Long-term Hedging of Foreign Exchange Risk

Long-term exposure to foreign-exchange risk arises from the impact of changes in foreign exchange rates on the present value of the firm's assets and thus on the market value of the firm. Suppose a United States company has invested £10 million in plant and equipment in a British subsidiary. How will a change in the dollar–sterling rate affect the present value of the parent company? If we could assume that expected changes in spot rates are governed by purchasing power parity, there would be no effect on the present value of foreign assets when measured in the home currency, as we have already shown. Thus, there would be no foreign exchange exposure risk (even in the short term) for the value of fixed assets held abroad. Because interest rates are governed only loosely by inflation rate differentials and purchasing power parity is an inexact description of the real world, exchange rate exposure for foreign fixed assets remains a problem. The present value of the assets translated into the home currency can be affected by departures from purchasing power parity.

How do companies cover for long-term foreign exchange risk exposure? The usual method is to try to match assets and liabilities in the same currency. If a company wishes to invest £10 million in Britain, it will seek to raise as much of the money as possible in that country. As earnings from the project could be used to repay principal and interest in the same currency, the project might bear no more exchange risk on its cost than any locally owned asset. Of course, the project's net present value and its equity or net worth still would remain exposed to foreign exchange risk. Also, if the project fails and its present value is reduced, the value of the assets and of the liabilities will no longer match.

Central banks in most countries ordinarily do not permit 100 percent local financing by foreign companies. Because income from the project net of the cost of local financing eventually will be converted to a foreign currency, central banks often specify the minimum proportion of the total equity that must be supplied by the foreign company. International companies use a number of measures to minimize exposure when local financing is limited by a central bank. Joint ventures with nationals of the host country are one way of increasing permitted local financing. Another way is to engage in leasing arrangements to the extent possible; a local company actually owns the assets, but puts them at the disposal of the foreign company through leasing contracts.

Summary

We have discussed major influences affecting the relationship between spot and forward rates of exchange, interest rates, and inflation. We have shown how methods described earlier in Chapter 7 to value capital project cash flows in an inflationary environment can be adapted to deal with simultaneous cash flows in several currencies. We have discussed briefly some of the problems of project analysis that are peculiar to international business. Finally, we have shown some ways managers can try to hedge their exposure to exchange rate risk.

Problems

*1. On a particular date a United States investor can invest in a one-year United States government bond yielding 11.5 percent. At the same time she can invest in a comparable one-year United Kingdom government bond yielding 12.5 percent. The spot rate of exchange between sterling and the dollar on that day is $1.3000/£1.00. At what one-year forward rate of exchange would the investor be indifferent between the two bonds if she paid no taxes?

*2. The ninety-day Treasury bill rate in the United Kingdom is 12 percent (annualized) at a time when in the United States the ninety-day Treasury bill rate is 15 percent. What would the three-month forward rate of exchange be if the spot rate between sterling and dollars were $1.3000/£1.00?

*3. If the pound sterling and the Deutschmark are quoted at $1.2690/£ and DM2.9405/$ in New York, what is the value of the the Deutschmark in terms of the pound?

*4. Given a spot rate of DM1.75/$, and expected inflation rates of 5 percent and 12 percent (for the coming twelve months) in West Germany and the United States, respectively, what is the expected future spot rate at the end of the twelve months?

*5. The rate of inflation in country A is 10 percent and in country B is 30 percent. The real rate of interest in country A is 2 percent, in B it is 5 percent. The spot rate of exchange is 1.5 units of B's currency for each unit of A's currency.

   (a) Estimate the interest rate on one-year government bonds in both countries.

   (b) Estimate the one-year forward rate of exchange.

   (c) Estimate the spot rate of exchange at the end of one year.

   (d) Can you reconcile the answers to (b) and (c)?

In each case name the theories that you use to obtain your answers.

6. The rate of inflation in country A is 10 percent, while in country Z the rate is 200 percent per year. The annual real rate of interest in country A is zero and in country Z is 25 percent.

   (a) What would you expect to be the difference in the one-year nominal rates of interest for the two countries?

   (b) How large would be the discount or premium on the twelve-month forward rate of exchange, given that one unit of A's currency is worth ten units of B's currency at present?

*7. Country Y trades extensively with country A. The spot rate of exchange between their two currencies is ten units of Y's currency for each unit of A's currency. A price index composed of an appropriately weighted average of the prices of the basket of goods traded between the two countries is inflating at the rate of only 5 percent in country Y and at 10 percent in country A. What spot rate of exchange would the purchasing power parity theorem predict at the end of five years?

8. Country A's only product is bananas, and it sells most of its product to country W. The current price of a ton of bananas in W's currency is 500 units. The equivalent price in A's currency after adjusting for transportation and other expenses is 1,500 units. Country W's rate of inflation is 50 percent, while in A the rate is only 10 percent. Using the purchasing power parity theorem, forecast the exchange rate for currency A per unit of currency W for the next three years.

9. An international company in country A would like to invest in country B. The expected nominal (currency B) cash flows (after country B corporate taxes) for the proposed project in country B are given below. The rate of inflation in country B is 100 percent per year. The required *real* rate of return for the project, considering its risk, is 20 percent. The

current spot rate of exchange between the two currencies is three units of B's currency for each unit of A's. The company pays no taxes in the home country. Using method 1 from the chapter, estimate the net present value of the project in currency A. State the assumptions justifying the method.

End of year	0	1	2	3	4	5
Net incremental cash flow after	−1,000	744	1,487	2,975	5,950	11,899

*10. Suppose that remittances to the home country A for the project in Problem 10 are taxed at 15 percent but that no remittances can be paid until the end of five years. By that time a new government may be in power that might freeze all remittances indefinitely; the probability of this happening is judged to be 30 percent. When remittances are paid, they will be taxed again by the home country at 50 percent. The home country tax authorities give a credit for foreign withholding taxes on remittances and foreign corporate income is not taxed. The home country A rate of inflation is 15 percent. Estimate the net present value of the project. State your assumptions in using the method.

11. Use method 2 from the chapter and the data in Problems 9 and 10 to estimate the annual tax credits available in the home country A for withholding taxes in the host country B on remittances, assuming now that all after-tax cash flows will be remitted in the years they are earned.

References

Agmon, T., and S. Bronfeld, "International Mobility of Short Term Covered Arbitrage Capital," *Journal of Business Finance and Accounting,* 2, no.2 (Summer 1975): 269–78.

Alamouti, K., "An Empirical Study of the Relationship between Security Returns, Exchange Rates and Inflation Rates," unpublished Ph.D. thesis, London Business School, August 1981.

Aliber, R. Z., *Exchange Risk and Corporate International Finance,* New York: Halsted Press, 1978.

Cooper, I., and D. R. Lessard, "International Capital Market Equilibrium with Deadweight Costs to Foreign Investments," London Business School, September 1981.

Cornell, W. B., and J. K. Dietrick, "The Efficiency of the Market for Foreign Exchange Under Floating Exchange Rates," *Review of Economics and Statistics,* 60, no. 1 (February 1978).

Eiteman, D. K., and A. I. Stonehill, *Multinational Business Finance,* 3rd ed., Reading, Mass.: Addison-Wesley, 1982.

Feiger, G., and B. Jacquillat, *International Finance: Text and Cases,* Boston, Mass.: Allyn and Bacon, 1982.

Grauer, F. A., R. A. Litzenberger, and R. E. Stehle, "Sharing Rules and Equilibrium in an International Capital Market Under Uncertainty," *Journal of Financial Economics* (June 1976): 233–56.

Lessard, D. R., "Evaluating Foreign Projects—An Adjusted Present Value Approach," in D. Lessard, ed., *International Financial Management: Theory and Application*, Boston, Mass.: Warren Gorham & Lamont, 1979.

Lessard, D. R., "The Structure of Returns and Gains from International Diversification," in N. Elton and M. Gruber, eds., *International Capital Markets*, Amsterdam, North Holland: 1976.

Levich, R. M., "Tests of Forecasting Models and Market Efficiency in the International Money Market," in *The Economics of Exchange Rates: Selected Studies,* edited by J. Frenkel and H. G. Johnson, Reading, Mass.: Addison-Wesley, 1978.

Lietaer, B. A., *Financial Management of Foreign Exchange: An Operational Technique to Reduce Risk,* Cambridge, Mass.: M.I.T. Press, 1971.

Solnik, B. H., "An Equilibrium Model of the International Capital Market," *Journal of Economic Theory,* 8 (1974): 500–24.

Appendixes: Compound, Present Value, and Annuity Tables

APPENDIX A.   Future value of 1 dollar after n periods

$(1+R)^n$

Rate (percent)

Period (n)	1.0	1.5	2.0	2.5	3.0	3.5	4.0	4.5	5.0	5.5	6.0	6.5
1	1.01000	1.01500	1.02000	1.02500	1.03000	1.03500	1.04000	1.04500	1.05000	1.05500	1.06000	1.06500
2	1.02010	1.03023	1.04040	1.05063	1.06090	1.07123	1.08160	1.09203	1.10250	1.11303	1.12360	1.13423
3	1.03030	1.04568	1.06121	1.07689	1.09273	1.10872	1.12486	1.14117	1.15762	1.17424	1.19102	1.20795
4	1.04060	1.06136	1.08243	1.10381	1.12551	1.14752	1.16986	1.19252	1.21551	1.23883	1.26248	1.28647
5	1.05101	1.07728	1.10408	1.13141	1.15927	1.18769	1.21665	1.24618	1.27628	1.30696	1.33822	1.37009
6	1.06152	1.09344	1.12616	1.15969	1.19405	1.22926	1.26532	1.30226	1.34010	1.37884	1.41852	1.45914
7	1.07213	1.10985	1.14869	1.18869	1.22987	1.27228	1.31593	1.36086	1.40710	1.45468	1.50363	1.55399
8	1.08286	1.12649	1.17166	1.21840	1.26677	1.31681	1.36857	1.42210	1.47746	1.53469	1.59385	1.65500
9	1.09368	1.14339	1.19509	1.24886	1.30477	1.36290	1.42331	1.48610	1.55133	1.61910	1.68948	1.76257
10	1.10462	1.16054	1.21899	1.28009	1.34392	1.41060	1.48024	1.55297	1.62889	1.70815	1.79085	1.87714
11	1.11567	1.17795	1.24337	1.31209	1.38423	1.45997	1.53945	1.62285	1.71034	1.80209	1.89830	1.99915
12	1.12682	1.19562	1.26824	1.34489	1.42576	1.51107	1.60103	1.69588	1.79586	1.90121	2.01219	2.12910
13	1.13809	1.21355	1.29361	1.37851	1.46853	1.56396	1.66507	1.77220	1.88565	2.00578	2.13293	2.26749
14	1.14947	1.23176	1.31948	1.41298	1.51259	1.61870	1.73168	1.85195	1.97993	2.11609	2.26090	2.41488
15	1.16097	1.25023	1.34587	1.44830	1.55797	1.67535	1.80094	1.93528	2.07893	2.23248	2.39655	2.57184
16	1.17258	1.26899	1.37279	1.48451	1.60471	1.73399	1.87298	2.02237	2.18287	2.35527	2.54035	2.73901
17	1.18430	1.28802	1.40024	1.52162	1.65285	1.79468	1.94790	2.11338	2.29202	2.48481	2.69277	2.91705
18	1.19615	1.30734	1.42825	1.55966	1.70243	1.85749	2.02582	2.20848	2.40662	2.62147	2.85433	3.10666
19	1.20811	1.32695	1.45681	1.59865	1.75351	1.92250	2.10685	2.30786	2.52695	2.76565	3.02559	3.30859
20	1.22019	1.34686	1.48595	1.63862	1.80611	1.98979	2.19112	2.41172	2.65330	2.91776	3.20713	3.52365
21	1.23239	1.36706	1.51567	1.67958	1.86029	2.05944	2.27877	2.52024	2.78596	3.07824	3.39956	3.75269
22	1.24471	1.38757	1.54598	1.72157	1.91610	2.13152	2.36992	2.63365	2.92526	3.24754	3.60353	3.99661
23	1.25716	1.40838	1.57690	1.76461	1.97359	2.20612	2.46471	2.75217	3.07152	3.42616	3.81974	4.25639
24	1.26973	1.42951	1.60844	1.80873	2.03279	2.28333	2.56330	2.87602	3.22510	3.61460	4.04892	4.53306
25	1.28243	1.45095	1.64061	1.85395	2.09378	2.36325	2.66584	3.00544	3.38635	3.81340	4.29186	4.82771
26	1.29526	1.47272	1.67342	1.90030	2.15659	2.44596	2.77247	3.14068	3.55567	4.02314	4.54937	5.14151
27	1.30821	1.49481	1.70689	1.94780	2.22129	2.53157	2.88337	3.28201	3.73345	4.24441	4.82233	5.47571
28	1.32129	1.51723	1.74103	1.99650	2.28793	2.62018	2.99870	3.42970	3.92013	4.47785	5.11167	5.83163
29	1.33450	1.53999	1.77585	2.04641	2.35657	2.71188	3.11865	3.58404	4.11613	4.72414	5.41837	6.21068
30	1.34785	1.56309	1.81136	2.09757	2.42726	2.80680	3.24340	3.74532	4.32194	4.98396	5.74347	6.61438

APPENDIX A. Future value of 1 dollar after n periods

$(1+R)^n$

Rate (percent)

Period (n)	7.0	7.5	8.0	8.5	9.0	9.5	10.0	10.5	11.0	11.5	12.0	12.5
1	1.07000	1.07500	1.08000	1.08500	1.09000	1.09500	1.10000	1.10500	1.11000	1.11500	1.12000	1.12500
2	1.14490	1.15563	1.16640	1.17723	1.18810	1.19903	1.21000	1.22102	1.23210	1.24323	1.25440	1.26563
3	1.22504	1.24230	1.25971	1.27729	1.29503	1.31293	1.33100	1.34923	1.36763	1.38620	1.40493	1.42383
4	1.31080	1.33547	1.36049	1.38586	1.41158	1.43766	1.46410	1.49090	1.51807	1.54561	1.57352	1.60181
5	1.40255	1.43563	1.46933	1.50366	1.53862	1.57424	1.61051	1.64745	1.68506	1.72335	1.76234	1.80203
6	1.50073	1.54330	1.58687	1.63147	1.67710	1.72379	1.77156	1.82043	1.87041	1.92154	1.97382	2.02729
7	1.60578	1.65905	1.71382	1.77014	1.82804	1.88755	1.94872	2.01157	2.07616	2.14252	2.21068	2.28070
8	1.71818	1.78348	1.85093	1.92061	1.99256	2.06687	2.14359	2.22279	2.30454	2.38891	2.47597	2.56578
9	1.83846	1.91724	1.99900	2.08386	2.17189	2.26322	2.35795	2.45618	2.55803	2.66363	2.77308	2.88651
10	1.96715	2.06103	2.15892	2.26098	2.36736	2.47823	2.59374	2.71408	2.83942	2.96995	3.10585	3.24732
11	2.10485	2.21561	2.33164	2.45317	2.58042	2.71366	2.85311	2.99906	3.15175	3.31149	3.47855	3.65324
12	2.25219	2.38178	2.51817	2.66169	2.81266	2.97146	3.13842	3.31396	3.49845	3.69231	3.89598	4.10989
13	2.40984	2.56042	2.71962	2.88793	3.06580	3.25375	3.45227	3.66193	3.88327	4.11693	4.36350	4.62363
14	2.57853	2.75245	2.93719	3.13341	3.34172	3.56285	3.79749	4.04643	4.31043	4.59038	4.88712	5.20158
15	2.75903	2.95888	3.17216	3.39975	3.64248	3.90133	4.17724	4.47130	4.78458	5.11827	5.47357	5.85178
16	2.95216	3.18080	3.42594	3.68872	3.97030	4.27195	4.59497	4.94079	5.31089	5.70687	6.13040	6.58325
17	3.15881	3.41936	3.70001	4.00227	4.32763	4.67779	5.05446	5.45957	5.89508	6.36116	6.86605	7.40616
18	3.37993	3.67581	3.99601	4.34246	4.71712	5.12218	5.55991	6.03283	6.54354	7.09493	7.68998	8.33193
19	3.61652	3.95149	4.31569	4.71157	5.14166	5.60879	6.11590	6.66628	7.26333	7.91084	8.61278	9.37342
20	3.86968	4.24786	4.66095	5.11205	5.60440	6.14162	6.72749	7.36623	8.06229	8.82059	9.64631	10.54509
21	4.14055	4.56645	5.03382	5.54658	6.10880	6.72508	7.40024	8.13969	8.94915	9.83496	10.80387	11.86323
22	4.43039	4.90893	5.43653	6.01804	6.65859	7.36396	8.14026	8.99436	9.93355	10.96598	12.10033	13.34613
23	4.74052	5.27710	5.87145	6.52957	7.25787	8.06353	8.95428	9.93876	11.02624	12.22707	13.55238	15.01440
24	5.07236	5.67288	6.34117	7.08458	7.91107	8.82957	9.84971	10.98233	12.23913	13.63319	15.17866	16.89120
25	5.42742	6.09835	6.84846	7.68677	8.62308	9.66838	10.83468	12.13548	13.58543	15.20101	17.00010	19.00260
26	5.80734	6.55573	7.39633	8.34015	9.39915	10.58688	11.91815	13.40970	15.07982	16.94912	19.04012	21.37793
27	6.21385	7.04741	7.98804	9.04906	10.24507	11.59263	13.10996	14.81772	16.73861	18.89827	21.32494	24.05017
28	6.64882	7.57596	8.62708	9.81823	11.16712	12.69393	14.42095	16.37358	18.57985	21.07158	23.88393	27.05644
29	7.11424	8.14416	9.31725	10.65278	12.17216	13.89986	15.86605	18.09281	20.62363	23.49480	26.75000	30.43849
30	7.61223	8.75497	10.06263	11.55827	13.26766	15.22034	17.44935	19.99255	22.89222	26.19671	29.96000	34.24330

APPENDIX A. Future value of 1 dollar after n periods

$$(1+R)^n$$

Rate (percent)

Period (n)	13.0	13.5	14.0	14.5	15.0	16.0	17.0	18.0	19.0	20.0	25.0	30.0
1	1.13000	1.13500	1.14000	1.14500	1.15000	1.16000	1.17000	1.18000	1.19000	1.20000	1.25000	1.30000
2	1.27690	1.28822	1.29960	1.31102	1.32250	1.34560	1.36890	1.39240	1.41610	1.44000	1.56250	1.69000
3	1.44290	1.46214	1.48154	1.50112	1.52088	1.56090	1.60161	1.64303	1.68516	1.72800	1.95313	2.19700
4	1.63047	1.65952	1.68896	1.71879	1.74901	1.81064	1.87389	1.93878	2.00534	2.07360	2.44141	2.85610
5	1.84244	1.88356	1.92542	1.96801	2.01136	2.10034	2.19245	2.28776	2.38635	2.48832	3.05176	3.71293
6	2.08195	2.13784	2.19497	2.25337	2.31306	2.43640	2.55516	2.69956	2.83976	2.98598	3.81470	4.82681
7	2.35261	2.42645	2.50227	2.58011	2.66002	2.82622	3.00124	3.18548	3.37932	3.58318	4.76837	6.27485
8	2.65845	2.75402	2.85259	2.95424	3.05902	3.27842	3.51145	3.75886	4.02139	4.29982	5.96046	8.15730
9	3.00404	3.12581	3.25195	3.38259	3.51788	3.80296	4.10683	4.43546	4.78545	5.15978	7.45058	10.60450
10	3.39457	3.54779	3.70722	3.87306	4.04556	4.41144	4.80683	5.23384	5.69468	6.19174	9.31323	13.78584
11	3.83587	4.02675	4.22624	4.43466	4.65240	5.11727	5.62399	6.17593	6.77667	7.43009	11.64153	17.92160
12	4.33453	4.57036	4.81791	5.07768	5.35026	5.93603	6.58007	7.28760	8.06424	8.91610	14.55192	23.29808
13	4.89802	5.18736	5.49242	5.81395	6.15279	6.88579	7.69868	8.59937	9.59645	10.69933	18.18990	30.28749
14	5.53476	5.88765	6.26135	6.65697	7.07571	7.98752	9.00746	10.14725	11.41977	12.83919	22.73737	39.37374
15	6.25428	6.68248	7.13794	7.62223	8.13707	9.26553	10.53872	11.97376	13.58953	15.40703	28.42171	51.18586
16	7.06734	7.58462	8.13726	8.72745	9.35763	10.74801	12.33031	14.12904	16.17154	18.48843	35.52714	66.54163
17	7.98609	8.60854	9.27647	9.99293	10.76128	12.46769	14.42646	16.67227	19.24413	22.18612	44.40892	86.50410
18	9.02428	9.77069	10.57518	11.44191	12.37547	14.46252	16.87896	19.67328	22.90052	26.62334	55.51115	112.45534
19	10.19744	11.08974	12.05571	13.10098	14.23179	16.77653	19.74838	23.21447	27.25162	31.94802	69.38895	146.19193
20	11.52311	12.58685	13.74351	15.00062	16.36657	19.46077	23.10561	27.39308	32.42942	38.33762	86.73618	190.04950
21	13.02112	14.28608	15.66760	17.17571	18.82155	22.57450	27.03356	32.32384	38.59101	46.00515	108.42023	247.04636
22	14.71386	16.21469	17.86106	19.66619	21.64478	26.18642	31.62926	38.14213	45.92330	55.20618	135.52527	321.18365
23	16.62667	18.40368	20.36161	22.51778	24.89151	30.37624	37.00624	45.00771	54.64874	66.24742	169.40659	417.53870
24	18.78814	20.88817	23.21224	25.78286	28.62523	35.23644	43.29730	53.10911	65.03198	79.49690	211.75824	542.80029
25	21.23059	23.70808	26.46195	29.52138	32.91902	40.87428	50.65785	62.66875	77.38808	95.39627	264.69781	705.64038
26	23.99058	26.90866	30.16663	33.80198	37.85687	47.41416	59.26968	73.94913	92.09181	114.47554	330.87231	917.33240
27	27.10936	30.54134	34.38996	38.70326	43.53542	55.00043	69.34554	87.25998	109.58925	137.37067	413.59033	1192.53223
28	30.63358	34.66441	39.20456	44.31524	50.06573	63.80050	81.13426	102.96678	130.41119	164.84479	516.98792	1550.29199
29	34.61594	39.34412	44.69320	50.74094	57.57558	74.00858	94.92709	121.50082	155.19933	197.81378	646.23499	2015.37915
30	39.11602	44.65556	50.95025	58.09837	66.21193	85.84996	111.06470	143.37097	184.67529	237.37650	807.79358	2619.99268

APPENDIX B. Present value of 1 dollar

$1/(1+R)^n$

Rate (percent)

Period (n)	1.0	1.5	2.0	2.5	3.0	3.5	4.0	4.5	5.0	5.5	6.0	6.5	7.0
1	.99010	.98522	.98039	.97561	.97087	.96618	.96154	.95694	.95238	.94787	.94340	.93897	.93458
2	.98030	.97066	.96117	.95181	.94260	.93351	.92456	.91573	.90703	.89845	.89000	.88166	.87344
3	.97059	.95632	.94232	.92860	.91514	.90194	.88900	.87630	.86384	.85161	.83962	.82785	.81630
4	.96098	.94218	.92385	.90595	.88849	.87144	.85480	.83856	.82270	.80722	.79209	.77732	.76290
5	.95147	.92826	.90573	.88385	.86261	.84197	.82193	.80245	.78353	.76513	.74726	.72988	.71299
6	.94205	.91454	.88797	.86230	.83748	.81350	.79031	.76790	.74622	.72525	.70496	.68533	.66634
7	.93272	.90103	.87056	.84127	.81309	.78599	.75992	.73483	.71068	.68744	.66506	.64351	.62275
8	.92348	.88771	.85349	.82075	.78941	.75941	.73069	.70319	.67684	.65160	.62741	.60423	.58201
9	.91434	.87459	.83676	.80073	.76642	.73373	.70259	.67290	.64461	.61763	.59190	.56735	.54393
10	.90529	.86167	.82035	.78120	.74409	.70892	.67556	.64393	.61391	.58543	.55840	.53273	.50835
11	.89632	.84893	.80426	.76214	.72242	.68495	.64958	.61620	.58468	.55491	.52679	.50021	.47509
12	.88745	.83639	.78849	.74356	.70138	.66178	.62460	.58966	.55684	.52598	.49697	.46968	.44401
13	.87866	.82403	.77303	.72542	.68095	.63940	.60057	.56427	.53032	.49856	.46884	.44102	.41496
14	.86996	.81185	.75787	.70773	.66112	.61778	.57748	.53997	.50507	.47257	.44230	.41410	.38782
15	.86135	.79985	.74301	.69046	.64186	.59689	.55526	.51672	.48102	.44793	.41727	.38883	.36245
16	.85282	.78803	.72845	.67362	.62317	.57671	.53391	.49447	.45811	.42458	.39365	.36510	.33874
17	.84438	.77638	.71416	.65719	.60502	.55720	.51337	.47318	.43630	.40245	.37137	.34281	.31657
18	.83602	.76491	.70016	.64117	.58739	.53836	.49363	.45280	.41552	.38147	.35034	.32189	.29586
19	.82774	.75361	.68643	.62553	.57029	.52016	.47464	.43330	.39573	.36158	.33051	.30224	.27651
20	.81954	.74247	.67297	.61027	.55368	.50257	.45639	.41464	.37689	.34273	.31181	.28380	.25842
21	.81143	.73150	.65978	.59539	.53755	.48557	.43883	.39679	.35894	.32486	.29416	.26648	.24151
22	.80340	.72069	.64684	.58086	.52189	.46915	.42196	.37970	.34185	.30793	.27751	.25021	.22571
23	.79544	.71003	.63416	.56670	.50669	.45328	.40573	.36335	.32557	.29187	.26180	.23494	.21095
24	.78757	.69954	.62172	.55287	.49193	.43796	.39012	.34770	.31007	.27666	.24698	.22060	.19715
25	.77977	.68920	.60953	.53939	.47761	.42315	.37512	.33273	.29530	.26223	.23300	.20714	.18425
26	.77205	.67902	.59758	.52623	.46369	.40884	.36069	.31840	.28124	.24856	.21981	.19450	.17220
27	.76440	.66898	.58586	.51340	.45019	.39501	.34682	.30469	.26785	.23560	.20737	.18262	.16093
28	.75684	.65910	.57437	.50088	.43708	.38165	.33348	.29157	.25509	.22332	.19563	.17148	.15040
29	.74934	.64936	.56311	.48866	.42435	.36875	.32065	.27901	.24295	.21168	.18456	.16101	.14056
30	.74192	.63976	.55207	.47674	.41199	.35628	.30832	.26700	.23138	.20064	.17411	.15119	.13137

APPENDIX B. Present value of 1 dollar

$$1/(1+R)^n$$

Rate (percent)

Period (n)	7.5	8.0	8.5	9.0	9.5	10.0	10.5	11.0	11.5	12.0	12.5	13.0	13.5
1	.93023	.92593	.92166	.91743	.91324	.90909	.90498	.90090	.89686	.89286	.88889	.88496	.88106
2	.86533	.85734	.84946	.84168	.83401	.82645	.81898	.81162	.80436	.79719	.79012	.78315	.77626
3	.80496	.79383	.78291	.77218	.76165	.75131	.74116	.73119	.72140	.71178	.70233	.69305	.68393
4	.74880	.73503	.72157	.70843	.69557	.68301	.67073	.65873	.64699	.63552	.62430	.61332	.60258
5	.69656	.68058	.66505	.64993	.63523	.62092	.60700	.59345	.58026	.56743	.55493	.54276	.53091
6	.64796	.63017	.61294	.59627	.58012	.56447	.54932	.53464	.52042	.50663	.49327	.48032	.46776
7	.60275	.58349	.56493	.54703	.52979	.51316	.49712	.48166	.46674	.45235	.43846	.42506	.41213
8	.56070	.54027	.52067	.50188	.48382	.46651	.44989	.43393	.41860	.40388	.38974	.37616	.36311
9	.52158	.50025	.47988	.46043	.44185	.42410	.40714	.39093	.37543	.36061	.34644	.33288	.31992
10	.48519	.46319	.44229	.42241	.40351	.38554	.36845	.35218	.33671	.32197	.30795	.29459	.28187
11	.45134	.42888	.40764	.38753	.36851	.35049	.33344	.31728	.30198	.28748	.27373	.26070	.24834
12	.41985	.39711	.37570	.35553	.33653	.31863	.30175	.28584	.27083	.25667	.24332	.23071	.21880
13	.39056	.36770	.34627	.32618	.30734	.28966	.27308	.25751	.24290	.22917	.21628	.20416	.19278
14	.36331	.34046	.31914	.29925	.28067	.26333	.24713	.23200	.21785	.20462	.19225	.18068	.16985
15	.33797	.31524	.29414	.27454	.25632	.23939	.22365	.20900	.19538	.18270	.17089	.15989	.14965
16	.31439	.29189	.27110	.25187	.23408	.21763	.20240	.18829	.17523	.16312	.15190	.14150	.13185
17	.29245	.27027	.24986	.23107	.21378	.19784	.18316	.16963	.15715	.14564	.13502	.12522	.11616
18	.27205	.25025	.23028	.21199	.19523	.17986	.16576	.15282	.14095	.13004	.12002	.11081	.10235
19	.25307	.23171	.21224	.19449	.17829	.16351	.15001	.13768	.12641	.11611	.10668	.09806	.09017
20	.23541	.21455	.19562	.17843	.16282	.14864	.13575	.12403	.11337	.10367	.09483	.08678	.07945
21	.21899	.19866	.18029	.16370	.14870	.13513	.12285	.11174	.10168	.09256	.08429	.07680	.07000
22	.20371	.18394	.16617	.15018	.13580	.12285	.11118	.10067	.09119	.08264	.07493	.06796	.06167
23	.18950	.17032	.15315	.13778	.12402	.11168	.10062	.09069	.08179	.07379	.06660	.06014	.05434
24	.17628	.15770	.14115	.12641	.11326	.10153	.09106	.08171	.07335	.06588	.05920	.05323	.04787
25	.16398	.14602	.13009	.11597	.10343	.09230	.08240	.07361	.06579	.05882	.05262	.04710	.04218
26	.15254	.13520	.11990	.10639	.09446	.08391	.07457	.06631	.05900	.05252	.04678	.04168	.03716
27	.14190	.12519	.11051	.09761	.08626	.07628	.06749	.05974	.05291	.04689	.04158	.03689	.03274
28	.13200	.11591	.10185	.08955	.07878	.06934	.06107	.05382	.04746	.04187	.03696	.03264	.02885
29	.12279	.10733	.09387	.08215	.07194	.06304	.05527	.04849	.04256	.03738	.03285	.02889	.02542
30	.11422	.09938	.08652	.07537	.06570	.05731	.05002	.04368	.03817	.03338	.02920	.02556	.02239

APPENDIX B. Present value of 1 dollar

$$1/(1+R)^n$$

Rate (percent)

Period (n)	14.0	14.5	15.0	16.0	17.0	18.0	19.0	20.0	22.0	24.0	26.0	28.0	30.0
1	.87719	.87336	.86957	.86207	.85470	.84746	.84034	.83333	.81967	.80645	.79365	.78125	.76923
2	.76947	.76276	.75614	.74316	.73051	.71818	.70616	.69444	.67186	.65036	.62988	.61035	.59172
3	.67497	.66617	.65752	.64066	.62437	.60863	.59342	.57870	.55071	.52449	.49991	.47684	.45517
4	.59208	.58181	.57175	.55229	.53365	.51579	.49867	.48225	.45140	.42297	.39675	.37253	.35013
5	.51937	.50813	.49718	.47611	.45611	.43711	.41905	.40188	.37000	.34111	.31488	.29104	.26933
6	.45559	.44378	.43233	.41044	.38984	.37043	.35214	.33490	.30328	.27509	.24991	.22737	.20718
7	.39964	.38758	.37594	.35383	.33320	.31392	.29592	.27908	.24859	.22184	.19834	.17764	.15937
8	.35056	.33850	.32690	.30503	.28478	.26604	.24867	.23257	.20376	.17891	.15741	.13878	.12259
9	.30751	.29563	.28426	.26295	.24340	.22546	.20897	.19381	.16702	.14428	.12493	.10842	.09430
10	.26974	.25819	.24718	.22668	.20804	.19106	.17560	.16151	.13690	.11635	.09915	.08470	.07254
11	.23662	.22550	.21494	.19542	.17781	.16192	.14757	.13459	.11221	.09383	.07869	.06617	.05580
12	.20756	.19694	.18691	.16846	.15197	.13722	.12400	.11216	.09198	.07567	.06245	.05170	.04292
13	.18207	.17200	.16253	.14523	.12989	.11629	.10421	.09346	.07539	.06103	.04957	.04039	.03302
14	.15971	.15022	.14133	.12520	.11102	.09855	.08757	.07789	.06180	.04921	.03934	.03155	.02540
15	.14010	.13120	.12289	.10793	.09489	.08352	.07359	.06491	.05065	.03969	.03122	.02465	.01954
16	.12289	.11458	.10686	.09304	.08110	.07078	.06184	.05409	.04152	.03201	.02478	.01926	.01503
17	.10780	.10007	.09293	.08021	.06932	.05998	.05196	.04507	.03403	.02581	.01967	.01505	.01156
18	.09456	.08740	.08080	.06914	.05925	.05083	.04367	.03756	.02789	.02082	.01561	.01175	.00889
19	.08295	.07633	.07027	.05961	.05064	.04308	.03670	.03130	.02286	.01679	.01239	.00918	.00684
20	.07276	.06666	.06110	.05139	.04328	.03651	.03084	.02608	.01874	.01354	.00983	.00717	.00526
21	.06383	.05822	.05313	.04430	.03699	.03094	.02591	.02174	.01536	.01092	.00780	.00561	.00405
22	.05599	.05085	.04620	.03819	.03162	.02622	.02178	.01811	.01259	.00880	.00619	.00438	.00311
23	.04911	.04441	.04017	.03292	.02702	.02222	.01830	.01509	.01032	.00710	.00491	.00342	.00239
24	.04308	.03879	.03493	.02838	.02310	.01883	.01538	.01258	.00846	.00573	.00390	.00267	.00184
25	.03779	.03387	.03038	.02447	.01974	.01596	.01292	.01048	.00693	.00462	.00310	.00209	.00142
26	.03315	.02958	.02642	.02109	.01687	.01352	.01086	.00874	.00568	.00372	.00246	.00163	.00109
27	.02908	.02584	.02297	.01818	.01442	.01146	.00912	.00728	.00466	.00300	.00195	.00127	.00084
28	.02551	.02257	.01997	.01567	.01233	.00971	.00767	.00607	.00382	.00242	.00155	.00100	.00065
29	.02237	.01971	.01737	.01351	.01053	.00823	.00644	.00506	.00313	.00195	.00123	.00078	.00050
30	.01963	.01721	.01510	.01165	.00900	.00697	.00541	.00421	.00257	.00158	.00097	.00061	.00038

APPENDIX C.   Present value of 1 dollar per period for n periods

$$(1/R)(1-(1/(1+R))^n)$$

Rate (percent)

Period (n)	1.0	1.5	2.0	2.5	3.0	3.5	4.0	4.5	5.0	5.5	6.0	6.5	7.0
1	0.99009	0.98523	0.98039	0.97561	0.97087	0.96618	0.96154	0.95694	0.95238	0.94787	0.94339	0.93897	0.93458
2	1.97039	1.95590	1.94156	1.92743	1.91347	1.89970	1.88609	1.87267	1.85941	1.84632	1.83339	1.82063	1.80802
3	2.94038	2.91223	2.88388	2.85603	2.82861	2.80164	2.77509	2.74896	2.72325	2.69794	2.67301	2.64848	2.62431
4	3.90196	3.85442	3.80774	3.76198	3.71710	3.67309	3.62989	3.58753	3.54595	3.50516	3.46510	3.42580	3.38721
5	4.85342	4.78269	4.71346	4.64584	4.57971	4.51507	4.45182	4.38998	4.32947	4.27029	4.21236	4.15568	4.10019
6	5.79546	5.69723	5.60144	5.50813	5.41719	5.32856	5.24213	5.15788	5.07569	4.99554	4.91732	4.84102	4.76653
7	6.72816	6.59828	6.47199	6.34940	6.23028	6.11456	6.00205	5.89270	5.78637	5.68297	5.58237	5.48452	5.38929
8	7.65159	7.48599	7.32549	7.17016	7.01969	6.87397	6.73274	6.59589	6.46321	6.33457	6.20978	6.08876	5.97129
9	8.56599	8.36058	8.16225	7.97089	7.78611	7.60770	7.43533	7.26879	7.10782	6.95220	6.80168	6.65611	6.51523
10	9.47126	9.22227	8.98260	8.75208	8.53020	8.31662	8.11090	7.91272	7.72173	7.53763	7.36008	7.18884	7.02358
11	10.36758	10.07121	9.78686	9.51423	9.25262	9.00157	8.76047	8.52892	8.30641	8.09254	7.88686	7.68905	7.49867
12	11.25505	10.90760	10.57536	10.25779	9.95401	9.66335	9.38507	9.11858	8.86325	8.61853	8.38383	8.15873	7.94268
13	12.13369	11.73164	11.34839	10.98322	10.63495	10.30276	9.98564	9.68286	9.39357	9.11709	8.85267	8.59975	8.35765
14	13.00306	12.54339	12.10626	11.69093	11.29607	10.92054	10.56312	10.22283	9.89864	9.58966	9.29497	9.01385	8.74546
15	13.86501	13.34335	12.84928	12.38100	11.93794	11.51743	11.11838	10.73955	10.37966	10.03759	9.71224	9.40267	9.10791
16	14.71783	14.13139	13.57773	13.05503	12.56110	12.09414	11.65229	11.23402	10.83777	10.46217	10.10588	9.76777	9.44664
17	15.56220	14.90777	14.29189	13.71223	13.16612	12.65134	12.16567	11.70719	11.27406	10.86462	10.47725	10.11058	9.76322
18	16.39832	15.67272	14.99205	14.35330	13.75351	13.18971	12.65929	12.15999	11.68958	11.24608	10.82759	10.43247	10.05908
19	17.22596	16.42632	15.67848	14.97892	14.32380	13.70986	13.13393	12.59330	12.08532	11.60766	11.15811	10.73472	10.33559
20	18.04551	17.16878	16.35146	15.58920	14.87747	14.21243	13.59032	13.00794	12.46221	11.95039	11.46991	11.01851	10.59401
21	18.85693	17.90029	17.01123	16.18459	15.41502	14.69800	14.02916	13.40473	12.82115	12.27525	11.76406	11.28499	10.83552
22	19.66032	18.62098	17.65807	16.76545	15.93691	15.16715	14.45111	13.78443	13.16300	12.58318	12.04157	11.53520	11.06124
23	20.45577	19.33103	18.29222	17.33208	16.44361	15.62044	14.85684	14.14778	13.48857	12.87505	12.30337	11.77014	11.27218
24	21.24332	20.03057	18.91395	17.88552	16.93554	16.05839	15.24696	14.49548	13.79864	13.15119	12.55035	11.99074	11.46933
25	22.02309	20.71977	19.52348	18.42442	17.41315	16.48154	15.62208	14.82821	14.09394	13.41394	12.78335	12.19788	11.65358
26	22.79514	21.39881	20.12106	18.95065	17.87684	16.89038	15.98277	15.14662	14.37518	13.66250	13.00316	12.39238	11.82577
27	23.55955	22.06780	20.70692	19.46405	18.32703	17.28539	16.32958	15.45130	14.64303	13.89811	13.21052	12.57500	11.98671
28	24.31637	22.72680	21.28130	19.96493	18.76411	17.66705	16.66306	15.74288	14.89812	14.12143	13.40615	12.74648	12.13711
29	25.06572	23.37627	21.84441	20.45359	19.18845	18.03579	16.98371	16.02189	15.14107	14.33311	13.59071	12.90749	12.27767
30	25.80764	24.01602	22.39648	20.93003	19.60044	18.39207	17.29203	16.28889	15.37245	14.53375	13.76482	13.05868	12.40904

APPENDIX C. Present value of 1 dollar per period for n periods

$$(1/R)(1-(1/(1+R))^n)$$

Rate (percent)

Period (n)	7.5	8.0	8.5	9.0	9.5	10.0	10.5	11.0	11.5	12.0	12.5	13.0	13.5
1	0.93023	0.92593	0.92166	0.91743	0.91324	0.90909	0.90498	0.90090	0.89686	0.89286	0.88889	0.88496	0.88106
2	1.79557	1.78326	1.77111	1.75911	1.74725	1.73554	1.72396	1.71252	1.70122	1.69005	1.67901	1.66810	1.65732
3	2.60053	2.57710	2.55402	2.53129	2.50891	2.48685	2.46512	2.44371	2.42262	2.40183	2.38134	2.36115	2.34125
4	3.34933	3.31213	3.27560	3.23972	3.20448	3.16986	3.13586	3.10244	3.06962	3.03735	3.00564	2.97447	2.94383
5	4.04589	3.99271	3.94064	3.88965	3.83971	3.79078	3.74286	3.69589	3.64988	3.60477	3.56057	3.51723	3.47474
6	4.69385	4.62288	4.55359	4.48592	4.41983	4.35526	4.29218	4.23054	4.17030	4.11141	4.05384	3.99755	3.94250
7	5.29660	5.20637	5.11852	5.03295	4.94961	4.86842	4.78930	4.71219	4.63704	4.56376	4.49230	4.42261	4.35463
8	5.85731	5.74664	5.63919	5.53482	5.43344	5.33492	5.23919	5.14612	5.05564	4.96764	4.88205	4.79877	4.71774
9	6.37889	6.24689	6.11907	5.99524	5.87529	5.75902	5.64632	5.53704	5.43107	5.32825	5.22848	5.13166	5.03765
10	6.86408	6.71007	6.56135	6.41766	6.27880	6.14456	6.01477	5.88923	5.76777	5.65023	5.53643	5.42625	5.31952
11	7.31543	7.13896	6.96899	6.80519	6.64731	6.49506	6.34821	6.20651	6.06975	5.93770	5.81016	5.68694	5.56786
12	7.73528	7.53607	7.34469	7.16072	6.98384	6.81369	6.64996	6.49235	6.34058	6.19438	6.05348	5.91765	5.78666
13	8.12584	7.90377	7.69006	7.48690	7.29118	7.10335	6.92304	6.74987	6.58348	6.42355	6.26976	6.12181	5.97743
14	8.48916	8.24423	8.01010	7.78615	7.51185	7.36668	7.17018	6.98186	6.80133	6.62817	6.46201	6.30249	6.14928
15	8.82712	8.55947	8.30424	8.06069	7.82818	7.60608	7.39382	7.19087	6.99671	6.81087	6.63289	6.46238	6.29893
16	9.14151	8.85136	8.57534	8.31256	8.06226	7.82371	7.59622	7.37916	7.17194	6.97399	6.78479	6.60388	6.43077
17	9.43396	9.12163	8.82520	8.54363	8.27604	8.02155	7.77939	7.54879	7.32909	7.11963	6.91982	6.72909	6.54694
18	9.70601	9.37189	9.05548	8.75562	8.47127	8.20141	7.94514	7.70161	7.47004	7.24967	7.03984	6.83991	6.64928
19	9.95908	9.60359	9.26772	8.95011	8.64956	8.36492	8.09515	7.83929	7.59645	7.36578	7.14652	6.93797	6.73946
20	10.19450	9.81814	9.46334	9.12854	8.81238	8.51356	8.23091	7.96333	7.70982	7.46944	7.24135	7.02475	6.81890
21	10.41348	10.01680	9.64363	9.29224	8.96108	8.64869	8.35376	8.07507	7.81150	7.56200	7.32565	7.10155	6.88890
22	10.61719	10.20074	9.80980	9.44242	9.09688	8.77154	8.46494	8.17574	7.90269	7.64465	7.40058	7.16951	6.95057
23	10.80669	10.37105	9.96295	9.58020	9.22089	8.88322	8.56556	8.26643	7.98447	7.71843	7.46718	7.22966	7.00491
24	10.98297	10.52876	10.10410	9.70661	9.33415	8.98474	8.65662	8.34813	8.05782	7.78432	7.52638	7.28288	7.05279
25	11.14695	10.67477	10.23419	9.82258	9.43758	9.07704	8.73902	8.42174	8.12361	7.84314	7.57901	7.32999	7.09497
26	11.29949	10.80997	10.35410	9.92897	9.53204	9.16094	8.81359	8.48806	8.18261	7.89566	7.62578	7.37167	7.13213
27	11.44138	10.93516	10.46460	10.02558	9.61830	9.23722	8.88108	8.54780	8.23552	7.94255	7.66736	7.40856	7.16487
28	11.57338	11.05107	10.56646	10.11613	9.69708	9.30657	8.94215	8.60162	8.28298	7.98442	7.70432	7.44120	7.19372
29	11.69617	11.15840	10.66033	10.19828	9.76902	9.36960	8.99742	8.65011	8.32554	8.02181	7.73717	7.47009	7.21914
30	11.81039	11.25778	10.74685	10.27365	9.83472	9.42691	9.04744	8.69379	8.36372	8.05518	7.76638	7.49565	7.24153

APPENDIX C.   Present value of 1 dollar per period for n periods

$$(1/R)(1-(1/(1+R))^n)$$

Rate (percent)

Period (n)	14.0	14.5	15.0	16.0	17.0	18.0	19.0	20.0	22.0	24.0	26.0	28.0	30.0
1	0.87719	0.87336	0.86957	0.86207	0.85470	0.84746	0.84034	0.83333	0.81967	0.80645	0.79365	0.78125	0.76923
2	1.64666	1.63612	1.62571	1.60523	1.58521	1.56564	1.54650	1.52778	1.49153	1.45682	1.42353	1.39160	1.36095
3	2.32163	2.30229	2.28323	2.24589	2.20959	2.17427	2.13992	2.10648	2.04224	1.98130	1.92344	1.86844	1.81611
4	2.91371	2.88410	2.85498	2.79818	2.74324	2.69006	2.63859	2.58874	2.49364	2.40428	2.32019	2.24097	2.16624
5	3.43308	3.39222	3.35216	3.27429	3.19935	3.12717	3.05763	2.99061	2.86364	2.74538	2.63507	2.53201	2.43557
6	3.88867	3.83600	3.78448	3.68474	3.58919	3.49760	3.40978	3.32551	3.16692	3.02047	2.88498	2.75938	2.64275
7	4.28831	4.22358	4.16042	4.03857	3.92238	3.81153	3.70570	3.60459	3.41551	3.24232	3.08332	2.93702	2.80211
8	4.63887	4.56208	4.48732	4.34359	4.20716	4.07757	3.95437	3.83716	3.61927	3.42122	3.24073	3.07579	2.92470
9	4.94637	4.85711	4.77159	4.60654	4.45057	4.30302	4.16333	4.03097	3.78628	3.56550	3.36566	3.18421	3.01900
10	5.21612	5.11591	5.01877	4.83323	4.65860	4.49409	4.33893	4.19247	3.92318	3.68186	3.46481	3.26892	3.09154
11	5.45273	5.34140	5.23371	5.02864	4.83641	4.65601	4.48650	4.32706	4.03540	3.77569	3.54350	3.33509	3.14734
12	5.66029	5.53834	5.42062	5.19711	4.98839	4.79323	4.61050	4.43922	4.12737	3.85136	3.60595	3.38679	3.19026
13	5.84236	5.71034	5.58315	5.34233	5.11828	4.90951	4.71471	4.53268	4.20277	3.91239	3.65552	3.42718	3.22327
14	6.00207	5.86056	5.72448	5.46753	5.22930	5.00806	4.80228	4.61057	4.26456	3.96160	3.69485	3.45873	3.24867
15	6.14217	5.99116	5.84737	5.57546	5.32419	5.09158	4.87586	4.67547	4.31522	4.00129	3.72607	3.48339	3.26821
16	6.26506	6.10634	5.95424	5.66850	5.40529	5.16235	4.93770	4.72956	4.35673	4.03330	3.75085	3.50265	3.28324
17	6.37286	6.20641	6.04716	5.74870	5.47461	5.22233	4.98966	4.77463	4.39077	4.05911	3.77052	3.51769	3.29480
18	6.46742	6.29381	6.12797	5.81785	5.53385	5.27316	5.03333	4.81220	4.41866	4.07993	3.78613	3.52945	3.30369
19	6.55037	6.37014	6.19823	5.87746	5.58449	5.31624	5.07002	4.84350	4.44152	4.09672	3.79851	3.53863	3.31053
20	6.62313	6.43680	6.25933	5.92884	5.62777	5.35275	5.10086	4.86958	4.46027	4.11026	3.80834	3.54581	3.31579
21	6.68696	6.49502	6.31246	5.97314	5.66476	5.38368	5.12677	4.89132	4.47563	4.12117	3.81615	3.55141	3.31984
22	6.74295	6.54587	6.35866	6.01133	5.69638	5.40990	5.14855	4.90943	4.48822	4.12998	3.82234	3.55579	3.32295
23	6.79206	6.59028	6.39884	6.04425	5.72340	5.43212	5.16685	4.92453	4.49854	4.13708	3.82725	3.55921	3.32535
24	6.83514	6.62907	6.43377	6.07263	5.74649	5.45095	5.18223	4.93710	4.50700	4.14281	3.83115	3.56188	3.32719
25	6.87293	6.66294	6.46415	6.09709	5.76623	5.46691	5.19515	4.94759	4.51393	4.14742	3.83425	3.56397	3.32861
26	6.90608	6.69252	6.49056	6.11818	5.78311	5.48043	5.20601	4.95632	4.51962	4.15115	3.83670	3.56560	3.32970
27	6.93516	6.71836	6.51353	6.13636	5.79753	5.49189	5.21513	4.96360	4.52428	4.15415	3.83866	3.56688	3.33054
28	6.96066	6.74093	6.53351	6.15204	5.80985	5.50160	5.22280	4.96967	4.52810	4.15657	3.84020	3.56787	3.33118
29	6.98304	6.76063	6.55088	6.16555	5.82039	5.50983	5.22924	4.97472	4.53123	4.15853	3.84143	3.56865	3.33168
30	7.00267	6.77785	6.56598	6.17720	5.82939	5.51681	5.23466	4.97894	4.53379	4.16010	3.84241	3.56926	3.33206

Glossary

Abandonment decision The decision to sell or to discontinue operating an asset or project, usually if the present value of its cash flows is less than its resale value.

Accelerated depreciation The rapid write-off of the cost of an asset, at a rate greater than under the straight-line method of depreciation.

Accounting rate of return The ratio of accounting earnings for a period to the book value of assets employed during the period.

Acquisition The taking over of one company by another.

Adjusted present value (APV) The net present value of the operating cash flows of a project discounted at its unlevered cost of equity, plus the present value of financing benefits attributable to the project.

Agency cost The cost of monitoring the actions of managers to ensure that they are operating within the contractual agreements among management, shareholders, and debtholders.

Aging schedule An analysis of the periods for which accounts receivable relating to sales in different months have been outstanding, for the purpose of evaluating the collection system.

American option An option that is exercisable at any time before its expiration date.

Amortization schedule The repayment schedule for a loan.

Annuity An investment that gives equal cash flows each period for a specified number of periods.

Annuity factor A factor representing the present value of an annuity that gives a cash flow of one dollar per period.

Arbitrage The earning of a riskless profit by simultaneously buying and selling the same (or equivalent) security or currency in different markets.

Arbitrage pricing model A model of the relative pricing of assets that assumes investors' arbitrage transactions eliminate market anomalies.

Ask price Price at which dealers are willing to sell a security.

Automatic dividend reinvestment (ADR) An agreement in which the shareholders automatically reinvest all dividends distributed by the company.

Banker's discount basis A way of expressing the return from a Treasury bill as an annual return that would be earned over 360 days if the bill were reinvested at simple interest.

Barriers to entry Impediments that present difficulties to firms entering a market or industry.

Basis points 100 basis points equals one percentage point of interest, e.g., 85 basis points equals 0.85 percent.

Bear market A declining market in security prices.

Best efforts distribution An arrangement whereby underwriters agree to sell an issue of shares or a distribution at the best price that they can obtain.

Beta coefficient A coefficient that measures the tendency of a security's returns to change with changes in the returns on the market portfolio.

Bid price Price at which dealers are willing to buy a security.

Bond A security representing long-term debt.

Bond equivalent yield The actual dollar discount on a Treasury bill, expressed as a percentage of the bill's price and annualized on the basis of a 365-day year.

Book value The depreciated value of an asset that is recorded in a company's accounts. This value may differ from the amount the asset could fetch in the open market.

Break-even analysis The analysis of an enterprise to determine the level of activity at which total revenue equals the total of fixed and variable expense and no profit is earned.

Bridging finance Short-term loan to finance activities until long-term funds have been secured.

Bull market A rising market in security prices.

Call option A security that permits the holder to buy a company's stock at a fixed price over some future period.

Call price on a bond The price(s) at which the corporation can repay or redeem the bond before maturity.

Capital asset An asset with a useful life of more than one year.

Capital asset pricing model (CAPM) A model that relates the rate of return that investors expect from an asset to a measure of its systematic risk.

Capital market line A line derived from the equation for the capital asset pricing model describing investors' trade-off between risk and return.

Capital projects Investments in commercial activities.

Capital rationing A condition in which a firm has only a limited amount of funds available for further investment in commercial activities.

Capital structure The proportions of different financial instruments that are being used by a company to finance its assets.

Capitalization rate The rate applied to future cash flows to obtain their present value; also called a *discount rate*.

CBOE Chicago Board Options Exchange.

Certainty equivalent The dollar amount of the certain cash flow that is treated as equivalent to an uncertain cash flow.

Characteristic line The line which relates a security's expected return to the expected return on the market; the slope of the line is measured by the value of the beta coefficient.

Charter The contract between a private corporation and the state identifying the articles of association that describe the objectives of a corporation and the relationships between the stockholder, the management, and the corporation itself. Powers and privileges that are granted by the state to the corporation are included.

Clientele effect Consequence arising from the preferences of investors in different marginal tax brackets for different securities.

Closed-end fund An investment company which has a fixed number of common stocks outstanding.

Collateral The assets given to the lender as security for a loan.

Collection float The average number of dollars collected from customers each day multiplied by the average number of days taken up in the collection process.

Commercial paper Unsecured notes with maturities of up to nine months issued by large, high-credit-rated firms.

Commitment fee A one-time lump sum payment to a lender, typically related to the unused portion of a line of credit.

Common stock A security certifying the stockholder's proportionate ownership in a corporation and his or her claim on declared dividends.

Compound factor The future value of $1.00 invested at a given rate of interest compounded (reinvested) each period for a specified number of periods.

Concentration account A bank account to which a company transfers daily all cash balances.

Contingent project A project that cannot be undertaken independently of some other project(s).

Convertible securities Bonds or preferred stocks that are convertible on a predetermined basis to common stock in the issuing company.

Correlation coefficient Measure of the comovement between security returns, which can have values from −1 to +1. Also referred to as the *normalized covariance*.

Coupon The interest payment on a note or a bond.

Coupon bonds Bonds that pay interest, typically twice yearly.

Covariance A statistical measure of the comovement between the returns on two securities.

Covenant The specific terms of a loan agreement for the protection of lenders.

Covered interest arbitrage Simultaneous borrowing and lending in two currencies, covered in the forward exchange market for the risk of changes in the rate of exchange between the two currencies.

Credit terms A part of the terms of sale specifying payment conditions.

Cum-dividend A term that indicates that the buyer of a stock is entitled to a previously announced dividend.

Cum-rights A term that indicates that the buyer of a stock is entitled to a previously announced rights distribution.

Cumulative preferred stock Stock that takes preference over common stock for distribution of dividends; furthermore, no dividends can be paid on common stock until any arrears in cumulative preferred stock dividends have been paid first.

Current ratio Current assets divided by current liabilities; a measure of the firm's ability to pay its short-term debts.

Current yield The yield obtained by dividing the annual interest on a bond by its current price.

Date of record The specific date on which an investor must be registered as a shareholder on the stockbook of the company in order to be entitled to a declared dividend or to vote on company affairs.

Debenture bonds Bonds that are unsecured by specific assets of the firm.

Deep discount Exercise price or striking price on an equity rights issue that is set well below the market price per share for the stock.

Default premium The excess of the price at which a bond is bought or sold compared with the corresponding price on a risk free security that would be comparable in all other respects.

Detachable A security is detachable when it is sold with another security but subsequently can be traded separately.

Direct financing The raising of capital by a company without the use of underwriters.

Disbursement banks Banks through which corporate cash payments are made.

Disbursement float The average number of dollars paid to suppliers each day multiplied by the average number of days taken up in the payment process.

Discount bonds Bonds selling below par value; includes zero coupon bonds.

Discount factor The present value of $1.00 to be received at a future date.

Discounted cash flow (DCF) method Comparison of investments in terms of their net present values. Also, comparison of the internal rate of return on a project with a hurdle rate.

Discounted cash flow (DCF) rate of return See internal rate of return.

Discounted payback period The point in time when the cumulative sum of discounted cash flows for a project first becomes positive.

Disintermediation Withdrawing funds from a financial institution for direct investment.

Diversified portfolio Investment in a collection of different risky assets chosen such that the risk of the portfolio as a whole is less than the value-weighted average of the risks of the individual assets in the portfolio.

Dual purpose funds Investment companies that provide dividend paying shares for those investors who prefer dividend income and capital shares for those investors who prefer capital gains.

Duration A measure of the average maturity of a bond's cash flows.

EBIT Earnings before interest and taxes.

Economic depreciation The amount of an asset's present value used up during a period.

Economic life The length of time during which a project is economically viable.

Economic order quantity (EOQ) The reordering quantity for stocks that minimizes the sum of ordering costs and holding costs for the inventory.

Economic rationale for merging Reasoning that emphasizes the positive opportunities to strengthen the commercial viability of combined businesses and to introduce efficiencies through acquisitions and mergers.

Economic rents Returns greater than those that would be earned in a perfectly competitive market environment.

Economic value The market value of an asset or the present value of its future cash flows.

Efficient capital market A market in which current securities prices reflect all available relevant information.

Efficient markets hypothesis The hypothesis that security prices reflect all relevant information instantaneously.

Efficient set of portfolios Portfolios that minimize the risk for each level of expected return and maximize expected return for each level of risk.

Equity Net worth; common and preferred stock.

Eurobond A bond sold in a country other than the one in whose currency the bond is denominated; generally sold in Europe in U.S. dollar denominations.

Eurodollars Dollar deposits in foreign banks.

European option An option that is exercisable only on the final exercise date.

Ex-dividend A term that indicates that stock is sold without entitlement to the previously announced dividend.

Exercise price The price at which an option, a right, or a warrant may be exercised; also called the *striking price*.

Expected return The mean value of the probability distribution of possible outcomes for returns on a security.

Ex-rights A term indicating that the buyer of the stock is not entitled to a previously announced rights distribution.

Face value The value of a security shown on the certificate; also called *par value*.

Factor A company that purchases and/or collects accounts receivable on behalf of a firm.

Financial Accounting Standards Board (FASB) The public accounting industry board that operates as an accounting standards-setting body in the United States.

Financial assets Financial claims on an economic entity's cash flow and assets; mainly stocks and bonds.

Financial intermediary An institution that operates in financial markets by transferring funds from those with excess funds to those that need funds.

Financial lease A rental contract in which the lessee is granted the use of an asset in exchange for the commitment to make regular payments that will recompense the lessor for the full purchase price of the asset and all the associated (after-tax) financing costs.

Financial rationale for merging Reasoning that emphasizes the positive financial aspects of merging, e.g., savings in corporate taxes.

Fisher effect As originally proposed by Irving Fisher, the hypothesis that interest rates fully reflect anticipated rates of inflation.

Fisher open proposition The hypothesis that states that the difference between the interest rates on similar bonds in two countries equals the expected difference between the inflation rates in the two countries.

Flotation costs The costs associated with issuing new securities.

Forward currency market A market in which foreign currency can be purchased at a rate agreed upon now for delivery at a specified future date.

Forward discount See forward premium.

Forward interest rate The interest rate fixed today on a loan to be made at some future time.

Forward premium or forward discount The difference between the forward and spot rates of exchange.

Forward rate of exchange The rate contracted now for the exchange of two currencies at a future date.

Free cash flow The after-tax cash flow that is generated from operations net of replacement expenditures and increases in net working capital.

Gordon model A model that relates the expected rate of return on a stock to the sum of the dividend yield and the expected dividend growth rate.

Growth stock A company that is expected to earn returns somewhat in excess of the company's cost of capital on new investments; also called a *growth company*.

Hedging Covering or preventing risk by means of offsetting financial transactions.

Holding period rate of return The rate of return that is obtained by dividing the sum of dividends and capital gains over a period by the amount invested at the beginning of the period.

Hurdle rate The minimum rate of return that is acceptable on capital projects.

In the money A call option is said to be in the money when the exercise (or striking) price is lower than the current price for the asset. A put is in the money if its exercise price is higher than the current price.

Income stock A company that earns only its cost of capital on new investments.

Incremental borrowing capacity A company's additional borrowing capacity that would result from investment in a project.

Incremental yield method The comparison of the internal rate of return on the difference between the cash flows for two projects with the cost of capital or hurdle rate.

Indenture A formal agreement between a company that isues a bond and the bondholders.

Intangible assets Assets that do not have tangible or physical properties; examples are goodwill, trademarks, and patents.

Interest rate parity The theorem stating that the difference between short-term interest rates for two countries determines the difference between the spot and forward rates of exchange for their currencies.

Intermediation The process whereby funds are invested through a financial institution.

Internal rate of return (IRR) The discount rate that would make the net present value for an investment equal to zero.

Investment tax credit (ITC) The portion of a new capital investment that can be deducted from the firm's federal income taxes.

IRR See internal rate of return.

ITC See investment tax credit.

Lead time The time that is expected to elapse between the placing of a replenishment order and the receipt of the goods in stock.

Lessee and lessor Parties to a leasing contract providing for the use of an asset by the lessee in exchange for rental payments to the lessor.

Letter of credit A letter issued by a bank guaranteeing checks drawn on the bank or on other banks by a named buyer, thus reducing the credit risk in a commercial transaction.

Letter stock A stock sold to small groups of private investors, which is not registered with the SEC upon issue and which cannot legally be sold in the secondary market by the purchaser for at least two years from date of issue.

Leverage The extent to which variations in a company's earnings per share are magnified as a result of interest expense.

Leveraged leasing Leasing transactions in which the lessor (owner of the leased asset) raises part of the purchase price of the asset by borrowing (leveraging) from other financial institutions or from individual investors.

Lien A lender's claim on assets that are pledged as security for a loan.

Limited liability The legal exemption of stockholders from financial liability for the debts of the corporation beyond the amount that they individually have invested.

Line of credit A credit facility offered by a bank or other lender up to a specified amount for a specified period.

Liquidity preference theory A theory stating that if the capital market is dominated by risk-averse lenders, each forward interest rate will include a risk premium and the spot interest rates will tend to increase with maturity.

Liquidity risk The risk of not being able to pay creditors on time.

Listed securities Securities listed on an organized securities exchange.

Loan balance method A method of valuing a lease by determining the amount of money deposited in a bank at the start of the lease that, together with earned interest, would be sufficient to pay for the lease rentals over the lease period.

Lock box A mail box under the control of a bank that collects and deposits payments from customers of a firm.

Marginal productivity of capital The rate of return that would be obtainable from additional investment in capital projects.

Market capitalization rate The expected or required rate of return on a security.

Market imperfection A market condition in which competition is insufficient to reduce all net present values for investments to zero.

Market risk The part of a security's risk that cannot be eliminated by portfolio diversification; also known as *systematic risk*.

Market value The price that a security or other asset will fetch on the open market.

Material requirements planning (MRP) An approach to determining factory requirements and inventory based on a detailed analysis of the materials that are required to fill known and anticipated customers' orders.

Maturity The date at which a negotiable instrument becomes due for payment.

Merger A corporate combination that is the result of a friendly arrangement between the managements of companies that are of roughly equal size or strength.

Money market The financial market for securities with short maturity periods.

Money market fund   A mutual fund that invests exclusively in short-term low-risk securities, such as Treasury bills.

Moral hazard   The possibility that the borrower may not abide by the terms of the loan contract, which could lead to a default on the loan obligation.

Mortgage   The conveyance of a title to a property as security to a lender until the debt is paid.

Mortgage bond   A bond that is secured by a mortgage on all properties of the issuing corporation.

Mutual fund   An investment company that ordinarily stands ready to sell or to buy back its shares at their current net asset value.

Mutually exclusive projects   Two projects that offer a clear choice and would not be undertaken simultaneously.

Negotiated underwriting   An underwriting for which the fee payable to the underwriter is negotiated.

Net incremental cash flow   The difference between a company's cash flows with and without a capital project.

Net present value (NPV)   The difference between the present value of a project's after-tax operating cash flows and the present value of its after-tax investment expenditures.

Net working capital   The excess of a company's current assets over its current liabilities.

Net worth   The book value of the common stockholders' investment in a corporation.

Nominal interest rate   Interest rate expressed in money-of-the-day terms, i.e., not corrected for the expected rate of inflation.

Nondiversifiable risk   The remaining risk in a well-diversified portfolio that cannot be reduced further by increasing the number of different securities in the portfolio.

Normal distribution   A symmetric, bell-shaped probability distribution containing 68 percent of the probability of outcomes within plus or minus one standard deviation from the mean.

Note   Unsecured debt, usually with a maturity of less than fifteen years.

NPV   See net present value.

Open position   A holding of foreign currency that has not been hedged for the risk of changes in exchange rates.

Operating lease   A leasing contract committing the lessee to the payment of rentals that are not expected to compensate the lessor for the full cost of the leased asset including financing costs, in contrast to a financial lease. The lessor normally expects to take possession of the asset before the end of its useful life in order to re-lease the asset or to sell it.

Operating leverage The degree to which the cost structure of a project may magnify the effect of its revenue sensitivity on the net cash flow and the present value of the project.

Operating leverage factor The ratio of the sum of the present value of the project and of its fixed operating expenditure divided by the present value of the project.

Opportunity cost The rate of return that can be earned in another equally risky investment.

Option A contract that gives the option holder the right to buy (call option) or to sell (put option) an asset at a fixed price during some future (prespecified) period.

Option pricing models (OPM) Model formulas such as Black and Scholes's and the binomial model, widely used for estimating the expected prices of options.

Out of the money A situation where the exercise of an option would result in a financial loss owing to an unfavorable relationship between the exercise price and the price of the underlying asset.

Paid-in capital Equity funds received in excess of par value by a company issuing stock.

Par value The value of a security shown on the certificate.

Payback period The time required to recover a project's initial investment from a project's after-tax operating cash flows.

Payout ratio Annual dividends divided by annual earnings.

Perpetuity An equal sum of money to be paid in each period forever. An annuity with an infinite life.

Pooling of interest A method of accounting for merged companies in which the consolidated financial statement is a simple combination of the statements of the two merged firms.

Portfolio An investment in a collection of different securities or other assets selected for the purpose of reducing risk.

Portfolio effect The effect of portfolio diversification when the standard deviation of the returns on a portfolio is less than the value weighted average of the individual securities' standard deviations.

Portfolio theory A theory concerning the relationships between risk and expected return in portfolios of assets.

Preemptive right A right granted to common stockholders to any valuable distribution by the company; usually applies to further issues of new common stocks.

Preferred habitat approach The theory of the term structure of interest rates based on the assumption that investors have bond maturity preferences.

Preferred stock A security that pays a (normally fixed) stated dividend that must be paid before common stock dividends can be paid.

Present value factor See present values of a dollar.

Present values of a dollar Sums of money invested today that will compound to $1.00 at specified periods in the future assuming different rates of interest.

Price-to-earnings (PE) ratio The market price per share of a stock divided by the company's earnings per share; also called the *earnings multiple*.

Primary market The market where new issues of securities are first issued and sold.

Prime rate The rate at which banks lend to their most favored customers.

Private placements The issue of securities directly to financial institutions at negotiated prices.

Probability distribution The function describing the probabilities of outcomes for different ranges of values for outcomes.

Profitability index (PI) The ratio of a project's present value of operating cash flows to the present value of investment expenditures.

Project finance Debt issued to finance a specific project and where the lender's claim to interest and principal repayment is limited to the financial resources of the particular project.

Prospectus A written offer to sell a security that provides information concerning the quality of the issue summarized from the registration statement that must be filed with the SEC.

Proxy statement A document that authorizes another person to act on behalf of the signatory, usually to vote on behalf of a common stockholder at meetings of the stockholders.

Public offering The offer of a new issue of securities to the general public.

Purchasing power parity (PPP) The theorem stating that the rate of change in the spot rate of exchange is related to the difference between the rates of inflation for the two countries.

Pure expectations hypothesis The assumption that the term structure of interest rates reflects only the bond market's expectation of what interest rates will be in the future.

Put option An option that permits the holder of the put to sell a common stock at a predetermined price during some future (prespecified) period.

Random walk Price changes are said to follow a random walk if all future prices represent random departures from the current price.

Real option The opportunity to invest in a commercial activity in the future contingent upon future revisions of expectations.

Refunding The sale of new debt securities to replace existing debt.

Reorder level The level of stock in an inventory signifying that more stock should be ordered.

Repurchase agreement An arrangement whereby a lender can purchase, hold, and resell government securities to a bank for a flexible period, usually less than 89 days.

Residual value See salvage value.

Return on capital employed (ROCE) The accounting rate of return calculated by dividing an asset's accounting income for a period by the book value of the assets that are employed during the period.

Revenue sensitivity The degree to which a project's cash income changes with changes in general economic conditions.

Revolving credit agreement A loan contract in which a lender allows the firm to borrow at any time any amount up to some dollar limit specified in the agreement.

Rights issue Stock offered by a corporation to each existing stockholder in proportion to the number that he or she already holds.

Rights on A term indicating that buyers of the stock are entitled to a previously announced rights issue.

Risk-averse investor An investor who attaches greater weight to the possibility of a loss than to an equal possibility of a gain.

Risk premium The investors' required rate of return on a risky investment in excess of the risk-free rate of return.

Safety stock Extra inventory that is carried in order to prevent running out of stock when actual sales exceed forecasted sales.

Salvage value The expected resale value of an asset at the end of its economic life.

Scenario A hypothetical chain of possible future events that is constructed to test the viability of plans in different future circumstances.

SEC See Securities and Exchange Commission.

Secondary market The market where securities that have already been issued are traded.

Securities and Exchange Commission (SEC) The U.S. government agency that regulates the issuance and trading of marketable securities.

Security A document that certifies legal ownership of an asset or a claim on the wealth of an individual or corporation.

Security market line (SML) The line that reflects the relationship between market rates of return and risk for individual securities; also called the *market line*.

Segmented markets approach The theory of the term structure of interest rates based on the assumption that investors prefer absolutely to hold bonds of particular maturities to the exclusion of other maturities.

Semistrong form efficient market hypothesis The hypothesis that security prices adjust rapidly to all publicly available price sensitive information.

Senior debt Debt that ranks in front of subordinated debt in its claim on the firm's income and assets should a default occur.

Sensitivity analysis A method of assessing a project's risk by estimating the range of net present values for the project corresponding to a range of possible future conditions or scenarios affecting costs and revenues.

Separation theorem A theorem stating that the optimum portfolio of risky assets can be chosen without regard to the individual investor's risk preferences.

Short sale The sale of a security that the seller does not yet own.

Sinking fund An account administered by independent trustees for the purpose of repaying outstanding bonds.

Specialist A member of an organized stock exchange acting as a dealer, quoting bid and asked prices for a stock.

Spot currency market A market in which foreign currency can be purchased or sold immediately.

Spot rate of interest The interest rate fixed today on a loan beginning today for a specific maturity.

Spread The difference between the asked and bid prices.

Standard deviation A measure of risk; the square root of the variance.

Stock dividend A free issue of additional shares to existing stockholders in proportion to the number of shares already held.

Stockout Exhaustion of an inventory before the stocks are replenished.

Stock splits Division of the outstanding shares of a corporation into a larger number of shares.

Striking price See exercise price.

Strong-form efficient market hypothesis The hypothesis that prices reflect rapidly all price sensitive information (both public and nonpublic information).

Subchapter S corporation A small business corporation that is permitted by the Internal Revenue Code to have profit taxed directly at the shareholder level rather than at the corporation level.

Subordinated debentures Bonds that rank behind both mortgage bonds and debentures in their claim on the firm's income and assets should default occur.

Syndicate See underwriting syndicate.

Synergy Extra returns that result when the commercial activities of companies are combined.

Takeover The acquisition by a company of a sufficient proportion of another company's shares to control its decisions.

Takeover bid A tender offer to buy common stock made directly to the existing shareholders of a company in an attempted takeover.

Target company A company that has attracted attention for possible acquisition by another company.

Taxable income The difference between revenue and tax deductible expenses.

Tax clientele effect An effect attributable to the preference for particular stocks or particular bonds by investors who pay different marginal rates of tax.

Tender offer An offer made directly to the existing shareholders for the acquisition of their shares.

Term structure of interest rates The relationship between interest rates on bonds of different maturities. The relationship is measured in terms of interest rates on equivalent portfolios of zero coupon bonds of different maturities.

Trading crowd Floor brokers at an organized exchange buying and selling a stock among themselves.

Trading post The area in an organized exchange at which a security is traded.

Treasury bills Short-term zero coupon securities representing claims on the U.S. Treasury with maturities of up to one year.

Treasury stock Common stock that has been repurchased by the issuing company.

Trustee An agent who acts on behalf of the bondholders.

Underwriter An investment banking firm or securities dealer that buys a firm's issue of securities for purposes of resale to the public.

Underwriting syndicate A group of investment bankers and securities dealers who join together to distribute a new issue of securities for a corporation.

Value additivity A proposition that the economic value of a firm is equal to the sum of the economic values of its individual commercial activities.

Variance The probability-weighted average of squared deviations from the mean of a distribution of outcomes.

Warrants Securities giving the holder the right to buy the company's common stock directly from the company at potentially advantageous prices. Warrant terms specify the number of shares, prices, and dates when the warrant can be exercised.

Weak-form efficient market hypothesis The hypothesis that security prices adjust rapidly to any information contained in the pattern of past price changes; security prices under this hypothesis follow a random walk.

Weighted average cost of capital (WACC) The discount rate obtained from a weighted average of the after-tax costs of debt and equity instruments that are used to finance an asset, where the weights reflect the proportions contributed by each instrument.

White knight A potential acquirer that is preferred by the management of the target company to another acquirer attempting a takeover.

Working capital Cash and other current assets such as receivables and inventories that can be converted into cash fairly quickly.

Yield curve The plot of yields to maturity against maturities for bonds of similar quality.

Yield to maturity The bond's internal rate of return (IRR) reflecting its price, coupons, and redemption value.

Zero coupon bond A bond that does not pay any interest and is issued or sold at a price that is below its face (par) value.

Solutions

Chapter 3 Solutions

1. Using the table of Future Values in Appendix A, the future value $= \$5,000 \times F_{5, 0.15}$

$= \$5,000 \times 2.01136$

$= \$10,057$

2.

End of year	Discount factor at 12.5 percent
0	1.0 $= 1.0$
1	$1.0/(1+0.125)$ $= 0.88889$
2	$1.0/(1+0.125)^2 = 0.79012$
3	$1.0/(1+0.125)^3 = 0.70233$
4	$1.0/(1+0.125)^4 = 0.62430$
5	$1.0/(1+0.125)^5 = 0.55493$

4. Calculate the NPV of cash flows using the discount factors

End of year	0	1	2	3	4	5
Net incremental cash flow (dollars)		5,000	4,000	3,000	2,000	1,000
Discount factor		0.8696	0.7561	0.6575	0.5718	0.4972
Present value (dollars)		4,348.00	3,024.40	1,972.50	1,143.60	497.20

Total present value at 15 percent = \$10,985.70.

The maximum amount the company could pay for the machine to break even is \$10,985. Any amount less than this will mean a positive increase in the present value of the company.

5. Net present value = $-5,000 + 1,200\, A_{5,0.10}$

$$= -5,000 + (1,200 \times 3.79078)$$

$$= -451.06$$

The investment is not profitable, as its net present value is $-\$451.06$.

6. The present value of the project is given by:

Present Value = Annual Cash Flow

$\times$ Annuity Factor for n Years at 13%

$$PV = C \times A_{N,R}$$

We can solve for the annuity factor

$$A_{N,R} = \frac{PV}{C} = \frac{1,200}{250} = 4.8$$

What life would produce an annuity factor of 4.8 for each dollar of annual cash flow at 13 percent? Looking down the 13 percent column in Appendix C we find

$A_{8,0.13} = 4.79877$ in row 8 ($N = 8$ years).

Thus the break–even life for the project is approximately eight years.

8. The present value of a perpetual stream of cash flows, C, is C/R where R is the discount rate.

$$\text{Present value} = \frac{\$1,000}{0.12} = \$8,333.33$$

9. The annual rate of interest when the quarterly rate is 3.5 percent $= (1 + 0.035)^4 - 1 = 0.1475$, or 14.75 percent.

   The quarterly rate of interest when the annual rate is 15 percent $= (1.15)^{1/4} - 1 = 1.0356 - 1 = 0.0356$, or 3.56 percent.

11. (a) The present value at 15 percent for the project can be obtained using a two-year annuity factor and a three-year present value factor.

$$PV = -1,000 + (200 \times A_{2,0.15}) + (1,200 \times P_{3,0.15})$$

$$= -1,000 + 200 (1.6257) + 1,200 (0.6575)$$

$$= \$114.14$$

The project appears to be profitable with a present value of $114.14 at a discount rate of 15 percent or $114.66 to five places.

(b) At 0% discount factor $PV = -1,000 + 200 + 200 + 1,200 = 600$

At 10% discount factor $PV = -1,000 + (200 \times A_{2,0.10})$
$$+ (1,200 \times P_{3,0.10})$$
$$= -1,000 + (200 \times 1.7355)$$
$$+ (1,200 \times .75131)$$
$$= 249$$

At 30% discount factor $PV = -1,000 + (200 \times 1.3609)$
$$+ (1,200 \times .45517)$$
$$= -182$$

(See figure on page 790.)

Interpolation PV at 15% = 114.14

   PV at 30% = - 182

$$IRR = 15\% + \frac{114}{114 + 182} \times 15\%$$

$$= 20.8\%$$

12. (a) Annual Interest Payment $= 0.12 \times 10,000 + \$1,200$

$$\text{Annual Capital Repayments} = \frac{10,000}{5} = 2,000$$

Total Annual Payment $= \$3,200$

(b) Interest payable on the reducing balance of the loan is equivalent to an annuity. (See solution to Problem 7.) The annuity factor for five years at 14 percent $= 3.4331$, so in this circumstance, annual payment would be

$$\frac{\$10,000}{3.4331} = \$2,912.82$$

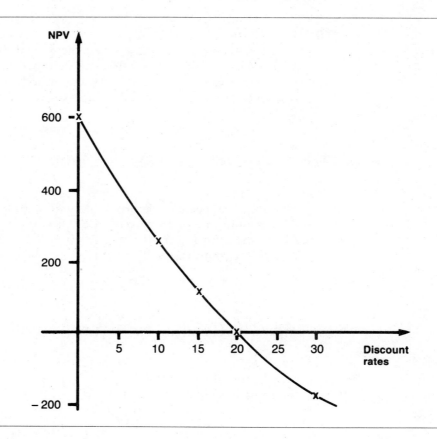

It is more favorable to pay interest at a higher rate (14 percent) on a reducing balance basis than at a lower rate (12 percent) on the initial loan, especially as the term of the loan increases.

17. (a) $-1000 + (265 \times 3.60478) = -44.73$

(b) $-1000 + (66.25 \times A_{20,r}) = NPV$

Quarterly rate $= (1 + R)^4 - 1 = 0.12$

$$R = 2.8737\%$$

Thus, $-1000 + (66.25 \times A_{20,0.028737}) = NPV$

$$NPV = -2.76$$

Chapter 4 Solutions

1. Calculate the present value of the after-tax cash flows

End of year	Cash flow	Discount factor at 15%	Present value
0	−$2,400	1.0000	−$2,400.00
1	−500	0.8696	−434.80
2	2,000	0.7561	1,512.20
3	2,000	0.6575	1,315.00
Net present value			−$7.6

The project would not be financially attractive.

2. At an initial cost for the fixed assets of $2 million, the ITC on five-year assets amounts to:

$$0.10 \times 2/3 \times \$2,000,000 = \$133,333$$

With reference to Table 4.4, the basis of the ACRS depreciation is:

$$\$2,000,000 - 0.5\,(\$133,333) = \$1,933,333$$

First prepare the tax statement, rounding to the nearest thousand dollars.

End of year	1	2	3	4	5
Operating cash flow	800	1,200	1,600	1,400	1,000
ACRS depreciation	−290	−425	−406	−406	−406
Taxable income	510	775	1,194	994	594
Corporate taxes at 46%	−235	−356	−549	−457	−273
Investment tax credit	133				
Net corporate income tax effect	−102	−356	−549	−457	273

Calculate the present value of net incremental cash flows (thousands of dollars)

End of year	0	1	2	3	4	5
Cash flow	−2,200	800	1,200	1,600	1,400	1,000
Working capital						200
Taxes		−102	−356	−549	−457	−273
Net cash flow	−2,200	698	844	1,051	943	927
Discount factors at 15%	1.0	0.8696	0.7561	0.6575	0.5717	0.4972
Present values	−2,200	606.98	638.15	691.03	539.11	460.90

$$\text{Net present value} = -2{,}200 + 606.98 + 638.15$$
$$+ 691.03 + 539.11 + 460.90$$

$$= 736.17$$

The company should undertake the project as it has a positive net present value of $736,170. The market value of the company might be expected to increase by this amount when sufficient information about the project is received by the market.

4. (a) Using straight-line depreciation:

Depreciable amount = $20,000 − 2,000

$$= \$18{,}000$$

Calculate the tax shields

End of year	1	2	3	4	5
Depreciation	3,600	3,600	3,600	3,600	3,600
Tax shield at 46%	1,656	1,656	1,656	1,656	1,656

(b) Using ACRS:

Depreciable amount = $20,000

Calculate the tax shields (with reference to Table 4.4)

End of year	1	2	3	4	5
Depreciation	3,000	4,400	4,200	4,200	4,200
Tax shield at 46%	1,380	2,024	1,932	1,932	1,932
Residual value in excess of unrecovered ACRS*					2,000
Tax at 46%					−920

*No excess residual value occurs in the case of straight-line depreciation because the depreciable amount is based on cost minus residual value. There is an excess under ACRS because the full amount has been depreciated according to rates in Table 4.4.

Present value of tax shields

End of year	Discount factor at 15%	(a) Straight-line		(b) ACRS	
		Tax shields	Present values	Tax shields	Present values
1	0.8696	1,656	1,440.1	1,380	1,200.0
2	0.7561	1,656	1,252.1	2,024	1,530.3
3	0.6575	1,656	1,088.8	1,932	1,270.3
4	0.5717	1,656	946.7	1,932	1,104.5
5	0.4972	1,656	823.4	1,012*	503.2
Present value of tax shields			5,551.1		5,608.3

*(1,932 − 920 = 1,012)

The ACRS depreciation policy will result in higher tax shields for the company, therefore in lower taxes.

6. (a) The cash flows for the first 3.5 years add to zero:

$$-\$5,000 - \$4,000 - \$3,000 + \$7,000 + 0.5\,(\$10,000) = 0$$

Therefore the payback period is 3.5 years.

(b)

End of year	0	1	2	3	4
Cash flow	−5,000	−4,000	−3,000	7,000	10,000
Discount factor at 10%	1.0	0.9091	0.8264	0.7513	0.6830
Present value	−5,000	−3,636.4	−2,479.2	5,259.1	6,830.0

$$-\$5,000 -\$3,636.4 -\$2,479.2 +\$5,259.1 +0.8575(\$6,830) \simeq 0$$

The cash flows for the first 3.8575 years add to approximately zero. Therefore the discounted payback period at 10 percent is 3.86 years. The discounted method is preferred because it takes the time value of money into consideration within the payback period.

7. Investment tax credit $= \$500,000 \times 0.10 \times 1/3$

$$= \$16,667$$

Depreciable amount $= \$500,000 - 1/2\,(16,667)$

$$= \$491,667$$

Prepare the income statement (in dollars)

End of year	1	2	3
Pre-tax cash flow	200,000	200,000	200,000
ACRS depreciation	−122,917	−186,833	−181,917
Taxable income	77,083	13,167	18,083
Corporate taxes at 46%	−35,458	−6,057	−8,318
Investment tax credit	16,667		
Value written off			−8,333
Net income after tax	58,292	7,110	1,432

Calculate the book value (in dollars)

End of year	0	1	2	3
Value of asset at beginning of period		500,000	368,750	181,917
Less 1/2 ITC		−8,333		
Less depreciation		−122,917	−186,833	−181,917
Book value of assets at end of period	500,000	368,750	181,917	0

Calculate the accounting rate of return (in dollars)

End of year	1	2	3
Accounting income	58,292	7,110	1,432
Book value of asset	500,000	368,750	181,917
ARR (%)	11.66	1.93	7.87

Average accounting rate of return = $(11.66 + 1.93 + 7.87)/3 = 7.15\%$

8. (a) Payback period
   Project: $-15,000 + 4,500 + 4,500 + 4,500 + 0.333(4,500) = 0$
   Payback period is 3.333 years

   (b) NPV
   Using a discount rate of 10%:

   NPV of project $= -15,000 + 4,500 (3.1699)$

   $$= -\$735.45$$

   The project should be rejected and Whiz Kid should invest in bonds. Note the NPV of bonds is zero.

   (c) To calculate break-even payback use the formula

   $I = PV = CA_{N,R}$
   where I = Investment, C = Annual Cash Flow, and $A_{N,R}$ is the annuity factor

   $$\frac{I}{C} = A_{N,R} = \text{Break-even Payback}$$

The above break–even payback formula depends upon both N and R, and the cash flows must be in the form of an annuity. The break–even payback is a function of the cash flow profile of the asset.

In our example,

$$\frac{I}{C} = 3.333$$

Using annuity tables, break–even payback (at 10 percent) is between four and five years.

11. (a) The depreciation shields are carried forward until the company is in a taxpaying position, as is the ITC.

Prepare the tax statement (thousands of dollars)

End of year	1	2	3	4	5
Pre-tax operating cash flow	1,600	2,400	3,200	2,800	2,000
Adjusted ACRS depreciation			−2,242*	−812	−812
Taxable income	1,600	2,400	958	1,988	1,188
Corporate taxes at 46%			−2,281†	−914	−546
ITC			+266		
Net corporate income tax effect			−2,015	−914	−546

*2,242 = 580 + 850 + 812   †2281 = (1,600 + 2,400 + 958) × 0.46

Calculate the present value of net incremental cash flows (thousands of dollars)

End of year	0	1	2	3	4	5
Cash flow	−4,000	1,600	2,400	3,200	2,800	2,000
Taxes				−2,015	−914	−546
After-tax cash flow	−4,000	1,600	2,400	1,185	1,886	1,454
Discount factor at 15%	1.0	0.8696	0.7561	0.6575	0.5717	0.4972
Present value	−4,000	1,391.36	1,814.64	779.14	1,078.23	722.93

Net present value $= -4,000 + 1,391.36 + 1,814.64 + 779.14 + 1,078.23$
$\qquad + 722.93$

$\qquad = 1,786.30$

(b) If the company is in a taxpaying position now, it is able to use the depreciation shields as they arise.

Prepare the tax statement (thousands of dollars)

End of year	1	2	3	4	5
Pre-tax operating cash flow	1,600	2,400	3,200	2,800	2,000
ACRS depreciation	−580	−850	−812	−812	−812
Taxable income	1,020	1,550	2,388	1,988	1,188
Corporate taxes at 46%	−469	−713	−1,098	−914	−546
ITC	266				
Net corporate income tax effect	−203	−713	−1,098	−914	−546

Calculate the present value of net incremental cash flows (thousands of dollars)

End of year	0	1	2	3	4	5
Cash flow	−4,000	1,600	2,400	3,200	2,800	2,000
Taxes		−203	−713	−1,098	−914	−546
After-tax cash flow	−4,000	1,397	1,687	2,102	1,886	1,454
Discount factor at 15%	1.0	0.8696	0.7561	0.6575	0.5717	0.4972
Present value	−4,000	1,214.83	1,275.54	1,382.06	1,078.23	722.93

Net present value $= -4,000 + 1,214.83 + 1,275.54 + 1,382.06$
$\qquad + 1,078.23 + 722.93$

$\qquad = \$1,673.59$

The project is more profitable in the first instance because no tax is paid until the third year, despite the delay in using the tax shields.

Chapter 5 Solutions

1. If the IRR rule is used, project A with an IRR of 80 percent would be selected. If the company's required rate of return is 20 percent, this should be used to discount the cash flows for each project.

End of year	Cash flow	Discount factor at 20%	Present value of cash flow
PROJECT A			
0	−25,000	1.0000	−25,000.0
1	25,000	0.8333	20,832.5
2	30,000	0.6944	20,832.0
3	10,800	0.5787	6,250.0
NPV			$22,914.5
PROJECT B			
0	−25,000	1.0000	−25,000.0
1	10,000	0.8333	8,333.0
2	10,000	0.6944	6,944.0
3	60,800	0.5787	35,185.0
NPV			$25,462.0

Using the NPV method, Project B would be selected, as it has the higher net present value; the two rules are in conflict in this case. The NPV rule should be used to make the choice. At a discount rate of over 27.7 percent, the NPV of A is greater than B.

2. Calculate the NPV:

End of year	Cash Flow A	Cash Flow B	Discount Factor A	Discount Factor B	Present Value A	Present Value B
0	−15,000	−15,000	1.0000	1.0000	−15,000.0	−15,000.0
1	10,000	6,000	0.9091		9,091.0	
2	8,000	6,000	0.8264		6,611.2	
3	6,000	6,000	0.7513		4,507.8	
4	0	6,000	0.6830		0	
5	0	6,000	0.6209	3.7908	0	22,744.8
Net present value					5,210.0	7,744.8

On the NPV basis, at a discount rate of 10 percent, Project B should be chosen.

Calculate the IRR:

$$\text{NPV of A at } 25\% = -15{,}000 + 10{,}000(0.8000) + 8{,}000(0.6400) \\ + 6{,}000(0.5120)$$

$$= \$1{,}192.0$$

$$\text{NPV of A at } 35\% = -15{,}000 + 10{,}000(0.7407) + 8{,}000(0.5487) \\ + 6{,}000(0.4064)$$

$$= -\$765.0$$

$$\text{A's IRR} = 0.25 + \frac{1{,}192}{1{,}192 + 765} \times (0.35 - 0.25)$$

$$= 31.09\%$$

$$\text{NPV of B at } 20\% = -15{,}000 + 6{,}000(2.9906) = \$2{,}943.6$$

$$\text{NPV of B at } 30\% = -15{,}000 + 6{,}000(2.4356) = -\$386.4$$

$$\text{B's IRR} = 0.20 + \frac{2{,}943.6}{2{,}943.6 + 386.4} \times (0.30 - 0.20)$$

$$= 28.84\%$$

Project A should be selected on the basis of the IRR rule.

5.

End of year	Project A	Project B	Project A-B
0	−4,750	−4,572	−178
1	1,000	900	100
⋮	⋮	⋮	⋮
9	1,000	900	100
10	0	1,000	−1,000

(a) NPV of Project A

NPV at 0% = $4,250

NPV at 10% = −4,750 + 1,000(5.7590) = $1,009.0

NPV at 20% = −4,750 + 1,000(4.0310) = −$719.0

NPV of Project B
NPV at 0% = $4,528
NPV at 10% = $-4,572 + 900(5.7590) + 1,000(0.3855)$
              = $996.6
NPV at 20% = $-4,572 + 900(4.0310) + 1,000(0.1615)$
              = $-782.6

(b) NPV of A-B cash flows
    NPV at 0% = $-$278
    NPV at 10% = $-178 + 100(5.7590) - 1,000(0.3855)$
                  = $+$12.4
    NPV at 20% = $-178 + 100(4.0310) - 1,000(0.1615)$
                  = $63.6
    Graph not given.

(c) The IRR of the (A-B) cash flows is about 15 percent, which implies
    that we would accept A if the company's required rate of return is
    less than 15 percent. The incremental yield method will not always
    provide an unambiguous criterion because the projects may *not* have
    the same risk and therefore the same required rates of return. This
    leads to the difficult if not impossible problem of choosing an appro-
    priate discount rate for the incremental cash flow. Also there are two
    solutions to the IRR (9.06 and 49.78 percent). Without the NPV the
    wrong decision may be made.

6. NPV at various discount rates

End of year	0	1 through 9	10	NPV
Cash flow	-178	81	-919	
Discount rate				
0%				-368.0
10%				-65.8
20%				0.1
25%				3.8
30%				-0.1

(a) NPV at 20% = $0.1
    NPV at 30% = $-$0.1
(b) Internal rates of return are 19.956 percent and 29.902 percent.
(c) NPV at 15% = $-178 + (81 \times 4.7716) - (919 \times 0.2472)$
                  = $-$18.7
(d) The IRR, by definition, is the rate that makes the NPV equal to zero.
    In this case, there are two IRRs because of the large cash outflow in

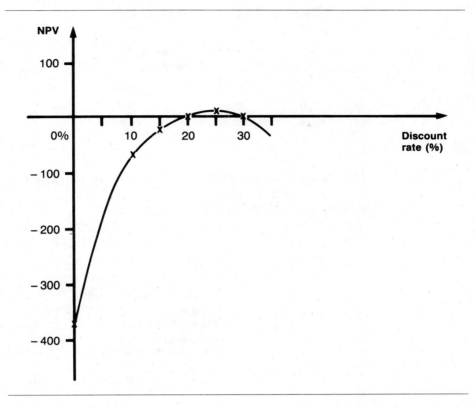

year 10. The project has a very small positive NPV between 20 percent and 30 percent; if the required rate of return is less than 20 percent or greater than 30 percent, the project's NPV is negative, and therefore the project is unacceptable.

8. Calculate NPV and Profitability Index

Project	NPV	PI
A	$-2{,}000 + 700 \times (3.0373) = 126.11$	1.06
B	$-1{,}000 + 380 \times (3.0373) = 154.17$	1.15
C	$-1{,}000 + 330 \times (3.0373) = 2.31$	1.00
D	$-\ 900 + 320 \times (3.0373) = 71.94$	1.08

Projects ranked by profitability index

Project	NPV	Investment	PI	Cumulative investment
B	154.17	1,000	1.15	1,000
D	71.94	900	1.08	1,900
A	126.11	2,000	1.06	3,900
C	2.31	1,000	1.00	4,900

With a budget of $2,000, the company can invest in Projects B and D and will have $100 left over.

9. Calculate NPV and Profitability Index

Project	Discounted cash flow at 15%	NPV	Profitability index
A	$-900 + 495 \times (2.2832) =$	230.2	1.256
B	$-400 \times (0.8696)$ $+ 205 \times (2.8550 - 0.8696) =$	59.2	1.170
C	$-900 \times (0.8696)$ $+ 495 \times (2.8550 - 0.8696) =$	200.1	1.256
D	$-1500 \times (0.7561)$ $+ 735 \times (3.3522 - 1.6257) =$	134.8	1.119

Cumulative net funds requirements and capital budget:

End of year	A	B	C	D	Cumulative capital budget
0	−900.0				1,000.0
1	−495.0	−400.0	−900.0		1,300.0
2	−49.5	−235.0	−495.0	−1,500.0	1,630.0
3	440.5	−53.5	−49.5	−915.0	1,793.0
4		146.1	440.5	−271.5	1,972.3
5				436.3	2,169.5

Cumulative fund requirements for different combinations of projects compared with the cumulative budget; asterisks indicate infeasible project combinations.

End of year	A	AB	AC	AD	B	BC	BD	C	CD	D	Cumulative capital budget
0	900										1,000.0
1		895	1,395*		400	1,300		900			1,300.0
2				1,549.5			1,735*		1,995*	1,500	1,630.0
3											1,793.0
4											1,972.3
5											2,169.5

NPV for combinations of projects:

Projects with:	A	B	C	D
A	230.2	(230.2 + 59.2)		(230.2 + 134.8)
B		59.2	(59.2 + 200.1)	
C			200.1	
D				134.8

The best combination of projects to be accepted is the one with the highest NPV: Projects A and D with a combined NPV of $365.

11. Cumulative cash flow:

Cash flow	−25	125	−75	25	−500
Cumulations					
Stage 1	−25	100	25	50	−450
Stage 2	−25	75	100	150	−300

Using the Pratt and Hammond technique, you find that there are no more than two changes of sign in both stages and therefore no more than two IRRs. One might have guessed there to be as many as four by counting the number of changes of sign in the original cash flow.

Chapter 6 Solutions

1. NPV of cash flow of existing contracts:

End of year	Cash flow	Discount factor at 13%	Present value
0	−15,000	1.0000	−15,000.0
1	6,000	0.8850	5,310.0
2	8,000	0.7832	6,265.6
3	10,000	0.6931	6,931.0
NPV			3,506.6

Expected cash flow of new contract:

End of year	Cash flow
0	−8,500
1	4,000
2	4,000
3	4,000

As the new project will reduce the cash flows from the existing contracts and is also dependent on the initial investment, the new project should be evaluated together with the current contracts.

NPV of incremental cash flow:

End of year	Cash flow	Discount factor at 13%	Present value
0	−15,000 − 8,500 = −23,500	1.0	−23,500.0
1	6,000 + 4,000 − 800 = 9,200	0.8850	8,142.0
2	8,000 + 4,000 − 800 = 11,200	0.7832	8,771.8
3	10,000 + 4,000 − 800 = 13,200	0.6931	9,148.9
NPV			2,562.7

Mr. Jay should not take the new contract as it reduces the NPV of his current contracts from $3,506.6 to $2,562.7 for the new combination of contracts; he has also to spend more of his spare time on this new contract.

2. Cost to company of producing 20,000 units = $64,000
Cost to company of buying 20,000 units = $60,000
Cash flows from decision to buy from suppliers:

End of year	0	1	2	3	4	5
Cost saving		4,000	4,000	4,000	4,000	4,000
Tax on cost savings at 46%		−1,840	−1,840	−1,840	−1,840	−1,840
Inventory	−10,000					10,000
Sale of machine	5,000					
Tax on sale	−2,300					
Net incremental cash flow	−7,300	2,160	2,160	2,160	2,160	12,160

NPV at 20% = −7,300 + 2,160(2.5887) + 12,160(0.4019)
= $3,178.7

Subcontracting is cheaper.

It has been assumed that the discount rate of 20 percent is a good approximation of the rate of return required for this project, given the company's required rate of return from the product (i.e., that there is no increased risk from using an outside supplier). If the risk of manufacturing is not the same as that of subcontracting, the two decisions must be evaluated with different discount rates.

It would be useful to determine why subcontracting is cheaper than manufacture. It may be that the subcontractor does not have a cost advantage but is lowering its price only temporarily.

4. Cash flow expected from adapting machine:

End of year	0	1	2	3	4	5	6	7	8
Capital expenditure and cost saving	−5,000	1,500.0	1,500.0	1,800.0	1,800.0	1,800.0	1,800.0	1,800.0	1,800.0
Depreciation*		625.0	625.0	625.0	625.0	625.0	625.0	625.0	625.0
Tax on cost saving minus depreciation		−402.5	−402.5	−540.5	−540.5	−540.5	−540.5	−540.5	−540.5
Net cash flow	−5,000	1,097.5	1,097.5	1,259.5	1,259.5	1,259.5	1,259.5	1,259.5	1,259.5

*Depreciation = 5,000/8 = 625

NPV of incremental cash flows

$$= -5,000 + 1,097.5(1.7355) + 1,259.5(5.3349 - 1.7355)$$
$$= 1,438.1$$

The cost savings make it worthwhile to spend \$5,000 to adapt the machine.

6. Opportunity cost of keeping the equipment = \$60,000

NPV of cash flow if company continues producing X:

End of year	Cash flow	Discount factor at 16%	Present value
0	−60,000	1.0	−60,000.0
1	35,000	0.8621	30,173.5
2	25,000	0.7432	18,580.0
3	10,000	0.6407	6,407.0
NPV			−4839.5

The company should sell the equipment to the competitor, as continuing to produce X results in a negative NPV.

8. Schedule of operating and maintenance costs and scrap values:

End of year	0	1	2	3	4	5	6
Cost	50,000						
Operating cost		12,000	14,400	17,280	20,736	26,957	35,044
Scrap value				(10,000)	(7,500)	(5,625)	(4,219)

Present value of all costs if equipment is scrapped:

End of year	Discount factor at 15%	Costs if scrapped at end of:			
		3 years	4 years	5 years	6 years
0	1.0000	50,000	50,000	50,000	50,000
1	0.8696	12,000	12,000	12,000	12,000
2	0.7561	14,400	14,400	14,400	14,400
3	0.6575	17,280–10,000	17,280	17,280	17,280
4	0.5717	—	20,736–7,500	20,736	20,736
5	0.4972	—	—	26,957–5,625	26,957
6	0.4323	—	—	—	35,044–4,219
Present value of total costs		76,109.6	90,251.6	105,145.7	121,268.1

Obviously, the present value of total costs increases as the life of the equipment increases. The following equation determining the equivalent annual costs will make them comparable:

Present Value of Cost = Equivalent Annual Cost
$$\times \text{(Annuity Factor for } n \text{ years at 15\%)}$$

$$\text{Equivalent Annual Cost} = \frac{\text{Present Value of Cost}}{\text{Annuity Factor}}$$

Therefore,

$C_3 = 76,109.6/2.2832 = 33,334.6$
$C_4 = 90,251.6/2.8550 = 31,611.8$
$C_5 = 105,145.7/3.3522 = 31,366.2$
$C_6 = 121,268.1/3.7845 = 32,043.4$

The lowest equivalent annual cost occurs for a machine that is to be scrapped in the fifth year, so the company should plan to replace the units at the end of the fifth year. The NPV of the decision to invest in these five units should be based on a five-year life and the cash flows associated with this time period.

9. (a) Depreciation on straight-line basis = 600/5 = 120

From the equation in Chapter 6,

$$PV\,[(p - v)Q(1 - T) + TD - F(1 - T)] - I = 0$$

The cash flows $[(p - v)Q(1 - T) + TD - F(1 - T)]$ for each year are as follows (where p = break-even price):

End of year	Cash flows
0	−600
1	$(p - 8.0)$ 80(1 − .46) + (.46 × 120) − 30(1 − .46)
2	$(p - 7.5)$ 90(1 − .46) + (.46 × 120) − 30(1 − .46)
3	$(p - 7.0)$ 100(1 − .46) + (.46 × 120) − 40(1 − .46)
4	$(p - 6.0)$ 80(1 − .46) + (.46 × 120) − 40(1 − .46)
5	$(p - 6.0)$ 60(1 − .46) + (.46 × 120) − 40(1 − .46)

These cash flows reduce to:

End of year	Cash flows
0	−600
1	$43.2p - 345.6 + 55.2 - 16.2 = 43.2p - 306.6$
2	$48.6p - 364.5 + 55.2 - 16.2 = 48.6p - 325.5$
3	$54.0p - 378.0 + 55.2 - 21.6 = 54.0p - 344.4$
4	$43.2p - 259.2 + 55.2 - 21.6 = 43.2p - 225.6$
5	$32.4p - 194.4 + 55.2 - 21.6 = 32.4p - 160.8$

Discount the cash flows at 25%:

End of year	Cash flow	Discount factor	Present value
0	− 600	1.0000	− 600
1	$43.2p - 306.6$	0.8000	$34.56p$ − 245.280
2	$48.6p - 325.5$	0.6400	$31.104p$ − 208.320
3	$54.0p - 344.4$	0.5120	$27.648p$ − 176.333
4	$43.2p - 225.6$	0.4096	$17.695p$ − 92.406
5	$32.4p - 160.8$	0.3277	$10.617p$ − 52.694
Net present value			$121.624p$ − 1,375.033

To get the break-even point, NPV = 0

$$121.624p - 1,375.033 = 0$$

$$p = \$11.306$$

The price in the first three years (before competitors enter the market) will be $(11.31 \times 1.2) = \$13.57$, and $(11.31 \times 1.1) = \$12.44$ in the last two years.

(b) From $p' \times Q (1 - T)/(1 + r)^n$, calculate the present values of the incremental cash flow.

$p' = $ price charged $-$ break-even price

Price differences and calculation of NPV:

End of year	Price difference	Incremental cash flow × discount factor	Present value
1	2.26	(2.26)(80) (1 − .46) 0.8000	78.106
2	2.26	(2.26)(90) (1 − .46) 0.6400	70.295
3	2.26	(2.26)(100)(1 − .46) 0.5120	62.484
4	1.13	(1.13)(80) (1 − .46) 0.4096	19.995
5	1.13	(1.13)(60) (1 − .46) 0.3277	11.998
Net present value			242.878

The net present value from the investment of $600 is $242.88. This represents a substantial return because of the unique advantage in being first in the market, and the inability of competitors to sell the product until the fourth year.

(c) The ACRS depreciation will be less beneficial to the company than the straight-line policy above. More tax is paid in the first year as the tax shield (15% depreciation under ACRS when compared to 20% straight-line depreciation) is lower. The slightly higher tax shields in later years under ACRS are less valuable when discounted back to year 0. Effectively, the NPV of the project will be reduced slightly.

Chapter 7 Solutions

1. From Fisher's proposition,

    (1 + Nominal Rate of Interest)

    $$= (1 + \text{Real Rate of Interest})(1 + \text{Expected Rate of Inflation})$$

    Nominal Interest Rate $= (1 + 0.02)(1 + 0.08) - 1$

    $$= 0.1016 \text{ or } 10.16\%$$

2. From Fisher's proposition,
    Required Nominal Rate of Interest
    $$= (1 + 0.01)(1 + 0.15) - 1$$

    $$= 1.1615 - 1.0$$

    $$= 0.1615 \text{ or } 16.15\%$$

    It is possible to borrow at the nominal rate of interest of 12 percent and to invest the proceeds in real assets expected to increase in nominal value 15 percent annually. Increased borrowing would push interest rates up until they fully reflect the expected inflation rate and the required real rate of interest, that is, about 16 percent.

4. As the asset is fully depreciated after five years, the disposal proceeds of $100 \times (1.08)^5$ are fully taxable. Assuming that the net proceeds are taxed at 46 percent, the residual value net of taxes $= \$146.93(1 - 0.46)$
    $$= \$79.34$$
    Present value of residual value discounted at 9 percent $= \$79.34$
    $$\times 0.6499$$
    $$= \$51.56$$

5.

End of year	0	1	2	3	4	5
(a) FIFO						
Economic value of inventory used		550.00	605.00	665.50	732.05	805.26
Value charged to cost of goods sold		500.00	550.00	605.00	665.50	732.05
FIFO stock gain		50.00	55.00	60.50	66.55	73.21
Federal and state taxes at 46%		−23.00	−25.30	−27.83	−30.61	−33.68
Discount factor at 19%		0.8403	0.7062	0.5934	0.4987	0.4190
Present value		−19.33	−17.87	−16.51	−15.27	−14.11
Present value of taxes paid = −$83.09						

(b) **LIFO**

Economic value of inventory used	550.00	605.00	665.50	732.05	805.26
Value charged to cost of goods sold	550.00	605.00	665.50	732.05	500.00
LIFO stock gain	0	0	0	0	305.26
Federal and state taxes at 46%					−140.42
Discount factor at 19%					0.41905

Present value of taxes paid = −$58.84, which is lower than when FIFO is used.

6. Compute the real required rate of return:

$$(1 + R) = (1 + r)(1 + 1)$$

$$(1 + 0.19) = (1 + r)(1 + 0.10)$$

$$(1 + r) = \frac{1.19}{1.10} = 1.0818$$

Real required rate of return, $r = 1.0818 - 1 = 0.0818$, or 8.18%. Note: The discount factor for 8.18 percent is not given in the Appendix but can easily be calculated.

End of year	Discount factor at 8.18%
1	$1.0/(1 + 0.0818) = 0.92439$
2	$1.0/(1 + 0.0818)^2 = 0.85449$
3	$1.0/(1 + 0.0818)^3 = 0.78988$
4	$1.0/(1 + 0.0818)^4 = 0.73015$

Discount real cash flows at the real required rate of 8.18%:

$$NPV = -1,500.00 + 450.00(0.92439) + 600.00(0.85449) +$$
$$750.00(0.78988) + 500.00 (0.73015)$$
$$= \$386.15$$

Adjust cash flows for inflation of 10 percent:

End of year	0	1	2	3	4
Cash flow	−1,500	$450(1.1)$	$600(1.1)^2$	$750(1.1)^3$	$500(1.1)^4$
		= 495.00	= 726.00	= 998.25	= 732.05

Discount nominal cash flows at the nominal required rate of 19 percent

$$NPV = -1,500.00 + 495.00(0.84034) + 726.00(0.70616)$$
$$+ 998.25(0.59342) + 732.05(0.49867)$$
$$= \$386.07$$

The NPVs for each method are only approximately equal because of rounding. If the company paid taxes, the two results would be very different.

9. Cash flows from inflated sales and costs:

End of year	0	1	2	3	4	5
Sales	—	127,680	156,957	193,880	160,302	160,373
Operating costs	—	−25,080	−30,280	−36,736	−29,831	−29,311
Labor cost	—	−8,512	−10,788	−12,644	−14,162	−14,099
Other costs	−20,000	−5,500	—	—	—	−6,442
Depreciation		−50,000	−40,000	−30,000	−20,000	−10,000
Before-tax profit	−20,000	38,588	75,889	114,500	96,309	100,521
Tax at 46%	9,200	−17,750	−34,909	−52,670	−44,302	−46,240
Profit after-tax	−10,800	20,838	40,980	61,830	52,007	54,281
Inventories	0	−6,270	−7,570	−9,184	−7,320	0

Cash flows:

End of year	0	1	2	3	4	5
Capital investment	−160,000					10,000
Inventories	0	−6,270	−7,570	−9,184	−7,320	0
After-tax cash flow from operations	−10,800	70,838	80,980	91,830	72,007	64,281
Net cash flow	−170,800	64,568	73,410	82,646	64,687	74,281
Discount factor	1.00000	0.83333	0.69444	0.57870	0.48225	0.40188
Net present value = $42,860						

The economic rents available in this new product market make it worthwhile for the company to invest in this project, which has an NPV of $42,860 for an investment of $160,000.

$$\text{Profitability index} = (42,860 + 160,000)/160,000$$
$$= 1.27$$

10. Real cash flows for project (millions of dollars):

End of year	0	1	2	3	4	5
Capital expenditure	−150		−200			
Labor cost		−50	−50	−50	−50	−50
Material and other costs		−100	−100	−100	−100	−100

Expected price increases:

Capital expenditure $\quad = 12\%$
Labor costs $\qquad\qquad = 15\%$
Material and other costs $= 10\%$ for first two years and 13% for last three years

Expected general rate of inflation $= 12\%$

Real rate of return for company $= 8\%$

Nominal rate of return $= (1 + 0.12)(1 + 0.08) − 1$
$\qquad\qquad\qquad\qquad = 1.2096 − 1$
$\qquad\qquad\qquad\qquad = 0.2096$ or 20.96%

Nominal cash flows (millions of dollars):

End of year	0	1	2	3	4	5
Capital expenditure	−150.00		−250.88			
Labor cost		−57.50	−66.13	−76.04	−87.45	−100.57
Material and other costs		−110.00	−121.00	−136.73	−154.50	−174.59
Total cost	−150.00	−167.50	−438.01	−212.77	−241.95	−275.16
Discount factor at 12%	1.00000	0.89286	0.79719	0.71178	0.63552	0.56743
Cash flow deflated by inflation rate	−150.00	−149.55	−349.18	−151.45	−153.76	−156.13
Discount factor at 8%	1.00000	0.92593	0.85734	0.79383	0.73503	0.68058
Present value (at real rate of return of 8%)	−150.00	−138.48	−299.36	−120.22	−113.02	−106.26
NPV	−927.34					

The same present values can be calculated by discounting the nominal cash flows at the nominal rate of 20.96 percent.

To break even, the present value of the annual rental over fifty years should equal the present value of the costs of construction (i.e., $927.34 million).

If R is the annual revenue (in real terms) to be received, starting from year 6, the annual rental over fifty years can, as an approximation, be treated as a perpetuity.

$$\text{Present value of rentals} = \frac{R}{0.08} \times (1.08)^{-5} = 8.50729R$$

For break-even:

$$8.50729R = \$927.34 \text{ million}$$

$$R = \$109.005 \text{ million}$$

Annual rental for building in real terms, r, can be calculated as follows:

$$(50 \times 0.6 \times 1.5r) + (50 \times 0.4 \times r) = \$109.005 \text{ million}$$

$$r = \$1.677 \text{ million}$$

Annual rental for basic buildings should be $1.677 million and rental for larger buildings should be $2.516 million.

Treating the rentals as a fifty-year annuity, the formula above becomes,

$$\text{Present Value of Rentals} = \left[\frac{R}{0.08}\left(1 - \frac{1}{(1.08)^{50}} \right) \right] \times (1.08)^{-5}$$

This increases the required rentals by over 2 percent.

Chapter 8 Solutions

1. First, calculate the mean return, then the variance, using the equations:

$$R_i = \frac{1}{n} \sum_{t=1}^{n} R_{i,t}$$

$$s_i^2 = \frac{1}{n-1} \sum_{t=1}^{n} (R_{i,t} - R_i)^2$$

Observations, t	$R_{i,t}$	$(R_{i,t} - R_i)$	$(R_{i,t} - R_i)^2$
1	1.08	1.08 − 0.674	0.1648
2	1.43	1.43 − 0.674	0.5715
3	0.76	0.76 − 0.674	0.0074
4	−1.80	−1.80 − 0.674	6.1207
5	−0.54	−0.54 − 0.674	1.4738
6	2.20	2.20 − 0.674	2.3287
7	0.84	0.84 − 0.674	0.0276
8	−0.36	−0.36 − 0.674	1.0692
9	1.24	1.24 − 0.674	0.3204
10	1.29	1.29 − 0.674	0.3795
11	0.88	0.88 − 0.674	0.0424
12	1.07	1.07 − 0.674	0.1568
	8.09		12.6628

Mean return $R = R_{i,t}/n = 8.09/12 = 0.674$

$$\text{Variance} = \frac{1}{n-1} \sum_{t=1}^{n} (R_{i,t} - R_i)^2 = \frac{1}{12-1} (12.6628) = 1.1512$$

Standard deviation $= \sqrt{1.1512} = 1.0729$

3. If funds are invested equally in the two securities, the expected return of the portfolio $= (0.10 + 0.12)/2$
$$= 0.11 \text{ or } 11\%$$

Variance of portfolio $= (x_1s_1)^2 + (x_2s_2)^2 + 2r_{1,2}(x_1s_1)(x_2s_2)$

$x_1, x_2 =$ proportions of portfolio invested in securities 1 and 2, respectively

$s_1, s_2 =$ standard deviations of returns on securities 1 and 2, respectively

$r_{1,2} =$ correlation coefficient

Variance $= (0.5 \times 0.3)^2 + (0.5 \times 0.4)^2 + 2(0.2)(0.5 \times 0.3)(0.5 \times 0.4)$

$$= 0.0745$$

Standard deviation, or risk of portfolio $= \sqrt{0.0745} = 0.273$ or 27.3%
4. The market return is obtained by adding the risk premium to the risk-free interest rate.

Expected return on portfolio = $[(0.05 + 0.07) + (0.08 + 0.10)]/2$

$$= 0.15 \text{ or } 15\%$$

Standard deviation = $\sqrt{\text{Variance of portfolio}}$

$$= \sqrt{(x_1 s_1)^2 + (x_2 s_2)^2 + 2r_{1,2}(x_1 s_1)(x_2 s_2)}$$

$$= \sqrt{(0.5 \times 0.2)^2 + (0.5 \times 0.5)^2 + 2(0.3)(0.5 \times 0.2)(0.5 \times 0.5)}$$

$$= \sqrt{0.0875}$$

$$= 0.2958$$

Standard deviation = 29.6%

The expected rate of return on the portfolio is exactly midway between the expected rate of return on each fund, but the standard deviation of 29.6 percent is less than midway (35 percent) between the two standard deviations. This is because the correlation between each fund's returns is less than 1.00.

6. Standard deviation of returns on SME stock = 0.75
Standard deviation of returns on market index = 0.25
Standard deviation of returns on mutual fund = 0.30
Correlation between returns on SME stock and the market = 0.15
Correlation between returns on mutual fund and the market = 0.30
Correlation between returns on SME stock and on mutual fund = 0.30

We can use the equations $\beta_i = \dfrac{c_{i,M}}{s_M^2}$, where $c_{i,M}$ = covariance, s_M^2 = variance of returns on the market portfolio, and $c_{i,M} = r_{i,M} s_i s_M$, where $r_{i,M}$ = correlation between returns on assets i and m

(a) Value of beta for mutual fund = $\dfrac{0.30 \times 0.30 \times 0.25}{(0.25)^2} = 0.36$

   Value of beta for SME stock = $\dfrac{0.15 \times 0.75 \times 0.25}{(0.25)^2} = 0.45$

(b) Value of beta for mutual fund if 5 percent of its assets are invested in SME stock

   $\beta_{MF} = (0.05 \times 0.45) + (0.95 \times 0.36)$

   $= 0.0225 + 0.342$

   $= 0.3645$

(c) Standard deviation of new portfolio =

$$s_{MF} = \sqrt{(0.05 \times 0.75)^2 + (0.95 \times 0.30)^2 + 2(0.30)(0.05 \times 0.75)(0.95 \times 0.30)}$$

$$= 0.2984$$

Standard deviation of the mutual fund (if 5 percent of its assets are invested in SME stock) is 29.8 percent.

8. The securities are A, B, and C, $\beta_A = 1.0$, $\beta_B = 0.5$, and $\beta_C = 0.8$ and the variance on the market portfolio = 0.0625.

(a) From the equation $\beta_i = \dfrac{c_{i,M}}{s_M^2}$ we can calculate the covariance $c_{i,M}$ between the security i and the market:

$$c_{A,M} = \beta_A \times s_M^2 = 1.0 \times 0.0625 = 0.0625$$

$$c_{B,M} = \beta_B \times s_M^2 = 0.5 \times 0.0625 = 0.03125$$

$$c_{C,M} = \beta_C \times s_M^2 = 0.8 \times 0.0625 = 0.05$$

(b) The beta value of a portfolio composed equally of the three securities

$$\beta_p = (1.0 + 0.5 + 0.8)/3$$

$$= 0.7667$$

(c) The covariance between the portfolio's returns and the market returns can be calculated by:

$$c_{p,M} = x_1 c_{1,M} + x_2 c_{2,M} + \cdots + x_n c_{n,M}$$

$$= (1/3) \times 0.0625 + (1/3) \times 0.03125 + (1/3) \times 0.05$$

$$= 0.0479$$

The covariance can also be calculated by using the equation,

$$c_{p,M} = \beta_p \times s_M^2$$

$$= 0.7667 \times 0.0625$$

$$= 0.0479$$

9. Risk–free rate = 0.10

Risk premium on market = 0.0825

(a) Use the equation, $\beta_p = x_1\beta_1 + x_2\beta_2 + \cdots + x_N\beta_N$

   We know that there is virtually no risk associated with Treasury bills, so $\beta_{TB} = 0.0$. If investor A invests x in Treasury bills,

$$0.08 = x\,(0.0) + (1 - x)(1.2)$$

$$x = \frac{1.2 - 0.80}{1.2}$$

$$= 0.3333$$

The investor should invest one-third of his funds in Treasury bills and two-thirds in the mutual fund in order to limit portfolio beta to 0.80.

   Calculate the portfolio returns:

$$R_p = xR_f + (1 - x)R_{MF}$$

$$R_{MF} = R_f + \beta_{MF}(E(\tilde{R}_M) - R_f)$$

$$= 0.10 + 1.2\,(0.0825)$$

$$= 0.199$$

$$R_p = (1/3 \times 0.10) + (2/3 \times 0.199)$$

$$= 0.0333 + 0.1327$$

$$= 0.166$$

The expected return from the portfolio (with a beta of 0.80) is 16.6 percent.

(b) If she borrows x and assuming β of debt = 0.0 the weighted average beta is,

$$1.5 = x(0.0) + (1 - x)(1.0)$$

$$1.5 = 1.0 - x$$

$$x = -0.5$$

She should borrow $5,000 to add to her $10,000 invested in the mutual fund to maximize her expected return, subject to the beta of her portfolio being 1.5.

Calculate the returns from her portfolio, assuming that she can borrow at the risk-free rate of 10 percent.

$$R_{M,F} = 0.10 + 1.0(0.0825)$$

$$= 0.1825$$

$$R_p = (-1/2 \times 0.10) + (3/2 \times 0.1825)$$

$$= 0.22375$$

The expected return on her portfolio (with a beta of 1.50) is 22.4 percent.

Chapter 9 Solutions

1. As investment in an average common stock is risky when compared to a risk-free asset such as a ninety-day Treasury bill, the required rate of return for such an investment must be larger than for a Treasury bill.

   Shareholders' Required Rate of Return = Risk-free Rate of Interest
   + Risk Premium

   The risk-free rate of interest is 10 percent; we have to estimate the risk premium. Using Ibbotson and Sinquefield's estimate for the risk premium of 8.3 percent based on fifty-six years' data, the required rate of return is $(0.10 + 0.083) = 0.183$, or 18.3 percent.

2. From Gordon's model

$$R = \frac{D_1}{P_0} + g$$

where P_0 is the initial price

D_1 is the dividend in year 1

g is the growth rate of dividends

Assuming that the growth rate g is constant for every future period, the expected average growth rate

$$g = R - \frac{D_1}{P_0}$$

$$= 0.15 - 0.05$$

$$= 0.10 \text{ or } 10\%$$

4. To estimate the shareholders' required rate of return of the common stock of U.S. Goldmines, use the equation:

$$\begin{array}{c} \text{Required Rate} \\ \text{of Return} \end{array} = \begin{array}{c} \text{Risk-free Rate} \\ \text{of Interest} \end{array} + \begin{array}{c} \beta(\text{Expected Risk Premium} \\ \text{on Market Portfolio}) \end{array}$$

Risk-free rate   = 0.05

Beta coefficient = 0.50

Using the historical estimates of the risk premium,

Required Rate of Return = 0.05 + 0.5(0.083)

$$= 0.0915, \text{ or } 9.15\%$$

5. If we assume that the market risk premium is in the region of 8.3 percent (from the study of Ibbotson and Sinquefield), the required rates of return for companies A and B can be calculated using the equation:

$$\begin{array}{c} \text{Required Rate} \\ \text{of Return} \end{array} = \begin{array}{c} \text{Risk-free Rate} \\ \text{of Interest} \end{array} + \begin{array}{c} \beta(\text{Expected Risk Premium} \\ \text{on Market Portfolio}) \end{array}$$

For company A,

Required Rate of Return = 0.10 + 1.20(0.083)

$$= 0.1996, \text{ or } 19.96\%$$

As the only difference between the companies is the value of beta, the difference between their required rates of return will be:

(Difference Between Betas) × (Risk Premium)

Difference in Required Rates of Return = (1.20 − 0.90)(0.083)

$$= 0.0249, \text{ or } 2.49\%$$

7. Given that the common stock of Advanced Projects, Inc., is of average risk, we can assume that the beta of the common stock (and therefore of the company, as it is all-equity financed) is about 1.0. We are told that

Asset A has twice the systematic risk as Asset B. Given that:

$$\frac{\text{Beta of}}{\text{Company}} = \frac{\text{Beta of}}{\text{Asset A}} \times \left(\frac{PV_A}{PV_A + PV_B}\right) \times \frac{\text{Beta of}}{\text{Asset B}} \left(\frac{PV_B}{PV_A + PV_B}\right)$$

$$1.0 = 2 \times \text{Beta of Asset B} \times (0.5) + \text{Beta of Asset B} \times (0.5)$$

$$\text{Beta of Asset B} = \frac{1.0}{1.5} = 0.667$$

$$\text{Beta of Asset A} = 2 \times \text{Beta of Asset B} = 2 \times 0.667 = 1.334$$

Assuming that the expected risk premium on the market portfolio is 8.3 percent,

$$\text{Required Rate of Return on Asset A} = 0.10 + (1.334 \times 0.083)$$

$$= 0.2107, \text{ or } 21.07\%$$

$$\text{Required Rate of Return on Asset B} = 0.10 + (0.667 \times 0.083)$$

$$= 0.1554, \text{ or } 15.54\%$$

9. As the money raised from the debt issue will be used for replacement of existing assets, there will be no change in the risk of the assets. That is, the risk of the assets should remain the same as before the issue of bonds, at 0.80.

   If we assume that beta of debt = 0.0, from the equation

$$\text{Asset Beta} = \text{Equity Beta} \left(\frac{E}{B + E}\right) + \text{Debt Beta} \left(\frac{B}{B + E}\right)$$

we can estimate the beta for the stock of the company after the bond issue. If we assume that the market value of the bonds is equal to par value, then:

$$0.80 = \text{Equity Beta} \left(\frac{100}{150}\right) + 0.0 \left(\frac{50}{150}\right)$$

$$0.80 = 0.6667 \times \text{Equity Beta}$$

$$\text{Equity Beta} = \frac{0.80}{0.6667}$$

$$= 1.2$$

The beta value of the equity is changed from 0.8 to 1.2 by the issue of the $50 million long-term debt. As we stated previously, the asset beta remains the same.

11. Market Value of Debt   = (40 × 85/100) million
                                    = $34 million

    Market Value of Equity   = $(5 × 36) million
                                    = $180 million

    Total Value of Company = $(34 + 180) million
                                    = $214 million

As the quoted beta represents the equity beta, we must calculate the asset beta.

Assuming the beta of Elban's debt equals 0, and using the equation:

$$\text{Asset Beta} = \text{Equity Beta} \left(\frac{E}{B + E}\right) + \text{Debt Beta} \left(\frac{B}{B + E}\right)$$

$$= 1.32 \left(\frac{180}{214}\right) + 0.0 \left(\frac{34}{214}\right)$$

$$= 1.11$$

Chapter 10 Solutions

1. Calculate the beta value of the existing projects, assuming beta of debt = 0.

$$\beta_{\text{Assets}} = \left(\frac{\text{Equity}}{\text{Equity} + \text{Debt}}\right) \beta_{\text{Equity}} + \left(\frac{\text{Debt}}{\text{Equity} + \text{Debt}}\right) \beta_{\text{Debt}}$$

$$\beta_{\text{Assets}} = \left(\frac{4}{1 + 4}\right) \times 1.36$$

$$= 1.088$$

The beta of the new project = 1.5 × 1.088

$$= 1.632$$

Calculate the required rate of return for the new project.

$$R_p = R_f + \beta_p(E(\tilde{R}_M) - R_f)$$

$$= 0.08 + 1.632\,(0.10)$$

$$= 0.2432 \text{ or } 24.3\%$$

2.

Project	β Value	Expected Return (%)
A	0.5	10.0
B	0.7	12.5
C	1.5	14.0

(a) Average of β for the 3 projects $= (0.5 + 0.7 + 1.5)/3$

$$= 0.9$$

Required rate of return $= R_f + \beta(E(\tilde{R}_M) - R_f)$

$$= 0.05 + 0.9\,(0.09)$$

$$= 0.131$$

If a single test discount rate of 13.1 percent is used, projects A and B would be rejected, and C would be accepted. This practice will not permit net present value maximization.

(b) The estimated required rate of return for each project is:

Project	β Value	Required rate
A	0.5	0.05 + 0.5(0.09) = 0.095
B	0.7	0.05 + 0.7(0.09) = 0.113
C	1.5	0.05 + 1.5(0.09) = 0.185

Projects A and B should be accepted as the expected returns are higher than the required rates of return (i.e., they are positive NPV projects); project C should be rejected as the expected return is much lower than the required return (for its risk level).

(c) These results show that a wrong decision is made if a single required rate of return is used; that is, a high-risk unprofitable project (C) is accepted, and the net present value of the firm is not maximized.

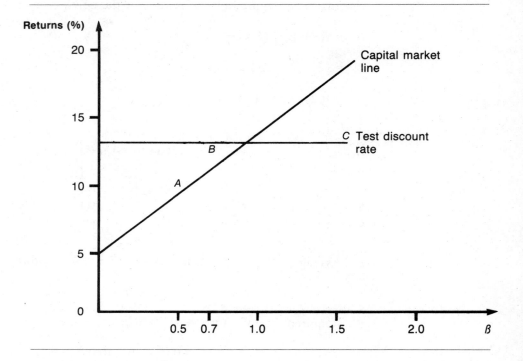

(d) If a company persists in accepting type-C investments, it will be making losses in the long run.

3. The beta value of debt is normally assumed to be 0 unless default risk is present.

$$\beta_{\text{Asset}} = \left(\frac{\text{Equity}}{\text{Equity} + \text{Debt}}\right) \beta_{\text{Equity}} + \left(\frac{\text{Debt}}{\text{Equity} + \text{Debt}}\right) \beta_{\text{Debt}}$$

On a book value basis,

$$\beta_{\text{Asset}} = \left(\frac{9.5}{9.5 + 1.5}\right) \times 1.2 + \left(\frac{1.5}{9.5 + 1.5}\right) \times 0.0$$

$$= 1.036$$

On a market value basis,

$$\beta_{\text{Asset}} = \left(\frac{17.2}{17.2 + 1.3}\right) \times 1.2 + \left(\frac{1.3}{17.2 + 1.3}\right) \times 0.0$$

$$= 1.116$$

Beta is a market value measure of risk, so the calculations used in ungearing β should be based on market values of equity and debt, and thus the asset β of 1.116 is the right one to use.

5. With the information provided, calculate the operating leverage factor. Treating the cash flows as perpetuities discounted at the same discount rate (which therefore cancels),

Operating Leverage
 Factor

$$= \frac{\text{Revenue} - \text{Variable Costs}}{\text{Revenue} - \text{Variable Costs} - \text{Fixed Operating Expenditure}}$$

$$\text{Operating Leverage Factor for A} = \frac{24.26 - 15.58}{24.26 - 15.58 - 5.32}$$

$$= \frac{8.68}{3.36} = 2.58$$

$$\text{Operating Leverage Factor for B} = \frac{24.26 - 17.84}{24.26 - 17.84 - 3.20}$$

$$= \frac{6.42}{3.22} = 1.99$$

Equipment B has a slightly lower cash flow but a much lower operating leverage factor compared to equipment A; B has higher variable operating costs but lower fixed operating expenditures. As the company is not expecting any large increases in production, the company might prefer to invest in B. It would be preferable to choose equipment A if the company were expecting increased production as it has lower variable costs, and the higher fixed operating expenditures can be absorbed by a larger number of units of production. However, should demand fall, B is less risky because its fixed operating expenditure is lower.

7. From the break-even chart, the cash flow break-even point for Fixit is $200,000, i.e., when 100,000 units of Fixit are sold (revenue is $2 × 100,000). This is just sufficient to cover the fixed operating expenditure of $100,000 and variable costs ($1 × 100,000).

Operating Leverage
 Factor

$$= \frac{\text{Revenue} - \text{Variable Costs}}{\text{Revenue} - \text{Variable Costs} - \text{Fixed Operating Expenditure}}$$

$$= \frac{(150,000 \times 2) - (150,000 \times 1)}{300,000 - 150,000 - 100,000} = 3.0$$

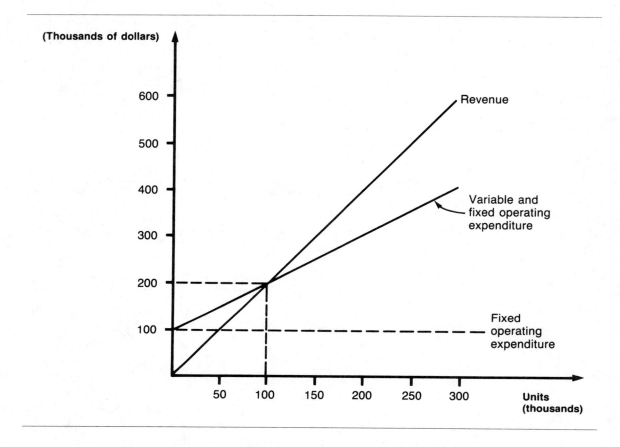

(b) If fixed operating expenditure increases to $150,000 per year, the operating leverage factor of Fixit is

$$\text{OLF} = \frac{\text{Revenue} - \text{Variable Costs}}{\text{Revenue} - \text{Variable Costs} - \text{Fixed Operating Expenditure}}$$

$$= \frac{(2 \times 200,000) - (1 \times 200,000)}{400,000 - 200,000 - 150,000} = 4.0$$

The operating leverage factor increases from 3.0 to 4.0 (or by 33 percent) because of the increase in fixed operating expenditure.

8. The company should accept the waste reduction project because it is of somewhat lower than average risk, yet the rate of return anticipated for the project is very near the average. The expected rate of return for the waste reduction project almost certainly is greater than the required rate of return for the project's risk class. The scale expansion project, on the

other hand, is relatively risky because it depends upon a larger market for the project, which might not materialize if economic conditions deteriorate. As the scale expansion project in this example promises very little extra return for its relatively large risk, it should not be accepted.

The expected rates of return for each project may be estimated more specifically by using the risk premium for each class.

9. Project risk classes are defined as follows:

A: Below-average risk
B: Average risk
C: Above-average risk
D: High risk

The projects may be classified as:

1. D
2. A or B
3. C
4. A or B
5. B
6. A or B
7. D
8. A
9. C (as result of research project is unknown)
10. D
11. D
12. D (as results of prospecting can be very uncertain)
13. A
14. A

In ambiguous cases such as 2 and 4 risk factors based on revenue sensitivity and relative operating leverage can be used to aid the choice of risk class.

12.
$$\alpha_t = \left(\frac{1 + R_f}{1 + R}\right)^t$$

(a) When the discount rate is 12 percent,

$$\alpha_1 = \left(\frac{1.04}{1.12}\right) = 0.9286$$

$$\alpha_2 = \left(\frac{1.04}{1.12}\right)^2 = 0.8622$$

$$\alpha_3 = \left(\frac{1.04}{1.12}\right)^3 = 0.8007$$

$$\alpha_4 = \left(\frac{1.04}{1.12}\right)^4 = 0.7435$$

(b) When the discount rate is 18 percent,

$$\alpha_1 = \left(\frac{1.04}{1.18}\right) = 0.8814$$

$$\alpha_2 = \left(\frac{1.04}{1.18}\right)^2 = 0.7768$$

$$\alpha_3 = \left(\frac{1.04}{1.18}\right)^3 = 0.6846$$

$$\alpha_4 = \left(\frac{1.04}{1.18}\right)^4 = 0.6034$$

The certainty equivalence method adjusts the cash flows for risk, while the CAPM adjusts the discount rate for risk. Once the certainty equivalence of a period's cash flow has been calculated, it is then discounted at the risk-free rate. If a constant risk-adjusted discount rate is used, risk is assumed to increase with time when this discount rate is used for all periods. We can say this because the corresponding certainty equivalence coefficients decline by the same proportion in each succeeding period.

Chapter 11 Solutions

1. Cost of investment = $1,000
   Value of portfolio at end of year = $1,350
   S & P Index has risen 30 percent during the same period

   (a) Return on Portfolio = $\dfrac{(1,350 - 1,000) + \text{Dividends}}{1,000}$

   Assuming no dividends were received, the return on the portfolio is 35 percent.
   This return can be compared to the 30 percent increase in the market index. If an electronics industry portfolio has a beta of 1.5, the performance of the portfolio should be $10 + 1.5\,(30 - 10) = 40\%$ (when the Standard & Poor's index has a β of 1.0). Therefore, the portfolio has not performed quite as well as expected.

   (b) The electronics industry is susceptible to economic cycles and other factors outside the control of management. Abnormally bad or good

performance may have occurred by chance. Using a longer time
period would help to reduce the effect of chance on the data.

2. (a) Assuming no residual value and using straight-line depreciation over
five years:

End of year	0	1	2	3	4	5
Cost	−1,000					
Depreciation		200	200	200	200	200
Book value at end of year	1,000	800	600	400	200	0
Cash flow	−1,000	335	335	335	335	335
PV of future cash flow at 20%	1,001.8	867.2	705.7	511.8	279.2	0

The economic value of the asset at the end of each year is higher than
the book value in each year. The book value is reduced each year by
a constant $200, whereas the economic value depends on changes in
the present value of the future cash flows. Accounting depreciation
is reducing the book value of the asset faster than economic depreciation is reducing its present value.

(b) The forecast ROCEs differ from the IRR of 20.08 percent because
straight-line depreciation differs from economic depreciation.

End of year	0	1	2	3	4	5
Cash flow		335	335	335	335	335
Accounting income		135	135	135	135	135
Book value	1,000	800	600	400	200	0
ROCE (%)		13.5	16.9	22.5	33.8	67.5

4. The IRR of the project cash flows is 20 percent.
   Calculate economic income

End of year	0	1	2	3	4	5
Cash flow	−5,000	1,200	1,500	1,800	2,168	2,168
Present value of cash flow at 20%	5,000.1	4,800.2	4,260.2	3,312.2	1,806.7	0
Change in present value (economic depreciation)		−199.9	−540.0	−948.0	−1,505.5	−1,806.7
Economic income		1,000.1	960.0	852.0	662.5	361.3
Economic ROCE (%)		20.0	20.0	20.0	20.0	20.0

The economic ROCE is 20 percent for each year. Note that the expected economic ROCE always equals the discount rate that is used to calculate the economic depreciation, except where economic depreciation is based on the cost of the asset and changes in secondhand values.

5. Calculate accounting ROCE

End of year	0	1	2	3	4	5	6
Net cash flow	−18,000	7,000	6,000	5,000	2,000	1,000	5,663
Depreciation		3,000	3,000	3,000	3,000	3,000	3,000
Book value of asset at end of year	18,000	15,000	12,000	9,000	6,000	3,000	0
Accounting income		4,000	3,000	2,000	−1,000	−2,000	2,663
Accounting ROCE (%)		22.2	20.0	16.7	−11.1	−33.3	88.8

Calculate economic ROCE

End of year	0	1	2	3	4	5	6
Net cash flow	−18,000	7,000	6,000	5,000	2,000	1,000	5,663
Economic value at 15%	18,000.4	13,700.4	9,755.5	6,218.8	5,151.6	4,924.3	0
Economic depreciation		4,300.0	3,944.9	3,536.7	1,067.2	227.3	4,924.3
Economic income		2,700.0	2,055.1	1,463.3	932.8	772.7	738.7
Economic ROCE (%)		15.0	15.0	15.0	15.0	15.0	15.0

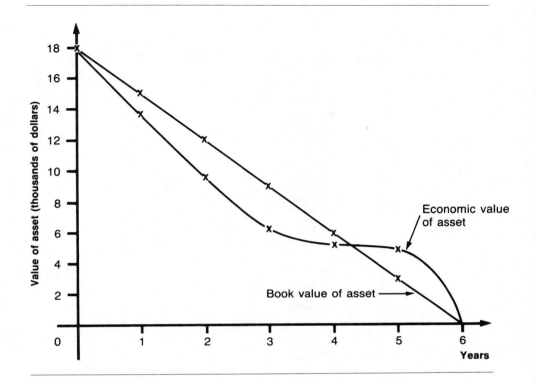

The difference between economic values and book values is due to the difference between economic and accounting depreciation.

The accounting rate of return ranges from -33.3 percent to 88.8 percent and cannot be used as a uniform measure of performance. A sum-of-the-years' digits depreciation policy will reduce the book value by larger amounts in the first few years and will be a closer approximation to the economic value of the asset than a straight-line policy, in this particular example.

7. (a) IRR $= 34.66\%$

Assume straight-line depreciation and no residual value or ITC for parts (b) to (d)

End of year	0	1	2	3
Cash flow	$-1,000$	587.0	587.0	587.0
Depreciation		333.3	333.3	333.4
Taxable income		253.7	253.7	253.6
Tax at 50%		126.85	126.85	126.8

(b) Cash flows after-tax   −1,000,   460.15,   460.15,   460.2.
(c) The after-tax IRR is 18.03 percent.

End of year	0	1	2	3
Cash flow	−1,000	587.0	587.0	587.0
Depreciation		333.3	333.3	333.4
Accounting income pre-tax		253.7	253.7	253.6
Book value at end of year	1,000	666.7	333.4	0.0
(d) Before-tax accounting ROCE (%)		25.4	38.1	76.1

End of year	0	1	2	3
Cash flow	−1,000	587.0	587.0	587.0
Accounting income after-tax		126.85	126.85	126.80
Book value at end of year	1,000	666.7	333.4	0.0
(e) After-tax accounting ROCE (%)		12.7	19.0	38.0

The before-tax ROCE ranges from 25.4 to 76.1 percent compared to the before-tax IRR of 34.66 percent. These are the target ROCEs which, if attained, will yield the before-tax IRR of 34.66 percent and (assuming that the company's taxpaying position does not change) will simultaneously yield the after-tax IRR of 18.03 percent.

10. Profit from sales = (430 − 100 − 167 − 100) × \$1,000
      = \$63,000 each year

Tax on profits each year = \$63,000 × 0.5
                      = \$31,500

Cash flows after-tax = \$163,000 − 31,500
                    = \$131,500

NPV of project cash flows at an after-tax discount rate of 5 percent to a competitor with the same costs would be,

= −\$800,000 + 131,500 (7.7217)
= + \$215,403.5

The NPV of Division X depends upon prices and the current market value of its assets. If the market value is less than $800,000, for example, its NPV would be greater than $215,403.5 given existing product prices. When the competitor enters the market, his break–even after–tax cash flow is only $800,000/7.7217 = $103,604. The corresponding break–even prices for the competitor could affect Division X's cash flow and NPV, if Division X cannot maintain its product price advantage.

Chapter 12 Solutions

1. If the serial correlation coefficient is positive 0.2, you would buy the security when its price is rising, because the price changes in the next period would be positively related to price changes in this period.

   If the coefficient is negative, however, price changes in a period tend to reverse changes in the preceding period; thus you would sell the security when the price is rising.

3. If the beta coefficient is 1.5, the security would tend to increase by 15 percent when the market increases by 10 percent. The actual security price change is 15 percent (13.80 − 12.00)/12.00. Since there are no abnormal returns, there is no incentive to buy or to sell the security. If the market is efficient, however, there is no incentive either to buy or sell the security even when there are abnormal returns.

5. (a) On average, the expected score of the second 500 trials is zero; the running total score is still expected to be +50 on average. The actual score will almost certainly be very different, however.

   (b) Share price changes follow a random walk. That is, changes in price are random and unrelated to past price changes. Forecasting the direction of a price change is similar to forecasting the outcome of flipping a coin—there is a 50 percent chance that you may be right, and a 50 percent chance that you may be wrong. Also, the outcome of one flip will not affect future outcomes, i.e., the outcomes are independent. This is why we describe price changes as being uncorrelated over time (i.e., serial correlation coefficient is equal to zero).

Chapter 13 Solutions

1. Valuation of equity and liabilities

Security	Number outstanding	Price	Value
Common stock	10,000,000	$16.50	$165,000,000
Preferred stock	1,000,000	5.50	5,500,000
Debentures	1,500,000	97.00	145,500,000
Market value of securities			316,000,000
Present value of accounts payable			18,200,000
Total value of equity and liabilities			$334,200,000

In order to take over the company, Swanning has to purchase the common stock, for which it would have to offer at least $165 million, or $16.50 per share. The acquiring company probably would have to pay a bid premium of at least 20 percent to acquire a sufficient shareholding to gain control.

3. Earnings attributable to common stockholders

$$= \text{Earnings after tax} - \text{minority interests} - \text{preferred dividends}$$
$$= \$115,000 - 5,000 - 2,500$$
$$= \$107,500$$

$$
\begin{aligned}
\text{Number of shares} &= 300,000/5 \\
&= 60,000 \\
\text{Earnings per share} &= 107,500/60,000 \\
&= \$1.79 \\
\text{Price-to-earnings ratio} &= 19.50/1.79 \\
&= 10.9
\end{aligned}
$$

5. Depreciation for each year $= \dfrac{\$10,000}{10} = \$1,000$

Income statement

Sales		$20,000
Less		
Cost of goods sold	17,000	
Depreciation	1,000	18,000
Profit for the year		2,000
Tax at 46%		920
Profit after-tax		$ 1,080

Analysis of free cash flow

Total receipts (sales)		$20,000
Cost of fixed asset	$10,000	
Cost of goods sold	17,000	
Tax	920	
Total expenditure		$27,920
Free cash flow (deficit)		$ (7,920)

7. Market value of building in five years' time

$$= \$10,000,000 \ (1.08)^5$$

$$= \$14,693,000$$

Written–down value of building in five years' time
$$= \$3,500,000 - 5 \times \$250,000$$
$$= \$2,250,000$$
Expected capital gains $= \$14,693,000 - \$2,250,000$
$$= \$12,443,000$$
Expected capital gains tax $= 0.28 \times \$12,443,000$
$$= \$3,484,000$$
Present value of capital gains tax $= \$3,484,000/(1.08)^5$
$$\simeq \$2,371,000$$
Present value of building to Jarvis Retail Co.
$$= \$10,000,000 - 2,371,000$$
$$= \$7,629,000$$

9. Assuming a risk premium on the market portfolio of 8.3 percent per year and a beta value of 0.8 on existing assets,

Required rate of return $= 0.10 + 0.8 \ (0.083)$

$$= 0.1664$$

To value the cash flows from existing assets, calculate the free cash flow for each year.

Free cash flow = After-tax earnings + depreciation − capital expenditure

Free cash flow $= \$100,000 + 100,000 - 100,000$
$$= \$100,000$$

If we assume this will continue as a perpetuity,

$$\text{PV of free cash flow} = \frac{\$100,000}{0.1664} = \$600,962$$

The present value of existing assets is greater than the book value of $500,000, but we have assumed optimistically that the profitability of existing products will not be diminished by future competition.

From the average profitability index of 1.33, we can calculate the NPV of the three new investments.

$$PI = (I + NPV)/I = (1 + 0.33)/1$$
$$NPV/I = 0.33$$

The expected payoffs from new investment are found as follows:

End of year	Capital budget (I) (thousands of dollars)	NPV = I × 0.33		Probability of outcome		Expected payoff (thousands of dollars)
1	100	33.0	×	0.75	=	24.75
2	150	49.5	×	0.50	=	24.75
3	100	33.0	×	0.25	=	8.25

The betas of the expected payoffs (NPVs) from the future new investments are given by

$$\frac{\text{Beta of}}{\text{NPV (payoffs)}} = \frac{(I + NPV)}{NPV} \times \frac{\text{Beta of}}{\text{project}} \times \frac{\text{Probability}}{\text{of investment}}$$

The discount rate for each future NPV is given by

$$\frac{\text{Required rate}}{\text{of return}} = \frac{\text{Risk-free}}{\text{rate}} + \frac{\text{Risk premium}}{\text{on market}} \times \frac{\text{Beta}}{\text{of NPV}}$$

$$= 0.10 \quad + 0.083 \quad\quad \times \text{Beta of NPV}$$

Therefore the discount rates for the future new investments are obtained as follows:

End of year	$\dfrac{I + NPV}{NPV}$	Beta of project	Probability of investment		Beta of NPV	Required rate of return
1	(1.33/0.33)	× 0.80	× 0.75	=	2.42	0.3009
2	(1.33/0.33)	× 0.80	× 0.50	=	1.61	0.2336
3	(1.33/0.33)	× 0.80	× 0.25	=	0.81	0.1672

The discounted present value of the new investment NPVs is therefore

$$\text{PV of new investments} = \left(\frac{24.75}{1.3009} + \frac{24.75}{(1.2336)^2} + \frac{8.25}{(1.1672)^3}\right) \times \$1,000$$

$$= \$40,477$$

Based on the above figures, the total economic value of Jims Company is $600,962 + 40,491 = $641,453.

11. Book value of machine = $50,000

Inventory and accounts receivable = Total assets − book value of machine

$$= 100,000 - 50,000$$

$$= \$50,000$$

As a new machine costs $300,000 now, the written-down replacement cost of the machine should be:

$$\text{WDRC} = \text{Current cost of asset} \times \left(1 - \frac{\text{Age of existing asset}}{\text{Economic life of asset}}\right)$$

$$= \$300,000 \times \left(1 - \frac{7}{10}\right)$$

$$= \$90,000$$

Value of total assets, assuming that the value of inventory and accounts receivable can be realized immediately for $50,000, is therefore $50,000 + 90,000 = $140,000.

Total liabilities of Dregs Company = $50,000 + 23,000 = $73,000

The net worth of the company is $140,000 − 73,000 = $67,000. In the absence of other information, Leak may be willing to pay up to $67,000 plus the value of goodwill if it wishes to buy all the equity of Dregs Company, Inc. An important assumption is that WDRC provides a better estimate of the secondhand value of the assets than the book value based on historic costs. Naturally, it would be better to have the market price for the secondhand machine and the present value of the future cash flows in existing uses. We could use the higher of the two values. In principle the receivables should be discounted for the period of credit given.

Chapter 14 Solutions

1. Assuming total production remains at 2 million units (the capacity of the new plant):

Cost savings = ($1.20 − 0.96) × 2,000,000

$$= \$480,000$$

Therefore, merger benefits in the amount of $480,000 will accrue to the new merged company in the form of savings of operating costs. This is likely to be distributed equally between the two companies as they are of the same size.

2. The market value of company Y's stock currently stands at

($50 × 5,000,000) = $250,000,000

The total merger benefits are:

($50,000,000 + 15,000,000 + 3,500,000 − 18,000,000) = $50,500,000.

The maximum price X should pay for Y's stock is $250,000,000 + 50,500,000 = $300,500,000 or $60.10 per share. The maximum premium would be $60.10 − 50.00 = $10.10 per share.

4. The cash flows associated with building the facilities are as follows (in millions of dollars).

End of year	1	2	3
Cost of building	−0.85	−0.42	−0.35
Forgone sales	−0.48	−0.36	−0.24
Total cash flow	−1.33	−0.78	−0.59
Discount factor at 15%	0.8696	0.7561	0.6575
Present value	−1.1566	−0.5898	−0.3879

Present value of building the facilities = −$2,134,300

Present value of buying the facilities = −$2,250,000

Therefore, the company should build the facilities as it saves $115,700 by doing so.

6. In the six months, the market index has risen 25 percent from 1,000 to 1,250. Given that the beta coefficient for the company equals 1.25, the expected price rise for the share over the last six months was

$$1.25 \times 0.25 = 0.3125, \text{ or } 31.25\%$$

and the expected share price at the end of six months (without bid prospects) was

$$\$50(1.0 + 0.3125) = \$65.625$$

The actual price is $90 and the likely bid premium being paid by the acquiring firm per share is:

$$(\$100 - 90) + (\$90 - 65.625) = \$100 - 65.625 = \$34.375$$

The bid premium is calculated by comparing the price paid with the expected price for the acquired share. However, this assumes that the difference between the actual price $90.00 and the expected price of $65.625 is due to anticipation of the bid. If the difference can be attributed to other favorable price-sensitive information (for example, unexpectedly good earnings), the premium would be only $100 − 90 = $10.

8. The following points should be among those considered in acquisition valuation:

The value of the acquisition as it exists now.

The cost and value of the merger benefits expected by the acquirer's management.

The alternatives to merging.

The price that will be adequate to gain control of the acquiree company.

The net present value of the expected merger benefits acts as an upper bound on the premium that should be paid over the value of the acquisition as it exists now. If there are alternatives to merging (e.g., to expand production by buying new machines if factory space is available in present circumstances), the difference between the NPV of the merger benefits and of the alternative opportunity provides the maximum bid premium.

As to the value of company B, management's claim that the bid should be $175 per share is not correct. The use of the average PE ratio of 7 for the industry is not appropriate, as company B is a small company that may not have the same risk and dividend growth expectations as the other companies in the industry. You can illustrate this point using Gordon's model.

9. Assuming no transactions costs are incurred, the market value of the combined company should be:

$6,540,000 + 14,230,000 + 3,600,000 = $24,370,000

Assuming that the systematic risk of the new company is a value-weighted average of its constituent parts, the beta of the combined company will be:

$$\frac{6.54}{24.37}(1.1) + \frac{14.23}{24.37}(0.9) + \frac{3.6}{24.37}(1.3)$$

$$= 0.2952 + 0.5255 + 0.1920$$

$$= 1.01$$

Chapter 15 Solutions

1.

	Company X	Company Y
After-tax rate of return	12%	12%
Opening share price	X	Y
Closing share price	X_1	Y_1
After-tax income	$0.12X$	$0.12Y$
Capital gain after-tax	$(X_1 - X)(1 - 0.15)$	$(Y_1 - Y)(1 - 0.15)$
	$= 0.85(X_1 - X)$	$= 0.85(Y_1 - Y)$
Dividend after-tax	$(0.05X)(1 - 0.30)$	$(0.2Y)(1 - 0.30)$
	$= 0.035X$	$= 0.14Y$
Income after-tax	$0.12X = 0.85(X_1 - X) + 0.035X$	$0.12Y = 0.85(Y_1 - Y) + 0.14Y$
	$0.935X = 0.85X_1$	$0.83Y = 0.85Y_1$
Final share price	$X_1 = 1.1X$	$Y_1 = 0.9765Y$
Before-tax rate of return	$\dfrac{(X_1 - X) + 0.05X}{X}$	$\dfrac{(Y_1 - Y) + 0.2Y}{Y}$
(Substituting for X_1 and Y_1)	$\dfrac{(1.1X - X) + 0.05X}{X}$	$\dfrac{(0.9765Y - Y) + 0.2Y}{Y}$
Rate of return before tax	0.15 or 15%	0.1765 or 17.65%

3. Using Elton and Gruber's model,

$$(P_B - P_A)(1 - T_G) = D(1 - T_P)$$

$$(100 - P_A)(1 - 0.4T_P) = 10(1 - T_P)$$

$$100 - P_A = 10(1 - 0.4)/(1 - 0.4 \times 0.4)$$

$$P_A = 100 - 6/0.84$$

$$= \$92.86$$

where P_B and P_A are the prices of the stock with dividend and ex-dividend, respectively, T_G and T_P are the marginal capital gains tax and personal tax rates, respectively, and D is the dividend.

5. From

$$(P_B - P_A)/D = (1 - T_P)/(1 - T_G)$$

$$(50 - 46.5)/5 = (1 - T_P)/(1 - 0.5T_P)$$

$$0.7(1 - 0.5T_P) = (1 - T_P)$$

Implied marginal tax rate, $T_P = 46.15\%$

6. If the company pays corporate tax at 46 percent, and the average shareholder's marginal tax rate is 30 percent, it is more beneficial for the shareholder to receive the dividend immediately and invest it. The opposite holds true when the marginal tax rate of the average shareholder is 50 percent, in which case some form of distribution or return of capital is more beneficial.

As an example, if the company has $1,000 in cash, and Treasury bills yield 10 percent, the two positions at the end of the year are as follows:

Company invests in Treasury bills, then pays dividend at end of year:

Proceeds from Treasury bills = $1,000 + 100 (1 - 0.46) = $1,054

Dividends after-tax to shareholder = $1,054 (1 - 0.3) = $737.8

Company pays dividend, and shareholders invest in Treasury bills for a year:

Dividends after-tax = $1,000 (1 - 0.3) = $700

Proceeds from Treasury bills after-tax = $700 + 70(1 - 0.3) = $749.00

It is better for the company to pay the dividend immediately if the shareholders' average marginal rate of personal tax is lower than the company's tax rate.

If the shareholder's marginal tax rate is 50 percent:

Dividends after-tax to shareholders after company's initial investment in Treasury bills = $1,054 (1 − 0.5)

$$= \$527$$

Dividends after-tax to shareholders if they invest in Treasury bills themselves = $1,000 (1 − 0.5) + $40 (1 − 0.5)

$$= \$520$$

8. Current price-to-earnings ratio = 90/6 = 15

    After the repurchase of shares, 400,000 shares will be outstanding. As the number of shares outstanding is less, the earnings per share will have risen to $3,000,000/400,000 = $7.50.
    If the PE remains the same, Price per share = $7.5 × 15 = $112.50. The price is expected to rise to $112.50 after the repurchase, if the PE ratio remains the same. We assume that the share repurchase does not convey price-sensitive information to the market and therefore does not change the PE ratio.

Chapter 16 Solutions

1. From the *Wall Street Journal* of August 10, 1983, a three-month Treasury bill matures on November 10, 1983. The following information is shown:

Maturity date	Bid Discount	Asked	Yield
11 − 10	9.53	9.49	9.89

The bid and asked quotations are based on a banker's discount, which is the percentage difference between the face value of the bill and its market price annualized on a 360-day basis.
    The bid quotation is the annualized discount at which a dealer is

willing to buy the security, and the asked quotation is the annualized discount at which he is willing to sell it.

The yield is the bond equivalent yield, which is the actual dollar discount on the bill expressed as a percentage of the bill's price and annualized on a 365-day basis (see answer to Problem 3).

3. To calculate the bond equivalent yield, first calculate the price P of the bond as follows. On an asked quotation on a banker's discount basis,

$$\$9.49 = \frac{360}{90} \, (\$100 - P)$$

$$(\$100 - P) = 9.49 \times \frac{90}{360} = 2.3725$$

Price of bond $(P) = \$97.6275$

The bond equivalent yield Y can be calculated as

$$Y = \frac{365}{90} \times \left(\frac{\$2.3725}{\$97.6275} \right) \times 100$$

$$= 9.86\%$$

which is equal to the 9.86% yield quoted in the *Wall Street Journal*.

4. (a) The two notes have the same maturity but they have different coupons: one pays 9.875% annually (4.9375% semiannually) on the face value of $100 while the other pays 14.375% annually (7.1875% semiannually).

While there is a difference of nearly ten dollars between the coupons, the yields on the two notes are more nearly equal, because the low-coupon note is selling at a price that provides a capital gain, while the high-coupon note sells at a price that provides a capital loss.

(b)

	9⅞% Note	14⅜% Note
November 15, 1983	4.9375	7.1875
May 15, 1984	4.9375	7.1875
November 15, 1984	4.9375	7.1875
May 15, 1985	104.9375	107.1875

Chapter 17 Solutions

1. The July coupon is already paid, leaving only the January 15 coupon and the July 1984 coupon and redemption to be paid. On a calendar basis, 26 days have elapsed since the last coupon. The buyer of the bond must pay 26 days' accrued interest to the seller in addition to the quoted price. There will have been 184 days between coupons. The accrued interest is $(26/184) \times \$6.5625 = \$0.9273$. The buyer pays the ask price $102\frac{6}{32} = 102.1875$ plus accrued interest or $102.1875 + 0.9273 = 103.1148$.

   The January 15 coupon will be paid in only $184 - 26 = 158$ calendar days. This remaining period represents $(158/184) = 0.85870$ semiannual periods. The final July 15, 1984 coupon and redemption take place after 1.85870 semiannual periods. Thus the semiannual yield to maturity is obtained from the internal rate of return Y in

$$103.1148 = \frac{6.5625}{(1 + Y)^{0.85870}} + \frac{106.5625}{(1 + Y)^{1.85870}}$$

   The internal rate of return $Y = 5.284$ percent. The corresponding quoted annual yield to maturity would be $2Y = 10.57$ equalling the 10.57 percent quoted by the *Wall Street Journal*.

3. The table below sets out the cash flows for the bond, together with the spot rates for each year.

End of year	Cash flow	Spot rate	Discount factor	Present value
1	12	0.114	0.89767	10.7720
2	12	0.122	0.79435	9.5322
3	12	0.128	0.69674	8.3609
4	112	0.130	0.61332	68.6918
				97.3569

   The bond should be priced at around $97.36.

6. Duration of bond A can be calculated as follows:

$$\frac{1 \times 10/(1.1284)}{93.28} + \frac{2 \times 10/(1.1284)^2}{93.28} + \frac{3 \times 110/(1.1284)^3}{93.28}$$

$$= 2.725 \text{ years}$$

For bond B, the duration is:

$$\frac{1 \times 12/(1.1284)}{98} + \frac{2 \times 12/(1.1284)^2}{98} + \frac{3 \times 112/(1.1284)^3}{98}$$

$$= 2.687$$

Equation 17.6 suggests that bond A is more risky than bond B since its duration is slightly longer while the yields on the two bonds are the same. Thus bond B would be more attractive.

If two bonds have the same maturity, the bond with the longer duration should have the higher yield when the slope of the term structure of spot interest rates is rising. Since the long-term duration bond A does not have a higher yield as it should, bond B would be preferred. If the bond market is operating efficiently, however, both bonds would be fairly priced and the choice would depend on considerations such as the investor's tax position and risk preferences.

Chapter 18 Solutions

1. With reference to the *Wall Street Journal* of July 15, 1983:

	ITT Series K	ITT Series O
Current price	$72	$66⅞
Dividend yield	5.6	7.5

Series K pays a dividend of $4 while Series O pays a dividend of $5.

$$\text{Dividend yield} = \frac{\text{Dividend}}{\text{Market price}}$$

For Series K, dividend yield = 4/72 = 5.56%
For Series O, dividend yield = 5/66.875 = 7.48%

The difference in yield arises in part because of differences in the capital gain on redemption, and in part because of differences in the priority of claims.

3. The *Wall Street Journal* of July 15, 1983, gives the following for ITT common:

Current price	44½
Dividend yield	6.2
PE ratio	10

Earnings per share can be calculated if you know the market price per share and the price-to-earnings ratio.

$$\text{Price-to-earnings ratio} = \frac{\text{Market price per share}}{\text{Earnings per share}}$$

$$\text{Earnings per share} = \frac{\text{Market price per share}}{\text{Price-to-earnings ratio}}$$

$$= \frac{\$44.50}{10}$$

$$= \$4.45$$

The dividend per share can be calculated similarly.

$$\text{Dividend yield} = \frac{\text{Dividend per share}}{\text{Market price per share}}$$

$$\text{Dividend per share} = \text{Dividend yield} \times \text{Market price}$$

$$= 0.062 \times \$44.50$$

$$= \$2.759$$

5. Market value of $XYZ = 10{,}000{,}000 \times \$100$

$$= \$1{,}000{,}000{,}000$$

In a one-for-two rights issue, the number of shares to be issued is

$1/2 \times 10{,}000{,}000 = 5{,}000{,}000$

Money to be raised from issue $= 5{,}000{,}000 \times \$85$

$$= \$425{,}000{,}000$$

Rights-on price $= \$100$

$$\text{Ex-rights price} = \frac{\$1{,}000{,}000{,}000 + 425{,}000{,}000}{15{,}000{,}000}$$

$$= \$95$$

Minimum value of rights $= \$95 - 85$

$$= \$10$$

7. Market value of company = 200,000 × $40
   = $8,000,000
   Book value of company = $4,828,000

   Book value per share = $\dfrac{4,828,000}{200,000}$ = $24.14

   Price of share in private placement = $40.00 − (0.10 × 40)
   = $36.00
   New issue will raise   50,000 × $36.00
   = $1,800,000

   Number of shares = 200,000 + 50,000
   = 250,000

   Post-issue market value = $\dfrac{8,000,000 + 1,800,000}{250,000}$

   = $39.20

   Post-issue book value = $\dfrac{4,828,000 + 1,800,000}{250,000}$

   = $26.51

   The book value per share increases from $24.14 to $26.51 while the market or economic value per share decreases from $40 to $39.20 because the new issue is placed at a fairly large discount of 10%. The moral of the tale is, don't trust changes in book value as a signal of the value of new issues or new investment opportunities.

Chapter 19 Solutions

1. (a) The call option with a striking price of $35 is in the money, as the stock price is greater than the striking price.
   (b) At an exercise price of $35, the option is priced at $5¼ when the stock price is $38¾. A call option becomes more valuable when the exercise price is set further below the stock price. If the exercise price is increased, the stock price has to increase correspondingly more for the option to be exercised.

(c) The call option price increases as time increases because there is a greater opportunity for the stock price to rise above the exercise price. The longer the period to maturity, the more valuable the put option.

(d) A put option becomes more valuable when the price of the stock falls below the exercise price. In this case, the exercise prices of $40 and $45 are higher than the stock price of $38¾, and the puts therefore have value. The $40 put option is valued higher than the $35 put option because the possibility of selling the stock at $40 is more valuable compared with selling the stock at $35. For puts, a higher exercise price means a greater payoff.

2. Assuming that no dividend is paid, the minimum price of the option must be greater than the stock price less the PV of the exercise price, or

$$\$100 - 85/(1.0095)^3$$

$$= \$100 - 82.62$$

$$= \$17.38$$

Note: A 12 percent annual rate is equivalent to a monthly rate r of 0.95 percent, $(1 + 0.12) = (1 + r)^{12}$.

4. (a) Call option: Exercise price of $80

	Ms. Buyer	Mr. Seller
Price increases to $90	Exercises option and gains (+)	Loses (−), as he has to deliver the stock at a lower price than market
Price decreases to $70	Option worthless and loses price of option by not exercising (−)	Gains (+), as option is not exercised

(b) Put option: Exercise price of $70

	Ms. Buyer	Mr. Seller
Price increases to $85	Option worthless and loses price of option by not exercising (−)	Gains (+), as option is not exercised
Price decreases to $60	Exercises option and gains (+)	Loses (−), as he has to buy the stock at a higher price than market

8. (a) If the call option were priced at $3, you would sell the call options and buy the shares.

   As an example, if you buy the shares in the hedge ratio of 0.25 (calculated as $5/$20), you would buy one-fourth share for every call option sold.

   If the stock price rises from $100 to $110:

   payoff on stock = $27.50

   payoff on option = − $5

   If stock price falls to $90:

   payoff on stock = $22.50

   payoff on option = $0 because option will not be exercised.

   Combined payoffs from option and stock are the same ($22.50) regardless of outcome. However, you have obtained $3 for the call option sold at the beginning of the period, so

   $$(\$25 - 3)(1 + r) = \$22.50$$

   $$(1 + r) = \$(22.50/22.00)$$

   $$= 1.0227$$

   $$r = 2.27\%$$

The return for the period is 2.27 percent compared with the riskless rate of interest of 1 percent per period, so this strategy will be profitable.

(b) If investors bought the shares and sold the call options, the share price will increase, while the price of the call options will fall; this arbitrage will bring prices back into equilibrium.

9. Using the Black–Scholes formula:

$$C = SN(d_1) - \frac{E}{e^{rt}} N(d_2)$$

$S = \$100$

$E = \$80$

$r = 0.10$

$\sigma = 0.30$

$t = 44/365 = 0.12055$

$$d_1 = \frac{\ln (S/E) + (r + \tfrac{1}{2}\sigma^2)t}{\sigma\sqrt{t}}$$

$$= \frac{\ln (100/80) + (0.10 + \tfrac{1}{2}(.30)^2)0.12055}{0.30\sqrt{0.12055}}$$

$$= \frac{0.22314 + 0.01748}{0.10416}$$

$$= 2.31010$$

$$d_2 = d_1 - \sigma\sqrt{t}$$

$$= 2.31010 - 0.10416$$

$$= 2.20594$$

Calculate $N(d_1)$ and $N(d_2)$ using linear interpolation from Table 19.2.

$$N(d_1) = N(2.31010) = 0.9893 + \left[\frac{2.31010 - 2.30}{2.35 - 2.30}\right] \times (0.9906 - 0.9893)$$

$$= 0.9893 + 0.00026$$

$$= 0.98956$$

$$N(d_2) = N(2.20594) = 0.9861 + \left[\frac{2.20594 - 2.20}{2.25 - 2.20}\right] \times (0.9878 - 0.9861)$$

$$= 0.9861 + 0.00020$$

$$= 0.98630$$

$$C = SN(d_1) - \frac{E}{e^{rt}} N(d_2)$$

$$= 100 \, (0.98956) - \left(\frac{80}{e^{0.10 \times 0.12055}} \times 0.98630\right)$$

$$= 98.956 - \left(\frac{80}{1.01213} \times 0.98630\right)$$

$$= 98.956 - 77.95837$$

$$= 20.99763$$

Price of the option = \$20.99763 or \$21.
(b) Using the put-call parity formula:

$$C = P + (S - Ee^{-rt})$$

$$P = C - (S - Ee^{-rt})$$

$$= 20.99763 - (100 - 80/1.01213)$$

$$= 20.99763 - (20.95877)$$

$$= 0.03886$$

Price of the put option is \$0.04.

The put option value is so much lower because the call option is in the money (i.e., the share price can fall by \$20 before the exercise price is reached). The put option is out of the money and will not be exercised unless the share price falls by more than \$20.

Chapter 20 Solutions

1. (a) Value of the rights offer = Value of the call option to buy the share at the price of $90.

$$\text{The ex-rights price of the stock} = \frac{(\$120 \times 2 + 90 \times 1)}{3}$$

$$= \$110$$

This price reflects the effects of the issue of new shares at a discount on the current market price. Using the Black–Scholes model (Chapter 19), where

$S = \$110$

$E = \$90$

$t = 30/365 = 0.08219$

$\sigma = 40\%$

$r = 15\%$

$$d_1 = \frac{\ln(110/90) + [0.15 + \frac{1}{2}(0.4)^2]0.08219}{0.4\sqrt{0.08219}}$$

$$= \frac{0.20067 + 0.01890}{0.11468}$$

$$= 1.91463$$

$$d_2 = 1.91463 - 0.11468$$

$$= 1.79995$$

Interpolating Table 19.3:

$$N(d_1) = N(1.91463) = 0.9713 + \left[\frac{1.91463 - 1.90}{1.95 - 1.90}\right](0.9744 - 0.9713)$$

$$= 0.9713 + 0.00091$$

$$= 0.97221$$

$$N(d_2) = N(1.7995) = 0.9641 + \left[\frac{1.7995 - 1.80}{1.85 - 1.80}\right](0.9678 - 0.9641)$$

$$= 0.9641 + 0.000004$$

$$= 0.96406$$

$$C = 110\,(0.97221) - \left(\frac{90}{e^{0.15 \times 0.08219}} \times 0.96410\right)$$

$$= 106.9431 - \left(\frac{90}{1.0124} \times 0.96410\right)$$

$$= 106.9431 - 85.7062$$

$$= 21.2369$$

The value of the rights offer of one share at \$90.00 for every two held is \$21.24.

(b) The price would be \$20.00.

3. In eight years' time, shareholders will have to repay the loan of \$8 million if they wish to own the company.

(a) Using the Black–Scholes model,

$$E = \$8$$
$$S = \$12$$
$$\sigma = 40\%$$
$$r = 10\%$$
$$t = 8 \text{ years}$$

$$d_1 = \frac{\ln(12/8) + [0.10 + \tfrac{1}{2}(0.4)^2]8}{0.40\sqrt{8}}$$

$$= \frac{0.40547 + 1.44}{1.13137}$$

$$= 1.63118$$

$$d_2 = 1.63118 - 1.13137$$

$$= 0.49981$$

Interpolating Table 19.3:

$$N(d_1) = N(1.63118) = 0.9452 + \left[\frac{1.63118 - 1.60}{1.65 - 1.60}\right](0.9505 - 0.9452)$$

$$= 0.9452 + 0.00331$$

$$= 0.94851$$

$$N(d_2) = N(0.49981) = 0.6736 + \left[\frac{0.49981 - 0.45}{0.50 - 0.45}\right](0.6915 - 0.6736)$$

$$= 0.6736 + 0.01783$$

$$= 0.69143$$

Value of equity = Value of call option

$$= 12(0.94851) - \left(\frac{8}{e^{0.1\times8}} \times 0.69143\right)$$

$$= 11.38212 - 2.48544$$

$$= 8.89668$$

Value of equity is $8,896,680

Value of debt = Value of assets − Value of equity

$$= (12 - 8.89668)$$

$$= 3.10332$$

Value of debt is $3,103,320

(b) To calculate the default premium, you have to calculate the price of riskless debt with an eight-year maturity, with repayment of $8 million at the end of eight years, when the riskless rate of interest is 10 percent.

$$\text{Price of riskless bond} = \frac{8}{e^{0.1\times8}}$$

$$= \frac{8}{2.22554}$$

$$= \$3.59463$$

Therefore, the risk premium is ($3.59463 − 3.10332) = 0.49131, or $491,310.

5. The information for company X is identical to that for the company in Problem 3, where the value of debt has been shown to be $3.10332 million.

Calculate the value of debt for company Y by first calculating the value of the equity as a call option:

$$d_1 = \frac{\ln(12/8) + [0.10 + \frac{1}{2}(0.6)^2]8}{0.6\sqrt{8}}$$

$$= \frac{0.40547 + 2.24}{1.69706}$$

$$= 1.55885$$

$$d_2 = 1.55885 - 1.69706$$

$$= -0.13821$$

$$N(d_1) = N(1.55885) \quad = 0.9394 + \left[\frac{1.55885 - 1.55}{1.60 - 1.55}\right](0.9452 - 0.9394)$$

$$= 0.9394 + 0.00103$$

$$= 0.94043$$

$$N(d_2) = N(-0.13821) = 0.4602 + \left[\frac{-0.13821 + 0.10}{-0.10 + 0.15}\right](0.4404 - 0.4602)$$

$$= 0.4602 - 0.01513$$

$$= 0.44507$$

$$C = 12\,(0.94043) - \left(\frac{8}{e^{0.1 \times 8}} \times 0.44507\right)$$

$$= 11.28516 - \left(\frac{8}{2.22554} \times 0.44507\right)$$

$$= 11.28516 - 1.59986$$

$$= 9.68530$$

Value of equity is $9,685,300

Value of debt = ($12 − 9.68530)

= 2.31470, or $2,314,700

The value of Y's debt is much lower than that of X, because Y is more risky (because of the higher standard deviation).

To calculate the standard deviation of the merged firm's assets, we use:

$$s_{xy}^2 = (x_x s_x)^2 + (x_y s_y)^2 + 2r_{x,y}(x_x s_x)(x_y s_y)$$

$$s_{xy}^2 = (0.5 \times 0.4)^2 + (0.5 \times 0.6)^2 + 2(0.3)(0.5 \times 0.4)(0.5 \times 0.6)$$

$$= 0.166$$

$$s_{x,y} = \sqrt{0.166}$$

$$= 0.40743$$

For the merged firm, calculate the value of the equity for XY:

$$d_1 = \frac{\ln(24/16) + [0.10 + \tfrac{1}{2}(0.40743)^2]8}{0.40743\sqrt{8}}$$

$$= \frac{0.40547 + 1.46400}{1.15239}$$

$$= 1.62225$$

$$d_2 = 1.62225 - 1.15239$$

$$= 0.46986$$

Interpolating Table 19.3:

$$N(d_1) = N(1.62225) = 0.9452 + \left[\frac{1.62225 - 1.60}{1.65 - 1.60}\right](0.9505 - 0.9452)$$

$$= 0.94756$$

$$N(d_2) = N(0.46986) = 0.6736 + \left[\frac{0.46986 - 0.45}{0.50 - 0.45}\right](0.6915 - 0.6736)$$

$$= 0.6736 + 0.00716$$

$$= 0.68071$$

$$C = 24(0.94756) - \left(\frac{16}{e^{0.1 \times 8}} \times 0.68071\right)$$

$$= 22.74144 - \left(\frac{16}{2.2255} \times 0.68071\right)$$

$$= 22.74144 - 4.89381$$

$$= 17.84763$$

Value of equity is $17,847,630.

Value of debt $= 24 - 17.84763$

$$= 6.15237 \text{ million, or } \$6,152,370$$

Value of:	X Inc.	Y Inc.	XY Inc.	
Debt	3.10332	2.31470	$\frac{6.15237}{2}$	= 3.076185
Equity	8.89668	9.68530	$\frac{17.84763}{2}$	= 8.923815
Total	12.0	12.0	12.0	

The value of debt for X is decreased because the standard deviation of returns on the assets of the merged company is slightly higher (0.40743) than that for X alone (0.40). The value of debt for Y is increased as it becomes less risky after the merger: this is because of the coinsurance effect. The equity stockholders of company Y suffer the loss in value, as the value of the assets remains the same.

Chapter 21 Solutions

1.

	With debt financing			
Earnings before interest	Interest charges (Millions of dollars)	Earnings after interest	EPS	EPS With all-equity financing
−0.5	1.2	−1.7	−0.17	−0.033
0.0	1.2	−1.2	−0.12	0.000
0.5	1.2	−0.7	−0.07	0.033
1.0	1.2	−0.2	−0.02	0.067
1.5	1.2	0.3	0.03	0.100
2.0	1.2	0.8	0.08	0.133
2.5	1.2	1.3	0.13	0.167

The break–even point for the company
(a) With debt of $10 million at 12 percent is $1.2 million
(b) Without debt is $0 million
The range of EPS with only equity is 0.20, which is smaller than the range of 0.30 with debt.

3. If the company wishes to borrow, it should have minimum earnings of $1.2 million to pay interest on the borrowings.
   (a) To repurchase 30 percent of the equity with debt financing:

$$\text{Amount of debt raised} = 0.30 \times \$15,000,000$$

$$= \$4,500,000$$

Given perpetual debt, present value of
tax savings = $0.46 \times \$4,500,000$

$$= \$2,070,000$$

(b) To repurchase 50 percent of its equity with debt financing:

$$\text{Amount of debt raised} = 0.50 \times \$15,000,000$$

$$= \$7,500,000$$

Given perpetual debt, present value of
tax savings $= 0.46 \times \$7,500,000$

$$= \$3,450,000$$

The increase in the value of the firm in MM's world due to increased debt in the capital structure would be $2,070,000 with 30 percent debt and $3,450,000 with 50 percent debt. We are ignoring any expected costs of financial distress.

5. (a) Present value of taxes saved $= \dfrac{B i T}{(1 + i)} \dfrac{B i T}{(1 + i)^2} + \cdots + \dfrac{B i T}{(1 + i)^n}$

Taxes saved each year $=$ Interest $\times$ Tax rate

$$= (\$100 \times 0.15) \times (0.46)$$

$$= \$6.9, \text{ or } \$6,900,000$$

(i) If Gearmore pays taxes

$$\text{Present value of tax savings} = \dfrac{6.9}{(1 + 0.15)} + \dfrac{6.9}{(1 + 0.15)^2} + \dfrac{6.9}{(1 + 0.15)^3}$$

$$+ \dfrac{6.9}{(1 + 0.15)^4} + \dfrac{6.9}{(1 + 0.15)^5}$$

$$= \$6.9 \text{ million} \times \text{Annuity factor of } 3.3522$$

$$= \$23.130, \text{ or } \$23,130,180$$

(ii) If Gearmore starts paying taxes in year 3

$$\text{Present value of tax savings} = 0 + 0 + \dfrac{3 \times 6.9}{(1.15)^3} + \dfrac{6.9}{(1.15)^4} + \dfrac{6.9}{(1.15)^5}$$

$$= \$20,986,203$$

The increase in the value of the firm caused by tax savings is larger when the company already is taxpaying.

(b) Miller's arguments suggest that the company should not borrow in the first two years when it is not paying taxes, for the before-tax cost of debt is greater than the cost of equity. It should use equity financing for the first two years, or it could consider leasing (Chapter 23). When it resumes taxpaying, the company will be indifferent between debt and equity financing.

7. In Miller's world, where there is no risk, we can use the following equation to calculate the before-tax cost of debt.

$$\text{WACC} = i(1 - T_c) \frac{B}{B + E} + R_L \frac{E}{B + E}$$

$$0.12 = i(1 - 0.5) \frac{0.6}{1.6} + (0.12) \frac{1.0}{1.6}$$

$$i = 0.24$$

The before-tax cost of debt is 24 percent.

When the tax rate is reduced to 35 percent, assuming the cost of equity and WACC remain the same

$$0.12 = i(1 - 0.35) \frac{0.6}{1.6} + (0.12) \frac{1.0}{1.6}$$

$$i = 0.1846$$

The before-tax cost of debt falls to 18.46 percent.

The above results also can be obtained by using the equation $i(1 - T_c) = R_E = R_L$ in Miller's world where the equity is assumed to be risk-free.

8. From the equation that describes the NPV of net incremental income to securityholders due to debt financing in an MM world

$$L = B \left(1 - \frac{(1 - T_c)(1 - T_{ps})}{(1 - T_{pb})} \right)$$

$$= \$100,000,000 \left(1 - \frac{(1 - 0.46)(1 - 0.15)}{(1 - 0.30)} \right)$$

$$= 100,000,000 \, (1 - 0.6557)$$

$$= 34,430,000$$

If the personal tax rates on dividend and bond income are the same,

$$L = BT_c$$

$$= 100,000,000 \ (0.46)$$

$$= 46,000,000$$

The NPV is reduced when $T_{pb} > T_{ps}$

9. MM's propositions in a world without taxes and in a world with taxes hold if there are no costs of default, even if the risks of default lead to higher interest rates.

   If costs of default lead to higher interest rates, MM's propositions must be qualified, and there is some rationale for an optimal capital structure. (See the figure on the next page.)

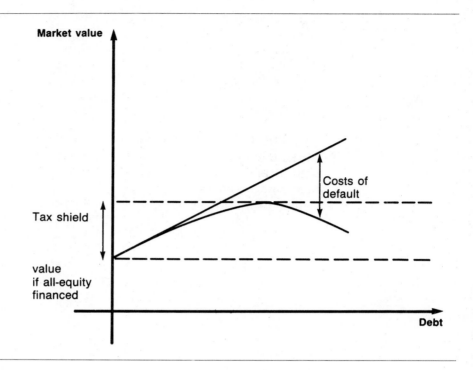

Chapter 22 Solutions

1. On a book value basis,

$$\text{WACC} = \text{Cost of debt} \left(\frac{B}{B + E}\right) + \text{Levered cost} \left(\frac{E}{B + E}\right)$$

$$= 0.12 \, (1 - 0.46)(0.5) + 0.16(0.5)$$

$$= 0.1124$$

The WACC is 11.24 percent on a book value basis.
  On a market value basis,

$$\text{WACC} = 0.12(1 - 0.46)(0.35) + 0.16(0.65)$$

$$= 0.12668$$

The WACC for Kingston, Inc., is higher at 12.67 percent on a market value basis because of the larger proportion of equity and its higher cost.

3. Return on W.E.T.'s stock $= R_f + \beta[E(\tilde{R}_M) - R_f]$

$$= 0.10 + 1.27(0.10)$$

$$= 0.227$$

$$\text{WACC} = 0.10(1 - 0.46)(0.4) + 0.227(0.6)$$

$$= 0.1578$$

The NPV of the project, using the WACC of 15.78 percent as the discount rate is equal to

$$-\$500 + \frac{250}{1.1578} + \frac{250}{(1.1578)^2} + \frac{250}{(1.1578)^3} + \frac{250}{(1.1578)^4} + \frac{250}{(1.1578)^5}$$

$$= \$322.792$$

5. (a) The NPV of the project, using the unlevered cost of equity of 15 percent

$$= -\$1,000 + 350 \times \text{(Present value of an annuity for five years at 15 percent)}$$

$$= -\$1,000 + 350 \times 3.35216 = \$173.26$$

Calculation of the present value of tax benefits

End of year	0	1	2	3	4	5
Operating cash flow		350.00	350.00	350.00	350.00	350.00
PV of remaining cash flow at 15%	1173.25	999.24	799.13	569.00	304.35	0
Borrowing at 25% of project's PV	293.32	249.81	199.78	142.25	76.09	0
Interest at 7%		20.53	17.49	13.98	9.96	5.33
Tax benefit at 46%		9.44	8.05	6.43	4.58	2.45

Present value of tax benefits discounted at 15 percent

$$= \left(\$ \frac{9.44}{1.15} + \frac{8.05}{(1.15)^2} + \frac{6.43}{(1.15)^3} + \frac{4.58}{(1.15)^4} + \frac{2.45}{(1.15)^5} \right)$$

$$= \$22.36$$

Adjusted net present value for the project

= \$173.27 + 22.36

= \$195.63

(b) Percentage of present value of tax benefits:
(i) As a proportion of the PV of the project

$$= \frac{22.36}{1,000 + 195.63}$$

= 0.0187 or 1.87%

(ii) As a proportion of the NPV of the project

$$= \frac{22.36}{195.63}$$

= 0.114 or 11.4%

7. (a) Cost of levered equity capital = 0.09 + 1.2(0.10)

$$= 0.21$$

$$\text{WACC} = (0.12(1 - 0.46) \times 0.3) + (0.21 \times 0.7)$$

$$= 0.01944 + 0.147$$

$$= 0.16644$$

$$= 16.64\%$$

$$\text{NPV of project} = -\$1,000 + \frac{250}{1.1664} + \frac{350}{(1.1664)^2}$$

$$+ \frac{450}{(1.1664)^3} + \frac{550}{(1.1664)^4}$$

$$= \$52.32$$

(b) Levered beta = 1.2

Unlevered beta = 1.2 × 0.7

$$= 0.84$$

Unlevered cost of equity = $0.09 + 0.84(0.10)$

$$= 0.174$$

NPV of the project discounted at the unlevered cost of equity

$$= -\$1,000 + \frac{250}{1.174} + \frac{350}{(1.174)^2} + \frac{450}{(1.174)^3} + \frac{550}{(1.174)^4}$$

$$= \$34.52$$

The present value of the tax benefits of debt is the difference between the two NPVs, i.e. ($52.32 - 34.52) = \$17.80$.

8. (a) Present value of loan $= \left(\dfrac{100,000}{1.12} + \dfrac{100,000}{(1.12)^2} + \dfrac{100,000}{(1.12)^3} \right.$

$$\left. + \frac{100,000 + 2,000,000}{(1.12)^4} \right)$$

$$= \$1,574,771$$

Value of the loan subsidy $= \$2,000,000 - 1,574,771$

$$= \$425,229$$

Alternatively, the present value at 12 percent of (12%–5%) of $2,000,000 equals \$425,229$.

(b) The value of the loan subsidy would increase if interest rates increase, as the interest and capital repayments would be discounted at higher rates, thereby lowering the present value of the loan.

10. Levered beta = 1.27

Unlevered or asset beta = $1.27(0.6)$

$$= 0.762$$

Unlevered cost of equity = $0.10 + 0.762(0.10)$

$$= 0.1762$$

The residual income accruing to the equity holders should be discounted at the levered cost of equity capital R_L of 22.7 percent:

$R_L = 0.10 + 1.27(0.10)$

$$= 0.227$$

$$\text{NPV of project} = \left(-\$171.35 + \frac{184.36}{1.227} + \frac{179.31}{(1.227)^2} \right.$$

$$\left. + \frac{173.51}{(1.227)^3} + \frac{166.76}{(1.227)^4} + \frac{158.98}{(1.227)^5} \right)$$

$$= \$322.67$$

The NPV is close to the answer to Problem 3, which used the WACC as the discount rate. The difference is due to rounding error.
Cash flows accruing to equity shareholders:

End of year	0	1	2	3	4	5
(1) Net operating cash flow	−500	250	250	250	250	250
(2) PV of remaining cash flow at unlevered cost of equity at 17.62%	788.57	677.52	546.89	393.26	212.55	0
(3) Borrowing at 40% of project's PV	315.43	271.01	218.76	157.30	85.02	0
(4) Interest at 10%		−31.54	−27.10	−21.88	−15.73	−8.50
(5) Tax benefits at 46%		14.51	12.47	10.06	7.24	3.91
(6) Present value of tax benefits discounted at 17.62%	33.05	24.37	16.19	8.98	3.32	0
(7) Total PV including value of tax benefits (2) + (6)	821.62	701.89	563.08	402.24	215.87	0
(8) Borrowing at 40% of total PV	328.65	280.76	225.23	160.90	86.35	0
(9) Loan	328.65					
(10) Loan repayments		−47.89	−55.53	−64.33	−74.55	−86.35
(11) Interest payments at 10%		−32.87	−28.08	−22.52	−16.09	−8.64
(12) Tax shields on interest charges at 46%		15.12	12.92	10.36	7.40	3.97
(13) Equity residual income (1) + (9) + (10) + (11) + (12)	−171.35	184.36	179.31	173.51	166.76	158.98

Chapter 23 Solutions

1. Lease payments each year = $125,000
   Tax shields from lease payments = $0.46 \times \$125,000$
   = $57,500
   If the computer costs $600,000 and lasts five years,
   the investment tax credit = $\frac{2}{3} \times 0.10 \times \$600,000$
   = $40,000
   ACRS depreciable amount = $600,000 - \frac{1}{2}(40,000)$
   = $580,000
   Calculation of depreciation tax shield

End of year	Depreciation schedule (%)	Depreciable amount (Dollars)	Depreciation (Dollars)	Depreciation tax shield (Dollars)
1	15		87,000	40,020
2	22		127,600	58,696
3	21	580,000	121,800	56,028
4	21		121,800	56,028
5	21		121,800	56,028

Hammond can borrow at 12 percent but is fully taxpaying, so its after-tax cost of borrowing
= $0.12 (1 - .46)$
= 6.48%
Cash flows of Hammond Manufacturers, Inc., if it leases the computer

End of year	Lease payment	Tax shield from lease payment	Purchase cost	ITC	Tax shield from depreciation	Total cash flow	Discount factor at 6.48%	Present value
0	−125,000	57,500	600,000	−40,000		492,500	1.00000	492,500
1	−125,000	57,500			−40,020	−107,520	0.93914	−100,976
2	−125,000	57,500			−58,696	−126,196	0.88199	−111,304
3	−125,000	57,500			−56,028	−123,528	0.82832	−102,321
4	−125,000	57,500			−56,028	−123,528	0.77791	−96,094
5	−125,000	57,500			−56,028	−123,528	0.73057	−90,246

Net present value of leasing versus purchase = −8,441

(a) As the NPV of the lease is negative, Hammond should purchase rather than lease the computer.

(b) The lessor would have a positive NPV of $8,441.

4. For year 5, the after-tax interest rate will be $0.15 (1 - 0.46) = 0.081$ or 8.1%. For year 4, the interest is tax-deductible only in year 5, so the after-tax rate will be (to four decimal places)

$$0.15 - \frac{0.15(0.46)}{1.081} = 0.0862$$

For year 3, the after-tax interest rate will be

$$0.15 - \frac{0.15(0.46)}{(1.081)(1.0862)} = 0.0912$$

For year 2, the after-tax interest rate will be

$$0.15 - \frac{0.15(0.46)}{(1.081)(1.0862)(1.0912)} = 0.0961$$

For year 1, the after-tax interest rate will be

$$0.15 - \frac{0.15(0.46)}{(1.081)(1.0862)(1.0912)(1.0961)} = 0.1009$$

Calculation of discount factors:

End of year	After-tax interest rate		Discount factor
1	0.1009	1/(1.1009)	= 0.9083
2	0.0961	1/(1.1009)(1.0961)	= 0.8287
3	0.0912	1/(1.1009)(1.0961)(1.0912)	= 0.7594
4	0.0862	1/(1.1009)(1.0961)(1.0912)(1.0862)	= 0.6992
5	0.0810	1/(1.1009)(1.0961)(1.0912)(1.0862)(1.0810)	= 0.6468

6. The loan balance method is an iterative process which you can start with an arbitrarily chosen loan balance of say $610,000 (near the asset cost of $600,000).

We use the data in the table in the answer to Problem 1 to obtain the lease obligations in the table below.

End of year	Lease obligation	Interest income (12%)	Tax on interest income (at 46%)	Net change in bank balance	New bank balance
0					610,000
0	−125,000			−125,000	485,000
1	−125,000	58,200		−66,800	418,200
2	−125,000	50,184		−74,816	343,384
3	−89,744	41,206	−68,811	−117,349	226,035
4	−123,528	27,124	−12,477	−108,881	117,154
5	−123,528	14,059	−6,467	−115,936	1,218

The final loan balance of 1,218 is greater than zero, so you must reduce the initial balance of 610,000 slightly.

After a number of such trials with the aid of interpolation we try an initial bank loan of $609,120, which gives a near-zero ending balance.

End of year	Lease obligation	Interest income (12%)	Tax on interest income (46%)	Net change in bank balance	New bank balance
0					609,120
0	−125,000			−125,000	484,120
1	−125,000	58,094		−66,906	417,214
2	−125,000	50,066		−74,934	342,280
3	−89,744	41,074	−68,648	−117,318	224,962
4	−123,528	26,995	−12,418	−108,951	116,011
5	−123,528	13,921	−6,403	−116,010	1

It would be better for Hammond to pay $600,000 for the asset than to sign a lease which would be equivalent to putting $609,120 into the bank to meet the liabilities of the lease.

Chapter 24 Solutions

1. The average collection period is

$$\frac{\$14,000}{\$132,000} \times 365 = 38.712 \text{ days}$$

The average collection period exceeds the thirty-day maximum credit period by nearly nine days. This difference, while not necessarily serious, raises some potentially important questions. Is the disparity increasing or being reduced? If it is increasing, is the credit department really in control of the situation? Which customers are the slow payers, and how far, individually, are they behind? Are any of them possible nonpayers? Are the appropriate collection procedures being followed? Management should seek the answers to such questions and take the implied actions.

2. By forgoing the 1 percent discount for payment within seven days, the customer can get $28 - 7 = 21$ days' credit. The effective annual interest rate is given by

$$(1.01)^{365/21} - 1 = (1.01)^{17.381} - 1$$

$$= 0.1888$$

$$= 18.88 \text{ percent per year}$$

As long as the customer can borrow at the lower rate of 15 percent per year, he or she should take the discount.

If the customer can take forty-five days to pay, the credit period is $45 - 7 = 38$ days, and the effective annual interest rate is given by

$$(1.01)^{365/38} - 1 = (1.01)^{9.605} - 1$$

$$= 0.1003$$

$$= 10.03 \text{ percent}$$

At forty-five days to pay, trade credit at an effective rate of 10.03 percent is preferable to borrowing at 15 percent.

3. The discounts that are expected to be taken for payment within seven days equal $0.01 \times 150 = 15$. The new after-discount receipts from payment within seven days are $150 - 15 = 135$. The net incremental cash flow for the credit policy decision is the difference between the cash flows with the trade discount and those without the discount (in thou-

sands of dollars):

	7 days	1 month	2 months	3 months	4 months	5 months
With	135	280	70	50	10	10
Without	0	400	100	50	10	10
Net	135	−120	− 30	0	0	0

The net incremental cash flow represents a \$135,000 reduction of trade credit starting in seven days' time, offset by corresponding increases of \$120,000 in one month and \$30,000 in two months' time. Because we have no information to suggest that trade credit to these customers is less risky than lending to them, the appropriate discount rate must be no less than 12 percent per year, or an equivalent monthly rate of

$$(1.12)^{1/12} - 1 = (1.12)^{0.08333} - 1$$

$$= 0.00949$$

$$= 0.949 \text{ percent}$$

Discounting at this equivalent monthly rate of interest,

$$\text{NPV} = \frac{135}{(1.00949)^{7/28}} - \frac{120}{(1.00949)^1} - \frac{30}{(1.00949)^2}$$

$$= 134.682 - 118.872 - 29.439$$

$$= -13.629$$

The trade discount has a negative net present value of −\$13,629 and therefore represents an unsatisfactory alternative to the existing credit policy.

4. The expected effective monthly interest rate received is

$$\frac{\left(\text{Discount} \times \text{Monthly Sales} - \frac{\text{Service}}{\text{Cost}}\right)(1 - p) - p \times \frac{\text{Cash Value of}}{\text{Credit Granted}}}{\text{Cash Value of Credit Granted}}$$

$$= \frac{(0.10 \times 10,000 - 0)(1 - 0.035) - 0.035 \times (2 \times 10,000)}{2 \times 10,000}$$

$$= \frac{965 - 700}{20,000} = 0.01325$$

or 1.325 percent per month. This monthly rate is equivalent to an annual rate of

$$(1 + 0.01325)^{12} - 1 = 0.1711$$

$$= 17.11 \text{ percent per year}$$

Although X can borrow at 10 percent, it would not lend to Y for less than 20 percent per year. The expected effective monthly interest rate received is not attractive, because it is less than 20 percent.

5. The expected monthly rate of return received is

$$\frac{\left(\dfrac{\text{Net Cash}}{\text{Flow}} - \dfrac{\text{Service}}{\text{Cost}} - \dfrac{\text{Inventory}}{\text{Carrying Cost}} \right)(1 - p) - p \times \dfrac{\text{Cash Value}}{\text{of Credit}}}{\text{Receivables} - \text{Payables} + \text{Inventory}}$$

$$= \frac{(0.50 \times 2,000 - 100 - 0.50 \times 4,000 \times 0.02)(1 - 0.01) - 0.01 \times (0.5 \times 6,000)}{(2,000 + 4,000) - 3,000 + 0.50 \times 4,000}$$

$$= 0.1643 \text{ or } 16.43 \text{ percent per month}$$

This is an exceptionally high rate of return, because it is assumed that the extension of credit creates extra business utilizing spare capacity and that the probability of nonpayment is not high. Extending credit in this situation appears to be the best use of scarce funds.

Chapter 26 Solutions

1. Operating income and expense items are identical to those given in Table 26.7. The new items are:

			(Millions of dollars)		
	1985	1986	1987	1988	1989
Interest expense	1.645	1.359	1.270	1.022	0.399
Earnings before taxes	4.555	8.541	9.030	14.178	15.801
Corporate income taxes	2.232	4.185	4.425	6.947	7.742
Net income	2.323	4.356	4.605	7.231	8.059

The new balance sheet numbers are:

	(Millions of dollars)				
Cash	3.000	3.000	3.000	3.000	3.000
Total assets	40.500	43.900	48.800	55.000	58.900
Short-term borrowing	7.877	6.321	6.416	5.185	0.827
Equity	16.223	19.979	23.984	30.615	38.073

In dollar terms, the income lost in order to provide greater liquidity is small. Whether the change would be desirable depends on the value of improved liquidity.

4. Management policies and bank requirements are inconsistent (the following figures are in millions of dollars):

   (a) If cash = 2.0 and dividends = 0.6, short-term borrowing = 6.812 (the original solution in Table 26.6). The maximum interest allowed should be \$1.24 (equals Earnings 6.2/5), which is exceeded if the above situation prevails. Using the equation,

   $$0.7 + 0.12 \times STB(1985) = 1.24$$
   $$STB(1985) = 4.5$$

   The maximum short-term borrowing has an upper limit of \$4.5 million.

   (b) If dividends = 0.6 and short-term borrowing $STB(1985) = 4.5$, then (using the notation in the text),

   $$E(1985) = 14.500 + [6.200 - 0.700 - 0.12 \times 4.500](1 - 0.49) - 0.6$$
   $$= 16.430$$

   Then Cash(1985) + 7.000 + 5.800 + 20.700 + 4.000
   $$= 10.400 + 4.5000 + 6.000 + 16.430$$
   or Cash(1985) = -0.17, which violates the lower limit of 2.0.

   (c) If Cash(1985) = 2.0 and STB(1985) = 4.5
   then 2.000 + 7.000 + 5.800 + 20.700 + 4.000
   $$= 10.400 + 4.500 + 6.000 + E(1985),$$
   or E(1985)   = 18.600
   and E(1985)   = $14.500 + [6.2 - 0.7 - 0.12(4.500)](1 - 0.49)$
   $$- \text{Dividends}(1985)$$
   or Dividends(1985) = $-18.600 + 17.030 = -1.570$
   which violates the requirement that dividends be at least 0.6.

   The policy alternatives open to Post Mills Controls in this case involve: (a) an equity issue; (b) reduction of the planned asset growth that has generated the need for equity funds; and (c) renegotiating credit agreements with the bank. A complete analysis would indicate the value of increased debt capacity (reduced interest coverage requirement) in terms of net present value from (now) feasible asset expansion.

Chapter 27 Solutions

1. For each dollar that the investor invested in the one-year United States bond the return would be $1.115. If she converted the dollars into sterling, she would get £0.7692 per dollar, so the return from this investment in the one-year United Kingdom bond would be (£0.7692) × 1.125. However, she should cover the exchange risk with a forward contract to sell the pounds for dollars at the one-year forward rate.

   If she pays no taxes, she would be indifferent between the two bonds only if she ended up with the same number of dollars with both the United States and the United Kingdom investments, or

$$1.115 = 0.7692 \times 1.125 \times f$$

   where f is the forward exchange rate measured in dollars per pound. Thus,

$$f = \frac{1.115}{0.8654} = 1.2884$$

   The forward exchange rate at which the investor would be indifferent is $1.2884/£1.00.

2. If the annualized rate on ninety-day Treasury bills in the United Kingdom is 12 percent, the three-month return = $(1.12)^{3/12} = 1.02874$. Similarly, the three-month return for the United States ninety-day Treasury bill is $(1.15)^{3/12} = 1.03556$.

   Given the interest rate parity theory,

$$(1.15)^{3/12} = \frac{(1.12)^{3/12} \times f}{1.3000}$$

   Thus the forward rate of exchange f is

$$f = \frac{1.03556 \times 1.3000}{1.02874}$$

$$= 1.3086$$

   The three-month forward rate of exchange would be $1.3086/£1.00.

3. ($1.2690/£) × (DM2.9405/$) = DM3.7315/£

4. The quote given in the problem is an indirect quote. The direct quote is given by 1/(DM2.9405/$) = $.3401/DM.

   From the equation for purchasing power parity,

   Expected Future Spot Rate at Time t

$$= \text{Current Spot Rate} \times \left[\frac{1 + \text{US Inflation Rate}}{1 + \text{WG Inflation Rate}}\right]^t$$

$$= 0.3401 \times \left(\frac{1 + 0.12}{1 + 0.05}\right)^1$$

$$= 0.3628$$

Expected spot rate at the end of twelve months is $.3628/DM

5.

	Country A	Country B
Inflation	10%	30%
Real rate of interest	2%	5%

The spot rate of exchange is B1.5/A

(a) Using Fisher's (closed) proposition,

Nominal rate of interest for A $= (1 + 0.10)(1 + 0.02) - 1$
$= 12.2\%$

Nominal rate of interest for B $= (1 + 0.30)(1 + 0.05) - 1$
$= 36.5\%$

The interest rates on one-year government bonds in countries A and B should be 12.2 percent and 36.5 percent, respectively.

(b) The return on one unit of A invested in a one-year bond in A is 1.122. One unit of currency A converts into 1.5 units of B. The return on the one-year bond in B $= 1.5 \times 1.365$. At the end of the year, if f is the forward rate of exchange, and if interest rate parity holds:

$$1.122 = \frac{1.5 \times 1.365}{f}$$

$$f = \frac{1.5 \times 1.365}{1.122}$$

$$= 1.825$$

Therefore, the forward rate of exchange is 1.825 units of B's currency for each unit of A's currency.

(c) Under the purchasing power parity theorem (using the indirect quotes),

Expected Future Spot Rate at Time t

$$= \text{Current Spot Rate} \times \left[\frac{1 + \text{Country B's Inflation Rate}}{1 + \text{Country A's Inflation Rate}}\right]^t$$

$$\text{Expected Spot Rate at End of One Year} = 1.5 \times \left[\frac{1 + 0.30}{1 + 0.10}\right]^1$$

$$= 1.7727$$

The expected spot rate at the end of one year will be 1.7727 units of B's currency for each unit of A's currency.

(d) The pure expectations hypothesis suggests that the currently quoted forward rate equals the expected future spot rate of exchange. The results reached in (b) and (c) do not agree; the forward rate of 1.825 units of B per unit of A does not equal the future spot rate of 1.7727. The difference is explained by the difference in real rates of interest for the two countries—the purchasing power parity theorem assumes that real rates of interest are the same.

7. The spot rate of exchange is Y10/A, and the inflation on the index for Y is 5 percent, for A 10 percent. Using the purchasing power parity theorem,

Expected Future Spot Rate at Time t

$$= \text{Current Spot Rate} \times \left[\frac{1 + \text{Country Y's Inflation Rate}}{1 + \text{Country A's Inflation Rate}}\right]^t$$

$$= 10 \times \left[\frac{1 + 0.05}{1 + 0.10}\right]^5$$

$$= 7.925$$

The rate of exchange between countries Y and A decreases from ten units of Y to 7.925 units of Y for each unit of A at the end of five years. This is because of the higher rate of inflation in country A compared with country Y.

10. Calculation of project NPV in currency A

End of year	0	1	2	3	4	5
CURRENCY B						
Nominal after-tax cash flow	−1,000	744	1,487	2,975	5,950	11,899
Total remittance (assuming reinvestment at 20% real)						88,555
Probability of remittance						0.7
Expected value of remittance 0.70 × 88,555 =						61,989
Withholding taxes at 15%						9,298
After-tax remittance						52,691
Foreign exchange rate[a]						47.7290
CURRENCY A						
Remittance received						1,104
50% tax on actual remittances						−195
Foreign tax credit on withholding tax						909
After-tax cash flow	−333					
NPV at 26.5%[b]	−52					

[a]Current spot rate = 3B/A

$$\text{Spot rate at end of year 5} = 3 \times \left[\frac{1 + 1.0}{1 + 0.15} \right]^5 = B47.7290/A$$

[b]Nominal discount rate = $(1 + 0.10)(1 + 0.15) - 1 = 26.5\%$

NPV of project = −52 units of A

Index